SCENARIOS OF POWER

SCENARIOS OF POWER

Myth and Ceremony in Russian Monarchy

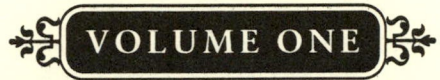

VOLUME ONE

FROM PETER THE GREAT
TO THE DEATH OF NICHOLAS I

Richard S. Wortman

PRINCETON UNIVERSITY PRESS · PRINCETON, NEW JERSEY

Library of Congress Cataloging-in-Publication Data

Wortman, Richard.
Scenarios of power : myth and ceremony in Russian monarchy / Richard S. Wortman.
p. cm. — (Studies of the Harriman Institute)
Includes bibliographical references and index.
Contents: v. 1. From Peter the Great to the death of Nicholas I.
ISBN 0-691-03484-2
1. Russia—Court and courtiers. 2. Russia—Kings and rulers. 3. Russia—Social life and
customs—1533–1917. I. Title. II. Title: Myth and ceremony in Russian
monarchy. III. Series.
DK127.W67 1995
394'.4'0970903—dc20   94-21537 CIP

Publication of this book has been supported by a grant from the National Endowment for
the Humanities, an independent federal agency.

This book has been composed in Sabon Typeface

C O N T E N T S

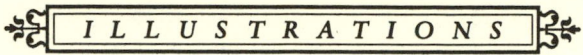
ILLUSTRATIONS

Unattributed photographs are by the author.

⚜ *A C K N O W L E D G M E N T S* ⚜

I OWE A GREAT DEBT of thanks to all those who have assisted me during my many years of work on this project. I have received generous assistance from the Social Science Research Council and the Guggenheim Foundation for free time to pursue methodological interests and research on new areas of the study of Russian monarchy. The International Research and Exchanges Board succeeded in overcoming a fifteen-year official exclusion from the Soviet Union and provided me with the assistance to return to research there. The research programs of Columbia University and Princeton University provided funds that made possible visits to Helsinki and the Soviet Union. The archivists in the former Central State Archive (TsGIA) in St. Petersburg, and the former Central State Archive of the October Revolution in Moscow, were most helpful and patient in helping me to find materials. I also thank the Avery Architectural and Fine Arts Library, Columbia University; the Columbia University Law Library; the State Pushkin Museum of Fine Arts, Moscow; the Slavic and Baltic Division, and the Spencer Collection, of the New York Public Library; and the Library of Congress for permission to use illustrations from their collections.

I am especially grateful to Edward Kasinec, who has gone out of his way to find rare books and illustrations in the excellent and expanding collections on Russian monarchy in the Slavic and Baltic Division of the New York Public Library. Our collaborative efforts made it possible to explore the potentialities of coronation albums as a historical source. Eugene Beshenkovskii and Ellen Scaruffi of the Columbia Library and the Bakhmeteff Archive were also generous with their time and their advice. I also thank my research assistants, Thomas Beck, Alberto Masoero, and Anna Tavis, for their help.

Those who read and commented on all or part of versions of this manuscript deserve special gratitude. Their patience and astute criticisms have helped me to revise a long and complex study. Peter Brown, Leopold H. Haimson, Dr. George Moraitis, Alfred J. Rieber, Michael Safonov, and Mark Von Hagen have given me invaluable suggestions. Laura Engelstein's exhaustive critique and enthusiastic encouragement guided me during the last stage of turning a manuscript into a book. I owe my greatest thanks to Marlene Stein Wortman, my in-house Maxwell Perkins. Her careful reading of the many drafts, her critical acumen and eye both for evasions and potentialities, and finally her unfailing understanding carried me through this project.

BE	*Entsiklopedicheskii slovar' Brokgauz i Efron*, 41 vols. (St Petersburg, 1890–1914).
DRV	*Drevniaia Rossiiskaia Vivliofika* (Moscow, 1788).
IGK, ts. Al. I	Stoletie Voennogo Ministerstva: *Imperatorskaia glavnaia kvartira; istoriia gosudarevoi svity; tsarstvovanie Imperatora Aleksandra I* (St. Petersburg, 1904).
IGK, ts. Nik. I	Stoletie Voennogo Ministerstva: *Imperatorskaia glavnaia kvartira; istoriia gosudarevoi svity; tsarstvovanie Imperatora Nikolaia I* (St. Petersburg, 1908).
IGK, ts. Al. II	Stoletie Voennogo Ministerstva: *Imperatorskaia glavnaia kvartira; istoriia gosudarevoi svity; tsarstvovanie Imperatora Aleksandra II* (St. Petersburg, 1914).
KFZ	*Kamer-fur'erskii tseremonial'nyi zhurnal.*
PSZ	*Polnoe sobranie zakonov Rossiiskoi Imperii.* Sobranoe 1, 45 vols. (St. Petersburg, 1830). Sobranoe 2, 55 vols. (St. Petersburg, 1830–1884).
RBS	*Russkii Biographicheskii Slovar'*, 25 vols. (St. Petersburg, 1868–1918).
TsGAOR	Tsentral'nyi Gosudarstvennyi Arkhiv Oktiab'rskoi Revoliutsii.
TsGIA	Tsentral'nyi Gosudarstvennyi Istoricheskii Arkhiv.

SCENARIOS OF POWER

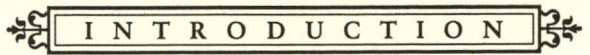

Scenarios of Power

> It would be necessary to add (not as a concession but as a truth)
> that the government is still the only European in Russia . . .
>
> —*Alexander Pushkin, Draft of letter to Peter Chaadaev,*
> *October 19, 1836*[1]

FROM THE SEVENTEENTH century until the demise of Russian monarchy in the twentieth, the ceremonies and celebrations of the imperial Russian court invariably produced a lasting impression on European visitors. These events conjured up what the Bavarian ambassador at Nicholas II's coronation, Count Carl Moy, described as "an overwhelming picture of Russian power and greatness."[2] Indeed, they were intended to impress Western governments and public opinion with the taste and resplendence of Russian monarchy. But they also were intended to impress Russians with the loftiness of the monarch's power. "Power in Russia," noted the astute and often critical observer of the life of the court, Anna Tiutcheva, a Lady-in-Waiting of Empress Maria Aleksandrovna, "is so very complete and majestic while elsewhere, in other countries, only the word remains. Here it bears a religious, and, one may say, supernatural character that acts on the imagination."[3]

At first sight, it may seem that Russian emperors and empresses, who disposed of a formidable administration and army, were least in need of such demonstrative displays. Imperial Spain and Hohenzollern Prussia are examples of absolute monarchies that ruled without elaborate ceremonies.[4] The sumptuous, highly ritualized presentations of Russian monarchy, produced at enormous cost of resources and time, indicate that Russian rulers and their advisers considered the symbolic sphere of ceremonies and imagery intrinsic to their exercise of power. This study argues that such presentations, by "acting on the imagination," tied servitors to the throne as much as

---

[1] A. S. Pushkin, *Polnoe sobranie sochinenii* (Leningrad, 1949), 15:261.

[2] Carl Graf Moy, *Als Diplomat am Zarenhof* (Munich, 1971), 61.

[3] Anna Fedorovna Tiutcheva, *Pri dvore dvukh imperatorov. Vospominaniia, Dnevnik, 1853–1882* (Moscow, 1928–1929), 1:36.

[4] On Spanish kingship, see Teofilo F. Ruiz, "Unsacred Monarchy: The Kings of Castile in the Late Middle Ages," in Sean Wilentz, ed., *Rites of Power: Symbolism, Ritual and Politics since the Middle Ages* (Philadelphia, 1985), 109–44; and J. H. Elliot, "Power and Propaganda in the Spain of Phillip IV," in Wilentz, ed., ibid., 145–73. On Prussia, see Karl Hammer, "Die preussischen Könige und Königinnen im 19 Jahrhundert und ihr Hof," in Karl Ferdinand Werner, *Hof, Kultur, und Politik im 19 Jahrhundert* (Bonn, 1985), 87–98.

the perquisites and emoluments they received from state service. To understand the persistence of absolute monarchy in Russia and the abiding loyalty of the nobility, we must examine the ways that these feelings were evoked and sustained. My work is meant as a first effort at exploring this problem, which has been all but ignored in the extensive scholarship on prerevolutionary Russia.

Although the imperial court represented an ongoing theater of power, we must not confuse the proceedings with what we currently understand by the word *entertainment*. To be sure, the ceremonies of the court frequently appealed to the sense of the delightful and wondrous. But the participants in these events, who were to a large extent also its audience, did not attend for amusement, as their frequent grumbling about tedious ceremonial obligations indicates. Rather, they were all participating in an intentional and often painstaking effort to present the ruler as supreme and to vest him or her with sacral qualities.[5] David Cannadine's remark, "Ritual is not the mask of force, but is itself a type of power," pertains with especial force to Russian monarchy.[6]

This process, which I call "elevation," lifted the sovereign into another realm where he or she displayed the superior qualities of a being entitled to rule. The elite that surrounded the monarch took on something of the sacral aura as well. By elevating those who ruled, though not to the extent of the monarch, the ceremonial sphere established a crucial symbolic distance between them and the ruled, making the exercise of power and the possession of privilege appear rooted in the natural order of things. At the Russian imperial court, nobles serving the sovereign shared something of the charisma of unlimited, unquestioned authority. Tiutcheva observed, "The supreme power in Russia is a historical fact, the service of which one must consider an honor, the more so that the dignity confers a certain charm that acts on the imagination."[7] By revering the idealized image of the sovereign, the nobility exalted their own self-image and their mastery over their subordinates and serfs.

Although the ceremonies of the Russian court of the eighteenth century superficially resemble those of the Versailles of Louis XIV, they dramatized a completely different historical relationship between throne and nobility. Versailles encouraged and displayed the submission of a once fractious nobility to the throne. The Russian nobility lacked traditions of feudal rights or local

[5] The creation of a charismatic appeal and a sacral, noumenal aura around monarchs is discussed in Clifford Geertz, "Centers, Kings, and Charisma: Reflections on the Symbolics of Power," in Wilentz, ed., *Rites of Power*, 13–16. This charismatic aura is reproduced in the ruler's appearance and gestures, the *numen*, that Roland Barthes says "produces a phantasmagoria of a power alien to man" (in Susan Sontag, ed., *A Barthes Reader* [New York, 1983], 70–71).

[6] David Cannadine, "Introduction: The Divine Rites of Kings," in David Cannadine and Simon Price, eds., *Rituals of Royalty: Power and Ceremonial in Traditional Societies* (Cambridge, 1987), 19.

[7] Tiutcheva, 1:36.

autonomy: they owed their standing, wealth, and influence to service to their sovereign. Imperial favor brought rewards of lands with serfs, large loans, and access to clientele networks that extended to provincial Russia. As the empire expanded to include non-Russian areas, the Baltic provinces, the cossacks, Muslim khanates, their elites too joined the service of the emperor, and, by the end of the eighteenth century, achieved the rights and privileges granted to Russian noblemen.

In this respect, imperial Russia represents an example of what Ernest Gellner has described as an "agro-literate society," that is, a traditional society organized horizontally, where the privileged groups seek to separate themselves as much as possible from the lower classes.[8] They create this separation by propagating myth—narratives that dramatize their difference from other mortals and their affinity with saints, heroes, or gods. The ceremonies of the court enact or refer to these narratives. The theater of power, in the period covered by this book, is a play performed principally for the participants. It is the various strata of the elite who gather to celebrate their collective domination, justifying it, Max Weber pointed out, first of all *to themselves*; the myths then would be accepted by "the negatively privileged layers."[9] They create and perform what Marshall Sahlins called their "heroic history," while the masses remain in a state of "historylessness," following the overarching symbolic patterns of their society unknowingly.[10]

The animating myth of Russian monarchy from the fifteenth to the late nineteenth centuries associated the ruler and the elite with foreign images of political power. In this respect, Russian political imagery resembles the patterns of mythology of Polynesian kingship analyzed by Sahlins. The "heroic history," of Polynesian dynasties identified kings with gods or godlike men who arrive from outside—strange and powerful foreigners, who subdue or are welcomed by the native population and found a new political order. The myths made clear that "royalty is the foreigner."[11]

By displaying themselves as foreigners, or like foreigners, Russian monarchs and their servitors affirmed the permanence and inevitability of their separation from the population they ruled. The devices of identification with foreign sources of power were varied—tales of foreign origin, analogies with or imitation of foreign rulers. Ceremonies of conquest in the eighteenth and early nineteenth centuries reaffirmed and reinforced the separation between the realms of the ruler and the ruled. In all cases, the source of sacrality was distant from Russia whether it was beyond the sea, whence the original Viking princes came, or located in the image of Byzantium, France, or Germany. To be sure, a national subtheme runs through Russian political imagery and myths, but, until the late nineteenth century, only as an antithesis

---

[8] Ernest Gellner, *Nations and Nationalism* (Ithaca, N.Y., 1983), 11.

[9] Max Rheinstein, ed., *Max Weber on Law in Economy and Society* (New York, 1967), 335–37.

[10] Marshall Sahlins, *Islands of History* (Chicago, 1985), 35–51.

[11] Ibid., 73–103.

that was repeatedly submerged by a dominant foreign motif. In expressing the political and cultural preeminence of the ruler, foreign traits carried a positive valuation, native traits a neutral or negative one.[12]

The princes of Moscow who consolidated power over a unified Russian state in the fifteenth and sixteenth centuries understood sovereignty in terms of foreign images. Their forebears had looked to the Byzantine emperor and the Mongol khan as sovereign. With the fall of Byzantium in 1492, they sought to display to the West the attributes of Christian sovereign represented in the image of the Byzantine emperor. Thus the assertion of foreignness became an assertion of an aspiration to empire. The word *empire* carried several interrelated though distinct meanings. First, it meant imperial dominion or supreme power unencumbered by other authority. Second, it implied imperial expansion, extensive conquests, encompassing non-Russian lands. Third, it referred to the Christian Empire, the heritage of the Byzantine emperor as the defender of Orthodoxy. These meanings were conflated and served to reinforce one another. The expansion of empire confirmed the image of supreme power and justified the unlimited authority of the Russian emperors. The religious, eschatological element enhanced their moral dominion, a theme emphasized by Boris Uspenskii and other scholars of the Tartu school.

Like monarchical power everywhere in Europe, imperial rule was consecrated by divine sanction. The tsar was known as the chosen-of-God, and the anointed-of-God. But neither religious sanction nor the force of tradition proved sufficient to ground the secular pretensions of Russian monarchs. Imperial Russian imagery expressed a historical and cultural dynamic in which each ruler had to demonstrate his or her foreign character and distance from the parochial interests of the ruled. I use the term *scenarios* to describe the individual modes of performance of the imperial myth. The scenario was disclosed in the manifestos and ceremonies that opened each reign. At the imperial coronation, it received ecclesiastical consecration and public ritual acclamation. Its principal themes were elaborated on the occasions of church holidays and secular celebrations.

During the eighteenth and nineteenth centuries—the chronological focus of this volume—myth usually took the form of an epic drama of conquest, the new ruler as conqueror, bringing to Russia the benefits of civilization and progress. The scenarios produced an illusion of irresistible dynamism, of constant renewal, presenting the ruler as deliverer whose selfless heroism saved Russia from despotism and ruin. The scenarios also played a tutelary role, disclosing the forms of comportment, deference, and cultural expression that defined a civilized monarchy.

Literature, art, and architecture were used to express the themes of the

[12] On the symbolic force of foreignness, see Ju. M. Lotman and B. A. Uspenskii, "The Role of Dual Models in the Dynamics of Russian Culture (Up to the End of the Eighteenth Century)," in Ju. M. Lotman and B. A. Uspenskii, eds., *The Semiotics of Russian Culture* (Ann Arbor, Mich., 1984), 3–35.

scenario in a current cultural idiom and glorify the monarch as an esthetic and cultural ideal. The arts described patterns of life and manners that became authoritative and shaped the semioticized behavior of noblemen analyzed in the works of Iurii Lotman. Ceremonial texts described the events, distilled their higher meaning, and prescribed the responses they should evoke. They disseminated the image of the ruler to a broader audience among the elite. The writers and artists who prepared such texts availed themselves of the array of current literary and artistic devices to give the ruler and the court the character of otherness: to show that ceremony represented something greater than the stately but ephemeral magnificence on view at the court. My study pays special attention to the various means employed to produce the illusion of the foreign and superordinate. The illustrations that I have included are meant to reveal not the actual appearance of individuals and events, but how they were supposed to be perceived by the participants and the audience.

The literary and dramatic presentations of the monarch were mythic in two senses of the word: they imitated or made reference to heroic and legendary archetypes, and they provided an animating political myth of rule. They presented the ruler in terms of what Michael Bakhtin called "the world of the epic." This was "a world of 'beginnings' and 'peak times' in the national history, a world of fathers and founders of families, a world of 'firsts' and 'bests.'" The epic is not an accurate reflection or product of the past, but rather a "transferal of a represented world onto the past." It confers "epic distance" on the present, canonizing current events and figures by incorporating them into a mythical past. Most important, this world is "absolute": it banishes doubt, and precludes all individual points of view.[13] Epic presentations were closed, "monologic" in Bakhtin's terminology, excluding questioning or, indeed, any response besides affirmation. Those who belonged to the culture of monarchy inhabited an epic, monologic world, where the incontrovertible truth of the monarch's supremacy had constantly to be displayed and witnessed.

The forms of cultural expression that I examine in this study confirmed the foreign character of the elite. Fireworks displays, engravings, odes, Baroque, Rococo, and neoclassical architecture, regardless of their content, were signs of belonging to the West. The presence of women in social events, their increasing role in the royal family, indicated advanced European culture, and the Russian empress became an exemplar of Western comportment and taste. The empresses took an active role in introducing advanced Western ideas of pedagogy into the upbringing of the heirs to the throne. They encouraged new approaches to the exercise of power in Russia, posing an alternative, philosophical model to the ceremonial image of triumphal conqueror.

The ceremonial setting, this book argues, ultimately shaped the heirs to

[13] M. M. Bakhtin, *The Dialogic Imagination* (Austin, Tex., 1981), 13–16.

the throne. Children of the imperial family grew up in a world of performance. The ritual, literary, and artistic expressions of the court constituted their psychological reality, defining their relationship to their parents and their servitors and shaping their conceptions of government. Separating "person" from "persona" in biographical material about Russian monarchs is often impossible, for the heirs' personal selves were entangled with the images that they were expected to project.

How far did this culture extend? The available materials permit only an approximate answer. The inner circle comprised the sovereigns themselves, the members of the imperial family, court officials, and the highest ranks of the military and officialdom. Their numbers were small, but their influence extended from the capital through family and personal connections; they constituted what Norbert Elias called the "core group" of the monarchy.[14] Important ceremonial functions were also attended by noble officers in guards' regiments, lesser officials, leaders of the church and the merchant estates as well. Major events in the eighteenth and nineteenth centuries, such as balls and fêtes, were great assemblages including three thousand or four thousand guests. This was scarcely a mass audience, but such events fulfilled the requirement of celebration—the participation and bearing witness by large numbers of people.

In the second quarter of the nineteenth century, Nicholas I widened the number of those exposed to imperial presentations by involving increasing numbers of officials from the growing Russian administration. He used print media to disseminate news about events in the court and the imperial family. Semiofficial periodicals brought Nicholas's scenario to a broader public. The press, dominated by the state, extended the monologic world of the court in an effort to discourage the dialogue and dissent that had accompanied the development of journalism in the West.

A more difficult question concerns the extent of credence that members of the elite lent to these various idealizations. Memoirs and diaries give some sense, but such affirmations of belief often have a ritualized character that may impugn their validity. Any evaluation of belief ultimately comes down to the question of what we mean by belief. It is clear, Paul Veyne has argued in his inquiry, *Did the Greeks Believe Their Myths?*, that belief can mean many different things. Veyne demonstrates that it was quite possible for the Greeks to regard their myths as fable and yet to accept them as expressing a fundamental truth. Veyne calls the latter "rhetorical truth," which expresses certain norms on a literary plane and is not subject to the test of common sense. The heroic mythology of the city-states instilled in the Greeks a sense of dignity and sharing in the great tradition of their cities. Belief expressed a feeling of belonging to the polity and set the citizens of the city apart from outsiders to its political tradition. Acceptance of myths was based on neither

---

[14] Norbert Elias, *The Court Society* (Oxford, 1983), 117–29.

calculation nor credulity. Nor was it the result of ideological manipulation from above.[15]

Despite the evident differences between the Greek city-states and Russian monarchy, both were based on traditions of political involvement of the elite. In the city-states, the involvement took the form of participation in the city's institutions; in Russian monarchy, of state service. Belief signaled a form of affiliation with the political core group and set the members apart from those who could not or would not participate. In both, the person was defined by his political role. Like Athenian citizens, Russian noblemen at once believed and disbelieved presentations of a rhetorical truth that elevated them into the superior realm of majesty and empire. They were at the same time participants in and audience for imperial ceremonies, their involvement demonstrating the truths enshrined by power. Their memoirs, often reflecting literary ambitions, reproduce the themes of imperial presentations; they describe the sense of exaltation experienced by their authors in the court and the efforts to reproduce such feelings on the stages of their estate theaters.[16]

To be sure, not all noblemen shared these attitudes or pretensions. The scenarios encompassed only those who wanted to believe or who found it to their advantage to believe. There were clearly different degrees of belief or indifference, as is always the case with the accepted myths that animate a political system. But until the early nineteenth century, the system and the various artistic and literary forms of expression successfully precluded alternative conceptions of the truth—dialogue, discussion, not to speak of opposition. When limited freedom was allowed, as in the journals of Nicholas Novikov during the reign of Catherine the Great, questioning the mythical and moral supremacy of the monarch continued to be forbidden. Only with the generation of the Decembrists do members of the nobility find another myth, a romantic myth, that they can set against the epic world of the court and that allowed them to approach everyday life with a sense of dignity. With the rise of the intelligentsia in the 1840s, noblemen trained at the university and exposed to German idealist philosophy embraced a different conception of the truth—truth as authenticity rather than rhetoric.[17] It was this type of thinking that would provide the basis for the Great Reforms of the 1860s.

The pervasiveness of imperial presentations combined with the evocative

[15] Paul Veyne, *Les grecs, ont-ils cru à leurs mythes?; essai sur l'imagination constituante* (Paris, 1983), 89–101.

[16] Priscilla R. Roosevelt, "Emerald Thrones and Living Statues: Theater and Theatricality on the Russian Estate," *Russian Review* 50, no. 1 (January 1991): 20–22; G. R. Derzhavin, *Sochineniia* (St. Petersburg, 1871), 6:578–80.

[17] Iurii Lotman gives insights into the Decembrists' patterns of thought and behavior in Lotman and Uspenskii, 71–124. On the noble idealists of the last decades of the reign of Nicholas I, see my *The Development of a Russian Legal Consciousness* (Chicago, 1976), 204–34.

force of the most important displays to produce an ongoing, iterative effect. In each reign, we witness not a series of separate dramas, but a single drama of many acts—the scenario—with the same themes developed in response to particular occasions and circumstances. The scenario provides the symbolic context for the individual events. For this reason, to the extent that space has permitted, I have given brief descriptions of the most important or evocative presentations elaborating the scenario of each reign.

My approach is historical, that is, I focus on the evolution of presentation over time, and the interplay between continuity and change. Although ceremonies always purport to permanence, there were striking changes of two types: first, changes in the types of ceremonies or celebrations that were regarded as most important, for example, from religious ceremonies, to advents, to court fêtes, to parades; second, changes introduced within the ceremonies, as in the coronation, that evolved over time to provide in each period a consecration of monarchy that reflected current goals and preoccupations.

Most important, a chronological approach reveals how the transformations of the myth in the scenarios responded to specific historical contexts. As Sahlins has argued, myth can provide a structure for understanding and accepting change. Russian emperors and empresses were constantly looking abroad to the latest exemplars of powerful monarchy, thereby encouraging a propensity to reform. But at the same time, court presentations expressed an ethos of domination and the willingness to wield force ruthlessly in defense of the interests of the elite. The chronological approach reveals the changing forms of elevation of the elite and the results when those forms did not conform to the elite's expectations. The evolution of the myth reflects an ongoing tension between the aspiration of the monarchy to strike an image of Westernness and its determination to maintain the existing political and social order.

Part One, "Borrowed Signs," reviews the period of the formation of the Russian state, tracing the development of the myth of foreignness from Kiev until the final adoption of Western models under Peter the Great. Part Two, "Olympian Scenarios," deals with the adoption of European Baroque and enlightenment patterns of presentation, following the example of Peter the Great. Part Three, "Mortal Sovereigns," is devoted to the attempts to adapt the myth to an era of revolutionary change, when the image of remote and godlike monarch had lost its hold. Part Four, "The Dynastic Scenario," examines Nicholas I's restoration of the primacy of the conquest motif and the image of heroic sovereign—the reconstitution of the myth to answer the nineteenth-century challenges of liberalism and nationalism.

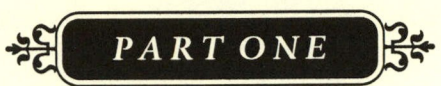

Borrowed Signs

The European Background

IN RUSSIA, sovereignty early became and remained identified with empire: the only true sovereign was an emperor who exercised complete and extensive dominion. From the tenth to the eighteenth centuries, empire evoked the two conflicting images of Rome and Byzantium. Until Peter the Great, the principal model was Byzantium, and the name for Russian emperor, "tsar," expressed his role as an Orthodox sovereign, the protector of his flock. Yet, from the late fifteenth century, the tsars of Moscow also sought Roman sources to express their parity with the Holy Roman Emperor and with Western kings who claimed descent from Rome. By the end of the seventeenth century, Russian imperial imagery had become an uneasy composite of both models, with the Byzantine and religious connotations of tsar still predominating.

The adoption of the title *imperator* by Peter the Great identified Russia with pagan Rome and the monarch with the image of triumphant military leader, the exemplar of force. Peter discovered his models of monarchical rule not in Rome itself, but in the representations of Rome that had reached him from the West. Russia found Rome through Europe, then appropriated classical symbols as signs of its own Western character. With the formation of unified absolutist states, Western monarchs had turned to the imagery of Rome for expressions of sovereign rule unencumbered by ecclesiastical intervention. Roman advents and tales of descent from Troy glorified their power, while art and literature lifted them into the company of the rulers and gods of antiquity. In this section we shall review the emergence of the absolutist imagery and ceremony in sixteenth- and seventeenth-century Europe that redefined the meaning of sovereignty for Peter and his successors.

The principal ceremony of kingship during the Western middle ages had been the coronation. Western coronations elevated the king not as ruthless wielder of force, but as a Christian monarch who ruled his land under the religious and moral guidance of the church. The hierarchs of the Roman Catholic Church composed elaborate liturgies to anoint and crown the kings of England and France and give the monarch's rule religious sanction. They negotiated or imposed what Jacques Le Goff has described as a contract between church and king: the church consecrated the king in return for his promised protection of the faith and the people, and for his vow to be a Christian king. Anointment ceremonies consecrated the identification of king with the nation by creating a biblical analogy. The holy unction made the king, like the kings of Israel, the ruler of a chosen people.[1]

---

[1] Jacques Le Goff, "A Coronation Program for the Age of Saint Louis: The Ordo of 1250," in Jànos M. Bak, ed., *Coronations: Medieval and Early Modern Monarchic Ritual* (Berkeley,

The Roman advent identified the monarch with the original sense of the word *imperator*—the triumphant military leader. The king rode into a city on horseback, wearing armor, as a conqueror, in a procession demonstrating his capacity to wield force. The Roman advent conferred dominion on the basis of demonstrated prowess. Its consecration of power, the anthropologist A. M. Hocart observed, fulfilled the same function as a coronation.[2] Lavish reenactments of the Roman advent glorified Charles V's short-lived universal empire. Charles's entry into Bologna before his coronation as emperor in 1529 served as the model for future royal advents. A woodcut of the time presents him in armor riding through the streets on horseback, with armored men marching by his side. He passed through triumphal arches decorated with classical figures, Bacchus and Neptune; the entry gate had pictures of Caesar, Augustus, Vespasian, and Trajan.[3] The kings of France followed Charles V's example, decking themselves out as warriors and using art, allegory, and poetry to associate themselves with a classical past.[4]

Mythical genealogies showed the descent of the monarch from the legendary Trojan founders of Rome. Such genealogies had been claimed by Holy Roman Emperors from the time of Charlemagne; now they were elaborated as necessary attributes of absolute power. Maximilian I (1493–1519) created a grandiose ancestor cult to buttress his claims to rule as both universal emperor and pope. He commissioned the most distinguished humanists and artists to construct a genealogy that included Noah and Christ, Hector, Priam, and other heroes of Troy.[5] By drawing on medieval tales of origin, the kings of England and France also claimed descent from the heroes of Troy. English kings traced their descent to one Brut, a relative of Aeneas. The Capetians boasted the Trojan Francus, a son of Hector, whose descendant Pharamond became the ostensible ancestor of Charles IX, who was called the French Augustus. These figures were incorporated in mythical histories of dynasties, and their pictures appeared on the arches at various coronations, supplementing the ecclesiastical consecration with a secular imperial legacy.[6]

Writers and artists revived classical themes as allegories of empire. The myth of the return of Astraea symbolized the renewal, *renovatio*, brought

---

1990), 48; Janet Nelson, "Ritual and Reality in the Early Medieval *Ordines*," in her *Politics and Ritual in Early Medieval Europe*, 329–39; Janet L. Nelson, "The Lords Anointed and the People's Choice: Carolingian Royal Ritual," in Cannadine and Price, *Rituals of Royalty*, 137–80; Ralph Giesey, "Models of Rulership in French Royal Ceremonial," in Wilentz, *Rites of Power*, 43–46.

[2] A. M. Hocart, *Kingship* (London, 1969), 86–89.

[3] For a description and illustrations of the advent, see Roy Strong, *Splendor at Court: Renaissance Spectacle and the Theater of Power* (Boston, 1973), 23–37, 86–99.

[4] Giesey, "Models of Rulership," 52–53; Frances A. Yates, *Astraea: the Imperial Theme in the Sixteenth Century* (London, 1985), 144–46, 209–11.

[5] Marie Tanner, *The Last Descendant of Aeneas: The Hapsburgs and the Mythic Image of Emperor* (New Haven, Conn., 1993), 70–71, 101–7.

[6] Yates, *Astraea*, 50, 130–32; Richard Jackson, *Vive le roi!: A History of the French Coronation from Charles V to Charles X* (Chapel Hill, N.C., 1984), 178–79.

about by a revival of imperial rule. The reference was to the fourth eclogue of Virgil's *Aeneid*, where the appearance of Astraea, the virgin goddess, signaled the dawn of "the age of gold" accompanying the reign of Augustus. The return of Astraea would inaugurate an era of secular rather than religious redemption—peace by dint of wise and courageous action of a savior-king or queen. Both Henry IV of France and Elizabeth of England were presented as Astraea, monarchs restoring the glories of imperial Rome. The figure of the "Gallic Hercules" with sword in hand, chains descending from his mouth, adorned the entry arches for the advents of the French kings; the sword symbolized the triumph of the king, and the chains, his skill in eloquence and his role in promoting literature and the arts.[7] Baroque paintings identified monarchs with the denizens of Olympus—with Hercules, in his various forms, with Perseus and Mars, as well as other gods. The association was metaphorical—a god allegorizing the king's greatness. The connection between the person of the king and the mythical referent became increasingly explicit. Portraits showed Mars, Perseus, Alexander the Great, and Caesar with the features of Henry IV and later Louis XIII.[8]

During the seventeenth century, the book, the brochure, and the engraving became increasingly important means to transmit and to elevate the image of the king. The published descriptions and illustrations of royal ceremonies—what Christian Jouhaud has called the "publicization" of ceremonies—created "an official version of a celebration of power." The texts describing the event became as important as the ceremony itself, both disseminating knowledge of the event, and explaining its official meaning. They marked it as worthy of inclusion in history, as "immortal in the memory of future ages."[9]

The role of the text grew with the consolidation and institutionalization of the power of the absolute monarch in the seventeenth century. The advent, radiating a charisma of conquest, did not provide a sufficient expression for strong and stable rule, especially for kings who showed no distinction on the battlefield. In the course of the seventeenth century, triumphal entries fell out of fashion, and the halls and the palace became the principal scene of royal ceremonies. Louis XIV (1654–1715), who was at best a mediocre commander, exercised a new type of charisma, what Norbert Elias described as that of the "conserving monarch." The "conserving" monarch unites the elite by observation of public conduct, and the manipulation of sentiments and benefits in a "court society."[10]

[7] Yates, *Astraea*, 29–87, 210–11.

[8] Françoise Bardon, *Le portrait mythologique à la cour de France sous Henri IV et Louis XIII; mythologie et politique* (Paris, 1974), 7–25, 53, 255–60, 278–79. On the perception of objective parallels in the sixteenth and seventeenth centuries, see Peter Burke, *The Fabrication of Louis XIV* (New Haven, Conn., 1992), 127–28.

[9] Christian Jouhaud, "Printing the Event: From La Rochelle to Paris," in Roger Chartier, ed., *The Culture of Print: Power and the Uses of Print in Early Modern Europe* (Princeton, N.J., 1989), 298, 302.

[10] Norbert Elias, *The Court Society* (Oxford, 1983), 128–29, 117; John B. Wolf, "Louis

In fact, Louis XIV continued to exercise the charisma of the conquering monarch, but symbolically, in ceremonial settings, where his command was open to display and publicization. Military parades and pageants presented him as Louis the invincible and Louis Augustus. A medal commemorating a review of 1666 shows the king, his sword raised, before eighteen thousand troops arrayed symmetrically.[11] At the great carousel of June 1662, Louis appeared in the center of the horsemen dressed as a Roman emperor, on horseback, holding a shield with the device of the sun emerging from behind the clouds, and the words, "I saw and I conquered." Brochures circulating in Paris explained the meaning of the emblems. A well-known engraving shows him in the center of concentric horsemen, his chevaliers, and quadrilles of five "nations," Romans, Persians, Turks, Indians, and "savages of America." The five peers of the realm who led the five "nations" were likewise portrayed in engravings.[12]

The boudoir became another symbolic substitute for the battlefield. Celebrations presented spectacles of the king's amorous powers, of his very public "private life." At the *fêtes d'amour*, Louis appeared surrounded by women and made known his latest mistresses and favorites. *Gazette de France* or *Le Mercure galant* published officially released accounts of the event that mentioned those in attendance, slyly alluding to the presence of a new mistress.[13]

Chivalric conceptions of women as symbols of weak and oppressed territories rescued by the king's conquests—as in the sixteenth- and seventeenth-century emblems of Andromeda saved by Perseus, or the maiden by St. George—were replaced by ideal female forms in neopagan celebrations of love. The figure of Venus embellished Louis's court, along with figures of the gods. "Woman" became the object and source of higher feelings, both esthetic and amorous. She represented the peaceful virtues, the king's transcendent taste and understanding of beauty, as well as his powers to captivate. Louis assembled a museum "dedicated to beauty," a culmination of the history of culture in the Hall of Mirrors. Among the eight antique statues were Diana and the famous "Venus of Arles," which stood face to face in the gallery.[14]

Versailles became Louis's Olympus, the scene of an allegorical drama that

XIV, Soldier-King," in John C. Rule, ed., *Louis XIV and the Craft of Kingship* (Columbus, Ohio, 1969), 196–220.

[11] Michel Foucault, *Discipline and Punish: The Birth of the Prison* (New York, 1979), 187–89, Plate 1.

[12] Jean-Marie Apostolidés, *Le roi machine; spectacle et politique au temps de Louis XIV* (Paris, 1981), 41–42; Marie-Christine Moine, *Les fêtes à la cour du roi soleil, 1653–1715* (Paris, 1984), 25–29. Illustrations of the carousel may be found in Émile Magne, *Les fêtes en Europe au XVII siècle* (Paris, n.d.), 128–32.

[13] Moine, *Les fêtes à la cour*, 142–47. The "*fêtes d'amour*," are described in Magne, *Les fêtes en Europe*, 143–90.

[14] Édouard Pommier, "Versailles, l'image du souverain," in Nora, ed., *Les lieux de mémoire* (Paris, 1986), vol. 2, pt. 2: 221.

began in the morning and lasted into the night. At his rising from bed, *le lever du roi*, Louis identified himself with Apollo, facing the rising sun, looking out on the park dedicated to the god. This was a spectacle witnessed by members of the royal family and the officials and noblemen who enjoyed royal favor.[15] Set apart in the country, the palace and parks of Versailles emphasized the king's remoteness from the everyday life of Paris, creating distance between him and his subjects. At night, festivals produced an aura of the otherworldly, stunning the imagination with wondrous effects. These miracles of the festival, Louis Marin observed, represented the king's triumph over the past, a symbolic coup d'état. Fireworks over Versailles showed that the king's power reached to the sky, that he was capable of rivaling divinities in producing what Jürgen Freiherr von Kruedener described as "a secularization of heaven." Engravings then captured the explosions of light, making known the evidence of prodigies produced by a godlike king.[16] Although removed from the city, Versailles was hardly a private, sequestered sphere. The palace and other buildings in the area housed ten thousand people, and free access to the palace and grounds permitted visitors to witness the king's daily appearances.[17]

For the nobility, Versailles provided an induction into the tastes and symbols of the royal court. Page corps and books on conduct and behavior bred young noblemen in the manners and attitudes appropriate to an Olympian realm. De Bourdonné wrote in *Le courtesan désabusé* that the air of the court "softens what remains of the savage and rude that comes from breathing the air of the provinces. Nature changes nature there. One becomes subtle, adroit, polite, spiritual, as if the presence of the sovereign influences those who have the honor of approaching him." The games of the court, *récréations galantes*, such as "arts and sciences" and "the three sirens," initiated the court nobility in the knowledge of antique literature. The labyrinth of the palace took the noblemen through paths ornamented by statues from Aesop's fables. Each statue held a meaning that had to be discovered. André Félibien composed a guide to the layout and to the meanings encoded in the labyrinth, enshrining the park itself in a literary work.[18]

The final stage in the evolution of Louis's image came in the 1670s, when historical painting began to depict Louis's reign as the culmination of the nation's history. Louis no longer presented himself only as Louis-Auguste, the monarch descendent from Pharamond and Augustus, but as the incomparable embodiment of the French state, *Louis le Grand*, whose glory ex-

---

[15] Elias, *The Court Society*, 83–85.

[16] Louis Marin, *Le portrait du roi* (Paris, 1981), 241; Jürgen Freiherr von Kruedener, *Die Rolle des Hofes im Absolutismus* (Stuttgart, 1973), 11, 35–39, 65; Magne, *Les fêtes en Europe*, 177, 199.

[17] Hélène Himelfarb, "Versailles, fonctions et légendes," in Nora, ed., *Les lieux de mémoire*, vol. 2, pt. 2: 243–45; Burke, *Fabrication of Louis XIV*, 153–55.

[18] Kruedener, *Die Rolle des Hofes im Absolutismus*, 65–70; Apostolidés, *Le roi machine*, 55–57; Marin, *Le portrait du roi*, 249–50.

ceeded theirs.[19] Charles Le Brun's paintings in the halls portrayed the unprecedented victories of French armies under Louis's leadership. These successes were attributed to the king himself—even when he did not in fact command. Félibien's text systematically identified the king with the successes of the nation. The paradox explored by Louis Marin, "the portrait of the king is the king," is no paradox: the king has become an abstract figure at the head of state.[20]

By the end of the seventeenth century, secular ceremonies and representations had replaced the coronation as the principal means of elevating the figure of the king.[21] Louis asserted in his diary that the consecration did not make him king, but simply declared that he was king. But the coronation ceremony did enhance his sacred image, making his kingship "more august, more inviolable and more holy."[22] "In the popular mind," Richard Jackson concluded, "the coronation made the king."[23]

The coronation continued to be an indispensable ceremony, but it was increasingly embellished by the secular symbols and imagery of the Baroque court. Classical themes and motifs cast the royal mysteries in the language of allegory and panegyric. During the coronation entries into Reims, the various myths of kingship—the oil of Clovis, the Trojan descent, and the connection with Augustus—appeared in *tableaux vivants* and cartouches on the arches. Poets heralded Louis XV as Caesar and Louis XVI as Ludovicus Augustus. Both were greeted with solar imagery and depictions of the theme of renewal and the return of Astraea and the age of gold. At the coronation of Louis XVI in 1775, neoclassical arches and Corinthian columns decorated the interior of Reims Cathedral.[24]

The coronation entry revealed the shift from Renaissance to Baroque images of kingship. The key moment in this respect was Louis XIV's entry to Reims in 1654. The king rode not on horseback, but in a carriage. The royal carriage, with increasingly lavish decorations, was the surrogate for the dashing image of the equestrian king. Louis XV and Louis XVI, as well as other European monarchs, would follow this example. The carriage became a sign of prestige and a means of propaganda. Its sumptuous gilt decoration

---

[19] Apostolidés, *Le roi machine*, 49–57; Burke, *Fabrication of Louis XIV*, 131–32.

[20] Pommier, "Versailles," 206–16; Gérard Sabatier, "Imagerie héroique et sacralité monarchique," in Alain Boureau and Claudio-Sergio Ingerflom, eds., *La royauté sacrée dans le monde chrétien* (Paris, 1992), 125–26; Marin, *Le portrait du roi*, 7–22, 251–60.

[21] R. E. Giesey, "Inaugural Aspects of French Royal Ceremonials," in Bak, ed., 35–45.

[22] Cited in Burke, *Fabrication of Louis XIV*, 42–43. The coronation maintained, Roger Chartier said, "in its effectuation, its representation, its trace, the belief in the irreducible singularity of the royal mystery" (Roger Chartier, *Les origines culturelles de la révolution française* [Paris, 1990], 158).

[23] Jackson, *Vive le roi!*, 10.

[24] Ibid., 175–87; Alain Charles Gruber, "Le décor des derniers sacres a Reims," in *Le sacre des rois*, 273–75; Françoise Waquet, *Les fêtes royales sous la restauration ou l'ancien régime retrouvé* (Geneva, 1981), 107.

1. *Anointment Ceremony.* Coronation of Louis XV of France, 1722. Artist, Antoine Danchet.

dazzled the eyes of the onlookers, and its allegorical representations replaced the advent's symbolic show of force.[25]

Ceremonial texts specified the event's current secular meaning. The elaborate volume describing the coronation of the twelve-year-old Louis XV in 1722 contained not only descriptions but also allegorical explanations and illustrations of the individual ceremonies.[26] The mystery of the anointment is turned into a moral lesson, celebrating a goddess, resplendent with the glories of power and civilization, who represents the nation (figs. 1, 2). Allegorized France rises to the heavens where, "penetrated with recognition and admiration," she meets the descending figures of the Virtues—Justice, Prudence, Power, and Temperance. Writhing under the arch of the heavens are Heresy, Duel, and Discord, whom "the heavenly oil has sworn to proscribe." The person of the king has been omitted from an allegory whose significance

[25] Anton Haueter, *Die Krönungen der französischen Könige im Zeitalter des Absolutismus und in der Restauration* (Zurich, 1975), 83–86; Rudolf H. Wackernagel, *Der französische Krönungswagen von 1696–1825* (Berlin, 1966), 233, 320–29.

[26] *Le sacre de Louis XV, roi de France et de Navarre dans l'Église de Reims* (Paris, 1732). The volume is not paginated.

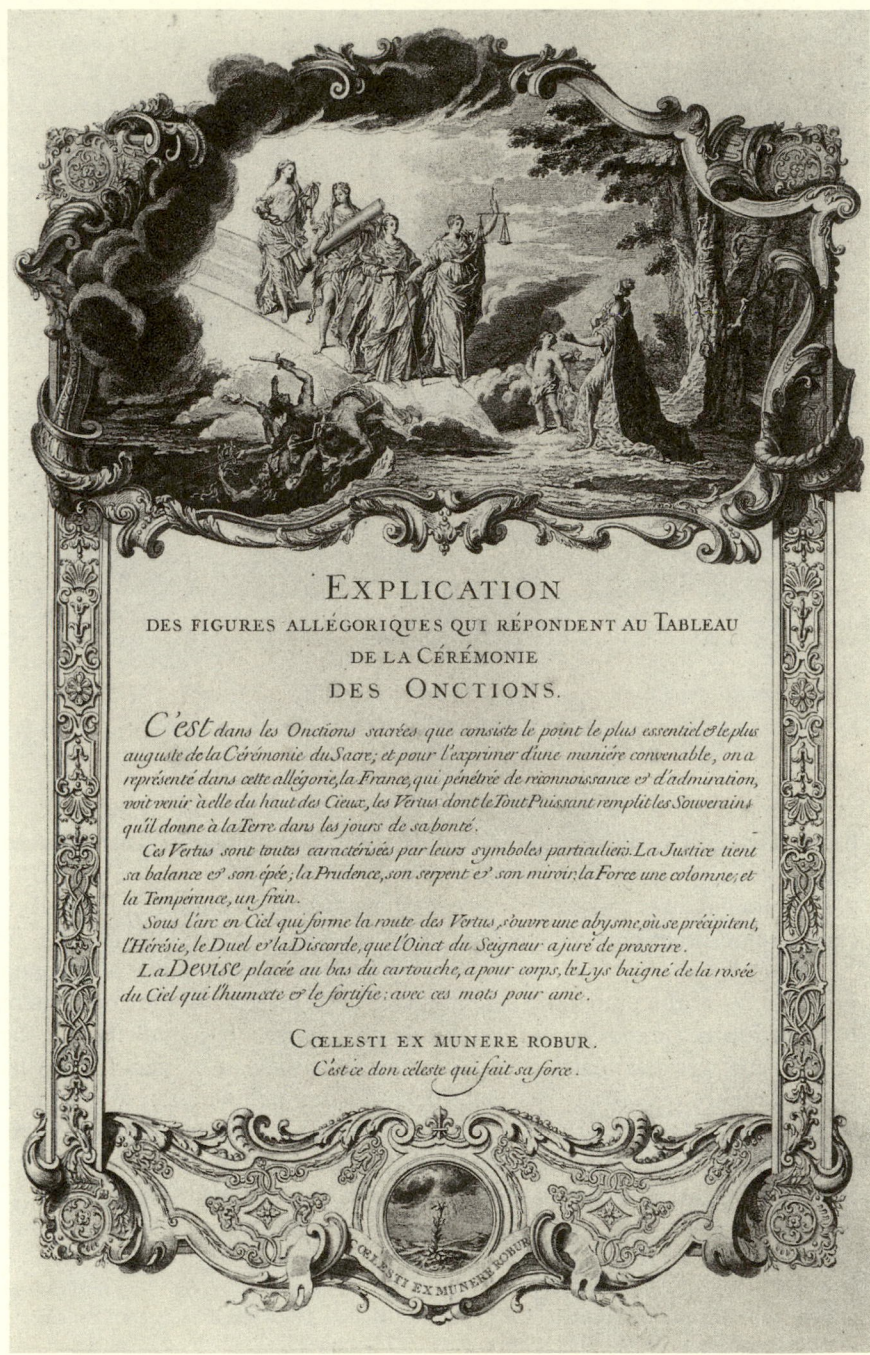

2. Allegory of anointment of Louis XV in 1722. Artist, Antoine Danchet.

pertains principally to the moral benefit of the nation. The same explanations and illustrations were reproduced in Louis XVI's coronation album published in 1775.[27]

Just as the symbols and myths of the Holy Roman Empire provided models for royal presentation in the sixteenth and seventeenth centuries, the court of Louis XIV displayed the festive events and forms of representation taken on by rulers of the eighteenth century. The monarch's court became the symbol of sovereignty and culture, especially in Central and Eastern Europe. The princes of the small German states created by the Treaty of Westphalia built their own little Versailles, the magnificence of their courts and the beauty and abundance of their mistresses proving their sovereignty and international significance. They introduced detailed rules of costumes, horses, etiquette, precedence, and protocol that were still more complicated than Versailles's—demonstrating that even a minor prince could be elevated as a monarch.[28] For Russian rulers beginning with Peter the Great, Versailles represented the exemplification of absolute power, a realm where the absolute monarch could display the godlike qualities and the foreign character expected of the ruler of an empire.

[27] *Le sacre et couronnement de Louis XVI, roi de France et de Navarre* (Paris, 1775).

[28] Adrien Fauchier-Magnon, *The Small German Courts of the Eighteenth Century* (London, 1958), 24–25, 34–39; Moine, *Les fêtes à la Cour*, 168–69.

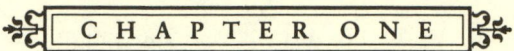

CHAPTER ONE

Viking Princes and Byzantine Emperors

The tributaries of the Varangians drove them back beyond the sea and, refusing them further tribute, set out to govern themselves. There was no law among them, but tribe rose against tribe. Discord then ensued among them, and they began to war one against another. They said to themselves, "Let us seek a prince who may rule over us and judge us according to the Law." They accordingly went overseas to the Varangian Russes: these particular Varangians were known as Russes, just as some are called Swedes and others Normans, English and Gotlanders, for they were thus named. The Chuds, the Slavs, the Krivichians, and the Ves' then said to the people of Rus', "Our land is great and rich, but there is no order in it. Come to rule and reign over us."

—Russian Primary Chronicle[1]

And now, in the most recent year, as in the earlier, may God bless the righteous and Christ-loving great prince, Ivan Vasil'evich, sovereign and autocrat of all Rus', the new tsar Constantine of the new city of Constantine—Moscow, and the sovereign of the entire Russian land and many other lands, as God blessed his kin [St. Vladimir], who was renowned in orthodoxy.

—*Metropolitan Zosima, Preface to* Izlozhenie Paskhalii, *1492*[2]

DESCENT AND ANALOGY

"Royalty is the foreigner" was an overarching motif of Russian political rhetoric and imagery from the beginnings of the Russian state. Kievan princes in the eleventh and twelfth centuries, then the princes of Moscow from the fifteenth century, set the pattern of looking abroad for exemplars of sovereignty that would elevate them above their subjects and give them parity with other monarchs. Their two principal referents were the Varangians, the Scandinavian princes who ostensibly founded Rus', and the Byzantine

---

[1] Samuel Hazard Cross and Olgerd P. Sherbowitz-Wetzor, eds., *The Russian Primary Chronicle: Laurentian Text* (Cambridge, Mass., 1973), 59. Henceforth referred to as Cross.

[2] Quoted in A. L. Gol'dberg, "K predystorii idei 'Moskva-tretii rim,'" in *Kul'turnoe nasledie drevnei rusi; istoki, stanovlenie traditsii* (Moscow, 1976), 114–15.

emperor, who represented the image of Christian sovereign. The monks compiling Russian chronicles availed themselves of devices of descent and analogy to draw such connections. Descent linked the princes with a primal intervention from abroad, marking the dynasty with a foreign origin. Analogy, through metaphor, dress, and architecture, gave the Kievan prince the semblance of the Byzantine emperor.

The Kievan monks who compiled the Russian *Primary Chronicle* in the eleventh and twelfth centuries began the heroic history of the family of Kievan princes with two tales of origin. Both of these emphasized the benefit of forceful rule imposed from outside on a native population deprived of political order and true religious faith. The tale of the invitation of the Varangians, cited in the epigraph, described the legendary beginning of Kiev Rus'. The native Russians, the "tributaries of the Varangians" had recalled the Viking princes to establish order among themselves. Whether this was a true invitation or the justification for an invasion is unknown. A. D. Stendar-Peterson has shown that the legend of an invitation was common in Viking sagas. Most important, the monk compiling the chronicle over two centuries after the event retained the tale of strong rule imposed by outsiders as the beginning of the Kievan dynasty. The Russians then received not only their government but their name, Rus', from the foreign rulers.[3]

The second event was the adoption of Eastern Orthodoxy by Prince Vladimir Sviatoslavich, later Saint Vladimir, in 988. The chronicler presents the conversion of Rus' as a form of conquest—a violent imposition, enforced by a Russian prince, but involving the rejection of native pagan beliefs. The legends included in the chronicle tell that Vladimir consulted representatives of the principal religions—the Muslim, Jewish, Roman Catholic, and Orthodox faiths—before his decision to accept Eastern Orthodoxy. The conversion made possible his marriage to the Byzantine princess Anna, and, according to the chronicle, Vladimir insisted that she arrive in Kherson in time for his baptism. His return to Kiev became the occasion for a public symbolic destruction of the pagan faith. He ordered the idols to be smashed, burned, or cast into the river. The weeping townspeople watched as Perun, the god of thunder and rain, was dragged to the Dnepr. Like later cultural transformations, the conversion of Rus' took the form of a sudden and traumatic imposition from above. Vladimir Solov'ev described it as a form of national self-rejection.[4]

Analogy set Russia in the context of sacred history and allowed the chronicler to state an equivalence between Prince Vladimir and the Emperor Constantine. "He [Vladimir] is the new Constantine of mighty Rome, who baptized himself and his subjects; for the prince of Rus' imitated the acts of

[3] A. D. Stendar-Petersen, *Die Varägersage als Quelle der altrussischen chronik* (Copenhagen, 1934), 42–76; M. D. Priselkov, *Nestor, letopisets* (Petrograd, 1923), 105; D. S. Likhachev, *Russkie letopisi* (Moscow; Leningrad, 1947), 160.

[4] Cross, 112–13, 116; George Florovsky, *Ways of Russian Theology* (Belmont, Mass., 1979), 1:3.

Constantine himself."[5] Kievan coins show princes sometimes as patricians, sometimes as emperors. Kievan cathedrals followed the model of the Byzantine domed-cruciform church, the prince sitting, like the Byzantine emperor, above the congregation in the tribune. The Kievan prince thus emulated the Byzantine emperor without challenging his supremacy.[6] If the myth of the Varangians set the prince above the population, figurative resemblance to the Byzantine emperor provided religious and symbolic sanctions for his pretensions to power and grandeur.

Both these legends from the chronicle convey a tale of the benefits of strong princely rule. The Varangians bring political order at the request of a people incapable of laying their dissension to rest. Vladimir imposes religious truth on a people living in error; he then introduces an organized church, brings books, and founds a cathedral. The motif of the civilizing role of force exerted from above became paradigmatic for both the Muscovite and the Petrine state.

Kiev Rus' was a confederation of towns united by the family of princes who governed them and led by the prince of Kiev. By the end of the twelfth century, this fragile unity had fragmented, the princes settling and ruling in their individual towns. The center of Rus' shifted to the north, to the Vladimir-Suzdal principality, whose princes claimed the title of Great Prince of Kiev. The Mongol invasions in 1220 and 1238 subjected Russia to the domination of the Golden Horde. The khan, at Sarai, was the true sovereign of Russia, and was described with the term *tsar*. But as a Muslim, the khan could not be a referent for Russian images of rule. The Mongol influences that may have affected the exercise of power in Russia had to remain concealed beneath the representations of a Christian monarch. The Mongol conquest could not be a tale of origin and had to be painstakingly denied by the chroniclers, hagiographers, and preachers of Rus'.[7]

The unity of Rus' and the possibility of a Russian sovereign accordingly were little more than memories until the end of the fifteenth century. It was the princes of Moscow, a junior line of the Vladimir princes, who succeeded in "gathering the Russian lands," in the fourteenth and fifteenth centuries. This process culminated during the reign of Ivan III (1462–1505). Ivan subjugated Novgorod in 1478 and renounced his subordination to the khan in 1480. He began to rule Russia as a unified monarchy. He introduced his own coinage, a law code, and created a military force of conditional landowners that provided him with a reliable source of manpower.

Ivan ruled Russia, but as Great Prince of Moscow, lacked the symbols and titles of a sovereign ruler. At this point, Ivan, guided by the hierarchs of the Russian church, began to lay claim to the symbolic heritage of the Byzantine

[5] Cross, 124.

[6] Michael Cherniavsky, "Khan or Basileus: An Aspect of Russian Mediaeval Political Theory," in Cherniavsky, ed., *The Structure of Russian History* (New York, 1970), 66.

[7] Charles J. Halperin, *Russia and the Golden Horde: The Mongol Impact on Medieval Russian History* (Bloomington, Ind., 1985), 61–74.

Empire, which had fallen to the Turks in 1452. He assumed the emperor's titles of tsar and autocrat. The word *tsar*, designating the Byzantine emperor—as well as other foreign sovereigns—derived from the Greek *kaisar*, but was considered the translation for *basileus*, or emperor. It came to connote a Christian emperor as distinguished from the pagan emperors of antiquity, such as Augustus, who was described as *kesar*'.[8]

The designation of a prince as emperor expressed the sense, fundamental to later Russian political attitudes, that imperial sovereignty was the only true sovereignty. The first use of the term *autocrat* (*samoderzhets*) for the Moscow prince occurred in the passage by Metropolitan Zosima cited in the epigraph to this chapter. Zosima turned the analogy between the Moscow prince and the Byzantine emperor into a virtual equivalence.[9] *Samoderzhets*, a calque of the Greek *autocrator*, expressed the supremacy of the Muscovite tsar and his freedom from overlordship: for the first time there was no higher earthly power than the ruler of Moscow.[10]

Ivan III also took on signs of sovereignty from the Western monarchs with whom he claimed parity. In emulation of the seal of the Holy Roman Empire—a double-headed eagle—he introduced his own imperial seal—a crowned Byzantine double-headed eagle, with lowered wings.[11] He married the Byzantine princess Sofia Paleologus, who had been residing in Rome and had cultivated Western artistic tastes. He then set about constructing cathedrals and palaces that would lend his capital a monumental grandeur. Architects from Italy gave the Moscow Kremlin an aspect of Renaissance magnificence. Pietro Solari designed new Kremlin walls and towers in the manner of an Italian walled town. Rodolfo Fioravanti's Assumption Cathedral added greater dimensions and splendor to the domed-cruciform pattern of the Vladimir Assumption Cathedral. Venetian architects decorated the exterior of the Archangel cathedral with a shell motif. The Palace of Facets, the first

---

[8] Vladimir Vodoff has shown that the term *tsar* was frequently attached to princes in the chronicles before Ivan III, usually to designate their religious virtues and religious role (Vladimir Vodoff, "Remarques sur la valeur du terme 'tsar' appliqué aux princes russes avant le milieu du XVe siècle," *Oxford Slavonic Papers* 11 [1978]: 1–41). Also see Gianfranco Giraudo, "*Car', carstvo*, et termes corrélatifs dans les textes russes de la deuxième moitié du XVIe siècle," *Da Roma alla Terza Roma* (Rome, 1983), 3:550–51.

[9] A. L. Gol'dberg, "K predystorii idei 'Moskva-tretii rim,'" 114–15. But I see no justification in the text for Gol'dberg's claim that the comparison now assumed the character of an opposition between Moscow and Constantinople with Moscow overshadowing Constantinople.

[10] Marc Szeftel, "The Title of Muscovite Monarch up to the End of the Seventeenth Century," *Canadian Slavic Studies*, vol. 13, nos. 1–2 (Spring–Summer, 1979): 65–66.

[11] Gustave Alef concludes that the double-headed eagle, a symbol but never a seal in Byzantium, was adopted to give Ivan an imperial symbol equal to the double-headed eagle on the seal of the Holy Roman emperor. See Gustave Alef, "The Adoption of the Muscovite Two-Headed Eagle: A Discordant View," in his *Rulers and Nobles in Fifteenth-Century Muscovy* (London, 1983), Section 9; G. V. Vilinbakhov, "Vsadnik russkogo gerba," *Trudy Gosudarstvennogo Ermitazha* 21 (1981): 117–18; E. N. Voronets, *Chetyrekhsotletie Rossiiskogo Gosudarstvennogo Gerba* (Kharkov, 1898), 16–29; *BE*, vol. 17, 405–8, 411–13; A. B. Lakier, *Russkaia Geral'dika* (Moscow, 1990), 141–42.

stone residence of a Russian ruler, was an imitation of a Renaissance palace.

Like the Holy Roman Emperors and other Western monarchs, the Moscow princes supported their claims to sovereignty with mythological genealogies that showed their illustrious imperial descent. "The Tale of the Vladimir Princes," composed in the first half of the sixteenth century, introduced into the historical record a brother of Augustus, Prus, who presumably ruled the Prussian lands and was a direct ancestor of Riurik. It then traced the lineage of the Moscow princes back to Riurik. The "Tale" was entirely a ruler myth—that is, unlike the myths of Trojan origin common in Europe, it gave no hint of a connection between the Russian people and a mythical Trojan migration.[12] It became a principal justification for the imperial pretensions of Muscovy during the sixteenth century. Ivan IV, boasting of his "German" descent from Riurik, asserted that he was no "Russe."[13] He explained the eagle on the imperial shield by referring to his blood relationship to Augustus. Russian diplomats cited the "Tale" to bolster their claims against the Polish-Lithuanian state. This reconstruction of the past provided the basis for the first Muscovite "historical" work, the *Book of Degrees* (*Stepennaia Kniga*) and the collection of Saints' lives (*Chet'ia-Minei*), both composed under the metropolitan Macarius's direction in the mid-sixteenth century.[14]

The authors of the "Tale of the Vladimir Princes" also drew a direct connection with the Byzantine Empire. The second part, "The Legend of Monomakh," described a long tradition and "ancient" regalia for the Russian imperial coronation. According to the legend, Vladimir Monomakh received imperial regalia from the Emperor Constantine Monomakh—the prince's grandfather, who had actually died before his accession—to forestall an attack against Byzantium. The regalia of Monomakh comprised the "life-giving cross," a pectoral cross with a piece of the wood from the cross of the crucifixion; the *barmy*, a counterpart to the Byzantine emperors' shoulder pieces; the crown, "Monomakh's cap," which was probably of Tatar origin; and a chain of the "gold of Araby."[15]

---

[12] See Edward S. Reisman, "The Absence of a Common-Descent Myth for Rus'," *Russian History/Histoire russe*, vol. 15, no. 1 (1988): 9–19; Susan Reynolds, "Medieval *Origines Gentium* and the Community of the Realm," *History*, vol. 68, no. 224 (October 1983): 375–90.

[13] R. P. Dmitrieva, *Skazanie o kniaziakh vladimiriskikh* (Moscow-Leningrad, 1955), 5; Edward Keenan, "Royal Russian Behavior, Style and Self-Image," in Edward Allworth, ed., *Ethnic Russia in the USSR: The Dilemma of Dominance* (New York, 1981), 15.

[14] V. O. Kliuchevskii, *Sochineniia* (Moscow, 1957), 2:122–30; Dmitrieva, 5–6, 154–55; Robert Lee Wolff, "The Three Romes: The Migration of an Ideology and the Making of an Autocrat," *Daedalus*, vol. 88, no. 2 (Spring 1959): 301–2.

[15] Giuseppe Olshr, "La Chiesa e lo Stato nel cerimoniale d'incoronazione degli ultimi sovrani Rurikidi," *Orientalia Christiana Periodica* 16 (1950), fasc. 3–4:283, 292–93. I am most indebted to Alberto Masoero for his translation of this work. On the regalia, see also D. I. Prozorovskii, "Ob utvariakh pripisyvaemykh Vladimiru Monomakhu," *Zapiski otdeleniia russkoi i slavianskoi arkheologii Imperatorskogo russkogo arkheologicheskogo obshchestva* 3 (1882): 1–64; Dmitrieva, *Skazanie o kniaziakh vladimiriskikh*, 116–17; Robert Craig Howes, ed., *The Testaments of the Grand Princes of Moscow* (Ithaca, N.Y., 1967), 97–103.

While Western monarchs used such tales to free themselves from the domination of the Roman Catholic church, the Russian legends were created by the church hierarchs themselves. They elevated the clergy, with the tsar, as heirs to the Byzantine imperial mission of defending the faith. The symbiotic relationship between tsar and church reflected the late Byzantine concept of the "symphony" between secular and ecclesiastical spheres as elaborated in the Byzantine book of canons, *Kormchaia Kniga*. In Roman Catholic states, we see a separation between secular and ecclesiastical authority, reflected in the contractual relationship Le Goff has described in regard to the French coronation. In Russia, the interests of church and throne were indivisible, and the early Russian coronation served as a lavish avowal at the outset of each reign of their mutual fealty.

The Russian coronation was a ceremony of absolutism, with none of the medieval holdovers of the French or English coronations. The metropolitan Macarius composed the first coronation of a Russian tsar in 1547 to consecrate and make known the imperial identity of the seventeen-year-old Ivan IV. Macarius adapted his ceremony from late Byzantine rites of the fourteenth century.[16] The regalia of Monomakh were the sacred items conferring the imperial succession on the princes of Moscow and now the tsar of Russia. The investiture of the tsar with the regalia constituted the principal moment of Ivan's coronation, which did not include an anointment ceremony.[17] The rite opened with a dialogue between the tsar and metropolitan, Ivan asking Macarius to consecrate his hereditary claims to the title of Russian tsar. Ivan announced that since Vladimir Monomakh, all his ancestors had been crowned. He also mentioned his father's command that he be crowned, "according to our ancient rite" (*po drevnemu nashemu tsarskomu chinu*). The metropolitan replied by confirming the tsar's ancestral rights to the imperial crown. He then lowered the life-giving cross around the tsar's neck, placed his hands on the tsar's head and pronounced the benediction, as in a clerical ordination. This gesture, the metropolitan declared, achieved the act of consecration.[18]

After conferring the "holy *barmy*," Macarius crowned Ivan, then handed

---

[16] G. A. Ostrogorskii, "Evoliutsiia vizantiiskogo obriada koronovaniia," in *Vizantiia, iuzhnye slaviane i drevniaia rus', Zapadnaia Evropa* (Moscow, 1973), 38–39; David B. Miller, "The Coronation of Ivan IV of Moscow," *Jahrbücher für Geschichte Osteuropas* 15 (1967): 559–74.

[17] The anointment was added to a later coronation order that served as a program for future coronations. See B. A. Uspenskii, "Tsar i Patriarkh: kharizma vlasti v Rossii (Visantiiskaia model' i eia russkoe pereosmylenie)," manuscript article.

[18] M. V. Shakhmatov, "Gosudarstvenno-natsional'nye idei 'chinovnykh knig' venchaniia na tsarstvo moskovskikh gosudarei," *Zapiski russkogo nauchnogo instituta v Belgrade* 1 (1930): 250–51, 259–60; Miller, "The Coronation of Ivan IV," 559–61; Dmitrieva, *Skazanie o kniaziakh vladimiriskikh*, 44–52, DRV 7:1–4; E. V. Barsov, *Drevnerusskie pamiatniki sviashchennogo venchaniia tsarei na tsarstvo v sviazi s grecheskimi ikh originalami* (Moscow, 1883), 72–75; Olshr, "La Chiesa e lo Stato nel cerimoniale d'incoronazione degli ultimi sovrani Rurikidi," 295–97.

him the scepter. He concluded the first part of the ceremony by delivering the precept (*pouchenie*). Written by Macarius and derived from the homily of the Deacon Agapetus to the Emperor Justinian, the precept was an extended admonition on the tsar's obligations to the church and his subjects. It ended on an eschatological note; the metropolitan envisioned the tsar's ascent into the heavens where the Russian tsar would rule with Christ and all the saints in recompense for his "imperial exploits (*tsarskie podvigi*) and labors."[19]

The legend of Monomakh was the guiding myth of the early Russian coronation, and the regalia of Monomakh became the sacred insignia of the power of the tsar that were consecrated by the Russian Orthodox Church. The coronation took place in the Assumption Cathedral (*Uspenskii Sobor* means more precisely Dormition Cathedral, but I have retained the customary translation) in the Moscow Kremlin—the see of the metropolitans who had allied themselves with the princes of Moscow since the fourteenth century. The coronation ceremonies surrounded the regalia with gestures of liturgical veneration. The tolling of the church bells, the darkness of the cathedral and aroma of incense, the saints looking down from the walls and the iconostasis all combined to produce an atmosphere of timeless mystery, as if the generations of princes and emperors had joined the living in the consecration of power.[20] Ceremony turned the fiction of imperial succession into sacred truth.

The legend of Monomakh played the same role as the legend of the Holy Ampulla in the French coronation. Both evoked sources of the charisma transmitted to the bearer of power by sacred articles—the regalia in Russia, the oil in France. Both invoked descent to establish the historical connection of the present ruler to the recipients of the initial charismatic gift. But their motifs suggest the different character of the charisma they bestowed. The vial containing the oil of Clovis that consecrated the power of Capetian kings, according to the French legend, was borne in the beak of a dove sent from heaven. It attested to the providential origins of French monarchy; God bestowed his sanction directly on the clergy and kings, without imperial mediation. The legend expressed an early sense of the continuity of the realm and the unity of the nation around the king.[21]

The Monomakh legend accentuated the derivative character of Russian

---

[19] Barsov, *Drevnerusskie pamiatniki*, 80–84; Miller, "The Coronation of Ivan IV," 567–69; Ihor Ševčenko, "A Neglected Source of Muscovite Political Ideology," in Michael Cherniavsky, ed., *The Structure of Russian History*, 92; Douglas Joseph Bennet, Jr., "The Idea of Kingship in Seventeenth-Century Russia," Ph.D. dissertation, Harvard University, 1967, 91–94.

[20] On the early Russian notion of time, according to which "descendants repeat their forbears like an echo," see A. M. Panchenko, "Istoriia i vechnost' v sisteme kul'turnykh tsennostei russkogo barokko," *Trudy otdela drevnei russkoi literatury* 34 (1979): 189–99.

[21] Ralph E. Giesey, "Models of Rulership in French Royal Ceremonial," 43; Janet L. Nelson, "The Lord's anointed and the people's choice: Carolingian royal ritual," in David Cannadine and Simon Price, eds., *Rituals of Royalty: Power and Ceremonial in Traditional Societies* (Cambridge, 1987), 137–80.

sovereignty: sanction came not from God directly, but through the mediation of the Byzantine Empire, and political and ecclesiastical authority strove to recapture a Byzantine image. The oil of Clovis, descending from heaven, bestowed miraculous powers, like the power to cure scrofula on the French kings. The Monomakh legend was a secular myth; it invoked neither miracle nor pretensions to supernatural powers. Rather, it derived from the Kievan prince's valor in his invasion or threatened invasion of Constantinople. The prince, according to the precept, would rule in heaven as a result of his deeds on earth, his "imperial exploits (*tsarskie podvigi*) and labors." The Muscovite coronation, in this way, gave the image of conqueror religious sanction. It united the destiny of the orthodox church with the success of the secular empire. Ivan IV considered his coronation a justification for his use of the title of tsar and mentioned it frequently to defend challenges to his sovereignty, especially from Poland.[22]

The first Russian imperial coronation consisted of a ceremony of investiture and a mass. Uspenskii and Tikhoniuk have shown that the original ceremony did not include a rite of anointment. But a coronation order, composed probably in the mid-1550s, contained a description of his anointment during the mass. Like the investiture, the anointment was a ceremony of absolutism, introduced to ensure recognition of the Moscow tsar's sovereign status. Anointment was added as an afterthought, perhaps to secure the blessing of the Patriarch of Constantinople. It took place *after* the investiture, unlike the French, English, and Byzantine coronations, and played no role in the consecration of the tsar's secular power. Rather, Uspenskii has argued convincingly, it was endowed with sacramental meaning, for the Russian clerics composing the ceremony confused the coronation anointment with the *sacrament* of anointing at baptism. It endowed the tsar with a special charisma that set him apart as the most holy of laymen, and, in the eyes of some, identifying him with Christ.[23] Once again, a foreign form was borrowed and given heightened and purified meaning to stress the claims of the Russian tsar to absolute power.

The myths of derivation were accompanied by efforts to realize the imperial vision of rule over extensive realms and other peoples. Ivan's conquest of Kazan and Astrakhan brought the first non-Russian territories under Muscovite suzerainty. The victory over Kazan was marked by a triumphal pro-

---

[22] Barsov, *Drevne-russkie pamiatniki*, xxiii–iv; Olshr, "La Chiesa e lo Stato nel cerimoniale d'incoronazione degli ultimi sovrani Rurikidi," 293.

[23] Whereas the Byzantine patriarch uttered the words "Holy, Holy, Holy . . ." at the moment of oiling, the Russian declaimed, "The seal and the gift of the Holy Ghost . . ." This difference, Uspenskii remarks, is the difference between Old and New Testament consecrations: the Byzantine signifying the God-chosen monarch, like the kings of Israel, and the Russian, the tsar in the image of Christ (B. A. Uspenskii, "Tsar i Patriarkh: kharizma vlasti v Rossii [Visantiiskaia model' i eia russkoe pereosmylenie]," unpublished manuscript; I. A. Tikhoniuk, "O Vizantiiskom obraztse tsarskoi koronatsii Ivana Groznogo," unpublished manuscript; see also Olshr, "La Chiesa e lo Stato nel cerimoniale d'incoronazione degli ultimi sovrani Rurikidi," 296–97).

gress through Russian towns, culminating in a ceremonial entry to Moscow. These processions celebrated the victory of the conqueror, but unlike Roman triumphs, attributed Ivan's successes to God and the clergy. The principal references were to Byzantium and the "Legend of Monomakh." Before Ivan entered Moscow, he removed his armor and dressed himself in the Monomakh cap, the *barmy*, and the life-giving cross.[24]

Ivan's imperial designs were thwarted by the defeat of his efforts to expand to the West during the Livonian Wars. But the imperial pretensions remained. He began to use the word *Rossiia*, greater Russia ruled by the Russian tsar, instead of *Rus'*, which referred to the core territories of the Muscovite principality. Ivan elaborated the imperial seal. He added a shield on the eagle's breast that depicted "the rider," the Moscow prince on horseback holding a lance. The seals of the various principalities and territories ruled by Moscow surrounded the eagle.[25] The establishment of a patriarchate in Russia under Tsar Fedor in 1589 gave the head of the Russian church the supreme ecclesiastical title in Greek Orthodoxy and brought the Russian empire closer to the Byzantine model.

The patriarch of Constantinople, confirming the title of tsar in a charter of 1561, likened Ivan IV to a Byzantine emperor, "tsar and sovereign of Orthodox Christians of the whole universe from the East to the West and as far as the ocean."[26] But in stating their claims to parity, the Russian tsars did not echo the Constantinople patriarch's vision of dominion over the "whole universe." The imperial heritage set Russian monarchy on the same symbolic plane as Western monarchs and gave them the religious, cultural, and historical grounds to rule absolutely in Russia. It showed that Russia possessed the symbolic heritage that demonstrated sovereignty in the West.[27]

•

The seventeenth century began with the "Time of Troubles," the cataclysmic social and political breakdown following the demise of the dynasty that had ruled Moscow. The country fell into civil war between the various social groups and reunited only after invasion by Swedish and Polish armies. A movement of national unity, summoned by the hierarchs of the church, was led by Kuz'ma Minin, a merchant, and Prince Dmitrii Pozharskii, a military servitor. The movement culminated with the convening of an assembly

[24] Michael Cherniavsky, "Russia," in Orest Ranum, ed., *National Consciousness, History, and Political Culture in Early-Modern Europe* (Baltimore, Md., 1975), 125.

[25] Giraudo, "*Car', carstvo*, et termes corrélatifs," 563–68; Alef, "The Adoption of the Muscovite Two-Headed Eagle," sect. 9; G. V. Vilinbakhov, "Vsadnik russkogo gerba," *Trudy Gosudarstvennogo Ermitazha*, vol. 21 (1981): 117–18; Lakier, *Russkaia Geral'dika*, 141–42, 149.

[26] Marc Szeftel, "The Title of Muscovite Monarch up to the End of the Seventeenth Century," *Canadian Slavic Studies*, vol. 13, nos. 1–2 (Spring–Summer, 1979): 70–71.

[27] See the analysis of the theme of empire in the *Stepennaia kniga*, in Peter Nitsche, "Translatio imperii? Beobachtungen zum historischen Selstverständnis im Moskauer Zartum um Mitte des 16. Jahrhunderts," *Jahrbucher für Geschichte Osteuropas* 35 (1987), 321–38.

of all the estates of the realm, which, after considerable intrigue, elected Michael Romanov tsar.

The end of the Troubles and the election of Michael, the historian Vasilii Kliuchevskii wrote, brought a new national consciousness to Russian political life. Russians no longer regarded their country as the possession of the Muscovite tsar, but as a state ruled by a tsar and including the people. At the time, Kliuchevskii believed, this was only an idea, but in the future it could inspire the development of a state devoted to its people.[28] The introduction of the "state" as a category in Russian political discourse indeed proved to be a major change. During the seventeenth century, the Russian administration expanded and became more complex. The armed forces also grew, and increasing numbers of them were regular, barracked troops. At the same time, the orthodox church came under increasing state control.

But the Romanov monarchy of the seventeenth century restored and even widened the distance between ruler and ruled. The social disturbances of the Troubles continued through the first half of the century, and the tsar succeeded in restoring his earlier control only in the first decade of the reign of Alexei Mikhailovich (1645–1676). Alexei summoned an Assembly that drafted a law code, the *Ulozhenie* of 1649, which addressed the social grievances of the various groups and at the same time created service obligations that strengthened and extended the power of the central state. The establishment of a state-sponsored system of serfdom cemented the alliance between military servitors and the throne. For the next two centuries, both nobles and townspeople would seek their advantages by addressing the throne.[29]

The Law Code laid to rest the principal grievances of the middle serving class and townspeople. The peasantry, subjected to bondage, was helpless. The peasants' discontent would erupt in bloody revolts over the next century, which served only to strengthen the landlords' power over them and deprive them of their few remaining rights. The landlords and governmental officials became the tsar's partners in rule, dominating the subjugated population on the land. They also participated in presentations of his power that elevated them above the melee of social interests as servants of the Russian tsar. With Alexei Mikhailovich's reign, the Russian court begins to resemble the courts of Western monarchs, where the tsar's servitors joined in collective expressions of devotion to the monarchical myth and in displays that set them in a higher mythical realm.

Rather than seek rapport with the people, the Romanovs strove to reclaim the imperial dignity of their predecessors. The principle of election compromised the tsar's absolute power and never became one of the theoretical grounds of the monarchy. Official sources explained Michael's election as an

[28] Kliuchevskii, *Sochineniia* 3: 14–17, 68–69.

[29] A brief account of the terms and effects of the law can be found in Richard Hellie, *Readings for Introduction to Russian Civilization: Muscovite Society* (Chicago, 1970). See also Richard Hellie, *Enserfment and Military Change in Muscovy* (Chicago, 1971), 135–37.

act of divine intervention.[30] At Michael's coronation, it was announced that he, too, was descended from the "Great Riurik" and St. Vladimir, with no indication that the succession had been broken. Later in the seventeenth century, the *Great State Book*, an illustrated collection of brief biographies of the princes and tsars, repeated the genealogy of the "Tale of the Vladimir Princes." The volume began with portraits of Augustus and Riurik. Paintings on the walls of the Palace of Facets included Augustus, with his three sons, seated on thrones, and Riurik in a pictorial genealogy of the dynasty.[31]

But, during the seventeenth century, the new dynasty increasingly played down its tenuous mythical origins and emphasized resemblances to imperial models. Analogy overshadowed descent in the search for appropriate images of sovereignty, a process that culminated at the end of the century when Peter the Great adopted the symbols and ceremonies of the Baroque. The annexation of the eastern parts of Little Russia, including Kiev, and of White Russia, including Smolensk, during the 1650s and 1660s, gave new territorial grounds for imperial claims. The Russian tsar now could claim to be "tsar of all the Russias." The word *Rossiia* (greater Russia) increasingly replaced *Rus'* in official documents and ceremonies. The seal was expanded to reflect the new imperial grandeur like those of Western monarchs. The "state seal" that Alexei Mikhailovich introduced in 1667 was composed under the supervision of the Austrian Heraldry-Master Lavrentii Khurulevich. The eagle's wings were raised as on the seal of the Holy Roman Empire. Three crowns above the eagle's heads symbolized the possession of Kazan, Astrakhan, and Siberia, while three sets of columns on the borders represented the "cities," Great, Little, and White Russia. The eagle held the orb and scepter in its talons, which signified, according to a decree of 1667, "the most gracious Sovereign, His Imperial Majesty (*Tsarskoe Velichestvo*), Autocrat, and Possessor."[32]

During the first years of Alexei's reign, while the tsar was still a youth, the Patriarch Nikon dominated the government, as "co-sovereign." A gifted individual with grandiose dreams, Nikon saw himself embodying the imperial legacy and making Russia the center of a universal Christian Empire. Such a vision required the establishment of an imperial religion, set above the local peculiarities of Russian liturgy and books, which had been declared canonical at the church councils of the sixteenth century. In 1653 Nikon introduced reforms that imposed the original Byzantine liturgy and books, which he found in Greek and Ukrainian sources, on the Russian church. Nikon

[30] Bennet, "The Idea of Kingship," 45–69.

[31] Nikita Chakirov, ed., *Tsarskie koronatsii na Rusi* (New York, 1971), 52–62; Michael Cherniavsky, *Tsar and People: Studies in Russian Myths* (New Haven, Conn., 1961), 59; Frank Kämpfer, *Das russische Herrscherbild von den Anfangen bis zu Peter den Grossen* (Recklinghausen, 1978), 84, 218–20.

[32] Lakier, *Russkaia Geral'dika*, 142–50; V. Lukomskii, "Gosudarstvennyi gerb," *Novyi entsiklopedicheskii slovar'*, vol. 14 (St. Petersburg, ?), 471–72; E. N. Voronets, *Chertyrekhsotletie Rossiiskogo Gosudarstvennogo Gerba*, 27; PSZ, 421, 1667.

achieved his goal of creating an imperial religion, with claims to universal rather than parochial truth, and his reforms brought into the fold the Ukrainian clergy, who had been educated in Western, often Jesuit seminaries. The Nikonian reforms were the cultural and political equivalent of the original conversion to Christianity. Ruthlessly enforced, they alienated large numbers of those faithful to the "Old Belief," who resisted or immolated themselves rather than submit to what they perceived as a foreign heresy.

Although Alexei turned against Nikon after 1658, he preserved the reforms. He also remained faithful to the image of Byzantine emperor that Nikon had taught him to emulate. Nikon had insisted that Alexei receive communion wearing imperial vestments rather than the traditional Russian communion robes, and initiated the tsar into a severe liturgical routine that he believed exemplified the Christian emperor. Alexei maintained this hieratic manner even after Nikon's fall from grace. He ordered opulent golden *barmy*, as well as an orb and scepter from Istanbul patterned on the models of Greek emperors. The tsar's performance of elaborate rituals, ensuring the salvation of his flock, revealed the timeless holiness of his power, his preeminence before his subjects and servitors. He was described as "most serene," a translation of the Greek *Galenotetos*. The word *holy, sviatoi*, included in the title of the Byzantine emperor, was now attached to Alexei's title.[33]

The tsar thus placed himself above his subjects by appearing as the supreme worshiper of the realm, whose piety exceeded theirs. Michael Cherniavsky and A. N. Robinson have pointed out the new personal element of Alexei's performance of the tsar's role.[34] Alexei's piety was presented not as a feature of an abstract image of tsar but as a distinctive personal quality, demonstrating spiritual and therefore political preeminence. His almost monastic regimen of worship was the first clear example of an imperial scenario, a concerted and organized demonstration of an individual tsar's embodiment of a foreign image of rule. He was called "the young monk."

Like the nobilities of other emerging monarchies, the Russian service elite set themselves apart from the ruled by claiming, often fictional, foreign ancestries, both Tatar and European. According to the "Felt Book," which listed the families of high Russian servitors at the close of the seventeenth century, only 75 of 1,758 noble families, or less than 5 percent, admitted to Russian origins.[35] The tsar's servitors demonstrated their adherence to his

[33] I. E. Zabelin, *Domashnii byt Russkikh tsarei v XVI i XVII st.*, vol. 2 (Moscow, 1915), 489–90; I. A. Bobrovnitskaia et al., *Gosudarstvennaia oruzheinaia palata* (Moscow, 1988), 350–51; Kliuchevskii, *Sochineniia* 3:320–26; Bennet, "The Idea of Kingship," iii; V. M. Zhivov and B. A. Uspenskii, "'Tsar' i Bog; Semioticheskie aspekty sakralizatsii monarkha v Rossii," in B. A. Uspenskii, ed., *Iazyki kul'tury i problemy perevodimosti* (Moscow, 1987), 74–75.

[34] A. N. Robinson, *Bor'ba idei v russkoi literature XVII veka* (Moscow, 1974), 73–76; Cherniavsky, *Tsar and People*, 62–64.

[35] Nikolai Zagoskin, *Ocherki organizatsii i proiskhozhdeniia sluzhilogo sosloviia v dopetrovskoi rusi* (Kazan, 1876), 176–78; Halperin discusses the invention of fictitious noble

sovereign power by joining his displays of piety. They shared his devotional regimen as if they, too, were monks, his brethren. They took part in all the services, processions, and receptions under threat of punishment, showing their self-abnegation as "the tsar's slaves."[36] In keeping with the monastic regime, women, with rare exceptions, were barred; the tsarevna watched ceremonies, including the coronation, through a concealed window.[37]

The servitors joining Alexei in his ceremonies constituted an imperial court, a collective presentation of the tsar and the elite who assisted him in the exercise of power and the extension of his empire. The servitors' positions in the ceremony revealed their status in the court, their closeness to the tsar, and the power and influence they could wield. Ceremonial rules (*chiny*) were issued for many functions, such as ambassadorial receptions, weddings, and banquets. Alexei broke with the tradition of determining position at official functions by "place," set by the servitor's lineage (*mestnichestvo*). Now the tsar himself determined the arrangement of his servitors. At his wedding, Alexei demanded absolute discipline from the members of the court in following the prescribed action and had the chief servitors sit in a new order.[38]

Most imperial ceremony remained within the precincts of palace and cathedral, where only those high in the service could behold the tsar's "bright eyes."[39] On major religious holidays, however, the tsar displayed the grandeur of his court in a procession that left the palace and vested spiritual ascendancy in attributes of secular magnificence. These processions dis-

---

ancestries and the difficulties of determining actual origins (*Russia and the Golden Horde*, 111–13.

[36] Robert O. Crummey, *Aristocrats and Servitors: The Boyar Elite in Russia, 1613–1689* (Princeton, N.J., 1983), 140–42, 170–71, 253; I. E. Zabelin, *Domashnii byt russkikh tsarits v XVI i XVII st.* (Moscow, 1901), 289.

[37] Nancy Shields Kollmann, "The Seclusion of Elite Muscovite Women," *Russian History*, vol. 10, pt. 2 (1983), 170–87. The Tsarevna, Sofia Alekseevna, educated by Western tutors, broke with this tradition when she followed her brother Fedor's casket in his funeral procession in 1682. C. Bickford O'Brien, *Russia under Two Tsars, 1682–1689: The Regency of Sophia Alekseevna* (Berkeley and Los Angeles, 1952), 21–22.

[38] Crummey, *Aristocrat and Servitor*, 169–72; Robinson, *Bor'ba idei v russkoi literature*, 105–7. For a different view, see Nancy Shields Kollmann, *Kinship and Politics: The Making of the Muscovite Political System, 1345–1547*, 146–48. While Kollmann's arguments about the complexity of boyar marital politics and the maintenance of an image of harmonious relationships are convincing, I see no evidence of procedures, either formal or informal, that allowed them to participate as a group in legislation or decision making or that allowed them to determine key appointments. One could argue equally that the "harmony" of the court was a "facade" or "fiction" concealing the domination of the elite by the ruler. In her treatment of the seventeenth-century court (Nancy Shields Kollmann, "Ritual and Social Drama at the Muscovite Court," *Slavic Review*, vol. 45, no. 3 [Fall, 1986], 490, 500), Kollmann shows how ceremony indicated the boyars' right "to be accorded high social status and benefit economically from authority." But I see no evidence of "a traditional right to share in power."

[39] Robert O. Crummey, "Court Spectacles in Seventeenth-Century Russia: Illusion and Reality," in Daniel Clarke Waugh, ed., *Essays in Honor of A. A. Zimin* (Columbus, Ohio, 1985), 130–31.

played Alexei in his newly fashioned Monomakh regalia, the Great Array (*Bol'shoi nariad*) that marked the tsar as the equivalent of the Byzantine emperor, whether or not they were of Byzantine origin themselves (fig. 3). He wore new ornately wrought gold crowns, copies of "Monomakh's cap," with countless gems crafted by foreign workmen in his service or imported from abroad.[40] His gold-embroidered robes had emerald buttons, and his gold bracelets were strung with pearls. His servitors were also dressed in rich clothing with gems.[41] The processions, in the company of the clergy, presented a hieratic image of Christian emperor, surrounded by his servitors and the clergy. The most sumptuous of these was the Blessing of the Waters, which took place each year on the celebration of Epiphany on January 6. The tsar and patriarch proceeded to the Moscow River where the patriarch blessed the waters, through a hole in the ice, and blessed the tsar with the water. This ceremony had little resemblance to its Byzantine prototype, which remained within the confines of the palace. The emperor played the central role in the Byzantine ceremony, whereas in the Russian version of the sixteenth century, the metropolitan dominated the proceedings, sitting on the throne while the tsar stood. In the early seventeenth century, these positions were reversed, and in later decades the ceremony depended on the power balance between tsar and patriarch.[42]

Regardless of its origins, by the close of the seventeenth century, the Blessing of the Waters had become a celebration of the unity of an imperial elite set apart from the ruled by symbols of power and sumptuous dress. The tsar appeared in elaborate robes, thought to resemble Byzantine dress and called the purple (*porfiry*); they were of Venetian gold cloth, lined with ermine, with buttons set with precious stones. He wore the *barmy*, and a crown set with a ruby. He carried the golden imperial scepter, also studded with gems. The "life-giving cross" from the regalia of Monomakh hung on a golden chain. Accounts mention that the tsar was supported under the arm by two boyars who helped him to bear the great weight of his attire. His slow and laborious movement at the end of a long procession emphasized the remote and static character of his power.[43] The courtiers also marched in rich robes; those dressed in ordinary cloth caftans could witness the ceremony but could not participate in the procession.

It was an imposing show of domination. But perhaps the most striking

[40] These were made in the shape of the "Monomakh cap," but with considerably more elaborate gold work and many more gems. Bobrovnitskaia et al., *Gosudarstvennaia oruzheinaia palata*, 344–47.

[41] Zabelin, *Domashnii byt Russkikh tsarei* 1:376–79; 2:481–82; Robinson, *Bor'ba idei v russkoi literature*, 100.

[42] Bushkovitch argues that the ceremony arose from folk rituals with the church seeking to co-opt and transform rites it was banning. Paul A. Bushkovitch, "The Epiphany Ceremony of the Russian Court in the Sixteenth and Seventeenth Centuries," *The Russian Review* (January 1990), vol. 49, no. 1: 1–18.

[43] On this aspect, see the remarks by A. K. Baiburin and A. L. Toporkov, *U istokov etiketa* (Leningrad, 1990), 66.

3. *Tsar Alexei Mikhailovich*. Portrait.

aspect of the Blessing was the massive presence of armed forces, particularly the musketeers (*strel'tsy*), the regular barracked troops who served as the palace guard and internal police force. Two hundred of them, dressed in bright uniforms and carrying gilded muskets, golden spears, and harquebuses plated with mother-of-pearl, led in the procession, while 150 accompanied the tsar. Another regiment, with drums and standards, guarded the route. At the end of the seventeenth century, a detachment of brightly dressed cannoneers stood guard at their guns during the ceremony.[44] The ceremony of the Blessing of the Waters had begun to resemble a European triumph.

Other ceremonies gave shows of the harmony between the secular and the religious leaders. On New Year's Day in September, the tsar and the patriarch led processions to Red Square, where they met and kissed.[45] Foreigners were especially impressed with the annual Palm Sunday procession from the Assumption Cathedral in the Kremlin to the Cathedral of the Intercession (Vasilii the Blessed) on Red Square. The procession reenacted Christ's entry into Jerusalem. The tsar, bedecked in the finery of his imperial robes, holding the scepter in his right hand, led the patriarch, who, sitting side-saddle on a horse, played the role of Christ on the donkey. This ceremony has received several interesting readings that differ on the relative significance of the tsar and the patriarch. But in the context of other seventeenth-century ceremonies, like the Blessing of the Waters and the coronation, it appears as another occasion to display the unity of the elite before the social turmoil threatening the state order. The tsar gave a show of deference to the patriarch as the successor to Christ, even as his government was bringing the church under increasing governmental control. Again the musketeers figure in the presentation. An engraving of the time shows them, not the citizens of Moscow, prostrating themselves before the procession.[46]

Late-seventeenth-century coronation ceremonies introduced additional analogies between the Russian tsar and both the Byzantine emperor and Western monarchs. At his coronation in 1676, Fedor Alekseevich appeared in the entry procession wearing the *opashen'*, a golden caftan that Aleksei had worn in emulation of the Byzantine emperor. The investiture began with the tsar reciting the creed, following the example of the Byzantine, as well as the French and English coronations.

The eloquent opening consecration of the tsar's hereditary claims to the legacy of Kiev and Byzantium now included a statement of the extent of the tsar's rule. Standing before his throne on the dais, Fedor proclaimed that all "Great Sovereigns" of "all Great Russia," going back to Riurik, had been

[44] Zabelin, *Domashnii byt Russkikh tsarei*, 1:397–98.

[45] Samuel Baron, ed., *The Travels of Olearius in 17th-Century Russia* (Stanford, Calif., 1967), 67.

[46] Crummey "Court Spectacles," 132–36; Ernst H. Kantorowicz, "The 'King's Advent' and the Enigmatic Panels in the Doors of Santa Sabina," *Art Bulletin* 26 (1944): 229–30. The Palm Sunday procession had been introduced in the sixteenth century, when the heads of the church sought to elevate the metropolitan by creating a ceremony based on Roman Catholic sources. Recently, Michael Flier set forth a compelling argument for an apocalyptic and eschatological reading of the procession in the sixteenth century. He argues that Ivan IV and the hierarchs of the church employed the analogy with Christ to demonstrate the messianic, theocratic character of the tsar himself (Michael S. Flier, "Emperor as Mythmaker: Ivan the Terrible and the Palm Sunday Ritual," manuscript article).

crowned, including Michael Feodorovich. He used the term *Great Russia*, the word *Rossiia* having replaced the word *Rus'*, to describe the extent of the tsar's imperial authority. This change had occurred in seventeenth-century *chiny* (coronation orders) and expressed the unity of all the Russian areas— Great, Little, and White Russia, as well as Kazan, Astrakhan, and Siberia. But Fedor's *chin* went a step further and referred to the Great Russian Tsardom, *Velikorossiiskoe Tsarstvie*, a term denoting an imperial, absolutist state, subordinating Russian as well as non-Russian territories.[47]

For the first time at a coronation, Fedor Alekseevich received communion at the altar with the clergy, a practice begun during the reign of Alexei. The patriarch and two metropolitans handed him the wafer and the chalice, but he was not allowed to approach the altar or to take communion directly from the paten and chalice as were priests and hierarchs of the church. He received communion as a lesser member of the clergy, like the Byzantine emperors, and thus attained dignities equal to the French kings', who partook of communion of both kinds, like the clergy, at their coronations. All future Russian sovereigns took communion at the altar at their coronations.[48]

The Assumption Cathedral is small. Its floor space is about one-quarter that of Reims Cathedral or Westminster Abbey, and only the highest servitors could witness the services. But many more could see the resplendent processions to and from the cathedral of the assembled elite of the empire— the tsar, the clergy, the serving people—all guarded by the military force of large numbers of musketeers. The opening processions accompanied the regalia, and then the tsar himself, from the Palace of Facets to the cathedral. The tsar followed a priest, who blessed his path with holy water, and a long line of serving people. Officers of the musketeers marched alongside the procession and guarded the staircase leading from the palace, as well as the path to the cathedral. As the tsar entered the cathedral, a chorus intoned "many years." The coronation order emphasizes again and again the "decorum" (*blagochinie*) of the procession and the powerful emotional response of those on the square. The spectators, the *chin* indicates, attest to the international renown of the Russian tsar. The throng before the cathedral was "an all-national great multitude of orthodox Christians and foreigners, who serve the Great Sovereign, and many ranks of different people from neighboring states," who stand in "fear and trembling, praising God for so great a deed, and marveling at the miraculous Imperial origins."[49]

The recessional from the cathedral was longer and even more imposing. Tsar Fedor emerged in full regalia from the south doors of the Assumption Cathedral. As he left the cathedral, a boyar threw gold coins before him, a custom probably borrowed from wedding ceremonies, where it betokened

---

[47] DRV 7:328–37; Shakhmatov, "Gosudarstvenno-natsional'nye idei," 256–58.

[48] Uspenskii, "Tsar i patriarkh"; Giuseppe Olshr, "La Chiesa e lo Stato nel cerimoniale d'incoronazione degli zar Romanov," *Orientalia Christiana Periodica* 18:357–60.

[49] DRV, 7:324–27.

prosperity for the newlyweds.[50] Accompanied by his family, entourage, and clergy, he moved slowly across the square to the Cathedral of Archangel Michael, where he paid his respects to his ancestors, and to the Annunciation Cathedral, the imperial family's private church. Fedor's coronation order describes the equivalent of a popular acclamation, staged to be sure, for the event. It mentions "an innumerable multitude of orthodox Christians," now specifying "both men and women," who stood "in fear and trembling." There is also "cordial joy (*serdechnaia radost'*) and thanksgiving, offering glory to all-powerful God, glorifying and praising the Pious Tsar, crowned by God" and "marveling at the wonderful Imperial event."[51]

The coronation order pointedly mentions the vestments of the hierarchs glittering with jewels and the magnificent robes of the boyars. It refers by name to the servitors who participate in the ceremony and praises their rich attire. It mentions the serving people who prepare the cathedral for the ceremony, lead the procession, bear the regalia to and from the cathedral, and toss coins before the tsar during the recessional.[52] Like the Byzantine coronation of the tenth century, the Russian ceremony provided "a visual sign of the hierarchy of officialdom."[53] Those who stand by the tsar hold positions in the Boyar Duma. Several come from old families with considerable wealth, but they, too, must hold high administrative office. There is no counterpart to the French peers of the realm, whose lineage alone entitled them to play an important role in the investiture of French kings.

The coronation ceremonies concluded with the banquet, which followed the recessional. The banquet was a sedate occasion that gave another demonstration of the solidarity between church and secular authorities. The ceremonies in the cathedral had begun with the metropolitan or patriarch welcoming the tsar at the portal into his domain, ecclesiastical space. The banquet in the Muscovite coronation was an occasion for the tsar to receive the presiding cleric in secular space, the Palace of Facets. Thus Fedor Alekseevich began the ceremony by sending a special invitation to the patriarch and the leading hierarchs, the "Sacred Council," who then proceeded to the palace. The church hierarchs were placed at one table, the boyars at another to the right of the tsar.[54]

•

By the last decades of the seventeenth century, the identification of the tsar with the clergy and the conception of his role as a defender of orthodoxy increasingly clashed with the secular demands of his rule. From the sixteenth

[50] Barsov, *Drevnerusskie pamiatniki,* xxxii.

[51] *DRV* 7:362–69.

[52] *DRV* 7:310–25.

[53] "The Construction of Court Ritual: The Byzantine *Book of Ceremonies,*" in David Cannadine and Simon Price, eds., *Rituals of Royalty: Power and Ceremonial in Traditional Societies* (Cambridge, 1987), 130–32.

[54] *DRV* 7:370–72.

century, a stream of foreign specialists came to Russia, recruited to introduce new military and technology and to train mercenary units in the use of the latest firearms. With Nikon's reforms, Ukrainian monks educated in the Baroque culture of the West began to dominate the Russian church hierarchy. The growth of the administration, with the development of a system of chancelleries, created a contingent of officials who understood the state as a secular institution whose interests had little to do with the liturgical imagery of rule.

A second symbolic system, with themes and imagery borrowed from the West, increasingly glorified the tsar as secular leader. Official rhetoric, like Western absolutist writings, began to praise the tsar's advancement of the secular well-being of his subjects—not only his concern for the salvation of their souls.[55] The image of the ruler as "god on earth," capable of producing secular prodigies, began to appear in official presentations. Simeon Polotskii, a Kievan monk educated in Italy and Poland, brought Baroque panegyrics to Russia. Polotskii's odes proclaimed that Aleksei's glory extended to the whole world; all Europe and Asia, as well as Constantinople, revered him.[56] Alexei's successor, Tsar Fedor Alekseevich, not only spoke Polish and composed Polish verse, but, it is said, issued a decree abolishing old Russian dress and requiring foreign, probably Polish-style clothing.

Clerks in governmental offices composed translations or adaptations of European histories of the great "tsars" of antiquity, from Assyria to Greece and Rome, whom they extolled as secular leaders. They noted exploits of Russian princes and tsars that placed them in the company of the great monarchs of the past. The first foreign play, *The Play of Esther*, known in Russia as *The Play of Ataxerxes* (*Ahasuerus*), drew a connection between the ancient Persian and the Russian court. The presentation, adapted from Western versions by a German Lutheran pastor, Johan Gotfried Gregory, and translated by clerks in the administration, was performed before Alexei's court in the 1670s, but only after Alexei had received assurances from his confessor that Christian rulers, including the Byzantine emperors, had permitted such presentations. A courtier addresses Ataxerxes, "Oh universal tsar, you are an earthly god!" The king's speaker, Mamurza, announced to the tsar that King Ataxerxes was rising from the grave. The King then bowed before Alexei, giving, as it were, his recognition to the glory and power of the emperor of Russia.[57]

Representations of the tsar, following Western practices, increasingly emphasized his personal characteristics, prefiguring the scenarios of the eighteenth century that presented the emperors' and empresses' personal features as political virtues. Polotskii's *Scepter of Rule* broke with tradition and pre-

[55] Bennet, "The Idea of Kingship," 207–65.

[56] S. M. Solov'ev, *Istoriia Rossii s drevneischikh vremen*, 15 vols (Moscow, 1959–1966), 7:182–83; Zabelin, *Domashnii byt russkikh tsarei*, vol. 1, pt. 2: 442.

[57] Crummey, "Court Spectacles," 139–40; Robinson, *Bor'ba idei v russkoi literature*, 133–34, 137–39, 143; N. L. Rubinshtein, *Russkaia istoriografiia* (Moscow, 1941), 41–42.

ceded the word *tsar* with individual qualities, "most serene" and "most pious." These qualities did not belong to the official title but were used during church services and in the court and pleased the tsar greatly. Portraits executed by or under the influence of Western artists (*parsuny*) began to show the tsar's personal likeness. The rider on the seal of Moscow set on the breast of the two-headed eagle now bore the features of the reigning tsar.[58]

The image of the monarch as conqueror, as bearer of foreign attributes, had been fundamental to the mythology of Russian power from the earliest chronicles. The Varangian lineage, the descent from Augustus, the seizure of the Byzantine regalia, and the discovery of an affinity with the kings of antiquity all defined rulers as wielders of an autonomous, political authority based on the capacity to exert force. The mythology of empire indicated that the Russian tsar's authority was supreme and universal and endowed service to him with majesty and amplitude. But the term *tsar* designated a Christian ruler. The exertion of secular power was balanced by the tsar's ecclesiastical role, as the defender of the faith and a participant in the "symphony" of ruler and patriarch, which was expressed in the image of the orthodox Byzantine Empire. By the end of the seventeenth century, the forms of the Christian Empire and the Christian emperor no longer fit the needs of an autonomous, dynamic, monarchical rule. Alexei's son, Peter, brought this development to its culmination. He embarked on another violent act of cultural imposition, like Prince Vladimir's, like Nikon's, and recast the image of tsar and elite in terms of a Western myth of conquest and power.

[58] Robinson, *Bor'ba idei v russkoi literature*, 73–76; G. K. Frideburg, *Portrety i drugie izobrazheniia Petra Velikogo* (St. Petersburg, 1872), 3; G. V. Vilinbakhov, "Vsadnik russkogo gerba," 119–20; G. H. Hamilton, *The Art and Architecture of Russia* (Kingsport, Tenn., 1983), 254–55.

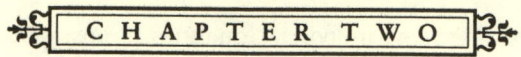

CHAPTER TWO

Peter the Great

General! Admiral! The chief of all naval forces,
You came, you saw, you conquered the proud foe,
The commander's courage defeated the Turks,
Deprived them of weapons and stores,
Fierce battle subdued the Moslems,
Crushed their ambitions, set their ships aflame.

—*Verse read by Andrei Vinius on the triumphal entry of Russian forces
into Moscow after the conquest of Azov, September 30, 1696*

What has been the custom among both neighboring and distant peoples
but not in Russia has now come to pass. Not that there have not been
women worthy of this honor among us. But since there be great inequality in merits, the judgment of God has postponed this until there appeared a very most worthy Heroine, so that the Russian people may
have not a vain, but a righteous glory about Her most joyous coronation. We behold such justice in this deed, accomplished by our very most
wise Emperor that I cannot dream of finding her equal in history: I even
venture to declare that among other peoples who have the ancient custom of crowning their [women] Monarchs, never has there been one
more deserved and just than this first Russian coronation of its kind.

—*Feofan Prokopovich, Sermon on the coronation of
Empress Catherine Alekseevna, May 7, 1724*

REDEFINITION BY ANALOGY: THE PETRINE TRIUMPHAL ENTRY

On September 30, 1696, Peter the Great staged a Roman advent to celebrate
his victory over the Crimean Tatars at Azov. His armies passed through a
classical arch, built at his own command. An enormous relief figure of Hercules held one side of the vault and pediment, under the words "with Her-
culean strength." On the other side stood a figure of Mars beneath the inscription "with the courage of Mars."[1] In the very year of the death of his

---

[1] M. M. Bogoslovskii, *Petr I; Materialy dlia biografii* (Leningrad, 1940), 1:344–47; V. P.
Grebeniuk, "Publichnye zrelishcha petrovskogo vremeni i ikh sviaz 's teatrom," in *Novye
cherty v russkoi literature (XVII-nachalo XVIII v.)* (Moscow, 1976), 134.

half-brother Ivan, when he began to rule himself, Peter announced a new symbolic language and political imagery taken from the repertoire of Western absolutism. Hercules and Mars signified the irresistible, superhuman force that Peter attached to a modern army. Semblances of classical gods rather than pious Byzantine emperors elevated his image as tsar. Hercules and Mars confronted Russians with the Western metaphors of monarch-hero, monarch-god, marking the abandonment of the humble and effacing mien of the Muscovite tsar.

The inscriptions on the vault trumpeted the extent of Peter's own superhuman achievement. The words, "I have come, I have seen, I have conquered," were inscribed in three places on the arch, an identification with the figure of Julius Caesar that would be repeated frequently during Peter's reign. The inscriptions on the pediment made clear the role of human agency in the achievement. "God is with us, no one can attack us, the unheard of," one of these read. But it was not God who deserved the credit; "He who has wrought this is worthy of his reward," a phrase from a letter of Peter, ornamented the pediment, and beneath a figure of a winged Victory held a laurel crown and a green branch. Two gilt tapestries on the side carried legends comparing Peter to the emperor Constantine. But the phrases described the warrior Constantine, not the pious believer: "The return from victory of Tsar Constantine," and "The triumph of Tsar Constantine over the impious Roman tsar, Maxentius."[2]

The procession through the city lasted from nine in the morning to nightfall. It celebrated the exploits of the commanders, General and Admiral Lefort and General Shein, and, by implication, of Peter himself, who appeared as "The Great Captain." The Duma clerk and postmaster, Andrei Vinius, stood on the arch and shouted the panegyric verse cited in the epigraph to the accompaniment of cannon salvos. Peter walked behind Lefort's sleigh, at the head of the sailors. He wore a black German coat and a hat with a white feather and carried a halberd. Turkish prisoners were displayed along the way. The Semenovskii Regiment was led in by Colonel Chambers, while General Patrick Gordon marched at the head of his troops and the regiments of *strel'tsy* brought up the rear. The procession also included Imperial and Brandenburg engineers, as well as Franz Timmerman with his shipwrights and carpenters.[3]

The verses delivered by Vinius made known the shift from a Byzantine to a Roman imperial model. Peter was bringing Renaissance political spectacle to Russia, staging an advent in the manner of Charles V and Henry IV of

---

[2] V. M. Zhivov, "Kul'turnye reformy v sisteme preobrazovanii Petra I," unpublished manuscript. Zhivov emphasizes the prominence of Constantine in Petrine art and celebrations. On this question, however, I tend to agree with Lotman and Uspenskii that the Roman images, embodied in Julius and Augustus Caesar, are dominant (Ju. M. Lotman and B. A. Uspenskii, "Echoes of the Notion 'Moscow as the Third Rome,'" in "Peter the Great's Ideology," Ju. M. Lotman and B. A. Uspenskii, *The Semiotics of Russian Culture*, 53–67). The figure of Constantine in Peter's reign rather seems to be an effort to turn Byzantium into a mirror image of Rome.

[3] Bogoslovskii, *Petr I*, 346–48.

France. He was emulating a European monarch's emulation of a classical model. But the innovation here was far more sudden and shocking. Moscow had never seen a true classical advent. European triumphs had combined the military celebration of the triumph with the ceremonies of the medieval entry, during which the townspeople displayed great pageantry and staged ceremonies of welcome. Peter's first entry had no trappings of welcome; it showed the raw power of arms, the conquest of the capital celebrating his conquest of new lands for the empire. Such advents also followed his major victories over the Swedes in the Northern War.

The advent replaced Peter's coronation as the defining ceremony of his reign. The coronation, with his half-brother Ivan in 1682, could not justify his rejection of the past and the sacrifices he demanded to introduce a new, more powerful Russian state. Georges Florovsky observed that Peter "was inclined to exaggerate anything new. He wanted everything refurbished and altered until it passed beyond all recognition."[4] In this respect, symbolic change was anterior to political and social change: Peter redefined the meaning of his rule, and presented a new image of monarchy before he embarked on his reforms. The advent consecrated his power in the sense noted by Hocart: conferring dominion upon the ruler as the military leader, *imperator*.[5] Peter's advents gave notice that the Russian tsar owed his power to his exploits on the battlefield, not to divinely ordained traditions of succession. The Roman arches, too, gave his power new meaning. They marked what Arnold Van Gennep has described as a passage from the profane to the sacred, the general or ruler entering his own domain, earned by the feat of conquest.[6]

The image of conqueror disposed of the old fictions of descent. The conqueror presents himself as the founder, a godlike figure who defiles old forms of authority to create new ones, reproducing what Sahlins called "an original disorder." Then, "having committed his monstrous acts against society, proving he is stronger than it, the ruler proceeds to bring system out of chaos."[7] The primitive founder came from outside and invaded as a conqueror, denying the prevailing moral order to assert a new form of authority more ruthless and irresistible than the old. Although Russian, Peter assumed foreign features from childhood. He never appeared with a beard, the traditional orthodox sign of godliness. In the early 1690s, he began wearing Western clothing. To the horror of the hierarchy, he ate meat during fasts and remained indifferent to their strictures. Rumors spread among the people that he was a son not of Tsar Alexei, but of a German, and had been substituted for a daughter born to the tsaritsa. Others called him a Swedish pretender from Stockholm.[8]

[4] Florovsky, *Ways of Russian Theology*, 1:114.

[5] A. M. Hocart, *Kingship* (London, 1969), 86–89.

[6] Arnold Van Gennep, *The Rites of Passage* (Chicago, 1960), 15–21. Article "Triumphus," in *Paulys Encyclopaedie der classischen Altertumswissenschaft* (Stuttgart, 1939), 31:496.

[7] Sahlins, *Islands of History*, 80.

[8] Solov'ev, *Istoriia Rossii*, 8:99–100; N. Pavlov-Sil'vanskii, *Proekty reform v zapiskakh sovremennikov Petra Velikogo* (St. Petersburg, 1897), 1.

At Preobrazhensk, Peter had lived in his own foreign enclave. He trained his "play regiments" of adult soldiers with the aid of foreign officers, the regiments that would enforce his changes ruthlessly on the hostile and reluctant. Even before he took active charge of government, he openly displayed his contempt for traditional religious ceremonies. He made the Palm Sunday procession the pretext for drunken and blasphemous masquerades. In 1692 he staged a wild drunken parody of the procession, his "Most Comical and Most Drunken Council." The "Council" remained one of Peter's favorite amusements for the duration of his reign. As Victor Zhivov has shown, the council's ribaldry reversed the meanings of signs, designating what was holy absurd, and what was profane sacred. It was a rare example of a monarch's exploitation of the subversive possibilities of the carnivalesque.[9]

Peter ridiculed the old solemnities to make way for ceremonies that glorified him and his elite as conqueror. Rather than young monk, he displayed himself as young commander, brother to mercenary soldiers, not to prelates, Caesar's successor and the protégé of Hercules and Mars. Wearing Western dress, he gave indication that his servitors, too, would have to change guise and assume a new cultural persona. After Azov, Peter decorated Lefort with what was the first European-style military order. During his trip to Europe in 1697 and 1698, he founded the Order of Andrew the First Called, imitating the examples and decorations of the English Order of the Garter, the legendary Order of Constantine, and the French Order of the Holy Spirit.[10]

His first ceremonial spectacles surrounded his power with the stage effects of the battlefield. For Peter as Louis XIV, the festivals were a symbolic equivalent to a coup d'état, creating miracles previously allowed only to God. Displays of fireworks, often staged by Peter himself, demonstrated the conquest of the heavens. A show of fireworks at the village of Voskresensk in 1693 glorified his comrade-in-arms, Generalissimo Romanodovskii, whom he had declared the commander of his "play" regiments and admiral of his fleet. Three salvoes from fifty-six cannons heralded the event, while the sky was illuminated with the generalissimo's initials. Peter himself played the humble officer, working his way up the ranks, but an officer, as the displays showed, who was akin to the gods. A blazing picture of Hercules tearing apart the jaws of the lion symbolized the power of Peter's forces and his irresistible, superhuman will. The figures of Hercules and Mars were also illuminated during the fireworks' display marking the victory at Azov.[11]

Peter followed the ceremonial celebration with a pictorial celebration of

[9] V. M. Zhivov, "Kul'turnye reformy v sisteme preobrazovanii Petra I"; James Cracraft, *The Church Reforms of Peter the Great* (Stanford, Calif., 1971), 11–19; Kliuchevskii, *Sochineniia*, 4:39–42; Friedrich Wilhelm von Bergholz, *Dnevnik kammer-iunkera Berkhol'tsa* (Moscow, 1858), 2:18–19. On the "carnavalesque," Mikhail Bakhtin, *Rabelais and His World* (Bloomington, Ind., 1984), 270–71; L. N. Semenova, *Ocherki istorii byta i kul'turnoi zhizni Rossii; pervaia polovina XVIII v.* (Leningrad, 1982), 194–96.

[10] G. V. Vilinbakhov, "K istorii uchrezhdeniia ordena Andreia Pervozvannogo i evoliutsiia ego znaka," in *Kul'tura i iskusstvo petrovskogo vremeni*, 144–58; "Istoricheskii obzor," in *Pridvornyi kalendar' na 1892 g.* (St. Petersburg, 1892), 302–3, 308, 412.

[11] V. N. Vasil'ev, *Starinnye feierverki v Rossii* (Leningrad, 1960), 15.

the events. Engravings lifted his achievements into the category of Western monarchies', and created a mythic history of his reign. The Dutch master Adrian Schoonebeck visited Moscow in 1696 and 1697 and made engravings of the fireworks celebrating the Azov victory. Schoonebeck entered the Russian service in 1698 and began training Russian apprentices in the new techniques.[12] Engravings and then paintings made known the new military image and Roman persona of the Russian tsar. Schoonebeck's panorama of the battle of Azov included individual portraits of the generals Shein, Lefort, and Gordon, as well as of Peter himself. Another engraving celebrating the battle, executed shortly after the event by Jacob Nachtglass, presents Peter on a throne, in classical dress, surrounded by allegorical figures and soldiers in Roman helmets grasping spears. At Peter's feet, the captive Turks offer their crowns.[13]

A series of portraits by Gottfried Kneller, executed during Peter's visit to Holland in 1697, presented the emperor as a young warrior in armor. A crown in Western style is set before him (fig. 4). In subsequent years, his portraits, most of them by European artists, presented him in a conventional manner—dressed in armor, surrounded by laurel wreaths, weapons, state shields, and imperial regalia. Several carried the title of *imperator* before Peter officially adopted it in 1721.[14]

As we have seen in chapter 1, absolute monarchies did not leave the understanding of visual symbols to the imagination. Explicit verbal explanations ensured that pictures would enhance the sovereign image in specific ways. Classical and mythical figures were turned into emblems that were decoded in emblem books. The book, *Symbols and Emblems*, a favorite of Peter's, was published for him in Amsterdam in 1705 and republished in Russia in 1719. The frontispiece of the volume showed Peter surrounded by emblems set in medallions. The inscription read, "Beauty and Defence from Him."[15]

As in the West, the emblems and symbols were decoded in texts by symbol specialists. In Russia, this task was taken on by scholars at the Moscow Academy, who both planned the triumphs and subsequent displays of fireworks and composed program books elaborating their meanings.[16] From 1700, Stepan Iavorskii, the Riazan metropolitan and pro-rector of the acad-

---

[12] M. A. Alekseeva, *Graviura petrovskogo vremeni* (Leningrad, 1990), 15–17, 20–22.

[13] B. F. Borzin, *Rospisi petrovskogo vremeni* (Leningrad, 1986), 151, 153; E. S. Shchukina, "O sozdanii medali v pamiat' vziatiia Azova raboty Ia. Boskama," in *Kul'tura i iskusstvo petrovskogo vremeni* (Leningrad, 1977), 159–62.

[14] These portraits were reproduced in engravings. Rovinskii, *Podrobnyi Slovar' russkikh gravirovannykh knig* (St. Petersburg, 1889), 3:1536–41; N. A. Baklanova, "Otrazhenie idei absoliutizma v izobrazitel'nom isskusstve pervoi chetverti XVIII v.," in *Absoliutizm v Rossii (XVII–XVIII vv.)*, 497–98.

[15] Borzin, *Rospisi petrovskogo vremeni*, 30; Stephen L. Baehr, " 'Fortuna Redux': The Iconography of Happiness in Eighteenth Century Courtly Spectacles," in A. G. Cross, ed., *Great Britain and Russia in the Eighteenth Century: Contacts and Comparisons* (Newtonville, Mass., 1979), 110–11; Vasil'iev, 25, 40.

[16] Grebeniuk, "Publichnye zrelishcha," 133–45.

4. *Tsar Peter Alekseevich*. Portrait by Gottfried Kneller, 1697.

emy, recruited scholars from the Kiev Academy, and shifted the emphasis in the school's teaching from Greek to Latin. This, too, came at Peter's instance. On July 7, 1701, he issued a decree with the order: "bring *Latin* scholars to the Academy." The Kievan scholars provided the Roman symbols and imagery of the Baroque that Peter used to create his new imperial manner.[17]

The arches for the 1703 triumph after the victory over Sweden were decorated with the classic motif of Perseus rescuing Andromeda from the sea monster; the accompanying text explained that Perseus represented Russia; Andromeda, the conquered territory of Ingermanland; and the sea monster,

[17] Max J. Okenfuss, "The Jesuit Origins of Petrine Education," in J. G. Garrard, ed., *The Eighteenth Century in Russia* (Oxford, 1973), 113–20; Sergei Smirnov, *Istoriia Moskovskoi Slaviano-Greko-Latinskoi Akademii* (Moscow, 1855), 78–80.

of course, Sweden.[18] On the gates of the 1703 procession, Peter was personified as Ulysses, Perseus, and Hercules, the text explained, holding "the defeated Swedish lion by a chain." The infant Hercules destroying two serpents symbolized Peter's crushing of the *strel'tsy* rebellion. Sermons, speeches, and paintings presented Peter as Mars, Agamemnon, Neptune, Jupiter, and Hercules.[19]

The prefect of the academy, Iosif Turoboiskii, explained the meaning of the new likenesses of power. The gods, he wrote, were meant "not in their literal but their allegorical sense." The allegories came "not from sacred texts, but from secular histories, and are not sacred icons, but figures invented by poets." Turoboiskii defended the use of allegory. It was known to all that "great things cannot be depicted exactly, that lesser things can do this, as a circle describes the sun." But despite such strictures, the devices were often taken as objective parallels as they had been in Europe during the previous century.[20]

Peter presented himself as the founder of Russia, a hero, set apart from the past, the *casus sui*, his own father. He insisted that he be addressed without patronymic, an honor previously reserved for the clergy or saints.[21] The panegyric plays given by the pupils of the Academy emphasized the difference between previous times, *prezhde*, when Russia was in dishonor, bondage, and darkness, and nowadays, *nyne*, when it had become glorious. To be sure, his Romanov ancestors were presented and praised, but only as precursors, harbingers of his own greatness. On the arches for the 1703 triumph, Michael was depicted as a pacifier of the realm. Alexei extended the boundaries of Rus'; he was the "new Russian Philip of Macedon," preparing the way for Russia's Alexander the Great.[22]

Peter's glorification by allegory and illustration in picture resembles that of Louis XIV. But whereas Louis was creating a fictional persona of king, Peter's heroism and achievements were real. There was no separation between the mortal and the political body: the glorification of the sovereign was not a glorification of the state or nation personified but of Peter's own superhuman feats undertaken for the benefit of the nation. In this respect, Peter's decisive victory over Charles XII at Poltava in 1709 was a great symbolic divide. He then threw off his restraint and began openly asserting im-

[18] Grebeniuk, "Publichnye zrelishcha," 135–36.

[19] *Panegiricheskaia literatura petrovskogo vremeni* (Moscow, 1979), 20–21, 63–65, 93; Borzin, *Rospisi petrovskogo vremeni*, 153–55.

[20] Grebeniuk, "Publichnye zrelishcha," 136; *Panegiricheskaia literatura*, 21; *P"esy shkol'-nykh teatrov Moskvy* (Moscow, 1974), 25; Vasil'ev, 23–24. Victor Zhivov and Boris Uspenskii have described the coming into use of this "sacral semantics," literary figures that expressed the ruler's transcendance and that came to be taken as descriptions of the truth in the eighteenth century. See Zhivov and Uspenskii, "Tsar' i Bog," 72, 121–22.

[21] Boris Uspenskii, "Historia sub specie semioticae," in D. P. Lucid., ed., *Soviet Semiotics* (Baltimore, 1977), 109.

[22] *P"esy shkol'nykh teatrov Moskvy*, 39; *Opisanie izdanii napechatannykh pri Petre I; svodnyi katalog* (Moscow-Leningrad, 1958), 91.

perial and godly pretensions. Analogy gave way to direct statements of similarity and even equivalence. Peter wrote in a letter after the battle that "an entire army of Phaetons has been defeated," seeing himself as Zeus subduing the refractory son of Helios. He thought in terms of mythical symbols, made up his own emblems, and understood his own deeds in terms of their symbolic meaning. The dreams he recounted, E. V. Anisimov has observed, cast his experience in the simple figures of allegories.[23] After Poltava, the visual arts openly characterized Peter as emperor and god. G. V. Vilinbakhov's analysis of Petrine standards shows how Peter ceased concealing his person in the figures of his patron saints, Peter and Andrei: he began to place an imperial crown and his own initials on his standards.[24] We observe the shift from allegorical identification with gods to visual resemblance. In 1711 and 1712 the painting on the ceiling of the Menshikov Palace, *The Triumph of Mars*, portrayed the god with Peter's features.[25]

The Poltava triumph, the most grandiose of the Northern War, marked Peter's assumption of the persona of military leader, *imperator* in its original sense. Peter entered, now on horseback, not the captain but the military leader, behind the Preobrazhenskii Regiment, guarding Swedish captives. The seven arches that decorated the way presented Peter in various guises. On the Synodal Arch, he was depicted as Mars in Roman battle dress, holding laurels. Turoboiskii's description of the arches built by the Moscow Academy refers to Peter as "the all-Russian Hercules," who surpassed even Hercules in his achievements, "for [Hercules] seized his greatest glory from triumph over dumb animals, while you, most radiant monarch, have tamed not the chief of the animals, the lion, but all animals, with the strength and severity of outstanding men."[26] Hercules, for Peter, remained a symbol of armed might and had none of the intellectual implications that the "Gallic Hercules" had in French advents. (See the prologue to part 1).

The Poltava entry demonstrated that the triumphal entry had displaced the religious procession as the central public ritual of Russian monarchy. During the entry, Peter took over the religious imagery that had been reserved for the Patriarch. He was greeted with the chant previously sung to Christ—the Patriarch—on Palm Sunday, "Blessed is He that cometh in the Lord's name, Hosanna the highest, God, the Lord appear before us."[27] Peter's victory was couched in Old Testament analogies. A play presented him

[23] Vasil'ev, *Starinnye feierverki*, 40; Alekseeva, *Graviura petrovskogo vremeni*, 126, 188; E. V. Anisimov, *Vremia petrovskikh reform* (Leningrad, 1989), 49.

[24] G. V. Vilinbakhov, "Otrazhenie idei absoliutizma v simvolike Petrovskikh znamen," in *Kul'tura i iskusstvo Rossii XVIII veka* (Leningrad, 1981), 17–21.

[25] Borzin, *Rospisi petrovskogo vremeni*, 173, 52–54.

[26] N. I. Pavlenko, *Petr pervyi* (Moscow, 1975), 180–81; Solov'ev, *Istoriia Rossii*, 8:286; Borzin, *Rospisi petrovskogo vremeni*, 160–61; M. A. Alekseeva, "Brat'ia Ivan i Alexei Zubovy i graviura petrovskogo vremeni," in N. I. Pavlenko, ed., *Rossiia v period reform Petra I* (Moscow, 1973), 347, 351; *Panegiricheskaia literatura*, 63–65.

[27] Zhivov and Uspenskii, "Tsar' i Bog," 114–15; Uspenskii, "Historia sub specie semioticae," 110.

as David, slaying Goliath—Charles XII of Sweden. Absalom's betrayal of David allegorized Mazeppa's betrayal of Peter; political treachery became infamy, the violation of a biblical commandment.[28] Peter's victories began to be marked on church calendars as holidays celebrating events in a new heroic history. Peter had left the office of patriarch vacant after Patriarch Adrian's death in 1700, and the Poltava triumph prepared the way for the abolition of the office and secularization of the church administration in 1721.

The master of the panegyrical use of biblical imagery was the prefect of the Kiev Academy, Feofan Prokopovich, and Prokopovich's *Panegirikos*, pronounced at Saint Sofia cathedral only two weeks after the battle of Poltava, amply displayed his gifts as a rhetorician in the service of the throne. The battle took place, Prokopovich observed, on the day of St. Samson "not I imagine without the watchfulness of God," and he used the occasion to compare Peter to the biblical Samson breaking the jaws of the lion, now representing Sweden. The analogy with Samson became general in the panegyrical literature. In 1735 B. K. Rastrelli's bronze statue of Samson struggling with the lion was placed in the center of the great cascade of fountains of Peterhof.[29]

The remarkable engraving executed in 1711 by Alexei Zubov, Schoonebeck's most gifted student, fixed the Poltava triumph as one of the prodigies in the evolving Petrine myth (fig. 5).[30] Zubov's first version had been turned down by Peter. The second is less graphic and detailed, and perhaps less artistically unified. But by presenting the parade more schematically, it makes the individual figures more visible and prominent. The procession stretches like a ribbon across the page, following a familiar pattern of Western engravings. The Russian troops, in 115 rows, wind snakelike through the streets of Moscow, past the seven arches, hundreds of tiny, identical figures in uniform, carrying rifles, with a detachment of huddled Swedish captives. The various units, generals, and the emperor himself are marked by numbers, which are identified on a large plaque that occupies the foreground with the figures of two captive Swedes in chains lying at the side. In the middle ground, the center of the scene, we see Peter, number twenty-seven, rearing on his horse, riding at the head of the Preobrazhenskii Regiment. Before him walk the Swedish generals, and his prize captive, the Swedish prime minister, Count Karl Piper. The city of Moscow and the population of Moscow are not present; the original version had included buildings but apparently Peter did not care for this distraction. Aside from a few tiny

[28] *Panegiricheskaia literatura*, 66–67.

[29] Ibid., 22–25, 197; *Pamiatniki arkhitektury prigorodov Leningrada* (Leningrad, 1983), 380. On Prokopovich, see James Cracraft, "Feofan Prokopovich and the Kiev Academy," in Robert L. Nichols and Theofanis George Stavrou, eds., *Russian Orthodoxy under the Old Regime* (Minneapolis, Minn., 1978), 44–66.

[30] D. A. Rovinskii, *Podrobnyi slovar' russkikh graverov XVI–XIXvv.* (St. Petersburg, 1895), 1:353–54, 362–63.

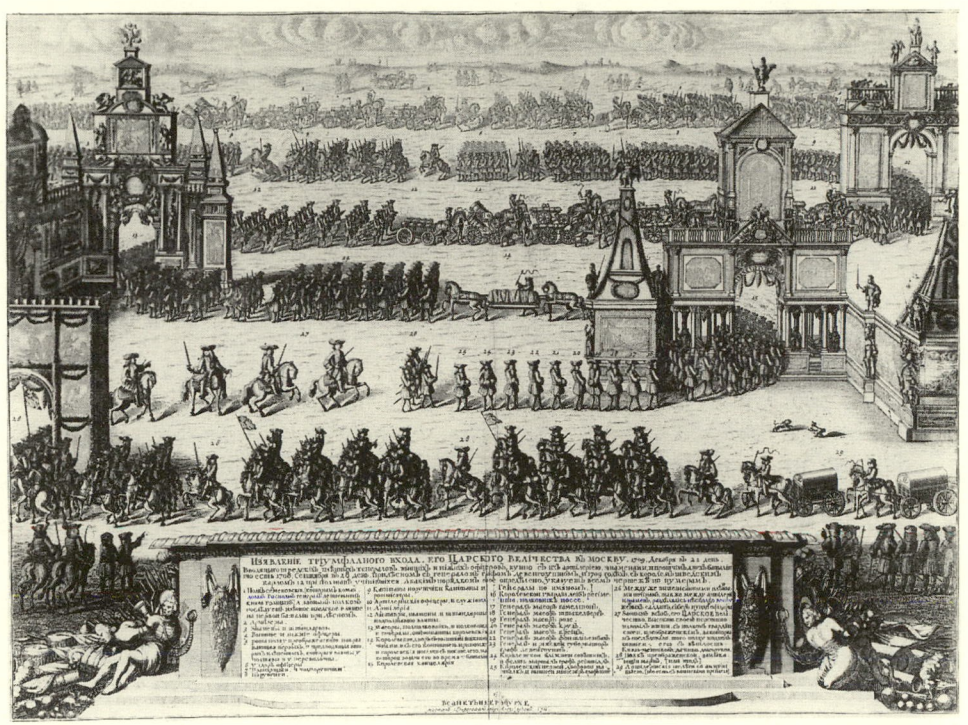

5. *Triumphal Entry of Russian Armies into Moscow, 1709.*
Engraving by Alexei Zubov.

figures sketched in the rear ground, the only people are the soldiers and their captives; the only structures are the arches. Zubov has dispensed with the population and buildings of Moscow to depict the significant figures, the higher reality of the political order, the tsar with his army trooping proudly through the capital of Russia.[31]

VENUS AND MINERVA: THE SYMBOLIC ASCENDANCE OF WOMEN

These startling innovations in the presentation and representation of the Russian monarch followed the pattern of Russian political mythology. Peter elevated the authority of the monarch and the state by vesting himself in new foreign forms exemplifying sovereignty. He redefined the ruler as a foreign force in a way that permitted him to embark on far-reaching changes. Ceremonies prepared the way for reform as the beginning of a new tradition.

Peter's new foreign image of rule announced colossal changes he introduced into the Russian state, economy, and culture. In the first years of the

---

[31] Alekseeva, *Graviura petrovskogo vremeni*, 116–19.

eighteenth century, he completed the transformation of the Russian army into a regular standing army and founded a Russian navy. He developed a native iron and cloth industry that made Russia self-sufficient in the production of arms and uniforms. Russian armies, supported by impressive artillery power, engaged Sweden, the major power of Northern Europe, in grueling hostilities for twenty-one years that resulted in the conquest of the Baltic littoral and the establishment of Russia's new capital, St. Petersburg on the Neva.

The great transformations that Peter introduced helped to consolidate and strengthen the service state structure that had taken form in the previous two centuries. He enforced a requirement of lifetime service for the landholding classes and established a Table of Ranks, based on European models, which would attach status more to service than to birth. The introduction of the head or poll tax, following a French example, eliminated distinctions between different groups of the peasantry, subjecting them all to bondage, and preparing the way for their further debasement in the course of the eighteenth century. Westernization, and the modernization of the military, economic, and political structure of Russia, thus proceeded at the cost of subjecting Russia's rural population to a system of state-sanctioned serfdom.

After the battle of Poltava, during the last fifteen years of his reign, Peter set about providing Russian monarchy with the institutions of Western absolutism. This was the period of the establishment of the colleges and new local governmental institutions, and the introduction of a system of procuracy headed by a procurator-general who presided over the Senate. The new institutions followed Western examples, particularly the Swedish model, recommended by the Holsteiner Heinrich Fick, formerly an official in the Swedish service. Peter apparently expected that these institutions would work as they had in Sweden.[32] The differences in social organization, particularly the existence of an enserfed peasantry and the absence of a tradition of local self-government and an educated officialdom in Russia, make Peter's hopes seem fanciful. But the governmental reforms also had a symbolic meaning: they provided Russia with governmental institutions that resembled those of the other major powers, a state to befit a European monarch.

Having given the Russian state the semblance of a Western administration, Peter set about creating a Western court culture to unite and to educate his servitors. Peter's contempt for the pomp and luxury of the Muscovite court only prepared the way for a new, more lavish magnificence modeled on Europe. In his "paradise," St. Petersburg, Peter built palaces designed by Dutch and French architects. At Peterhof, he created his own version of the

---

[32] Claes Peterson, *Peter the Great's Administrative and Judicial Reforms: Swedish Antecedents and the Process of Reception* (Stockholm, 1979), 416–17, passim; S. M. Troitskii, *Russkii absoliutizm i dvorianstvo v XVIII v; formirovanie biurokratii* (Moscow, 1974), 48–77; E. V. Anisimov, *Podatnaia reforma Petra Velikogo* (Leningrad, 1982), 48–58.

palaces and gardens at Versailles. Petersburg embodied the idea of regularity (*reguliarnost'*), the symmetry, order, and control of the Baroque city. The public buildings and homes of the Petrine aristocracy were built of stone in styles borrowed from Europe, in Count Francesco Algarotti's words, "a kind of bastard architecture, one which partakes of the Italian, the French and the Dutch."[33] Like the triumphal entries, the capital had to be represented as well as created; it had to be celebrated by being depicted. Engravings showed the vast spaces of the Neva and made known the symbolic meaning of Peter's new city. Alexei Zubov's Petersburg landscape of 1716 lines up the residences of the emperor and his high officials. The buildings corresponded in length to the number of serfs held by each owner, like a "ceremonial group portrait."[34]

During Peter's visit to France in 1717, he was impressed by the art and palaces that surrounded the French monarchy. He commissioned his own, more elaborate version of François Girardin's equestrian statue of Louis XIV and gave the sculptor, Carlo Bartolommeo Rastrelli, instructions to prepare several models. In one project, completed under Peter's close supervision, the figure of Victory confers a crown of laurels on an equestrian figure of Peter. It was rumored that these monuments, none of them completed during Peter's lifetime, were to be larger than Girardin's statue.[35]

Most of all, Peter was impressed by the layout and culture of Versailles and immediately ordered measurements taken of the garden.[36] Like Versailles, his gardens were schools in mythology and literary references to teach the nobility taste and refinement. Peter had a Russian translation of Aesop's *Fables*, published in Holland in 1700, and he placed figures from the fables, as well as figures and emblems from classical mythology, in labyrinths of the Summer Garden and in the gardens at Peterhof and Tsarskoe Selo.[37] He began to take on the conservative attributes of Louis's image, while retaining his charisma as invincible military leader. Indeed, he pursued the goal of creating a new elite responsive to his conception of the state with the same ruthless ferocity that accompanied his military reform. Peter replaced the old decorum of humility (*blagochinie*) with a decorum based on Western social norms.

These norms would distinguish one who was "well-born," that is, "noble" (*blagorodnyi*), from one who was "base"(*podlyi*). Peter's *Table of Ranks*, issued in 1722, made state service the determinant of rank, and Western taste and appearance the expression of noble status. The Table was

[33] James Cracraft, *The Petrine Revolution in Russian Architecture* (Chicago, 1988), 193, 240–41, 258.

[34] Grigorii Kaganov, "'As in the ship of Peter,'" *Slavic Review*, vol. 50, no. 4 (Winter, 1991): 755–67.

[35] Baklanova, "Otrazhenie idei absoliutizma," 502–3.

[36] Ibid., 494.

[37] D. S. Likhachev, *Poeziia sadov; k semantike sadovo-parkovykh stilei; sad kak tekst* (St. Petersburg, 1991), 127–31.

meant to be the counterpart of European rank systems that created an order and hierarchy for the display of aristocrats, church hierarchs, and officials, bearing witness to the monarch's glory. Instead, it introduced a hierarchical ordering based on progress in service, and prescribed official and public behavior according to a servitor's rank. Parallel tables of military and civil ranks defined standing by office, and conferred hereditary nobility on nonnobles who reached the eighth rank in the civil hierarchy and the fourteenth (the lowest officer's rank) in the military. A servitor's rank designated where he and his wife would stand at church services, ambassadorial audiences, ceremonies, and celebrations. It also determined the richness of the clothing he was to wear. The last article of the Table decreed that "each should have the attire, equipage and livery demanded by his rank and character. All must act accordingly, and be deterred by an announced fine and greater punishment." External signs of Western character—Western wardrobes, gestures, and language—demonstrated the nobility's participation in the Europeanized world created by the monarch.[38]

The nobleman was to learn to defer before his sovereign in Western manner. Peter instructed his servitors in courtly manners. No longer were they simply to debase themselves before the ruler as "obedient slave." They had to display their beauty; to become men in the image of gods rather than monks. They would assume the tastes, manners, and ways of speaking that would allow them to frequent Western court society. To acquaint them with Western standards of civility, Peter had published *The Honorable Mirror of Youth*, a collection of instructions from Western courtesy books prepared under the supervision of Count Jacob Bruce and issued in 1717. The volume instructed Russian youth in the genteel manners of Western courts—how to eat and speak properly and, in general, to distinguish themselves from peasants. It urged them to converse with one another in foreign tongues, both to practice the languages and to avoid eavesdropping by servants.[39]

The new deportment had to be taught and demonstrated in public. St. Petersburg, the city epitomizing the principle of regularity, would breed an elite accustomed to act according to the secular principle of decorum expressed by the idea of "police." In 1718 Peter established the Chief-Magistracy of the Police in imitation of the French Lieutenant-Général de Police, an office meant to make Paris a secure and orderly city. He appointed to the position Anton Divier (Di Vier), the son of a Portuguese Jew who had moved to Holland. Divier, on the basis of police supervision, set about creating the polite society that would inhabit the governmental city of Petersburg.[40]

In 1718, Divier issued a decree announcing a new type of gathering, the

[38] *PSZ*, no. 3890, January 24, 1722; Troitskii, *Russkii absoliutizm*, 112–13.

[39] P. Miliukov, *Ocherki po istorii russkoi kul'tury* (Paris, 1930), 3:244–46; Semenova, *Ocherki istorii byta*, 102–3.

[40] Sidney Monas, "Anton Divier and the Police of St. Petersburg," in *For Roman Jakobson; Essays on his Sixtieth Birthday* (The Hague, 1956), 361–66.

assamblei. "Assembly is a French Word which cannot be rendered into Russian by a single Word," the decree stated. The *assamblei* was described as a gathering, intended both for diversion and business, which was not to start before 4:00 or end after 10:00 P.M. The guests would "freely sit, walk and play" without the elaborate etiquette of official occasions. The gathering would include guests from different levels of society, ranging from the highest ranks of the aristocracy to rich merchants and masters of workshops, their wives and even their children—but no servants or attendants.[41]

The police chief continued to supervise the *assamblei.* He issued invitations, inspected the premises on the day of the event, and his officials ensured that those admitted had been invited. Arrangements had to be made quickly. Peter ordered many of them to take place at the residences of his favorites, sometimes with as little as two days' notice. As a result, his servitors had to keep spacious homes, furnished according to Western aristocratic tastes suitable for an *assamblei.*[42]

In contrast to Peter's drunken feasts, the *assamblei* introduced a new standard of polite behavior. The guests chatted, played cards or chess, partook in soft drinks, and danced. The men were to adopt a new gallant manner, to pay homage to the fair sex, whose beauty complemented their contribution to the state. They performed graceful Western dances, and under Peter's watchful eyes, the leading figures of government, some of them old and decrepit, dutifully executed endless minuets, English dances, and polkas. If a guest failed to behave properly, there was the threat of blows from the fists of the emperor himself. During the evening, the host awarded a bouquet to the most distinguished lady, who then took charge of the dances. Later on, she passed the bouquet to her favorite cavalier, who on the next day was obliged to send her a fan, a pair of gloves, and a bouquet.[43]

Peter thus brought women of the elite out of seclusion, and presented them as embodiments of Westernized nobility, both at official functions and the less formal *assamblei.* The public presentation of women had great significance for Peter's and subsequent reigns. As we have seen in the prologue to this part, the devotion to the world of the sublime and genteel in late-seventeenth-century France took the form of worship of idealized feminine forms. Just as the images of might—Hercules, Perseus, and Mars—symbolized military conquest, Venus and Minerva, and throngs of women around the monarch, symbolized the conquest of the sphere of love, beauty, and civilization. This tendency became even more pronounced in eighteenth-century France, which the Goncourts described as "the century of woman and her caressing domination over manners and customs."[44]

[41] *PSZ*, no. 3246, November 26, 1718.

[42] Brenda Meehan-Waters, *Autocracy and Aristocracy: The Russian Service Elite of 1730* (New Brunswick, N.J., 1982), 103–4; Semenova, *Ocherki istorii byta*, 204.

[43] E. Karnovich, "Assamblei pri Petre Velikom," *Drevniaia i novaia Rossiia* 1 (1877): 81–82.

[44] See the comments on the importance of women in eighteenth-century art and architecture

Peter adopted the feminine allegorical idiom of Louis XIV's court. In Russia, what Jean Starobinski called the "fictitious ascendancy of women," took on prescriptive force, for it designated the most sublime stage of Western monarchical rule.[45] If the principal analogues of valor were the gods and heroes, Venus and Minerva became the analogues of the new Western culture. In place of the self-abnegation and Christian love inspired by the Mother-of-God, the goddesses introduced a Western Neoplatonic concept of love, comprising beauty, strength, and wisdom. They represented love as supreme beauty, tamer of discord, the inspiration for a poetry of terrestrial bliss.[46] Woman represented man's higher faculties rather than the snares of the passions. Marriage became the consummation of love rather than the acceptance of a hierarchy of divinely ordained paternal authority.

The figures of goddesses and female allegorical figures decorated the first Petersburg palaces. The ceiling paintings of the Summer Palace, *The Triumph of Russia, The Triumph of Minerva, The Triumph of Morpheus*, and *Peace and Tranquillity*, present ample female figures surrounded by Cupids as allegories of power and civilization. In the Summer Garden, Peter placed the famous *Tauride Venus*, a Roman copy of the statue of Praxiteles acquired in Rome, his answer to Louis XIV's *Venus of Arles*. To line the alleys of the garden, Peter's agents in Italy purchased seminude statues of the virtues. Pietro Baratta's *Mercy* writes in her book, "Justice condemns the criminal, mercy shows him grace" (fig. 6). Marino Groppelli's *Truth* leans her foot on a globe, holds the book of wisdom, and gazes upon the sun as the symbol of enlightenment (fig. 7).[47] Female beauty becomes a symbol of virtue and wisdom, the erotic and intellectual combined in an aspiration to a higher world of reason. The statues violated at once traditional moral sensibilities and orthodox suspicions of three dimensional representation.

Crude and artless when he wished to be, Peter nonetheless presented an example of the cultivated worship of the feminine. His romance with Catherine Skavronka, the Lithuanian peasant girl, placed love above considerations of social background and religion. His marriage to her, in secret in 1711, then publicly in 1712, was a studied affront to traditional Russian susceptibilities. Not only had the emperor married a commoner, but he had done

in Debora L. Silverman, *Art Nouveau in Fin-de-siècle France: Politics, Psychology, and Style* (Berkeley, Calif., 1989), 25–28.

[45] Jean Starobinski, *The Invention of Liberty, 1700–1789* (New York, 1987), 55–57.

[46] Strong, *Splendor at Court*, 225–32; Baehr, "'Fortuna Redux,'" 109–22.

[47] On the statuary of the summer garden, see S. O. Androsov, *Zapadnoevropeiskaia skul'ptura v Rossii petrovskogo vremeni; avtoreferat dissertatsii* (Moscow, 1990); S. O. Androsov, "Skul'ptura letnego sada," in *Kul'tura i iskusstvo Rossii XVIII veka*, 44–58; O. Ia. Neverov, "Pamiatniki antichnogo iskusstva v Rossii petrovskogo vremeni," in *Kul'tura i iskusstvo petrovskogo vremeni*, 48–49. Later in the century, these sculptures evoked scorn and contempt from those who were less disposed to see half-nude women as symbols of virtue and civilization. Casanova commented to Catherine II in 1764 that he presumed the statues "had been placed there to impose on fools or to excite the laughter of those acquainted with history" (Hamilton, *Art and Architecture*, 438).

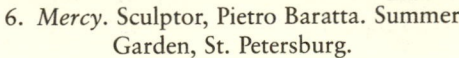

6. *Mercy*. Sculptor, Pietro Baratta. Summer Garden, St. Petersburg.

7. *Truth*. Sculptor, Marino Groppelli. Summer Garden, St. Petersburg.

so while his first wife was alive. Their wedding had taken place without a priest, according to the ceremony of a rear admiral, not of a tsar. But the greatest desecration was of the traditional norms of kinship. At her baptism into orthodoxy, Peter's son, Alexei, had served as her godfather, and provided her patronymic, Alekseevna. This meant, according to spiritual kinship, that Peter had married his granddaughter. It was taken by traditionalists, Uspenskii writes, as "a kind of spiritual incest, a blasphemous flouting of fundamental Christian laws."[48]

The wedding itself was another act of declaration, making known to the public that the old conventions no longer held, and that the tsar boasted of his amorous inclinations. Peter himself provided the example of the behavior he tried to impose by legislation. He had sent his first wife, the tsaritsa Evdokiia who opposed his Western ways, into a monastery. He now showed that individuals should marry the person of their choice, not their parents'. But he also introduced a contradictory norm—that the Russian ruler and members of his family, regardless of their inclinations, must marry non-Russian, European spouses. This principle served the practical goal of elevating the monarch above his servitors. He freed himself from dependence on the noble families who had previously supplied the brides of tsars, and raised his own family to an international, European plane. In the seventeenth century, it had been taboo for tsareviches to marry a non-Russian, and the tsar's daughters, the *tsesarevny*, had not been permitted to marry at all, in order to avoid creating interest groups among the aristocratic clans seeking their hands. Peter married for love, but he arranged marriages for his children and niece with members of European royalty, initiating a practice that brought Russia into the marital politics of the West and imprinted a European character on all future members of the imperial family. From Peter's reign, the sovereign's children, now designated as grand dukes or grand duchesses, married only foreign royalty, setting them apart from the aristocratic families that had supplied the brides of the tsars of Moscow.[49]

The promulgation of Peter's wedding was as important as the event itself. Peter invited the leading figures of state, foreign ambassadors, representatives of the estates to a feast, ball, and fireworks display. He issued numerous announcements of the event, whose significance was made clear by an engraving of the feast, apparently completed before the event, by Alexei Zubov (fig. 8). The guests sit around a large oval table. Their names are enumerated in the cartouche at the bottom. Peter is at the far end of the table facing his ministers and flanked by foreign ambassadors. Catherine, at the near end, has turned to face the viewer. Alexander Menshikov stands behind the tsar with a staff, the marshall of the ceremony. The engraving avoids the exaggerated perspective common at the time; it is foreshortened, drawing the eye to the figures who were supposed to play the important roles at the wedding.[50]

---

[48] Uspenskii, "Historia sub specie semioticae," 121.

[49] On the changing political meaning of marital bonds, see Edward L. Keenan, "Muscovite Political Folkways," *Russian Review*, vol. 45, no. 2 (April 1986), 160; Kollmann, "Ritual and Social Drama at the Muscovite Court," 486.

[50] The engraving follows the model of an engraving of feast by Schoonebeck. Alekseeva, *Graviura petrovskogo vremeni*, 122–23; Semenova, *Ocherki istorii byta*, 25, 68–70; A. Bychkov, "O svad'be Imperatora Petra Velikogo s Ekaterinoiu Alekseevnoiu," *Drevniaia i novaia Rossiia* (1877), 3:323–24; Rovinskii, *Podrobnyi slovar'*, 1:362–63.

8. *The Wedding of Peter I and Catherine Alekseevna.* Engraving by Alexei Zubov.

In the evening, illuminations lit up a transparency with an allegory of marriage as love, which was reproduced in an engraving of the design of the spectacle. Two entwined columns occupy the center. At one side stands Hymen grasping a flaming torch; at the other the bride, with Catherine's features, holding a burning heart. At her feet, two pigeons are kissing. Above is the all-seeing eye.[51]

At the *assamblei,* Peter and Catherine together gave an example of courtly behavior. They often danced on indefatigably, with great zest, after the devoted servitors had collapsed in exhaustion. Catherine partnered others as well, but perfunctorily, giving a conspicuous sign of her fidelity.[52] She appeared as Peter's creation, his Galatea, who represented the new European woman, all appearance, gaiety, charm. She came elaborately dressed, in contrast to Peter in his usual simple attire. Elegant ladies-in-waiting and pages

[51] D. A. Rovinskii, *Obozrenie ikonopisaniia v Rossii do kontsa XVII veka; opisanie feierverkov i illuminatsii* (St. Petersburg, 1903), 189; Vasil'ev, 51, Plate 29.

[52] Karnovich, "Assamblei," 78; Semenova, *Ocherki istorii byta,* 204.

in green uniforms with gold embroidery accompanied her; Peter arrived with a single orderly. The other ladies tried to follow her example; they were clothed in the latest fashions, heavily bedecked in jewels, and made up with rouge and powder.

The lavish celebrations in Petersburg in 1721, following the signing of the Treaty of Nystadt, became an occasion to demonstrate the worship of feminine beauty. To be sure, Peter did not pass up the opportunity to have a drunken masquerade, which lasted a week. But he also insisted on proper European attire. All attending were to come in fine clothes, under threat of a fifty-ruble fine. Catherine and her daughters, Elizabeth and Anna, set the standards of dress. Catherine wore a red gown, embroidered with silver, and a priceless tiara of gold and silver, set with gems. The grand duchesses appeared in white dresses, with gold and silver trimming, and tiaras also covered with gems. The French ambassador noted that Peter himself had commanded that the compulsory drinking rule, which he enjoyed enforcing at public functions, be suspended during the banquet. The banquet was followed by a European-style ball, and Peter walked through the halls, making sure that his aristocracy behaved in a European manner, though there is no indication that he danced himself.[53]

The same eye to sartorial ostentation was shown at the even more elaborate celebrations of the Peace of Nystadt in Moscow during the winter of 1721–1722. Catherine changed her gowns frequently, each more lavish than the last, "appearing now in red felt richly embroidered with silver, then in light blue, with different camisoles and other articles." She wore a sword studded with diamonds and her Order of Catherine. In subsequent years, Peter himself appeared in dress befitting his status as European monarch. In 1723 he astonished onlookers by greeting returning ambassadors while wearing an elegant dress coat and riding in a fancy carriage. At Catherine's coronation ceremony in 1724, he wore a light blue summer caftan embroidered with silver, red stockings, and a hat with a white feather. He received his greetings on his fifty-second birthday a few weeks after the coronation "again playing the dandy," according to Friedrich-Wilhelm von Bergholz, in a smart red caftan, with silver embroidery, which was tailored in the French style with large lapels, but with a small Swedish collar.[54]

By the last years of Peter's reign, the images of the conqueror and the goddess were dominant figures in the representation of Russian monarchy. The guards' regiments and the ladies of the imperial family and of the court had become the main participants and ornaments of official ceremonies and celebrations. The descriptions of the Blessing of the Waters of 1722, which took place during the court's sojourn in Moscow for the Nystadt celebra-

[53] Reinhard Wittram, *Peter I; Czar und Kaiser* (Göttingen, 1964), 2:465; Bergholz, *Dnevnik kammer-iunkera Berkhol'tsa,* 1:196.

[54] Meehan-Waters, *Autocracy and Aristocracy,* 104; Bergholz, *Dnevnik kammer-iunkera Berkhol'tsa,* 4:51–52, 61; N. Belozerskaia, "Tsarskoe venchanie v Rossii," *Russkaia Mysl',* vol. 5 (1883): 5–6.

tions, give a sense of a new mode in the observance of traditional religious holidays. The celebration began in the palace before the Blessing itself. Women, far from being concealed, were proudly in evidence.[55] Bergholz described how his sovereign, the Duke of Holstein, kissed the hand of the empress who, "as almost always was dressed magnificently." Vodka, chocolate, and coffee were served in unlimited quantities. The ladies in waiting, dressed more modestly, approached the empress one by one, and kissed her dress, her hand, and her dress again. Then all crowded to the windows to watch the service outside.

The military presence, already prominent in the last decades of the seventeenth century, now overshadowed the clergy during the ceremony itself. The clergy marched in procession, dressed as before in their magnificent ceremonial robes, with gold and silver embroidery. But Peter's guardsmen dominated the landscape. Eight regiments, numbering fourteen thousand troops, many of them chosen for their appearance, lined up along the river. Bergholz wrote, "The view was marvelous, because the regiments consisted entirely of handsome men, especially the first six regiments, the Preobrazhensk, Semenov, Kapor, Lefort, Butyrsk, and Shlusselberg."

But most striking was the role performed by the tsar. Peter was not a faithful worshiper participating in the liturgy, but its organizer. Although the archbishop formally officiated, Peter took charge. He did not march in the procession of the cross to the river, but strode back and forth before his troops "not stopping for a minute." During the Blessing of the Waters, he remained with his troops and himself gave orders for resounding salutes.

The Reproduction of Divinity: The Petrine Coronation and Funeral

Despite the panoply of images and allegory, Peter continued to justify his power by referring to achievement, whether military or civil. In this respect, Petrine ideology was very much of the age of rationalism, his contribution to the "general welfare" of Russia legitimating his rule. The preambles to his laws, as M. M. Bogoslovskii noted, always referred to the principle of reason. The *ponezhe* (inasmuch as) explained why a given statute would work to the benefit of Russia, the *obshchee blago* (general well-being) or *obshchaia pol'za* (general welfare). The principle of utility was the philosophical equivalent of victory on the battlefield, turning the monarch into the savior of his people, enhancing his charisma as a figure from beyond who wrought prodigies. Feofan Prokopovich elaborated the rationalist propositions he found in the writings of Samuel Pufendorf and other Natural Law theorists into an ideology that made the emperor God's chosen to rule his people for their good. It was the Erastian rationale for the extension of

---

[55] Bergholz, *Dnevnik kammer-iunkera Berkhol'tsa*, 2:22–25.

power of the police state. Petrine ideology created what Georges Florovsky called "'police pathos,' the pathos of order and paternalism," which "proposes to institute nothing less than universal welfare and well-being, or quite simply 'universal happiness.'"[56]

With Peter, Russian monarchs presented themselves as embodiments of the ideal, as well as the reality of Western monarchy. Seventeenth-century ceremonies and rhetoric had portrayed the tsar as an exemplar of sanctity, elevated by a fictive imperial tradition. The new principle of utility disposed of tradition and ensured that history began with Peter's accession. The hierarchs of Peter's church expounded a theology of utility, guided by the monarch's rational understanding of the state's general welfare. The utilitarian argument justified the church's direct subordination to the emperor, realized in Prokopovich's Spiritual Regulation of 1721, which replaced the Patriarchate with the Holy Synod, a state office organized on collegial principles. The organization followed the model of the Protestant states of Germany, where the prince was uncontested head of the ecclesiastical administration of his realm. Prokopovich, and other clerics trained in Kiev, dominated the early years of the Synod, while Great Russians were in the minority. In June 1724 the Synod consisted of five Ukrainians, three Great Russians, two Greeks, and one Serb.[57]

The figure of St. Alexander Nevskii provided an image of princely religious virtue for the Petrine church. Nevskii, whose victories afforded historical grounds for the claims to the Neva land, was glorified as patron saint of St. Petersburg. In 1723 his remains were removed from Vladimir to the Nevskii Monastery in the capital. The sanctification of Nevskii transformed the prince into Peter's image, emphasizing his military exploits and downplaying his piety. The feast day of Alexander Nevskii was moved to the anniversary of the Treaty of Nystadt, which concluded the Northern War, thus commemorating Peter's victories more than his own. In 1724 the Synod ruled that the saint should be depicted not in monk's but in princely attire. Prokopovich's sermon on Nevskii ridiculed monks who were concerned only for their own blessedness and salvation, and presented the prince as an exemplar of civic duty. But Prokopovich made clear that even Nevskii's achievements could not make him the equal of Peter, whose exploits surpassed all of his predecessors' combined.[58]

As in Europe, the church publicized the events of the new heroic history. It marked Peter's major victories, as well as the day of his accession and coronation, as holidays on the religious calendar. According to a decree of 1721, issued on the anniversary of Peter's coronation, the church was to celebrate

[56] M. M. Bogoslovskii, *Oblastnaia reforma Petra Velikogo* (Moscow, 1902), 1–13; N. I. Pavlenko, "Idei absoliutizma v zakonodatel'stve XVIII v.," in *Absoliutizm v Rossii* (Moscow, 1964), 389–427; Florovsky, *Ways of Russian Theology*, 1:115

[57] Cracraft, *The Church Reform of Peter the Great*, 165–218; Alexander V. Muller, *The Spiritual Regulation of Peter the Great* (Seattle, Wash., 1972), ix–xxxviii.

[58] Cherniavsky, *Tsar and People*, 84–85; *Panegiricheskaia literatura*, 86–88.

his birthday and name day with public prayers. From this time on, the personal holidays, and the birth and name days of the members of the imperial family, were placed on the list of official holidays (*tabel'nye*, or *vysokotorzhestvennye dni*) in the manner of German princes. According to Zhivov, the official register included mention of forty-four such observances for 1723.[59]

Metaphor created the image of a monarch without debt to the past. Peter was compared to the Apostle Andrew and the emperors Augustus and Constantine.[60] But most of all, Peter wished to be identified as creator. When he accepted the title of *imperator* from the Senate in October 1721, the rhetoric of the speeches raised him to a supreme being. Chancellor Gavriil Golovkin lauded Peter for taking Russia "from the darkness of Ignorance into the Theater of the World, so to speak from nothingness into being, into the company of political peoples." As V. Iu. Matveev has shown, Peter actively developed the theme of Pygmalion and Galatea from a Baroque emblem into a personalized glorification of his achievements. Peter emblazoned his standard and seal with the image of himself as a sculptor shaping Russia.[61]

Golovkin heralded Peter as "Father of the Fatherland, Peter the Great, All-Russian Emperor (*Imperator*)," giving him the highest dignities accorded to Western monarchs. *Imperator* placed him in the company of the pagan emperors of antiquity rather than the Christian emperors of the Byzantine Empire. The adoption of the title of emperor (*imperator*) turned a *tsarstvo* into an *imperia*. The renaming marked a cultural transformation. It meant, as Golovkin suggested, a coming into being, escaping ignorance and barbarism, for the company of "political peoples." "All-Russian" (*Vserossiiskii*) now designated not only rule over many peoples, but a new political identity, those belonging to the imperial category, those who were part of the Westernized, elite culture, who had made themselves in the image of their sovereign.

The title, "Peter the Great," made Peter the equal of Louis le Grand; the title, "father of the fatherland" "(*Otets otechestva*), the equivalent of the Latin *pater patriae*, stated the new meaning of the tsar's role as father of his

[59] Zhivov, "Kul'turnye reformy"; Zhivov and Uspenskii, "Tsar' i Bog," 118–19; Cracraft, *The Church Reform of Peter the Great*, 211.

[60] The order of St. Andrew was the first he established, and a golden arc with relics of the Saint was buried in the ground beneath the Peter-Paul fortress. At the same time, Peter, like his predecessors, was described as "a new Constantine," as the first Christian emperor. Peter continued the cult of Constantine's cross, which adorned nearly all the regimental standards of his reign. Vilinbakhov, "K istorii uchrezhdeniia ordena Andreia Pervozvannogo i evoliutsiia ego znaka," 144–58; "Istoricheskii obzor," *Pridvornyi kalendar' na 1892 g.* (St. Petersburg, 1892), 302–3, 308, 412; G. V. Vilinbakhov, "Osnovanie Peterburga i imperskaia emblematika," in Iu. M. Lotman, ed., *Semiotika goroda i gorodskoi kul'tury (Trudy po znakovym sistemam)* 18: 49–52; Lotman and Uspenskii, "Echoes of the Notion of 'Moscow the Third Rome,'" 57–58.

[61] Vilinbakhov, "Osnovanie Peterburga i imperskaia emblematika," 49, 52; Solov'ev, *Istoriia Rossii*, 9:321; *Panegiricheskaia literatura*, 298; V. Iu. Matveev, "K istorii vozniknoveniia i razvitiia siuzheta 'Petr I—vysekaiushchii statuiu Rossii,'" in *Kul'tura i iskusstvo Rossii XVIII veka* (Leningrad, 1981), 26–43.

flock. Now the relationship between sovereign and subjects was to be based not on hereditary right and personal obligation, but on the obligation to serve the state. The title was bestowed, declared the Senate decree of October 22, 1721, because Peter was the model of such service: "for the supreme mercy, paternal solicitude, and efforts he has shown for the prosperity of the state for the entire length of his most glorious reign and especially during the recent Swedish wars."[62]

The principle of utility rather than blood thus defined the metaphor of tsar as father. Peter was the paternalistic father: one who was obeyed and revered because of his care for his subjects, his direction of their lives. For the elite, the paternalistic image of domination by solicitude replaced the patriarchal image—domination justified by biblical injunction to revere the father. Peter's successors would assume an office vested with enormous power and sacral qualities, but they, too, had to justify their power by their deeds; they, too, had to emulate the gods, to prove their efficacy, and to show themselves dedicated to the common weal.

But creating a successor proved vastly more difficult than constructing a mythology of rule. Involved in his military campaigns, Peter left his son in the care of his first wife, Evdokiia. Alexei received a traditional religious education, and showed little interest in military or civil service. In vain did Peter implore him to learn to serve as an officer and an official. After Alexei's poor performance in a bombardier company at Narva in 1704, Peter both admonished and cajoled him. "You should love everything that serves the weal and honor of the fatherland, should love faithful advisers and servants, whether they are others or your own, and not spare labors for the common good. If my advice is so much air and you do not do what I wish, then I do not recognize you as my son: I will pray god that he punish you in this life and the next." Alexei kissed his father's hand and vowed to imitate him.[63]

But the son of a founder cannot himself be a founder unless he destroys his own legacy. Alexei assumed his father's posture of rebellion on behalf of everything his father rejected. Aside from Alexei's own predilections and weakness, there was an intrinsic contradiction between Peter's ruling myth and his demand for obedience to his will. Peter commanded Alexei to follow his example, but his example was one of the furious god, engaged in destruction and re-creation, the image of the conqueror, with contempt for everything that preceded him. Adopting Peter's role in the myth, Alexei would have to stand apart from the new order and wield the same type of destructive force.

From 1715 on, Peter began to bring his second, his Western family into his scenario, displaying Catherine and her children in public and using engravings to exalt their image. The genre he employed, the *konkliuziia*, had been developed at the academies in Kiev and Moscow at the end of the seven-

---

[62] *PSZ*, no. 3840, October 22, 1721; Cherniavskii, *Tsar and People*, 82–87.
[63] Solov'ev, *Istoriia Rossii*, 9:111.

teenth century to illustrate allegorically the program of a learned dispute. Typically, it depicted the firmament, with figures of saints and gods at the side of mortals; beneath were earthly scenes of towns, battles, and ceremonies. The scenes had a theatrical character; the figures stand, looking out from a proscenium, as if posing to demonstrate the heights of glory they had attained.[64]

Such Baroque analogies between mortals and divinities elevated Peter's second family into the company of saints and gods, removing the stain of blasphemy left by the baptism of Catherine and then the marriage. This was the clear purpose of P. Pikart's and Alexei Zubov's *konkliuziia* of 1715, "The *Konkliuziia* dedicated to the Most Radiant Tsarist union, united by God." The engraving marked the birth of two heirs to Peter, Peter's own son, Peter Petrovich (who died in 1719), and his grandson, Peter Alekseevich, the future Peter II. Both of the latter are shown at the side, fully grown, next to Anna and Elizabeth, Peter's daughters by Catherine. Peter stands on one side in Roman dress, on the deck of a ship. On the opposite side, Catherine is shown next to St. Catherine. She is taller than the saint, a practice characteristic of the *konkliuziia* and unlike icons, which always presented mortals smaller than saints. St. Alexei looks down on the scene from the heavens, holding a picture of one of the tsareviches, but it is impossible to tell which. The regalia, in the middle of the picture, indicate that the succession is an important issue.[65] Alexei Zubov's "*Konkliuziia* on the Succession" of 1717, executed for Catherine's name day, eliminates all reference to the tsarevich Alexei. She is illuminated by a heavenly ray, with the caption, "Loving mother of the Tsarevich, Peter Petrovich."[66]

Alexei Petrovich could find no place in the reigning myth, and the conflict ended with the trial and murder of the heir in 1718. The result was the succession law of 1722, which sought to remove the mishaps of biology from the process.[67] It deemed succession by seniority "an evil custom." The oldest son could be poisoned by "Absalom's malice." The principal argument was from utility. Peter claimed he acted out of "solicitude for the integrity of the state," whose borders he had greatly extended. He commanded, as a result, that "the ruling tsar always have the freedom (*volia*) to designate whom he wishes, and to remove the one who has been designated, if [the tsar] sees in him such debauchery, so that children and posterity, having this check upon them, do not fall into such malice, described above."

[64] Alekseeva, *Graviura petrovskogo vremeni*, 186, passim; M. A. Alekseeva, "Zhanr konkliuzii v russkom iskusstve kontsa XVII-nachala XVIII veka," in *Russkoe iskusstvo barokko; Materialy i issledovaniia* (Moscow, 1977), 7–29.

[65] Alekseeva, *Graviura petrovskogo vremeni*, 139–40, 188.

[66] Ibid., 181–83.

[67] See G. Gurvich, *"Pravda voli monarshei" Feofana Prokopovicha i eia zapadnoevropeiskie istochniki* (Iur'ev, 1915); Mikhail Zyzykin, *Tsarskaia vlast' i zakon o prestolonasledii v Rossii* (Sofia, 1924), 72–82. For a Freudian interpretation, see Alain Besançon, *Le tsarévitch immolé; la symbolique de la loi dans la culture russe* (Paris, 1967), 109–22.

In fact, Russian tsars had possessed this freedom, and the law referred to the precedent of Ivan III, who had designated his grandson, Dmitrii, then his son Vasilii, as heir. But Peter's decree was understood as abolishing the principle of seniority and requiring the reigning monarch to designate his or her successor. The law concluded with an oath, to be taken by all servitors, to abide by the emperor's choice. The change in the law was defended by the tract "The Law of the Monarch's Will" (*Pravda voli monarshei*), which set forth additional examples from history and natural law arguments of Hobbes and Pufendorf.[68]

Peter never designated a successor. But increasingly in his last years, he advanced his helpmeet, Catherine, as preserver of his values and incarnation of the new secular order. Catherine was his counterpart in the reigning myth. She was a player in his scenario, acting as his creature, his Galatea, a symbol of the European woman, and thus the Westernized character of Russian monarchy. She had taken on the tasks spurned by Alexei, participating in battles and even riding at the head of the troops on the Pruth campaign. She was credited with inventing the scheme that freed Peter from captivity after the defeat on the Pruth. To celebrate this deed, Peter introduced the Russian honorary order for women, the Order of St. Catherine, November 14, 1714, the order of "Liberation." Each member had to "redeem one Christian from barbarian servitude with her own money."[69]

Peter's reign and his succession law had the effect of making a woman, and in the long run, women his successors. For only women could both present themselves as absolutely faithful to Peter's Western legacy, and at the same time quiet fears of a return of the coercive energy of the founder. Whether or not Peter had decided to make Catherine his successor, and the evidence is ambiguous, in 1723 he announced his intention to proceed to crown her Empress of Russia. The coronation of a woman was another open transgression of Russian Orthodox norms, another violation committed and displayed in order to establish a completely new order. (The only previous crowning of a tsarevna had taken place in 1606, when the First False Dmitrii, supported by the Poles, was crowned at the side of his Polish wife, Marina.)

Peter's manifesto again invoked an analogy to place Russian monarchy on the plane of universal monarchy and to justify the break with tradition. It began with the typical Petrine rationalist explanatory *ponezhe* (inasmuch as): "inasmuch as it is known to all that in all Christian states it is the

[68] *PSZ*, no. 3893, February 5, 1722; Olshr, "La Chiesa e lo Stato nel cerimoniale d'incoronazione degli zar Romanov," 371–73. The tract is customarily attributed to Feofan Prokopovich, but James Cracraft has thrown doubt on Prokopovich's authorship of the *Pravda*. See James Cracraft, "Did Feofan Prokopovich Really Write *Pravda Volei Monarshei*?" *Slavic Review*, vol. 40, no. 2 (Summer, 1981): 173–94.

[69] On Catherine's role in Peter's reign, see J. T. Alexander, "Favourites, Favouritism and Female Rule in Russia, 1725–1796," in Roger Bartlett and Janet Hartley, eds., *Russia in the Age of Enlightenment: Essays for Isabel de Madariaga* (New York, 1990), 106–7.

indispensable custom for Potentates to crown their spouses." The manifesto then cited Byzantine tradition, providing examples of four emperors who had crowned their wives. The second argument, from utility, defended Catherine's qualifications to rule. The manifesto extolled her service both to Peter and the fatherland, particularly her valor in the Northern War, when she had "put aside female weakness, and willingly stayed at Our side and helped as much as possible." A specific reference was made to the episode in the Pruth campaign. At a "desperate moment," the manifesto declared, she had "acted as a man and not a woman."[70]

The coronation manifesto introduced a new note of sexual ambiguity into the image of empress, which sounded again in Prokopovich's coronation sermon and would characterize the reigning empresses later in the century. The female monarch combined loyalty to Peter's model of heroism and sacrifice with the elegance and taste now symbolizing the higher values of the West. The classical Western concept of fundamental identity of the sexes, described by Thomas Laqueur, here enters Russian imagery. Queen Elizabeth of England used this concept "to play the alluring but inaccessible virgin queen and warrior prince," and Catherine I and her female successors would affect a similar duality.[71]

The iconic form of this monarchical persona was the goddess Minerva, who conjoined power with wisdom, beauty, and high culture. The wall and ceiling paintings of the Summer Palace, completed in 1713 and 1714, presented Minerva in both military and peaceful dress. She wielded a sword, and her victory was celebrated by Cupids holding a wreath of stars. A carved wall panel of Catherine as Minerva adorned Peter's study at Peterhof. The ceiling of the throne room of the Summer Palace, *The Triumph of Catherine*, painted in the 1720s, probably after Peter's death, completed Catherine's ascension to the heavens. Wearing a decolleté gown, she rides in a golden carriage drawn by a double-headed eagle and holds a scepter in her right hand and the figure of a warrior with lance and shield in her left. She is accompanied by Cupids, while the figures of Perfidy and Ignorance lie defeated beneath.[72]

On the day of the coronation, in the Palace of Facets, the Moscow Academy made a presentation of a *konkliuziia* by Ivan Zubov, Alexei Zubov's older brother (fig. 9). The scene, the surviving section of a four-panel engraving, is set as if on a stage. Cupids raise the curtains on the emperor, dressed in armor and a cape, and wearing a laurel wreath. At his right stand Neptune and Hercules. Peter points to the great expanse of Russia on a globe; at its left lie two crowns in the new Western style, his and Catherine's. Cather-

---

[70] *PSZ*, no. 4366, November 15, 1723.

[71] Thomas Laqueur, *Making Sex: Body and Gender from the Greeks to Freud* (Cambridge, Mass., 1990), 122–23.

[72] Bardon, *Le portrait mythologique*, 49–50; Borzin, *Rospisi petrovskogo vremeni*, 108–12; Cracraft, *The Petrine Revolution in Architecture*, 187. The scepter in her right hand suggests that the painting was completed after she had succeeded Peter.

9. *Konkliuziia on the Coronation of Empress Catherine Alekseevna.*
Engraving by Ivan Zubov.

ine approaches from the right, followed by the allegorical figures of Glory, Truth, Piety, and Foresight. A goddess, unidentified, descends from the missing upper panel, greets Catherine, and hands the crown to two cherubs who announce that God has found Catherine worthy. At the foot of the stage, a female figure wearing a crown and mantle, and presumably representing Russia, asks God to give her a blessing.[73]

Unlike the early *konkliuziia*, the setting is entirely secular, without the appearance of saints or religious symbols. It has the spirit of love and cele-

---

[73] Alekseeva, *Graviura petrovskogo vremeni*, 99, "Zhanr konkliuzii v russkom iskusstve kontsa XVII-nachala XVIII veka," 12. The engraving, Alekseeva indicates, repeats many of the motifs of the school play, *Russian Glory*, which was performed by the student theater at Moscow Hospital for Peter and Catherine after the coronation. Catherine was apotheosized as "Russian Virtue." The Russian text was interspersed with Latin texts, many of them from the *Aeneid*. In the second act, "About the Coronation," Cupid greets Catherine with the words, "Your love attracts the Russian people," and asserts that that is why she was being crowned. See B. V. Varneke, *History of the Russian Theater* (New York, 1951), 55–56; *P"esy shkol'nykh teatrov Moskvy* (Moscow, 1974), 256–83, 507–8.

bration. In the lower right, a genius, and Cupids, play music, under the legend "the joy of all the people" (*radost' vsenarodnaia*). A cartouche nearby, held by a muse, has the words of the Academy's dedication. The engraving, it says, is for Catherine's coronation and with it the whole land is rejoicing. The chief of the merriment "is God himself." The dedication extols her heroism, and virtues, especially her courage and inspiration in battle, much as do other documents at the moment, and attests to the "national joy" about her crowning.

The center cartouche displays the Latin theses expounded at a scholastic dispute at the Academy on the occasion of the coronation.[74] The theses elaborate on the nature of God, sin, and repentance, the attainment of truth, justice, and beauty. The final thesis connects the act of celebration with God. True beatitude, it states, is only God, which can be intuited through the works of reason. But beatitude is formally to be found in the concrete manifestations of God—love, friendship, and joy (*per amorem amitiae et gaudium*). The theses confirm the divine nature of the celebration and the conjugal union that symbolizes the new secular state.[75]

·

The coronation of Catherine I at the Assumption Cathedral in Moscow on May 7, 1724, was a consecration of Peter's new order. It laid claim to Muscovite ceremonies, but changed them freely to give religious sanction to the principle of utility, Western ways, and the unchallenged supremacy of secular power. Just as the Muscovite coronation disclosed the prince of Moscow as the bearer of the signs of Byzantine sovereignty, the Petrine coronation adapted Muscovite rituals to sanctify the Westernized emperor as the successor of the tsars. It was the Petersburg empire's ceremonial taking possession of the Muscovite past. Modifications of the ceremonies in the Petrine spirit, introduced at the coronation of Anna Ioannovna in 1730 and of Elizabeth Petrovna in 1742, completed the evolution of the imperial coronation ceremony.

After the coronation, Peter issued the first published *Opisanie (Description)* of a Russian coronation.[76] Unlike the *chin venchaniia* (coronation order), the *Opisanie* encompassed the many events that Peter added before and after the religious ceremonies: the arrival of the emperor, the promulgation of the coronation and announcement of the date, and the parades and celebrations after the religious services. The *Opisanie* made the religious ritual

---

[74] On the curriculum, see Okenfuss, "Jesuit Origins," 116–20; Vishnevskii was the rector of the Academy. He was one of the Kievan monks whom Iavorskii brought to Moscow after 1700. Smirnov, *Istoriia Moskovskoi Slaviano-Greko-Latinskoi Akademii*, 196.

[75] I would like to thank Elena Rabinovich for her explanations of the Latin text and the classical allusions in the engraving.

[76] *Opisanie koronatsii e. v. Ekateriny Alekseevny* (St. Petersburg, 1724; Moscow, 1725). For complete titles, see *Svodnyi katalog russkoi knigi grazhdanskoi pechati XVIII veka* (Moscow, 1964), 2:356.

an event of secular import, justifying and glorifying every movement of the all-Russian emperor. With it, the coronation became a state act that figured in the historical mythology of Petrine absolutism.[77]

The "textualization" of the coronation followed the European pattern, defining the meanings the ceremonies were supposed to convey and the feelings they were supposed to evoke. The *Opisanie* established the new cultural context in which the coronation was to be understood. The title was *Opisanie koronatsii*, the borrowed word *koronatsiia* supplanting the Muscovite term for crowning (*venchaniia*). The opening of the account made clear the new textual focus: the first subject was not the cathedral, or the regalia, but the emperor and empress themselves, whose movements before and after the ceremonies set the coronation in the chronicle of their lives. The *Opisanie* mentioned the new ceremony of promulgation, borrowed perhaps from Prussia, which it called "the usual ceremony," though it had never been performed in Russia. Two days before the coronation, heralds in Western costumes appeared "everywhere in Moscow," and "with horns and drums made public announcement" of the date of the event.[78]

That the volume addressed a non-Russian audience—though it appeared in no foreign language—became clear from the elementary description of the Kremlin—"the fortress in the middle of the city where previous all-Russian emperors, the ancestors of His Imperial Majesty, now ruling happily, had their customary residence." The depiction of the cathedral included an explanation that "Greek law" forbade holy images to be covered by tapestries and other decorations. It proudly mentioned the opulence of the interior and particularly of the silver chandelier in the center, "which may be admired as one of the most remarkable in all Europe for its great height, size, and marvelous work."[79]

Like the *chiny*, the *Opisanie* gave details on the preparation of the cathedral for the ceremony. Now two thrones stood before the altar, replacing the "tsar's place." A canopy was placed above them, embroidered with the imperial coat of arms, and the cross of St. Andrew, sewn entirely of gold thread, "of only the best work." But much of the description of the interior was devoted to the arrangement of the galleries erected along the walls—to emphasize the visibility of the ceremonies to the elite, their involvement in the proceedings. In the galleries sat state dignitaries, generals, "the most notable ladies and maidens," foreign ambassadors, and foreign gentlemen and cavaliers, "who wanted to watch this glorious ceremony."

[77] For a general description of coronation accounts and albums in eighteenth- and nineteenth-century Russia, see Edward Kasinec and Richard Wortman, "The Mythology of Empire: Imperial Russian Coronation Albums," *Biblion: The Bulletin of the New York Public Library*, vol. 1, no. 1 (Fall, 1992): 77–100.

[78] *Opisanie koronatsii e. v. Ekateriny Alekseevny* (St. Petersburg, 1724; Moscow, 1725), 3; Chakirov, *Tsarskie koronatsii*, 87, 89; Barsov, *Drevne-russkie pamiatniki*, 154–55; Bergholz, *Dnevnik kammer-iunkera Berkhol'tsa*, 4:43.

[79] *Opisanie*, 5.

The ceremony was performed by the elite, for the elite. From the start, it had the aspect of a triumph, now expressing the conquest of the ceremony of consecration by the Western Petersburg court. The *Opisanie* presented the troops not merely as guards but as principal actors in the celebrations and ceremonies, far more prominent than the clergy. Cannon salvoes resounded through the city to announce the moments of the crowning and anointment. Before the ceremonies began, the guards' regiments and other battalions invested the Kremlin square. Grenadiers of the guards, their hats decorated with plumes, lined the way from the Palace of Facets to the Assumption Cathedral. The *Opisanie* made no mention of spectators.[80]

The reception of the regalia in the palace, which opened earlier coronations, was eliminated, an indication that their importance in the ceremony would be somewhat reduced. The opening procession from the Kremlin palace to the Assumption Cathedral was apparently planned with the assistance of Catherine's son-in-law to be, the Duke of Holstein. A new ceremonial division of the guards, the *drabanty*, led and closed the procession. The *drabanty*, later called Cavalier Guards, were modeled on European guards' regiments, most likely the *drabants* of Charles XII of Sweden. They wore bright green uniforms, decorated with gold braid and golden imperial coats-of-arm, and boots with spurs; their musicians played silver drums and horns.[81]

The drums and horns provided a martial counterpoint to the tolling of the bells of the churches of Moscow, as the imperial family and the court proceeded from the Palace of Facets to the Assumption Cathedral. The court dignitaries who followed now bore the titles and wore the dress of a European court—a Hofmeister, a dozen pages, then four of Peter's young adjutants. The *tseremoniimeister*, Shuvalov, was followed by Lifland, Estland, and other provincial deputies. Generals and officials marched in their uniforms. A Prince Golitsyn, Baron Ostermann, Prince Dolgorukii, Count Musin-Pushkin, and Count Bruce bore the regalia on pillows. The marshall of the court, Count Peter Tolstoi, held the new silver state mace, crowned by a double-headed eagle and an immense emerald.

The emperor marched behind the grand marshall, flanked by the field marshalls Prince Menshikov and Prince Repnin. He wore his elegant blue summer caftan embroidered with silver, the work, it was said, of the empress herself. Catherine, walking arm and arm with the Duke of Holstein, showed that Russia could rival Western splendor. She wore a lavish purple robe in Spanish style, decorated with gold embroidery. Five "State Ladies" carried the train. Her hat was studded with gems and pearls.[82] They then entered

---

[80] *Opisanie*, 16–17.

[81] S. Panchulidze, *Istoriia kavalergardov, 1724–1799–1899* (St. Petersburg, 1899), 1:2–8. Though disbanded after the coronation, the Cavalier Guards were reconstituted for funerals and coronations and, in 1800, became a permanent regiment.

[82] *Opisanie*, 19–25; Bergholz, *Dnevnik kammer-iunkera Berkhol'tsa*, 4:50–52; Belozerskaia, "Tsarskoe venchanie," 5–6; S. S. Dmitriev and M. V. Nechkina, ed., *Khrestomatiia po*

the cathedral, to the accompaniment of choral singing. Now the choir intoned not the traditional "many years" but Psalm 100 (101 in the Western Bible): "I will sing of mercy and justice unto Thee Oh, Lord." The psalm proclaimed the king's vow to extirpate evil and promote justice, announcing a Western, Protestant conception of the monarch's assumption of supreme moral guidance of the population.[83]

The scene that the *Opisanie* depicted inside the cathedral resembled no previous Russian coronation. Westernized courtiers and foreign diplomats were arrayed in glittering magnificence in the gallery along the walls. German royalty occupied prominent places in the cathedral. The Duchess of Mecklenburg and the Duchess of Courland, both nieces of Peter, sat on thrones near the empress. Behind them, in cloth of gold, was the seat of the Duke of Holstein, the fiancé of Peter's daughter, Anna. The placement of the courtiers and the Duke of Holstein at the throne followed European practice, probably at the duke's instance. The court officials, the ceremony masters, and the heraldry masters stood on the steps. The marshall of the court, Tolstoi, led Peter up the steps. The empress was accompanied to the throne by the duke. For the first time at a coronation, emperor and empress sat on thrones side-by-side; above them was a golden canopy, with the state arms embroidered in black and the cross of St. Andrew.[84]

Peter introduced new items of regalia and purged the ceremony of the symbols of descent connected with the Monomakh legend. A European crown and mantle replaced the "Monomakh cap" and the sacred *barmy*. The lavish new crown of gold was in European style. It impressed Bergholz, the chamberlain of the Duke of Holstein, who looked upon "Monomakh's cap" and other old Russian crowns with some contempt. He remarked approvingly in his diary that it "far surpassed all the [other crowns] in its elegance and opulence," and had been made "as an imperial crown ought to be made." It weighed four pounds and was decorated with hundreds of gems, including an enormous ruby acquired by Tsar Alexei from China, which, the *Opisanie* boasted, was "the very most expensive" (*naidragotsenneishii*) and "of a size larger than a pigeon egg." Above the ruby was an orb with a diamond cross. The new imperial mantle was no less extravagant. It was of gold and purple cloth, ornamented like the mantles of European kings, with ermine, and, according to the *Opisanie*, "a multitude of large diamonds." Bergholz was amazed at its size and costliness; it was said to

istorii SSSR (Moscow, 1953), 106–7. Bergholz may have been referring to the crimson coronation robe of Catherine I, embroidered with silver, that is now preserved in the Kremlin Armory. It was apparently made in Paris at a cost of 4,000 rubles (Bobrovnitskaia et al., *Gosudarstvennaia oruzheinaia palata*, 338–39).

[83] *Opisanie*, 26.

[84] *Opisanie*, 10, 15, 27–30. My account also uses material found in Bergholz, *Dnevnik kammer-iunkera Berkhol'tsa*, 4:53–56; Chakirov, *Tsarskie koronatsii*, 84–90; Belozerskaia, "Tsarskoe venchanie," 4–6; V. I. Zhmakin, "Koronatsii russkikh imperatorov i imperatrits," *Russkaia Starina*, vol. 37 (1883): 501–7.

weigh 150 pounds, and the broach alone, he asserted, cost nearly 100,000 rubles. The scepter and orb, as mentioned above, had been made in the sixteenth and early seventeenth centuries in Western Europe. The *Opisanie* stressed that the orb "recalls imperial orbs," and claimed that its work was "ancient Roman."[85]

The first part of the ceremony, the conferral of the regalia, had also been changed beyond recognition; Peter, together with the Archbishop Feodosii, worked out the changes. Although Catherine was being crowned, and Feodesii and the archbishop of Pskov, Feofan Prokopovich, officiated, Peter himself was the central figure in the ceremony, directing the proceedings and conferring the regalia. Once all had taken their places, Peter gave the order to begin. He rose from the throne and took the scepter, the symbol of supreme authority, in his right hand and brandished it throughout the ceremony. Turning toward the clergy, he pronounced in loud tones, "Since our intention to crown our dearest wife has been known to all, may we proceed to complete this according to the church ceremony."

The rites opened with Catherine's reciting of the creed. Feodesii then proceeded to bless her, laying his hand on her head; the introductory exchange between tsar and presiding cleric concerning hereditary rights to the throne had been deleted. Peter took the mantle from Feodesii and Feofan and placed it on her shoulders. Observers reported that she wept and bent before him to kiss his feet, but Peter, hardly one for displays of sentiment, smiled and raised her to her feet. Ceremony for him was a display of majesty, power, and dignity, not of personal emotion.

Then, in the central episode of the coronation, Catherine fell to her knees and Peter placed the crown on her head, the emperor replacing the clergy as the agent conferring the principal symbol of power. At the moment of the crowning, two cannons, placed before the cathedral, were fired and answered by a salvo of all the guns of the city and a volley from the guards lined up on the square. Peter handed Catherine the orb. Since the precept had also been removed from the ceremony, Catherine proceeded directly to the Imperial Doors. There she kneeled and was anointed according to the earlier ritual, on the brow, lips, and arms. But as consort, she was not given communion at the altar with the clergy, but before the holy doors. Another cannon salute announced the anointment.[86]

The Petrine coronation thus heightened the split in the dramatic action between the investiture and the liturgy that had characterized Russian coronation rituals since the sixteenth century. The investiture carried the political and cultural content of the ceremony, elevating the sovereign, in this case in the person of his spouse, as the ruler of an empire of a European type. The

---

[85] *Opisanie*, 80–81; *BE*, 31:318–19; Chakirov, *Tsarskie koronatsii*, 88; Bergholz, *Dnevnik kammer-iunkera Berkhol'tsa*, 4:33–34, 51; Belozerskaia, "Tsarskoe venchanie," 5; Olshr, "La Chiesa e lo Stato nel cerimoniale d'incoronazione degli zar Romanov," 365; Evgenii Karnovich, "Koronovanie gosudarei," *Russkii Arkhiv* 1 (1990): 38.

[86] *Opisanie*, 32–42.

liturgy—the anointment and communion—retained its Muscovite character. The clergy continued to exercise the dominant role that they had lost in the investiture. The anointment and communion at the altar conferred an ambiguous sacerdotal designation that made Russian monarchs members of the clergy but did not empower them to hold services or minister the sacraments.

The elimination of the precept made clear that the monarch no longer looked to the clergy for moral guidance. It was replaced by a sermon or oration (*Slovo Bozhiia*), which at this coronation followed the communion. Feofan Prokopovich delivered the sermon, and little in his message was religious.[87] He justified Catherine's coronation by citing her virtues: she had earned the right to be crowned by her merits and accomplishments; she was "a collection of all virtues." In other countries, Prokopovich declared, it was common to crown wives of monarchs. Russia also had women worthy of coronation, but God awaited the moment when there would be one who was "very most worthy," a "Heroine," before the Russian people could adopt the custom. Prokopovich's analogies from legend and world history removed her, like Peter, from the Russian past and placed her in a universal context. He compared her to the Babylonian Semiramis, the Scythian Tamira, the Amazon Penfesileia, the Byzantine Elena, Pulkheria, and Evdoxia, but each of these, he declared, excelled at only one of the qualities that Catherine exemplified. As in the manifesto on the coronation, Prokopovich's sermon attributed male virtues to her: "This great Heroine is so strong in this respect that few men can compare to her, on campaigns, bad weather, adversity, boiling heat, frigid weather, storms, hard crossings, noisy rooms, and other such difficulties harmful to the health." But she also excelled in her wifely duties. She gave Peter rest, entertainment, and companionship.

The procession in full regalia from the Assumption Cathedral to the Archangel Cathedral for the prayer over the graves of the tsars was a great display of Catherine's glory and magnificence. Peter did not remain with her, but indicating that he felt weak and tired, returned to the palace. She walked under an enormous canopy carried by six major-generals, and her train was borne by five ladies-in-waiting. The custom of tossing gold and silver coins before the monarch was abandoned. Instead, Prince Menshikov threw gold and silver coins into the crowd, a practice that had been followed at Byzantine and many Western coronation ceremonies.[88]

Catherine did not proceed to the Annunciation Cathedral, but set off in a resplendent procession for the Voznesenskii Convent for prayers at the graves of Peter's female ancestors. At the coronation banquet, the emperor and the empress replaced the ruler and patriarch as the principal figures. In

[87] Ibid., 45; Feofan Prokopovich, *Slova i rechi pouchitel'nye, pokhval'nye, i pozdravitel'nye* (St. Petersburg, 1761), 2:103–11.

[88] Belozerskaia, "Tsarskoe venchanie," 6–7; Zhmakin, "Koronatsii russkikh imperatorov," 506–7.

attendance were the assembled courtiers, notables, as well as members of the clergy. The court officials stood through the meal to serve the emperor and empress, then took the repast themselves. During the banquet, a feast of roast ox was served to the "people" in the square outside, an innovation apparently following Holsteinian custom. Two fountains spouted red and white wine. According to Bergholz, Peter left the banquet for a short while to watch the scene on the square.[89]

Catherine's coronation was the first to be surrounded by the elaborate and spectacular secular celebrations that would overshadow the ceremony itself over the next century. The festivities gave ceremonial confirmation to the utilitarian scenario: displays of merriment and joy indicated that the emperor's efforts for the benefit of the realm were appreciated. The celebrations, however forced and regimented, provided symbolic consent for the enormous sacrifices of service the emperor was exacting. These festivities comprised only the elite surrounding the emperor. The people of Moscow kept their distance, behind the lines of soldiers, and showed little sympathy for the celebrations. Nor did Peter show especial clemency in honor of the coronation. Two decrees granting extensions of several years on arrears owed the treasury were the only perfunctory gestures toward popular feeling.[90]

The day after the coronation, a gala reception took place at the Kremlin, which was resumed two days later. The receptions were followed by a ball and a lavish two-hour fireworks display on Tsaritsyn Meadow. "I do not believe there have been many comparable to it on earth," Bergholz wrote.[91] The *Opisanie* gave the textual celebration of the gala events. The festivities on the last day were celebrated "with magnificence and richness (*s magnifitsentsieiu i bogatstvom*)" and concluded "deep at night . . . with the igniting of splendid and really skillful fireworks." An engraving of the fireworks shows eight fountains of light and numerous rockets traced against the night sky. In the foreground is an illuminated figure of Neptune on horseback.[92]

•

It is a measure of Peter's impact on Russian ceremonies that he, in effect, created his own funeral solemnities. Muscovite obsequies were modest events, religious observances in keeping with the ecclesiastical tenor of the tsar's life. They began with a simple cortege of clergy, courtiers, and the

[89] Bergholz, *Dnevnik kammer-iunkera Berkhol'tsa*, 4:58.

[90] Both foreign and native merchants in Moscow were disgruntled by a decree ordering them to send all horses, without compensation, to Prince Menshikov for the new Cavalier Guards (Zhmakin, "Koronatsii russkikh imperatorov"; *Russkaia Starina* [March 1883]: 507–9; Bergholz, *Dnevnik kammer-iunkera Berkhol'tsa*, 4:38; Belozerskaia, "Tsarskoe venchanie," 8–9).

[91] Bergholz, *Dnevnik kammer-iunkera Berkhol'tsa*, 4:59.

[92] *Opisanie koronatsii e. v. Ekateriny Alekseevny*, 77–78; Vasil'ev, *Starinnye feierverki*, 55, Plate 31.

tsar's family, which proceeded from the Kremlin Palace to the Archangel Cathedral on the day of the tsar's death or the day after.[93] Peter broke with the old traditions when, in 1699, he staged the funeral ceremonies for Admiral and General Lefort and General Gordon patterned on European knightly funeral processions. Here, the deceased's horse and battle paraphernalia, displayed in his procession, showed his achievements on earth. Officers had already replaced the clergy as the principal participants in the ceremony.[94]

The field marshall, Count Jacob Bruce, composed Peter's ceremony, apparently on the model of French, German, and Swedish royal funerals. Bruce patterned Peter's rites on funerals for generals, adding elements of Western royal ceremonies, notably the regalia and the standards of the provinces of the empire.[95] The elaborate ceremonies of lying in state, probably based on French practice, supplanted the Muscovite custom of immediate burial. As with the coronation, an *Opisanie*, published shortly after the funeral by the Senate press, recorded the details of the ceremonies and established the event in the new mythology of empire.[96]

The *Opisanie* opened with a depiction of the elaborate decorations in the hall in the Winter Palace, where Peter's body lay in state for more than thirty days after his death on January 28, 1725. Emblems announced the Western and supranational character of his empire, without a trace of the orthodox past. Over the entry hung an immense state coat of arms. The ceiling was decorated with an enormous St. Andrew's cross. Imperial crowns, items of regalia, and medals of St. Andrew and Danish and Polish orders surrounded the coffin. Shields of all the provinces of the empire ornamented the walls.

The account described the statues set about the room, many acquired by Peter himself, and left no doubt about the triumph of Western culture. Two figures in full height sat in mourning beside each provincial shield. They represented "different peoples of the Russian empire." Four bronze statues, placed on the steps of the throne, Russia, Europe, Mars, and Hercules, mourned Peter's death. The same theme was repeated in four marble pyramids, representing Faith, Time, Glory, and the Founding of the Fleet. At the base of each was a mourning genius. At the side of each pyramid stood statues symbolizing the emperor's virtues. Opposite the coffin, skeletons and geniuses held Peter's initials, his coat of arms in bronze, and a golden medallion with his portrait. The tsar lay in his coffin clad in a crimson coat em-

---

[93] *Opisanie pogrebeniia blazhennoi pamiati imperatora Nikolaia Igo s prisovokupleniem istoricheskogo ocherka pogrebenii tsarei i imperatorov vserossiiskikh i nekotorykh drugikh evropeiskikh gosudarei* (St. Petersburg, 1856), 1–6.

[94] Ibid., 6–7.

[95] Ibid., 9–29; Strong, *Splendor at Court*, 111, 113. The funeral of King Karl Gustave of Sweden, which introduced large numbers of soldiers, and the French funeral, during which the body had to lie in rest for forty days, appear to have also been the most direct influences on the Russian ceremony.

[96] *Opisanie poriadka derzhannogo pri pogrebenii blazhennyia vysokoslavnyia i vechno dostoineishiia pamiati . . . Petra Velikogo* (St. Petersburg, 1725; Moscow, 1726). My account is based on this text, and the account in *Opisanie pogrebeniia*, 30–58.

broidered with silver, boots with spurs, a sword, and the medals of St. Andrew.

The funeral cortege on March 8, 1725, as recounted in the *Opisanie*, was a massive demonstration of Peter's imperial achievements. More than a thousand musketeers, and more than ten thousand troops of the guard, fleet, and local garrisons, as well as Cavalier Guards, lined the way from the palace to the Cathedral of Peter and Paul. The procession opened with trumpeters and drummers, officers and courtiers. It also included deputies from towns, and the Lifland and Estland nobility. Peter's favorite horse, the *Leib-Pferde*, wearing red and white feathers and a rich saddle, was led by two lieutenant colonels.

Walking behind the coffin was the empress Catherine, with Menshikov and Apraksin at her side, her train carried by chamberlains, then Peter's daughters and other members of the imperial family, with the ladies-in-waiting. At their sides marched lines of Cavalier Guards, and behind them marched a group of magnates, including the chancellor, Count Golovkin, Prince Romanodovskii, and wives and daughters of servitors of the first eight classes of the Table of Ranks. There followed rows of officers and officials, members of the Russian nobility, Little Russian officers, and forty-five Russian merchants, all carrying candles. The *Opisanie* thus confirmed the presence and participation of representatives of the entire Russian state. Officers, officials, nobles, clergy, and merchants joined the imperial family on the way to the emperor's resting place. They all bore witness to his achievements and made the observance a show of national grief and respect.

Peter was buried in the cathedral in the Peter-Paul Fortress. The regiments were lined up along the city wall. After the service, Archbishop Prokopovich delivered his famous funeral oration. The speech itself was brief, but according to one eyewitness, cited by Golikov, it was so often interrupted by weeping and crying that it lasted nearly an hour. At his opening words, "What is this? What have we lived to witness, oh Russians!" Prokopovich and all the mourners wept. They then approached the coffin for their final farewells, which concluded, according to the *Opisanie*, "with great sobbing and indescribable howling." When Peter's coffin was lowered into the ground, three volleys from the thousands of troops along the way, answered by three salvoes from all the cannons of the admiralty and the Peter-Paul Fortress, announced the passing of the founder.[97]

The sermons of Prokopovich and others in the Petrine church hierarchy had extolled Peter as an exemplar of spiritual as well as worldly virtue.[98] They had employed religious imagery and rhetoric to glorify purely secular achievements. So it was in Peter's funeral oration: Prokopovich invoked bib-

[97] *Opisanie poriadka derzhannogo pri pogrebenii*, 30–31; I. I. Golikov, *Deianiia Petra Velikogo, mudrogo preobrazatelia Rossii* (Moscow, 1837–1843), 10:160; *Panegiricheskaia literatura*, 127.

[98] Nicholas V. Riasanovsky, *The Image of Peter the Great in Russian History and Thought* (New York, 1985), 12–17.

lical analogies to eulogize Peter as a pagan god, not a sinful mortal. He cited biblical figures not to trace the divine origins of monarchical power, but to give Peter's accomplishments biblical significance and magnitude.[99] Peter was Russia's Samson: he found feeble forces "and made your [Russia's] power stone, adamantine, as befits his name." He was Russia's Japheth, for building a fleet; Moses, for giving laws; and Solomon, for advancing wisdom, knowledge, craft, and civil institutions. David and Constantine, the only nonbiblical figure he mentioned, were his symbols for reorganizing the church and combating superstition.

For Prokopovich, the Bible figured as another sign of beginning, the ultimate denial of predecessors and origins. He mentioned no previous Russian ruler. Peter had created Russia, and he had also created his successor in his wife Catherine. It was appropriate that she had come from humble origin, for Peter, Prokopovich emphasized, molded Catherine. The female sex did not prevent her from being like Peter, for not only cohabitation, but association with Peter's wisdom, labors, and misfortunes had made her like him. Out of "gold refined in a crucible," Prokopovich declared, Peter had fashioned an heir to his crown, orb, and throne.

Prokopovich's eulogy held out the consolation that Peter's spirit lived on. It lived on in Russia, which Prokopovich now made the object of emotions. Peter had made Russia lovable, fearful to her enemies, "glorious throughout the world." It lived on in his religious, civic, and military reform. "For leaving us with the ruins of his body, he has left us his spirit." Finally, Peter's spirit lived on in the empress, "your [Russia's] sovereign and mother," and his descendants. Peter could not reproduce his own superhuman persona. But in Catherine he created his new image of the Russian monarch, who resembled European monarchs, embodied the same values, and earned the same admiration as they. During the following decades, women would represent and preserve the image of civilized Western monarchy in Russia. The stage manager, director, and leading actor withdrew from a scenario of heroic conquest and change, leaving the role of founder vacant.

---

[99] *Panegiricheskaia literatura*, 279–82. A good translation of the oration can be found in Marc Raeff, *Peter the Great Changes Russia* (Lexington, Mass., 1972), 39–43.

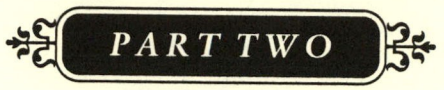

PART TWO

Olympian Scenarios

The Noble Monarchy and the Petrine Heritage

PETER THE GREAT bequeathed to his successors a daunting image of emperor as hero and god. His Succession Law and other legislation established a utilitarian measure of justifying rule by dedication to the general good. The right to rule did not emanate from the imperial office, whether acquired by heredity or usurpation, but by achievement, real or pretended. Just as Prokopovich's funeral oration made Catherine I Peter's spiritual heir, the sermons, odes, and festivals that inaugurated subsequent reigns portrayed new rulers as benefactors, who, like Peter, had subdued the forces working for personal interests against the welfare of all. Their scenarios presented them as godlike saviors of the realm, the emanations of Astraea, inaugurating an era of universal justice and happiness.

The practical effect of Peter's law was to leave the succession clouded by doubt. Peter himself designated no one, and the conflicting directives of his successors held little force. In the half-century after Peter's death, aspirants to the throne called on regiments of the guards to decide the outcome of struggles for the throne. Even before Peter's death, the empress Catherine ordered out the guards. Officers filled the hall where the leading officials conferred as Peter lay dying on the night of January 28, 1725, and lined the square outside the palace. Catherine's claims were supported by Alexander Menshikov, Peter Tolstoi, and other members of the Petrine elite. Citing grounds neither of heredity nor of her predecessor's designation, the decree named her ruling empress on the basis of her coronation.[1]

Similar scenes opened the reign of empresses Anna Ioannovna in 1730 and Elizabeth Petrovna in 1741. The guards' regiments and the court elite advanced the interests of the entire nobility in defending an alliance with the crown that lasted until the accession of Paul I in 1796.[2] These decades saw the increase of the nobles' power over their serfs, who, by the last decades of the century, had lost almost all possibility of redress of grievances, declining almost to the condition of chattel. Although the Table of Ranks, in principle, allowed lesser officials to gain noble status, the landed nobility dominated high positions in the administration. They usually began service in the military, often after being registered in guards' regiments at birth, then transferred to high positions in the administration, preferably in the capital.[3] The

---

[1] Kliuchevskii, *Sochineniia*, 4:259–61.

[2] On the guards' role as representatives of noble interests, see Dietrich Beyrau, *Militär und Gesellschaft im vorrevoliutsionären Russland* (Cologne, 1984), 190–93.

[3] S. M. Troitskii, *Russkii absoliutizm i dvorianstvo v XVIII v.; formirovanie biurokratii* (Moscow, 1974), 298–304; Wortman, *The Development of a Russian Legal Consciousness*, 18–20.

eighteenth-century state was a shared system of domination between a monarch, whose personal power was unlimited by institutions, and a nobility, who dominated the bureaucracy and ruled their estates in a manner resembling their sovereign's.

In this system, the term general welfare came to mean the advancement of noble interests.[4] Peter's secular, rationalist scenario of power was recast to express the harmony between sovereign and nobility. Accession decrees and coronations presented the empresses as benefactresses of the realm, while the ensuing celebrations displayed the concord between them and the ruling elite. If Peter exercised what Elias described as the leadership of the conqueror, the empresses of eighteenth-century Russia epitomized the conservative rule of the later stages of absolutism, exemplified by the Versailles of Louis XIV. Rather than lead the nobility in selfless deeds, the empresses maintained their positions in a stable system by manipulating the relations between the great families, disposing of honors and skillfully exercising intrigue and fear.[5]

Yet, at the same time, they maintained the ethos and image of conqueror. The presentations of their assumption of power emphasized the heroic display of violence producing the rupture with the previous reign, which stood for injustice and despotic self-interest. The show of force set them within the Petrine myth of monarch seizing his or her rule with ruthless violence in order to attain the utility of the realm. The demonstration of force was a symbolic requisite of enthronement, revealing the empress as the possessor of unbridled authority—one who had the power to act in behalf of the general good, without regard to the scruples of the previous ruler or cliques. Each seizure of power, therefore, was not concealed but publicly enshrined in public statements and displays as a heroic act. Accession manifestos justified the coup, the empress appeared at the head of guards' regiments, paintings glorified the show of force. The empresses presented themselves as the perpetuators of Peter's work of transformation, maintaining the image of what Cynthia Whittaker has called "the reforming tsar."[6]

The myth of renewal, of *renovatio*, endowed the victor with the aspect of a goddess descendant, inaugurating an age of gold. The second episode of the myth, after the seizure of power, was the acclamation: the nobility greeted the dawn of the new era by joining in festive celebration. The scenarios of the eighteenth century thus glorified change while they maintained and reinforced the stability that would preserve the predominance of the serf-holding

---

[4] On this shift of meaning see, Pavlenko, "Idei absoliutizma v zakonodatel'stve XVIII vek."

[5] The role of the networks in the Russian political system at this time has been masterfully examined by John LeDonne. See John P. LeDonne, *Absolutism and the Ruling Class: The Formation of the Russian Political Order, 1700–1825* (New York, 1991), 81–87, and John P. LeDonne, "Ruling Families in the Russian Political Order, 1689–1825," *Cahiers du Monde russe et soviétique*, vol. 38, nos. 3–4 (July–December 1987), 233–322.

[6] Cynthia Whittaker, "The Reforming Tsar: The Redefinition of Autocratic Duty in Eighteenth-Century Russia," *Slavic Review*, vol. 51, no. 1 (Spring, 1992): 77–98.

nobility. The conqueror was also the conserver, who helped defend and extend the elite's authority. At ceremonies and celebrations, the nobility appeared as a unified group, the diverse economic and national constituents of the empire displaying their common allegiance to their sovereign.

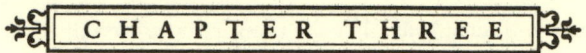
The Return of Astraea and the Demonstration of Happiness

It is true that now, at the rumor of the visit of HER IMPERIAL MAJESTY to Moscow for the acceptance of the crown, all of Russia, hearing of such good fortune, rejoices as never before. But this ruling city has been especially delighted with the joy and happiness at the sight of the face and the sojourn of HER IMPERIAL MAJESTY. It is like a person, who when happy, all his parts, his eyes, ears, tongue and lip, hand and leg, give sign of joy, though the true happiness resides in the heart. So, in truth, although now all Russia celebrates with joy, this city, which is like the heart of all Russian cities, feels the greatest joy because it contains all the causes and prerogatives (*prerogativy*) of joy. Here is the residence of the throne of the ancestors and parents of HER IMPERIAL MAJESTY. Here She is adorned with the Monarchical crown and the Imperial purple, here the scepter and orb await Her native hands. For she came to the ineffable joy of all Her faithful subjects. She came to receive what Christ himself, the Tsar of tsars, the Lord of rulers, has prepared for Her. She came, the God-chosen autocrat, who has adorned the All-Russian throne with Her kindness and Her beauty. And all wish, with one voice and one heart, with the grace and blessing of God, that she rule Her fatherland for innumerable years in endless joy and eternal prosperity.

—*Welcoming oration of Ambrosii, Archbishop of Novgorod to Empress Elizabeth Petrovna, in the Assumption Cathedral, Moscow, on her gala entry to Moscow, February 28, 1742*

THE RUSSIAN EMPRESSES AND THE AGE OF GOLD

The compact between throne and nobility was sealed during the struggle surrounding the accession of the empress Anna Ioannovna in 1730. Peter's death in 1725 had left the government without a strong leader and clear political goals. The Senate, the institution dedicated to Peter's concept of the absolute state, now became subordinated to the figures close to the empress. Alexander Menshikov, who had secured the throne for Catherine I, dominated the government from his position in a five-member Privy Council until her death in 1727. Catherine I was succeeded by Peter II, Alexei Petrovich's eleven-year-old son, whom she had designated in the testament she had agreed to shortly before her death.[1] Peter II replaced Menshikov as the principal favorite with Ivan Dolgorukii, who turned the council into a stronghold of the Muscovite aristocracy under the sway of two members of the Dolgorukii family and Prince Dmitrii Golitsyn. At Peter II's death in 1730, the council ignored Catherine's testament. They invited Anna, Duchess of Courland, the daughter of Peter the Great's half-brother Ivan, under conditions stipulating that she share power with the council.

The ensuing struggle quickly showed that only an unlimited monarch could win the trust of the various groups within the nobility. The large number of noblemen who had gathered in the capital for the wedding of Peter II to Princess Ekaterina Dolgorukaia rallied to the cause of absolute monarchy. On February 11, the day after she arrived from Courland at Vsesviatskoe outside Moscow, she had declared herself colonel of the Preobrazhenskii Regiment and captain of the Cavalier Guards before battalions of the two regiments. She served each of the Cavalier Guards a *riumka* of vodka. This was an open and demonstrative violation of the fourth of the conditions, which had placed the guards under the authority of the council.[2] Two weeks later, "before all the people," she tore up the "points" that she had agreed to as a condition of rule. Anna's assumption of power, her enthronement and coronation, established the pattern followed by Elizabeth and Catherine II. She presented herself as champion of the Petrine cause of the "general good," as opposed to the specific interests of the aristocrats on the council. In this respect, she had the backing of the principal spokesmen of Petrine absolutism, Prokopovich, V. N. Tatishchev, and A. P. Volynskii, all of whom wrote forcefully in defense of absolute monarchy. Anna then proceeded to extend to the nobility the privileges they had sought from the council, among them the reduction of service to twenty-five years and the establishment of a Noble Cadets Corps to provide them with an easy, elite path of advancement in the service. But at the same time, noblemen retained the ethos of state service as stated by Peter. The sacrifices and exactions of his reign had ceased, but service remained what Marc Raeff has described as "the expression of a social and moral ideal."[3]

It is no accident that women rulers proved able to fuse the personae of conquering and conserving monarchs, for only they could claim to defend Peter's heritage without threatening a return of his punitive fury. From 1725 until 1796, Russia was ruled by empresses, except for the brief interludes of

---

[1] After Peter II, Catherine designated her daughters, Anna—then Duchess of Holstein—and Elizabeth (Solov'ev, *Istoriia Rossii*, 10:80–81).

[2] D. A. Korsakov, *Votsarenie Imperatritsy Anny Ioannovny* (Kazan, 1880), 243–44; Solov'ev, *Istoriia Rossii*, 10:214–15; P. Miliukov, "Verkhovniki i shliakhetstvo," in his *Iz istorii russkoi intelligentsii* (St. Petersburg, 1903), 41, 48.

[3] Marc Raeff, *Origins of the Russian Intelligentsia: The Eighteenth Century Nobility* (New York, 1966), 119–20.

the reigns of Peter II (1727–1730), Ivan VI (October–December 1741), and Peter III (December 1761–June 1762). Empresses served as exemplars of both cathartic force and disarming mildness and love, reflecting a classical conception of the identity of the sexes and sexual ambiguity.[4]

The Olympian scenarios presented the symbolic and artistic forms that reconciled the antinomies of conqueror and conserver, turning the conqueror into the deliverer initiating an era of tranquillity, cultivation, and grace. The androgynous image of Minerva fused the violence, on which the authority of the monarch rested, with classical reason and wisdom, and identified the Russian empress with the royal figures glorified as denizens of Olympus in the West. In this respect, eighteenth-century empresses continued the role of Catherine I and served as symbols of Western culture and taste. They exemplified the dominant feminine imagery of Western courts of the eighteenth century. In Paris, aristocratic women held salons and received amorous praise. At Versailles, the mistresses of Louis XV, and later Marie Antoinette, wielded considerable influence. In Petersburg, empresses employed Western tastes and manners as signs of imperial rule, receiving the deference of their servitors' praise and imitation.

The Russian court was to become a semblance of the West; but it had to be a semblance, Russians acting as Europeans, performing the metaphor and behaving "like foreigners." Status accrued to noblemen through service; they displayed their standing by imitating Europeans while remaining Russian. It was the very division between Russian origin and Western manners that entitled them to rule. In eighteenth-century Russia, theatricality was an attribute of power. Indeed, the esteem for things Western, Iurii Lotman observed, could actually intensify animosity to foreigners, whose Western features were real and not idealized and also not subject to political and social validation.[5]

Foreigners might be recruited for the Russian service, but their rule or domination of the court violated patriotic pride. Although Peter recruited many foreigners to serve in his new institutions, he restricted them to certain positions to ensure their subservience. They could not be chosen presidents of colleges and were not allowed to see details of the state budget.[6] The breach of this principle during the reign of Anna Ioannovana (1730–1740) violated the patriotic feelings of the nobility. Anna's German favorites, particularly her lover, Ernst-Johann Biron, dominated the government. After her death, Biron tried to establish a regency for the infant tsar, Ivan VI, whom she had designated. Ivan VI was the son of Anna Leopoldovna, the niece of the empress Anna. Biron was quickly overthrown by Burckhard Münnich, who established the regency of Anna Leopoldovna. On November 25, 1741, Peter's daughter, Elizabeth, led a coup supported by members of

---

[4] See Laqueur, *Making Sex*, especially chapter 4.

[5] Lotman and Uspenskii, *The Semiotics of Russian Culture*, 233.

[6] Meehan-Waters, *Autocracy and Aristocracy*, 29.

the guard that deposed Ivan VI. The guardsmen claimed to be animated by patriotic hatred against the German tyranny. As Sergei Solov'ev put it, favorites had also caused discontent during the reigns of Peter, Catherine I, and Peter II, "but they were ours, they were Russians."[7]

Elizabeth came to the throne as a "native" (*prirodnaia*) empress and elaborated the forms of Westernized presentation and celebration that Catherine II later used to glorify her own reign. The accession manifesto portrayed Elizabeth as savior of the realm. The previous regime was using violence in the name of the infant tsar, subjecting the population and herself to "extreme oppressions and insults," and bringing the state to ruin. As a result, her subjects, "especially the regiments of the Guard," had asked her to ascend the throne. Finally, she declared that the throne was hers by legal right. Future decrees asserted her claims entirely on the basis of inheritance. But the presentations also emphasized her selfless act for the well-being of the fatherland. In the three years after her accession, numerous sermons elaborated this theme—E. Anisimov counts more than a hundred—and proclaimed her victor over "the wicked wreckers of the fatherland," a heroine who had wrested "Peter's heritage from the hands of foreigners."[8]

The victory ushered in the celebration of the "age of gold." The nobility expressed their happiness in festivities and odes greeting the empress in the name of all Russians. They performed rituals of acclamation following the pattern of the Pindaric ode, which evoked theatrical scenes of the empress's subjects rejoicing in praise of their sovereign. The celebrations consisted of hero and chorus, as if set on a proscenium: the audience was as much a part of the performance as the players, the subjects responding exultantly to the benevolence of the monarch.[9]

The odes of Michael Lomonosov and Alexander Sumarokov presented these shows of adulation as a collective ritual. The individual voice of the poet expressed the collective "we" of Russia (*Rossiia*).[10] Thus Lomonosov greeted Elizabeth's return to Petersburg in 1742, and also the recent victory over the Swedes, with an ode acclaiming the dawn of the "age of gold," repeating a theme common to the members of the German poets of the "school of reason," at the Academy in St. Petersburg.[11] The "age of gold"

---

[7] E. V. Anisimov, *Rossiia v seredine XVIII veka; bor'ba za nasledie Petra* (Moscow, 1986), 27; Solov'ev, *Istoriia Rossii*, 10:652–53.

[8] *PSZ*, no. 8473, November 25, 1741; no. 8476, November 28, 1741; Anisimov, *Rossiia v seredine XVIII veka*, 28–29, 42, 46, 134–35.

[9] On the relationship between ode and court ritual, see James von Geldern, "The Ode as a Performative Genre," *Slavic Review*, vol. 50, no. 4 (Winter, 1991), 927–39; V. M. Zhivov, *Kul'turnye konflikty v istorii russkogo literaturnogo iazyka XVIII–nachala XIX veka* (Moscow, 1990), 58–62.

[10] I. Z. Serman writes that the poet of the 1730s and 1740s "expresses general thoughts and feeling as his own personal feelings" (I. Z. Serman, *Russkii klassitsizm; poeziia, drama, satira* [Leningrad, 1973], 40–42).

[11] L. V. Pumpianskii, "Lomonosov i nemetskaia shkola razuma," *XVIII vek; sbornik 14* (Leningrad, 1983), 21–22.

was the expression of the joy of the elite. The monarch, the Goddess, drives away the storms and clouds and brings the spring,

> She resurrects the universe,
> Renews nature for us,
> Covers the fields with flowers again:
> And so kindness and love,
> And the bright gaze of Peter's daughter
> Enlivens us with new life.

The sun breaking through the clouds is hailed with choral approval from the empire and the world. What L. V. Pumpianskii called Lomonosov's "rapture (*vostorg*) before the West," which turned into "rapture over oneself as a Western country."[12]

> Shouts rise to the East and the West!
> Different peoples declare to their Monarch:
> "May the Lord to the end of our days
> Multiply Your cherished years
> To the joy and defence of the world!"[13]

Metaphor created analogies that presented Elizabeth as the equivalent of Western monarchs. Poets placed her in the classical pantheon along with European royalty. In their odes, the Christian God ruled pagan gods. Lomonosov has God on Mount Olympus address the empress as "the Russian Goddess," to whom he had entrusted "thunder" to defeat the Swedes. Elizabeth became, as it were, God's own icon: "Peoples will worship My image in you," the Lord says. Lomonosov's God was a secular force. God had poured his soul into the empress, who would bring justice and felicity to Russia.[14]

The Russian court performed allegories of a political Olympus where the ruler, joining the company of European monarchs, bestowed benefactions upon his or her subjects. It presented what Baehr has described as "an ideal world where man can control his fate and harness the natural forces of the world to give him an ideal life."[15] Court ceremonial, literature, and religious sermons celebrated her transcendent accomplishments and glory. The empresses were shown as heroines delivering and showering their bounty on the people, not helping to redeem their sins or to ensure their afterlife. The

---

[12] L. V. Pumpianskii, "K istorii russkogo klassitsizma (Poetika Lomonosova)," *Kontekst* 14 (1982): 310.

[13] M. V. Lomonosov, *Polnoe sobranie sochinenii* (Moscow, 1959), 8:96, 101.

[14] Ibid., 8:85; Zhivov and Uspenskii, "Tsar' i Bog," 125–30. On Lomonosov's use of the metaphor of the tsar as icon of the divinity, see Baehr, "Regaining Paradise: The Political Icon in Russia," 153.

[15] Stephen L. Baehr, "'Fortuna Redux': The Iconography of Happiness in Eighteenth-Century Courtly Spectacles," in A. G. Cross, ed., *Great Britain and Russia in the Eighteenth Century: Contacts and Comparisons* (Newtonville, Mass., 1979), 110.

"iconography of happiness" was expressed in pageants, like those of Renaissance England, that portrayed the empress as the epitome of the virtues. The resemblance is hardly accidental. In both cases, classical imagery strengthened the legitimacy of female monarchs whose rights to the throne were fragile.

But the absolutist ceremonies of the Renaissance and Baroque were hardly empty repetitions of dead European forms. They conveyed contemporary, enlightenment meanings necessary to the elevation of the empress's image. The "happiness," in official rhetoric, expressed the eudaemonistic ethic of the enlightenment. By promising the felicity of her subjects, the Russian empress defined herself as a European monarch. The nobility, in turn, understood service as the realization of the idea of enlightenment, of acting for the general good.[16] In an era when, Jean Starobinski has observed, "pleasure became the universal justification," ceremonial displays of pleasure, indicating general "happiness," gave public confirmation to the monarch's devotion to Western conceptions of the general good.[17]

THE CORONATION OF EMPRESS ELIZABETH PETROVNA AND THE SCENARIO OF REJOICING

In the eighteenth century, the Russian imperial coronation became the most elaborate of these displays of happiness. It combined solemn reverence for the past with the enforced gaiety of the Olympian scenario. The coronation consecrated the claims of each of the empresses, and the accompanying celebrations glorified her in terms of the Petrine myth. It was regarded as an urgent requirement of rule, and preparations began immediately after the seizure of power.[18] In this respect, eighteenth-century Russian coronations, like English coronations of the sixteenth and seventeenth centuries, confirmed the uncertain claims to the throne.[19]

---

[16] See the article by S. O. Shmidt, "Obshchestvennoe samosozanie *noblesse russe* v pervoi treti XIX vv," *Cahiers du monde russe et soviétique*, vol. 34, nos. 1–3 (January–June 1993), 20.

[17] Stephen Lessing Baehr, *The Paradise Myth in Eighteenth Century Russia: Utopian Patterns in Early Secular Russian Literature and Culture* (Stanford, 1991), 58–60; Jean Starobinski, *The Invention of Liberty, 1700–1789* (Geneva, 1964), 53–56. Some modification is required of Isabel de Madariaga's characterization of Russian court spectacle as no more than "a belated echo of the political use of court spectacle as it had developed in the Renaissance and which reached its apogee at the court of Louis XIV" (Isabel de Madariaga, *Russia in the Age of Catherine the Great* [New Haven, Conn., 1981], 534).

[18] The coronation of Anna Ioannovna took place just over two months after her accession; Elizabeth's, five months after she ascended the throne; and Catherine II's, three months after her accession. Only Peter III tarried, ignoring warnings by Frederick the Great, and was overthrown before he had set a date for his coronation.

[19] D. Sturdy, " 'Continuity' versus 'Change': Historians and English Coronations of the Medieval and Early Modern Periods," in Bak, ed., *Coronations*, 238–42.

The coronation of Elizabeth Petrovna in 1742 incorporated the innovations introduced at the coronations of Catherine I and Anna. It represents the final state of evolution of the ceremonies of the Russian imperial coronation. When Elizabeth removed the crown from the hands of the archbishop and crowned herself, she culminated the changes that had turned the Muscovite coronation into the consecration of an absolute monarch, beholden to no earthly power, not even the church. The speeches and celebrations also set the ceremony in an Olympian scenario of joy, giving a lavish initial display of the happiness of her subjects.

The secular and religious events of the coronation elevated the leading figures of the elite, presenting them with the empress as champions of the empire's well-being. The upstarts from the guards, who had helped Elizabeth to power, joined the scions of old families to bear witness to the consecration of the new reign. The entry into Moscow, the solemn processions to and from the cathedral, the banquet in the Hall of Facets were inspiring shows of solidarity of all the ranks of the state—the vel'mozhi of the Senate and the court, the officials in the colleges—with the monarch and her allies in taking the throne. The conquest was celebrated as a defense of the existing social hierarchy, now ostensibly renewed by deliverance from the despotism of the previous reign. The prolonged celebrations following the religious ceremonies provided strenuous, often feverish shows of acclamation by the elite for a monarch dedicated to the well-being of Russia as they understood it.

The result was that the coronation assumed a new amplitude, reaching out to the population beyond the Kremlin and demonstrating, in the context of staged and anticipated responses, a consensus in favor of the new monarch. Elizabeth's coronation in February 1742 opened with an elaborate entry into Moscow, a practice repeated at all subsequent coronations.[20] Elizabeth also remained in Moscow for eight months after the end of the coronation. She ruled from the old capital, holding court, appearing at balls and masquerades and visiting religious shrines, particularly the Trinity Monastery.[21] In this way, she strengthened her connections with the nobility and officials

---

[20] Peter II's coronation in February 1728 was the first to open with a great triumphal entry to Moscow, with Roman arches and a speech of welcome from the governor. (Anna was in Moscow in 1730, dispensing with the need for an entry.) Peter II's entry was briefly described in a supplement to Sankt-Peterburgskie Vedomosti, February 17, 1728, with mention of the names of the members of the Supreme Privy Council, but it seems not to have been assigned the significance of the coronation entry of Elizabeth. No description of the coronation ceremonies themselves was published.

[21] Peter II remained in Moscow after his 1728 coronation, temporarily restoring its status as capital. In 1730 Anna indicated that she intended to keep her principal residence there. The court moved to Petersburg only at the end of 1731, or about a year-and-a-half after the coronation. Elizabeth arrived in Moscow at the end of February, and left the following December, spending eight months there. Catherine II remained in Moscow from September 13 to June 14, or for nine months after the crowning.

in the old capital, where many central institutions maintained their head-quarters until the last decades of the century.[22]

The understanding of the coronation's intended meaning was not left to the imagination of those witnessing the various events. The *Opisanie* defined what the events meant, how they were to be perceived, and how they should be celebrated by the elite. Like other *Opisaniia*, Elizabeth's purported to provide an account of what occurred. It was written in the past tense to make known the symbolic and historical significance of the event. But, in fact, it portrayed not so much what occurred as what was supposed to have occurred. It was prescriptive, as well as descriptive, setting the tone and rhetoric of celebration for the forthcoming reign.

Elizabeth's *Opisanie*, like Anna's, was an elaborate leather-bound album, illustrated with numerous engravings.[23] Its model, in this respect, appears to have been the lavishly illustrated account published in 1732 for the coronation of the twelve-year-old Louis XV in Paris (see above, chapter 1). Like the Louis XV album, hers was to be the "first monument of a reign," to glorify and publicize the majesty of her rule. The content and design of the album was assigned to Procurator-General Nikita Trubetskoi.[24] The librarian of the Academy of Science, Johann Daniel Shumacher, directed the production of the album and tried to ensure a broad circulation. He suggested that volumes be sent to colleges, offices, chancelleries, and monasteries, "in which these books will be kept for the eternal honor and glory of Her Imperial Majesty."[25]

The album opens with a magnificent full-length frontispiece of the empress standing proudly, decolletée, in full regalia (fig. 10). The scene is the palace. A Baroque painting of an angel decorates the wall behind her. There are no allegorical descriptions, such as those appended to the description of the French coronations (fig. 2). The personal figure of the empress literally embodies and defines the political order. The ceremonies elevate and glorify

[22] As late as 1763, of eighteen major central agencies, eleven had their headquarters in Moscow (John P. LeDonne, *Ruling Russia; Politics and Administration in the Age of Absolutism, 1762–1796* [Princeton, N.J., 1984], 36–37).

[23] *Opisanie koronatsii Eia Velichestva Imperatritsy i Samoderzhitsy Vserossiiskoi Anny Ioannovny torzhestvenno otpravelennoi v tsarstviushchem grade Moskve, 28 aprelia, 1730 g.* (St. Petersburg, 1730); *Obstoiatel'noe opisanie torzhestvennykh poriadkov blagopoluchnogo vshestviia v tsarstvyiushchii grad Moskvu i sviashchenneishei koronovaniia eia Avgusteishego imperatorskogo velichestva vsepresvetleishiia derzhavneishiia velikiia gosudaryni Elisavet Petrovny, samoderzhitsy vserossiiskoi* (St. Petersburg, 1744).

[24] LeDonne, "Ruling Families in the Russian Political Order," 299. John LeDonne describes Trubetskoi as the leading member of the dominant "Naryshkin group."

[25] *Materialy dlia istorii Imperatorskoi Akademii Nauk* (St. Petersburg, 1889), 5:1025; (St. Petersburg, 1895), 7:620–21. The album was initially to be published in an edition of 1,200 copies, 600 in Russian, 300 in French, and 300 in German. Shumacher reasoned, however, that because the plates were ready, the cost of individual volumes could be reduced by increasing the edition to more than 2,000. *Svodnyi Katalog* indicates a final total of 1,550 copies.

10. *Empress Elizabeth Petrovna*. Engraving by Johannes Stenglin after a drawing by Louis Caravaque.

her personal role, without the abstractions of state and nation. The engravings of the processions and ceremonies distinguish the empress by the highlighting and detail from the tiny identical figures around her (figs. 11, 12, 13). The albums also include engravings of the masquerades and fireworks, making clear that these now were considered integral parts of the coronation events.

Procurator-General Nikita Trubetskoi, who supervised the production of the album, instructed the editorial committee in the Academy of Sciences that the volume begin with a scene of Moscow and end with a vignette of the final masquerade.[26] The album encompassed the total event of the coronation, the entry, the promulgation, the various processions, balls, and audiences, in addition to the rites in the cathedral. Twenty-seven of the fifty-two engravings are of the processions, triumphal columns, celebrations, and fireworks; twenty-five depict the coronation ceremonies, items of regalia, and plans of the cathedral. The crowning is the only rite in the cathedral to be illustrated.

The opening description of the entry procession to Moscow and welcoming ceremonies takes up 21 of the 128 pages, almost a sixth of the total text of the *Opisanie*.[27] The account reveals that the entry has become a principal part of the coronation, a spectacle whose symbolic meaning is almost as important as the rites in the Assumption Cathedral. The procession on February 28 reenacted the Petrine triumph, making clear that military leadership elevated the sovereign and consecrated her authority no less than the blessings bestowed by the clergy.

The triumphal entry was a glorification of force, an unambiguous statement that the monarch's power derived from a heroic act of conquest that anteceded consecration. It presented the Westernized elite of the new capital, in Clifford Geertz's words, as "taking possession" of Moscow. The rows of guards' regiments, the massive array of horses, elaborate sumptuous Western dress and carriages showed the conquest of the old capital by the new.

The album described the various groups of noblemen who marched through the Moscow streets. Grenadiers on horseback and courtiers in livery led in the ornate carriages of the court aristocracy. Thirty members of the "aristocratic nobility" followed in twos on richly decorated horses. Then forty cavalrymen of the guard led forty chamberlains and junkers of the chamber on horseback. A chief master of the stables, Peter Spirodovich Sumarokov, a scion of an old family who had been an ally of Anna in 1730, rode before the resplendent carriage of the empress, drawn by "a most handsome team of eight Neapolitan horses." Her escorts riding by the carriage epitomized the ceremonial union unveiled by the coronation. On one side

[26] *Materialy dlia istorii Imperatorskoi Akademii Nauk* (St. Petersburg, 1895), 7:36.

[27] This description is based on *Obstoiatel'noe opisanie*, 3–26. See also Solov'ev, *Istoriia Rossii*, 11:157–58; Anisimov, *Rossiia v seredine XVIII veka*, 151–52; I. Tokmakov, *Istoricheskoe opisanie vsekh koronatsii rossiiskikh tsarei, imperatorov i imperatrits* (Moscow, 1896), 83–85.

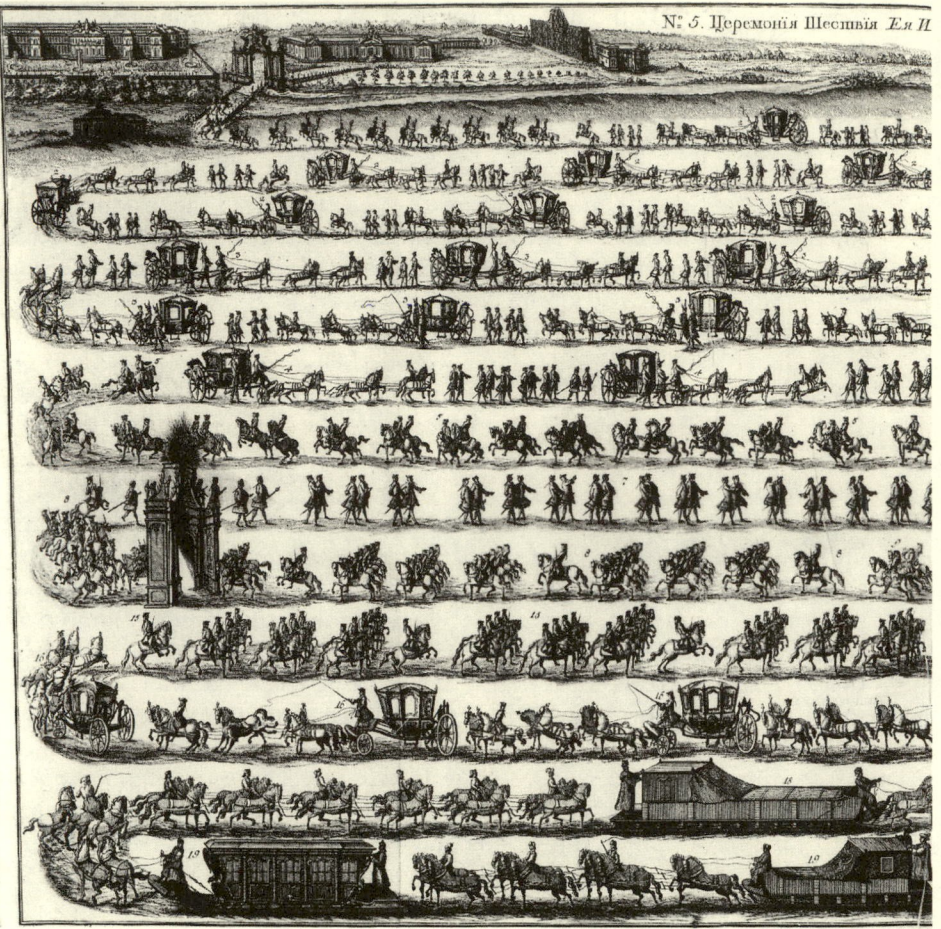

11. *Entry Procession of Elizabeth Petrovna to Moscow.* Engraving by Ivan Sokolov.

was the chief master of the stables, Prince Alexander Kurakin, a relative of the powerful Lopukhin clan and the son of Peter the Great's brother-in-law. On the other side marched Elizabeth's favorite, the chamberlain Michael Vorontsov.[28] Two rows of footmen carrying sabers strode beside the carriage. Six pages of the empress on horseback were followed by the carriage of Elizabeth's fourteen-year-old nephew, Peter Fedorovich of Holstein, the son of Grand Duchess Anna Petrovna, whom the empress had just designated heir. Behind him rode another forty horsemen of the guard and four carriages of ladies-in-waiting. Regiments of the guards lined the entire way from the first arch, on Tver Street, to Red Square.

[28] LeDonne, "Ruling Families in the Russian Political Order," 299; Alexander, "Favourites, Favouritism and Female Rule in Russia," 112.

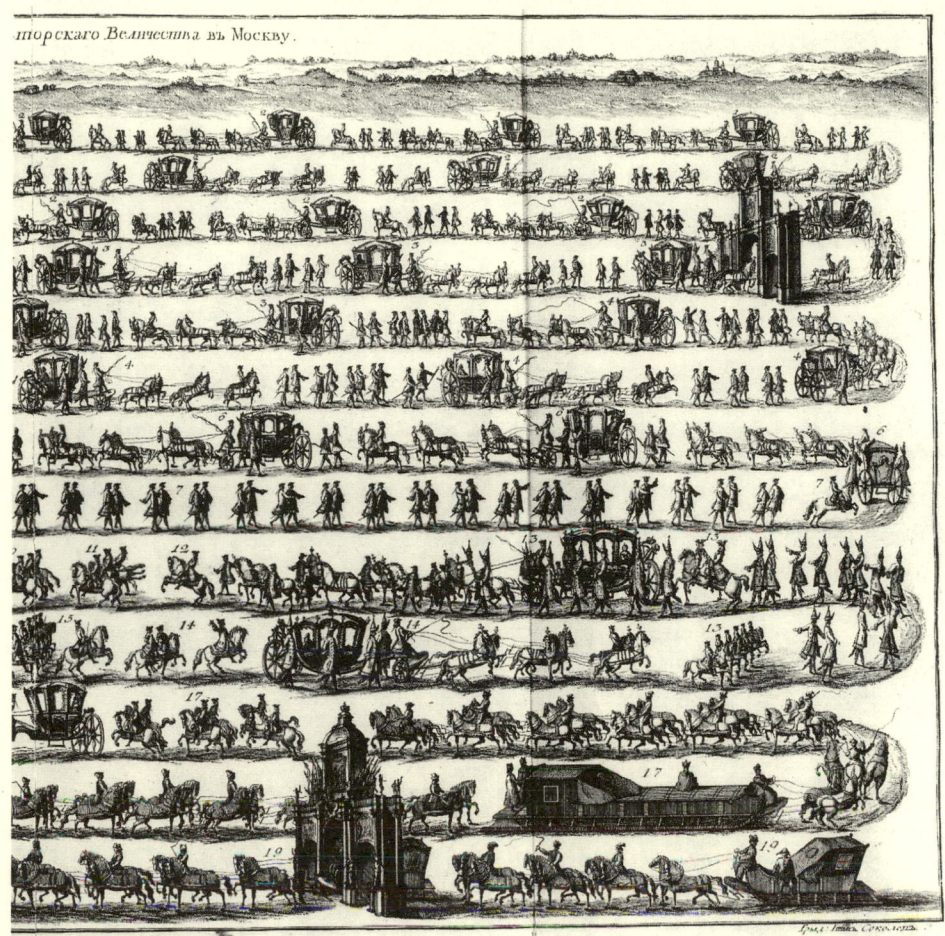

торскаго Величества въ Москву.

The magnificent engraving by Ivan Sokolov deliberately recalled the Petrine triumph (fig. 11). Sokolov had been instructed by Trubetskoi to follow the example of the engraving of the Poltava entry of 1709, and depict the entire procession on a single page. The editorial committee also insisted that he avoid the use of perspective, which would obscure the "free look" of the ceremony.[29] The effect is to take the entry procession out of the ordinary and give it a sense of otherness.

We see several hundred tiny figures wind in a snaking line across the space of the foldout. There are covered sledges, hundreds of horsemen, carriages, marching guardsmen, noblemen, courtiers, and servants in livery. All figures

[29] *Materialy*, 7:37; 5:1026.

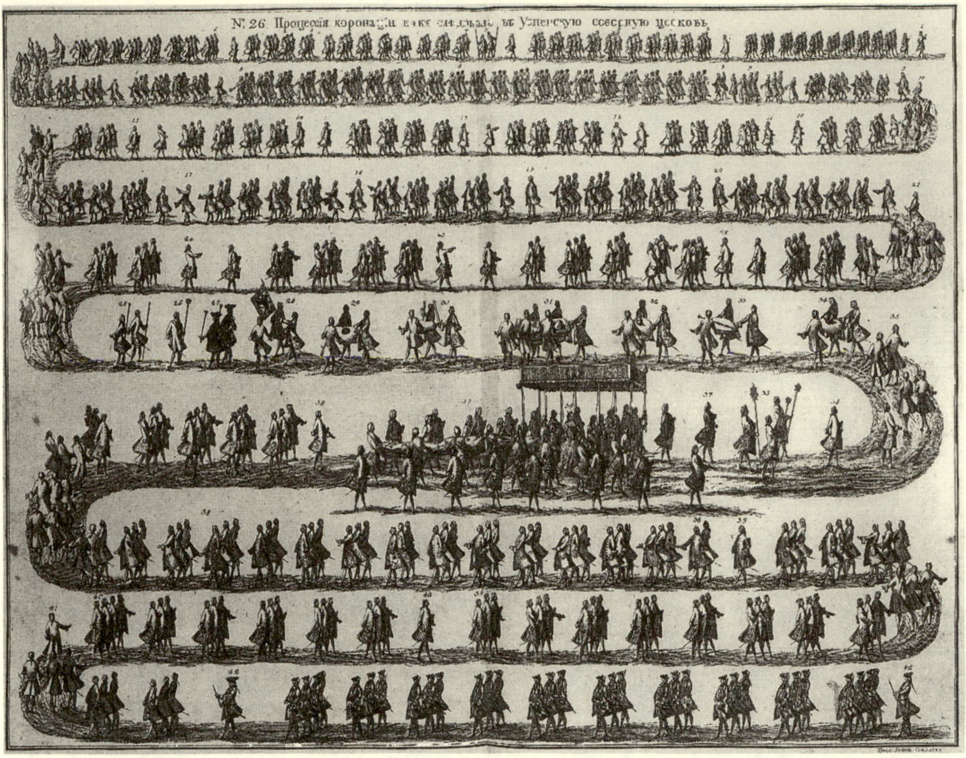

12. *Procession to the Assumption Cathedral.* Engraving by Ivan Sokolov.

13. *Crowning Ceremony, Empress Elizabeth Petrovna.* Engraving by Grigorii Kalachev.

are rendered in profile except for the empress, who is shown full face, in her carriage. A separate engraving gives an enlarged detail of the empress's carriage and escort. The figures march in a single line without background. The empress, the court, the military panoply are in their own realm, the realm of art and power. The earthly setting, the Kremlin, the spectators, even Moscow itself are invisible. But the imperial palaces, the realm of the Olympian elite, appear at the top of the page. Indeed, despite the title of the engraving, "The Procession of HER IMPERIAL MAJESTY into Moscow," the procession is moving *toward* the palace on its return from the Kremlin, the moments of initial acclaim and celebration preparing the way for a festive ball in the evening.

In imitation of European entries, welcoming speeches were presented at four arches constructed along the route. But these ceremonies, staged according to orders from the authorities in St. Petersburg, had an official character. The Senate decreed that arches be erected on Tver Street by the Moscow Provincial Chancellery, in Kitai-Gorod by the Synod from the funds of the Moscow Province, and on Miasnitskii Street, paid for by the merchantry, but supervised also by the Provincial Chancellery.[30] The welcoming parties consisted of officials, clergy, and merchants holding administrative posts in the magistracy.

The album contains Grigorii Kalachev's engravings of the facades of the four arches, with explanations in the text. The illustrations convey the principal themes of celebration, especially the image of the empress as God-appointed savior of her people.[31] The arch on Tver Street, built by the Moscow Provincial Administration, proclaims the absolute supremacy of the empress's power (fig. 14). The notes point out that this is a Roman arch with Corinthian capitols. Battle standards flaring out at the top mark the glory of the empress's martial exploits. Two angels on pedestals on the cornice point to her picture above; the other figures nearby represent the virtues. The arches are guarded by statues of Jupiter, Mars, Neptune, and Minerva. Above, God hovers over a large figure of Elizabeth, who awaits the people coming from the city to meet her. The words descending from God's lips, "You come to save my people," designate the empress the divine agent of her people's renewal. Beneath, figures of Judith and Deborah place her in the company of heroines who had delivered their peoples.

Elizabeth's agency, the pictures made clear, was direct, unmediated by clerical or other human powers. A picture above the passageway of the Tver arch, not among the illustrations, showed a hand extending from the heavens to place a crown on Elizabeth's head. The legend, "the true sovereign is crowned not from earth but heaven," prefigured the empress's self-crowning. This image was repeated on the coronation medal: a figure of Providence crowned the empress, who wore a decolleté gown exposing an

---

[30] Solov'ev, *Istoriia Rossii*, 11:157.
[31] *Obstoiatel'noe opisanie*, 93, 131–35, Plate 34.

14. *Triumphal Arch on Tver Street*. Engraving by Grigorii Kalachev.

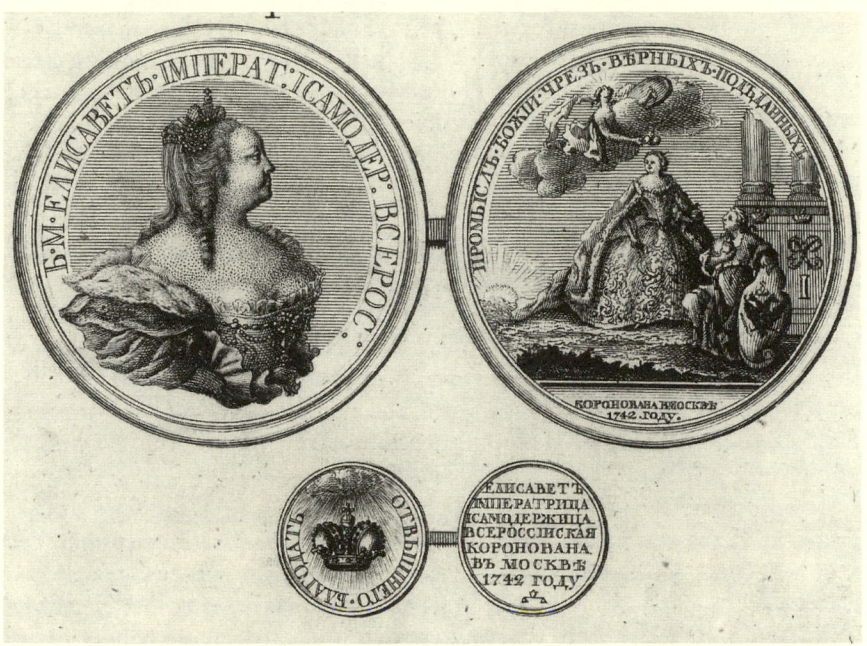

15. *Coronation Medal*. Engraving by Grigorii Kalachev.

ample bosom (fig. 15). The legend read, "Divine Providence through faithful subjects."

The procession ended at the Kremlin, where Elizabeth and her entourage attended a welcoming service in the Assumption Cathedral. The oration of Archbishop Ambrosii in the Assumption Cathedral emphasized the tone of happiness and rejoicing characteristic of the scenario of renovation.[32] Elizabeth was "the actual and true Mother of the Fatherland." Even though she had been on the throne only a short time, Ambrosii declared "how much good, joy, benefit, and happiness and security has she wrought." He described the rejoicing of all the groups in society, the clergy, the army and the administrative ranks. The "great multitude of the nation" (*vsenarodnoe mnozhestvo*) were jubilant, and most of all "the poor and defenceless" at the advent of "the true mother of mercy."

The archbishop then, in the passage cited in the epigraph to this chapter, gave the empress the welcome of Moscow. The speech expressed the joy of Moscow as a city, using what would become the conventional metaphor of Moscow as the heart of Russia. Moscow was both personified as a collective and made a symbol of all of Russia, the heart of all Russian cities. The personification of the city allowed its ruling institutions to speak for the city as a whole. The encomia of the bishops and officials substituted for ceremo-

[32] Ibid., 11–13.

nies of mutual recognition between the town fathers and the monarch characteristic of traditional European festive entries. Ambrosii, the ranking cleric of Moscow, thus added the voice of the Moscow ruling elite to the chorus of approval ordained and composed from above.

The coronation ceremonies took place two months later, on April 25. The procession from the Hall of Facets to the Assumption Cathedral was composed of forty-nine groups (compared to nineteen at the coronation of Anna Ioannovna) and presented a magnificent display of the social and national components of the Russian elite. It opened with a detachment of the Cavalier Guards, led by the empress's favorite, Lieutenant, now Chamberlain, Peter Shuvalov. They were followed by pages in livery with the chief marshal of the court and two masters of ceremony carrying their maces. Then came representatives from the various parts of the empire, merchant deputies from Estland, Lifland, and foreign countries, cossack *starshiny* from the Ukraine, noblemen from Smolensk, Lifland, and Estland.

The procession made the presence of the state institutions more prominent than was the case at previous coronations. Following the noblemen marched senators, then, for the first time, officials from each of the twelve colleges. Three new items of "state regalia" that had appeared during the late seventeenth and early eighteenth centuries revealed the sacred character now attributed to the imperial state. The state banner (*panir*) emblazoned with the imperial arms—the double-headed eagle with the insignia of the parts of the empire—was carried by General in Chief Volkov.[33] The vice chancellor, Alexei Bestuzhev-Riumin, and a General Naryshkin held the state seal and state sword. The hilt of the sword was in the form of two double-headed eagles, and another double-headed eagle adorned its tip.[34]

The bearers of the imperial regalia were major figures of the governmental elite from the past reign, and their role in the coronation demonstrated their solidarity with Elizabeth and the restoration of the Petrine spirit. The album identifies several of them as senators, indicating that they had the honor to be appointed to the restored Petrine Senate. The highest-ranking civil official, the chancellor, Senator Prince Alexei Cherkasskii, carried the crown.[35]

Elizabeth followed the regalia under the baldachin, which was held by

---

[33] This probably refers to Matvei Fedorovich Volkov, who rose to rank under Peter (Meehan-Waters, *Autocracy and Aristocracy*, 200).

[34] *Obstoiatel'noe opisanie*, Plate 18.

[35] Ibid., 35–39. The mantle was carried by two of Anna's cabinet ministers, Field Marshall Münnich—shortly to be exiled to Siberia—and the keeper of the stables, Prince Alexander Kurakin. Andrei Ivanovich Ushakov, the director of the Secret Chancellery since 1730, followed with the orb. The scepter was carried by General Grigorii Chernyshev, who had assisted with the mantle at Anna's coronation. Cherkasskii had carried the orb at Anna's coronation and had also served as one of her ministers.— Chernyshev, Kurakin, Ushakov, and Cherkasskii, who had been appointed to the Senate on December 11, 1741, in an effort to restore the institution to its glory under Peter I, were clearly identified as senators in the text (Solov'ev, *Istoriia Rossii*, 11:142–43).

sixteen court officials, generals, and senators.[36] Behind the empress marched rows of generalitet, Russian nobility, and Moscow merchantry. The magnates, the institutions, and the social and national constituents of empire bore witness to the blessing of the empress and gave recognition to those who enjoyed her favor.[37] Sokolov's engraving depicts a procession that winds from the Kremlin Palace to the Assumption Cathedral (fig. 12). Neither the palace nor the cathedral appears in the scene, but the numerous delegations and notable personages are all present and identified. The figures are presented in profile, distinguishable only by their dress, except for the empress, who faces outward, from under the canopy.

The investiture remained the principal moment of the coronation ceremony. Changes introduced since 1724 had only enhanced the focus on the sovereign as absolute monarch and ruler of the empire. After reading the credo and assuming the mantle, Elizabeth received the benediction from the archbishop. Then, at her command, the crown was brought to her; she lifted it, and placed it on her head. After the conferral of the scepter and the orb, she sat on the throne and listened to a protodeacon recite her full title. The recitation included the principalities and lands that made up her realm, a proclamation of the vast extent of her imperial dominion. The bells in the Kremlin tolled, accompanied by a 101-gun salute. The clergy then greeted the empress with a triple bow. Kalachev's engraving presents the empress as if on a stage (fig. 13). Elizabeth, her features delicately delineated, sits in the vast space, all eyes fixed upon her. Indeed, the editorial committee for the album had insisted on the proper use of perspective in this illustration and requested the court stage designer, Girolamo Bon, to revise the drawings.[38]

The drama of the investiture now culminated with two prayers that Prokopovich had introduced at Anna's coronation to express the absolute monarch's relation to God and to her people. Elizabeth first pronounced a supplication for guidance from above, the prayer of Solomon. She occupied center stage and addressed the Lord directly rather than through the mediacy of the officiating prelate. In full regalia, she delivered a supplication for guidance, a turning to God for wisdom. She beseeched the Lord to teach her (*nastavi*), to give her understanding (*vrazumi*), and to guide her (*upravi*) "in this great service." She asked for His help in governing "for the welfare of the people entrusted to me and to your great glory."

---

[36] Among the eight chamberlains, carrying her train, were favorites who had supported her coup, Alexander Shuvalov, and her lover, the young cossack, Alexei Razumovskii. Her escorts included a mix of old and new: Field Marshall Vasilii Dolgorukii, the new president of the War College, who had held the position in 1730 and 1731, and then had been imprisoned; Prince Nikita Trubetskoi, the Procurator-General of the Senate since 1740, and her favorite, Michael Vorontsov.

[37] *Obstoiatel'noe opisanie*, 39–49; Belozerskaia, "Tsarskoe venchanie," 21–22; *BE*, vol. 17, 397–98; vol. 51, 445–46; Tokmakov, 85–86.

[38] *Materialy dlia istorii Imperatorskoi Akademii Nauk*, 5:1027; 7:40, 776.

The supplication established the empress, rather than the church, as the primary moral guardian of the people. Ambrosii now kneeled and delivered the prayer, "from the entire people" (*ot litsa vsego naroda*), which replaced the pre-Petrine precept. He begged forgiveness for lawlessness and called on the Lord to instruct Elizabeth to work in "her great service" to God. He also asked God to bestow reason upon her to judge people fairly, and repeated many of the admonitions that had been contained in the pre-Petrine precept, to subdue enemies, to open her heart to the poor and afflicted, to instill in her subjects a sense of justice and avoid partiality and bribery. No reference was made to the role of the church, and Jesus Christ, whose name had dominated the precept, was mentioned only once, in the closing sentence. The church had become the spiritual voice of the people, supporting the monarch's entreaties, rather than an instrument of divine will bestowing authority upon her.

Then Ambrosii delivered a sermon hailing the empress's courage and heroism, following the example of Prokopovich's encomium at Catherine I's coronation.[39] He described Elizabeth as the embodiment of Peter's courage and foresight. All of Russia, he declared, was rejoicing because "in You our Most Radiant God-Crowned Autocrat lives the soul of Peter the Great, who astounded all the world with his victories and triumphs." Peter lived in his daughter. Like Catherine, she had forgotten "the delicacy of her sex" and had put her life at risk for the fatherland. As "the leader and cavalier of the troops," she had succeeded in "wresting the heritage of Peter the Great from the hands of foreigners and delivering the sons of Russia from slavery." She had brought the return of the prosperity of her father's reign.

Ambrosii employed the choral mode as justification for the comparison with Christ. "When I present my speech at our present, general celebration, I hear joyous exclamations from the other side, I hear the singing of all and rejoicing and I ask, what is the jubilation for?" His answer was that it was for the triumph of Christ, and both Christ and Elizabeth were saviors enjoying the adulation of their people. She had freed the Christian faith from the foreigners, and thus she was worthy of anointment. God had sent her to govern her country, and he had designated the orthodox church to assist her.

The ceremonies of the liturgy remained unchanged from the pre-Petrine coronation. Indeed, the *Opisanie* assigns them little importance, devoting only one page to the description of the anointment and communion and making no mention of the response of those present.[40] It thus deemphasizes the sacramental aspect of the coronation, reflecting the general downgrading of the clergy in eighteenth-century ceremonies. The anointment and communion have become obligatory rites without symbolic resonance: the empress and the court had no wish to stress their affinity with the clergy.[41]

---

[39] *Obstoiatel'noe opisanie*, 62–65.

[40] Ibid., 66–70.

[41] Indeed, several memoranda were composed for Catherine the Great's coronation in 1762,

After congratulations from "ecclesiastical and secular personages," the empress left the cathedral in full regalia accompanied by the clergy and her courtiers to the thunder of the troops' guns on the square, the musical sounds of horns and drums, and the tolling of church bells. She made the traditional procession around the square to prayer services in the Archangel Cathedral for the pre-Petrine tsars, and in the Annunciation Cathedral. Behind her walked the chancellor, Prince Cherkasskii, who tossed coins into the crowd.

The coronation banquet had become another event celebrating the Westernized elite around the empress. The clergy, no longer honored guests, were but one of the service groups joining in the celebration. Court, civil, and ecclesiastical ranks moved together in procession to the hall in the Palace of Facets and awaited the empress's arrival. Elizabeth opened the proceedings by awarding coronation medals to leading figures at the court and bishops of the Holy Synod, thus making clear that clerical positions were equivalent to state offices. She then gave the signal to be seated. Twelve colonels brought the dishes to the table, under the direction and with the assistance of the grand marshall and the ceremony masters of the court. Her favorites, Vorontsov and one of the Shuvalov brothers, stood at the side of her throne as Cavalier Guards. During the banquet, the *Opisanie* indicated, Elizabeth rose from her throne to toss coins from the window to the people standing outside.[42]

The ceremonies in the Kremlin began a round of festivities. "The celebration of the coronation of Her Imperial Majesty continued with various joyous diversions for a whole week," the *Opisanie* declared. Church bells tolled and the city was illuminated. In the evening on the day after the coronation, April 26, the empress held the first of a series of audiences, to receive congratulations from the members of the various estates, the bureaucracy, military officers, and foreign ambassadors. During the first audience, the feast for the people took place before the palace. Wine in the fountains gushed from the mouths of Cupids; figures of Bacchus and Ceres symbolized joy and plenty. An engraving (fig. 16) shows the square filled with masses of people, the oxen laid out on four plinths. The *Opisanie* states that "Her Imperial Majesty deigned to throw silver coins from the window to the people." This was the first official mention of an appearance of a Russian monarch before the people's feast.[43]

On April 29 Elizabeth moved in another elaborate procession from the Kremlin to her palace, her "winter house," on the river Iauza. The decora-

---

confirming that Anna and Elizabeth had taken communion in the sanctuary, indicating that there was considerable uncertainty about whether that had taken place (*Opisanie Vshestviia v Moskvu i Koronovaniia Gosudaryni Imperatritsy Ekateriny II*, printed in *KFZ* for 1762 [St. Petersburg, 185?], 196–206).

[42] *Obstoiatel'noe opisanie*, 85–89.

[43] Ibid., 94–112.

N:30. Видъ въ проспектив Успенской соборной церкви и передъ оной площади и прочему спроенно

16. *Feast for the People*. Engraving by Ivan Sokolov.

tions on the Iauza palace, figures of nude gods and goddesses, set the tone for the coming days. There were gala dinner balls and performances of the Italian opera. On May 7 the regalia were put on exhibition in the Kremlin palace. The *Opisanie* reported that 100 "notables" (*znatnye*), and 136,158 of those "of other ranks besides commoner," visited the exhibition. There were frequent masquerades, held at the winter house, eight listed for May alone. From eight hundred to a thousand tickets were given out. The vignette on the last page of the account is a scene of the dance floor, with costumed figures deftly turning legs and torsos (fig. 17).[44] The preface to the description of the fireworks in the *Opisanie* explained the significance of the celebrations. Elizabeth's coronation had "produced so many pleasant and amusing feelings" that appeared only "with the general joy at the attainment of all the most perfect and desired prosperity. Surprise and reverence, love and hope (*nadeianie*), pleasure and joy, merriment and exclamation, hope (*nadezhda*) and firm trust." These thoughts about the coronation, it continued, "correspond completely with the inner feelings and public recognition of all loyal residents of the Russian empire."[45]

[44] *Materialy*, 7:36; *Obstoiatel'noe opisanie*, 128.
[45] Ibid., 161–63.

17. *Vignette of Masquerade.* Engraving by Ivan Sokolov.

Firework displays marked the official end of the celebrations, nearly six weeks after the coronation ceremony. The engravings show the heavens lit up with fountains of light that illuminate the entwined initials of the empress. Beneath sits Genii, symbolizing justice, courage, prosperity, and "the joy of the empire." An illumination followed revealing a grove of trees before a mountain. The pomegranate tree, the *Opisanie* explained, was of special significance. Although the pomegranate tree was known as a symbol of fertility, the *Opisanie* presented it as a symbol of innate and incipient royalty, justifying the self-crowning. The pomegranate, though it has a crown from its first shoots, only displays it at complete maturity and "therefore with its innate (*prirodnaia*) force must place the crown on itself, that is, *Meam mihi reddo coronam* or 'I lay the crown on myself.' "[46]

The summer after the coronation Elizabeth went on a pilgrimage to the Trinity Monastery; a visit to the shrine would conclude all future imperial coronations. Elizabeth was known for her piety; along with the bon vivante,

[46] Ibid., 162–65.

and pagan reveler, she could appear as a devout believer, displaying her orthodox, "native" persona. At the moment of her coup, she is said to have
fallen to her knees before an icon of the Mother-of-God and prayed with
great fervor. This was the piety of a lay believer, not the monastic piety of the
seventeenth-century court. Elizabeth liked to have clerics in attendance, even
at balls, operas, and masquerades, and her exact observance of the many
fasts of the church won the admiration of the hierarchs. She thus succeeded
in avoiding Anna's identification with Europeans and fulfilled the symbolic
imperative of the myth: to affect a foreign role, while remaining Russian.[47]

Elizabeth's many pilgrimages to monasteries during her reign were performed more in the spirit of rejoicing than of solemn devotion. They combined worship with pleasure, turning religious observance into a type of
festivity. This is the tone of the official description of her visit to the Trinity
Monastery in March 1744. The empress was hailed by the monastic clergy
who joined in the celebration of her visit. She was greeted at the gates by all
the brothers who held crosses. Then the abbot delivered a welcome speech.
Seminary students, dressed in white, with golden wreaths on their heads,
and palm branches in their hands, recited verses, much as they had at the
coronation entry, to the tolling of bells and the thunder of cannon salutes. In
the evening she was entertained by a fireworks display. On subsequent days
she attended feasts in the abbot's cells in the company of members of her
court, with toasts to the empress, vocal music from the seminarists, and
cannon salvoes. In the evening there were illuminations.[48]

•

The coronation introduced the scenario of demonstrative rejoicing that continued through the first years of Elizabeth's reign. The rejoicing was for the
return of Petrine Russia. Peter the Great displaced all other Russian princes
and tsars as the subject of odes.[49] But Elizabeth had inherited neither her
father's vision nor his destructive energy. After restoring the Senate and
other institutions of Peter's reign, she tended to leave government in the
hands of her favorites. The momentum of change and the ethic of sacrifice in
service had largely dissipated. In this respect, Elizabeth's reign represents a
period of restoration, and the heroic act of accession, a reassertion of the
compact between crown and nobility sealed in 1730.

Elizabeth evoked her father not only to legitimize her position, but to

---

[47] Anna did make a show of piety by visiting the Trinity Monastery, where, according to the
brief report in *Sankt-Peterburgskie Vedomosti*, July 16, 1730, 227–28, "she worshiped with
great reverence." But otherwise no descriptions of demonstrative piety appeared in the texts.

[48] P. Bartenev, ed., *Osmnadtsatyi vek* (Moscow, 1869), 2:221–28; F. Ternovskii, *Religioznyi
kharakter russkikh gosudarei XVIII veka* (Kiev, 1874), 15–16; Philip Longworth, *The Three
Empresses: Catherine I, Anne and Elizabeth of Russia* (London, 1972), 180.

[49] Whittaker mentions that of 129 panegyric works reviewed, 125 named no other previous
ruler (Whittaker, "The Reforming Tsar," 90). See also Riasanovsky, *The Image of Peter the
Great*, 25–34.

provide a mythical charismatic basis for her own rule, the rule of a conserving monarch, whose principal goal was to maintain the existing social and political order. Neither Elizabeth nor her servitors yearned for a return to the furious and merciless dynamism of Peter's reign. The nobility looked back on him with respect, but the thought of a new Petrine era struck terror into their hearts.[50] They were the beneficiaries of Peter's successful act of conquest and had no reason to look forward to another.

They celebrated rather the return of Petrine forms of Westernized culture and institutions at least purportedly based on principles of law. Elizabeth resumed Peter's role as the leader of revelry. She revealed her devotion to the general good by effecting prodigies of transformation, dominating the imagination with a world of make-believe and delight, the festival as coup d'état. Peter had intended her to wed the young Louis XV, and she indulged her taste for the erotic playfulness and amorous intrigues of Versailles. A painting by Louis Caravaque, no longer extant, gave her the body of a naked Venus. Venus was the allegorical embodiment of gaiety and abandon, the leading figure in a scenario of unending joy. Elizabeth's beloved *metamorfozy* effected sexual transformations. All, including the empress, came in costumes of the opposite sex.[51]

Elizabeth played her roles with great ardor. Anisimov estimates that she spent nearly half her days at court diversions during the first decade of her reign. These functions were not exclusive gatherings for the highest elite; they encompassed lesser officials and noblemen, as well as the high aristocracy. More than a thousand guests reveled at her masquerades, which filled all the public halls of the imperial palace. The empress first played cards, then as the revelry rose, in the early hours of the morning, she wandered through the halls, changing masks along the way. Every day numerous plays were performed at the theater; every Sunday a ball.[52] But the indefatigable merrymaking was not simply the random pursuit of pleasure, like the princely festivals of the West.[53] Like Peter's *assamblei*, the masquerades were strictly regulated. Rejoicing was the ceremonial display of triumph and solidarity of the empress with her elite, a protracted, unmistakable affirmation of the principle of happiness.

The elite also expressed their sense of belonging by appearing in costly Western attire. Elizabeth enjoyed preeminence, wearing the most expensive gowns, following the example of her mother, Catherine. Her legendary wardrobe—ostensibly fifteen thousand dresses were found after her death— and her frequent changes of attire were not the result of mindless extravagance, but behavior prescribed by a scenario of demonstrative abandon

[50] See, for example, David Ransel, *The Politics of Catherinian Russia: The Panin Party* (New Haven, Conn., 1975), 264–65.

[51] Lotman and Uspenskii, *The Semiotics of Russian Culture*, 141–42; Anisimov, *Rossiia v seredine XVIII veka*, 157–58.

[52] Ibid., 154–56, 164–65.

[53] Starobinski, *The Invention of Liberty*, 85.

from the constraints of necessity. The nobility had to follow her example. According to the court jeweler, Pauzié, even ladies of relatively low rank had outfits of enormous cost, reaching 10,000 rubles. Elizabeth's decrees went into great detail about the style of women's hairdos and dress at the court, ensuring that the ladies would conform to Western fashion, but not so much that they would rival the empress.[54]

The palaces Elizabeth built provided vast and fantastic settings for court festivities. Bartolommeo Rastrelli's Summer Palace, and Smolny Convent, his redesign of the Great Palace at Tsarskoe Selo and the Winter Palace created an aura of Rococo magnificence. Rastrelli rendered the Rococo flourishes of feminine grace and elegance in monumental dimensions suitable to Russian monarchy. The immense facades of the Tsarskoe Selo Palace and the Winter Palace were themselves theatrical displays of sovereignty. The architectural historian John Summerson aptly compared the Winter Palace to a "brutally literal Bibiena stage design," which could be tolerated only in Russia where it gave "an effect of absolute, grim and careless dominion."[55]

Yet, it was not only in externals that Elizabeth preserved the spirit of Peter's reign. The historian, Sergei Solov'ev, wrote that Russia found herself in Elizabeth's reign. The restoration of the Senate and other Petrine offices indicated the intention to maintain a continuity of state institutions based on Peter's legislation. Efforts at codification of the laws continued, and the principle of advancement by merit was reaffirmed, even if honored more often in the breach. The government established banks for the advancement of trade and agriculture, and, at the instance of Peter Shuvalov, eliminated internal tariffs. Most important, the spirit of reform persisted, paving the way for changes introduced after her death. Powerful noblemen like Peter Shuvalov sought their own interest, but at the same time drafted projects for new laws that advanced "state interest," based on Western ideas.[56]

In the sphere of enlightenment, Elizabeth's reign prepared the way for the development of thought later in the century. Elizabeth herself was poorly educated and lacked intellectual interests. But many of her favorites, among them Ivan Shuvalov, Peter Shuvalov's brother, and Nikita Panin, read the works of the philosophes, and conceived of a monarchy based on law, staffed by officials who gained their positions on the basis of merit. It was Ivan Shuvalov who persuaded the empress to agree to the establishment of Russia's first university, Moscow University, in 1755. With the encouragement of Nikita Panin, a group of intellectuals and writers formed at the university to pursue ideas of enlightenment reform. Elizabeth appointed Panin tutor to the son of the heir, Paul Petrovich. In other areas as well, intellectual Westernization quickened during Elizabeth's reign. The first

---

[54] Geremie Pauzié, "Zapiski brillianshchika Poz'e," *Russkii Arkhiv*, no. 1 (1870): 86–87.

[55] William Craft Brumfield, *A History of Russian Architecture* (Cambridge, 1993), 228–49; John Summerson, *The Architecture of the Eighteenth Century* (London, 1986), 34; Hamilton, *Art and Architecture*, 283–88; Anisimov, *Rossiia v seredine XVIII veka*, 167–70.

[56] Solov'ev, *Istoriia Rossii*, 12:636–39; Anisimov, *Rossiia v seredine XVIII veka*, 54–56.

scholarly and intellectual journals began to appear, with small circulations to be sure, but harbingers of things to come. "A new generation was prepared, trained in different rules and customs from those dominant in earlier reigns," Solov'ev wrote. These noble intellectuals would become prominent after Elizabeth's death, a generation "that made the reign of Catherine II renowned."[57]

Elizabeth's reign was a prelude to the reign of Catherine the Great. The theme of deliverance contained the promise of betterment and reform, the approximating of the Western ideals, symbolized by the figure of Minerva. Panegyrics of her reign presented a goddess of war, but war tempered with wisdom and understanding, and striving toward peace. On Elizabeth's name day in 1747, a display of fireworks illumined Minerva in her Temple, "signifying the great wisdom of Her Majesty," and at the sides were "symbolic representations of peace and war." Lomonosov wrote an inscription:

> You shine with peace and war in the southern realms,
> And so you increase your people's merriment
> To You, Our Minerva, we fervently bear
> The radiance of joyous lights.[58]

In the course of her reign, Elizabeth took on Minerva's peaceful qualities as the protector of science and embodiment of civic virtue. The beneficent aspects were a prominent theme of the panegyrics of her last years. Lomonosov wrote, in 1758:

> As Minerva's Helmet shines on Your head,
> The hand of Science protects with Her shield.[59]

[57] Solov'ev, *Istoriia Rossii*, 12:639.
[58] M. V. Lomonosov, *Polnoe sobranie sochinenii* (Moscow, 1959), 8:194.
[59] Ibid., 8:643.

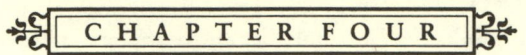

CHAPTER FOUR

Minerva Triumphant

Rejoice, Russian state!

World, hearken to our happiness!

And you, glory of Catherine,

Be proclaimed forever across the land!

What more can Russia desire?

Minerva is on her throne,

Bounty reigns!

Astraea has descended again from the heavens

Has returned to earth,

In her former beauty.

—*A. P. Sumarokov*, Ode on the Name Day of Catherine II,
November 24, 1762

THE DEMONSTRATIONS OF LOVE

On June 28, 1762, the empress, Catherine Alekseevna, dressed in the Pre-obrazhenskii Guards' uniform of Peter I's time, led a conspiracy that deposed her husband, Peter III. Catherine had initially given the impression that she was acting in behalf of her son, Grand Duke Paul, but it immediately became clear that she herself intended to rule. As the former Princess Sophia of Anhalt-Zerbst, Catherine had no legal claim to the throne—neither by heredity nor designation. She elevated her rule by reference to her achievements, real or putative, for the benefit of Russia.

Catherine's seizure of power was related as an act of heroic deliverance. The accession manifesto of July 6, 1762, written by Nikita Panin and Grigorii Teplov, painted Peter III's reign in the darkest colors. Monarchical power "unbridled by kind and altruistic qualities" was "an evil with many destructive consequences," the manifesto declared. The fatherland trembled seeing "a Sovereign and ruler who slavishly obeyed all his passions . . . before he began to think of the well-being of the state entrusted to him."[1] Like Anna, Peter III had taken on the appearance of a foreigner, rather than of a

---

[1] This manifesto was printed and circulated in both church and civil script. It was omitted from *The Complete Collection of Laws* in 1832. Peter Bartenev, *Osmnatstaty vek; istoricheskii sbornik* (Moscow, 1869), 4:217; Ransel, *The Politics of Catherinian Russia*, 70–71.

Russian acting as a foreigner. The manifesto accused him of "hatred for the fatherland." He had "no traces of the Greek orthodox church," in his heart, had shown contempt for the religion, its rites and icons, and had planned to begin the destruction of churches. Most important, the manifesto maintained, he had tried to corrupt everything that Peter the Great had accomplished, had scorned laws and justice, squandered state funds, begun costly and bloody wars. The strict Prussian discipline that Peter III had introduced in imitation of Frederick the Great prompted the charge that he had "conceived a hatred for the Guards' regiments," and had thrown the organization of the army into disarray.[2]

The coup brought the dawn of the new age. Catherine's selfless act of violence supported her claim to rule in the interests of all. The medal issued upon her accession depicts her in helmet, as a formidable, bellicose Minerva (fig. 18). Like Catherine I and Elizabeth before her, she exemplified male as well as female qualities, both prowess and graciousness. A painting of 1762 presents her in guards' uniform at the head of her troops. A drawing executed at her request shows her being greeted by troops at the balcony of the Winter Palace. She loved to ride about and appear at masquerades in guards' uniform (fig. 19).[3] "A man's dress is what suits her best," the British envoy, Lord Buckingham, remarked, "she wears it always when she rides on horseback." Later in her reign, she continued to wear men's costumes at balls and, on occasion, to play at pursuing young ladies.[4]

The assent for the coup came in the form of her subjects' expressions of affection. The reverse side of the medal shows Catherine receiving a crown from a kneeling allegorical figure of Petersburg; the presentations of her accession emphasized the popular support, the love her subjects had displayed. In fact, there is little evidence of widespread support for the leaders and guards' regiments that participated in the coup.[5] Catherine's scenario used the "love" of the people as a sign of the popular support that enabled her to depart from the norms of succession. Love became a leitmotiv of the rhetoric of the first years of her reign. The generalized "joy" of Elizabeth's scenario turns into the generalized "love" of Catherine's. The word *love* expresses her intention to act for the good of others rather than in her own interests, "the kind and altruistic qualities" that Peter did not exemplify. The manifesto of July 7, 1762, announcing the coronation for the subsequent

---

[2] Bartenev, *Osmnatstaty vek*, 4:217–19. For a rehabilitation of Peter that gives a good sense of the propagandistic success of Catherine's decree and subsequent statements, see Carol S. Leonard, "The Reputation of Peter III," *The Russian Review*, vol. 47, no. 3 (July 1988): 263–92, and *Reform and Regicide: The Reign of Peter III of Russia* (Bloomington, Ind., 1992).

[3] The pictures are reproduced in A. Brückner, *Istoriia Ekateriny vtoroi* (St. Petersburg, 1885), vols. 1 and 2.

[4] John T. Alexander, *Catherine the Great: Life and Legend* (New York, 1989), 65; de Madariaga, *Age of Catherine the Great*, 574.

[5] Leonard, *Reform and Regicide*, 138–47; Solov'ev, *Istoriia Rossii*, 13:89–103. Kliuchevskii, on the other hand, turns it into a veritable expression of the Russian nation (Kliuchevskii, *Sochineniia*, 4:348–58).

18. Medal issued on accession of Catherine II.

19. *Catherine II in Guards' Uniform.*

September, declared: "The entire world can see that zeal for religion, love for Our Russian Fatherland, and also the fervent wish of all Our loyal subjects to see us on the Throne, and through us to receive deliverance from those dangers that have occurred and even greater ones that were about to follow." If she had not acted, she would have had to answer before the Lord's judgment for the dangers threatening Russia, and having done so, she had received the Lord's blessing. She had liberated the fatherland from danger, "without bloodshed." She now had the pleasure of seeing the "love, joy, and gratitude" that her subjects had shown in accepting her and "the zeal with which they pronounced the solemn oath of loyalty to us, about which we had earlier been completely confident."[6]

"Love," as well as joy, purportedly greeted Catherine's act of deliverance, and during her reign her relations with her servitors were portrayed in terms of affection. Love implied inner dispositions that motivated the external displays of joy and exultation. Catherine's love for her subjects suggested a new type of rule informed with the sensibilities of the enlightenment. It was rule by humane feelings, if not by institutional guarantees. The monarch would reign with benevolence and care because it was in her heart to do so. Her subjects would show their appreciation with displays of love, confirming her right to rule. Love described what purported to be an independent prompting rather than an orchestrated response. This feeling of love particularly defined Catherine's relationship with the noble elite, who were awaiting confirmation of Peter III's decree of 1762 emancipating the nobility from service. As she expanded the nobility to include the elites of newly acquired territories, demonstrations of love proved the devotion that united the nobility of the Russian empire with the empress.

Catherine was also presented as Minerva, the embodiment of enlightenment, making known that the advancement of science and learning would accompany the impending process of renovation. In his accession ode, Michael Lomonosov wrote:

> Sciences, celebrate now:
> Minerva has ascended the Throne.
> Permessian Waters, rejoice,
> Swirl loudly into the golden distance,
> You rush into rivers and the sea
> And proclaim our joy,
> To meadows, mountains and islands;
> Say that for enlightenment,
> Everywhere she brings instruction,
> Founding magnificent temples to you.[7]

Catherine the Great's coronation put on display the leading themes of Catherine's reign—love and science—in the context of the myth of renova-

[6] Bartenev, *Osmnatstaty vek*, 4:223.
[7] Lomonosov, *Polnoe sobranie sochinenii*, 8:780–81.

tion. If Elizabeth's coronation proclaimed a "native empress" who revived her father's spirit, Catherine presented a humane empress, whose rule was distinguished by compassion and reason that won her subjects' hearts. They, in turn, responded with exultant celebration, which, the text and verse emphasized, was joy animated by a feeling of love.

The chorus of adulation extends beyond the elite to include the "people" as well. For the first time at a Russian coronation, references are made to shouts of "Hoorah!" from the crowds in the square during the procession. The proscenium as a distance-creating barrier is eliminated. No longer a stage performance with an inferred audience, the spectacle purports to be enacted in and among the people. The performance leaves the court, reaches the streets of Moscow, eventually goes to the provinces. But Catherine's scenario carries no democratic implications. The people are themselves only actors supporting the chorus of the elite and confirming the dawn of the new era with Catherine's accession. There is no hint that rule derives from or even is beholden to popular sentiment. Rather, the response confirms the derivation of her power from a higher realm that inspires altruism and wisdom, and allows her to bestow her virtues on her subjects.

The opening of the coronation *Opisanie* immediately reveals her relationship with the elite and the empire.[8] It tells how the elders of the Zaporozhets Cossack host, led by their commander, the hetman, Kiril Razumovskii—a former lover of Catherine—greet the empress at her suburban palace as their source of joy and their "true mother."[9] The speeches of welcome by the clergy during the entry procession repeated the themes and sometimes the words of those given by Archbishop Ambrosii at Elizabeth's coronation but included expressions of love. At the arch of the Kremlin's Nikolskii Gate, the metropolitan of Moscow, Timothy, declared that all the faithful were welcoming their empress, "the Russian deliverer," and that Moscow, "adorned with the true Christian faith," was rejuvenated in the joy of her appearance. Then students from the Moscow Academy—dressed in white and wearing wreaths, and holding forth laurel branches—sang a hymn welcoming Catherine as the chosen of God, who saw in her "a multitude of kindnesses, for the showing of her bounty."[10]

The oration of Dmitrii, Archbishop of Novgorod, at the Assumption Cathedral followed the form of Ambrosii's at Elizabeth's coronation. But after enumerating Catherine's virtues and extolling her mercy and maternal care, he emphasized that she was bearing the heavy burden of rule only because of her "love for the Fatherland." He asked how they should welcome her. Scat-

---

[8] The *Opisanie* of Catherine's coronation remained unpublished during her reign for unknown reasons, though the high costs may have figured in the decision (*Opisanie Vshestviia v Moskvu i Koronovaniia Gosudaryni Imperatritsy Ekateriny II*, printed in *KFZ*, 1762, vol. 63 [St. Petersburg, 185?]; henceforth, *Opisanie Vshestviia*. A brief account appeared in *Sankt-Peterburgskie Vedomosti*, October 1, 1762, no. 80, appendix).

[9] *Opisanie Vshestviia*, 7–11.

[10] Ibid., 23–28.

tering flowers and releasing incense like the ancient Greeks and Romans were insufficient expressions. "Instead of this, we bring our unfeigned love, our fervent wishes, instead of this, we dedicate our hearts in faithfulness."[11]

Catherine's coronation took place on September 22, nine days after the entry. The procession to the Assumption Cathedral was larger than before, consisting of fifty-one different sections. The *Opisanie* stressed the tranquility of the population during the entry procession to the cathedral. "There was no disorder but everyone, it seems, waited with impatience only for the crowning of Her Majesty as 'the beloved Most Kind Sovereign Autocrat.'" Delegations from the Zaporozhets and Don cossacks, each led by its ataman, made clear the broadening of the imperial elite. The bearers of the regalia were prominent figures from Elizabeth's reign, showing Catherine's loyalty to the dominant ruling families. The state banner (*panir*) was carried by Semen Kirilovich Naryshkin, an Eger-Meister, and Admiral Ivan Talyzin, who had commanded the troops in Catherine's coup. Senator Peter Sumarokov, who had served under Anna, Elizabeth, and Peter III, carried the state sword. The bearers of the imperial mantle were General Peter Saltykov, who had led Russian armies during the Seven Years War, and Field-Marshall Alexander Shuvalov, Elizabeth's favorite, who had been a senator under Peter III.

The crown was carried by one of Elizabeth's favorites, Alexei Razumovskii. His brother, Kiril, the hetman of Little Russia, was among the empress's escorts, along with Chancellor Alexei Petrovich Bestuzhev-Riumin, who had dominated Russian foreign policy in Elizabeth's reign until his fall in 1757 and now had returned to favor. To the side marched one (which one is not identified in the *Opisanie*) of the Orlov brothers, who had helped her seize the throne. The procession thus presented an impressive show of the members of the elite joining ranks in support of Catherine's usurpation.

Despite Catherine's frequent complaints about costs, she spent lavishly on the production of her regalia, making certain that their magnificence equaled or surpassed Western examples. Immediately after her accession, she preoccupied herself with the redesign of the imperial crown. Following her instructions, the court jeweler, Geremie Pauzié, fashioned a crown that he described as "the most opulent thing that exists in Europe." It weighed nearly five pounds and, in somewhat altered form, was worn at all subsequent coronations. It was studded with 75 large pearls, 2,500 diamonds, and 5,012 other precious gems. The cross on top rested on a ruby. Catherine's robe of silver brocade was embroidered with eagles and gold braid.[12]

Catherine's coronation observed the order of ceremonies followed by Elizabeth's. The speech of congratulations, delivered by the Novgorod Archbishop, Dmitrii, carried on the tradition of lauding the empress's personal

[11] Ibid., 30–33.

[12] Pauzié, "Zapiski brillianshchika Poz'e," no. 1, 112; Chakirov, *Tsarskie koronatsii*, 136; *BE*, 31:319; The robe is on display in the Kremlin Armory. I. A. Bobrovnitskaia et al., *Gosudarstvennaia oruzheinaia palata*, 340–41.

virtues and qualifications for rule, and used the appellation "Mother of the Fatherland," which would describe her concern for her citizens during her reign. Dmitrii spoke of her "pure heart" and her "blameless path" to power. She did not seek power or wealth by coming to the throne, he said, addressing her, "but only maternal love for the fatherland, only faith in God, and ardor for piety, only compassion for the suffering and oppressed Russian children impelled You to take on this great service to God." At the conclusion, he exclaimed, "Oh, Russians, you have received such a Mother of the fatherland, a Mother who cares for her flock and rejoices in them!"[13]

The recessional to the graves of the empress's "ancestors" at the Archangel Cathedral and to the Annunciation Cathedral, with the empress in full regalia, provided an occasion for a display of popular acclaim. When Catherine emerged from the Assumption Cathedral, "the regiments were standing on parade and all the assembled people shouted hoorah." The *Opisanie* text says that the shouts continued for half an hour until the empress gave a sign for the procession to continue. The account in *Sankt-Peterburgskie Vedomosti* remarked on the "pure heart, thought and spirit revealed by the countless people who have attained their wish and saw their most gracious sovereign invested in Purple and Crown." Their "noise and joyous exclamations, the tolling of the bells, the cannon fire and salutes seemed to shake the air."[14] After the procession, the empress retired to the Kremlin Palace where she ascended the throne for the granting of favors. She lavished awards, diamond swords, Orders of Nevskii, court ranks, especially on those "who showed outstanding service and fidelity to her and the fatherland on her accession to the throne."

The incomplete illustrations of the coronation by Louis de Veilly, express the personal drama of the ritual instead of the total spectacle.[15] Unlike the engravings for Elizabeth's album, they draw the viewer close to the ceremonies. Rather than a cavernous version of the Assumption Cathedral, the artist presents the empress and the courtiers clustered at her side. The procession to the Assumption Cathedral includes only the Red Staircase (*Krasnoe Kryl'tso*), leading from the Palace of Facets, and the figures in the immediate vicinity. After the crowning, the empress is shown standing proudly in full regalia at the "tsar's place"; her courtiers nod their greeting with studied nonchalance (fig. 20). For the first time, the reading of the credo, the anointment, and even communion in the sanctuary are illustrated, making clear that the former Lutheran princess had received the ecclesiastical status of

---

[13] *Opisanie Vshestviia*, 94.

[14] Ibid., 102; *Sankt-Peterburgskie Vedomosti*, October 1, 1762, no. 80, appendix, 2.

[15] The illustrations were published first in the 1790s, and republished during the nineteenth century. The engravings of de Veilly's drawing were by A. Ia. Kolpashnikov, S. Putimtsev, G. T. Kharitonov, and A. I. Kazachinskii. Ia. V. Bruk, *U istokov russkogo zhanra; XVIII vek* (Moscow, 1990), 77, 242; Rovinskii, *Pobdrobnyi Slovar'*, 2:535–36. V. A. Vereshchagin, *Russkie illiustrirovannye izdaniia XVIII i XIX stoletii* (St. Petersburg, 1898), 614. N. S. Obol'ianinov, *Katalog russkikh illiustrirovannykh izdanii, 1725–1860* (Moscow, 1914–15, 2:369.

20. *Catherine at the Tsar's Place*. Engraving after a drawing by Louis de Veilly.

21. *Coronation Banquet for Catherine II*. Engraving after a drawing
by Louis de Veilly.

previous monarchs. The coronation banquet is a scene of little solemnity, with the courtiers preoccupied with their own repast and conversations (fig. 21).

The completion of the coronation ceremonies set the stage for the celebrations. "The gala coronation of Her Imperial Majesty continued with various joyous diversions for eight days," the *Opisanie* declared. The official account only alluded to the festivities, but their magnificence and scale reconfirmed the European character of the Russian court and stunned foreign visitors. "An impartial description must seem an exaggeration," the English ambassador wrote of a magnificent amateur show at court, "which would do honor to its author in any country." Such elegance was doubly impressive in view of "how recently the fine arts were introduced to Russia." Celebrations at the homes of the great Moscow nobles, the Sheremet'evs, the Razumovskiis, the Saltykovs, and Golitsyns, were no less sumptuous. The balls, theatrical performances, and masquerades showed that the great families were following their empress in exemplifying Western taste. The French ambassador wrote that these events were "indeed of a magnificence that few countries would want to authorize." Catherine herself excelled in the merriment and, wearing an officer's uniform at the masquerades, flirted with Princess Dashkova.[16]

The postcoronation celebrations were given a broader scope to show the "love" of the common people for the new empress. On the evening of the coronation, the Kremlin was illuminated and people converged from all over Moscow to witness "the spectacle of fire." At midnight, both the *Opisanie* and the newspaper account reported, Catherine stepped out on the Red Staircase incognito to admire the illumination, and the people "recognized her and greeted her with a loud hoorah until she repaired to her chambers." At the popular feast on the day after the coronation, fountains again spouted red and white wine, and roast oxen were served to the people. Catherine threw gold and silver coins into the crowd, and, the *Opisanie* adds, "Each can imagine the rapture with which the people gazed on their anointed Sovereign." Catherine was "gladdened" by the joy of her subjects. On Saturday of that week, roast oxen with trimmings and bread were sent out on specially carved wooden stands to different streets in the city.[17]

While the balls and masquerades at Catherine's coronation were not publicized, the fireworks display on Tsaritsyn Meadow served as another occasion to demonstrate the popular approval of the new empress. At the signal of a 101-gun salute, a blazing shield revealed an allegorical figure of Russia "despairing and insulted" who had been brought back to life by a figure of "Providence descending from the heavens" through the name of Her Majesty. The allegory could be "seen more extensively," the *Opisanie* asserted,

[16] V. A. Bil'basov, *Istoriia Ekateriny Vtoroi* (London, 1895), 2:159–61; Alexander, *Catherine the Great: Life and Legend*, 65.

[17] *Opisanie Vshestviia*, 125, 135; *Sankt-Peterburgskie Vedomosti*, October 1, 1762, no. 80, appendix, 3; Bil'basov, *Istoriia Ekateriny Vtoroi*, 2:153–55.

in an illustrated and printed book, a copy of which was presented to the empress. The thunder of the guns and brilliance of the display, the account continued, so delighted the throng of people who gathered nearby that they could not contain exclamations of "Hoorah!"[18]

The celebrations of Catherine's coronation also proclaimed her intellectual intentions and ambitions. The world of education and scholarship gathered to hail the dawning era of wisdom. Speeches from the rostrums of the lecture halls of the Academy of Sciences and the recently founded Moscow University extolled the empress as a patron of learning and were duly published.[19] A fireworks display before the building of the university showed Catherine as Minerva, the bearer of peace and the protector of wisdom. The meaning of the symbols was explained in a published volume, with Russian, German, and French translations. The text declared that the Russian people were now thanking Providence for bringing the reign of Catherine and an end to the troubles and disturbances, and the beginning of a happy time. Moscow University expressed its recognition that "by gloriously putting aside weapons and battle, THE RUSSIAN MINERVA turns her most gracious gaze on [the university] and mercifully deigns to assist its growth."[20]

The festivities continued during the six months Catherine remained in Moscow, dramatizing Catherine in her role of moral instructor. The dawning golden age would not only bring just rule and prosperity, but the instruction of the people in virtue, under the guidance of a benevolent monarch. The golden age now was pictured as a time of honest and responsible behavior, when the population would learn civic virtue.

This was the theme of the extraordinary street masquerade staged in January during Shrovetide. The program booklet was entitled " 'Minerva Triumphant' in which the vileness of the vices and the glory of the virtues are presented."[21] The actor and theater director Fedor Volkov staged a cavalcade that lasted three days and comprised nearly four thousand individuals and two hundred floats. Choruses on the floats sang verses composed by Michael Kheraskov and Alexander Sumarokov, both supporters of Nikita Panin. The floats satirized stupidity and ignorance, drunkenness, deceit, ar-

---

[18] *Opisanie Vshestviia*, 150–51.

[19] At Moscow University, Professor Reichel's speech in Latin showed how rulers and states promoted learning. This theme was taken up by Gerard Friedrich Miller in an oration at a public meeting of the Academy of Sciences on the occasion of the coronation (*Torzhestvo blagopoluchno sovershivshegosia v Moskve koronovaniia i miropomazaniia Blagochestivshia Gosudaryni Imperatritsy Ekateriny Alekseevny . . . otpravlennoe Imperatorskoiu Akademieiu Nauk v publichnom sobranii 23 sentiabria, 1762* [St. Petersburg, 1762]; Bil'basov, *Istoriia Ekateriny Vtoroi*, 2:155).

[20] *Opisanie allegoricheskoi illiuminatsii predstavlennoi vo vseradostneishii den' koronatsii eia Imperatorskogo Velichestva Ekateriny Vtorye v Moskve pred Universitetskom gome v 1762 godu* (Moscow, 1762).

[21] The booklet was reprinted in 1850. "Torzhestvuiushchaia Minerva," *Moskvitianin* (October 1850), Otd. Nauki i khudozhestva, 109–28; Bil'basov, *Istoriia Ekateriny Vtoroi*, 2:161–65; Baehr, "Fortuna Redux," 117–18.

rogance, and prodigality. The masquerade was combined with extensive popular amusements, games, dances, puppet shows, and magicians.

Although it took the form of a carnival, Catherine's masquerade in the streets of the city was hardly a manifestation of "popular" or "low" culture. Rather, it used popular forms to display a moral transformation effected from above. "Minerva Triumphant" represented the myth of renovation in terms of the moral education of the population. The cavalcade of dwarfs and giants, satyrs, drunkards, and fools concluded with the figures of Vulcan and Jupiter and then a parade of the virtues accompanying Minerva herself. The choruses ended with invocations of Astraea and the Age of Gold. In Catherine's enlightenment scenario, knowledge and reason were to help the monarch overcome the flaws of humanity. Sumarokov's choruses concluded with an exultant apostrophe to Minerva calling on her to open the Palladian gates. Kheraskov, on the staff of Moscow University and director of its printing house, declared that learning and study were the answers to vice.[22]

The masquerade thus portrayed what would become Catherine's enlightenment version of the utilitarian ethos of the Petrine absolute state. The antinomy of sin and salvation has been replaced by that of vice and virtue, with virtue defined in civic terms. The empress saves her people from the despotism of her predecessor, and transforms them into citizens through laws and education. But she does not redeem their sins nor is she concerned for her own. She and her elite disport themselves in a firmament beyond the judgment of ordinary mortals, where personal probity and biblical morality had no special value. The result would be a state of increasing pleasure and happiness. The Muscovites, who stood at apartment windows and crowded the stands erected along the way, were delighted by the spectacle. Andrei Bolotov wrote, "Everything was so well arranged, decorated so wondrously and richly and all the songs and verses were sung with pleasant voices that one could watch only with great pleasure."[23]

At the same time, Catherine, like Elizabeth, put on demonstrative shows of her devotion to orthodoxy and the church. She made clear that she, unlike her husband, would respect the religious traditions of Russia, a gesture necessitated by her intention to proceed with the confiscation of monastery lands planned during his reign. Although she was devoid of piety, she, too, staged magnificent pilgrimages that gave her religious observance all the splendor of a court spectacle. Her first pilgrimage, to the Trinity Monastery, took place less than a month after the coronation. She traveled in a large convoy of carriages with a great suite. Her visit was described in an official account published that year, *A Description of the Most Joyous Entry of the Most Pious Sovereign Empress Catherine Alekseevna into the Holy Trinity Monastery*. The text described a gala reception that continued the scenario

---

[22] "Torzhestvuiushchaia Minerva," 115, 128.

[23] A. Bolotov, *Zhizn' i prikliucheniia Andreia Bolotova opisannye samim im dlia svoikh potomkov, 1738–1795* (St. Petersburg, 1871), 2:389–91.

presented at the coronation. After she entered the monastery to a hymn sung by a group of seminarians, Archimandrite Lavrentii welcomed her as "the Russian Delevratrix," who in piety was "the Second Helen," and in courage "the image of Judith of Israel." In the evening there was an illumination, which, with emblems and stories from the scriptures, "presented the joy that the Church and Russia had seeing ruling over it a monarch known for piety and wisdom," and gratitude to God, for his providence in protecting "his Israel."

The next day, she heard speeches proving the compatibility of reason and religion and lauding her as reason's defender. During a lengthy service, the abbot, Innokentii, delivered a sermon proving the "veracity of the Sacred scriptures." She toured the monastery buildings, and heard a speech by the rector, Platon, who praised her for the wisdom with which she watered "the vineyard of learning." Then Catherine listened "with the most evident signs of her love for Science," to a debate on the "existence and providence of God." As she inspected the monastery, seminarians intoned a song comparing the arrival of their "Dearest Mother" to the spring, bringing joy and water on a warm day.[24]

The following May, Catherine undertook a demanding pilgrimage on foot to Rostov. The purpose of the trip, which was also described in an official publication, was to pray at the recently opened remains of St. Dmitrii of Rostov. Peter the Great had forbidden the display and worship of the remains of saints, but Elizabeth had opened the remains of Dmitrii for veneration and ordered the construction of a silver shrine, which had not been completed at her death. Catherine insisted on attending the dedication to prove that she had taken the throne "for defence of orthodoxy."

Catherine walked to Rostov at the rate of about seven miles a day. Often she had to retire to a carriage, but apparently returned to the place where she had left off. Despite the bad weather, she completed the journey in eleven days. She patiently witnessed miracle cures and insisted that the shrine be kept open during her stay "so that the common people do not think that the remains are being hidden from me." Her effort won the admiration of Muscovites, who regarded the pilgrimage as a religious exploit. It showed Catherine's religious sensibilities shortly after she had succeeded in removing the Rostov metropolitan, Arsenii, the leading opponent of secularization of monastery lands.[25]

The Rostov trip, however, was more than a pilgrimage. It was the first of Catherine's many trips through the empire as she extended the ambit of her

---

[24] *Opisanie vseradostneishego vshestviia Blagochestiveishei Gosudaryni Imperatritsy Ekateriny Alekseevny v Sviatuiu-Troitskuiu Lavru* (Moscow, 1762); summarized in Bil'basov, *Istoriia Ekateriny Vtoroi*, 2:156–58. K. A. Papmehl indicates that Platon prepared the reception for Catherine at the monastery (K. A. Papmehl, *Metropolitan Platon of Moscow [Petr Levshin], 1737–1812* [Newtonville, Mass., 1983], 8).

[25] Bil'basov, *Istoriia Ekateriny Vtoroi*, 2:165–67; de Madariaga, *Age of Catherine the Great*, 113–17.

ceremonies to the provinces. Catherine was the first Russian ruler to exploit the ceremonial possibilities of travel, which showed the monarch's care for her subjects and their demonstrative appreciation for her concern. From Rostov she went to Iaroslavl, which pleased her greatly. The following fall she visited the Baltic provinces on a visit that allowed the nobility to demonstrate their devotion to the throne—in the hope of confirming their special privileges. The triumphal arches, balls, and fireworks brought the Baltic Ritterschaft into the rejoicing of the realm and displayed the unity of the elite of the empire.[26]

THE EMPRESS AS LEGISLATRIX

Catherine presented herself as "philosophe on the throne," identifying her rule not with present or historical models of Western monarchy, but the ideal she found in Western thought. As a young grand duchess, she had learned the importance of self-discipline and knowledge from a Swedish count, H. A. Gyllenborg, who had provided her with a reading list, including works of Plutarch, Tacitus, and Montesquieu. Before she came to the throne, she had read many of the principal works of the philosophes, and in the last years of Elizabeth's reign, she began to consider theoretical questions of politics under the tutelage of Nikita Panin.

Early on she made known her persona as the legislatrix, who brought the benefits of reason to her subjects through the instrumentality of the laws. Her principal endeavor was the establishment of a commission to codify the laws, which she convoked in Moscow in 1767. The commission consisted of deputies from the estates—nobility, townspeople, state peasants, and deputies from the "non-Russian tribes." The *Nakaz (Instruction)* that she composed to guide them consisted of precepts borrowed from enlightenment legal writers, particularly Montesquieu and Cesare Beccaria. The *Nakaz* was published in German, French, English, and Latin translations, giving it immediate notoriety. Six editions were published between 1767 and 1771, and four more during the remaining years of Catherine's reign.[27] The commission failed to produce a code. Instead, the various estates took the occasion to voice their particular grievances and demands, and showed little concern for the empress's lofty goals. Nonetheless, the expression of legal principles from the throne established an ideal and a measure for future legal reform in Russia.

Whatever their legal and institutional significance, the *Nakaz* and the subsequent commission were constituent events in Catherine's scenario of rule. They played a crucial role in defining her image as sovereign and presenting her within the Petrine motif of conquest and renovation. The effort at cod-

---

[26] Bil'basov, *Istoriia Ekateriny Vtoroi*, 2:290–92; Solov'ev, *Istoriia Rossii*, 13:315–22.

[27] William E. Butler, "The *Nakaz* of Catherine the Great," *American Book Collector*, vol. 16, no. 5 (1966): 19–20.

ification showed her as Astraea, realizing justice, bringing the golden age. Victor Zhivov writes, "The *Nakaz*, like the entire state ideology, entered the sphere of myth and fulfilled a mythological function. It was an attribute of the monarch establishing universal justice and creating harmony in the world."[28]

Yet, Catherine gave an entirely new presentation to the myth of universal justice and the golden age. This was not to be the Christian justice of the pious monarch, or Astraea defeating the forces of dissension identified with Satan. Catherine took on the image of legislatrix who realized her subjects' welfare by introducing legal norms found in the writings of the West. She thus gave a new interpretation to the myth of empire. In Russia, George Knabe pointed out, the image of Rome played a distinctive role, replacing Russian reality with an emblematic reality of classical antiquity.[29] If Peter assumed the aspect of Augustus, the military leader, Catherine appeared as the successor to Numa and Marcus Aurelius, a sovereign who embodied wisdom as well as military leadership. Catherine's exemplar was not the sun king, but the philosopher king. Accordingly, she filled the expectations of Western exemplars of the enlightenment. Voltaire described the *Nakaz* as "the finest monument of the age." Frederick the Great said it was worthy of a great man, concluding: "We have never heard of any Female being a Lawgiver. This Glory was reserved for the Empress of Russia."[30]

Ernst Cassirer wrote that the philosophy of the enlightenment held to an "apriority of law," to a "demand for absolutely universally valid and unalterable legal norms."[31] Catherine's *Nakaz* was a typical product of enlightenment thought, spelling out universal norms from which the deputies could choose in order to devise appropriate statutes for Russia. At the outset, in Articles 6 and 7, she expresses the conviction that gave rise to Lomonosov's "rapture" at joining the West. Russia was "a European state," because of Peter's great success in "introducing the Manners and Customs of Europe among the European People in his Dominions." The end of monarchy, Article 13 proclaims, was "Not to deprive People of their Natural Liberty; but to correct their Actions in order to attain the *supreme Good*." The Laws brought the wise influence of the sovereign to bear upon the courts. The judges must precisely apply the laws issued by the sovereign without interpretation, for "they are not Legislators" (Articles 20, 149, 151). The propositions of the *Nakaz* were totally new for Russia: "The Laws ought to be so framed, as to secure the Safety of every Citizen as much as

---

[28] V. M. Zhivov, "Gosudarstvennyi mif v epokhu Prosveshcheniia i ego razrushenie v Rossii kontsa XVIII veka," in *Vek Prosveshcheniia; Rossiia i Frantsia, Vipperovskie chteniia* (Moscow, 1989), 22:150.

[29] G. S. Knabe, "Rimskaia tema v russkoi kul'ture i v tvorchestve Tiutcheva," in Iu. Lotman, ed., *Tiutchevskii Sbornik; stat'i o zhizni i tvorchestve Fedora Ivanovicha Tiutcheva* (Tallin, 1990), 255–56.

[30] Citations from Alexander, *Catherine the Great*, 101.

[31] Ernst Cassirer, *The Philosophy of the Enlightenment* (Boston, 1951), 243–44.

possible" (Article 33). "The Equality of the Citizens consists in this; that they should all be subject to the same Laws"(Article 34). The document went beyond legal questions to make recommendations on the growth of the population, the development of commerce and trade, taxation, education, the family, and the conduct of the nobility.[32]

The commission was to open the reign of *eunomia*, when good laws, arrived at through enlightenment principles, would bring happiness to mankind. The *Nakaz*, Baehr observed, evokes the image of paradise. Article 520 declares, "For God forbid! that, after this Legislation is finished, any Nation on Earth should be more just; and, consequently, should flourish more than Russia." Article 521 expresses the expectation that codification would "render the People of Russia, humanly speaking, the *most happy* in themselves of any People upon Earth." The works of art and literature issued on the occasion of the commission portray Catherine in the company of classical lawgivers, particularly Numa and Lycurgus. In their company, she, too, takes on the sacrality of a founder and creator. An engraving of the time shows Catherine standing before the throne, flanked by Minerva and Mars, her right hand extended toward the open book, the *Nakaz* (fig. 22). The common people press toward the throne struggling to see the instructions bestowed on them. A large obelisk bears the inscription, "the good of each and all." In the background, on a column, stands the statue of an ancient legislator. Before the throne sit a couple with two infants, Romulus and Remus; behind them the face of a wolf is visible.[33]

The allegory places Catherine in a classical setting, showing her to be the founder, renewing Russia by incorporating Rome. Michael Kheraskov's allegorical novel, *Numa, or Flourishing Rome*, published in 1768, expanded on this theme, using the figure of Numa the lawgiver to glorify Catherine, as one whose laws would make Russia into a "flourishing Rome." Kheraskov portrayed Numa as a savior of his people and other lands. His laws would bring "truth triumphant, virtue rejoicing, and vices driven out."[34]

The allegorical engravings at the beginning and conclusion of the four-language 1770 edition of the *Instruction* place the *Nakaz* and the empress in an Olympian setting.[35] The frontispiece shows Catherine in a foreboding

---

[32] W. F. Reddaway, ed., *Documents of Catherine the Great* (New York, 1971), 216–17, 219.

[33] Ibid., 293; Baehr, *The Paradise Myth*, 120–21; Brückner, *Istoriia Ekateriny vtoroi* (opposite page 546). At the instance of Catherine's "factotum," Alexander Bezborodko, the painter Dmitrii Levitskii executed his own allegory "Catherine in the Temple of Justice" (1783); Catherine stands before the figure of Themis and a bas-relief of a classical lawgiver. M. M. Safonov comments on Bezborodko's role in his *Zaveshchanie Ekateriny II*, unpublished manusript, chap. 4, 110. The original is at the Russian Museum.

[34] Baehr, *The Paradise Myth*, 121–22; Stephen L. Baehr, "From History to National Myth: *Translatio imperii* in Eighteenth Century Russia," *Russian Review*, vol. 37, no. 1 (January 1978): 6.

[35] *Nakaz e.i.v. Ekateriny vtoryie . . . dannyi kommissii o sochinenii proekta novago ulozheniia* (St. Petersburg, 1770); Butler, "The *Nakaz* of Catherine the Great," 20.

22. *Allegory of Catherine as Legislator.*

setting in the embrace of Themis, awaiting the onset of a storm (fig. 23). The endpiece depicts the effect of enlightenment, the brilliant dawning (fig. 24). Catherine, in the radiant sunlight, points with her left hand to an obelisk with her initials, and with her right hand to a book at the base of the monument, presumably a book of laws or the *Nakaz*. Saturn sits on the other side

23. *Allegorical Frontispiece.* Drawing by Jakob von Staehlin.
Engraving by C. M. Roth.

24. *Allegorical Endpiece.* Drawing by Jakob von Staehlin. Engraving by C. M. Roth.

of the obelisk, while Minerva at his side prepares to subdue a gnome, symbolizing the forces of evil, with a spear.[36]

The solemn ceremonies that opened the commission on July 30, 1767, in the Moscow Kremlin established the codification as an act of historical significance in the mythology of state. Convoking the meeting in Moscow, a city not to the empress's liking, gave it a historical precedent in the Assemblies of the Land of the previous century, and also the consecration of the clergy of the principal cathedral of the Russian Orthodox Church.[37] The ceremonies began with a mass in the Assumption Cathedral and the signing of an oath by the 460 deputies.[38] The deputies then filed into the Audience Room of the Kremlin Palace where they saw Catherine, wearing the imperial mantle and the small crown, standing on the dais. On a table beside her lay the books displayed as significant in the work of legislation: the *Nakaz*, the procedure of the commission, and the *Instruction to the Procurator-General*. The metropolitan of Moscow, Dmitrii, delivered a speech declaring Catherine the successor to Justinian, and Russia the heir to the Byzantine legal tradition.

The ceremony brought the deputies into Catherine's scenario of renovation. The didactic goal of creating publicly minded participants was set forth in a speech delivered by the vice chancellor, Prince Alexander Golitsyn. Golitsyn declared that the deputies, too, would be participating in a great, heroic task undertaken by the empress. He called on them to show their concern "for the good of humanity, for instilling morality and altruism into the hearts of people, for tranquillity, calm, security and the good of your dear fellow citizens." He exhorted them "to glorify yourselves and your era and to gain the respect and gratitude of posterity." The oath they signed obliged them to act with the selflessness claimed by the empress herself. They promised to strive to begin and end the task, observing rules "pleasing to God" that would "instill altruism, good morals for the preservation of the felicity and the tranquillity of the human species." It was from these rules that "all justice flows." For this purpose they called on God for the strength to "avert the heart and thought from blindness arising from partiality, self-interest, friendship, enmity, and hateful envy, for such passions may breed severity in thought and cruelty in advice."[39]

After mass on Sunday, August 12, the deputies gathered in the palace for a display of personal recognition and homage. They offered Catherine the

---

[36] I am indebted to Andrew Day for his analysis of these engravings in his paper, "The *Nakaz* and Catherinian Monarchy: A Historiographical Discussion." Day argues convincingly that the central figure is not *Rossiia*, as Rovinskii had suggested, but Catherine herself. Considering the numerous other paintings of Catherine, surrounding the *Nakaz*, it seems likely that Catherine is at the very least confounded with *Rossiia*.

[37] Robert E. Jones, *The Emancipation of the Russsian Nobility, 1762–1785* (Princeton, N.J., 1973), 128.

[38] The ceremony is described in Solov'ev, *Istoriia Rossii*, 14:71–73.

[39] Ibid., 14:72.

titles of Great, Most Wise, and Mother of the Fatherland. She declined all three with studied modesty. Whether she was "great," she declared, could only be determined by posterity and the term *most wise* could only be used for God. The appellation of Mother of the Fatherland was superfluous, for "to love the subjects entrusted to me I consider the duty of my calling and to be beloved of them is my wish."[40]

The hopes for such sacrifice of self-interest in the cause of altruistic legislation, however, proved ill founded; the deputies above all sought to advance the interests of their particular estates, and the humanitarian sermons left them unmoved. The commission continued its deliberations until the autumn of 1768 when the outbreak of war against the Ottoman Empire provided an excuse for termination, though several of the subcommissions continued working into the 1770s. Catherine continued to believe, however, that the didactic purpose had been achieved. The *Nakaz*, she was convinced, brought unity of rules and discussions. "People began to judge colors by their color and not as blind people judge colors. At least they began to learn something of the will of the legislator and to act according to it."[41]

The Empress, the Nobility, and the Empire

A series of decisive victories for Russia's land and sea forces in the war against the Ottoman Empire enhanced the feeling of mutual admiration and dependence between Catherine and her leading military servitors. The successes of the Russian armies and the defeat and destruction of the Turkish fleet at Chesma by Russian ships under Catherine's favorite, Alexei Orlov, on June 24, 1770, established Russia's dominance in the south. Catherine understood the victory as a new confirmation of the Petrine heritage and glory, and the devotion of her servitors. In a letter to General P. A. Rumiantsev, she remarked that she had held a Te Deum and memorial service for Peter, "the founder of the Russian fleet and the initial cause for this new glory for Russia." Her rescript to Alexei Orlov dilated on the glories of Russian armies and the expectation that Orlov's achievement would arouse fear among Russia's enemies. She rewarded Orlov and his officers with decorations, and Orlov with the title of Chesmenskii.[42] In 1774 the treaty of Kuchuk-Kainardzhi gave Russia new territories along the Black Sea, augmented the province of New Russia, and established the right for Russian subjects, for the first time, to trade and to navigate on the Black Sea.

But the good feeling was considerably dimmed by the rebellion led by Emelian Pugachev, the massive uprising among the Iaik cossacks, Bashkirs, and other national groups that spread to the peasantry of central Russia in

---

[40] Ibid., 14:74.

[41] Ibid., 14:75, 119–20.

[42] Ibid., 14:382–83; de Madariaga, *Age of Catherine the Great*, 211.

1773 and 1774. Although ultimately defeated, the uprising revealed the nether side of the Age of Gold, the resentment of the enserfed population toward the noblemen who constituted the Westernized administration and culture of Petrine Russia. The initial recruits to Pugachev's cause were the cossack rank and file who had been reduced to near-serf conditions with the encroachments of the modern state and the development of local noble elites. The movement spread into a jacquerie in the Volga areas, as many peasants took the opportunity to even accounts with landlords—looting estates, stringing up their landlords, leaving thousands dead. Pugachev was beheaded and his assistants sentenced to either beheading or penal servitude.

The crushing of the rebellion was celebrated with a triumphal entry to Moscow, demonstrating a symbolic reconquest of the capital. The defeat of the internal enemy was no different from that of foreign countries. But the role of protector of the law was emphasized here as well. The scenes on the arches were allegories of Catherine dispensing law and justice. In fact, she showed leniency by issuing an amnesty for all offenses committed during the rebellion and mitigating the sentences of Pugachev's lieutenants.[43] Catherine appeared as the just monarch implementing a severe but nonetheless fair retribution.

But the costs of the war levied on the local population, and the state of anarchy brought about by the removal of military forces from the provinces, exposed the vulnerability of the absolutist edifice. The war had left the countryside virtually unpoliced, revealing the inadequate governmental presence in the countryside and a lack of attention to local needs. Catherine now turned to the reform of local government that had been her intention since her accession. The preamble presented the reform as a demonstration of the principle, pronounced in the *Nakaz*, that Russia was a European state. Peter had cited the precedents of other nations and empires in his laws. Catherine now claimed that Russia no longer needed such examples but had achieved parity with other states. The experience of past monarchies, she stated, had shown that an expansion of the boundaries of empire and a growth of population had necessitated changes in institutions. But now Russia did not need to investigate "remote times or foreign kingdoms," for, in considering Russia's rise, "every person can see, with the help of common sense and by the sense of history, how the Russian fatherland has shone with glory, benefit, and strength."[44]

The Provincial Reform of 1775 both established a serious administrative presence in the countryside and involved the local nobility in their own institutions. The reform created district and provincial elective offices that fulfilled judicial, police, and fiscal tasks. It divided the functions of governmental organizations according to specialization, and, through elections by local

---

[43] de Madariaga, *Age of Catherine the Great*, 268.
[44] *PSZ*, no. 14,392 (November 7, 1775).

gentry assemblies, ensured a supply of officials who would serve in offices that carried low prestige in the Russian social hierarchy. Catherine clearly understood the need to train such officials and viewed the reform as another example of the beneficent, tutelary role she exerted. In the preamble, she stated her hope that the new institutions would instill in those holding office a love for justice and virtue, and an aversion to "idle time spent in luxury and other vices corrupting to the morals." They should regard with shame laziness, carelessness, and, most of all, "dereliction of duty and indifference to the general good."[45]

The new institutions also stimulated local social life, bringing some of the display and pomp of the capital into sleepy provincial towns. The emancipation from service had freed many nobles to return to the countryside and to become involved in the assemblies and the offices created by the reform.[46] The governor-general or *namestnik* himself became a symbolic bond between them and the Petersburg court. A powerful high official with personal attachments to the empress, he sat in the Senate and appeared as her emissary in the provinces. He arrived with a convoy of twenty-four light cavalrymen and two adjutants, and was provided with an honor guard of young noblemen, one from each district. The arrival of the *namestnik* became the occasion for great balls and receptions that allowed the provincial nobility to participate in the life of celebration centered in the capital.

The founding of the new institutions became a special occasion for celebrations, which, Robert Jones observed, were used to attract the nobility into the new institutions. In Tver, for example, the elections were followed by a Te Deum in the cathedral, a banquet at the governor-general's house, and a ball. The empress sent her personal congratulations to the nobility of Novgorod. Provincial delegations came to St. Petersburg after the first election meetings and received a warm personal audience with the empress. Many of them proposed to erect statues to Catherine; the empress graciously declined and urged that the funds go instead to the local public welfare boards.[47]

The sense of mutual interest and sympathy between empress and the nobility led to an extension of the nobility's already considerable privileges. The concessions to the nobility, from the time of the emancipation from service by Peter III in 1762, were systematized in the charter Catherine bestowed in 1785. The charter confirmed their right to own serfs and landed property; their freedom from service; and their right to be tried in cases involving loss of life, property, or noble status, by a court of their peers. It

[45] Ibid.

[46] John P. LeDonne, *Ruling Russia: Politics and Administration in the Age of Absolutism, 1762–1796* (Princeton, N.J., 1984), 67–75; PSZ, no. 14,392 (November 7, 1775). For an assessment of the extent of the nobility's movement to the provinces, see Leonard, *Reform and Regicide,* 65–70.

[47] Jones, *The Emancipation of the Russsian Nobility,* 247–50.

vested the local nobilities with a corporate status that empowered them to certify and register noblemen as members of their assemblies.[48]

In the preamble to the charter, Catherine declared that "the most aristocratic and noble Russian nobility" had earned these rights and privileges by the especial devotion they had shown to the fatherland. She mentioned Russian successes in the south, particularly the treaty of Kuchuk-Kainardzhi concluded by Field Marshall Rumiantsev, and Potemkin's conquest of the Crimea. But it was not the feeling of obligation, she stressed, that had moved her to make so generous a grant, but her "own maternal love and splendid recognition of the Russian nobility."[49]

The nobility now began to go beyond choral participation and to stage their own ceremonies of fealty. They reproduced the spectacles of the court glorifying the empress and other members of the imperial family as the creators of empire and the patrons of the sciences. At a celebration of 1776, at the mansion of the procurator-general, Prince Viazemskii, the host's young daughter declared in French to the members of the imperial family that she believed the palace had been transformed into "a temple consecrated to your sacred names." Her apostrophe to them was printed in *Sankt-Peterburgskie Vedomosti*. "Dear object of our vows, you are our divinities," she recited. "Yes I see Minerva, goddess of knowledge, the sciences and the arts. Phoebus, god of light and Hebe, the ornament of empire. You are leaving Olympus to embellish these places. You will inspire that divine ecstasy and celestial joy that only the gods have the power to produce."[50]

Such displays gave a show of deference to the Olympian image that the nobility entertained of their sovereign. "Maternal love" expressed the new relationship between them and the throne. Noblemen no longer served out of formal duty imposed by imperial fiat, but out of an obligation displayed as mutual affection. Catherine evoked this feeling personally. Members of the nobility felt her endearing manner and reciprocated her sentiments. The countess Golovine wrote: "No one could be more imposing than the Empress at times of state. No one could be greater, kinder, or more indulgent than she in her private circle. She hardly made her appearance before fear yielded to a tender respect." The countess added, "She carried her attentions so far as to order a blind to be lowered if the sun was inconveniencing someone." The poet, Gavriil Derzhavin, wrote about scenes of the court that had "seemed godlike and kindled his spirit with fire" to serve, though the flame died when he experienced the intrigues and corruption firsthand.[51]

[48] For a useful discussion of the charter and its relationship to earlier legislation, see Jones, *The Emancipation of the Russsian Nobility*, 253–99.

[49] *PSZ*, no. 16,187 (April 21, 1785).

[50] The newspaper reported is cited in G. R. Derzhavin, *Sochineniia* (St. Petersburg, 1868), 1:287, 295.

[51] V. N. Golovine, *Memoirs of Countess Golovine* (London, 1910), 38; see also Shakhovskoi's appreciations of her kindness (I. P. Shakhovskoi, *Zapiski* [St. Petersburg, 1872], 194–95); G. R. Derzhavin, *Sochineniia* (St. Petersburg, 1871), 6:654, 693.

From the beginning of her reign, Catherine inspired an atmosphere of order and mutual affection in her court. She eliminated the wild excesses of Peter III's reign, had rules drafted on court ranks, and brought expenditures and palace housekeeping under strict control. At court functions, she appeared as an effacing and friendly companion of her servitors and favorites. After the first decade of her reign, she often withdrew to the side, with leading figures in the court or government, for a game of chess or cards, a retiring demiurge of the proceedings. On days when there was no reception, she played cards or heard a concert in her residence next to the Winter Palace in an atmosphere of complete informality.[52]

The celebration of the Feast of Epiphany in January 1777 gives a sense of Catherine's ceremonial style. She first attended mass in the palace church. The clergy made their traditional procession to the "Jordan" staircase on the Neva, where they completed the ceremony of the Blessing of the Waters and then consecrated the standards of the guards' regiments. Meanwhile, Catherine and other members of the imperial family remained in the palace and received congratulations, until holy water was brought to the empress by the court marshall. Then she played chess, with Procurator-General Viazemskii, Prince Sergei Bariatinskii, and Prince Nicholas Vasil'evich Repnin. At one she attended dinner, and at six she played cards, again with important noblemen. The solemn military character of the ceremony under Peter the Great had disappeared (see above, chapter 2); the celebration had turned into a comfortable social occasion. Likewise, her birthday celebration was spent receiving congratulations and playing chess; then there was a ball where she played cards. The evening of Christmas was an occasion for a ball during which she played cards, and at one point deigned to dance.[53]

Catherine introduced a personal note to the formal splendor of the court. Her displays of kindness and sympathy reflected the monarch's new beneficent tutelary role. Rather than Peter's method of prescribing conduct by law in the *assamblei*, Catherine herself provided a tone of conduct for the elite, a modal feeling that would unite all those marked with their sovereign's attentions. If furious merrymaking and rejoicing united Peter the Great and Elizabeth with their servitors, it was affection and considerate self-restraint that attached Catherine to hers, the sharing of sentiments felt by enlightened individuals. Russian noblemen were to deport themselves with a genteel enlightened cultivation, a civility that separated them from brutal combat or the crudeness of those deprived of breeding and education.

The empress's favorite played an important role in training the noble elite in genteel conduct. Like Louis XIV, she used her current favorite as an ornament of power; he rode in her carriage and stood at her side at important functions. In this respect, her amorous attraction was to be displayed as another attribute of her supreme power. But the favorite also was a tutelary

---

[52] de Madariaga, *Age of Catherine the Great*, 327, 573.
[53] *KFZ* (1777), 1–7, 20–24, 922–25, 987–1002.

image. Catherine sought out lesser noblemen from the provinces, whom she had turned into paragons of cosmopolitan grace.[54] She thus repeated and reversed the transformation that Peter had wrought with Catherine I, turning a creature of the opposite sex into a symbol of civilization and progress.

Whereas the form of Catherine's spectacles had something in common with those of earlier absolutist monarchs, like Louis XIV, the content of their presentation and the type of thought and behavior they encouraged were very much reflections of the enlightenment. Catherine was striving to create a new kind of man, shaped according to the Stoic image popular in the Panin circle and among other young intellectuals in the 1760s.[55] Only by acquiring such enlightenment could the nobleman become an honest and trustworthy official capable of serving the general good in Catherine's new institutions. The enlightening of the nobility was a central purpose of Catherine's writings. In her journal, *Vsiakaia Vsiachina*, she continued the tradition of Kheraskov and Sumarokov, using satire as a means of moral education. She wrote didactic comedies and works on history. She paid close attention to the education of the tsarevich Paul, and his firstborn Alexander, for whom she composed children's tales and a history primer (see below, chapter 6). Her collected works fill a dozen large volumes.

Catherine's writings and remarks projected her image of rule and conduct onto the past, making it an intrinsic character of Russian monarchy. Like Peter, she turned early Russian rulers into forerunners of herself, whom she portrayed as enlightened, refined individuals. Catherine's historical remarks on Prince Vladimir interpreted the prince as a "wise, sensible, merciful and just sovereign," surrounded by a magnificent court. Catherine sympathized with him as a bearer of enlightenment and stability to Russia. In 1782 she created the Order of Vladimir for those in the civil and military service who had "brought especial benefit, honor, and glory" to Russia. She saw in the prince, Karen Rasmussen comments, "a cosmopolitan sovereign who appreciated and participated in the world beyond the frontiers of Kievan Russia."[56]

But her most ambitious achievement in this respect was to reshape the image of Peter the Great. Her attitude to Peter, Rasmussen concludes, was ambivalent: in her effort to improve the dispensation of justice, though she may have sought out Peter's opinion, she tried to rely on "mercy rather than justice" and believed that her achievements exceeded his.[57] Catherine transformed Peter in her own image, much as Peter had transformed his predecessors. The transformation was accomplished in part through the medium

---

[54] Alexander, *Catherine the Great: Life and Legend*, 223–26.

[55] On the neo-Stoicism of the first part of Catherine's reign, see Walter J. Gleason, *Moral Idealists, Bureaucracy, and Catherine the Great* (New Brunswick, N.J., 1981), 90–92, 96–98.

[56] Karen Rasmussen, "Catherine II and the Image of Peter I," *Slavic Review* (March 1978), vol. 37, no. 1, 60.

[57] Ibid., 51–69; Riasanovskii, *The Image of Peter the Great*, 45–46.

25. *Monument to Peter the Great*, St. Petersburg. Sculptor, Etienne-Maurice Falconet. Photograph by William Brumfield.

of sculpture, in the famous statue on the Neva completed in 1782 by Étienne-Maurice Falconet.

Falconet created a new image of Peter. His Peter is not the intimidating commander, but what the art historian H. W. Janson called "a hero of virtue." The monumental equestrian figure in Roman toga, modeled on a statue of Louis XIV by Bernini, soars skyward, trampling a snake, triumphant over evil and human weakness (fig. 25).[58] Falconet wrote to Diderot that he had in mind "not the victor over Charles XII, but Russia and her reformer." He wanted to fashion "the person of the founder, legislator, benefactor of his country." He therefore put no scepter in Peter's hand and clothed him as a Roman emperor.[59] The inscription, "Petro primo, Catarina secunda," on one side of the rock, repeated in Russian on the other, declares Catherine's assumption of the Petrine heritage even as she presumes to re-

---

[58] Robert Rosenblum and H. W. Janson, *19th-Century Art* (New York, 1984), 98. Janson takes issue with the usual viewpoint that the statue was directly copied from the Marcus Aurelius statue in Rome.

[59] I. Grabar', *Istoriia russkogo iskusstva* (St. Petersburg, 1909), vol. 6:370–72.

shape it. The dedication of the statue on August 7, 1782, was a major cere-monial occasion. Deeply moved, Catherine wrote to Baron Melchior Grimm that Peter's image, "had a look of contentment which also passed to me and encouraged me to do better in the future."[60]

The conception of the statue as a symbol of the merciless, inhuman power of Peter's will was a nineteenth-century conceit, a product of the genius of Alexander Pushkin. In the eighteenth century, the statue marked the change from a Baroque symbolic of extravagant display to a classical ethos and esthetic of self-control and order. The image of Peter as reformer also marked a shift to male figures of political virtue. Just as Peter introduced female allegories of virtue, identifying political dedication with love and beauty, Catherine's principal statue represented civic virtue in the heroic form of the male ruler. If Peter's statues prefigured masculinized feminine rulers who carried on his tradition, Catherine's monument to Peter intro-duces the image of male power tamed by wisdom, whose courage subdues human as well as physical nature. Peter is no longer a god but a mortal hero achieving prodigies through knowledge and inspiration. This was the Stoic image of the emperor, and contemporaries, aware of the message, called the statue "Marcus Aurelius."[61]

•

The enormous expansion of the empire in Catherine's reign—to the south to include New Russia, to the west in the partitions of Poland—gave substance to the imperial myth of the ruler of savage peoples, what Zhivov describes as the "ethnographic myth" of empire. "In geographical space the monarch emerges as the hypostatization of Mars, while in ethnographic space, the monarch appears as the hypostatization of Minerva."[62] As her empire grew, Catherine's endearing manner expressed the unity of native elites with the throne in idealized form. The personal devotion to the sovereign and the adoption of her Westernized culture, Andreas Kappeler has concluded, be-came the principal bonds uniting the various nationalities of empire.[63]

Catherine's method of rule in the new territories was to co-opt native elites and to assimilate them into the Russian nobility. Thus the upper strata of the Don and Zaporozhets cossacks were made members of the Russian nobility in 1785.[64] The rank and file, completing a process of differentiation that was

---

[60] Ransel, *The Politics of Catherinian Russia*, 262.

[61] Baehr, *The Paradise Myth*, 50; see also the useful brochure about the changing meanings of the statue, G. S. Knabe, *Voobrazhenie znaka; Mednyi Vsadnik Falcone i Pushkina* (Moscow, 1993).

[62] Zhivov, "Gosudarstvennyi mif v epokhe prosveshcheniia," 154.

[63] Andreas Kappeler, *Russland als Vielvölkerreich; Entstehung, Geschichte, Zerfall* (Munich, 1992), 135–38.

[64] Kappeler, *Russland als Vielvölkerreich*, 50–51, 64–65; Bruce W. Menning, "The Emer-gence of a Military Administrative Elite in the Don Cossack Land, 1708–1836," in Walter McKenzie Pinter and Don Karl Rowney, *Russian Officialdom: The Bureaucratization of Rus-sian Society from the Seventeenth to the Twentieth Century* (Chapel Hill, N.C., 1980), 130–61.

underway during the previous century, declined into a condition approximating that of serfs. Likewise, she granted nobility to the Tatar aristocracy in the Crimea, who received the privileges and honors of Russian noblemen. The imperial nobility was revealed as an association of the powerful and the educated of Russian and other nationalities who rejoiced in their devotion to a supreme, beneficent ruler.[65]

At the imperial court, uniformity of dress showed the unity of the supranational court elite. Special notices (*povestki*) announced dress requirements for various official functions. But although the manner was cosmopolitan, the rhetoric and styles of Catherine's reign left little doubt about the predominance of the Great Russian nobility. Imperial patriotism with a Great Russian coloration was a theme of late-eighteenth-century history and literature. Catherine the Great, the only Russian ruler since Riurik to have no Russian parent, extolled the glory of the Great Russian elite, who had achieved the conquest of empire. Again, woman represented the cultural ideal, and Catherine introduced "the Russian dress" for the ladies-in-waiting and other highly placed women of the court to wear at important processions and holidays. The Russian dress attached native elements, taken from seventeenth-century robes, to a Western-style evening gown. It consisted of a white satin gown worn under a red velvet robe ending in a long train. The Russian dress was worn with a Russian-style tiara (*kokoshnik*) of red felt and gold, often set with gems. It became standard attire for women attending important formal occasions in the court during the nineteenth century.[66]

The vision of a vast multinational empire became especially important to Catherine's image as her reign progressed. Kappeler points out the great pride she took in the complete listing of the empress's title, which she cited frequently. The Charter of the Nobility opens with the enumeration of the titles to thirty-eight provinces and lands under her rule, including *tsaritsa* of the new "Kherson-Tauride" Province.[67] By the end of Catherine's reign, it was important to confirm that Russia was not only an empire, but the most imperial of nations, comprising more peoples than any other. Thus the academician Heinrich Storch boasted of the ethnographic variety of Russia in 1797, commenting that "no other state on earth contains such a variety of inhabitants. Russians, and Tatars, Germans, Mongols, Finns, and Tungus, live in an immense territory in the most varied climates." He went on to say

[65] John P. LeDonne, "Ruling Families in the Russian Political Order, 1689–1825," *Cahiers du monde russe et soviétique* (July–December 1987), vol. 38, nos. 3–4, 310–11; Alan W. Fisher, "Enlightened Despotism and Islam under Catherine II," *Slavic Review* (December 1968), vol. 27, no. 4, 547.

[66] On eighteenth-century national ideals, see Hans Rogger, *National Consciousness in Eighteenth-Century Russia* (Cambridge, Mass., 1960). Also see *KFZ* (1777), 24, 995; N. E. Volkov, *Dvor russkikh imperatorov v ego proshlom i nastoiashchem* (St. Petersburg, 1900), 2:43; M. A. Korf, "Iz zapisok Barona M. A. Korfa," *Russkaia Starina*, vol. 99, no. 8 (1899): 294–95.

[67] Kappeler, *Russland als Vielvölkerreich*, 99; PSZ, no. 16,187 (April 21, 1785).

that this was "a most rare phenomenon" and that "one seeks in vain another example in the history of the world."[68]

The expansion of the empire brought more emphatic and specific statements of Russia's equivalence with ancient Rome, even as Greek influence began to overshadow Roman in the West. Andrew Kahn has shown how Vasilii Petrov's translation of the *Aeneid*, begun in the early 1770s, turned Virgil's glorification of the Augustan Age into a panegyric to Catherine's empire. Petrov made the character of Dido a celebration of the female monarch, who, coming from abroad, extends her empire and enlightens her people.[69] Other panegyrics of the 1770s gave new force to the theme of *translatio imperii*. After the peace of Kuchuk-Kainardzhi, an Accession Day ode by V. I. Maikov proclaimed, "When we turn our gaze from the West, loud fame, flying there, voices the thought that the Russian state (*derzhava*) has spread out like ancient Rome." One P. P. Potemkin, in an ode to Catherine of 1772, declared that Russia has "soared with greatness like Rome in its flourishing days and extending the limits of its territories, has given laws to all and amazed the entire world." The metaphor at points merges into "eutopia," which "asserts that the 'good place' exists here and now and deserves praise."[70] Making Russia the semblance of the Roman Empire elevated the monarch and the serf-holding elite as heirs to the highest values of the classical West. Russia has "given its laws to all" and has amazed "the entire world."

Architects used the idiom of neoclassicism to build edifices that would give Russia its own imitations of Roman architecture, again following a European example. Jean-Baptiste Vallin de la Mothe, who had studied in Paris and Italy, taught the principles of neoclassicism in the Academy of Arts. With Alexander Kokorinov, he designed the building for the academy on the Neva, the Small Hermitage, and the New Holland Arch, providing the first examples of classical symmetry and austerity of decoration. The palaces of Rinaldi, Bazhenov, Cameron, Quarenghi, and Starov created an ambience of restrained elegance in contrast to the earlier Rococo flamboyance. Russian imitations of Italian buildings transposed the political spirit of Rome to St. Petersburg and its environs. Rinaldi's unfinished Cathedral of St. Isaac's was modeled closely on St. Peter's Cathedral; the Pantheon became the model for parts of Ivan Starov's Tauride Palace. Charles Cameron's Pavlovsk Palace and Giacomo Quarenghi's English Palace at Peterhof brought the style of Palladio to Russia. The great noblemen followed this example and built their own neoclassical mansions and manor houses.[71]

[68] Cited in Kappeler, *Russland als Vielvölkerreich*, 121.

[69] Andrew Kahn, "Readings of Imperial Rome from Lomonosov to Pushkin," *The Slavic Review*, vol. 52, no. 4 (Winter, 1993), 752–56.

[70] Baehr, "From History to National Myth," 10–12; Baehr, *The Paradise Myth*, 54–55, 113.

[71] Brumfield, *A History of Russian Architecture*, 261–347; Hamilton, *The Art and Architecture of Russia*, 289–313; Roosevelt, "Emerald Thrones and Living Statues," 3; for a disap-

Russia's expansion to the south was glorified not merely in terms of national greatness or interest, but as a re-creation of Hellenic antiquity. Poets invoked Greek referents to glorify the southern conquests. Ippolit Bogdanovich identified Ochakov with Greece and personified Russia as Achilles, the victors over Turkey, the new Troy. In the 1780s, Catherine envisioned a Russian restoration of the Greek Empire centered in Constantinople, "the Greek project." Greek names were given to sites in the new territories—Kherson, after the Greek Khersones; Odessa, after Odysseus; Tauris, the Greek name for the district of the Crimea. Catherine's second grandson was baptized Constantine, destining him to rule the new empire. The reverse side of the medal coined on Constantine's birth showed the cathedral of St. Sofia. His wet nurse, servant, and first childhood friends were Greek.[72]

Catherine presented her vision in an operatic drama she wrote in 1786, entitled, "The Early Reign of Oleg, an Imitation of Shakespeare, Without the Observance of the Usual Rules of the Theater." The play was performed before the court and the general public in 1790 at considerable effort and expense. It was a great extravaganza, with a cast of more than six hundred, and huge suites for the two emperors, the Byzantine and the "Emperor of Festivals." Greek choruses commented on the action and recited verses by Lomonosov. The play recounted Oleg's exploits: the founding of Moscow (!); his marriage to a Kievan Princess, Prekrasa (most beautiful); and, finally and most important, Oleg's foray into Constantinople.[73]

But although the play's action took place in tenth-century Byzantium, its spirit was of pagan Greece, or, more accurately, Rome. Catherine's Byzantium has not a hint of religion. There is no priest among the dramatis personae. Oleg's victory over the Greek defenders mainly provides the occasion for exultant festivities. The emperor Leo rejoices at his defeat and welcomes Oleg. "In this capital, with so renowned a guest, only happy celebrations shall occur, joyous exclamations, endless games, singing, dancing, merriment and gala feasts." Prince Oleg watches martial games in the Hippodrome on a dais next to Emperor Leo and Empress Zoya. Hercules and the Emperor of Festivals appear before the celebrations, which are portrayed in dance and choruses, the music composed by the *Kapellmeister*, Giuseppe Sarti. In the final scene, Oleg leaves Igor's shield in the Hippodrome for his descendants, and Emperor Leo declares him a wise and courageous prince.[74]

The empress followed the myth of empire, not of the universal Christian

---

proving evaluation of this transplantation, see Summerson, *The Architecture of the Eighteenth Century*, 94.

[72] Baehr, *The Paradise Myth*, 48–49; E. P. Karnovich, *Tsesarevich Konstantin Pavlovich* (St. Petersburg, 1899), 5–6, 9.

[73] *Sochineniia Imperatritsy Ekateriny II* (St. Petersburg, 1901), 2:259–304; Roosevelt, "Emerald Thrones and Living Statues," 3–4. The play referred to in Roosevelt's citation is Oleg not Ol'ga, as the notes in the *Sochineniia* indicate on 306–9.

[74] *Sochineniia Imperatritsy Ekateriny II*, 2:294–304.

Empire, but a Roman Empire, led by an enlightened monarch and an enlightened administrative elite, bringing the benefits of law and improved material life to the new territories, as well as to the Russian provinces. The actual conquest gave substance to analogies with Rome, demonstrating the monarch's power to work miracles, turning deserts into populated areas filled with gardens, as Potemkin had tried to bring civilization to the new territories.[75]

It was not sufficient, however, to propound the myth in odes and state rhetoric. The performative character of Russian monarchy required that the realization of Western ideals be demonstrated in constant ceremonial affirmations. Catherine had extended her scenario to all of Russia, going outside the capital, bringing the force of her personality and governmental institutions to the local level through the provincial reform of 1775. In 1787 she brought her scenario to the provinces and to the newly conquered territories on the Black Sea, on a six-month journey that dramatized the military and cultural successes of her reign.

•

Catherine's journey took her through the major provinces of European Russia, to Kiev, and down the Dnepr to New Russia, Sevastopol, and the newly founded towns of Kherson and Ekaterinoslav. The journey was a lavish and extended demonstration of the efficacy of her persona and her mind, showing attainment of the general good of the population, an apotheosis of the Petrine principle of utility. The medal that was to commemorate the trip carried the inscription, "the route to the beneficial" (*put' na pol'zu*).[76] The trip was described in a journal kept by Catherine's secretary, A. V. Khrapovitskii, and was published the same year.[77]

The administrative authorities in St. Petersburg sent down decrees to construct a spectacle of happiness along the route. Crowds of happy people, dressed in clean new clothing, singers in their best attire, abundant markets, and garlands of flowers were to stage pleasant scenes for the empress's gaze. Catherine believed that such displays would refute foreign beliefs that Russia was a great desert. Everything that did not please her imagination was to be removed from sight. In Moscow, in the midst of famine, beggars were driven from the city so as not to spoil the empress's impressions.[78] The spectacle of happiness and transformation was presented to an audience of court dignitaries and foreign envoys—of Britain, France, and Austria. The caravan holding servants and retinue was made up of 14 carriages and 124 sledges,

[75] On the garden motif, see Baehr, *The Paradise Myth*, 71–84.

[76] A. Brückner, "Puteshestvie Imperatritsy Ekateriny II v poludennyi krai Rossii v 1787 godu," *Zhurnal Ministerstva Narodnogo Prosveshcheniia*, pt. 2, vol. 162 (1872): 4.

[77] A. V. Khrapovitskii, *Zhurnal Vysochaishego puteshestviia eia Velichestva Gosudaryni Imperatritsy Ekateriny II Samoderzhitsy Vserossiiskoi v Poludennye Strany Rossii v 1787 g.* (Moscow, 1787).

[78] Brückner, "Puteshestvie Imperatritsy Ekateriny II," 8–9.

in addition to 40 auxiliary vehicles. In provincial towns, twenty-five apartments were prepared to house her suite. New magnificent palaces were constructed in Kiev and in towns in the conquered territories to accommodate the imperial party.[79]

On the way to and from the new territories, Catherine participated in numerous staged demonstrations of mutual fealty between herself and the Russian nobility. Widening the circle of her "maternal love," the trip gave the local nobility the opportunity to reciprocate with their own feelings of affection. Her sojourns brought court spectacles to provincial towns, performing a scenario of happiness and mutual affection that expressed the consummation of the alliance between a grateful nobility and a benevolent monarch who understood their needs. The nobility of each province, by official order, escorted the procession with a special convoy that accompanied the empress into the provincial capital with a gala welcome. All was to be presented in a holiday mood.[80]

Khrapovitskii's description of Catherine's sojourn in his native town of Smolensk dwells on the displays of recognition between nobility and sovereign. An honor guard of Smolensk noblemen and a hundred horsemen carrying torches escorted her into the town. After a welcome at the gates from the local garrison and members of the clergy, she rode along illuminated streets lined by pupils from the recently established national schools. Cannon salvoes from the local fortress greeted her arrival. The next day she awarded promotions and her new "Order of St. Vladimir" upon local officials. They, in turn, gave expressions of gratitude and devotion. Khrapovitskii quoted the welcoming words of the provincial marshall of the nobility, one Stepan Khrapovitskii: "We are happy with *You* [in the familiar form], and we prosper. *You* rule over our hearts, with the countless benefactions *You* have undertaken. So incomparably greater is our happiness, joy, and rapture, to see you, and to kiss the Hand that is so kind to us." There followed three days of exhausting balls, receptions, and church services.[81]

A more poignant and personal response to the empress's appearance in the provinces was recorded in the memoirs of the Tula nobleman, Andrei Bolotov, during her visit to the town of Tula in June 1787.[82] Bolotov describes the excitement of the preparations to meet the empress. Noble ladies spent lavishly on their uniforms and gowns to satisfy the empress's critical view. The noblemen were ordered to send the largest carp from their ponds for the festivities. Fireworks were prepared. A triumphal arch was erected on the main street of the town.

Bolotov recalled that the empress was the single object of the nobles' thoughts. All the greater was their dismay when Catherine, shocked by news that the Ottoman Empire had declared war, did not attend most of the func-

---

[79] de Madariaga, *Age of Catherine the Great*, 370.
[80] Khrapovitskii, *Zhurnal Vysochaishego puteshestviia*, 9–10.
[81] Ibid., 9–12; de Madariaga, *Age of Catherine the Great*, 370–71.
[82] Bolotov, *Zhizn' i prikliucheniia Andreia Bolotova*, 4:147–71.

tions. The ladies were distraught, feeling that their effort and expense had been in vain. When Catherine finally appeared at a gala performance, the moment of her arrival was "ravishing for everyone." The entire audience stared, and continued to stare at her during the play, "which hardly one in ten saw." But unable to make out her features, they left disappointed. Bolotov himself was crushed when he was not allowed to present a manuscript to her personally. But, finally, as a member of the escort accompanying her to her carriage at her departure, he and the others gained "the longed for opportunity to see the sovereign," gazing at her "to their heart's content" (*naliubovavshis' do syta*).

The objective of the journey, the southern region, was presented as a spectacular confirmation of the motifs of conquest and transformation. After a sojourn in Kiev, during which she worshiped and took communion at the Monastery of the Caves, Catherine traveled by boat down the Dnepr. This was a voyage not of exploration but of display, made up of a squadron of seven galleys, each provided with an orchestra, eighty ships resembling Roman galleons, and three thousand troops. Catherine and her entourage beheld the spectacle of happiness along the banks staged by Potemkin, the governor-general of Azov and New Russia, of the Crimea and Ekaterinoslav, "the Viceroy of the South." Groups of peasants, cossacks, and townspeople greeted her in villages decorated with wreaths of flowers and triumphal arches. Khrapovitskii took note of the acclaim of "the people, in great throngs along the shore," who met the empress with joyous cries.[83] In Ekaterinoslav, Archbishop Ambrosii's oration translated myth into fact. Catherine's rule had "turned infertile deserts into inhabited villages and cities, defending this country from foes, and securing the well-being of the subjects." At the banquet, afterward, an orchestra and 186 singers performed an Italian cantata written by Sarti. In the evening the town was lit with illuminations.[84]

The foreign guests, and particularly the emperor Joseph of Austria, were hardly persuaded by these transformations, though several were impressed by the number of settlements and the progress made in so short a period. Joseph called the trip a "hallucination," and observed that nothing was being completed and that the changes required the use of poorly fed servile labor. He remarked that fifty thousand had perished in the territory since the conquest. But even Joseph took notice of the fleet and harbor at Sevastopol. He and Catherine were welcomed to the port with an impressive naval review. Loud salutes came from the ships' guns, and the sailors on board shouted "Hoorah!" The display and subsequent inspection proudly demonstrated Russia's military presence on the Black Sea. Joseph declared it was the best port in the world, and that it awaited a great future.[85]

[83] Khrapovitskii, *Zhurnal Vysochaishego puteshestviia*, 36–44; de Madariaga, *Age of Catherine the Great*, 371–72.

[84] Khrapovitskii, *Zhurnal Vysochaishego puteshestviia*, 53, 56–57.

[85] Khrapovitskii, *Zhurnal Vysochaishego puteshestviia*, 77–78; Brückner, "Puteshestvie Imperatritsy Ekateriny II," 44–45, 51; de Madariaga, *Age of Catherine the Great*, 373.

The proverbial "Potemkin villages," it seems, were no more than a canard: with several dubious exceptions, the reports from foreign guests, most of whom hardly restrained their skepticism and even derision, make no mention of cardboard sets of flourishing towns. But the orders issued from the capital and Potemkin's feverish preparations leave no doubt about the determination to embellish reality. The stage effects of painted towns and singing peasants along the Dnepr reproduced the "eutopic" idiom of Catherine's court: the vision of transformation was glorified as if realized. The Age of Gold had reached the outlying territories, legitimizing conquest by the benefits and maternal care lavished, or to be lavished, on the joyous subjects.

The imperial theme was displayed repeatedly through the journey. The fortress at Kherson carried the device, "The Route to Byzantium." The city of Ekaterinoslav was to be Catherine's and Potemkin's counterpart to St. Petersburg, a perfect imperial city, to show the monarch's creation of a realm of cultivation and political order in a "new Russia."[86] Potemkin began construction of a cathedral that would be a replica of St. Peter's in Rome. He intended to transport a gargantuan statue of Catherine from Berlin. Building materials had been assembled to construct court houses on the model of ancient basilicas, a propylaeum like that of Athens, and twelve factories. Potemkin planned a musical conservatory in Ekaterinoslav to be placed under Sarti's direction. Russia, the agent of civilization, was going to restore classical culture to the southern steppes.[87]

Catherine's ceremonies also included ceremonies of recognition with the native leaders of the new territories. At Kremenchug, she met with a delegation of Tatar noblemen, the *murzy*. An escort of the *murzy* accompanied her into the town of Bachisarae where she met the assembled dignitaries of the region. At a banquet, she entertained the Austrian emperor, and the *mufti*— the chief cleric, now recognized as the administrative head of the territory— along with the highest civil and military ranks. The journey to New Russia arrayed the leaders of the conquered territories, along with the notables of the court, in ceremonial displays of the elite of the empire.[88]

THE PERSONAL VOICE

Catherine's ingratiating personal address and the genteel manner of address expected of her servitors gave rise to new forms of panegyric and ceremonial texts. The myth of the godlike monarch had to be brought down to earth.

[86] A. M. Panchenko has shown how the mythical grounds for Catherine's southern trip were rooted in the absolutist dream of constructing a "new Russia," in a new territory (A. M. Panchenko, " 'Potemskie derevni' kak kul'turnyi mif," in *XVIII vek* [Leningrad, 1983], 14:93–104).

[87] Brückner, "Puteshestvie Imperatritsy Ekateriny II," 31–32, 36, 44; Panchenko, " 'Potemskie derevni,' " 100–101.

[88] Khrapovitskii, *Zhurnal Vysochaishego puteshestviia*, 75–76.

The poet now responded with appropriate expressions of his gratification at the empress's humanity. Gavriil Derzhavin introduced a new personal style with his odes to Felitsiia. The Felitsiia cycle expressed the poet's infatuation with Catherine's own idealized image of herself as a sympathetic, sentient goddess, which she herself had portrayed in her tale, "The Tsarevich Khlor" (see below, chapter 6). Felitsiia, "the Kirghiz princess," also represented her imperial self, a ruler of exotic oriental lands. For Derzhavin, Felitsiia has all the qualities of a divinity, but a divinity who has enchanted the poet in human form. She is a goddess, at once Minerva, Themis, and Astraea. But most of all, as the name suggests, she is the personification of happiness, who captivates the individual nobleman, a "goddess of love." In "Portrait of Felitsiia," the poet feels "enraptured" by the princess and paints his picture, not on canvas, but in his heart.

> I see in my heart a diamond mountain:
> Upon it, divine qualities
> Shine before the ecstatic gaze;
> Upon it, in radiance, I see you, Felitsiia.[89]

Derzhavin presented the empress as an otherworldly figure, but one who had come down to earth and prompted human feelings. The poet's "I," his own voice, replaces the "we," the choral expression of assent of earlier odes.[90] Derzhavin used this voice to create a new type of ceremonial text, an account that purported to express the actual feelings of an individual observer. His description of Potemkin's celebration of the capture of the fortress of Izmail in 1791 in the recently completed Tauride Palace introduces the personal mode that would become common in ceremonial texts of the first decades of the nineteenth century.[91] In December 1790, the formidable Turkish fortress had fallen to Potemkin's armies, under the leadership of A. S. Suvorov, leading to negotiations for peace. Derzhavin composed both the description, which appeared the following year, and the choruses sung during the celebration, which were also published separately.

Derzhavin relates the celebration from the viewpoint of an individual responding with his own feelings of wonderment and admiration. He writes in the first-person singular, rather than plural, purportedly describing his own responses rather than the adulation of all. The worship and love of the monarch are thus the subject of an internal monologue of the poet himself. The account opens with Derzhavin sharing his admiration for Starov's neoclassical palace. The "poetry of columns" and avoidance of external ornament remind him of the ancient world, particularly the suburban homes that belonged to Pompeius and Maecenas. He admires the lack of sculpture and gilt decoration on the walls. "Its distinction is its ancient elegant taste. It is

[89] Derzhavin, *Sochineniia*, 1:190–92.
[90] Serman, *Russkii klassitsizm*, 80–82.
[91] Derzhavin, *Sochineniia*, 1:264–84. The title is *Opisanie torzhestva v dome kniazia Potemkina po sluchaiu vsiatiia Izmaila.*

simple but majestic."[92] The prodigies of transformation also evoke a personal response. The winter gardens in the palace remind him of the paradise myth of the garden. The singing of birds, the fragrance of the flowers, turn the building into "some kind of heavenly or enchanted country," and force everyone to ask himself, "Isn't this Eden?"[93]

Derzhavin briefly introduces "the people" into his account. They sit in an amphitheater outside the palace where they are treated to gifts and a feast. Articles of clothing, food, and "sweet drinks" are given out, and the people respond with "exclamations to the honor and glory" of the empress. "A simple 'hoorah' filled the air," Derzhavin writes, and indicates how this demonstration, however staged, was to be understood: "The greatest praise of a good ruler is the joyous cry of his people." But the people are merely the necessary props for the main event. Their acclaim supplies the background, as the host, Prince Potemkin, cordially welcomes the members of the imperial family—Catherine, Alexander, and Constantine Pavlovich, the heir Paul, and Paul's wife, Grand Duchess Maria Fedorovna.

The arrival of the imperial family in the palace is presented and described as an entry of the gods. An orchestra and choir of three hundred burst into a thunderous chorus of Derzhavin's verses, set to music by O. A. Kozlovskii. Twenty-four pairs of "the most notable [aristocratic] and splendid women, maidens and young men" dressed in white robes embroidered with diamonds, dance to Derzhavin's text. They are led by the young grand dukes, Alexander and Constantine Pavlovich, and the Prince of Württemburg. Derzhavin writes,

> In ancient times the gods,
> At Olympic celebrations,
> Leaving their mountain halls,
> And the bright thrones of divinity,
> Descended, concealing from the gaze of mortals,
> Their bright radiance.[94]

The poet now returns to the choral mode, portraying the ecstasy with which the "Russians" (*Rossiane*) greet the members of the imperial family. He describes the opening of the polonaise. The music is martial; the chorus extols the exploits of Russian armies, to the accompaniment of drums. The dancers move into a contredanse, a "tempestuous, intoxicated, comic spectacle." The loud music and the chorals, Derzhavin explains, "had as their only intention to inspire the youths to glory according to the example of the ancients." The chorus evokes Pindar as the inspiration to great deeds. Mars and Minerva look upon the young men and "see their own kind in them." One is Alexander the Great, another Constantine, both symbols of the new areas of conquest.

[92] Derzhavin, *Sochineniia*, 1:264; Hamilton, *Art and Architecture*, 302–3.
[93] Derzhavin, *Sochineniia*, 1:266–67; see Baehr, *The Paradise Myth*, 85, on winter gardens.
[94] Ibid., 1:268.

And in them the gods saw honor,
And all the glory of Hellas:
The former [Alexander] will bring thunder to the Persians,
The other [Constantine] will build Rome anew.[95]

The guests then return to the garden to behold an act of metamorphosis. What had been a garden was transformed into a stunning display of light. Crystal lamps cover the cornices, windows, and piers of the halls. Chandeliers and thousands of candles glitter with lights of different tones. "Rubies, emeralds, sapphires, topazes blaze." The plants that fill the halls, entwined "as if with stars . . . burn like flaming pillars." Groves of aromatic oranges and lemons add a translucent golden hue, which blends with the greens, reds, and yellows of a vineyard, lilies and tulips, and pineapples.

The empress herself confirms the marvel. Entering the garden, she asks, "Can it be that we are where we were before?" These words prompt Derzhavin to examine his own feelings. He himself experienced something "beyond the natural" (*chrez"estestvennyi*) that was hard to describe. He used the common comparison of "the enchanted palaces of Scheherazade." He, like the empress, is bewildered; he does not know where he is. The setting arouses "a new feeling." That feeling is heightened and expressed as gratitude as he gazes upon the statue of the empress now glowing in sapphire, pink, and amber lights.

Derzhavin makes clear that his feeling, though personal, is hardly unique. It pours out in his prose as the feeling of all Russians. "Every Russian will imagine and feel an incomparable pleasure from gratitude for the past, from love for the present and from hope for the expected good." If the Russian is sensible (*blagorazumen*), then he will say with tenderness of the heart (*umilenie serdtsa*), "This pure and clear flame is the true semblance of my zeal for her; this lilac and green flame, the image of my and my posterity's immortal hope in them [Alexander and Constantine]." If he is sensitive, the Russian will "shed angelic tears and by his bliss, approach the denizens of heaven, contemplating the incomprehensible, eternal radiance."[96]

Now, Derzhavin follows the script of the scenario and attributes his exaltation to the empress's amazing maternal powers. "Before her everything becomes more alive, everything takes on greater radiance. . . . Her bright face encourages smiles, dances, charades, games. This is the image of a mother, this is a monarch surrounded by glory, love, magnificence." He now records sentiments identical to his own, voiced by guests he overhears conversing in the garden:

How can I reply to her bounty?
My majesty is the creation of her hands;
All my happiness is her spirit of good,
And the glory of the celebration is hers not mine.[97]

[95] Ibid., 1:269–74.
[96] Ibid., 1:277–78.
[97] Ibid., 1:278–81.

The celebration is a grandiose metaphor of emanation. Catherine's Olympian influence has transformed the ordinary into the extraordinary and endowed her servitors with majesty. At the conclusion, as Catherine prepares to depart, Derzhavin portrays her as the goddess, Minerva, who has infused her male servitors with the spirit of the divine. Her farewell to Potemkin becomes a tutelary image. The chorus intones their regrets at the loss of the source of their happiness. Potemkin falls to his knees and kisses the empress's hand. Derzhavin likens Potemkin to a bereft Telemachus. "Thus the divine Minerva departed from the son of Ulysses."

> The goddess mounted
> The descending clouds,
> Climbing to the heights,
> She looked upon him with a smile.
> The sounds of armor came with the wind,
> The ray of her gaze flew;
> Lifting his hands to the sky,
> He silently gazed after her.[98]

[98] Ibid., 1:281–84.

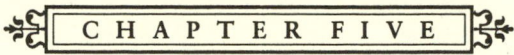

CHAPTER FIVE

Minerva and Telemachus: The Education of Princes

Mentor, speaking thus, continued along the road to the sea; and Telemachus, not strong enough to proceed on his own, allowed himself to be led without resistance. Minerva, at all times concealed within the form of Mentor, covered Telemachus invisibly with her aegis, and extending over him a divine ray, gave him a sense of courage that he had not felt since he had come to this island.

—*Fénelon*, Les aventures de Télémaque, *livre VI*

THE EDUCATION OF GRAND DUKE PAUL PETROVICH

The allegory of Minerva and Telemachus portrayed the tutelary relationship between the goddess-empress and the servitor lifting his hands to "the ray of her gaze." It presented Catherine as the enlightenment ideal, monarch as philosopher and pedagogue, uplifting her people. This image inspired I. I. Betskoi's efforts to found schools that would produce "a new type of man" and the measures Catherine introduced to create a national system of primary and secondary education that would train pupils in "quiet and useful citizenship."[1] The education of the heirs to the throne now assumed especial importance. The ruler could improve monarchy by training better monarchs, making them in the image of philosophers capable of ruling according to virtue and wisdom. It was this faith that inspired the dream of transforming the Russian political system by educating the heir to the throne, a dream entertained by tutors and their staffs from the mid-eighteenth century until the era of Great Reforms.

Eighteenth-century tracts on princely education emphasized the importance of education to the well-being of the state. Leibniz's "On the Education of a Prince" stressed the importance of careful cultivation of the prince's moral qualities and intellectual powers, and became widely read during the century.[2] The price of an incompetent ruler could be the destruction of the realm. A Russian extract from *l'Encyclopédie*, published in 1770, stated that "the ignorance and carelessness of sovereigns are the most common cause of

---

[1] de Madariaga, *Age of Catherine the Great*, 493–502; J. L. Black, *Citizens for the Fatherland: Education, Educators and Pedagogical Ideals in Eighteenth Century Russia* (Boulder, Colo., 1979).

[2] G. W. Leibniz's *De educatione Prinipis commentatio* (in French), in *Magazin für das Kirchenrecht die Kirchen und Gelehrten-Geschichte*, vol. 1 (1787), 177–96.

the catastrophes desolating their states." It asserted the necessity for the ruler to possess wide knowledge, the appropriate virtues, and the nobility of character that would dispose him to do good. All of these would result from his education.[3]

The absorption with the training of the prince reflected a general shift from a Baroque to a neoclassical conception of a monarch. Analogies with the gods could no longer aggrandize the image of a monarch (see the prologue to part 3). Rather, he or she had to realize the higher qualities that men could achieve by enlightenment. The future ruler was to be treated as a human being, but a human being with a higher calling. The extract from *l'Encyclopédie* emphasized that the ruler had to learn that he was a mortal, to obey as well as to command. He was not to be lauded as "an earthly god."[4]

Metaphor could transform Peter the Great into the image of Mars, Augustus, or Constantine. Paul I and Alexander I were taught to remake themselves in the image of the great men of the past, as understood and transmitted by their tutors. They were to be not gods, but "human beings on the throne," as prophesied in Derzhavin's ode on the birth of Alexander I. They and subsequent heirs to the throne grew up with constant reminders that their monarchical distinction was not inbred, natural, or an attribute of their future office, but the product of their own character and efforts. They were never allowed to forget the sobering admonition that emperors of Russia would be expected to represent the highest ideals of Western monarchy.

The enlightenment model referred to a new exemplar of the potentialities of kingship, Frederick the Great of Prussia. In many respects, Frederick's example was the opposite of Louis XIV's. The myth of sacred king and allegorical pageantry had no place in the formation of the Prussian state. Before Frederick, Prussian ceremony had been austere and reserved, and representation played little role. A dictionary of 1735 stated, "A Prince remains self-same whether he walks alone or has a large committee at his side." The court at Potsdam and Berlin made little effort at significant ostentation or show. Frederick, rather than seeking to embody the state, presented himself, as he declared, as its first servant, its first officer. His ascendancy, his elevation relied on his achievements, his personal discipline and qualities.[5]

The Prussian king projected the image of the humble organ of the state, an official and an officer, who slept on a camp bed. The humility, of course, was spurious, for Frederick represented himself as its *first* servant, capable of enduring privation and showing limitless dedication, an example for his servitors. The king is like all men, Frederick the Great says, but, Otto Brunner

---

[3] A. Lefevre, *O nadzirateliakh pri vospitanii iz Entsiklopedii* (St. Petersburg, 1770), 95, 100.

[4] Ibid., 96–97.

[5] Karl Hammer, "Die preussischen Könige und Königinnen im 19 Jahrhundert und ihr Hof," in Karl Ferdinand Werner, ed., *Hof, Kultur, und Politik im 19 Jahrhundert* (Bonn, 1985), 87–88; Thomas Stamm-Kuhlmann, "Der Hof Friedrich-Wilhelms III. von Preussen 1797 bis 1840," Karl Möckl, ed., *Hof und Hofgesellschaft in den deutschen Staaten im 19. und beginnenden 20. Jahrhundert* (Boppard am Rhein, 1990), 275–76.

pointed out, he must be a man who incorporates an ideal: "He must also be the most humane and the first citizen." The allegorical glorifications of the Baroque were discarded. The monarch instead aspired to live as a "human being," but a human being seeking a lofty, and largely unattainable Stoic ideal of a rational and humane ruler.[6]

Frederick replaced metaphorical transformations with exemplary displays of command and discipline on the parade ground. Like Peter, he exerted something of the charisma of the conqueror, leading his armies to victory on the battlefield. But he made the exercise of severe discipline and control of his army the fundamental principle of his success. The parade ground showed the king's power to bring about the well-being of the nation. The principle of strict discipline, the training of soldiers and officials in absolute obedience, made possible the enforcement of the king's rational will. The monarch is not a god but a commander, whose military and civil attainments are achieved by his wisdom and determination in imposing his will.

Catherine's imagery of transformation reversed Peter's sexual metaphor of power. Peter as Pygmalion had shaped a Russia in female form that epitomized the refined and civilized image of empire. Catherine as Minerva now strove to shape a future monarch into an exemplar of male ruler who realized Western classical ideals. The myth acknowledged that the principle of heredity must return as the basis of succession. But the principal influence on the heir from the start would be wisdom, incarnated in the female figure of a godlike ruler—the goddess who would protect the boy from the pernicious effects of the milieu, particularly from his parents, and replace them by wise and sympathetic teachers.

The principal statement of the Minerva-Telemachus myth for eighteenth- and early-nineteenth-century Russia was not the *Odyssey* itself, but the most popular tale of princely virtue of the era, François Fénelon's *Les aventures de Télémaque, fils d'Ulysse*, first published in 1699. An archbishop, Fénelon had become known as an educator, and was appointed tutor of the *dauphin*, the Duke of Burgundy—the grandson of Louis XIV. He approached the education of the *dauphin* as a training of a humane monarch for the throne, a king who would work for the welfare of his people, and *Télémaque* was the summation of his efforts. Numerous editions of *Télémaque*, four of them in translation, appeared during the eighteenth century in Russia.[7] Fénelon's

---

[6] Otto Brunner, "Vom Gottesgnadentum zum monarchischen Prinzip," *Das Königtum*, in the series *Vortrage und Forschungen, herausgegeben vom Institut für geschichtliche Land-esforschung des Bodenseegebietes in Konstanz, geleitet von Theodor Mayer*, Band III: 298–99.

[7] Black, *Citizens for the Fatherland*, 220; Gleason, *Moral Idealists*, 97–98. It is believed that *Télémaque* was actually written in the town of Carennac in the Dordogne, where Fénelon had served as abbot. The work was taken by intellectuals as a critique of the luxury of the imperial court, and Catherine's journal, *Vsiakaia Vsiachina*, treated the work unfavorably. But at the same time *Télémaque*'s code of princely conduct very much suited the empress, and she later gave the book to her grandson, Alexander. The view presented by A. S. Orlov that Catherine objected to the content of *Télémaque* seems absolutely unfounded (A. S. Orlov, " 'Tilemakhida'

tale remained an essential book for heirs to the throne and other grand dukes through the nineteenth century.

Télémaque presents an example of the ideal ruler and a utopian vision of an austere life of labor and dedication. It leads the boy into a fictive "world of a hero," realized in a mythical antiquity that had been envisioned by Fénelon, Bossuet, and other seventeenth-century writers on pedagogy. The book showed the heir how a virtuous monarch should think and feel. "First of all," Georges Snyders wrote of seventeenth-century pedagogy, "virtue was to be attained only by renunciation." It arose only from scorn for the world and its blandishments, from total devotion to civic ideals, liberty, and the state.[8] *Les aventures de Télémaque* dramatized the lesson that a prince had to stand above both family and personal entanglements, which prevented him from dedicating himself completely to the commonweal. Telemachus learned to be king not from his missing father, but from Mentor, his "second father," who makes wisdom and virtue rather than instinct and tradition his guides to behavior: Paul's tutors were to replace his dead father. Telemachus's search for his natural father leads him into danger, and it is Mentor's advice that saves him. When the boy encounters a storm, he realizes his error:

> Am I not unhappy for having believed myself at an age when one has neither anticipation of the future nor experience of the past, nor the moderation to improve the present! Oh! If ever we escape from this tempest, I will distrust myself as my worst enemy: it is you Mentor whom I will always believe.[9]

Patience is the most important virtue for Fénelon. The gods make Telemachus wait to find his natural father in order to teach him patience. "One must be patient in order to be the master of oneself and of others." It was impatience that allowed the passions to reign and kings to abuse their powers.[10]

The greatest danger to the boy came in the form of Eros. "Love is to be feared more than shipwrecks." Like Ulysses, Telemachus falls in love with a nymph on Calypso's island. He begins to waste away from his passion. Mentor makes clear that romantic love is the greatest danger. Modest beauty was far more dangerous than vice or brutality, for "in loving it, one believes that he is loving only virtue." Love diverts the monarch from true virtue, which

---

V. K. Trediakovskogo," *XVIII Vek* [Moscow, 1935], 5–57). Catherine, as well as other educated individuals, found Trediakovskii's translation ponderous and impenetrable. Indeed, according to Karamzin, it was prescribed as a playful punishment for those who did not speak Russian in the Academy (Orlov, " 'Tilemakhida,' " 23). But Catherine certainly approved of the work in general and it remained an important intellectual influence during her reign (de Madariaga, *Age of Catherine the Great*, 490).

[8] On the image of classical virtue among seventeenth-century writers on pedagogy, see George Snyders, *La pédagogie en France au XVIIe et XVIIIe siècles* (Paris, 1965), 74–83.

[9] *Les aventures de Télémaque*, in Francois de Fénelon, *Oeuvres complètes* (Geneva, 1971), 6:401–2.

[10] Ibid., 6:564.

can be attained only by ruling his people.[11] Fénelon expresses the secular asceticism of his era. Love was not sinful or evil; it was selfish. It led the prince away from his obligations to humanity, which for him, as for Catherine, was to be the only constant object of his attachment.

The Prince must resist and deny his own sexual impulse, to become less masculine in the interest of the good of all. In the final scene, reason takes on a feminine form. Mentor dematerializes and, in a blaze of azure and gold, reveals himself as Minerva. The goddess calls on Telemachus to restore the Age of Gold, and recites a final set of maxims. She exhorts him to love his people, and to do everything to win their love—to live in simplicity for the good of the people and not for his own glory.[12]

Télémaque carries a message of admonition. The tutor uses his warnings and his knowledge to tame the young man by showing him that power is a dangerous possession. This was the lesson that Paul's principal tutor, Nikita Panin, strove to convey to his pupil. Empress Elizabeth appointed Panin to take charge of Paul's education in 1760, and the outline he prepared expressed views close to those of Catherine, whom he helped to seize the throne two years hence. Drawing on pedagogical principles set forth by Leibniz, Panin sketched out a plan to instill a sense of civic virtue and duty in the heir.[13] This duty required the mastery or denial of the ruler's personal impulses. The heir had to learn to be a new kind of man, not the kind he saw in the court around him. Panin's outline emphasized that the heir must have "a tender soul and heart" before he could learn to think and reason. He had to develop the virtues of a sensitive (*chuvstvitel'noe*) understanding of his creator and his intentions and of man's duty to God. But there was little emphasis on religion in Panin's memorandum. The education he recommended focused on political morality. A good monarch, he stressed, could have no true interest apart from the well-being of the people entrusted to him.

For Panin, history was the repository of models that could guide the prince. History would provide lessons of past rule, allowing the prince, Leibniz had written, to "take council from ancient Emperors and Kings so that he one day will better preside in his own realm." Panin's project also stressed the importance of Russia's history, which would present the heir with "ex-

---

[11] Ibid., 6:436–44.

[12] Ibid., 6:565–66.

[13] N. I. Panin, "Vsepoddannaishee pred'iavlenie slabogo poniatiia i mneniia o vospitanii Ego Imperatorskogo Velichestva Pavla Petrovicha," *Russkaia Starina*, vol. 36 (1880): 315–17. Leibniz had taught that the prince should be a "good man," who exhibited "great sentiments of piety, justice and charity" and applied himself "firmly to do his duty." The most important virtue for a prince, according to Leibniz, was prudence. Prudence "ordains the manner in which the prince must act in all sorts of circumstances." Other virtues that Leibniz thought the prince should exemplify were valor, moderation, justice, and generosity (Leibniz, *De educatione*, 178, 191–92, 195–96; Patrick Riley, ed., *The Political Writings of Leibniz* [Cambridge, 1972], 92–103). For a summary of the entire proposal, see Ransel, *The Politics of Catherinian Russia*, 207–11.

amples of the great deeds of his sanctified ancestors." But Western models—particularly Henry IV and Frederick the Great—dominated Paul's education. Paul took notes on Sully's diary, and his library contained many volumes on Frederick's statecraft. The only "sanctified ancestor" of whom his teachers made an example was Peter the Great, who, as David Ransel has shown, became the symbol of their hopes for reform. Panin and his assistants evoked Catherine's tamed and seemly Peter, devoted to law and sympathetic to their constitutional goals. Paul's mathematics and science teacher, Semen Poroshin, distinguished between two types of courage: fearlessness and impudence. But, in his view, only fearlessness was governed by reason, and it was fearlessness that Peter exemplified. Peter's courage was an act of self-control. Peter, Poroshin informed his pupil, was not courageous by nature, but reasoning (*razsuzhdeniia*) had overcome his weakness.[14]

Paul's religious tutor, Platon Levshin, later the metropolitan of Moscow, presented Peter the Great as a model of piety. Platon posed the question whether Peter would be remembered more for his piety or his courage. He taught a humanitarian faith, based on the notion that the teachings of religion were supported by reason, the viewpoint that had recommended him to Catherine when he expounded his ideas during her visit to the Trinity Monastery in 1762. He told Paul that tsars had been commanded to love the people entrusted to them by God, that "the people is the flock, and the tsar their shepherd."[15]

Paul was introduced to the new principles of rule in the writings of Montesquieu, Voltaire, Diderot, Helvétius, and Hume. At the dinner table, he heard Panin converse with leading officials, foreign dignitaries, and writers. Later, under Panin's influence, he composed several memoranda that argued for the regularization and organization of government through the introduction of a rule of law and the reform of institutions. Paul wrote that legislative power should "repose in the hands of the ruler but with the agreement of the state, for otherwise it will turn into despotism." In these writings, Paul described a Stoic image of ruler who, subordinating his will to natural law, promoted the well-being of his people. The good ruler epitomized meekness, for he had it in his power to abstain from power, to refrain from abuse of the law. The tsar, as the extract from the encyclopedia suggested, should behave like a man rather than a demigod, and, ruling by law, induce his people to love him.[16]

[14] Semen Poroshin, *Zapiski* (St. Petersburg, 1881), 97–98, 292; Leibniz, *De educatione*, 192; Panin, "Vsepoddannaishee pred'iavlenie," 316; Ransel, *The Politics of Catherinian Russia*, 268, 282–83.

[15] I. M. Snegirev, *Zhizn' Platona* (Moscow, 1891), 1:39; Mitropolit Platon, *Pravoslavnoe uchenie ili sokrashchennaia khristianskaia Bogosloviia dlia upotrebleniia Ego Imperatorskogo Vysochestva Presvetleishego Vserossiiskogo Naslednika blagovernogo Gosudaria Tsesarevicha i Velikogo Kniazia Pavla Petrovicha* (Moscow, 1819), i–iv, ix, 228–29, 235–40.

[16] Hugh Ragsdale, ed., *Paul I: A Reassessment of His Life and Reign* (Pittsburgh, Pa., 1979), ix; David Ransel, "An Ambivalent Legacy: The Education of the Grand Duke Paul," in Ragsdale, *Paul I*, 4–5, 8–11; Lefevre, *O nadzirateliakh*, 96, 99. On the reception of Stoic and

The general lines of the education followed Catherine's recommendations, and she attended all of Paul's examinations. But Paul took different lessons from his readings than his tutors had intended and sought a strong masculine image in the monarchs of the past. From childhood, Paul admired the authoritarian, intimidating Peter, whose will brooked no limits, the second element in what David Ransel has described as his "ambivalent legacy."[17] Paul admired other authoritarian figures from the past, particularly King Henry IV of France, whom he extolled in a composition written when he was twenty years old. Paul describes Henry as a king totally devoted to the state, who strives to improve his people, as would befit Leibniz's and Panin's ideal ruler. But Henry's devotion, in Paul's presentation, is displayed as a distrust of everyone, a determination to take responsibility for everything himself, and as a will to punish swiftly when disobeyed. Henry refused to be deceived, Paul writes, and made it his business to know everything, down to the pettiest detail. He banished vassals who did not do service, and gave gifts and favors himself, not through ministers. He approached government not as a matter of abstract principles, but with the feelings of a father for the well-being of his family. And this paternal concern for "the good order of domestic life" distinguished him from gifted people who had profound minds. We see in Paul's vision of paternal control and supervision the impulses that inspired his passion as emperor to direct all Russian life from the throne.[18]

The quality Paul most esteemed in Henry was order (*poriadok*). Frugality came next on his list, followed by tenderness, patience, honesty, and fidelity to one's word. He admired Henry's ability to combine opposed characteristics, elevated feelings and simplicity, a soldier's courage and an abundance of love. But the strongest feeling expressed in this school exercise is a fear of weakness in the monarch. Paul saw Henry as an embodiment of strength. Though Henry was tender with friends, Paul emphasized, he had a strong will and was never weak. In a note on how a wise monarch could transform

---

natural law theories in Russia, see Gleason, *Moral Idealists*, 87–91; the theme of self-restraint is set forth most effectively in the works of Denis Fonvizin, and particularly his "Discourse on Permanent Laws of State." See Marc Raeff, *Russian Intellectual History: An Anthology* (New York, 1966), 101. For comments on the text, and other writings of Fonvizin, see Walter Gleason, *The Political and Legal Writings of Denis Fonvizin* (Ann Arbor, Mich., 1985).

[17] "Tsarevich Pavel Petrovich; istoricheskie materialy khraniashchiesia v biblioteke dvortsa goroda Pavlovska," *Russkaia Starina*, vol. 9 (1874): 674; Ransel, "An Ambivalent Legacy," 13–14; Snegirev, *Zhizn' Platona*, 1:22.

[18] "Tsarevich Pavel Petrovich; istoricheskie materialy," 676–82; John L. H. Keep, "Paul I and the Militarization of Government," in Ragsdale, *Paul I*, 100; Roderick E. McGrew, *Paul I of Russia*, (Oxford, 1992), 62–65. Ragsdale has argued that Paul's tendency to subject everything to rule and control fits the obsessive-compulsive personality type. Such traits are undoubtedly evident in his character, but it is important to note that the pattern of control from above exemplified by Frederick the Great was widely admired in Europe at the time. Paul merely took it to insane extremes. See Hugh Ragsdale, "The Mental Condition of Paul," in Ragsdale, *Paul I*, 17–30.

"the Russians," Paul reveals that he hoped by civilizing his people, to turn them into a more effective weapon. Once the wise monarch had "softened their ferocious spirit, their cruel and unsociable manners, this people [the Russians] would become terrifying for all their neighbors."[19]

Warfare had the greatest appeal for Paul and he found his principal examples of male behavior not in the classroom but at the military exercises he was allowed to attend. As a very young boy, he fantasized about serving in the ranks in the cavalry and infantry. Riding in uniform, wearing a saber, participating in reviews and maneuvers at Krasnoe Selo captured his imagination. It was not only the glamour and color of the events that he found enchanting. On the drill field, he escaped from the world of admonition and piety, and took his position as commander, issued orders, received reports, watched complicated exercises enacted for his approval. This was the real world of power that the abstract prescriptions of his classroom could scarcely rival. It is no wonder that his lessons suffered seriously in the following days.[20] Paul's military fantasies and exercises continued into his youth. Paul's biographers have noted his difficulty in distinguishing imagined events from real. Early on he was inspired by romantic histories of the crusades, especially of the Maltese Order. The role of knight appealed to his mystical longings to impose an order of virtue by warfare. After his marriage, he staged tournaments twice a week in costumes of medieval knights.[21]

In military exercises and discussions, Paul found a common interest with men of high station. His tutors spoke to him as a pupil, preaching and admonishing. Wearing military uniform, Paul, whom Catherine had appointed general-admiral at his birth, had to be treated on a more equal footing. Over the dinner table, he heard talk of war and armies. He listened intently to serious conversations about military matters and the military resources of Russia conducted by leading generals of the realm, among them Nikita Panin's brother, Peter. From them he heard complaints that the armed forces lacked order and discipline and pleas for more powerful and assertive leadership.[22]

During these conversations, Paul heard many complaints about Catherine's neglect of the army and the superiority of Prussian military organization; Peter Panin spoke with great admiration of the Prussian army. In 1765, at age eleven, Paul was most impressed by a description of the Prussian military camp at Breslau by a Colonel Mikhail Kamenskii. Kamenskii sneered at the philosophical character of Paul's education. What good, he asked, would the wisdom of Greece's philosophers have done at the battle of Marathon? Kamenskii's Peter the Great "gave his subjects an example in all things, was

[19] "Tsesarevich Pavel Petrovich; istoricheskie materialy," 682–83.
[20] Poroshin, *Zapiski*, 327–33, 416, 517–18; N. K. Shil'der, *Imperator Pavel Pervyi* (St. Petersburg, 1901), 61–64.
[21] Dmitrii Kobeko, *Tsesarevich Pavel Petrovich, 1754–1796* (St. Petersburg, 1887), 166–67; McGrew, "Paul I and the Knights of Malta," 45.
[22] Poroshin, *Zapiski*, 516; Shil'der, *Imperator Pavel Pervyi*, 59–60.

not ashamed to be a soldier or sailor, but never was a clerk, nor a protocolist in a single college or even the Senate." These thoughts troubled Paul's teacher, Poroshin, but Kamenskii's influence prevailed, and Paul later raised Kamenskii to the position of general field marshal. When Prince Henry of Prussia visited Russia in 1770, the two became acquainted, and Paul's fascination for Prussian ways increased.[23]

Like his father, Peter III, Paul idolized Frederick the Great. It was not Frederick the statesman but Frederick the commander and disciplinarian that captured his, as well as his father's, imagination. Paul's admiration only grew when he met Frederick in Berlin in 1776, and he could witness the king's compelling military control over his government. Discussions with Peter Panin, and Prince Nicholas Repnin, a cousin of the Panins, convinced Paul of the need to transform the Russian armed forces, particularly in the light of the difficulties in quelling the Pugachev rebellion. He drafted plans to improve the recruitment of soldiers into the army and the deployment of Russian armies along the borders. He hoped to form a special army of foreign soldiers under his own personal leadership.[24]

Catherine, fearing her son as a potential rival for power, allowed him no governmental responsibility. She forbade petitioners to approach him for assistance. In the early 1770s, when Panin's influence began to wane, Catherine began to see her son as a center of opposition. Paul became known as "the Russian Hamlet," the sensitive crown prince, brooding over the death of his father, nurturing hopes for revenge. He found support against his mother in his wives. Natalia Alekseevna, a *Landgräfin* from Hesse-Darmstadt, whom he married in 1773, formed her own circle and soon stirred the empress's suspicion and wrath. After she died in childbirth in 1776, Paul wed the Württemberg princess, Sophie, who was baptized Maria Fedorovna. As grand duchess, Maria Fedorovna was a submissive wife, who worshipped her husband and shared his passion for things Prussian. She bore him ten children, the first generation of the Romanov dynasty, as it was known in the nineteenth century.

Paul was the progenitor of the dynasty, but he hardly played the role of paterfamilias. The image of father was not morally elevated or sufficient in the context of eighteenth-century scenarios. Mentor's admonitions about romantic love taught not chastity, but wariness of deep involvements that would distract the monarch from his civic duty. In this respect, Paul followed the eighteenth-century model of the monarch who, devoted to the well-being of the people, was not limited by biblical injunctions meant for ordinary mortals. His return to the notions of dynasty and primogeniture during his reign did not inspire him with a devotion to marital fidelity, which he openly violated.

The officer, not the father, was Paul's principal image of power, and en-

[23] Ibid., 60–61.
[24] McGrew, *Paul I of Russia*, 97–98; Kobeko, *Tsesarevich Pavel Petrovich*, 171–79.

couraged by his wife, Paul gave the surrounding area the atmosphere of Potsdam. "As you entered Gatchina," one observer wrote, "it was as if you were entering a Prussian territory." At Gatchina, Paul indulged his love for drill, uniforms, and the trivial details of the parade ground—the mania that dominated his reign and became his abiding legacy for future generations. His Gatchina detachments, drawn from lesser nobility, many of them Little Russian, were coarse and rude, loyal only to Paul. They formed a reliable force that would make Paul independent of the guards' regiments of the capital after his accession. At the same time they bred suspicions and later provided proof of the despotic and alien nature of his rule.[25]

But Potsdam was not the only ideal that Paul entertained. In 1782 he and Maria Fedorovna had toured Europe, and on this trip, France made the greatest impression. Paul was a great success at Versailles. He seemed to know as much about the French court as the Russian, and his knowledge and tact impressed his hosts. Potsdam exemplified the effective exercise of authority for Paul, but it was too restrained and austere to suit the sense of majesty he identified with the imperial image. The Russian court in the eighteenth century had been patterned on Versailles or German imitations of Versailles. At Versailles, Paul was impressed by the extent and organization of ceremonies and the courtly bearing of the aristocracy.[26]

Paul had the parks of Gatchina laid out on the model of those at Chantilly. Gatchina became Paul's pleasure palace, as well as his military camp. He devoted his mornings to military exercises, his afternoons and evenings to diversions. In the first years at Gatchina, from 1783 to 1790, these pleasures were innocent—walks, games, theater, games of cards and lotto, sometimes a hunt. Paul and Maria Fedorovna led a happy family life. Catherine called them "*bons seigneurs de paroisse*" ("good lords of their parish"), who lived quietly taking care of their estate. But after 1790, relations between Petersburg and the "young court" of the heir became increasingly strained. Paul reacted with outbursts of irascibility and suspicion, the signs of paranoid behavior that would characterize his reign. It was the era of the so-called Gatchina terror when he became distrustful of all, banishing many of his close associates and bringing close to him the most severe and inhuman of the martinets of Gatchina, Alexei Arakcheev, the former Prussian hussar Fedor Lindener, and Paul's future procurator-general, Peter Obol'ianinov.[27]

From 1790 until his accession, Paul stayed away from the capital. Gatchina became the embattled enclave in which he reigned over his Prussian-style regiments. His diversions, meanwhile, lost their innocence. The repre-

---

[25] McGrew, *Paul I of Russia*, 152–63; Kobeko, *Tsesarevich Pavel Petrovich*, 102; Shil'der, *Imperator Aleksandr Pervyi*, 1:94.

[26] McGrew, *Paul I of Russia*, 132–34; E. S. Shumigorskii, *Imperatritsa Mariia Fedorovna, (1759–1828)* (St. Petersburg, 1892), 1:212–21; Shil'der, *Imperator Pavel Pervyi*, 157–76.

[27] N. Lanceray, "Po povodu Pavil'iona Venery," *Starye Gody* (July–September 1914): 192–93; S. Kaznakov, "Pavlovskaia Gatchina," *Starye Gody* (July–September 1914): 103–20.

26. *Ceiling of Pavilion of Love*, Gatchina. Painting by J. Mettenleiter.

sentation of sovereignty as erotic power that he had seen in France had not been lost on him. He began a romance with the maid of honor, Catherine Nelidova, which at first embittered relations between himself and Maria Fedorovna. This infatuation may have remained platonic, but Paul's public display of his partiality to Nelidova and the open expression of his feelings are indications that he shared the image of monarch as hero of romantic conquest. The year 1793, the height of his affair with Nelidova, also marked the completion of a Pavilion of Venus on an "Island of Love" at Gatchina, a replica of the pavilion he had seen at the chateau of Chantilly.[28] "The Triumph of Venus" on the ceiling is a final development of eighteenth-century feminine imagery, an "Olympus of the Ceiling" where floating goddesses charmed the senses without reference to the meaning or purposes of power (fig. 26).[29]

[28] Ibid., 115–17; Lanceray, "Po povodu Pavil'iona Venery," 192–93; N. Lanceray, "Arkhitektura i sady Gatchiny," *Starye Gody* (July–September 1914): 21, 30; *Pamiatniki Arkhitektury prigorodov Leningrada* (Leningrad, 1983), 298–99. On Nelidova, see McGrew, *Paul I of Russia*, 170–72.

[29] On the "Olympus of the Ceilings" in the eighteenth century, see Starobinski, *The Invention of Liberty*, 58.

Grand Duke Alexander Pavlovich

Paul's firstborn son, Alexander, supplanted Paul as the empress's hope for the future. Catherine doted on Alexander with a grandmother's affection and actively engaged herself in the planning of his education. She withdrew him at birth from his parents' care, just as Elizabeth had taken Paul away from her, and made every effort to shape Alexander according to her enlightenment ideal of humane ruler. Derzhavin's ode on Alexander's birth in 1777 carried a Stoic message. Thunder roared and the north glowed: "a god has been born." The geniuses bestowed on the infant all the gifts—plenty, joy, peace, beauty, reason—and all the talents necessary to a tsar. The last gift, that of virtue, utters an apostrophe that would be cited as Alexander's guiding ideal through his life:

> Be the ruler of your passions,
> Be a human being (*chelovek*) on the throne.

Derzhavin portrayed the enlightenment conception of a ruler who, rather than the semblance of a god, chose to be an ideal human being capable of overcoming his animal impulses and heeding the voice of reason. He would be a "father to his subjects," a "model to monarchs." But the Olympian image of Catherine remained to inspire him. The future tsar will be no ordinary mortal. Derzhavin concludes the ode,

> Becoming the equal of [your parents'] mother,
> You will be comparable to a divinity.[30]

Catherine set forth the principles that would turn her grandson into the ideal ruler she envisaged. Like Minerva disguised as Mentor, she sought to replace the absent father and teach her pupil to be a better man and a good ruler. She set forth a series of maxims on a copy of Fénelon's *Télémaque* that stressed the Stoic principles of reserve and self-control: "Be mild, humane, accessible, compassionate and liberal (*liberal'nyi*)." Good people should love him, evil fear him, and all should respect him. He should preserve the "ancient taste for honor and virtue." "Duplicity," she asserted, "is unknown to great people." She hoped he would become "a great person, a hero." But she did not want him to follow his father's military path. When he was four years old, she wrote in her notebook: "Listen, do not begin to imagine that I want to make of Alexander the one who cuts the Gordian knot. Literally, nothing of the kind. Alexander will be a splendid person but not at all a conqueror—he has no need to become one."[31]

The ruler Catherine envisaged stood apart from society. He made decisions on his own, prompted by his own conscience: "virtue does not make itself known in the crowd." He should avoid flatterers and contact with high

---

[30] G. R. Derzhavin, *Sochineniia Derzhavina*, 1:50–53. The ode was published in December 1779, in *Sankt-Peterburgskii Vestnik*.

[31] Shil'der, *Imperator Aleksandr Pervyi*, 1:27–28, 21.

society which might "darken the ancient taste for honor and virtue." Catherine dramatized this lonesome quest for virtue in her own version of *Télémaque*, *The Tale of the Tsarevich Khlor*.

The tsarevich, Khlor, in Catherine's tale, was the son of the kind tsar of Russia before the rise of Kiev. He was beautiful, intelligent, and lively, and his reputation spread far and wide. The Kirghiz Khan longed to have the wonderful boy. He had Khlor kidnapped, then gave him the task of finding the "rose without thorns," the symbol of virtue. Felitsiia, the personification of happiness—Catherine, herself—helped him in his quest. Felitsiia's son, Reason (*Razsudok*), guides Khlor to find the correct path to the rose.

The central theme of the tale was caution. Felitsiia warns Khlor about those who entice him from his path by flattery and merry diversions. Only Reason gives sound advice. Reason points to a hill far in the distance, but Khlor, impatient, ignores his directions and seeks a shorter way. This leads him to grief—a marketplace—and, frightened, he returns knowing that he must curb his impulsive nature. Reason, like Mentor, emphasizes the importance of patience. "Only by patience is work conquered." On the hill, Khlor meets an old man and an old woman, representing honor (*chestnost'*) and truth (*pravda*). At the temple of the rose, horns blare, drums resound, extolling the boy who discovered the rose at so young an age. At Tsarskoe Selo, Catherine built Alexander his own temple of the rose. The rose lay in an urn on an altar.[32]

Catherine listed the *Tale of the Tsarevich Khlor* (mentioning the title twice) among the books she recommended in the memorandum she wrote to Count Nicholas Saltykov, the governor of Alexander and Constantine. The precepts of the memorandum were drawn directly from enlightenment writers, and many of them, like the articles of her *Nakaz* to the codification commission, are direct quotations from her favorite philosophers, in this case, Comenius, Locke, and Fénelon.[33] The heir's education, she wrote, should create a kind, good person. Virtue, respect, and good conduct should be the chief concerns of his teachers. He should grow up learning the golden rule, to feel "benevolence to humanity," and have "tender and sympathetic attitudes to all,"—a "pure and grateful heart." The child should learn "justice," which she defined as not acting contrary to the laws, in addition to "love for truth, generosity, self-restraint, intelligence, based on reflection, wholesome ideas and reasoning combined with diligence." Throughout her reign, Catherine defended enlightenment ideas in her conversations with Alexander, and in her last years even read and explained to him the "Declaration of the Rights of Man."[34]

[32] Catherine II, *Skazka o tsareviche Khlore* (St. Petersburg, 1787). The ceiling of the temple was decorated with frescoes of Peter the Great looking down on an allegorical "Russia prospering," with symbols of wealth, science, and industry. Russia herself leaned on a shield carrying a picture of Felitsiia—Catherine (Shil'der, *Imperator Aleksander Pervyi*, 1:59–60).

[33] Black, *Citizens for the Fatherland*, 117.

[34] Shil'der, *Imperator Aleksandr Pervyi*, 1:32; "Sobstvennoruchnyi imennoi ukaz i nastavlenie Imp. Ekateriny II gen.-an-shefu Nikolaiu Ivanovichu Saltykovu o vospitanii velikikh

Alexander's tutor was the Swiss philosophe and republican Frédéric-César de La Harpe. La Harpe set before Alexander a model of civic virtue for a future sovereign: a ruler, he declared in a memorandum to Catherine, should not be a physicist or a naturalist or a jurist, but an "honorable man and enlightened citizen." He should use his knowledge to become conscious of the obligations of one responsible for the fate of millions. History would provide examples of the rulers who showed "the civic spirit," but, La Harpe emphasized, the instructor had to guide the heir to the proper models.

> One must never forget that Alexander the Great, gifted with wonderful genius and brilliant qualities, laid waste to Asia and committed so many atrocities merely from the desire to imitate the heroes of Homer. In the same way, Julius Caesar, emulating Alexander the Great, committed a crime by destroying the freedom of his fatherland.[35]

La Harpe explained in his memorandum that philosophy would help the prince to understand "civil societies" and "the principles which are their bases." Alexander would learn that men were once equal, and that there have been absolute monarchs "so generous and true" that they vowed publicly, "We have the glory to say that we exist only for our peoples."[36]

To acquire virtue, to become a "public man," Alexander had to isolate himself from his environment and engage in diligent, solitary work. La Harpe hoped that principles of philosophy and the examples of history would provide the guidance that would allow his pupil to escape traditional models of masculine conduct. La Harpe urged Alexander "to replace living friends by those who are dead, and these true friends you will find in the great models presented by history."[37]

Peter the Great's name was conspicuously absent from La Harpe's recommendations, and, Nicholas Riasanovsky has suggested, Alexander may have been the first Russian ruler not deeply concerned with Peter's image. The historical figures La Harpe approved of as Alexander's friends were not the conquerors but the great legislators—Solon and Numa, who had laid the bases of the institutions that had shaped their peoples' political life. His principal exemplar was Marcus Aurelius, and La Harpe liked to think of himself as Marcus's tutor, Seneca. Alexander, enlightened on the throne, could realize the Stoic ideal of virtue and introduce a just and egalitarian political order.[38]

---

kniazei Aleksandra i Konstantina Pavlovichei," *Sbornik imperatorskogo russkogo istoricheskogo obshchestva*, 27:307–20; A. Kornilov, *Kurs istorii Rossii XIX v.* (Moscow, 1918), 1:78–79.

[35] Shil'der, *Imperator Aleksandr Pervyi*, 1:36.

[36] Ibid., 1:37–39; Jean Charles Biaudet and Françoise Nicod, *Correspondance de Frédéric-César de la Harpe et Alexandre Ier* (Neuchatel, 1978), 1:12–13.

[37] Shil'der, *Imperator Aleksandr Pervyi*, 1:39; Biaudet and Nicod, *Correspondance*, 1:15, 90.

[38] A. Fatéev, "Le problème de l'individu et de l'homme d'état dans la personnalité historique de Alexandre I, empereur de toutes les Russies," in Russkii Svobodnyi Universitet v Prage, *Zapiski nauchno-issledovatel'skogo ob"edineniia* 3 (1936): 150–51.

La Harpe taught Alexander the Stoic notion of a supreme reason that would guide a philosophical elite to the natural law which would enable them to govern citizens equally. He introduced him to Montesquieu's notion of a "true monarchy," governed on the basis of unchanging laws and institutions respected by the ruler in his exercise of power. When Alexander was eight, he learned that "force established thrones, but to make them firm, to reconcile the strong with the weak, it is necessary to resort to fundamental laws, suited to the establishment of order and the rule of law." In 1790, at the age of thirteen, Alexander vowed to his tutor to "secure the well-being of Russia on immutable principles."[39]

When Alexander was fifteen years old and about to be married, La Harpe assigned him a colossal reading list, which might intimidate the most serious of students.[40] The history and thought of antiquity figured most prominently. La Harpe recommended many histories of the ancient world, by classical and modern authors, works of Greek and Roman poetry, with indications that some sections of the Latin texts should be read in the original. Many books on modern history were also assigned, including nearly every European country, the Ottoman Empire, and the United States. La Harpe was particularly insistent about *The Wealth of Nations*. "It is indispensable, sir, that you make the effort to read this classic, of which the principles, once well grasped, allow you to estimate what happens in matters of manufacture, trades, commerce and taxation." He assigned Cicero's writings on the Duties of Man, Ferguson's "Essay on Civil Society," Montesquieu, Mably, and Rousseau. He even recommended a collection of famous speeches that had been given in the English Parliament. But ultimately, he warned, Alexander must seek the true promptings of reason in himself.

> The immutable bases of morality have been placed in your heart by the creator of myriads of worlds. Accustom yourself, sir, to consult the infallible oracle who dwells in this temple and lend him an attentive ear in the silence of the passions. Books will teach you to organize according to different systems the truth evident to anyone who has not been perverted by prejudices or bad education.[41]

Alexander's religion tutor, Andrei Samborskii, taught him a religion of humanity and reason that complemented La Harpe's Stoic republicanism. Samborskii was a secularized cleric, educated in the principles of the enlightenment. He had been sent to England by Catherine with a group of priests in order to study agronomy so that when they returned, in addition to their pastoral obligations, they could teach the peasants how to till the land. Instead, Samborskii remained in London as chaplain to the Russian Embassy. He married an English woman, and was allowed to wear lay clothing and cut his beard. He conducted orthodox services in Greek and Latin for the bene-

---

[39] M. M. Safonov, *Problema reform v pravitel'stvennoi politike Rossii na rubezhe XVIII i XIX vv.* (Leningrad, 1988), 43, 128.

[40] He composed the reading list just before he left St. Petersburg for Switzerland. It is dated April 6, 1795 (Biaudet and Nicod, *Correspondance*, 1:111–39).

[41] Biaudet and Nicod, *Correspondance*, 1:135.

fit of Englishmen who wished to attend. His own religion was evangelical and universal. He preached, he claimed, not for Russia alone, "but for the whole world." His was a personal, mystical faith for all humankind, recognizing neither national bounds nor institutional limits. Samborskii also emphasized the role of religion in determining the relations between states and the maintenance of peace. He remained Alexander's instructor and confessor for fifteen years, and his teachings significantly influenced the vision of a Holy Alliance that Alexander entertained after 1812.[42]

La Harpe and Samborskii instilled in Alexander moral and political imperatives of a high order. But the enticements of the court proved difficult to resist. His cherubic countenance, poise, and charm evoked sighs of admiration from Catherine and the leading figures at court. His mathematics teacher, C.F.P. Masson, characterized him as "the ideal that enraptures us in Telemachus." French emigrés called him "the Greek Cupid." Potemkin compared him to Apollo. The ease of his social success distracted him from serious pursuits, lamented General A. Ia. Protasov, who supervised Alexander directly. Alexander's marriage, in 1793, to Princess Margaret of Baden, baptized Elizabeth Alekseevna, ended his tutors' supervision and brought his education to a close.[43]

Alexander took his tutors' admonitions seriously and constantly berated himself for failing to measure up. At the age of thirteen, he wrote to La Harpe: "Instead of urging myself on and doubling my efforts to profit from my remaining years of study, each day I become more nonchalant, more remiss, more incapable, and each day I surround myself with those like myself who stupidly consider themselves perfection only because they are princes." He castigated himself for being an egoist, uninterested in others, who out of excessive vanity wanted only to shine: "At thirteen, I am the same child as I was at eight, and the more I advance in age the closer I come to nil."[44]

He showed a far greater propensity for the military. As a child, during the 1780s, Alexander visited Gatchina once a week; in his teens, his visits became more frequent and his love of the military more open. His enthusiasm troubled his teachers. In 1793, when Alexander was fifteen, General Protasov deplored his fascination for gun practice.[45] After his marriage, Alexander began participating in exercises at Gatchina four times a week and experiencing the same joy at the maneuvers at Krasnoe Selo that his father had several decades before. During the summer of 1796, Alexander was

[42] Fatéev, "Le problème de l'individu," 3:159–63.

[43] A. N. Pypin, *Obshchestvennoe dvizhenie pri Aleksandre I* (Petrograd, 1918), 38; A. Ia. Protasov, "Dnevnye zapiski o vospitanii velikogo kniazia Aleksandra Pavlovicha," *Drevniaia i Novaia Rossiia* 3 (1880): 773–75; Mme la comtesse de Choiseul-Gouffier, *Réminiscences sur l'empereur Alexandre Ier et sur l'empereur Napoléon Ier* (Paris, 1862), 9; Shil'der, *Imperator Aleksandr Pervyi*, 1:44–46, 51–56.

[44] Biaudet and Nicod, *Correspondance*, 1:73–74.

[45] Protasov, "Dnevnye zapiski," 773.

occupied from six in the morning until afternoon. He wrote to La Harpe in October, of that year, "This summer, I can definitely say that I have served."[46] Alexander's first understanding of state service was military service. But the young Alexander, lacking in assurance and deaf in one ear, needed help in the techniques of command. He received generous advice and assistance from Paul's favorite, Colonel Arakcheev. Arakcheev, the provincial nobleman, the model of the brutal and ruthless martinet, became the heir's improbable friend and later favorite.

Alexander's service inured him to the military mode of subordination that enthralled his father. But at the same time, he began to develop a more informal, personal relationship with his close advisers and acquaintances. This relationship was characterized as "friendship," an affectionate bond between the young man and others who shared common ideas and feelings. Friendship brought the principle of equality into political relations and lifted them into an ideal literary sphere. Sentimental literature of the era extolled friendship as a feeling equivalent or superior to love. In a quatrain of 1797, Nicholas Karamzin wrote,

> Love is good for us,
> Only when it is like nice friendship;
> And friendship is dear to us,
> Only when it is equal with love.[47]

When Alexander was approaching his seventeenth birthday, La Harpe encouraged him to address his tutor as *mon cher ami*. Alexander began to use the phrase, *mon vrai ami*, in his letters to La Harpe, who responded with expressions of his own warm feelings. La Harpe confessed the deep imprint that Alexander's feelings had left in his soul: "Oh! My dear Alexander, permit me this expression, my dear Alexander, [*sic*] preserve this friendship, of which you have given me so many indications and which I will reciprocate until my last breath." Alexander evoked the same bonds of friendship in his acquaintanceships with the young aristocrats he drew around him as he grew into manhood. In 1792 he met Victor Kochubei, ten years his senior, who had just returned from revolutionary France. For Kochubei, he expressed "*amitié sans bornes*." In 1795 Alexander first met the young Polish aristocrat Adam Czartoryski, seven years older than he, and, in a conversation filled "with effusions of friendship on his part," confided his dreams to him.[48] Alexander also befriended two other "enlightened persons"—Paul

[46] Shil'der, *Imperator Aleksandr Pervyi*, 1:91–95, 98; Michael Jenkins, *Arakcheev* (New York, 1960), 50; Biaudet and Nicod, *Correspondance*, 1:179.

[47] N. M. Karamzin, *Polnoe sobranie stikhotvorenii* (Moscow, 1966), 234. At the beginning of the nineteenth century, Andrei Turgenev wrote: "Even a criminal can fall in love. But only a virtuous heart can feel friendship" (M. Raeff, "La jeunesse russe à l'aube du XIX siècle: André Turgenev et ses amis," *Cahiers du monde russe et soviétique*, vol. 8 (October–December 1967): 570n.

[48] Biaudet and Nicod, *Correspondance*, 1:88–89, 96, 141–43; Shil'der, *Imperator Aleksandr Pervyi*, 1:111–17.

Stroganov, only three years Alexander's senior, and Stroganov's cousin, Nicholas Novosil'tsev, the oldest of the group, who was already thirty-five when Alexander met him in 1795. Stroganov had been secretary of the "Friends of the Law" society in Paris, which had been founded by his tutor, Gilbert Romme, and in 1790 joined the Jacobin Club.

Alexander discussed political ideas with friends and, in 1796, confided his intention to La Harpe, Kochubei, and Czartoryski to abdicate. He would retire with his wife to a farm on the Rhine, "where I will live tranquilly as a private person, finding happiness in the society of friends and the study of nature." Alexander envisioned an idyll of a bucolic private life, inspired by the poetry of Solomon Gessner, whose grave he went out of his way to visit on his return from Paris in 1815.

But Alexander was also inspired by Western conceptions of government, which he believed, following previous Russian monarchs, should be embodied in Russian institutions. In this case the ideal was republicanism. He despaired at the inability of a single person to cope with the problems of the Russian administration. He wrote to Kochubei:

> Incredible disorder reigns in our affairs. There is stealing on all sides. All branches of the government are poorly administered. There is order nowhere and meanwhile the empire strives only to extend its border. In such a state of things, it is hardly possible for one person to administer a state, and all the more to correct the deeply rooted abuses. This is above the forces of a person like myself endowed with ordinary capacities, but even of a genius, and I have constantly maintained the rule that it is better not to take on a matter at all than to do it badly.[49]

If monarchical rule was responsible for the abuses of Russian administration, Alexander believed, then the end of monarchy was the logical next step. His "young friends," however, convinced him that it was his obligation first to grant Russia a constitution that would enable it to be governed well, then to reform the Russian political system. With him, they formed a circle to discuss the rights of man and plans for such a constitution. Alexander asserted that supreme power should depend not on hereditary succession but on votes of the people. According to Stroganov, he wanted a republic without a hereditary nobility. In a letter Novosil'tsev carried to La Harpe in England, Alexander described a revolution from the throne introducing representative government. The "young friends" also published a journal, *Sankt-Peterburgskii Zhurnal*, to further their ideas. In addition to sentimental and didactic verse, the journal printed a tract of A. F. Bestuzhev condemning class privileges, translations of selections from D'Holbach, an unpublished work by the playwright D. I. Fonvizin, as well as other articles in the spirit of enlightened monarchy.[50]

---

[49] Ibid.; Pypin, *Obshchestvennoe dvizhenie*, 36–37; Fatéev, "Le problème de l'individu," 5–8.

[50] Safonov, *Problema reform v pravitel'stvennoi politike Rossii*, 46–53.

The education of Paul and Alexander had acquainted them with high principles of behavior and with exemplary rulers, whom they were urged to approximate. They were expected to reconcile the ideals of enlightenment education with an image of authority that could express the transcendence of the Russian sovereign. In seeking the image they would embody and the virtues they would exemplify from the throne, they faced serious dilemmas of representation. Their search for suitable personae lent a strange and theatrical character to both of their reigns. The symbolic language of the enlightenment would be insufficient to elevate them to the heights expected of a Russian sovereign, and both father and son, though in different ways, had to struggle in public with the flaw of their mortality.

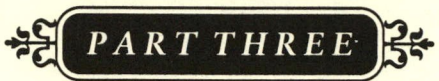

PART THREE

Mortal Sovereigns

The Dilemma of Neoclassicism

DURING THE REIGN of Catherine the Great, the imagery of triumphal goddess had kept alive the myth of conquering monarch. The empress was portrayed as perpetrator, or at the very least, initiator of prodigies of transformation. Joined by the leading members of the nobility, Catherine presented her rule as an exemplification of European monarchy, the Roman Empire reborn. She thus was able to appear as the successor to Peter the Great, the heroic sovereign transforming the elite and the Russian state into a semblance of Europe.

By the end of the eighteenth century, Baroque forms of idealization had lost their emotional force. The philosophes had dismissed the classical gods as rationalizations of political power or symbols of fertility. The gods survived, Hugh Honour wrote, as "types of physical beauty." But they no longer could serve as literary referents to transform the mortal sovereign into an emanation of supreme reason, beauty, or power. The upbringing of Paul I and Alexander I had impressed them with their obligation to act as men, following the examples of the great leaders of history. Despite the striking differences of personality and manner and conception of rule, both Paul and Alexander faced a common symbolic dilemma. At a time of the "desacralization" of monarchy, they had to appear as superhuman Western sovereigns who realized the Petrine image of emperor.[1]

The French Revolution dealt the final blow to the image of enlightened monarchs and made it impossible to justify absolute power by appropriating the most advanced models of Western polity. The revolution challenged the basic premises of the utilitarian justification of absolutism. The people themselves had arrogated the right to determine their own well-being, rejecting the image of the supreme, dispassionate rational sovereign. They had taken on the role of annihilating the vestiges of the past, including the monarchy and privileged estates. The emergence of the concepts of "nation" and the "people," often rendered in Russian with the same word, *narod*, brought discordant notes into political rhetoric. This "transfer of sacrality" to the people themselves threatened the symbolic distance that elevated the image of absolute monarch.[2]

---

[1] Hugh Honour, *Neo-classicism* (Middlesex, England, 1968), 43–44. On the "desacralization" of monarchy in Europe as a whole, see Heinz Dollinger, "Das Leitbild des Burgerkönigtums in der europäischen Monarchie des 19. Jahrhunderts," in Karl Ferdinand Werner, ed., *Hof, Kultur, und Politik im 19. Jahrhundert* (Bonn, 1985), 337, 341–43. On the transformation of the royal image in England, see Linda Colley, *Britons: Forging the Nation, 1707–1837* (New Haven, Conn., 1992), 203–7, 232–33.

[2] On the use of the word *nation* during the French Revolution, see Lynn Hunt, *Politics, Culture, and Class in the French Revolution* (Berkeley, Calif., 1986), 21–27. The concept of "a

Paul and Alexander followed opposite directions in their responses to this symbolic dilemma. Paul sought to restore the signs of absolute sovereignty, Alexander to make them disappear. Each engaged in an ultimately futile quest for images that could incarnate a Western ideal and the majesty of the Russian emperor. The single mortal image that could express supremacy for both was that of military leader. Napoleon exalted the image of military leader as the exemplar of all virtue, returning, Kantorowicz noted, to a symbol of early imperial Rome. The military uniform replaced mythical analogy as an expression of political transcendence and, at the end of the eighteenth and the beginning of the nineteenth centuries, uniforms became the accepted dress of European monarchs.[3] The magnificent uniform, bespangled with decorations, set the tone for a sartorial splendor that would unite the officer corps in admiration of their sovereign. Throughout the nineteenth century, Russian emperors would fuss over the details of their uniform and redesign them to fit their tastes and the fashion of each era. This passion, so troubling to sympathetic critics of the monarchy, ensured that the emperor's uniform would continue to define prowess, power, and beauty for the Westernized elite.

Indifferent battlefield commanders, the emperors of Russia revealed their valor and authority on the parade ground. During the reigns of Paul and Alexander, the parade became the principal ceremony of Russian monarchy and the role of parade commander the principal persona of the Russian emperor. The fascination with military drill to be sure was not limited to Russia at this time.[4] "Prussomania" had swept eighteenth-century Europe, but for Russia, in the absence of native images of male authority, it played a greater role. In Europe, the parade symbolized military organization and power; in Russia, it became a ceremony validating the persistence of the Petrine image. The parade demonstrated the authority and control of the emperor without invoking Olympian equivalents. The monarch, setting in motion the movement of vast numbers of men under the guidance of noble officers, presented a concrete rather than a metaphorical expression of domination. On the parade ground, the emperor directed ongoing, all-encompassing enactments of the conquest motif, reaffirming the efficacy of the Westernized ruler and elite. Successes on the battlefield—the victory over Napoleon, the expansion of the empire to include parts of the Caucasus and Finland—gave confirmation to the image of irresistible power. Paul and his sons, Alexander I and Nicholas I, turned the discipline of the parade ground into the paramount demonstration of imperial rule.[5]

---

transfer of sacrality" is developed by Mona Ozouf, in *Festivals and the French Revolution* (Cambridge, Mass., 1988), 262–82.

[3] Ernst H. Kantorowicz, "Gods in Uniform," in his *Selected Studies* (New York, 1965), 7–24.

[4] On the diffusion of the Prussian military pattern, see Christopher Duffy, *The Military Life of Frederick the Great* (New York, 1986), 246–47.

[5] On the military ethos in the imperial family, see John Keep, "The Military Style of the Romanov Rulers," *War and Society*, vol. 1, no. 2 (September 1983), 61–84.

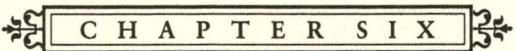

CHAPTER SIX

Paul I

And so the flatterer does not steal in with falsehood,
And the slanderer does not deceive,
[Paul] has taken everything into his own hands,
And with his own eye looked,
Looking at the artillery fire,
Looking at the cavalry charge,
At the fleets and the regiments he has looked;
Everywhere, where there was sleeping or dozing,
And the rules of office were unknown,
He turned everything around and set things right.

—*Stepan Russov, "Ode to the Sovereign Emperor Pavel
Petrovich," 1797*[1]

ACCESSION AND CORONATION

On the night before Catherine's death, the tsarevich, Paul Pavlovich, dreamed that he was being lifted into the heavens by an invisible and supernatural force.[2] During his reign, he struggled to vest himself in symbolic forms that would exalt his rule above the perils of revolution and court conspiracies. He appeared, at different moments, as the incarnation of Frederick the Great and Louis XIV and as leader of a crusading order. He performed these roles with a fanatic dedication, forcing the nobility's compliance without regard to their self-respect or sensibilities. His great lability of moods and shifting fancies of royal behavior struck the noblemen as a bizarre parody of the Petrine scenario that he believed he was reenacting.

Although legal heir to the throne—as he had been named in Catherine's manifesto of 1762—Paul followed the pattern of accession by violence, making a bold break with his mother's reign. But the display of military force revealed the intention to bring subjugation, in contrast to the signs of liberation that had surrounded the accessions of Elizabeth and Catherine. Derzhavin called Paul's accession an act of conquest (*zavoevanie*). The Winter Palace began to resemble a barracks, the sounds of boots and spurs echoing through the halls. The morning of November 7, the day after his accession,

[1] Bartenev, *Osmnatstaty vek*, 4:480.
[2] Kobeko, *Tsesarevich Pavel Petrovich*, 456.

at 11:00 A.M., Paul held his first *Wachtparade*, which he would repeat unfailingly during his reign. On November 29 he issued decrees imposing Prussian military rules upon the Russian army.[3]

Parades, Adam Czartoryski observed, became "the chief occupation of each day." Parades were not only shows of force to deter the opposition Paul feared to his rule. They presented a new image of foreign domination. Troops, lined up in battle array on the palace square, astounded the crowd by "the sight of soldiers entirely different from those it had been accustomed to seeing." Changes in dress and conduct accompanied the new military order. "In less than a day," Czartoryski wrote, "costumes, manners, occupations, all were altered." Gatchina troops were integrated with units of the guards under the command of Gatchina officers. Strict rules from above ended the old, nonchalant attitude toward military dress that had allowed dandies to tailor their uniforms as they wished and to leave them fashionably unbuttoned. The grenadier guards began to wear pointed hats; soldiers appeared with lances and halberds and other long-forgotten military paraphernalia. High collars gave way to low collars; mustaches, thickly dyed, became obligatory; and coiffures were strictly regulated.[4]

Paul's accession mimicked Peter the Great's shows of military force and imposition of foreign dress and manners. But his performance of the conquest motif violated the eighteenth-century script, which included leading members of the nobility and made the nobility as a whole the beneficiary of the act of violence. Paul excluded the nobility, turning them from comrades-in-arms into subjects of the conquest perpetrated by his Gatchina contingents in Prussian dress. Noblemen found themselves thrown down from their Olympian heights under Catherine to the position of subalterns at the mercy of Paul's henchmen. His military manner struck them not as an example of Western rule but as a throwback, which they compared to Germany of the sixteenth century or Turkish despotism.[5]

In response to the French Revolution, Paul presented himself as the defender of traditional authority. His succinct accession manifesto of November 6, 1796, written by Alexander Bezborodko, referred to "Our, Paternal (*Praroditel'skii*), hereditary, Imperial, All-Russian Throne." The principle of heredity had primacy over the principle of utility, which was mentioned only in the last line—an invocation for the Lord to help raise him to the task of "the well-being of the Empire and the prosperity of Our loyal subjects."[6]

In the weeks after Catherine's death on November 6, 1796, Paul set about

[3] Shil'der, *Imperator Pavel Pervyi*, 287–94; Derzhavin, *Sochineniia*, 6:700–701; N. Ia. Eidel'man, *Gran' vekov; politicheskaia bor'ba v Rossii, konets XVIII-nachala XIX stoletiia* (Moscow, 1986), 52–53.

[4] Shil'der, *Imperator Pavel Pervyi*, 295–300; McGrew, *Paul I of Russia*, 209–10; Adam Czartoryski, *Memoirs of Adam Czartoryski* (London, 1888), 1:141; V. M. Glinka, *Russkii voennyi kostium, XVIII-nachala XX veka* (Leningrad, 1988), 35, Plates 28, 29.

[5] Shil'der, *Imperator Pavel Pervyi*, 300–301.

[6] *PSZ*, no. 17,530, November 6, 1796; Safonov, *Zaveshchanie Ekateriny II*, chap. 7, 200.

restoring his father's memory to the history of the monarchy and exalting the symbols of hereditary monarchy. On November 19 he and the members of the imperial family attended a ceremony of disinterment of Peter III at the Alexander Nevskii Monastery. The coffin was opened and the members of the family proceeded to kiss the remains. On November 25 Paul staged the posthumous coronation of Peter III by placing the imperial crown on his dead father's casket. Then the imperial family returned to the Winter Palace. In the Throne Room, two *kamerdinery* (valets) lifted Catherine's corpse. Empress Maria Fedorovna then conferred the small crown on the head of Catherine, the same crown that Peter the Great had placed on the head of Catherine I. A week later, Peter III's casket was borne to the Winter Palace in a ceremonial procession through the capital accompanied by detachments of Cavalier Guards and horse guards. The eighty-year-old Alexei Orlov did penance for his part in the coup of 1762 by walking behind the funeral carriage and carrying the Great Crown. Peter the III and Catherine II were rejoined in death, their caskets placed side by side in the Great Gallery of the Winter Palace. An engraving of the catafalque showed the Great Crown on Peter's casket, the small one on Catherine's. The funeral procession to the Cathedral of Peter and Paul on December 6 demoted Catherine one further step. The imperial crown rested on Peter III's coffin, while Catherine's was bare.[7]

The scene symbolically and posthumously dethroned Empress Catherine the Great as ruling monarch and restored the direct connection between Paul and his father. In this way, Paul created a symbolic fiction of continuity and hereditary right, and began a process of sacralization of the regalia, which in his reign were to become symbols of hereditary right rather than opulent symbols of the imperial nature of Russian monarchy. A series of engravings gave graphic statement to Paul's intended reshaping of the myth. The most elaborate is an allegory of family unity (fig. 27). The figure of "Filial piety" holds medallions of Peter III and Catherine in the heavens. Beneath, Paul is about to kiss the urn containing Peter III's dust. "History" records the moment in her chronicle, thus restoring the family to the imperial myth, while "the united peoples contemplate the event." A relief on the sacrificial altar shows Peter I and Peter III welcoming Catherine II, a latecomer to the Elysian fields. Another shows the exhumation of Peter III, while a third is a scene of Paul on his knees before Peter III who has risen from the dead.[8]

Paul's coronation celebration in April 1797 presented the image and model of authority that Paul believed would impose order on the state. If Elizabeth and Catherine had played the role of deliveratrix and benefactress of a rejoicing fatherland, Paul descended on Moscow as the bearer of order and stability, the embodiment of discipline that would eradicate the laxity of "the spirit of Potemkin." Before the arrival of the court, Moscow was trans-

---

[7] This description is based on Safonov, *Zaveshchanie Ekateriny II*, chap. 8, 218–28; *KFZ* (1796), 788–91, 821–24, 860–68.

[8] D. A. Rovinskii, *Podrobnyi slovar' russkikh gravirovannykh knig* (St. Petersburg, 1889), 2:1224–26; Shil'der, *Imperator Aleksandr Pervyi*, 1:141.

27. *Allegory of Family Unity.*

formed. "Everything was made Prussian to please the new tsar." His triumphal entry into Moscow on March 28 was not a Roman advent, but a display of Prussian domination and conquest. Even the court servants were forced to ride horseback wearing what struck onlookers as odd imitations of Prussian uniforms. There was little show of rejoicing, forced or otherwise. The *Wachtparaden* took place daily, even during Holy Week. The military world of Gatchina now was put on display in Moscow, and the spectators, watching the troops march in Prussian uniform and partake in Prussian-style maneuvers, imagined that they were in Potsdam or Berlin.[9]

Because no official description was published for Paul's coronation, the reconstruction of the event must come from memoirs and the brief entries of the court journals.[10] Contemporaries witnessed an entry procession that presented the emperor as military commander and father. Paul rode down the street, hat in hand, waving to onlookers, the first Russian emperor to ride horseback in a coronation entry. Behind him rode his two oldest sons, Alexander and Constantine. The weather was cold, and several of the courtiers became completely frozen and had to be removed from their horses.[11]

Paul introduced an important innovation when the procession was about to enter Red Square. He halted at the Chapel of the Iberian Mother-of-God, the shrine holding the popular miracle-working icon. He descended from his horse and prayed before the icon. This was the first display of piety in an imperial entry procession, and it became a precedent that all future emperors followed.[12] Classical metaphors still supplemented these religious images. At the chapel, two very young pupils of the Trinity Seminary delivered a prepared conversation. Paul first was angered by the interruption, then embraced the boys and awarded them swords which they were supposed to wear throughout the coronation ceremonies. One asked, "Is it he, do you know?" The other replied,

> How can we not recognize Apollo,
> When he descends from the sky for us![13]

[9] Shil'der, *Imperator Pavel Pervyi*, 341–43.

[10] There is only a brief description of the entry in *KFZ*, which took place, it indicates, "by the established ceremonial" (*KFZ* [1797], 542–44).

[11] Shil'der, *Imperator Pavel Pervyi*, 343; E. F. Komarovskii, *Zapiski* (St. Petersburg, 1914), 118; Zhmakin, "Koronatsii russkikh imperatorov," 534.

[12] This demonstration of reverence for a popular, local shrine may have been made as a special gesture of recognition for Platon. See *Sochineniia Derzhavina* (St. Petersburg, 1869), 2:41; The Iberian Mother-of-God brought considerable revenues to the coffers of the Moscow Metropolitan. The popularity of the icon, Rovinskii pointed out, had little to do either with its historical significance or miracles connected with it. Rather, it was its location, close to quarters of the merchantry, noted for their piety, and to governmental judicial offices (D. A. Rovinskii, *Russkie narodnye kartinki* [St. Petersburg, 1900], 1:316–17; *Moskva zlatoglavaia; religioznoe zodchestvo Moskvy v proshlom i nastoiashchem* [Paris, 1979], 18).

[13] *Sochineniia Derzhavina*, 2:39–42. Upon the emperor's return to Petersburg, Derzhavin

The coronation celebrations presented Paul as a supreme religious leader favored with signs of Christian designation from above. The entry into Moscow took place on Palm Saturday, thus approximating Christ's entry into Jerusalem. Coronation odes appealed especially to Paul's sense of religious grandiosity; they compared him to Christ, citing the words addressed to Christ, and earlier to the patriarch, "Blessed is he that cometh in the Lord's name." Platon, the metropolitan of Moscow and Paul's former tutor, uttered this phrase when he welcomed Paul at the parvis of the Assumption Cathedral.[14]

The coronation ceremonies were held on Easter Sunday, April 5, 1797, in keeping with Paul's sense of his elevated religious mission. His succession law for the first time formally described the Russian sovereign as "the Head of the Church." While this merely stated what had been de facto the case since Peter had abolished the patriarchate, Paul took his role literally and believed that communion in the sanctuary actually bestowed priestly status upon him.[15] Here, too, he was not content with native signs of authority. He displayed his ambitions to an international religious mission by wearing the *dalmatic*—a clerical shoulder piece worn by Holy Roman emperors and French kings at their coronations and by archbishops on special occasions. The dalmatic indicated both Paul's priestly status and his universal pretensions. In the weeks after the coronation, Paul announced his wish to officiate at religious services and had sumptuous vestments made for that purpose. He also wished to serve as confessor to members of the imperial family and to his ministers but was dissuaded by arguments from the Holy Synod citing orthodox prohibitions against sacraments being administered by one who had remarried.[16]

It was as religious leader that Paul issued, also on the day of the coronation, a manifesto that prohibited landlords from forcing their peasants to work on Sundays. The manifesto, which was read in the Chamber of Facets just before the coronation feast, declared that it was taught in the Scriptures

---

adapted an ancient Greek hymn to Apollo to honor the new emperor. He identified the coronation with the coming of the spring. The concluding lines were his own,

> On your own separate throne,
> Your radiant kind light!
> Rise before the greedy gazes,
> Choruses of joyous sons of the father,
> Sing of glory, happiness and love!

[14] Zhivov and Uspenskii, "Tsar' i Bog," 108–9; Comte Fédor Golovkine, *La cour et le règne de Paul Ier; portraits, souvenirs et anecdotes* (Paris, 1905), 144.

[15] Zhivov and Uspenskii, "Tsar' i Bog," 108–9; Golovkine, *La cour et le règne de Paul Ier*, 144.

[16] E. S. Shumigorskii, *Imperator Pavel I; zhizn' i tsarstvovanie* (St. Petersburg, 1907), 121–22; Belozerskaia, "Tsarskoe venchanie v Rossii," 30; Golovkine, *La cour et le règne de Paul Ier*, 149; Zhivov and Uspenskii, "Tsar i Bog," 98; Karnovich, "Koronovanie gosudarei," 39; *KFZ* (1798), 1615.

that the seventh day of the week should be devoted to God, and that Paul considered it his duty to secure "the precise and unfailing implementation of this law." He also added that the remaining six days should be or could be divided evenly between work on peasants' and landlords' fields, a prescription whose purpose, meaning, and practical effects remain unclear.[17]

The proclamation of the Law of Succession took place after the communion. In an extraordinary gesture, Paul stepped forth and declaimed the law from the steps of the throne. The presentation of the law at the coronation sanctified it as a holy writ, the beginning of a new era. Paul then returned through the holy doors, placed the law in a silver arc, and declared that it would remain in the cathedral "for preservation for future times."[18] Paul thus created a new relic that would command respect and worship as an embodiment of supreme authority. For Peter and his successors, the regalia had been expressions of their Western character and the wealth, and therefore progress, of the Russian state. For Paul, the physical objects contained the sacred essence of monarchy commanding unquestioning obedience to the power of his descendants. In this sense, he returned to a Muscovite faith in the physical items of the regalia as the repository of the dynasty's charisma.

The law took the form, unprecedented in Russia, of a familial agreement.[19] It consisted of a covenant between husband and wife, which Paul and Maria Fedorovna had composed in 1788. The decree carried both signatures. The families of the German states often made such agreements, but they were not issued from the throne with only two signatures. It thus represented an element of private law given public force by the sovereign will. On the basis of their agreement, the emperor and empress designated their son Alexander heir, "by natural law." The statute introduced what was called the "Austrian system" of succession: male primogeniture of succession, with women following in line only in the absence of a male heir. The law required the ruler's permission for marriages of all those in line for the throne. It also spelled out the organization and conditions of regencies in case the heir had not reached maturity, in order to prevent a recurrence of the events that had kept Paul from the throne in 1762.

Despite the ecclesiastical trappings, the law still was expressed in the utilitarian rhetoric of the eighteenth century. The principle of heredity derived neither from religion or tradition. Justified by "natural law," it ensured "a tranquillity of the State," which was "based on a firm law of inheritance upon which every right-thinking person is certain." If Peter's succession law defended the monarchy against the scheming and perfidious son, Paul's took

---

[17] *PSZ*, no. 17,909, April 5, 1797; on the significance of the decree, see M. V. Klochkov, *Ocherki pravitel'stvennoi deiatel'nosti vremeni Pavla I* (Petrograd, 1916), 528–69.

[18] Belozerskaia, "Tsarskoe venchanie v Rossii," 31; Zhmakin, "Koronatsii russkikh imperatorov," 536–37; Nol'de, B. "Zakony osnovnye v russkom prave," *Pravo*, no. 9 (1913): 526, 532, 541.

[19] *PSZ*, no. 17,910, April 5, 1797; B. Nol'de, "Zakony osnovnye v russkom prave," *Pravo*, no. 9 (1913): 524–26.

care to support the claims of the son and to leave no room for the pretensions of an ambitious consort. Love now was to be defined, not as the mutual
affection of sovereign and ruled but as dedication and constancy, to be embodied in the members of the imperial family who identified their destinies
with those of the fatherland. The conclusion declared that the law provided
"proof before the whole World, of Our love for the Fatherland, the love and
harmony of our marriage, and love for Our Children and Descendants."

The Statute of the Imperial Family, promulgated the same day, made the
connection between the well-being of the imperial family and the well-being
of the state an explicit premise of Russian autocracy. It established the "increase of the Sovereign family (*familiia*)" as one of the grounds for the "illustrious condition" of the state. Russia had experienced the principal blessing,
"seeing the inheritance of the Throne confirmed in Our Family, which may
the All-High perpetuate to eternity." The statute specified the estates and
revenues that would accrue to the members of the family, the titles they held,
and the rules of inheritance they would observe. It established an Appanage
Department to manage the family's estates and income. On the day of the
coronation, Paul took another step honoring the family. He revived the Holstein Order of St. Anna that had been founded by Peter III.[20]

Paul's clerical aspirations did not overshadow his military predilections.
Rather, they indicated that he saw little distinction between the types of
governmental service and obedience. He appointed clerics to honorary orders, a practice that prompted angry objections from his teacher, the metropolitan Platon. He wore his sword during the ceremonies of crowning
and anointment. Only a reproof from Platon, "Here we bring bloodless sacrifices," deterred him from wearing it into the sanctuary when he took
communion.[21]

The fusion of commander and cleric took place in Paul's vision, growing
out of his boyhood dreams of himself as leader of a medieval knightly order
of Russian noblemen. On the day of the coronation, he issued a Statute on
Russian Imperial Orders, proclaiming their symbolic importance for his
reign.[22] The exalted rhetoric of the opening phrases recalled the glories of
the chivalric tradition.

> Soon after the time when the light of Evangelical teaching illuminated the uni-
> verse and when the true faith conquered error, Societies of Knights were foun-
> ded for the defence of piety and innocence and to promote deeds pleasing to
> God and useful to humanity. These, according to time and circumstances, being
> protected by the Supreme Authority, grew further and further.

Russia did not, however, have to look to foreign examples, the preamble
went on, for Peter the Great had established such orders, an allusion to the
orders of St. Andrew and St. Catherine. Paul thus confused the medieval

---

[20] *PSZ*, no. 17,906, April 5, 1797.
[21] Shil'der, *Imperator Pavel Pervyi*, 343; Papmehl, *Metropolitan Platon*, 70.
[22] *PSZ*, no. 17,908, April 5, 1797.

connotation of knightly orders with their more recent function as a reward for service to the absolute monarch. The orders would transform the noble-man's service to the state into Christian service, in which the emperor was the principal priest as well as sovereign. The statute did not neglect to indi-cate the great religious significance of the timing of the decree, "on the very day marking for every Christian the seal of Our common Salvation and on which We by Our Crowning for the All-Russian Tsardom and by Our Sa-cred Anointment are made worthy to receive the blessing of the Most Holy Spirit."

The statute went on to describe a reorganization of all these honorary orders into a single general order, "like a single body." In imitation of a Western custom, the emperor himself would confer the honor after touching the shoulders of each recipient three times with a sword. The statute also lists the emoluments, the number of serfs, that would be attached to the various ranks of the order. It indicated the charitable organizations to be placed under its care—foundling homes, hospitals, poor houses. Cavaliers of the order were supposed to visit educational and charitable institutions during their travels and make recommendations for improvements to the emperor.

Paul's passion for ceremonies was reflected in the elaborate prescriptions for the holiday celebrations of the various orders, for the rules for dress, and for the wearing of medals and ribbons included in the statute. He intro-duced a new holiday for all the branches of his new order, to take place on November 8, the day of the Archangel Michael. The Archangel was de-scribed with the term frequently used in orthodox texts, the *Sviatoi Ar-khistratig* (roughly the "Supreme Strategist of the Heavens") Michael. The Archangel, the heavenly champion of the militant faith, was a central inspir-ing symbol for Paul's mission.[23] The statute indicated that the new holiday was to take place in the Church of the Archangel Michael, in the Michael Castle, the construction of which Paul had begun to plan. Thus the knights of Paul's order took their place as a contingent of the church militant en-gaged in the struggle for universal salvation.

The postcoronation events were staged to present imposing spectacles of Paul's authority rather than of the joy of subjects ostensibly delivered from danger. Paul turned ceremonies into an enforced worship of his person, using the regalia to signify his exalted office. He wore the crown and impe-rial mantle at court processions and during the prolonged ceremonies of congratulations after the coronation. He continued this practice during his reign, holding crowning ceremonies during religious services on holidays and before he received communion.[24] He had the regalia reworked to make

---

[23] This dedication to the Archangel was explained by a vision of the Archangel Michael that a guard claimed to have seen on the evening of Paul's accession (Shumigorskii, *Imperator Pavel I*, 200).

[24] Roderick E. McGrew, "A Political Portrait of Paul I from the Austrian and English Diplo-matic Archives," *Jahrbücher für Geschichte Osteuropas*, Band 18, Heft 4 (December 1970),

them even more lavish than they had been. The new scepter of gold was studded with diamonds, the enormous Orlov diamond fixed at the end. The sapphire orb also glistened with diamonds. Catherine's crown was enlarged, and the small pearls replaced with larger ones. These three items became the traditional regalia for nineteenth-century emperors.[25]

In this respect, Paul was unlike Frederick the Great, whose manner was one of reserve and simplicity. Paul admired the elaborate ceremonies of the French court, which better defined the hierarchical relationship that he wished to establish between himself and the nobility. He upheld monarchical authority by elaborate and prolonged displays of homage and deference from the elite. The announcement of the awards of orders, promotions, and grants of serfs before the banquet turned into a painful show of deference as Paul himself, from the throne, affixed the medals and then had the recipients kneel and kiss his hand. The audiences on the days after the coronation were accompanied with elaborate and trying rules of etiquette invented by the emperor. The grand master of ceremonies, Czartoryski wrote, treated the courtiers like recruits, disciplining them to bow, kiss the emperor's or empress's hand, and withdraw precisely as commanded. The rules were extended to the balls and other celebrations, which also turned into tedious exercises in obedience.[26] But Paul's severity did not extend to his own personal morality, which continued to reflect the hedonistic spirit of the previous century. During the festivities, he amused himself with many of the young ladies present. One of them who caught his fancy, Anna Lopukhina, would later become his mistress; her father was shortly appointed procurator-general.[27]

After the coronation, Paul contrived excuses for additional ceremonies. He moved back and forth from the Kremlin to his suburban residence as often as possible in order to multiply the occasions for processions. He issued and rigorously enforced a rule that required all passersby to stop and kneel before all members of the imperial family whom they encountered. He tried the patience of the court with new ceremonies of his own invention. The French ambassador wrote, "It is unbelievable to what degree Paul loves great Ceremonies, the importance he attaches to them, and the time he uses at them." The grand master of ceremonies, he remarked, had become one of the most important posts in the empire.[28]

Paul fused the symbols of religious, military, and court supremacy, trying

---

515; Shil'der, *Imperator Pavel Pervyi*, 347–48, 377. See *KFZ*, vol. 1, no. 6 (1798), 44–45, for descriptions of Paul's appearance crowned at religious services (Duffy, *The Military Life of Frederick the Great*, 290).

[25] *BE*, vol. 31:319, vol. 51:445–46; xxxi.

[26] Golovine, *Memoirs*, 141; Shil'der, *Imperator Pavel Pervyi*, 347–48; Czartoryski, *Memoirs*, 155.

[27] Shil'der, *Imperator Pavel Pervyi*, 350; Eidel'man, *Gran' vekov*, 163.

[28] McGrew, "A Political Portrait of Paul I," 515; McGrew, *Paul I of Russia*, 213; Golovine, *Memoirs*, 153; Golovkine, *La cour et le règne de Paul Ier*, 148.

to exalt his power as an object of worship as well as obedience. His *Wacht-paraden* continued to take place every morning; exceptions were made only for his visits to the New Jerusalem Monastery and the Trinity Monastery. The military displays culminated with a parade and religious ceremony that took place on April 29, Mid-Pentecost (*Prepoloveniia Piatidesiatnitsy*). Paul commanded the parade in the Kremlin dressed in the dalmatic and crown. He was the first and only Russian emperor to command troops in regalia, and clad in clerical, sacerdotal, as well as imperial dress. When Metropolitan Platon blessed him, he decorated his teacher with the Order of St. Andrew.[29]

THE REPRESENTATIONS OF REGIMENTATION

During Paul's reign, the parade began to take on new meanings. It became a demonstration of the strength of the established order and an imperial cere-mony in its own right. The Blessing of the Waters on January 6, 1798, gives us a sense of the parade as a part of a religious ceremony. In the morning of January 6, 1798, the court journal reports, guard units lined up in the halls of the Winter Palace next to their regimental standards. Shortly after 9:00 A.M., Paul rode out with his generals and flugel-adjutants for his *Wacht-parade*, then "deigned to remain with His army, taking command and as-signing places" opposite the palace and all along the nearby streets. Grand Duke Alexander also commanded battalions. Meanwhile, the empress and the grand duchesses followed the Cavalier Guards and court ranks in proces-sion through the halls of the palace into the Palace Church for the mass led by Gavriil, the metropolitan of Novgorod and St. Petersburg. They were followed by the ladies-in-waiting and other highly ranked women of the court. They then joined a procession of the cross, led by the clergy in cha-subles carrying icons, which moved out to the Jordan landing on the Neva, where the rite of benediction took place. During the ceremony, Paul and Alexander remained with the troops. When the ceremony was over, they stood before the palace watching the regiments pass in review, a parade that lasted more than two hours. They returned for the drinking of holy water and dinner. In the evening, notables gathered to bring congratulations to the members of the royal family.[30]

The nonchalant, relaxed attitude of the Catherinian celebration is clearly gone, replaced by a regimented, military manner reminiscent of Peter. Like Peter, Paul remained with his troops during the blessing. But now the parade has become the dominating spectacle. Covering the squares and streets near the palace, the immense military assemblage gives the blessing a display of secular recognition that marks its importance as a state event. The parade

---

[29] Shil'der, *Imperator Pavel Pervyi*, 349; Snegirev, *Zhizn' Platona*, 1:96–97.

[30] *KFZ*, vol. 1 (1798), 33–40; the ceremony in 1797 followed a similar order, with Con-stantine Pavlovich also commanding the troops (*KFZ* [1797], 41–50).

became an essential element of holiday celebrations under Paul and Alexander I.[31]

The parade served as the ceremonial center of Paul's government, the setting where his power was displayed most dramatically. At each morning's *Wachtparade*, he received reports and announced favors and punishments. He made no exception for religious holidays, such as Easter Sunday or Christmas and, according to Roderick E. McGrew, spent two to three hours a day on the parade ground. He stood with bare head and without overcoat wearing a simple green uniform even in frigid weather and expected his trembling officers to do the same. In 1800 he issued a law prescribing the precise rules for the command and movement of troops in the *Wachtparade*, indicating that the details of parades were a fit subject for legislation.[32]

The drill field became his means to inculcate the nobility with a service ethos of absolute obedience. In some respects, Paul tried to enhance their position. He bolstered their exclusive position by prohibiting the promotion of commoners to officer ranks; he rewarded his favorites with huge numbers of serfs. But he also took measures to create an obedient corps of servitors. To replace the privileged elite of Catherine's reign, he insisted that the young noblemen who held court sinecures as chamberlains had to serve in a civil or military position. He disregarded various terms of the Charter of the Nobility, restoring compulsory service and forbidding the registry of infants in the guards and other evasions of the education requirements. He tried to make the local elective offices introduced by Catherine appointed positions. He eliminated provincial assemblies and withdrew the rights of personal petition and freedom from corporal punishment. The sentences he imposed for violations were severe, including loss of estates. By trying to strike his own image as the guardian of civic virtue, Paul offended the nobility's own sense of dignity, which under Catherine had become part of their cultural identity as Europeans.[33]

Paul's journeys brought his barracks scenario to the provinces. Whereas Catherine's travels were occasions for the display of mutual concord and love, Paul's trips were tours of inspection, designed to ensure the efficacy of subordination. On his return to St. Petersburg after the coronation, he conducted morning guards' parades and drills in the Russian towns along the way, then visited Vilnius and Grodno, where the condition of the troops pleased him. But in Kovno he found that his system of discipline had not been implemented and ordered Arakcheev to remain to train the troops properly. Arakcheev subjected them to harsh and unrelenting discipline for six weeks. To maintain his personal direction over the military administration during his trip, Paul established a special Military-Campaign Chancellery, staffed by his adjutants. He continued to use this as an agency of per-

---

[31] On the transformation of the parade in Russia from military exercise into ceremony, see Beyrau, *Militär und Gesellschaft*, 156–59.

[32] Shil'der, *Imperator Pavel Pervyi*, 287–88; McGrew, *Paul I of Russia*, 228.

[33] Kliuchevskii, *Sochineniia*, 5:190; Eidel'man, *Gran' vekov*, 86–104.

sonal supervision after the trip. The chancellery provided the nucleus for
Alexander I's imperial suite.[34]

Paul took special trips to ascertain that the Prussian military regulations
had been faithfully adopted. In 1798 he announced that he would visit Moscow and then proceed to Kazan to review the units in the Orenburg Military
Inspection. The news of the impending visit terrified the local commanders.
Traveling with the grand dukes Alexander and Constantine, he stopped in
Moscow for a massive review of nearly twenty-three thousand troops, which
so delighted him that it brought tears to his eyes. The review was followed by
three days of maneuvers that left the emperor, if few others, very pleased. He
declared that he felt honored to be "the founder and the chief of such an
army" and rewarded many officers with promotions and decorations.[35]

The accounts of Paul's journey indicate that he made no appeal for demonstrations of acclaim either from the elite or the "people." On his stops, he
exchanged cordial greetings with members of estates, but otherwise avoided
large gatherings. He prohibited ceremonial meetings and crowds of people
during his stay in Kazan and spent most of his time reviewing parades and
military exercises. But he did not have the people dispersed who gathered
before his house, and he seemed pleased by their enthusiasm. The reports
indicate that he appreciated the feelings expressed at receptions given by the
estates and a ball given by the nobility. At the ball, he and Grand Duke
Alexander, according to a contemporary journal, "uninterruptedly" danced
polonaises and contre-dances, "favoring many ladies and maidens in this
way." He was extremely gratified at a gathering with music in the court
garden. Aside from the drills and the ladies, he did not take special note of
local conditions. He announced that he had heard that the people in Kazan
were crude, but that he found "many who were well-mannered and enlightened, and especially among the ladies," and that he had found "few of the
like in Moscow."[36]

Paul made the principle of disciplinary subordination exemplified by the
parade ground a principle of governmental organization to be applied
ruthlessly and literally throughout the state apparatus. He imposed what
John Keep has called a "militarization of government," subordinating administrative offices to the discipline of his personal command. In the first
months of his reign, he issued decrees on the resolution of cases in state
offices, and asked for petitions to be addressed directly to himself. Corporal
punishment was introduced for wrongdoers of all estates. He took measures
to limit excessive expenditures among the nobility. The severe discipline instilled fear throughout the administration. Wrongdoers from all classes of
the population were summoned and sentenced without regard to law in the

---

[34] Shil'der, *Imperator Pavel Pervyi*, 355–56; *IGK, ts. Al. I,* 14–15.

[35] N. P. Zagoskin, *Imperator Pavel Pervyi v Kazani* (Kazan, 1893), 7–13; Shil'der, *Imperator Pavel Pervyi*, 386.

[36] Zagoskin, *Imperator Pavel Pervyi v Kazani,* 17, 23; Bartenev, *Osmnadtsatyi vek,* 4:466,
468; Shil'der, 384–88.

Senate's Secret Expedition, which was directly responsible to the emperor.[37]

Paul's efforts to control expressed a reform impulse, the desire to correct and improve by enlightened means. He took the first steps toward centralizing the governmental system in institutions that could bring supervision of local officials, a goal later realized in Alexander I's ministerial system.[38] But centralized control and regulation lacked any guiding principle, and the artifice of law became for Paul a means to direct everything himself. It was a crude effort to follow the example of Frederick the Great as he understood it. He tried personally to regulate everything down to the exact hours that governmental offices worked and the granting of leaves. The passion for regulation became an end in itself, an indiscriminate fascination with uniformity. His fear of revolution led him to prohibit the import of foreign books and to forbid travel abroad. Any straying from the prescribed norm was also considered a transgression of the bounds of legality. During 1799, the police chief of St. Petersburg, clearly at Paul's instance, forbade dancing the waltz and wearing certain styles: toupees over the forehead, any bright ribbons on women's attire that might resemble the ribbons of honorary orders, large curls, sideburns, as well as German coats and blue women's frock coats (*siurtuki*) with white skirts. During Paul's reign, more than five times as many laws were decreed per month than under Peter the Great, and twice as many as under Catherine. In 1797 alone, Paul issued forty-eight thousand orders. "The ardor for reform," the English ambassador wrote, "or more properly for change, extends even to the Provinces, where everything as in the Capital wears a military appearance."[39]

The all-seeing, all-controlling ruler, portrayed in Russov's ode, became Paul's principal image of power. This resembled the "ocular imperialism" of Louis XIV, in which the king's eyes became a metaphor for his control over the kingdom. But here the sovereign remained the center of attention even as he looked out upon his subjects, and the "omnispective" image became all embracing.[40] In Derzhavin's ode for New Year's day in 1797, there is no golden age imagery, no message of deliverance. The poem is full of straightforward praise for Paul's acts and the enormous tasks he had undertaken. Paul, following Atlas's model, had lifted the earth and, with steps of a giant, had entered the temple of honor fearlessly. He threatened opponents not with war, but with an olive branch. "He quiets the impudent with his gaze." He works to introduce speedy justice. He is both "severe and just," and yet merciful in his forgiveness. Derzhavin compares Paul to Marcus Aurelius and Titus.[41]

---

[37] McGrew, "A Political Portrait," 514; Keep, "Paul I and the Militarization of Government," 91–99.

[38] McGrew, *Paul I of Russia*, 210–24.

[39] McGrew, "A Political Portrait," 513–15; Eidel'man, *Gran' vekov*, 61, 68; Keep, "Paul I and the Militarization of Government," 100.

[40] Foucault, *Discipline and Punish*, 187–89; Apostolidés, *Le roi machine*, 46–47.

[41] Derzhavin, *Sochineniia*, 2:10–19.

Paul was guided by this image in his relations with his family, as well as the administration and the army. Indeed, he regarded his family as little more than another instance in the military-governmental hierarchy. His sons, the grand dukes Alexander and Constantine, stood at his side during many of the parades. According to the abbé Georgel, who visited Russia in 1799–1800, the grand dukes had to request the emperor's permission to see their mother, the empress. Alexander was placed in charge of the Seme-novskii Guards' Regiments, and later was appointed military governor of St. Petersburg. But he left the onerous task of introducing Prussian order into the regiment to Arakcheev, who also prepared his detailed daily reports on the capital.[42] Paul treated Maria Fedorovna as little more than an appur-tenance of power. There was none of Peter the Great's pretense of making his wife a companion in arms. Instead, he appointed her director of various charitable activities, a mission that she pursued with dedication throughout her life.[43]

Paul's dream was to bring discipline and morality to the nobility through a great Christian order. He had announced his plans at the coronation, and they grew only more grandiose during his reign. He demonstrated the uni-versal character of Russian sovereignty by assuming the role of defender of all Christianity, Roman Catholic as well as Orthodox. The occasion for this role arose when he accepted the offices first of protector, then of grand mas-ter of the knights at their request, after the island had fallen to the French. He wrote to the pope explaining that his acceptance of the grand mastership was part of his struggle against French aggression and his attempt to pre-serve the European nobility; it enabled him to "render the most signal ser-vice to the Universe." He introduced the Maltese Cross into the Russian Imperial Shield.[44]

The rites of the order provided Paul with another form of ceremonial exal-tation, a lofty display of the military-clerical signs of preeminence. The ritual of presentation of the knights' convention on November 29, 1797, was long and elaborate. Paul, wearing the costume of the order, stood on a dais beside a table on which lay the orb and scepter. He used the symbolism of the order to enhance the image of dynasty by knighting his sons, the grand dukes Alexander and Constantine, and bestowing the Order's grand cross upon the empress. Assembled for the ceremony were members of the government, the clergy, and the highest ranks of the court.[45]

At first, Paul acted as protector only of a Russian priory that admitted no one but Roman Catholic noblemen. In 1798, when he accepted the title of

[42] Eidel'man, *Gran' vekov*, 65–66; Jenkins, *Arakcheev*, 61–62.

[43] David Ransel, *Mothers of Misery; Child Abandonment in Russia* (Princeton, N.J., 1988), 70–78; *BE*, 22:867; 36:638–39.

[44] Roderick E. McGrew, "Paul I and the Knights of Malta," in Hugh Ragsdale, ed., *Paul I: A Reassessment of His Life and Reign* (Pittsburgh, 1979): 59–60; Eidel'man, *Gran' vekov*, 79–80.

[45] McGrew, "Paul I and the Knights of Malta," 50; Snegirev, *Zhizn' Platona*, 1:93.

Grand Master of the Order, he introduced a second priory, open to Russian noblemen. The second priory, McGrew concluded, was another means to transmit Paul's ideal of aristocratic service. Paul opened ninety-eight "commanderies," or chapters, for Russian Orthodox noblemen and filled them with great numbers of cavaliers of the order. The Knights of Malta began to overshadow all the other orders in Paul's dream of creating a single Russian chivalric order. He expected that it would indoctrinate the nobility in the principles of self-sacrifice, duty, and discipline. The laws and statutes of the order, Paul declared, "inspire love of virtue, contribute to strong morals, strengthen the bonds of subordination, and offer a powerful remedy against thoughtless love of novelty and unbridled license in thinking."[46]

Russia had known no knightly, chivalric tradition. The Knights of Malta introduced a grandiose Western ethical code to elevate the monarch and the elite and justify their precedence. The rites transformed the emperor and the knights into Russian counterparts of the crusading orders of the Middle Ages. He walked, in crown and full regalia, in procession with the guards' officers, who were dressed in uniforms of the knights—black velvet cloaks embroidered with the Maltese Cross. He then replaced the imperial crown with the crown of the grand master and donned a crimson felt dalmatic embroidered with pearls. He also wore a silk galoon embroidered with scenes of the passions of Christ. We see Paul in Vladimir Borovikovskii's portrait, wearing crown, mantle, dalmatic, and the Order of St. Andrei, over the Maltese Cross (fig. 28). The noblemen who were present felt uneasy. "There could be nothing stranger than the disguising of the Russian court as Maltese Knights," wrote Count Alexander Ribaupierre. Czartoryski compared it to a masquerade "which made the spectators and even the performers smile."[47]

At court ceremonies, Paul's model remained Louis XIV. The fascination for processions and particularly the ceremonial kissing of the monarch's hands, the *baisemain*, which often became crowded and unruly, continued throughout his reign. Gatchina, Paul's domain before his accession, became the principal scene of his court displays, spectacles, and celebrations. S. Kaznakov estimated that the emperor and empress spent all but three or four hours of the day before the eyes of the court. "All the merriment of Versailles and the Trianon" took place in its precincts, General Nicholas Sablukov recalled.[48] Gatchina became the theater of the family principle proclaimed at

[46] McGrew, "Paul I and the Knights of Malta," 50, 61–62; McGrew, "A Political Portrait," 521–22; I. G. Spasskii, *Inostrannye i russkie ordena do 1917 goda* (Leningrad, 1963), 29–30, 119.

[47] S. Kaznakov, "Pavlovskaia Gatchina," *Starye Gody* (July–September 1914): 163–64; Czartoryski, *Gran' vekov*, 189; O. A. Medvedkova, "Russkii paradnyi portret rubezha XVIII–XIX vekov: transformatsiia obraza," in *Aktual'nye problemy otechestvennogo iskusstva* (Moscow, 1990), 42.

[48] Golovkine, *La cour et le règne de Paul Ier*, 134–36; Sablukov's statement is cited by Kaznakov, "Pavlovskaia Gatchina," 141.

28. *Emperor Paul I.* Painting by Vladimir Borovikovskii.

the coronation. Paul's first visit after his accession was on his return trip from Moscow in the summer of 1797, and he used the opportunity to bring his family there for their first extended period together. Catherine had kept the grand dukes Alexander and Constantine away from Paul. Now the entire family participated in the presentations and celebrations.[49] Paul and the grand dukes devoted their mornings to military exercises. The afternoon and evening were taken up by audiences, "assemblies" (*sobraniia*), and sometimes plays or operas. All functions were governed by a severe, unrelenting etiquette devised by the empress.[50]

With the new importance assigned to the imperial family, Paul celebrated the "imperial days," the birthdays and name days of the members, with especial solemnity and magnificence. The congratulatory audiences began the evening before. Then there were diplomatic audiences and a "parade banquet" with chamberlains standing behind the chairs and serving the members of the imperial family. The balls in the evening were opulent affairs. The grand dukes partnered the grand duchesses to open the dances. The empress generally played cards, and the emperor engaged in conversations. They joined only the polonaise, the stately procession through the rooms of the palace.[51]

In 1799 the show of dynastic, familial unity was performed at Gatchina before a foreign audience. The weddings of Elena Pavlovna to Frederick-Ludwig, the Duke of Mecklenburg-Schwerin, and Alexandra Pavlovna to Archduke Joseph the Palatine of Hungary, brought an assemblage of European royalty and Russian and Western aristocracy. Foreign princes with their entourages, ambassadors, as well as the entire Petersburg court, crowded into Gatchina. There were countless balls and one masquerade. The grand dukes and duchesses gave their own balls that were smaller and less constrained.[52]

At Gatchina, Paul also showed himself a successor to Louis XIV in the realm of romantic conquest. By 1798, Lopukhina had replaced Nelidova as the chief mistress, awakening the empress's apprehensions about the loss of her position at court. Paul displayed his mistress proudly at the balls of Gatchina; the liaison clearly was not platonic. She loved to dance at balls and even performed the waltz, which Paul now permitted, despite its connotations of licentiousness. While she danced, he stood at the side listening for slights to her or himself, which could bring immediate disgrace. Balls and celebrations, Czartoryski wrote, were occasions when "one risked losing his liberty."[53]

But amid the circumstances, Paul constantly feared for his life. By the beginning of 1801, his distrust of his son, Alexander, as well as others near

[49] Kaznakov, "Pavlovskaia Gatchina," 126–27.
[50] Ibid., 134–38.
[51] Ibid., 139–41.
[52] Ibid., 151–58.
[53] Ibid., 149–50; Shumigorskii, *Imperator Pavel*, 152–58.

him, had become all-absorbing, undermining his faith in his dynastic principles. In October 1799 he had designated Constantine Pavlovich "Tsesarevich," although, according to his own Law of the Imperial Family, this title was to be held only by the heir to the throne. In 1801 he prepared a document to legitimize sons born to him from a mistress, Iur'eva, and spoke of banishing the empress. He mentioned to Maria Fedorovna that he was thinking of officially adopting her thirteen-year-old nephew, Eugene of Württemburg, who had won his favor, implying that he meant to make him heir. According to one memoir, Paul discovered a copy of Voltaire's *Brutus* on Alexander's desk and brandished before him Peter's decree condemning Aleksei Petrovich.[54] The plans for a stable dynasty were foundering on Paul's own fears and court intrigues.

Paul had planned his own Petersburg palace, the Michael Castle, to afford himself security from attacks and to express his medieval Christian vision. Over his family's objections, he moved from the Winter Palace to the Michael Castle on February 1, 1801. Appropriate festivities marked the event, including receptions, an opera, and a masquerade.[55] The court was most uncomfortable in the gloomy forbidding halls of the new palace, its plaster still dripping with moisture.

But the palace fulfilled Paul's vision. The architect Vincenzo Brenna gave the forbidding red building the aspect of a medieval castle, an impregnable fortress surrounded by a moat and guarded by twenty cannons. Three drawbridges, protected by guards, provided the only access. In the center of the parade ground before the palace, Paul placed Carlo Bartolommeo Rastrelli's equestrian statue of Peter, which had been kept hidden in a shed for half a century.[56] The statue presents a fierce and intimidating image of Peter as commander (fig. 29). The inscription, "From a Great-Grandson to a Great-Grand Father," was Paul's answer to Catherine's statement of descent on Falconet's statue.

The principal facade introduced the theme of the palace (fig. 30).[57] The inscription on the frieze, "Thy house is like the Lord's shrine for thy lifetime," was taken from Rinaldi's unfinished St. Isaac's Cathedral and immediately made known the religious reverence due the new residence. Two large obelisks with elaborate armatures at the side of the gate emphasize the mili-

[54] Eidel'man, *Gran' vekov*, 240–41; Shil'der, *Imperator Pavel Pervyi*, 478–79; E. P. Karnovich, *Tsesarevich Konstantin Pavlovich* (St. Petersburg, 1899), 74. The title was given as a reward for Constantine's exploits with Suvorov in Italy and Switzerland, but was motivated, in part, by Paul's suspicions of Alexander. I thank Mikhail Safonov for his observations on this matter.

[55] *KFZ*, vol. 1 (1801), 102–13.

[56] Grabar', *Istoriia russkogo iskusstva* (1909), 5:468–73; Brumfield, *A History of Russian Architecture*, 287–90; Hamilton, *Art and Architecture of Russia*, 314–15, 439; B. N. Kalinin and P. P. Iurevich, *Pamiatniki Leningrada i ego okrestnosti* (Leningrad, 1959), 124–26.

[57] The only description of the original interior is August Kotzebue, "Kratkoe opisanie Imperatorskogo Mikhailovskogo Dvortsa," *Russkii Arkhiv*, vol. 8, nos. 4–5 (1870): 969–98. The description is excerpted in Shil'der, *Imperator Pavel Pervyi*, 446–60.

29. *Monument to Peter I*, St. Petersburg. Sculptor, Carlo Bartolommeo Rastrelli.
Photograph by William Brumfield.

tary and imperial grandeur of Paul's achievement. The relief on the pediment makes clear that Panin's instruction of his pupil was not completely in vain: an allegorical figure of History enters the glorious deeds of the reign on her tablet.

The other elements of architecture and design reflected the capriciousness

30. Facade of Michael Castle, St. Petersburg. Architect, Vincenzo Brenna.
Photograph by William Brumfield.

of Paul's moods and tastes. The warren of intricate passageways inside, designed to secure Paul from attack, also recalled a medieval castle. On the
other hand, the principal halls had the splendor and breadth of eighteenth-
century palaces. Classical art was well represented. On the roof, female figures in crowns held the shields of Russian territories. There were elaborate
borrowings from Rome—statues of gods, a Laocoon, a Raphael gallery. Yet,
within the halls, as the playwright Kotzebue noted in his description, there
were jarring inconsistencies. The Laocoon gallery, in addition to a Roman
copy of the statue, had tapestries of St. Peter fishing, Christ driving the mon-
gers and money changers from the temple, the resurrection of Lazarus, and
Mary Magdalene at Christ's feet. Opposite these tapestries, Kotzebue was
surprised to see paintings of Diana and Endimion and of Amour and Psyche.
The ceilings, following the pattern of the Baroque, depicted allegories of
virtue and power. The theme of impending redemption was suggested by the
name of the entry gate, Resurrection (*Voskresenskii*), and also a Resurrection

Hall, in which the ceremonies of the Order of the Knights of Malta were to take place.[58]

Paul's own bedroom was hung with numerous landscapes. One corner held a painting he particularly cherished, a portrait of a knight standard bearer. The opposite corner was occupied by a plaster statue and a painting of Frederick the Great. A small camp bed stood in the middle—following the example of Frederick the Great. Above it hung a painting of an angel by Guido Reni. It was amid these signs of virtue, power, and holiness that Paul met his death by assassination, at the hands of leaders of his military forces, on the night of March 11, 1801, just over five weeks after he had moved to his castle.

In subsequent decades, Russians passed by the Michael Castle without daring to look and feared speaking of what had occurred there.[59] Paul's reign and his death left embarrassing memories for his successors. He had established the legal grounding of conservative dynastic rule as it came to be known in nineteenth-century Russia.[60] He was the progenitor of the ruling house. But he had also violated the traditions and forms of representation of Russian monarchy. He was remembered as a despot who had acted according to personal whim and ignored the rights and dignity of the members of the nobility. He had banished them from the circles of power and relegated them to the position of underlings. He had denied their identity as members of the ruling elite, comrades-in-arms of the conqueror. Paul I was a founder, but a founder manqué, whose furious and terrifying reign provided a distressing first chapter to the history of nineteenth-century monarchy.

[58] The Resurrection Hall is not named by Kotzebue. He describes it briefly before the Throne Room (Kotzebue, "Kratkoe opisanie," 975–76). I am grateful to Mikhail Safonov for this information.

[59] Le Marquis de Custine, *La russie en 1839* (Brussels, 1843), 2:53–56.

[60] For a discussion of Paul's role in the nineteenth century, see McGrew, *Paul I of Russia*, 354–57.

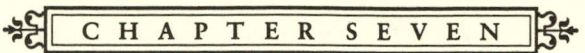

CHAPTER SEVEN

The Angel on the Throne

You shine like a divine angel
With goodness and beauty,
And your first words promise
Catherine's golden age.
Days of Happiness, Joy, Glory,
When the most wise statutes,
Maintained tranquillity,
And abroad, Russia was glorified,
Citizens sowed in peace,
And a citizen was a hero.

—*Nicholas Karamzin, "To His Imperial Majesty Alexander I,
All-Russian Autocrat, On His Ascension to the Throne," 1801*[1]

ACCESSION AND CORONATION

Alexander I confronted the fundamental contradiction between the image of
the Russian monarch as the realization of the highest values of the West and
the nature of Russian autocracy. Catherine's *Nakaz* could remain a figment
of the myth, an ideal guiding the empress and her servitors; Alexander, impatient with idealized forms, expected to take steps to change Russian government according to the wisdom of the philosophes. The ideal monarch, he
had learned from his reading of *Télémaque* and the historians of antiquity,
could contain his passions, forbear from power, in order to act in behalf of
his citizens. La Harpe had taught him the notion of "true monarchy," according to which the sovereign ruled, but only on the basis of fixed immutable laws. But the French Revolution had thrown doubt on the possibility of
increasing the people's happiness without the participation of the people
themselves. The absolute monarch's attainment of the enlightenment ideal
now involved the end of absolute monarchy, as well as the end of serfdom. In
the first decade of his reign, Alexander introduced governmental reforms,
but his efforts to promote legality and change the serf system reached an
impasse. After the Napoleonic wars, his gaze rose to the heavens, and while
not abandoning hope for reforms, he began to strive for the spiritual rather

[1] Karamzin, *Polnoe sobranie stikhotvorenii*, 261.

than the earthly betterment of his subjects. By the close of his reign, Alexander was a broken man. His personal despair announced the end of a heroic image of the Russian sovereign acting to transform his government into an image of a Western ideal.

On the first day of his reign, March 12, 1801, Alexander moved back into the Winter Palace and issued his accession manifesto. The manifesto did not emphasize the break with the previous reign. Indeed, responsibility for the death was assigned to "Divine Fates" that had brought an end to his father's life "suddenly with an apoplectic stroke." The new emperor proclaimed that he was ascending the throne by heredity (*nasledstvenno*). At the same time he declared that he assumed "the obligation to govern the people entrusted to Us by God according to the laws and the heart of Our late August Grandmother." He stated the hope "to raise Russia to the heights of glory and to provide for the indestructible good of all Our loyal subjects according to Her most wise intentions."[2]

The decree thus affirmed both the hereditary grounds for rule legislated by his father and the principle of acting in behalf of the subjects of the crown epitomized by his grandmother. Without condemning Paul, it intimated a scenario of deliverance and efforts to undo the despotism of the previous reign. Alexander's first steps indicated that he intended to fulfill such expectations. He restored the violated provisions of the Charter of the Nobility and summarily ended the administrative terror from the throne. He ordered the abolition of the hated Secret Expedition and the reinstatement of administratively discharged officers and officials. He issued an amnesty and a declaration that future cases must be prosecuted according to law. He also lifted the prohibition on foreign books and foreign travel.

The immediate reaction was relief and euphoria. Paul's funeral was later remembered as an occasion for boisterous merrymaking rather than weeping. Young people immediately exercised their freedom by wearing the round hats, and within several days the old caftans and camisoles vanished and Paul's long and clumsy uniforms gave way to tight-fitting ones closer to the French model. Before long, Russians began following the French imitation of Roman dress, though without the republican overtones. There were Roman hairdos "à la Titus and à la Caracalla" for the men, while women began to dress so that they resembled "Roman statues descending from their pedestals."[3]

But the presentation of the act of deliverance lacked the heroic overtones of the previous century. The coup had caused the death of a father, not of a hated husband or adversary, and feelings of bereavement and guilt allowed no statements of euphoria. Alexander abandoned the festive ceremonial presentations of the previous century, which he found tedious and useless. The

---

[2] *PSZ*, no. 19,779, March 12, 1801.

[3] Safonov, *Zaveshchanie Ekateriny II*, chap. 8, 216; A. S. Shishkov, *Zapiski, mneniia, i perepiska* (Berlin, 1870), 1:80; F. F. Vigel', *Vospominaniia* (Moscow, 1864), 1:190, 2:35–39.

accession was not accompanied by elaborate celebrations; there was no compulsory rejoicing or evocations of the love of the people. In part, the reserve was the result of his own ambivalence about his consent to the conspiracy. But it also reflected an attitude that he shared with his father: that the emperor's authority did not require validation by acclamation. Alexander's rule derived from hereditary right and his humane sympathy came from his own disposition and political principles.

Alexander also abandoned the ceremonial pretense of Paul's reign. As enlightened ruler, he could hardly posture as Louis XIV. He was a human being on the throne, as Derzhavin's ode had described. But a Russian emperor could hardly be a mere human being, any more than he could easily share power with his subjects. The office demanded elevation, and his person found its idealization in the metaphor of the angel. The angel exalted his humanity and humility; it raised him above ordinary mortals without claiming for him the attributes of a deity. Paul had found in the Archangel Michael a kindred spirit; Alexander's angelic form was the spirit of gentleness, beauty, and reason, qualities respected by the educated nobility at the beginning of the century. It also captured the melancholy and dissatisfaction with the world that set him off from the eighteenth-century monarchs inspiriting their subjects with joy.

The angelic persona was the leitmotiv of Alexander's scenario for the duration of his reign. It expressed a refined, otherworldly character that enabled him to captivate even those whose hopes he had deceived. His endearing qualities evoked love, but this was a more muted and ethereal love than the robust affirmations evoked by Catherine. Moreover, while he occasionally allowed himself to receive expressions of love from the elite or the people, he rarely asserted or displayed his love for them. He avoided any displays that might hint at the popular basis of his sovereign power.

Alexander's modal feeling was friendship. Announcing the end of the rift between emperor and nobility, Karamzin's ode declared that Alexander would surround himself with "friends, Russia's best sons." Friendship was more discriminating than love: it indicated a special affinity, singling out those who shared feelings and ideas with the monarch, like his "young friends." In June 1801, he formed with them an "Unofficial Committee" to consider plans for reform, which would be announced at his coronation in September. The coronation would present and consecrate the image of the self-abnegating monarch who accomplished the greatest act of heroism, surrendering his unlimited power for the good of his people.

The most radical of the committee's proposals was the project for a "Charter of the Russian People," a Russian version of the Declaration of the Rights of Man, which the members adapted from a project drafted by Count Alexander Vorontsov. In the opening article, the emperor vowed never to violate the terms of the charter. The charter not only confirmed the Charter of the Nobility, but extended to all citizens the right to property, and freedom of thought, speech, religion, and action. It promised reform of the courts and laws, and announced the principles of innocence until proven guilty and habeas corpus.[4] It even gave recognition to the principle of popular sovereignty. "The principle of all supreme power is found essentially in the nation (*natsiia*)." As Mikhail Safonov has shown, Alexander enthusiastically supported the project. He proposed that the committee first should reform the administration, then proceed to introduce a constitution that would preserve the laws. The newly created "Permanent" Council of high aristocrats approved the charter unanimously on September 9, 1801, the day after Alexander's coronation entry into Moscow.[5]

The Unofficial Committee also considered projects to improve the serfs' condition and to grant the Senate a greater role in legislation. But these young landlords were not enthusiastic about offending the nobility by abridging the rights of serf owners or diluting the emperor's power by giving the Senate the power to pass on laws. Novosil'tsev warned that laws that did not issue from the tsar at the present time would be regarded as acts of violence, for they would not bear "the sacred character that obliges the people to obey."[6] La Harpe, who had returned to Russia after Alexander's accession, added his voice of caution. In a letter to the emperor, he asserted that the Senate proposal "left the monarch only with the name [of monarch]." He exhorted Alexander "in the name of your people, preserve as inviolable the authority bestowed upon you, which you want to use for its supreme good. Do not allow yourself to be deterred by the aversion that unlimited power arouses in you." He urged him to show the courage to preserve his power "entirely and indivisibly," for the moment when it was necessary for "energetic government."[7]

When the time came, Alexander announced none of the coronation projects. Rather than a declaration of permanent laws and rights, Alexander's Manifesto of September 15, 1801, was a statement of kind intentions. The preamble asserted his obligations to his people, and his efforts from the beginning of his reign "to strengthen all statuses (*sostoianiia*) of the population in their rights and their immutable privileges." He summarized the first acts of his reign: the abolition of the Secret Expedition, the end of investigations over officials who had been wrongfully accused, and so on. On the other hand, he made clear that he believed that these measures were only the beginning, that only time would allow him to achieve the well-being of his empire. "By all these laws we wished only to indicate how sincerely we wish the happiness of our people, how pleasant it is for us to attest before the true sons of the fatherland to our love for the fatherland and attention to

[4] Marc Raeff, *Plans for Political Reforms in Imperial Russia* (Englewood, N.J., 1966), 75–84.

[5] Safonov, *Problema reform*, 128–41; on the "Permanent Council," see N. P. Eroshkin, *Istoriia gosudarstvennykh uchrezhdenii dorevoliutsionnoi Rossii* (Moscow, 1968), 152.

[6] Safonov, *Problema reform*, 146–55.

[7] Ibid., 155–64; Allen McConnell, *Tsar Alexander I, Paternalistic Reformer* (New York, 1970), 35–37.

its good." The message of the manifesto was inscribed in the column on the reverse side of the coronation medal: "Law is the guarantee of each and all."[8]

At the coronation, instead of specific reforms, Alexander revealed the particular charisma that would allow him to embody absolute power in forms consonant with his enlightenment ideas. His mildness was his understated expression of the break with the previous reign, showing him as his father's antithesis. If Paul had asserted his right to rule by displays of brute authority and force, Alexander would assert his by showing his restraint, power in suspension, as a result of the supreme beauty of the sovereign's soul. He now put a humane face on monarchical rule; he retained autocratic power by avoiding the appearances of power. And his very unassuming, modest manner substituted captivation for conquest and made it obligatory for his loyal servitors to react with gestures of affection and admiration rather than terrified submission.

Alexander's coronation unveiled a scenario of a kind and gentle monarch who ruled his subjects out of true concern for their well-being. The focus of the accounts was the emperor's own person, rather than the ceremonies consecrating him or the celebrations raising him to glory. The events, indeed, were modest in comparison with those of the previous century, in keeping with the enlightenment disdain for ceremony as a wasteful distraction from the business of wise government. Alexander proposed to the Unofficial Committee that the celebrations be brief. The committee agreed that his stay in Moscow should be limited to six weeks, so that his attention would not be burdened by "useless and onerous presentations." He carried out his intentions almost exactly, spending only forty days in the city. On the other hand, the event was performed to a larger audience than previous coronations. An enormous influx of noblemen from Moscow Province and other regions converged on the city to see the tsar.[9]

After his arrival in Moscow, Alexander appeared in the streets before the people near the Petrovskii Palace. Memoirs describe the people's reactions in the streets, worshiping him as a demigod. The crowds whispered "little father," the traditional words for the Russian tsar, "the native, beautiful sun." Vigel' described how the "simple people" mobbed him, kissed his horse and his boots, which had been consecrated by his touch. "Before the lords of the East people fall to the ground in terror. In the West, kings were regarded in respectful silence. Only in Russia are tsars sometimes worshiped."[10]

Alexander's extraordinary appearance before the people indicates the dual nature of his appeal. On the one hand, his manner during the celebrations

[8] Shil'der, *Imperator Aleksandr Pervyi*, 2:69–70; M. I. Bogdanovich, *Istoriia tsarstvovaniia Imperatora Aleksandra I i Rossii v ego vremia* (St. Petersburg, 1869), 1:49.

[9] Belozerskaia, "Tsarskoe venchanie v Rossii," 32–33.

[10] Vigel', *Vospominaniia*, 1:200.

was accessible, humble, and self-effacing. Yet, it was specifically the gracious humility and humanity of the sovereign that appeared supreme and transcendent. It was his act of being like a human being that made him superhuman as a sovereign. For this reason, we have the seeming paradox that the most apparently modest of Russian monarchs impressed his contemporaries and posterity as otherworldly, elusive, and remote. The metaphor of the angel was indeed apt, one who could not be described quite as a god, but too endearing to be considered simply mortal.

The poetry written for the event celebrates his personal sensitivity and kindness; his distinguishing feature is "gentleness" (*krotost'*), exemplified in the image of an angel. Derzhavin wrote a "Hymn to Gentleness" (*Gimn krotosti*) for the coronation. Gentleness was "the trait of angels that emanates from God himself!" When gentleness adorned the tsar, he was the "benefactor of the world," whose beauty equaled the sun. It was gentleness that substituted for force, elevating the emperor's authority, and the feature remained attached to his image throughout his reign.

> Thus, Gentleness, you win,
> The hearts of the people;
> More than all other qualities
> You make the tsar the father of the fatherland.[11]

Poets now extolled a more humane and accessible figure. Alexei Merzliakov's coronation ode, delivered at a gala assembly at Moscow University on September 25, began with the motif of renewal and creation, then referred to Alexander both as Russia's angel and as "Augustus on the throne." "Kindness" became the virtue that gave "wisdom" and "justice" the power to do good. Merzliakov evokes Apollo not as a symbol of beauty but in the company of Freedom, Piety, and Gentleness. It was the gentle virtues, combined with enlightenment, that gave Russia true power.

> May Russia (*Ross*) by science enlightened,
> And by kindness and good deeds,
> Conquer this world again![12]

Karamzin's coronation ode extolled the love for humanity that made him sensitive to his subjects' plight. One monarch was blinded by glitter, another saw only slaves in his subjects,

> But you, enlightened by the soul,
> Cannot bear the clang of their fetters;
> To you only love has charm,

---

[11] Derzhavin, *Sochineniia*, 2:244–47; for a list of thirty odes and other compositions to Alexander on the coronation, see M. N. Makarov, "Vospominaniia o koronatsii Aleksandra I," *Zaria* 3 (1870): 58, 83–85.

[12] A. Merzliakov, *Oda na vseradostneishee koronovanie Blagochestiveishego Gosudaria Imperatora Aleksandra Pervogo* (Moscow, 1801).

But can one love a slave?
Or be grateful to him?
Love cannot be with fear;
Only the free soul,
Is created for love's feelings.

Karamzin used the odic form to demonstrate that he was praising human, not divine, accomplishments. Alexander's greatness was to be sought not in analogies with divinities. Karamzin returns to the motif of Derzhavin's ode on Alexander's birth. The poet shouts that Astraea has arrived, or that Saturn's era has returned. But then Clio states the case for history. Alexander's immortality was not attained in Parnassus, but on earth. He left his imprint on men's hearts and the annals of the past. In the ode's most famous lines, Clio declares,

You have on the throne a human being!
The Most-Wise Alexander, born
To serve the fatherland, crowned
To live in hearts and chronicles![13]

Alexander was a human being (*chelovek*), but a human being in two senses. He shared human traits with his subjects, but at the same time he was a humane being, the model and exemplar of what human beings should be, in the Renaissance or enlightenment sense of "Man." In this sense, he was to be a superhuman, though not a god, an angel, deserving of worshipful admiration. The absence of a coronation album indicates Alexander's general shift to understatement, a refusal to indulge in the inflation of rhetoric and imagery on the part of the government.[14]

The speeches of Metropolitan Platon developed the themes of the coronation manifesto and the celebratory verse. Platon's welcome speech in the Assumption Cathedral after the entry to the capital portrayed the emperor's Christian self in a sentimental voice. The metropolitan first compared the church to the heart of Christ, then declared, "Thou bearest the image of the heavenly Tsar. We in thy visible glory contemplate His invisible glory, and this cathedral is the image of our hearts, for the external church creates the internal." He pronounced the words addressed to Christ on Palm Sunday, before Peter to the Patriarch in the Palm Sunday procession. "Blessed is he that cometh in the Lord's name."[15] His speeches, however, played down the messianic overtones of the image: his savior was Christ the compassionate lover of humanity rather than the image of God on earth. When he spoke at

[13] Karamzin, *Polnoe sobranie stikhotvorenii*, 265–68; on the thematic connection between Karamzin's and Derzhavin's odes, see Baehr, *The Paradise Myth*, 159.

[14] The only extended description of Alexander's coronation is in Makarov, "Vospominaniia o koronatsii," 47–94. Although the account purports to be contemporary, it was not published until after Alexander's death. An incomplete version appeared in *Vestnik Evropy* in 1827.

[15] Snegirev, *Zhizn' Platona*, 2:174; on the use of this phrase in the eighteenth century, see Zhivov and Uspenskii, "Tsar' i Bog," 107–9.

the welcoming reception that took place the next day, September 9, before the notables of Moscow at the Slobodskii Palace, Platon declared that in Alexander, God had given Russia, "a gentle, kind, enlightened Tsar." He called upon the emperor to rule for the sake of "truth, gentleness and justice."[16]

The coronation sermon that Platon delivered expatiated on the eighteenth-century theme of the heroism of the newly crowned sovereign.[17] His words echoed the reform conceptions voiced in the Unofficial Committee. Alexander's empire awaited "perfect harmony and good organization" from his wisdom. But Platon then went further, introducing the principle of the equality of men; his speech even caused grumbling in conservative circles. The most famous lines proclaimed, "Humanity itself will appear before thee in all its primal and naked simplicity without distinctions of birth or origin: behold, our common father, it cries out for the rights of humanity. We are all thy offspring." The speech was intended for circulation abroad. After the coronation, Alexander ordered it translated into Latin, Greek, French, Italian, and German. It appeared on the front page of the *London Chronicle*.[18]

The coronation introduced the scenario of a kind and gentle sovereign who expressed his relationship to his servitors by his concern for their welfare. The scenario permitted but did not encourage shows of popular enthusiasm. It evoked Catherine's scenario of mutual love, but did so in an understated manner, avoiding any hint that Alexander's power might derive from public acclaim. But when he felt it necessary, as before the invasion of Napoleon, Alexander reluctantly yielded to shows of popular affection. The first occasion occurred on his visit to Riga, in May 1802. The celebrations in Riga marked his confirmation in September 1801 of the privileges of the Estland, Livland, and Riga. He reaffirmed the special relationship between the throne and the Baltic provinces that had been breached by Catherine in 1783 and 1785 and then restored by Paul.[19]

Alexander himself refrained from open shows of affection during the trip and declared his intention to spurn "all honors and ceremonial occasions." But a brochure published at the time described the population's enthusiastic response: "The hearts of the inhabitants of Riga felt a necessary need [*sic*] to show their joy and recognition. Oh! He knew how ineffably we love Him!" It described a gala welcome procession to the city, greetings by the governor-general, the merchantry, and the joyous crowds. Several hundred members of merchant guilds asked to unharness the horse and pull the carriage themselves. Alexander at first refused, disliking such shows of emotion. But when

---

[16] Makarov, "Vospominaniia o koronatsii," 56; Snegirev, *Zhizn' Platona*, 2:175.

[17] The St. Petersburg metropolitan customarily officiated at coronations. Metropolitan Platon was asked to officiate as a gesture of special respect.

[18] Shil'der, *Imperator Aleksandr Pervyi*, 2:66, 274; Snegirev, *Zhizn' Platona*, 2:7–8; Papmehl, *Metropolitan Platon*, 122.

[19] Edward C. Thaden, *Russia's Western Borderland, 1710–1870* (Princeton, N.J, 1984), 25–27, 98–99.

they insisted, their eyes wet with tears, "the Emperor, touched, finally yielded to their entreaty." At the castle, Alexander was greeted by a hymn, praising him as "the Angel of Tsars!" An actress delivered an encomium proclaiming that their "heartfelt warmth depicts the feelings of tenderness and the zeal of love that burns in the heart and the blood, MONARCH, for thee." She concluded, "Sometime, You will be the Genius for the poet, who will sing eulogies to the world of the most wise monarch, of gentleness and goodness of the soul and kindness of heart."[20]

In Russia proper, he continued to evoke the love of the people in the eighteenth-century manner—as a ceremonial confirmation of the sovereign's beneficent rule. His acknowledgment of their acclaim showed his sensitivity and magnanimity, giving further cause for writers to praise his personal virtue. In December 1805, after an enthusiastic welcome to St. Petersburg, Alexander issued a decree declaring that "the love of my dear people is my best reward and the sole object of all my desires." A young nobleman, the would-be playwright S. P. Zhikharev, wrote: "These words express all of Alexander I. . . . How impatiently I long to gaze at the tsar—the soul of sacred mother Russia!" Zhikharev typically identified the love of the people with his own personal infatuation with the tsar. When he saw Alexander in Moscow, he exclaimed, "What a majestic appearance, what a beauty, and in addition what a soul!" He marveled at his "angelic face and captivating smile." The next month, returning from his work, he saw the tsar again, rejoiced at his "beautiful, tender and peaceful face," and his feelings again were stirred. "If it is sweet for any of us to be beloved by even one person, how must he feel who is worshiped by millions of people?"[21]

THE EXERCISE OF FRIENDSHIP: THE CHANCELLERY AND THE PARADE GROUND

Alexander continued to nurture hopes for a constitution that would involve some type of public participation. His principal aide, Michael Speranskii, in his project of 1809, expressed the dream of a constitution realized through absolutism: "The existence of a Russian constitution should be owing not to the inflammation of passions and the extremity of circumstances but to the beneficent inspiration of the supreme power, which, organizing the life of its people, can and has all means to give [that life] the most correct forms."[22] But the illusion of the autocrat's omnipotence met up against the everyday realities of wielding power. To produce change, Alexander had to centralize his administration and make it a more efficacious tool for change, to enhance his power before he curtailed it. Alexander's contributions to Russia's

---

[20] *Imperator Aleksandr v Rige; maia 24, 25, i 26 chisl 1802 goda* (St. Petersburg, 1802), 6–14; Shil'der, *Imperator Aleksandr Pervyi*, 2:88–89.

[21] S. P. Zhikharev, *Zapiski sovremennika* (Moscow, 1934), 1:203, 208, 362; 2:38.

[22] M. M. Speranskii, *Proekty i zapiski* (Moscow, 1961), 153.

political development were the reform and rationalization of the central administration and the lifting of the educational level of the officialdom. These changes merely increased the monarch's responsibility in decision making and his need to exert a personal, symbolic sway to make his rule effective.

Alexander, like his predecessors, looked abroad for the most advanced template of governmental organization. He found it in the administrative structure of Napoleonic France. For the members of the Unofficial Committee, Marc Raeff has shown, the notion of constitution took on the late-eighteenth-century sense of *l'esprit de système*, systematic, legal government. During its deliberations, the Unofficial Committee entertained an enlightenment eudomonaestic ideal of achieving subjects' happiness through forceful and rational reorganization imposed from above. Its means was to be "administrative regulations," expressing the sovereign's will and not the particular group interests in society. The committee followed the French model of a ministerial system, adopted after the Revolution and institutionalized by Napoleon.[23] Its project, signed by the tsar on September 8, 1802, divided government by function into eight ministries, headed by individuals who were to preside over the colleges. They were to be responsible to the tsar and the governing Senate. The reformers also envisaged an institution, a cabinet, that would unite the ministers in their decisions. This "united government" would ensure that all branches would pursue the same policies and be subject to the same rules. It required that the emperor deal with the ministers collectively, as a cabinet that could decide on coherent policies that would be implemented by all government branches.[24]

Alexander also took steps to staff his bureaucracy with qualified officials. He again looked to a European model. A university degree or examination had become a requirement for many administrative and judicial offices in the monarchies of the West. Alexander hoped that university education would supplant the Russian pattern of gaining high office through military service or connections. This task was undertaken by Alexander's most influential adviser at this time, Michael Speranskii. Speranskii resembled Western clerks and state secretaries—men of non-noble background who had administered Western administrations in the interests of their sovereign and state. The son of a priest, he exemplified the new official qualified by dint of his abilities and training.

Alexander took the initial steps toward building an educated officialdom. He founded four new universities and expanded Moscow University during the first two years of his reign. A decree of September 1803 introduced a requirement of completion of "private" or public school for those seeking appointment to civil posts "requiring judicial and other knowledge." This

---

[23] Marc Raeff, *Michael Speransky: Statesman of Imperial Russia, 1772–1839* (The Hague, 1969), 41–46; Raeff, *Plans for Political Reform*, 88–91.

[24] On the introduction of a ministerial system, see George L. Yaney, *The Systematization of Russian Government: Social Evolution in the Domestic Administration of Imperial Russia* (Urbana, Ill., 1973), 193–96; Eroshkin, *Istoriia*, 163–65.

had little effect, however, and Speranskii reported to Alexander that noblemen were continuing to avoid lower administrative positions. He pointed out that in France, England, and Austria, "no one can be a judge, lawyer or procurator without a certificate and test administered by specific offices." The result was the Examination Law of 1809, which made a university degree or the passing of an examination administered at a university a requirement for attaining the eighth civil rank.[25]

A second measure enacted in 1809 brought the administrative change to the level of the imperial court and reflected Alexander's approach to the representation of political power. The eighteenth-century court had been a display of the unity of the throne with the noble elite, the great families whether old or upstart who sought their interests through closeness to the throne. The court ranks of chamberlain and chamber junker were occupied by young noblemen who used them to transfer to comparable positions in the administration. This practice became particularly common in the tolerant atmosphere of the beginning of Alexander's reign: the number of chamberlains rose from 24 to 146 between 1802 and 1809. The law declared that "each type of service demands executors prepared by experience and gradual advancement." It eliminated the court ranks of chamberlain (*kamerger*) and chamber junker (*kamer-iunker*), which became instead court titles, carrying no rank, and as a result conferring no promotions on the holder. Instead, those who received such titles had to hold administrative positions.[26]

During the next half-century, the court was transformed into a showcase of the highest levels of the bureaucracy. The result was not only to ensure that the lower court ranks had performed administrative service, but to make court ranks rewards to officials who had shown especial loyalty to the tsar in the administration. As the administration became more educated and specialized and its procedures more defined, the court drew the officialdom into the scenario of power, extending the monarch's personal sway through the bureaucratic hierarchy.

The ministerial system that Alexander introduced during the first decade of his reign governed the Russian administration until the revolutions of the twentieth century. During the first half of the nineteenth century, it brought about the expansion and specialization of a centralized state bureaucracy. But the goal of constraining the emperor's personal influence or that of his powerful aides by law was never achieved. Indeed, Alexander continued to exercise his influence when he saw fit, and the attempt at systematization hardly reduced his own personal sway. The formal regulations might limit officials, but the emperor, as the personal embodiment of state power, remained an exception. And Alexander used the power of his personality unabashedly to neutralize, when he wished, the system that he himself had introduced.

[25] Wortman, *Development of a Russian Legal Consciousness*, 38–39.

[26] PSZ, no. 23,559, April 3, 1809; L. E. Shepelev, *Otmennennye Istoriei; chiny, zvaniia i tituly v Rossiiskoi imperii* (Leningrad, 1977), 121.

He appointed many of his personal favorites as ministers and to other important positions. He preferred to deal with his ministers directly and privately rather than through the Committee of Ministers. The rules on the ministers' accountability to the Senate quickly turned into a dead letter. He thus succeeded in introducing a system that resembled Western bureaucracies, but in a manner that sustained the monarch's preeminence and dominance. The emperor's image seemed only the more superordinate when he could breach the tangle of laws and ordinances that bound ordinary officials. High officials then established their own preeminence by reproducing his pattern of conduct.

Alexander exercised his personal sway by evoking the feeling of friendship —what Raeff called his "erotic tinge"—which tied his servitors to him more effectively than obligation or intimidation and allowed him to ignore formal procedures. The figures who did his bidding, his alter egos, executed his will and at the same time protected his angelic image. They were bound to him by ties of affection that could be withdrawn just as they were bestowed. Michael Speranskii and the Minister of Justice, Ivan Dmitriev, both described these feelings of affection. When Alexander removed them from office or made their positions untenable, there were tearful embraces and professions of continued attachment. Dmitriev recalled the tsar's tender look. Speranskii described him as "a veritable enticer."[27]

But many noblemen feared Alexander's effort to harness the nobility in the interests of bureaucratic rationalization. They felt their special relationship with the tsar threatened by Speranskii's influence and reforms, and their dissatisfaction led to the state-secretary's downfall and exile in 1812. Karamzin's *Memoir on Ancient and Modern Russia*, written in 1811, expressed the nobility's fear of losing their special relationship to the crown. Karamzin regretted that "eminent officials" with "long training and a strong sense of responsibility for their whole office" had come to be replaced by "insignificant officials, such as directors, filing clerks, desk chiefs, who, shielded by the Minister, operated with utter impunity." He insisted that rank should depend on noble status, for only noblemen had the wealth and desire for distinction necessary to serve well.[28] But though the examination laws could be evaded and the richest nobles could find other paths to the court, Speranskii's laws remained in effect and would help reshape the character of noble service and social identity in subsequent decades.

Karamzin called into question the fundamental premise of Alexander's

---

[27] The alter ego corresponds to what Alfred Rieber describes as the "free floater," a figure whom the emperor uses as an administrative device to circumvent bureaucratic formalities (Alfred Rieber, "Bureaucratic Politics in Imperial Russia," *Social Science History*, vol. 2, no. 4 [Summer, 1978]: 407–8). See also S. Mel'gunov, *Dela i liudi Aleksandrovskogo vremeni* (Berlin, 1923), 42; A. I. Gertsen, *Sochineniia* (Moscow, 1958), 7:446; Wortman, *Development of a Russian Legal Consciousness*, 124–25.

[28] Nicholas Karamzin, *Karamzin's Memoir on Ancient and Modern Russia* (New York, 1969), 149, 201.

reforms: that Western models should be used to transform Russian institutions. He called on the emperor to codify old laws instead of introducing new ones and to return to the institutions that had ruled Russia in the eighteenth century. There should be more, not less, personal intervention by the monarch. Alexander had to "keep an eye on the judges. . . . Russia is not England." Karamzin no longer extolled Alexander's mildness. "Not to fear the sovereign is not to fear the law!"[29] He was questioning the accepted notion that Russian monarchy and the values of the enlightenment were compatible. His words would have their greatest effect when Alexander's younger brother, Nicholas, ascended the throne in 1825 with Karamzin at his side.

•

The military was the other sphere of state activity where Alexander sought to prove his greatness as a leader. As commander, he displayed the efficacy of his rule. Although he disliked court ceremonies, reviews and great parades remained his passion. He resumed the *Wachtparaden* the day after his accession and continued them with his father's fanatic dedication.[30] He began each day with a review and made no exception for holidays. He even reserved time for his daily parade during the darkest moments of 1812. He shared his father's preoccupation with the details of drill and dress. Before 1807, Alexander introduced only one modification of Paul's statute on formations, and that was to define precisely the length and timing of his steps. In later years, his obsession with military exercises drew sardonic comments from both his wife and his mother. Maria Fedorovna remarked that such matters should be left to a subaltern.[31]

For Alexander, as for Paul, the parade ground served in part as a substitute for actual command on the battlefield. During the battle of Austerlitz, Alexander tested his skills at command, and, against General Michael Kutuzov's urging, insisted that his troops advance. The French counterattack sent them into rout and left Alexander confused and despairing, lost in the field, cut off from his adjutants. Alexander could scarcely live up to the model of his adversary, Napoleon. His self-deprecation on this matter was open and would continue throughout his reign. After the battle, Alexander refused to accept the Medal of George, first class, when offered it by the senior member of the order. He maintained that although he shared the dangers of the army, he had not commanded. He accepted the medal fourth class instead, in order to show his respect for the order.[32]

[29] Ibid., 197.

[30] *KFZ* 1 (1801): 230.

[31] Mel'gunov, *Dela i liudi*, 43–44; *IGK, ts. Al. I*, 3.

[32] When Alexander joined his armies during the Austrian campaign in 1805, it was the first time that a Russian ruler had appeared at the theater of war since Peter the Great. He arrived with his large suite and Arakcheev and made clear his contempt for General Kutuzov, who, unprepossessing and aging, did not fit his image of a general on horseback (*IGK, ts. Al. I*, 170–

If Alexander could not emulate Napoleon's genius, he could take on his military manner. He followed the Napoleonic model of making military displays, and military men, aesthetic objects. Napoleon closely attended to the minutiae of uniforms, giving the French military a flair and panache that made the military officer a model of style.[33] Alexander, too, concerned himself with the minutiae of military dress. At reviews he watched closely to make sure that socks were not worn too high, that the number of buttons followed the latest regulations. He replaced the ugly uniforms of his father's reign with the latest military styles of France. Powdered curls, an essential part of the Prussian appearance, were eliminated. Beginning in 1802, changes in the uniforms came with great rapidity. The typical Napoleonic bicornes were introduced in 1802, French shakos in 1803. Short, close-fitting vests replaced the earlier waist coats, and tight breeches were introduced, giving the officers the sleek style characteristic of the French army. The French ambassador, Armand Caulaincourt, wrote, in 1808, that in St. Petersburg talk was only of uniforms. "Everything is on the French model: the embroidery on generals' uniforms, the officers' epaulettes, shoulder belts instead of waist belts for the soldiers. French style music, French marches, French drill formations."[34]

Alexander staged his relationship with Napoleon and other monarchs within his scenario of friendship. His alliance with Prussia was presented in terms of his public flirtation with Queen Louise and the "eternal friendship" he and King Frederick William III professed for each other. At a meeting in 1805, Alexander kissed the grave of Frederick the Great, and he and Frederick William vowed eternal friendship. The meeting was commemorated by a painting and engraving of Frederick William and Alexander taking the vow; Alexander's left hand rests on the grave. The queen, wearing a flowing gown and headdress, stands between the two (fig. 31).[35]

The famous meeting between Napoleon and Alexander at Tilsit in 1807 was staged as a ceremony of mutual amity. The alliance was termed a *traité de paix et d'amitié*. Each morning, the French marshall of the court appeared before Alexander, the Russian marshall before Napoleon. The two emperors exchanged honors. Alexander was decorated with the Légion d'Honneur; Napoleon with the Medal of Andrew the First-Called. Napoleon provided Alexander with neckties and handkerchiefs. Alexander took a fancy to Napoleon's gold toilet case; Napoleon made him a gift of it. Each day, Alex-

71, 180–85). There is a good account of Alexander at Austerlitz in Alan Palmer, *Alexander I: Tsar of War and Peace* (New York, 1974), 98–110.

[33] Raoul Brunon, "Uniforms of the Napoleonic Era," *The Age of Napoleon: Costume from Revolution to Empire, 1789–1815* (New York, 1989), 179.

[34] See the useful introduction by G. V. Vilinbakhov, in V. M. Glinka, *Russkii voennyi kostium, XVIII-nachala XX veka* (Leningrad, 1988), 5–20. Also in this volume, pp. 38–57, Plates 31–37; Mel'gunov, *Dela i liudi*, 44; Velikii Kniaz' Nikolai Mikhailovich, *Diplomaticheskie snosheniia Rossii i Frantsii* (St. Petersburg, 1908), 4:3.

[35] Mel'gunov, *Dela i liudi*, 100; Shil'der, *Imperator Aleksandr Pervyi*, 2:90–92, 123, 132.

31. Frederick William of Prussia and Alexander I vow eternal friendship at the grave of Frederick the Great. Queen Louise witnesses the vow. Engraving by Friedrich Wilhelm Meyer from a painting by Franz Catel.

ander dined at Napoleon's camp. Napoleon's Guard Battalion gave a banquet for the Preobrazhenskii Regiment where the troops sat next to each other and wore each other's uniforms and hats. The parting was accompanied by embraces and Alexander's vows to visit Paris.[36] A portrait of the time shows Napoleon greeting Queen Louise (whose pleas to spare Prussia were spurned). Alexander stands slightly behind him (fig. 32).

But for all the effort to affect an affinity with Napoleon, Alexander's military display revealed a different image of monarchy. Except on special occasions, Napoleon wore simple attire, setting himself apart from his officers, who commanded a spectacle meant for the emperor's own eyes. Alexander remained the center of attention, dressed in brilliant uniforms, and allowed the same to those close to him, the members of his suite. The suite gained new importance in Alexander's reign, and they, like the emperor, were allowed to wear a bicorne hat, the aiguillette (aksel'bant)—the fancy gold braid draped smartly over the shoulder—as well as the emperor's initial on their shoulder belts. These were young men who owed their position to connections in the court that they had gained during Paul's reign. With the exception of I. V. Vasil'chikov, they were all opponents of governmental reform.[37]

The suite was Alexander's inner circle. Its members went out with him before his troops at his daily parade, accompanied him on his rides and his walks through the capital, appeared with him at balls and events of the court. They dined with him and were at his side in all his daily activities. Like his associates in the bureaucracy, they were favored with a bond of friendship and trust. Relations with them were easy and informal. The model of deportment was friendship. The countess of Choiseul-Gouffier observed that Alexander spoke differently to different people: "With men of a certain rank with great dignity and yet charm; with those in his suite with an air of kindness and familiarity."[38]

On the other hand, Alexander showed little sympathy for the other generals in the army or the officer corps as a whole. He prized refined conduct and proper appearance as the sign of status. He felt utter scorn for those who lacked it, like the raffish Kutuzov, whose dissolute ways and unkempt

---

[36] Shil'der, Imperator Aleksandr Pervyi, 2:191–92, 200–202; IGF, 1:196–98.

[37] Velikii Kniaz' Nikolai Mikhailovich, General-Ad"iutanty Imperatora Aleksandra I (St. Petersburg, 1913), 1–5, 29–32, 41, 45–46; IGK, ts. Al. I, 99–103. Fedor Uvarov, Alexander's inseparable companion during the first years of his reign, had been appointed adjutant to Paul at the instance of Anna Lopukhina, the mother of Paul's mistress. He was chief of the Cavalier Guards when the corps was raised to the level of a regiment. He played a minor role in the coup and, as a result, did not alienate the empress Maria Fedorovna. Others, like Illarion Vasilchikov and Peter Volkonskii, were also guards' officers close to Alexander in his father's court. Khristofor Lieven, whose mother had directed the upbringing of Maria Fedorovna's children, also was a general adjutant under Paul, and directed the tsar's Military Campaign Chancellery.

[38] IGK, ts. Al. I, 100, 185–86, 430–36, 475–80; Mikhailovich General-Ad"iutanty, 8–9; La Comtesse de Choiseul-Gouffier, Réminiscences sur l'empereur Alexandre Ier et sur l'empereur Napoléon Ier (Paris, 1862), 26.

32. *Napoleon Greets Queen Louise of Prussia, in the Presence of Alexander I, at Tilsit in 1807.* From a painting by Nicolas Gosse.

appearance blinded Alexander to his genius. Alexander received a cold and sullen reception when he arrived at the theater of war in November 1805. The severe and petty discipline and interminable drill on which he insisted had alienated the officers as well as the soldiers. As a rule, Alexander demonstratively kept his distance from the lower ranks in the military and displayed his camaraderie with a select few from the elite.[39]

Alexander aestheticized military ceremony in Russia. The parade ground identified the force of arms with civilized taste and culture, as they were represented in the West by Napoleon's armies. The masses of men, ranged by size in brilliant uniforms, moving in unison, created a spellbinding show. Lotman observed the similarity to a ballet: the soldiers were the corps, Alexander the producer.[40] But Alexander also remained the leading figure, much as Louis XIV had been at the first ballets staged at Versailles. The parade-ballet was more than entertainment. It put the emperor and his companions on display as exemplars of beauty, identifying the political with the aesthetic hierarchy. It was a demonstration of the order and harmony that had been created by the enlightened ruler.

During the first decade of his reign, Alexander I presented himself as a classical legislator and military leader. He inspired not joy but respect for the seriousness of his designs, the dedication to his governmental and military roles. The classical or neoclassical style in architecture expressed the gravity and lofty goals of his rule. He sought to reshape the center of St. Petersburg to express the new seriousness of state power. Now it was not the palace, the abode where the gods reveled, but the edifices of the ministries and the barracks and parade grounds of the guards' regiments that expressed the monarch's intentions. These buildings embodied the aspiration to exercise rational control over the government's wayward manner. Here, too, Alexander followed the Napoleonic model, the neoclassicism of *le style Ledoux*. *Le style Ledoux* reduced government buildings to the simple general principles that animated the reforms—the "Platonic ideals of architectural form" that "were thought to partake of natural laws."[41] The spacious and sweeping lines of the governmental buildings in St. Petersburg made forceful statements of the majesty and rational organization of power. Thomas de Thomon's Bourse and Bolshoi Theater, Adrian Zakharov's Admiralty, and Andrei Voronikhin's Academy of Mines marked the reception of French Empire architecture in Russia. Voronikhin's Kazan Cathedral, with its semicircular colonnades, was clearly inspired by St. Peter's in Rome, but heavily influenced by the architect's studies at the Paris Academy. The yellow color of many of these buildings, Georgii Vilinbakhov has suggested, represented the counterpart of imperial gold, which appeared on many imperial standards and the uniforms of the elite guards' regiments and the suite.[42]

[39] Shil'der *Imperator Aleksandr Pervyi*, 2:132–33, 283.

[40] Lotman and Uspenskii, *The Semiotics of Russian Culture*, 154–55.

[41] Honour, *Neo-classicism*, 110.

[42] On Alexander's neoclassicism, see Hamilton, *Art and Architecture of Russia*, 314–24; Brumfield, *A History of Russian Architecture*, 348–58; Albert J. Schmidt, *The Architecture and*

33. *Neptune*. The Stock Exchange, St. Petersburg. Sculptor, Samson Sukhanov.

The monumental statuary of Alexander's reign reversed the eighteenth-century aesthetics of gender. The statues built to grace the new buildings glorify the might of the male figure, an analog to the all-male ballet on the parade ground. They reveal the influence of late-eighteenth-century sculpture, the discovery of the Laocoon and Antonio Canova's sculptures, such as *Theseus* and *Hercules and Lichas*. Whereas Peter had seen the embodiment of the virtues in sleek, tumescent, and languorous goddesses, Alexander's sculptors expressed the power of the state in figures of mighty gods embodying a physical, rather than a moral ideal. Above the pediment of the stock exchange, Samson Sukhanov's Neptune raises his pitchfork over the sea, his open robe showing a powerful torso (fig. 33). At the rostral columns before the stock exchange, two other nearly nude male figures with impressive musculature are allegories of Russian rivers; the two female figures are discreetly covered. In groups by the staircase of the Mining Institute by Stepan

Planning of Classical Moscow: A Cultural History (Philadelphia, 1989), 1–3, 128; Albert Schmidt, "Architecture in Nineteenth-Century Russia: The Enduring Classic," in Theofanis George Stavrou, ed., *Art and Culture in Nineteenth-Century Russia* (Bloomington, Ind., 1983), 175, 180–81; Georgii Vilinbakhov, "Sankt-Peterburg—Voennaia Stolitsa," *Nashe Nasledie*, no. 1 (1989), 17.

34. *Hercules Subduing Antaeus*. Academy of Mines, St. Petersburg. Sculptor, Stephen Pimenov.

Pimenov and Demut-Malinovskii, a half-nude Hercules subdues Antaeus, while Pluto abducts Proserpina (fig. 34).[43]

The statues exalted Alexander's rule in the neoclassical forms dominating Western sculpture at the time. While drawing on mythological subjects, neoclassical statuary broke with the cosmic imagination of the Baroque. The virtues of the monarch were no longer to be glorified in the celestial images

---

[43] Rosenblum and Janson, *19th-Century Art*, 104–7; I. Grabar', *Istoriia russkogo iskusstva* (Moscow, 1909), 5:177–78.

35. *Dioscuri* (copy). Horse Guards' Manege, St. Petersburg. Sculptor, Paolo Triscorni.

of gods and goddesses, but in idealized figures of men themselves. Canova presented the male physique as a symbol of courageous resolution, the triumph of mind and will over nature. He even executed a nude sculpture of Napoleon, at Napoleon's request. Alexander did not go so far, but he did commission copies of the statues of the two Dioscuri—the messengers of the gods—that stand before the Quirinal Palace in Rome. The Dioscuri were a favorite subject of Canova and other classical artists of Revolutionary and Napoleonic Europe, who portrayed heroism in terms of grace and elevation of the soul. The two sleek, naked youths strain in the pattern of the "heroic diagonal" to subdue their horses (fig. 35). Intended for the steps of the horse guards' manege, where they now stand, the statues exemplify the military aesthetic of early-nineteenth-century Europe, force sublimated as beauty.[44]

[44] Rosenblum and Janson, *19th-Century Art*, 108; V. Ia. Kurbatov, *Peterburg* (St. Petersburg, 1913), 104, 190, 482, 516; Hamilton, *Art and Architecture of Russia*, 324–33; Shmidt, "Architecture in Nineteenth-Century Russia," 181–82; Kenneth Clark, *The Nude: A Study in Ideal Form* (Princeton, N.J., 1972), 188–90. The Dioscuri were sculpted in the studio of Paolo Triscorni to be placed at the front of the horse guards' manege. During the nineteenth century, they were kept discreetly in the court of the horse guards' barracks.

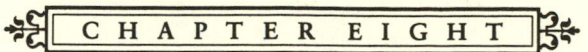

CHAPTER EIGHT

Blessed Tsar

Receive our free vow under the firmament:
For that most beautiful, imperial kindness of victory,
For the majesty you showed to the world,
The purple of your fathers, glorious from ancient days,
For your faith in your people in that terrible hour,
For the name given to them forever—
Here, surrounding your throne, Blessed!
We raise our arms to your sacred arm!
As before the horrible shrine of the altar,
We take our oath before it:
To sacrifice all for the tsar!

—*Vasilii Zhukovskii, "To Emperor Alexander," 1814*

> In that terrible year
> The late tsar still ruled Russia
> With glory. He walked sad,
> Bewildered out onto the balcony
> And said "It is not for tsars to tame
> God's elements." He sat
> And deep in thought
> Gazed at the horrid disaster
> With sorrowful eyes.

—*Alexander Pushkin, "The Bronze Horseman," 1833*

ALEXANDER I IN MOSCOW: THE INCLUSION OF THE PEOPLE

From the moment of his accession, Alexander avoided appeals to popular
sentiment and displays of popular acclaim. At the end of the decade, circumstances forced him to abandon his manner of reserve and to resort to such
appeals. The alliance with Napoleon and the economic costs of belonging to
the Continental System had caused widespread dissatisfaction among the
nobility. Speranskii's influence had aroused resentment and bitter criticism
in conservative circles; rumors circulated that he was a French agent. Alex-

ander now followed the example of Napoleon, "the emperor of the French," and began to seek popular support. The cosmopolitan, philosopher king appeared before crowds of exultant subjects and allowed himself to be depicted as the focus of popular and even national sentiment.

Moscow provided the setting for these displays of popular acclaim. Alexander inaugurated the nineteenth-century tradition of appearing in Moscow at moments of crisis to rally the nation and show popular support for the crown. As Archbishop Ambrosii's speech at Elizabeth's coronation had indicated, Moscow exemplified the spirit of the "native" and Russian. Moscow stood for Russia, a synecdoche of the nation, and its rejoicing was presented as the rejoicing of all Russians. Official descriptions explained the meaning and magnified the significance of the events. The ceremonial text returns, but in different form. It now purports not to be official at all, but the expression of an individual, often anonymous, author. Affecting a personal voice, the author describes the events, as much as possible, in terms of the emperor's scenario. He includes the people but the focus remains very much on the qualities of the emperor's person.

The anonymous account of Alexander's visit to Moscow in December 1809, *Journal of the Visit to Moscow of His Imperial Majesty Alexander I and His Brief Stay in This City of the First Throne in 1809*, described the people responding enthusiastically to the sign of recognition Alexander bestowed on their city. The news that he would appear in Moscow, "so long deprived of the sight of his face (*litsezrenie*)," prompted rapture and tears. The author described "general and unanimous sentiments of ineffable joy."[1]

The visit ostensibly celebrated the capture of Brailov from the Turks, which Alexander marked by depositing the keys to the city in the Kremlin Armory. But, the author asserted, military victories were not the real occasion for the celebration, for although victories impressed one's reason, they left the heart cold. "The soul" was delighted by "the kindness, goodness, understanding and bounty the Sovereign shows to his subjects, accompanied by their reciprocal feelings, as well as the tales resulting from them." He then generalizes what he claims are his personal feelings. The tsar's expressions of affection left memories that passed from generation to generation "and sow in hearts devotion to the SOVEREIGN, loyalty to the fatherland, and form true and good citizens."[2]

The *Journal* presents the "mutual sentiments" of love that unite tsar and people as feelings expressed between individuals. The people, as if one, greet his entry with delirious enthusiasm. They struggle to touch his horse, to wipe the sweat from its brow. The author records the emperor's response. "The merciful and sensitive SOVEREIGN, moved by these raptures of His people, shed precious tears, tears showing the tenderness of HIS Godlike soul." In Alexander's scenario, shedding tears was the sign of the tsar's ap-

---

[1] *Zhurnal poseshcheniia Moskvy ego Imperatorskim Velichestvom Aleksandrom I i kratkovremennogo prebyvaniia v sem pervoprestol'nom grade, v 1809* (Moscow, 1810), 4–5.

[2] Ibid., 3–4.

preciation of the displays of popular love. His appreciation shows the generosity of his heart, his extraordinary sensibility to their outburst of feelings, without, however, according the people a political role. Their enthusiasm merely confirms that he has been acting for their welfare.

The author marvels at Alexander's solicitude for his subjects, his children, as he halts his horse every few feet so as not to harm them. Alexander warns, "Be careful that the horse doesn't hurt you." The people shout in reply, "Little father! We will carry you and your horse on our shoulders; it will be easy to bear you!" "Oh the truth, pouring from souls feeling the blessing and the mild rule of a sovereign able to appreciate the attachment and love of the people!" The tsar, triumphal in war, had now conquered the hearts of his citizens. "Tsar! Thou enterst decorated by laurel and olive leafs, at the end of the war, crowned by a glorious peace and the expansion of thy borders. But to thy kind, sensitive heart the love of thy people is sweeter than all laurels!"[3]

At the end of the brochure, the author regrets the brevity of the stay of eight days and remarks that four weeks after the visit the people still felt the loss and thought only of the emperor. He then strikes a new national note that had not figured in Alexander's scenario. He explains the enthusiasm of the people not only as a response to the emperor's kindness, but as a monarchical sentiment distinctive to the Russian people. "Peoples of the world! Learn from the Russians (*ot Rossov*) devotion and love for your SOVEREIGN! Such sentiments will bring God's blessing upon you, and He will guard your borders against all invasions."[4]

The theme of the emperor's national appeal was expressed frequently and emphatically in 1812. Alexander's visit to Moscow in July of that year marked a major turning point—his assumption of the role of national leader who mobilized all the estates of the realm in the cause of defending the empire. This role offended Alexander's strongest inclinations. He agreed to go to Moscow only when defeat seemed imminent and after the urgent pleas of his advisers. Alexander still understood wartime leadership as command of armies on the battlefield. In the spring of 1812, while Napoleon's troops massed for invasion, he remained close to the armies, whose positions he inspected.

When news came of the invasion, Alexander issued a rescript in the name of Field Marshall Saltykov, concluding with his famous words, "I will not lay down arms while the last enemy soldier remains in my empire." The rescript indicatively referred to the empire as "my" and said nothing about the Russian people. It was Admiral A. S. Shishkov who finally prevailed on Alexander to leave the command of the armies and go to Moscow.[5] A conservative, nationalist poet, Shishkov had been appointed state secretary

[3] Ibid., 7–8, 29; Shil'der, *Imperator Aleksandr Pervyi*, 2:246.
[4] *Zhurnal poseshcheniia Moskvy*, 30.
[5] Shil'der, *Imperator Aleksandr Pervyi*, 3:80–87, 116; *IGK, ts. Al. I*, 113–19.

when invasion threatened. In subsequent months, Shishkov composed manifestos signed by Alexander that appealed to the people's patriotic and religious feelings and called on them to dedicate themselves to the struggle against the invader.

The trip to Moscow had practical as well as symbolic purposes. Alexander solicited money and recruits from the nobility and the townspeople. En route to Moscow, he received pledges of support from local nobilities. Enthusiastic welcomes greeted him all along the way, and throngs went out to meet him as he approached Moscow. But, wishing to avoid the crowds, Alexander arrived in the evening and declined a welcoming ceremony.[6] He found the morale in Moscow low. Oppositional sentiment among the nobility, who blamed Russia's situation on him, remained strong, and there was little sense of emergency or the need to sacrifice among the populace of the city. As Alexander entered the city, townspeople were being impressed into service, feeding feelings of fear and disquiet. On the next day, at a point late in the Kremlin ceremony, a rumor that the gates were being shut in order to conscript the spectators caused panicked flight, leaving the Kremlin Square empty.[7]

But the published texts described a wild and frenzied acclaim attesting only to utter devotion. The emperor's appearance would become a central episode in the myth of national sacrifice and unity woven around the events of 1812. At the moment, it gave a lofty purpose to the urgent and often brutal measures necessitated by the invasion. The most important contemporary text describing the event was the work of Sergei Glinka, a Moscow nobleman and the publisher of the journal, *Ruskoi Vestnik*. Glinka's account, ostensibly written in August 1812, was published in *Ruskoi Vestnik* in 1814 and provided the basis for later official portrayals of the event.[8]

Glinka's 1814 description is that of a rapt, innocent observer stunned by an explosion of popular enthusiasm for Alexander. Alexander emerged from his palace and "appeared on the Red Staircase like an Angel of god." He was greeted with shouts of "Hoorah!" and tears of joy. The rapture (*vostorg*), the pity, "the love for the gentle tsar," and anger at the enemy inspired the people creating a "spiritual outpouring." "Lead us Tsar-Sovereign! We will die or destroy the villain!" When the emperor proceeded through the crowd to the Assumption Cathedral, to the shouts of the people, Glinka recorded the people's shouts, accompanied by tears of "Our Father! Our Angel! May

---

[6] Ibid., 214–16; Komarovskii, *Zapiski*, 195.

[7] Mel'gunov, *Dela i liudi*, 129–33.

[8] S. Glinka, "Vospominanie o Moskovskikh proizshestviiakh v dostopamiatny 1812 god, ot 11 iulia do izgnaniia vragov iz drevnei Ruskoi Stolitsy," *Ruskoi Vestnik* 9 (1814): 3–21. For example, Glinka's description was the basis for the account in *Izbranneishiia cherty znamenitykh deianii, dostopamiatnykh deianii i dostopamatnykh izrechenii ili anekdoty, avgusteishego Imperatora Aleksandra I, mirotvortsa Rossii* (Moscow, 1814), 13–16. Glinka's embellished version of the event appeared in his *Zapiski o 1812 gode* (St. Petersburg, 1836), 6–14; excerpts of the 1836 version of the event were reprinted in V. V. Kallash, *Dvenadtsatyi god v vospominaniiakh i perepiske* (Moscow, 1912), 80–83.

God preserve you!" Glinka turned this expression of love into a superlative, denying anything comparable in human history. "Those Anointed by God ruled over peoples, no Tsar has ever been met and greeted as our Tsar was met, the Father of his subjects and Tsar of hearts!"[9]

Like the pamphlet of 1809, Glinka's description brings the people into Alexander's scenario of personal ingratiation. There is a natural love as well, a sense of national unity or patriotic upsurge. The Tsar is *both* "Our Angel," and "Our Father," both "the Tsar of Hearts" and the "Father of his subjects." The tie is both affection and blood. There is a suggestion that it is not only the virtues of the tsar, his achievements, that evoke enthusiasm, but a collective sense of the people themselves, an organic connection.

Glinka looked back to Muscovy for a national image and had placed portraits of Prince Dmitrii Donskoi and Tsar Alexei Mikhailovich at the front of the first issue of his journal; the spelling of the title, *Ruskoi*, is an apparent attempt to recall pre-Petrine *Rus'*.[10] Alexander's procession, after the Te Deum, to the shrines and the tombs of his ancestors allowed Glinka to portray the bond between tsar and people as a historical one distinctive to Russia. He compares Alexander's visit to the election of Tsar Michael in 1613. Again resorting to the unsubstantiated superlative, he quotes one "revered lover of the Fatherland," as saying, "Only in Moscow can one enjoy such an enrapturing coming together (*sblizhenie*) of the people with the Sovereign. The kind Russian Tsars thus built their palaces so they could see everyone and so that the Russian people could see them, and come close to them like children to their fathers."[11]

Glinka tries to bring an element of reciprocity into his account, a sign that the tsar recognizes the devotion of the people. To the shouts of enthusiasm, Alexander came out on the Red Porch and paused. "For a few minutes, his eyes and heart ran over (*obtekali*) the throngs of his loyal people." There is an intimation of reciprocity, but no more. Alexander stops to consider the spectacle, but his eyes remain dry. He weeps later, however, when he greets the merchant estate, in response to their loyal devotion. "The tears of the Tsar about his people are truly a priceless gift!" Glinka writes.[12]

The theme of nation and blood, apparent in Glinka's and several other texts of the time, was clearly incompatible with the tenor of Alexander's scenario. There was little in the ceremonies to present the tsar as a national rather than a personal leader. Archbishop Augustine's greeting to Alexander at the parvis of the Assumption Cathedral utilized the standard rhetoric of

[9] Glinka, "Vospominanie o Moskovskikh proizshestviiakh v dostopamiatny 1812 god," 11–12.

[10] Cherniavsky, *Tsar and People*, 130.

[11] Glinka, "Vospominanie o Moskovskikh proizshestviiakh v dostopamiatny 1812 god," 13–16.

[12] Ibid., 12–13, 19. Glinka added that Alexander on the Red Porch was "bowing to all sides," only in the 1836 account. Glinka, *Zapiski o 1812 gode*, 13–14. The gesture of bowing was introduced at the coronation of Nicholas I in 1826. See below, chapter 10.

Alexander's scenario, extolling him as a heroic conqueror of foes on the battlefield and of hearts among his people, who now would inspire them to fight for the fatherland.[13]

Metropolitan Platon sent a letter and an icon of St. Sergei of Radonezh to Alexander. His remarks were couched in the universalistic rhetoric of the Petrine tradition. "The first-throne city, Moscow, the New Jerusalem, receives its Christ, like a mother in the embrace of her zealous sons." He reiterated the phrase addressed to Christ, "Blessed is he that cometh in the Lord's name." "Gentle faith, that sling of The Russian David," he wrote, would "sever the head of the bloodthirsty arrogant" Goliath. St. Sergei was not a symbol of Russian religion but the "ancient devotee of the general good." Alexander's rescript to Platon stated that the icon would be entrusted to the Moscow militia with the hope that the Saint would preserve the fatherland "by his intercession at the throne of God." A poem in Glinka's *Ruskoi Vestnik*, published in 1812, evoked the historical parallel of Sergei's blessing of Prince Dmitrii before the battle of the Don. None of these texts mentioned the Russian people.[14]

Though Alexander was pleased by the mood of the people in general, the acclaim in the Kremlin seems to have made little impression on him. He was clearly ill at ease pressing through the crowds. Afterward he wept, he wrote his sister Catherine, but the tears were prompted by the "memories of happy times." The tears during the receptions for the merchants and the nobles appear to have been a response to the substantial donations and the volunteering of men for the militia, which he took as being "for the general good." He expressed his thanks in terms of personal trust. "I could expect nothing else from you. You have justified My opinion of you."[15]

While Rostopshchin and others issued appeals calling on Holy Russia to resist the invader, there was little national content in Alexander's own statements.[16] It is clear that he did not view himself as national leader. "This people," he said "needs a leader capable of leading them to victory, and I, unfortunately, have neither the experience nor the necessary gifts for this."[17] But the advance of Napoleon's armies forced the emperor to issue more emphatic statements of national leadership. After the fall of Moscow, Alexander resolved to continue the struggle, despite pressure to sue for peace from the court and the imperial family, particularly Grand Duke Constantine, the dowager, and Arakcheev.[18] It was at this point that he issued a

---

[13] I. Snegirev, *Ocherki zhizni Moskovskogo arkhiepiskopa Avgustina* (Moscow, 1848), 20–21; Shil'der, *Imperator Aleksandr Pervyi*, 3:90; Mel'gunov, *Dela i liudi*, 138.

[14] Snegirev, *Zhizn' Platona*, 2:42; V. K. Nadler, *Imperator Aleksandr I i ideia sviashchennogo soiuza* (Riga, 1886), 1:169–70; Zhivov and Uspenskii, "Tsar' i Bog," 108; *Ruskoi Vestnik* 9 (1812): 94–97.

[15] Shil'der, *Imperator Aleksandr Pervyi*, 3:90; Palmer, *Alexander I*, 235; *IGK, ts. Al. I*, 218.

[16] Cherniavsky, *Tsar and People*, 129–33.

[17] Shil'der, *Imperator Aleksandr Pervyi*, 3:92–93; Mel'gunov, *Dela i liudi*, 58.

[18] Shil'der, *Imperator Aleksandr Pervyi*, 3:112–13.

national appeal that addressed the people directly. On September 8 he signed a manifesto, written by Shishkov, calling on the Russian people to take up the cause of all peoples united in the struggle against the aggressor. The Russian people, led by the orthodox church, were presented for the first time as a force for salvation and liberation.

> It is pleasant and characteristic of the good Russian people to repay evil with good! Almighty God! Turn Thy merciful eyes on the Orthodox Church, kneeling in prayer to Thee! Bestow spirit and patience upon Thy faithful people fighting for justice! With this may they triumph over their enemy, overcome them, and, saving themselves, save the freedom and the independence of kings and kingdoms![19]

THE CHRISTIAN EMPIRE

A manifesto written by Shishkov and issued on November 24, 1812, to be read in all churches, gave generous recognition to the "Orthodox people" while asking the militia to surrender their arms. "You gave an example of the loyalty and courage characteristic of the Russian people. You took arms from the hands of the foe, joined militias against them, and helping our armies, everywhere annihilated and defeated the shaken forces of the brigands and evildoers. You laudably fulfilled your duty, defending Faith, Tsar and Fatherland."[20]

On Christmas day, 1812, Alexander issued Shishkov's famous manifesto proclaiming the expulsion of the invader from Russian territory.[21] This began with ringing praise of the Russian people, who had fulfilled the promise not to lay down arms until the foe no longer remained on Russian land. "We took this promise into Our heart, relying on the powerful valor of the people entrusted to Us by God, and we were not disappointed. What an example of daring, courage, piety, endurance and strength was shown by Russia!" But Alexander, chary of these addresses to the people, was careful to recognize divine intervention. The achievement was so staggering, the decree asserted, as to be beyond human powers. "In this deed we recognize Divine Providence itself." Salvation was to be found in religion, which the enemy had scorned. "We will learn from this great and terrible example to be mild and humble executor of the laws and will of God, not like those who have fallen away from the faith, those desecrators of the temples of God." Alexander then summoned all to give thanks to God in the cathedrals. On the same day he issued another decree, in which he vowed to build a cathedral to be named Christ the Redeemer, to show thanks to Divine Providence for Russia's salvation.[22]

[19] Shishkov, *Zapiski*, 1:156–59; Nadler, *Imperator Aleksandr I*, 2:54–57.
[20] Shishkov, *Zapiski*, 1:454.
[21] Ibid., 1:170–72; PSZ, no. 25,295, December 25, 1812.
[22] PSZ, no. 25,296, December 25, 1812.

The mention of Providence was scarcely formulaic. The people's involvement in the symbolic triumph of autocracy was Alexander's answer to Napoleon's claims to represent the French nation. The circumstances that forced the autocratic monarch into an alliance with the masses confronted him with the problem of reconciling autocratic rule with the principle of popular sovereignty. The people's involvement in the imperial scenario threatened the tsar's image as a superordinate force, whose title came from outside or from above, from foreign imposition, from divine mandate, or the emanations of reason. In social terms, it was impossible to present the people as a historical agent in a scenario that glorified the monarch's authority as the idealization of the ruling elite. The statements and panegyrics in the months after the expulsion of the French army displaced the responsibility for the victory from "the people" to Providence, turning the event from a national triumph into a religious miracle accomplished through the instrument of the Russian armies.

The victory also brought forth a revival of eighteenth-century classical odes, lauding the heroic emperor for his victory. Even poets of Karamzin's school, like Vasilii Zhukovskii and Peter Viazemskii, adopted the grandiloquent manner. In a widely quoted quatrain of 1814, Viazemskii greeted Alexander as hero and savior:

> A man firm in adversity and a modest victor,
> What kind of crown, what altar befits him?
> Universe fall before him; he is your Savior!
> Russia, take pride in him; he is your son, your tsar![23]

Popular literature seized on this theme of heroic emperor himself responsible for the victory. A pamphlet of 1814 related anecdotes about Alexander "depicting the great firmness of spirit, magnanimity, mercy, piety, military valor and virtues elevating Him above all the Monarchs of the World." It described his firmness of will as the source of the people's strength and called him the savior of Europe.[24] A popular print (*lubok*) of the time shows him leading Russian troops into Paris on March 19, 1814 (fig. 36). The verse beneath evokes all nations applauding the tsar of the northern lands, who was welcomed in Paris with open arms and worshiped. It was a call for deification.

> Extol Him as a Deity,
> He is a Tsar worthy of altars,
> His throne is above all others,
> And he is asked for laws,
> By all peoples and a throng of Tsars.[25]

[23] On the revival of the ode and secular messianism after Alexander's victory, see B. M. Gasparov, *Poeticheskii iazyk Pushkina kak fakt istorii russkogo literaturnogo iazyka* (Vienna, 1992), 83–89; Mel'gunov, *Dela i liudi*, 238.

[24] *Izbranneishiia cherty znamenitykh deianii . . . Imperatora Aleksandra Iogo*, 7–90; *Ruskoi Vestnik* 13 (1814): 74–76.

[25] *Otechestvennaia voina 1812 goda v khudozhestvennykh i istoricheskikh pamiatnikakh iz sobranii Ermitazha* (Leningrad, 1963), Plate 39.

36. Alexander I leads Russian armies into Paris on March 19, 1814.
Contemporary lubok.

Sergei Glinka's *Ruskoi Vestnik* also praised Alexander's triumphs as the emperor's own heroic achievement. An ode on Alexander's entry to Paris, by one D. Ermolaev, lauded the emperor as the deliverer of felicity to kingdoms, the restorer of law in France, and as friend and father protecting his subjects:

> And the voice of hearts will be heard:
> Monarch! The Chosen of God,
> Crowned by immortal glory!
> You are the friend of people (*drug liudei*)! You are a Father to them![26]

Alexander did not encourage the revival of the secular messianism of the previous century—the emperor as deliverer from misfortunes. He denied responsibility for the victory, calling for submission to the divine will. He endeavored to open an era of repentance and humble self-betterment. A decree of December 6, 1813, announcing the alliance of all the powers against Napoleon, declared this an event "that could not take place without the authority of God." "Who without Him is powerful? Who without his will is strong and firm?" The nation's true honor was "reverent humility before Him." Commenting on the decree in *Ruskoi Vestnik*, Glinka wrote

[26] D. Ermolaev, "Stikhi na vstuplenie v Parizh Gosudaria Imperatora," *Ruskoi Vestnik* 10 (1814): 75–76.

that Russia was strong and invincible "by the force of *faith* and *loyalty*." He once again compared 1612 to 1812, but drew a parallel between Alexander and Tsar Michael as tsars who were exemplars of humility. For him they were images of "the orthodox Tsar, the mild and pious Tsar." Napoleon had ignored the divine precept to be humble. "The proud one has been humbled, and gentleness exalted."[27]

Alexander's image of flamboyant humility reaffirmed the distance between ruling and ruled without resuming the Olympian imagery of the previous century. He presented himself as a humble believer acting as the instrument of Providence. Viazemskii, and other members of the literary society Arzamas, looked to him as a messiah bringing eternal peace.[28] But Alexander shrank from religious messianism as much as from secular; his humility was presented to exalt his imperial image. He took every opportunity to display a self-effacement in his work to effect the designs of God. The official medal commemorating 1812 carried the inscription, "Not for us, not for us, [*sic*] but for Thy name."[29] The phrase excluded both the people and himself from the glory of victory.

In July 1814 members of the Senate, Synod, and State Council approved a recommendation to offer Alexander the title "Blessed," (*blagoslovlennyi*) and proposed a coin and a monument in tribute to him. Alexander declined these honors. His reply, written by Shishkov, declared that he had not reached such heights and that the title would not be consistent with "the modesty" and "humility" he cherished. He rather importuned them, "May you erect a monument to Me in your feelings as they are enshrined in My feelings for you!" The pamphlet cited above, while glorifying his heroism, quoted Alexander's noble words with admiration.[30] The word *blessed*, however, continued to figure in expressions, official and unofficial, about Alexander, and by the end of his reign became as fixed an epithet as "angel."

On his return to Russia from England in July 1814, Alexander made a special effort to avoid public meetings. He wrote to General S. K. Viazmitinov, "Hating them always, I consider them even less proper now. The Most Supreme is the single cause of the notable events culminating the bloody struggle in Europe. We all must humble ourselves before Him." He rode inconspicuously into St. Petersburg, like an ordinary officer returning from

[27] *PSZ*, no. 25,488, December 6, 1813; "Mysli pri chtenii Vysochaishego Manifesta ot 6 Dekabria 1813 goda," *Ruskoi Vestnik* 11 (1814): 15–25.

[28] Gasparov, *Poeticheskii iazyk Pushkina*, 100–104.

[29] Mel'gunov, *Dela i liudi*, 241.

[30] *Izbranneishie cherty znamenitykh deianii . . . Imperatora Aleksandra Iogo*, 96–110; Shil'der, *Imperator Aleksandr Pervyi*, 3:246–48. Shil'der quotes Shishkov's memoirs to the effect that Alexander at first simply wanted to reject the proposal for the title "Blessed" and the "Monument," without explanation. Shishkov pointed out to Alexander that he was obliged to respond to the people's wish to call him "kind" or "good" tsar. Shishkov claims that he wrote the decree. This is a perfectly credible account and gives a rare illustration of how the tsar's manner of presentation takes on a life of its own that reflects the personal predilections of the sovereign, but does not necessarily express his own immediate sentiments.

the front, in a carriage led by a single cossack and without his suite. The next day he attended an almost private prayer service in the Kazan Cathedral. He called off the meetings and ovations planned for him and proceeded directly to Pavlovsk to see his mother. In the evening he made his first appearance at a ball.[31]

Alexander began to present himself as humble worshiper, a member of a Protestant priesthood of believers, rather than benevolent legislator bestowing laws and benefits on the people. To be sure, as Sergei Mironenko shows, Alexander continued until 1820 to consider plans for constitutional reforms and measures to begin the abolition of serfdom.[32] But he did not pursue these reforms and sought rather to attain the ethical well-being of the people to be brought about by their education in the Bible. Alexander's Christian mission, indeed, transformed the notion of the "general good" from a eudaemonistic to a spiritual goal. The burning of Moscow, Alexander said, had produced the revelation that his efforts on behalf of mankind were in vain and had given him knowledge of God. He realized at this point that he lacked the power to transcend his individual interest and to attain the general good. He told the German pastor Eylert that every person is an egoist. "Worst of all he tries to conceal this from others and himself. He tries to convince himself that he is serving the general good, (*obshchee blago*) while the true sources of his actions are either vanity, ambition, greed or other motives hidden deeply in his heart."[33] The Bible replaced philosophy as the source of ethical ideas that justified his imperial authority. With his friend, the chief procurator of the Holy Synod, Prince A. N. Golitsyn, Alexander read the Ninetieth Psalm and experienced a revelation. He listened intently to Admiral Shishkov reading passages from Jeremiah about the downfall of Jerusalem.[34]

Alexander wrote of his conversion, "From that time, I became a different person. The salvation of Europe from ruin became at once my salvation and my liberation." Alexander assumed the role as leader of world Christendom, the embodiment of the absolute values of humanity. The office of Russian emperor was filled with appropriate meaning—the instrument of God, the redeemer of humanity, and the defender of the legitimacy of monarchical government throughout Europe. But Alexander was not going to save humanity through his own Christlike suffering and martyrdom. His faith, Florovsky observed, was an amalgam of sentimentalism and pietism, a dreamy humanitarian religion.[35] His own role was missionary rather than exem-

[31] *IGK, ts. Al. I*, 274–76.

[32] S. V. Mironenko, *Samoderzhavie i reformy; politicheskaia bor'ba v Rossii v nachale XIX v.* (Moscow, 1989), 63–64, 75–78, 147–217; S. V. Mironenko, *Stranitsy tainoi istorii samoderzhaviia* (Moscow, 1990), 11–73.

[33] On Alexander's religious experience in 1812, see Nadler, *Imperator Aleksandr I*, 2:124–41; Shil'der, *Imperator Aleksandr Pervyi*, 3:117. Florovsky finds evidence that he harbored such mystical sentiments before 1812 (Florovsky, *Ways of Russian Theology*, 164–65).

[34] Ibid., 3:117; Nadler, *Imperator Aleksander I*, 2:124–33.

[35] Florovsky, *Ways of Russian Theology*, 1:164–70.

plary, to teach, and when necessary impose, the truth that had been revealed. Alexander put his mission on display in two grandiose military spectacles that he staged in France in 1814 and 1815.

The first of these took place in Paris on March 29, 1814, Easter Sunday on the Russian calendar. It was staged on the Place de la Concorde, previously named the Place de la Révolution. The military newspaper, *Russkii Invalid*, carried a detailed account of the event. Early in the morning, eighty thousand troops from the allied armies and the Paris national guard lined up on the square and the adjoining boulevards. Alexander reviewed the troops, then arrived with the Prussian king, Prince Karl-Philip Schwartzenberg, representing the Hapsburg Court, and a large suite. Seven regimental priests, in "rich vestments," stood at an altar erected on the site of Louis XVI's execution to lead the singing of the Te Deum. Alexander knelt at the altar for the prayer service. The French marshalls and generals pressed forward to kiss the Russian Cross. Then, once a prayer for the long life of the leaders of the alliance was pronounced, salvos sounded and the crowd shouted "Hoorah!"[36]

The ceremony deeply moved Alexander with a feeling that he had a providential mission to absolve the French of their misdeeds. He later said, "This moment was both touching (*umilitelen*) and awesome for me." He was convinced that he had come with his orthodox army "by the inscrutable will of Providence" to Paris to bring a "purifying and solemn prayer to the Lord." "The Russian tsar prayed together with his people, according to orthodox ritual, and it was as if they purified the bloodied place of defeat of the innocent royal victim." He believed the prayer had achieved its goal and had "instilled veneration in the hearts of the French." At the same time, it had demonstrated the triumph of Russia as the leader of the alliance. "I strongly sensed the apotheosis of Russian glory among the foreigners, and I myself even won their enthusiasm and forced them to share our national triumph with us."[37]

Vasilii Zhukovskii's poem, "To the Emperor Alexander," written the same year, dramatized the spectacle of purification and forgiveness for the Russian public:

> Oh, unforgettable day! See the victor,
> With forehead bare from horror,
> Knees bent, on that horrible place,
> Where the royal martyr beneath the sharp blade,
> In sight of the torn purple of his fathers,
> Prayed to the All-High for his poor people . . .
> On that horrible spot, the humble leader of tsars,
> Before the conciliating shrine of the altars,
> Commands his regiments to lower the standards of vengeance,
> And to bring a purifying offering to the heavens.

[36] Ibid., 5:183–85; *Russkii Invalid*, August 25, 1814: 243.
[37] Nadler, *Imperator Aleksander I*, 5:184–86.

Everything spread in ashes; all wept as one,
And look! The vessel of redemption rises . . .
And it sounded like thunder: the Redeemer hath risen![38]

The final apotheosis of Russian military glory occurred on the plains of Champagne near the town of Vertus, after "the hundred days" and the Congress of Vienna. Alexander intended a display that would prove to the world the perfection of discipline and training attained in the Russian army. The army itself would belie the notion of Russian barbarism and demonstrate the Western character of Russians: to show the Europeans, as he had said in Vienna "that we are not bears."[39] At the rehearsal, on August 25 (September 6, new style), 1815, he looked down on his troops from the hill, Mont Aimé, in admiration. He remarked to Alexander Mikhailovskii-Danilevskii, "I see that my army is the best in the world. Nothing is impossible for it, and from its external appearance no armies can compare with it."[40]

External appearance was indeed the emperor's principal concern, for beauty and symmetry signified order, and now the squares formed by the armies gave almost mystical confirmation of the divine source of his power. At the review on August 29, Alexander viewed the parade from the mount next to the Prussian king and the Austrian emperor, both in Russian uniform. The field below was covered with spectators. When the army shifted into squares, the three monarchs, surrounded by their suites, descended to the field and rode past the lines of troops standing at attention. The Duke of Wellington followed behind with his suite. Alexander's younger brothers, the grand dukes Nicholas and Michael, proudly commanded brigades and later cherished the memory of this coming of age at Vertus.

The displays had been scheduled to include Alexander's name day, August 30, the feast of Alexander Nevskii. The celebration provided the occasion for an immense religious ceremony, held a few miles from the site of the previous day's activity. Prayer services for the monarchs, the generals, and the armies took place in seven field chapels. The troops, more than 150,000, lined up without arms in a pattern of open squares pointing toward a nearby promontory, Mont Cormant, each side of the square formed by an entire division. Each unit moved in formation toward its altar. All were silent as the tsar knelt in prayer with the immense army lined up in symmetrical patterns in the field before him. Two days later the Russian armies began their return home.

As Alexander wished, the review demonstrated to a Western audience that Russia was a European power. It showed that Russia, the instrument of Prov-

---

[38] V. A. Zhukovskii, *Polnoe sobranie sochinenii* (St. Petersburg, 1902), 2:75.

[39] Throughout the struggle against Napoleon, Alexander had been concerned that his men act like Europeans. At Vienna, he showed increasing distaste for Russians and open preference for the company of foreigners. It was then, when warning the members of his suite to be polite with foreigners, that he said, "We must show them that we are not bears" (*IGK, ts. Al. I*, 282).

[40] Lieutenant-General Khatov, *Dva znamenitye smotra voisk vo Frantsii* (St. Petersburg, 1843), 50.

idence, had equaled and surpassed Napoleon's achievement. The model of Napoleon's massing of eighty thousand troops at Boulogne in 1805 was an example that Russians now claimed to have exceeded. For decades after, Russians could boast that Europeans were stunned: "They could hardly believe their eyes." The Duke of Wellington, himself a great advocate of strict discipline, was quoted as saying, "I never imagined that it was possible to raise an army to such great perfection." The English ambassador Sidney Smith declared that the review was a lesson to other nations.[41] The *London Times* reported that "all the evolutions were executed with astonishing precision. The soldierly appearance of the troops, the uniformity in each class, both in regard to the men and *materiel*, were such that no fault could be found by the most experienced judges."[42]

The symmetry, order, and coordination of the parade ground gave visual proof of Alexander's calling, proof that he could command men to act in accordance with a divine design. This discipline had ensured the good conduct of the Russian armies as they crossed Europe. Their humility and restraint identified Russia as a civilized Christian nation. *Le Moniteur universel* marveled at the absence of vengeance of the monarchs of Europe, who acted not as "our conquerors and enemies as we feared, but as our liberators." It was religion that had formed "that holy alliance for the bliss of peoples; religion whose sign of the cross is born on the brows of soldiers."[43]

After his return from Europe, Alexander continued to present parades as spectacles glorifying the authority of the Russian emperor. On vast parade grounds, the clergy blessed the army as the embodiment of the nation. The army became the symbolic substitute for the people, one more amenable to the emperor's wishes. At the same time, the elite units of the army, the guards' regiments, became the substitute for the army. The guards' units rose rapidly in numbers and in importance, especially after 1809. Guards' officers began to dominate command appointments, and the most handsome and able soldiers were removed from the army into the guards' regiments. By the end of Alexander's reign, the parade had become the central ceremony displaying the supremacy of the emperor and the noble elite as the exemplification of the nation.[44]

---

[41] Ibid., 58–61.

[42] *The Times of London*, September 23, 1815: 2.

[43] Cited in *Russkii Invalid*, August 25, 1814, 243. *Le Moniteur universel* also carried a report from *Journal de la Meurthe* describing a celebration by the Russian garrison in Nancy of Alexander's name day, during which cries from the population were heard of "vive, Alexandre" and "vive le Roi!" The population was thankful to the Russian troops for the help and sympathy. The journalist felt moved to "attest publicly how touched we were by the noble conduct and the strict discipline that they observed" (*Le Moniteur universel*, September 13, 1815: 1031).

[44] After the victory, Alexander continued an expansion of the guards' regiments that he had begun in 1809 and 1810 and elevated them above other ranks in the army. In 1809 and 1810, regular army units for the first time gained guards' status for bravery and heroism. They received privileges of "the young guard," that is, the officers enjoyed a one-rank advantage over

Alexander had elevated discipline to a spiritual absolute, an all-encompassing expression of providential designation and authority. This sense of divine mission gave support to what William C. Fuller, Jr., has called "the triumphalist myth," which produced the overconfidence that dominated Russian military thinking in subsequent decades.[45] Just as the army had replaced the people in official rhetoric, the review replaced the battle as the essential fact of the mythical past. The spectacle at Vertus demonstrated the divine source of all authority for Alexander and, in his mind, began to overshadow the experience of the war itself. He said, "The recollection of that review in which, before the Allied Sovereigns and their Generals, the regiments of the line and the artillery rivalled each other in the order and precision of their movements, and, in the condition of their arms and equipment, will always be present in my memory." When the army returned to Russia, Alexander insisted on increasing training in drill to bring its marching techniques to a new peak of virtuosity. New rules were introduced, and a committee began to formulate a new parade ground statute. A special model battalion was formed to train lower ranks in posture, length of step, and presentation of arms and dress. Grand Duke Constantine Pavlovich himself found the pettiness of these innovations bewildering, and remarked that "now drill has turned into such a study in dance (*tantsoval'naia nauka*) that you can make no sense of it." In Alexander's last years, during his travels across Russia, he staged reenactments of the Vertus parades and wearied his adjutants with constant reminiscing about it.[46]

The display at Vertus was a grandiose prelude to the final declaration of Alexander's divine mission, the announcement of the Holy Alliance. Alexander drafted the terms himself and prayed with the Baroness Krüdener that his allies would sign. The text of the Holy Alliance presents the principles of religion and the relations between nations in terms of Alexander's sentimental scenario. International salvation was to be attained by the application of the "Christian precepts of justice, charity and peace, which far from being uniquely applicable to private life" should direct the actions of princes. Monarchs should be united "by the bonds of true and unbreakable fraternity" and should rule their subjects, "like fathers of families, in the same

---

army officers, compared to the two-rank advantage of the older guards' regiments. At the beginning of Alexander's reign, the guards consisted of three infantry and four cavalry divisions and several battalions. At his death, there were ten infantry and eleven cavalry divisions (A. Popov et al., "Istoricheskaia spravka o naimenovanii 'Leib-Gvardiei,'" *Semenovskii Biulleten'* 20 [1950]: 5–7; Count A. Langeron, "Russkaia armiia v godu smerti Ekateriny II," *Russkaia starina* 83 [April 1895]: 174).

[45] William C. Fuller, Jr., *Strategy and Power in Russia, 1600–1914* (New York, 1992), 177–80.

[46] *IGK, ts. Al. I*, 282; Shil'der, *Imperator Aleksandr Pervyi*, 4:15–16, 459; *The Times of London*, September 26, 1815: 2. A repetition of Vertus, for example, was staged at Tulchin in 1824, where the entire second army, more than 100,000 troops, formed the three sides of a gigantic square. The tsar was touched, and wept (Bogdanovich, *Istoriia tsarstvovaniia Imperatora Aleksandra I*, 6:369–71; Shil'der, *Imperator Aleksandr Pervyi*, 4:284–86).

spirit of brotherhood, which animates them, for the preservation of faith, peace and justice."[47]

The declaration of the Holy Alliance denied the existence of distinctive national characteristics. The members of the alliance would be animated "by mutual benevolence and affection" and consider themselves members "of a single Christian nation." The "Autocrat of the Christian People," the document declared, was none other than Jesus Christ, in whom all love and knowledge resided.[48] Alexander, speaking in the name of Christ, drew his moral authority from above and detached himself from the forces of popular nationalism awakened during the war.

The New Year's Day Manifesto of 1816 marked the completion of the shift of Alexander's focus from the people to the divine agency assisting the Russian armies. Although the manifesto was termed an announcement of "Imperial gratitude," Alexander's principal purpose was to dispel the "pride" that the people might take in the victory, and indeed, he denied the importance of all human agency and sacrifice in the events of the previous years. It was the "The Hand of God," that had led the Russian people through the breakdown to order and tranquillity. Alexander thanked the Russian troops and the Russian people, but then added "the very greatness of the deeds shows that it was not we who achieved them." Summarizing the events of the previous years, the manifesto turned into a sermon on the dangers of revolution and the importance of religious faith. Alexander portrayed the war as punishment for the sins of the Russian people, calling for contrition rather than rejoicing. Napoleon, no longer the obliging friend, was the monster who represented moral decay and loss of faith, a condition that had affected all of Europe, including Russia. Alexander spoke of the destruction wrought by the war as if it expressed God's wrath, visited on the Russian people, who, having learned this lesson, acted as God's instrument to save Europe. "God chose us, to execute a great deed; He turned His just wrath with us into unheard of grace." Alexander condemned pride as "unjust, ungrateful and criminal" before a generous God. "Our humility will correct our morals, efface our guilt before God, bring us honor, glory, and show the world that we are fearsome for no one, but fear no one."[49]

The text of the Holy Alliance became a new holy writ. The Holy Synod ordered that it be posted on the walls of all churches. Every year the text was to be recited from church pulpits, "so that each and every person might fulfill his vow of service to the one Lord and Savior, who speaks through the person of the Sovereign for the entire people."[50] The emperor spoke the word of God for the people, but did not need their support, and his visits to

---

[47] Shil'der, *Imperator Aleksandr Pervyi*, 3:343–44.
[48] Nadler, *Imperator Aleksandr I*, 5:631–33.
[49] Shil'der, *Imperator Aleksandr Pervyi*, 4:1–2.
[50] Florovsky, *Ways of Russian Theology*, 1:166.

Moscow revealed his indifference to popular sentiment. In August 1816 he appeared in Moscow to inspect the devastated city. The reports in the pages of the official journal of the Ministry of Interior, *Severnaia Pochta*, give the general sense of rapture of the people who crowded around him. The account of August 30 stated that no eloquence could describe the emperor's feelings as he looked upon "this sincere proof of love and devotion to Him, of his Russian progeny."[51] But Alexander did not reveal such feelings. He remained aloof and even reproachful. His address to the Moscow nobility had an admonitory tone. "We saved Europe as well as Russia," he declared to the noblemen. But he cautioned them not to take the credit for themselves. "Everything occurred from God." They could not have achieved such heights without the divine law inscribed in the New Testament. He warned that he saw nations who lived without that law. "You know what consequences . . . arose . . . there. I am sure you too think about this."[52]

Most important, Alexander conspicuously avoided shows of national feeling and even public condolence for the suffering of the Moscow population. He visited none of the sites of the major events of 1812 as he had in Austria and Belgium. He ignored August 26, the anniversary of the Battle of Borodino, neither visiting the battlefield nor holding a mass for the victims in Moscow, but did find time to attend a ball. His bewildered adjutant, Mikhailovskii-Danilevskii, wrote in his diary, "It is worth mentioning that the tsar does not like to remember or talk about the Fatherland War though it makes up a magnificent page in his glorious reign."[53]

Instead of the people of Moscow, Alexander gave recognition to the city itself, in an "Imperial Charter, Given to the Capital City of Moscow." The charter declared that Alexander had come to Moscow not only to view the city's condition and needs, "but also to give a sign before the entire world, of her unquestionable services, blessed by God, respected by foreign States, and equally worthy of love and gratitude from us and the entire Fatherland. . . . Her zeal and fervor corresponded to our expectations. We saw her intense love for Us and the Fatherland, a love that spared no sacrifices." Moscow's destruction and defilement was the redemption of Russia and all of Europe. "In this way, Moscow, by its heroic exploits, loyalty and patience gave an example of courage and majesty."[54] The "Imperial Charter" follows the general pattern of displacing the responsibility for the victory from the people to other symbols. Alexander praised the city of Moscow as if addressing a human hero. The city of Moscow personified becomes an agent of history.

[51] *Severnaia Pochta*, August 30, 1816.

[52] Shil'der, *Imperator Aleksandr Pervyi*, 4:49–50. The elipses within the quote are Shil'der's.

[53] Ibid., 4:50; S. Glinka, "Stikhi na pribytie Gosudaria Imperatora v Moskvu," *Ruskoi Vestnik* 9 (1816): 5.

[54] *PSZ*, no. 26,417, August 30, 1816.

Symmetry and Cleanliness: The Imposition of Order

Catherine had given confirmation of her myth of godlike legislatrix by presenting provincial towns and conquered territories as semblances of paradise. Alexander, as divinely inspired commander, sought to use the order realized on the drill field to uplift the spiritual life of the empire. The appearance of symmetry, the fastidious beauty of the uniforms, denoted the presence of God and provided a model for the betterment of Russia. He sought to display this order in the buildings constructed in the capitals, in new, increasingly beautiful settlements to house the Russian army, and in the religious conversion of his subjects. Each of these undertakings aimed to bring universal principles of Christianity and reason into Russian life. Each involved the strengthening of administrative power and oversight over the population.

After the war, Alexander continued the renovation of the center of St. Petersburg in the spirit of French neoclassicism. In 1816 he appointed the Spanish military engineer and general, who had served under Napoleon, Augustin de Béthencourt, chairman of the Committee on Buildings of Petersburg, which also included the architects Carl Rossi and Vasilii Stasov. He formed the committee "to raise this capital's architecture to that level of beauty and perfection which, corresponding in all respects to its attributes, would unite the public and private good." The committee was concerned neither for the legality of private ownership nor for the durability of buildings; its assignment was to pass on the designs of facades to bring about "uniform exterior beauty." Such beauty was to express the harmony of the new public order and thus uplift private values as well.[55]

The spacious barracks and maneges that rose in the center of Petersburg made the city a majestic camp for the privileged guards' regiments. Vasilii Stasov's Pavlovsk Barracks near the field of Mars and Karl Rossi's General Staff added to the monumental military setting around the tsar's palace. This was a military paradise of straight lines, of men in order in the middle of vast geometrical spaces surrounded by yellow classical buildings, a demonstration of the emperor's invincible power over refractory reality. In Moscow, Béthencourt's manege was an immense military symbol located in the center of Moscow near the Kremlin. This huge building with a Doric colonnade could accommodate an entire infantry regiment, as well as cavalry. Foreigners reacted with admiration, as well as fear, to a structure that permitted training to proceed through the severe Russian winter. Ivan Martos's statue of the heroes of 1613, Minin and Pozharskii, on Red Square used oversized, powerful male figures in Roman dress to express heroic devotion to the fatherland (fig. 37).[56]

---

[55] Hamilton, *Art and Architecture of Russia*, 315; Shmidt, "Architecture in Nineteenth-Century Russia," 181.

[56] Schmidt, *The Architecture and Planning of Classical Moscow*, 156–58.

37. *Minin and Pozharskii.* Red Square, Moscow. Sculptor, Ivan Martos.

The institution that would bring Alexander's vision of beauty and order to the organization and quartering of the army was the "military colony." Alexander found his inspiration for the military colonies at Arakcheev's estate at Gruzino in Novgorod Province, which Alexander had visited in 1810. By exercising Draconian discipline and close supervision, Arakcheev had transformed his estate into a picture of rural well-being. He had replaced peasant huts with neat and symmetrical barracklike buildings, many of them of brick or stone, and brought new fields into cultivation. He had insisted that the peasants keep their homes tidy, and even forbade some villages to keep pigs. Alexander admired

> The order which prevails everywhere, the cleanliness, the construction of roads and plantations, the symmetry and elegance which we saw on all sides. The streets of the villages here have *precisely that kind of cleanliness* which I have been trying so hard to see established in the towns. The best proof that what I have been demanding is possible is that it can be found in the villages here.[57]

[57] Jenkins, *Arakcheev*, 88–89, 144–45.

In 1814 Alexander proceeded with his intention to create a system of such villages under Arakcheev's direction. He saw this as a humanitarian act that, he claimed, "would allow [the soldiers] to lead a settled life and make it possible for us to unite them with their families." Arakcheev used reports about a similar settlement in Austria on the Turkish border as the basis for a colony he formed among state peasants on swampland near his estate. Against the opposition of the army, Alexander expanded the Novgorod colonies and had new settlements established in the Ukraine and southern Russia. Over the next decade, nearly half the troops in the empire were placed under Arakcheev's direct supervision.

The soldiers in these colonies lived in symmetrical barracklike buildings arranged in squares around watchtowers for observation of each unit. Hospitals were built that were kept immaculate. The regiments lived in quarters with elegant furniture and silver services, but the soldiers and officers alike feared to use them lest they be worn out.[58] Arakcheev made sure that the colonies maintained their neatness and polish, and Alexander, on his numerous inspection trips to the various colonies, was treated to comforting sights of well-dressed and well-equipped soldiers living in well-appointed quarters, marching according to rule in bright clean uniforms. Everything gave the impression of "being in good order," the sense captured by the term (*blagoustroistvo*), which was frequently used at the time.[59] The military colonies represented what Richard Stites has aptly described as a "panegyric utopia, the geometrization of space, rationalism and the military ethos of order and obedience."[60]

The notion of paternal oversight became the pretext to issue countless regulations over the colonists. The result was discontent, strikes, and violent retribution. The inhuman Prussian punishment, the *spitz-ruten* (beating on the back by birch rods), often ending in death, was used to punish striking colonists. Despite their resistance, Alexander remained undeterred. He left their running of the colonies to Arakcheev's discretion and even encouraged the general to expand the Novgorod colonies in 1824 and 1825. On his visit to Gruzino in late June and July of 1825, he held parades and inspected the work that was underway.[61]

•

Alexander found another example of orderly life in the Protestant communities he had visited in England, particularly the Quakers' community. Their immaculate homes especially impressed him; he understood cleanliness as a sign of the purity he sought after.[62] His belief in the Bible as the source of

[58] Ibid., 191.

[59] Kizevetter, *Istoricheskie ocherki*, 350.

[60] Richard Stites, *Revolutionary Dreams: Utopian Vision and Experimental Life in the Russian Revolution* (New York, 1989), 22.

[61] Jenkins, *Arakcheev*, 194–96; Shil'der, *Imperator Aleksandr Pervyi*, 4:315–16, 335–36.

[62] Ibid., 4:459.

principles to regenerate mankind was another common ground he held with the Quakers. He prayed with them and invited them to open branches of the Bible Society and a network of Lancaster Schools in Russia.

The agent for Alexander's designs for spiritual regeneration was his friend Prince A. N. Golitsyn, the chief procurator of the Holy Synod, whom he named head of the Russian Bible Society in 1814. Before his own religious conversion in 1812, Golitsyn had been a rationalist, free thinker, and bon vivant. Under his direction, eighty-nine branches of the society opened throughout Russia and distributed more than 400,000 copies of the Bible. The Bible replaced the philosophes as obligatory reading for provincial governors, marshalls of the nobility, and even bishops. Officials quickly followed the example set above and formed their own chapters, well understanding that participation was essential to their future careers in the service. In 1816 Alexander indicated to Golitsyn that he wished Russians to be provided "with the means to read God's word in their native language, which for them is more comprehensible than the Church Slavic now used for the publication of the Holy Scriptures." Work began on a Russian translation of the Bible.[63]

In 1816 the Ministry of Education, the Synod, and the Administration of Foreign Creeds were amalgamated under Golitsyn's direction. Religion, the manifesto announcing the changes indicated, was merely another form of knowledge, "for Christian piety has always been the basis of true enlightenment." The ministry would permit no bigotry or religious intolerance. The Russian state began to promote an evangelical Protestantism that had little in common with the highly liturgical and institutionalized worship characteristic of Russian Orthodoxy. Alexander and Golitsyn prayed in silence together with Quakers visiting Russia. When the Quakers discovered extracts of Voltaire, Cicero, and other "heathen philosophers" in primers in one of the Lancaster schools and warned Alexander of such writings "harmful for their morality," these readings were replaced with selections from the Scriptures. Education was to be Alexander's way to transform mankind and create a utopia of believers.[64]

But the principles of religious tolerance and faith quickly became instruments of intolerance. Karamzin immediately noted that the combination of religion and education under a single ministry had the sinister potential of making hypocrisy a means for officials to proclaim their piety and crush independent thought. The movement's philanthropic goals and declarations of humility were accompanied by the persecution of secular philosophy and an effort to extirpate rationalist doctrines from the universities. Golitsyn's subordinates, such as another former free thinker and liberal, M. L. Magni-

[63] Ibid., 4:10–12; Mel'gunov, *Dela i liudi*, 244; Florovsky, *Ways of Russian Theology*, 1:188–91.

[64] Shil'der, *Imperator Aleksandr Pervyi*, 4:11, 134; Florovsky, *Ways of Russian Theology*, 1:166; Richenda C. Scott, *Quakers in Russia* (London, 1964), 89.

tskii, purged the universities of recently recruited philosophy professors and prescribed the teaching of religion. As curator of the Kazan educational district, Magnitskii dismissed eleven of twenty-one professors and introduced impossible requirements—such as basing the teaching of political economy on the Scriptures. He organized the students according to a military model, compelling them to march and sing in chorus. D. P. Runich, another of Golitsyn's appointees, introduced similar measures at Petersburg University.

The Orthodox Church finally responded to the Protestant challenge to its teachings and authority. In May 1824 members of the church hierarchy together with Arakcheev, who resented Golitsyn's influence, won a power struggle and forced the minister's resignation. He was replaced by Admiral Shishkov as head of a reinstated Ministry of Education. Shishkov promptly condemned efforts to translate the Bible into Russian as a foul heresy and had the text of the Russian Pentateuch burned at the brick factory of the Nevskii Monastery. Yielding to pressure from Shishkov and the hierarchy, Alexander forbade the translation of the Bible and ordered the Bible Societies closed.[65]

The Cathedral of Christ the Redeemer, which Alexander had promised to build on Christmas Day, 1812, was to be the principal monument to the spiritual truths he discovered. The church would commemorate the men who had lost their lives in 1812, and, in this respect, represent Alexander's response to what George L. Mosse has called "the nationalization of death" that began with the French Revolution.[66] To design and build the cathedral, Alexander chose a young Russian artist of Swedish ancestry, Alexander Vitberg, who shared his mystical conceptions of art. Vitberg had neither training nor experience in architecture, but Golitsyn, who had seen his drawings, urged him to undertake the building.

Vitberg planned a cathedral that was to be a soaring statement of eternal spiritual values, a demonstration that the emperor and the Russian people had conquered the beyond as well as the world. He wrote that he conceived of a church whose colossal size would correspond to the majesty of Russia. The cathedral was to be the largest edifice in the world, nearly 170 meters in height, or twice the size of the largest pyramid. Crowned with five pyramids, it would look down on Moscow from the heights of the Sparrow Hills.

Like Alexander, Vitberg believed that harmonious shapes, and classical geometrical forms, realized in the proper mass, could express spiritual truths. He designed the cathedral in three levels: the lowest, a square; the middle, a circle; the top, a tower crowned by a cross. The levels expressed three principles—body, soul, and spirit—and moments in the life of Christ—Birth, Transfiguration, Resurrection. A huge colonnade on the lower level was to carry the names of all the fallen in 1812, the story of

[65] Florovsky, *Ways of Russian Theology*, 194–202.

[66] George L. Mosse, *Fallen Soldiers; Reshaping the Memory of the World Wars* (New York, 1990), 36–37.

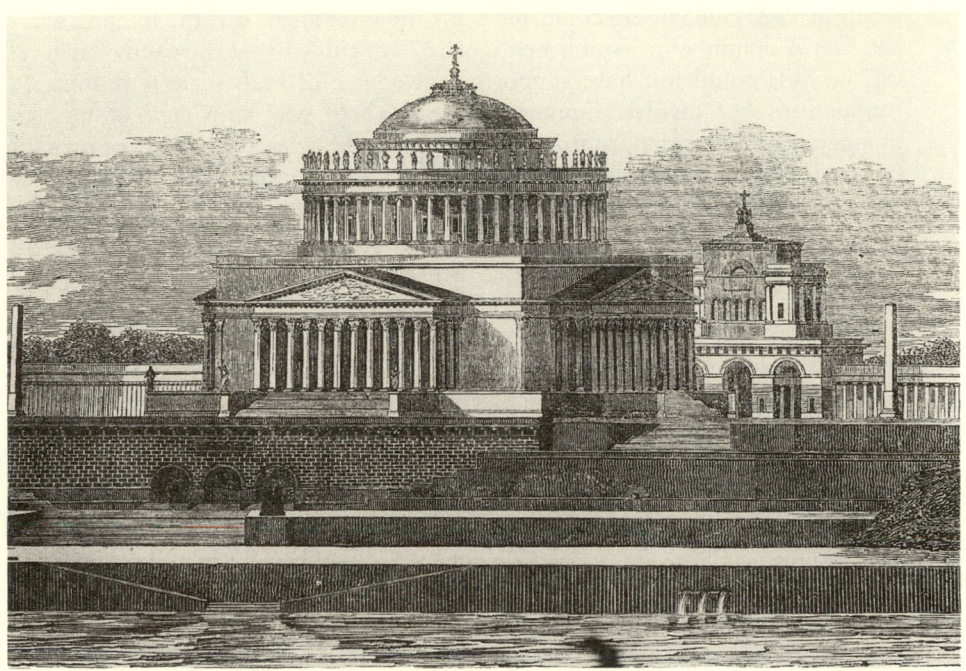

38. Project for Cathedral of Christ the Savior. Architect, Alexander Vitberg.

Russia's victory, the principal manifestos and statues cast from captured cannons. The middle level would be flooded with light and hold statues of Old Testament figures and illustrations of the gospels. The tower with the cross, as a pure expression of the spirit, was to be uncluttered by statues or ornamentation.[67]

But the cathedral, like Alexander's spiritual vision of a redeemed humanity, was destined to remain unrealized, thwarted by human imperfections and the limits of contemporary technology. Alexander provided funds to purchase 18,600 souls and made every effort to facilitate the construction. The cornerstone was laid in October 1817. By 1821, the commission had purchased 11,000 souls, and had water released from reservoirs to swell the river for the boats carrying stone to the site. But the efforts made little progress. More modest plans were drawn up for a smaller cathedral with only one cupola (fig. 38). The work still moved slowly. At the time of Alexander's

[67] Descriptions of the church vary, probably referring to the different projects advanced at successive stages of the cathedral. The account of Alexander Herzen (*Byloe i dumy* [Moscow, 1962], 1:246–53) is the most poetic if not necessarily the most accurate. See Shil'der, *Imperator Aleksandr Pervyi*, 4:79–80; *Istoricheskoe opisanie postroeniia v Moskve Khrama vo imia Khrista Spasitelia* (Moscow, 1883), 3–4; P. Petrov, "Khram Spasitelia v Moskve," *Zodchii* 1 (1880): 30–31; E. A. Borisova, *Russkaia arkhitektura vtoroi poloviny XIX veka* (Moscow, 1979), 105–6.

death in 1825, all Vitberg could show for the investment was the leveling of the site. A commission established in 1827 concluded that the sandy earth on the hills could not have supported an edifice of such scale without a foundation that involved immense cost. Vitberg was convicted of mismanagement and misappropriation of funds, and Nicholas I embarked on a completely different project for a cathedral to be placed in the center of Moscow (see below, chapter 12).[68]

THE FLIGHT FROM RESPONSIBILITY: ALEXANDER'S TRIPS THROUGH THE EMPIRE

In his last years, Alexander took extended trips both abroad and through the provinces. When in the capital, he participated in the usual court ceremonies and balls but with little relish or flair. His dissatisfaction with himself and what he had accomplished grew more extreme and began to affect his public image. He became increasingly peevish and distrustful, lashing out unaccountably at those who aroused his suspicions. He preferred to retreat whenever possible to Tsarskoe Selo where he could work in solitude and quiet. He relinquished the direction of day-to-day government to Arakcheev, who increasingly ruled in the emperor's name. Ministers waited for hours in the favorite's anteroom awaiting an audience. The division of functions established in the first decade of his reign became blurred, and affairs fell into the type of disarray that had so pained him in the years before his accession.

Alexander had always felt himself unable to live up to his image of the man required by the office of Russian emperor. He had called himself lazy when confronted with La Harpe's extensive reading list; he had felt himself sinful and weak when Moscow fell. At each stage he had responded with more ambitious designs of transformation of self and society, seeking new grounds for the superordinate image of emperor. But now the utilitarian scenarios, whether in secular or religious version, had lost their persuasive force. Enlightened despotism was no longer the most advanced form of polity in the West. Acting for the general good now was considered to involve the participation of some part of the population, which brought both the symbolic and the political preeminence of the autocrat into question.

In the years after the victory over Napoleon, liberal noblemen, many of them officers in the elite guards' regiments, took up the ideas of reform that Alexander seemed to have betrayed. In their eyes, his failure and apparent loss of faith in reform undermined the mythical figure of benevolent tsar, and fractured the monologic universe of heroic acts that had united the nobility with their sovereign. They had shared the apocalyptic frame of mind after the victory, which, expressed in poetry, identified Napoleon with the beast and Alexander with Christ. The rapid disappointment of these hopes, Boris

---

[68] *Istoricheskoe*, 4–5, 9–17; Shil'der, *Imperator Aleksandr Pervyi*, 4:80; Herzen, *Byloe i dumy*, 1:252–53.

Gasparov has shown, brought a reversal of the polarities and an identification of Alexander with the devil.[69] The granting of a constitution to Poland
but not to Russia in 1818, the brutality of the military colonies, and the
obscurantism of the mystical reaction led these noblemen to the conclusion
that they themselves would have to take up the cause of realizing the Western
political ideal in Russia. The monarchical myth was replaced by a revolutionary myth. The advanced members of the nobility, not the monarch, undertook the act of cathartic violence that would draw a sharp line between
the present and the past. At the end of the decade, they began to organize
secret societies to bring constitutional government to Russia.

Alexander knew of these societies, but he neither proceeded with reform
nor acted forcefully to suppress them. With the revolutions in Naples and
Spain in 1820, he finally relinquished his dreams of a constitution and the
abolition of serfdom. Despite the mutiny of the Semenovskii Regiment in
1820, and reports from his generals about widespread discontent and the
existence of revolutionary circles in the guards' regiments, Alexander did
nothing. His irresolution was one expression of his failing sense of the rectitude of his own power.

Alexander's frequent trips through the empire have accurately been described as a flight from responsibility. They also represent an innovation—
the use of trips to publicize the emperor's interest in and concern about
conditions in the provinces and non-Russian territories. Catherine's travels
had been displays of mutual admiration. Alexander's showed him trying to
learn about his subjects and to be in touch with the empire, much as the
English princes were doing for the ailing George III.[70] The descriptions of
Alexander's journeys emphasized this purpose. They stressed his rapport
with the people and his interest in the economic and military conditions and
civil institutions of each town. Alexander replayed his version of the scenario
of friendship away from the capital, where he found it easier to show himself
as simple mortal, to give touching displays of modesty and humility. He
continued to shun lavish presentations and even issued orders prohibiting
ceremonial meetings.[71]

The official descriptions of these trips presented Alexander not as the popular monarch receiving jubilant greetings but as the tragic hero, destined by
fate, the object of his subjects' sympathy and tears. A brochure describing
his visit to the town of Orel in 1823, on his way to the review at Tulchin,

---

[69] Gasparov, *Poeticheskii iazyk Pushkina*, 161–75.

[70] On England, see Colley, *Britons*, 233–34.

[71] Sometimes the authorities were told to announce his coming later than intended so he
could be alone in the palace when he arrived. Often he would ride about by himself, without a
suite. At the balls he loved to dance, to enjoy himself as an elegant cavalier unmindful of the
dignity of his office though, as Mikhailovskii-Danilevskii observed, a faraway look in his eyes
betrayed the fact that he had not forgotten. When at a ball in Poltava he saw his initials decorat-
ing the walls and heard a chorus sung in his honor, he immediately made known his displeasure
and prohibited the imperial initials, portraits, or statues, as well as choruses, in the ballrooms
(Shil'der, *Imperator Aleksandr Pervyi*, 4:75–76; *IGK, ts. Al. I,* 290).

portrayed him as a tender, caring tsar. It remarked on the inhabitants' joy at seeing him, "the creator of their well-being." The bishop delivered a sermon emphasizing the tsar's touching and painful concern for his subjects; the tsar himself was the object of sympathy, the tragic victim of fate. "TSAR! Your heart pains over Your loyal subjects, nurturing Your paternal love for them and therefore they will be illuminated all the more by YOUR most radiant and benevolent Countenance."[72]

In 1824 Alexander journeyed from late August through October, following an itinerary that took him as far as Orenburg and Perm in Western Siberia. Along the way he inspected mines and factories, as well as the local garrisons, making clear his concern for the economic betterment of the nation. Accounts were carried in the semiofficial journal, *Otechestvennye Zapiski*, edited by Pavel Svin'in. From Orenburg came "A Letter to the Publisher," written in the personal voice with great emotion by an anonymous correspondent.[73] The correspondent reported that the inhabitants were filled with joy when they heard of the tsar's planned visit, and eagerly awaited "the sight of his face" (*litsezrenie*). The correspondent followed this with the usual descriptions of services and officials, balls and parades, returning to the theme of joyous reception: "Exclamations of the people enjoying the sight of the face of the The Most Kind Monarch poured from their hearts."

The account also emphasizes the Russian sovereign's appeal even for subjects of the various nationalities. Even "foreign and crude peoples"—the Kirghiz, Bashkirs, and Tatars—were enraptured with his goodness (*blagost'*). The review at Orenburg included brigades of the Orenburg cossacks and three hundred Bashkirs. The author described a colorful scene of the soldiers, cossacks, and Bashkir warriors in their battle dress on the field surrounded by native Bashkirs, Khivans, Tatars, and Kirghiz. The tsar, riding through the ranks, praised the "cleanliness and neatness of the clothing and the even lines," and deigned to command himself. At the conclusion of the three-day visit, the correspondent described "a feeling of quiet despondency produced by the departure of the Blessed Emperor."

Reports of Alexander's visits to factories and mines focused on his interest in industrial work and his sympathy with the workers' lot. At Zlatoustov, he visited an arms factory and a gold mine.[74] He arrived at the iron refinery near the factory on a Saturday night and was surprised to hear the sounds of hammers and to see flames from the furnaces. Showing his concern for the laborers, he remarked that it was very late and that the next day was Sunday. The manager replied that the work of the factory itself had come to a halt,

---

[72] Shil'der, *Imperator Aleksandr Pervyi*, 4:282–83; *Puteshestvie ego Velichestva Gosudaria i Imperatora chrez Orlovskuiu guberniu v 1823 godu* (Orel, 1823), 3–7, 10–14, 16–21.

[73] "O prebyvanii Ego Velichestva Gosudaria Imperatora v Orenburge, (Pis'mo k izdateliu)," *Otechestvennye Zapiski* 21 (1825): 404–27.

[74] "Izvestie o vysochaishem prebyvanii ego Imperatorskogo Velichestva na Zlatoustovskikh zavodakh," *Otechestvennye Zapiski* 20 (1824): 265–95.

but the refinery workers, who were paid by the piece, wanted to wait until the molten iron had cooled in an hour, an answer that the tsar received favorably. At the arms factory, he admired the polished and smooth surface of one of the cannon balls. He then turned one of the lathes, which became, momentarily, "an invaluable monument of His Majesty's labor, designated to be preserved for posterity." Alexander also inspected the arms in the arsenal and commented on the quality of the weapons produced.

Alexander is portrayed as a sympathetic human being who displays his rapport with the workers. He chats with German craftsmen, whom he had brought from Solingen and Klingen in 1814, and receives thanks and greetings from them. He visits their homes and inquires why the winter window frames were not inserted. At the gold mine, he insists on working at a gold pit recently named in his honor. He holds a hack and shovel, announcing, "Now I will be a Berggauer," and begins to dig. "With sweat on his brow, the tsar worked for not less than a quarter of an hour when he was beseeched by the mine chief to stop." The very display of his humanity is a sign of his extraordinary virtue, his ability to sympathize with those so far beneath him, and confirmation of his superhuman nature. After his departure, the tools he used and the ore he unearthed were preserved "as sacred mementos" in the offices of the Mining Bureau and the spot was designated for the site of a monument.

In Ekaterinburg, Alexander visited an iron foundry and continued to give his opinion of the work. When some cannon balls split because they had been removed from their molds too early, he remarked that they were useless. The manager exclaimed, "You can't have bread without crumbs," at which the tsar laughed. When Alexander discovered that his order to permit Old Believers in the area to place a cross on their church had not been implemented, he gave a direct order that their wish be granted. In Perm, he visited a military hospital and a prison. He asked the provincial procurator about the crimes committed by each convict and forgave two who were being sent to Siberia. The account in *Otechestvennye Zapiski* gave special attention to his personal conversation with Archbishop Justin, who was seventy-six years old. On this occasion, as on others, Alexander approached clergy without ceremony, like an ordinary worshiper. The aged and ailing cleric was stunned to see the tsar humbly come to him in his cell. The old man, moved to tears, expressed fervent gratitude and uttered a prayer of thanksgiving.[75]

The reports sustain the scenario of humble mortal, but contain a message of fallibility. His efforts to descend to his subjects' level only diminish his imperial image. His visit to the iron foundry shows a fashionable genteel ignorance of technology in the guise of concern. He is sympathetic with the workers but cannot figure out the way to help them. His labor at the gold

---

[75] Bogdanovich, *Istoriia tsarstvovaniia Imperatora Aleksandra I*, 6:366–67; "Prebyvanie Gosudaria Imperatora v Permi," *Otechestvennye Zapiski* 23 (1825): 316–21.

mine is a theatrical display that is almost a parody of Peter the Great, though his tools are treated as relics. His directive to open the Old-Believer church had been simply ignored. He is persuasive only when seeking religious solace.

The accounts of his journey portray a sovereign in search of a role, caught between the heroic imperatives of the imperial myth and the unavoidable evidence of his own mortal fallibility. The human being on the throne could not give the necessary signs of advancing the well-being of his people. His hopes for constitutional reform and emancipation of the serfs had been still-born. The dream of creating a new humanity by spreading the Scriptures had turned into a bureaucratic nightmare and had to be discontinued. Discrepancies between myth and reality, of course, did not arise with Alexander I. But in the past, reality had not been allowed to spoil the allegorical evocations of transformation. Alexander, as the supreme but still flawed mortal, was without metaphorical armor. The final, emblematic proof of his mortality to him, and to many of his contemporaries, was the St. Petersburg flood of November 9, 1824.

Alexander's inability to fight the ravages of nature had implications beyond the disaster in the capital. It brought a realization that the human being on the throne could not spare his subjects incredible loss and suffering. His wife, the empress Elizabeth, expressed her and Alexander's common reaction in a letter: "The sight is terrifying because of the destruction that it represents; it is worse than a fire because one can do nothing to check it." Alexander felt able to accept the bloodshed of the battlefield, he declared, "that is the inevitable lot of war." But seeing the orphaned and dispossessed "deprived in one moment of everything that was dearest to them in life, that resembles nothing I have seen!"[76] The battle was an act of will and determination, and the soldiers entering the sphere of the military had left the sphere of the humane and secure. The military represented an area he believed he could control; the flood was a sign of an inscrutable tragic force of destruction that was beyond human power.

After the waters had receded, Alexander rode through the streets and witnessed the carnage. He left the carriage, stood and wept. The common people understood the flood as divine retribution; some thought it was revenge for the sinful gay life of the capital, others for failing to help the Orthodox Greeks in their rebellion against the Turks. Alexander made it clear to everyone that he viewed it as a sign of his own failings and doom. To a remark that God had punished the people for their sins, he purportedly replied, "No, for mine." After the flood, he became even more dejected and reclusive.[77]

The flood juxtaposed his image against the awesome memory of the founder. Peter had built a city on a swamp and had not been troubled with

[76] Palmer, Alexander I, 395–96; Shil'der, Imperator Aleksandr Pervyi, 4:327.

[77] Shil'der, Imperator Aleksandr Pervyi, 4:324, 327–28; Palmer, Alexander I, 396.

the death and suffering of those sacrificed to his task. Alexander displayed the acute sense of guilt and responsibility that went with the character of kindly, blessed tsar, the exemplar of his era as Peter had been of his. But Alexander could do nothing to save lives. Falconet's statue had apotheosized the enlightened ruler Alexander was to emulate. "The Bronze Horseman" was Pushkin's epitaph for the heroic myth. His sad tsar has been defeated by nature, chastened by an awareness of the limits of his powers. The flood in this respect marks the end of an era when claims of prodigies of progress and benefaction could elevate imperial authority.

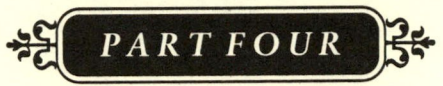

PART FOUR

The Dynastic Scenario

The Mother of the Dynasty

THE MONARCHIES that reemerged on the ashes of Napoleonic Europe differed fundamentally from those that had confronted the revolution at the end of the previous century. Once restored to their dominant position in domestic and international affairs, they had to adapt to the new social and political forces awakened during the revolutionary period. The principle of popular sovereignty may have been defeated, but only by calling on the principle of popular sovereignty itself to rally national feeling against Napoleon's forces. Nineteenth-century monarchs also found it necessary to seek what E. J. Hobsbawm called "a supplementary 'national' foundation" for their authority. They began to develop ways to represent themselves as the embodiments of national feeling rather than as distant figures whose title to rule stemmed from otherworldly origins.[1]

In certain respects, this change was the next step in the ongoing desacralization of European monarchy underway during the eighteenth century. But the new imagery could be as elaborate or fanciful as the old. The spinning of personal and historical mythology around the monarchs would continue over the next half-century, elevating rulers as figures revered or worshiped by the nation and uniting the nation's conservative elements during periods of rapid change. If the monarch could no longer be presented as a god, he or she could be idealized as a better kind of mortal, embodying the features that his people admired. Alexander I claimed the thoughts and sensibilities of an ordinary human being, but, performing the dominant myth, he was resacralized in the form of an angel, sustaining the image of a monarch with otherworldly qualities. George III of England, Frederick William III of Prussia, and Francis II of Austria embodied what Dollinger described as the "leading-image of bourgeois monarchy." Self-effacing, modest, averse to elaborate public presentations, they seemed to prefer the comfort of their private lives. An affectation of simplicity and equality replaced resplendent majesty as a royal ideal.[2]

While this image may have appealed to "bourgeois" values, European monarchs succeeded in divesting it of egalitarian connotations. They appeared as immanent rather than transcendent ideals: no longer gifts from the heavens, shedding benefactions on the land, they became exemplars of human conduct, of modest virtue, to be admired by their subjects. This vir-

---

[1] E. J. Hobsbawm, *Nations and Nationalism Since 1780: Programme, Myth, Reality* (Cambridge, 1990), 84; Dollinger, "Das Leitbild des Burgerkönigtums."
[2] Ibid., 345–52.

tue was demonstrated in the monarch's private life, and particularly in the realm of the family. Most European rulers of the eighteenth century had hardly been encumbered by biblical strictures. In the last decades of the eighteenth century, George III provided a model of personal rectitude that appealed to his subjects, a pattern that would be followed by Frederick William III and Francis II.[3]

The increasing autonomy of European bureaucracies encouraged this change. Administrative reforms of the early nineteenth century in Prussia and Austria created a separation between court and bureaucracy, limiting the monarch's powers over administrative institutions and making his symbolic role all the more significant. The Prussian king and the Hapsburg emperor, as the centers of aristocratic society and the emerging middle-class elite, epitomized common values of family and religion that appealed to both. The idealization of the monarch's family elevated the ruling dynasty as the historical embodiment of the nation.[4]

In Prussia, King Frederick William III became the model of the effacing king, who exemplified probity, constancy, and piety. In the austere tradition of Prussian royalty, he constructed no immense palaces. The single "palace" he built, at Paretz, hardly suited a court; he told the architect David Gilly, "Everything should be made very simple, just think that you are building not for a prince but an ordinary landlord." He hated public appearances, and preferred to walk alone in the woods. He disliked the court etiquette and would, unpredictably, ignore it. Only on the parade ground did Frederick William show a taste for show, but the symbolic value of his military leadership was destroyed by the debacle at Jena in 1806.[5]

From the outset of his reign, Frederick William presented himself as a model of familial rectitude. At his accession in 1797, he banned his predecessor's mistresses and introduced "almost the style of a German burgher home" to his court.[6] His family represented an ideal of romantic love to unite the nation. In the aftermath of the French Revolution, he sought to emphasize not the distance between king and nation but their common values. The first issue of the new journal, *Jahrbücher der Preussischen Monarchie unter den Regierung von Friedrich Wilhelm III*, published in 1798, identified the household of the king, which was "pervaded with the values of true domesticity," with the greater family of the people.[7]

The image of the family united the monarchs and subjects who "entered

---

[3] On George III, see Linda Colley, "The Apotheosis of George III: Loyalty, Royalty and the British Nation, 1760–1820," *Past and Present*, no. 102 (February 1984): 94–129. Also Colley, *Britons*, 196–236.

[4] Stamm-Kuhlmann, "Der Hof Friedrich-Wilhelms III, 277; Hannes Stekl, "Der Wiener Hof in der ersten Hälfte des 19. Jahrhunderts," in Karl Möckl, ed., *Hof und Hofgesellschaft*, 22–23.

[5] Stamm-Kuhlmann, "Der Hof Friedrich-Wilhelms III," passim; Hajo Holborn, *A History of Modern Germany, 1648–1840* (New York, 1964), 2:375–76.

[6] Ibid., 375.

[7] Wulf Wülfing et al., *Historische Mythologie der Deutschen* (Munich, 1991), 59.

into this beautiful sphere." The royal family now began to put on display the ideal of love in marriage. An essay in the June 1798 issue of *Jahrbücher der Preussischen Monarchie*, entitled "Belief and Love," averred: "We have seen in our time that a marvel of transubstantiation has come to pass. Has not the court turned into a family, the throne into heaven, a royal marriage into an eternal union of the heart?"[8] Dispossessed of his kingdom after the battle of Jena, forced to accept the reforms instituted by Baron Heinrich Stein, Frederick William indeed was left with the private realm as his only domain. He claimed no designation from above and even removed the words *from the grace of God* from his title. A painting depicting Frederick William and Queen Louise with their children typifies the Biedermeier style and became a model for subsequent royal family pictures.[9]

If Frederick William exemplified paternal feeling and morality, Queen Louise became the model of cultivated, selfless mother and spouse. She combined the elements of "true religiosity" and "true patriotism," epitomizing "the new Prussian wife." She participated in the German literary awakening of her day, though her first language remained French. From the pietism of Paul Gerhardt, she acquired a faith in the spiritual perfectibility of mankind, and, influenced by the theories of Jean Jacques Rousseau and Johann-Henrich Pestalozzi, she tried new approaches to the upbringing of her children. After her death in 1810, shortly after returning from exile to Berlin, she became the subject of a myth of the pure and holy woman. Poets sang her virtues; artists depicted her in terms of the transfiguration and with the features of the Virgin Mary. One adept of this myth was the queen's oldest daughter, Princess Charlotte, the future Empress Alexandra Fedorovna of Russia.[10]

•

Dynasty became a central theme of Russian monarchy during the reign of Nicholas I. Paul I had established the legal grounding for a dynastic tradition, but his laws could only attain their goal when they corresponded to the principal symbols and modes of public behavior that the monarch used to represent his power. Nicholas I identified the dynasty with the historical destinies of the Russian state and the Russian people. His scenario drastically changed, but at the same time reproduced, the imperial myth. It portrayed the emperor as exemplifying the attributes of Western monarchy, but now as a member of his family, as a human being elevated by heredity and his belonging to a ruling family that embodied the highest values of human-

[8] Ibid., 60.

[9] Holborn, *History of Modern Germany*, 2: 396; Dollinger, "Das Leitbild des Burgerkönigtums," 347.

[10] Wülfing et al., 61–78; Stamm-Kuhlmann, "Der Hof Friedrich-Wilhelms III," 318; Bogdan Krieger, "Erziehung und Unterricht der Königin Luise," *Hohenzollern Jahrbuch* (1910): 117–73; A. Th. Von Grimm, *Alexandra Feodorovna, Empress of Russia* (Edinburg, 1870), 1:51–54.

ity. In this respect, he reflected but magnified the image he emulated. Like his father-in-law, Frederick William III, Nicholas presented himself as a model of constancy, family values, and simple religious faith. Russian monarchy, however, did not permit the retiring, private life-style of the Prussian king. The royal family had to exemplify private virtue in a scenario, an ongoing dramatic performance of domestic dedication, to be admired and imitated by his servitors. As in France and England, the presentation of the monarch as the focus of national feeling required elaborate displays.[11] The private life of the tsar was lavishly staged to portray a Western ideal before the Russian public.

It was the dowager empress, Maria Fedorovna, who shaped the new scenario and instilled familial values in Nicholas during the last decade of Alexander's reign. Only forty-two years old at Paul's death, Maria Fedorovna retained precedence as the principal figure at the imperial court. While Alexander shunned public appearances, she presided over social functions, family dinners and outings, enforcing the strict etiquette she had observed in Paul's reign. Her palace at Pavlovsk became the social and cultural center of the monarchy. She brought to Russia Protestant notions of the altruistic mission of women and the image of empress as protector of the poor and bereft. She developed the network of foster homes and women's training institutes that she had founded under Paul and encouraged other charitable activities. Maria Fedorovna thus initiated the tradition of secular charity as a woman's concern in Russia.

Maria Fedorovna shared the religious and ethical values of the Prussian royal house. Her father, a Duke of Württemberg, had been in Prussian service, and she had been educated both in stern patriarchal Protestant values and the French manners and tastes of the eighteenth-century German courts. As grand duchess and empress, she maintained close family ties, intervening to ensure her parents and siblings marriage alliances, positions in Prussian and Russian service, and, when necessary, subsidies to avert financial disaster. Her attachment to her parents was encouraged by the sentimental literature of the late eighteenth century. She wrote to them in 1780 that she admired the Stoics' ability to remain indifferent to everything, but had no desire to emulate them. "The closer I come to maturity the more I become convinced that the ability to feel nurtures our soul: without it people become savage and cease being people."[12]

These sentiments remained with Maria Fedorovna, and she strove to instill them in the members of the Russian imperial family. At Pavlovsk, she planted a "family grove" of birch trees. The trees were dedicated to each member of the family, and each had a place with his or her name, birth date, and in some cases the date of marriage.[13] She introduced the practice of demonstrative mourning for deceased members of the house and the belief

[11] On England, see Colley, "The Apotheosis of George III," 113–21.
[12] Shumigorskii, *Imperatritsa Mariia Fedorovna*, 1:149.
[13] Likhachev, *Poeziia sadov*, 220, 229.

that family bonds grew stronger after death, elements of the "cult of memory" ascendant in the West. She hallowed the memory of her parents and her husband with two memorials at Pavlovsk, "To My Parents" and "To My Husband-Benefactor." Thomon's "To My Husband-Benefactor," completed in 1810, is a monument in the form of a Greek temple meant to express her sense of loss about Paul, for whom her feelings had been less than tender. The interior is occupied by Ivan Martos's statue of a mourning wife, her head resting at the side of an urn (fig. 39). The twenty-four weeping faces on the metopes express the feeling of sorrow due the father of the dynasty.[14]

Maria Fedorovna tried to show her children the importance of marriage and marital love, but her oldest sons remained deaf to her pleas. Both had strained relations with their wives and maintained the fashionable insouciance in matters of marital fidelity. Neither produced an heir. Alexander's two daughters with Elizabeth had died in infancy. Constantine's wife, the grand duchess Anna Fedorovna, left Russia in 1801 and saw her husband only during his European trips. Maria Fedorovna became the family conscience, warning her children that they served as personal models for their subjects. When, in 1803, the grand duke Constantine informed her that he wished to terminate his marriage with a divorce, the empress replied with an angry letter. After describing "wounds of the heart" he had inflicted on her, she pointed out the symbolic implications of such a step. It would bring "ruinous consequences for public morals as well as the lamentable and dangerous temptation for the entire nation." The humblest peasant far from the capital, noting the absence of the grand duchess's name next to his in church prayers, would lose respect for the sacrament of marriage and for religious faith itself.

> He [the peasant] will presume that faith is less sacred for the imperial family than for him and such an opinion is enough to tear the hearts and minds of subjects away from the tsar and the entire imperial house. How horrible it is to publicize the fact that this temptation is caused by the imperial brother, obliged to be the model of virtue for his subjects! Morals, already corrupted and spoiled, will decline into still greater depravity through the ruinous example on the steps of the throne, one who occupies the position next to the sovereign. Believe me, dear Constantine Pavlovich, only unwavering virtue will enable us to instill in the people confidence in our superiority, which together with the feeling of reverent respect, secures the tranquillity of the empire.

She was willing to relent if Constantine chose a respectable German princess for his wife. Constantine, however, had little taste for German princesses. In 1820 an imperial edict announcing the approval of his divorce permitted him to proceed with his morganatic marriage to a Polish noblewoman, Joanna Grudzinska.[15]

---

[14] *Pamiatniki arkhitektury prigorodov Leningrada*, 248–49.
[15] N. K. Shil'der, *Imperator Nikolai Pervyi*, 1:128.

39. Monument *To My Husband-Benefactor*. Scupltor, Ivan Martos.

Maria Fedorovna's romantic vision of family relations and connubial love was set forth by her protégé, the poet Vasilii Zhukovksii. Zhukovskii's verse shifted the referent of imperial virtue from a civic ideal, personified in figures of the gods, heroes, or Roman emperors, to the private ideals of the nursery and the hearth. Zhukovskii announced the new poetic theme in an ode to Maria Fedorovna of 1813:

> And where is a more glorious subject for the poet?
> Tsaritsa, mother, spouse, daughter of tsars,
> The beauty of tsaritsas, the joy of the hemisphere,
> Who can find the language proper for it?

Zhukovskii concluded the ode with an evocation of Alexander's imminent return to Russia. He presented the moment as a family event, not a mythical one, personal affection expressing imperial glory:

> Blessed hour! In the form of martial heroes,
> He bends his illustrious head,
> The Sovereign-son before the mother-tsaritsa,
> May their love bless this glory—
> And withal the saved world lies,
> At your sacred hand![16]

Maria Fedorovna presented lavish celebrations for the homecoming of Constantine and Alexander after the wars. A poem by Sergei Glinka, in *Ruskoi Vestnik*, described the reception of Constantine at Pavlovsk on June 17, 1814, as a touching reunion of mother and son. "Crowned Mother! You meet your Son in joy." Her maternal love became an expression of the feelings of all of Russia:

> Rejoice, Tender Mother! Everywhere
> Your joy is shared!
> The heavenly moment arrives;
> Soon you will see all your progeny!
> Your soul will come alive, MARIA!
> And Russia will come alive with YOU.[17]

The reunion of Maria and Alexander was the occasion for a great celebration staged by the Venetian artist Pietro di Gottardo Gonzaga. The spectacle was described on the pages of the official newspaper, *Severnaia Pochta*.[18] Alexander was met by dancing children and songs composed by Iu. A. Neledinskii. Young people in Russian dress, carrying sheaves of hay, walked behind ploughs, an allegory of peace and prosperity. Married women rocked their babies and called for the time when they would again see their beloved,

---

[16] Zhukovskii, *Polnoe sobranie sochinenii*, 2:24–25.

[17] "Prazdnestvo v Pavlovske, 17 Iunia 1814 goda," *Ruskoi Vestnik* 13 (1814): 37–38.

[18] *Severnaia pochta*, June 24, 1814, August 1, 1814; for a description in English, see Suzanne Massie, *Pavlovsk: The Life of a Russian Palace* (Boston, 1990), 87–89.

a scene, the newspaper indicated, that prompted expressions of joy on the faces of the emperor and empress. The evening ended with a ball and a show of fireworks, with the word *blessed* traced in letters of fire on the skies.

Maria Fedorovna's three youngest children—Nicholas, Michael, and Anna—grew up sharing strong feelings of family solidarity. Ignored by the court, they drew close to one another. They formed their own club, "triopathy," and wore special rings, one of which they gave to their mother as an honorary member. They maintained close ties throughout their lives, what Anna Pavlovna described as their "family union." Their later correspondence continued to express an intimacy of feeling and a common purpose that united the members of the house.[19]

Grand Duke Nicholas Pavlovich shared his mother's reverence for the institution of marriage and the inclination to regard marital vows as lofty and sacred. When Nicholas showed an interest in Princess Charlotte of Prussia on his return from France in 1814, Maria Fedorovna's esteem for him, previously none too high, rose appreciably. She herself had dreamed of such a match, and in 1809 had discussed the possibility with Queen Louise herself. Princess Charlotte worshiped the memory of the queen, whose bust she later kept in her boudoir. She made herself in her mother's image, adopting her romantic literary tastes and showing the same devotion to family and children. After Louise's death, which had occurred in Charlotte's thirteenth year, Charlotte took her mother's place at her father's side and learned at an early age the poise and confidence of a sovereign.[20]

The betrothal of Princess Charlotte to Grand Duke Nicholas in October 1815 turned the alliance between monarchies into a family bond. The sentimental rhetoric of the alliance identified political loyalty with personal dedication, but, as we can see from their letters to Frederick William in 1816, the emperor and his mother had different notions of personal dedication. Alexander praised the bond as an expression of the feeling of "sacred friendship" that had arisen between the monarchs. Maria Fedorovna dwelled on the qualities of the two young people, which seemed to promise a truly romantic marriage. Princess Charlotte struck her as the ideal spouse. But it was not Charlotte's beauty that impressed her: "The enchanting character of the young princess, her thorough and unaffected mind, the tenderness of her feelings clearly foretell the happiness of my son as well as my own." Nicholas had shown the traits of a good family man. He appreciated the honor of the princess's hand, "with all the warmth of a religious, pure, honorable and honest heart, totally given to his spouse and aware of all the responsibility carried by the obligation to make the happiness of his friend the constant preoccupation of his life."[21] It was this image of loving husband and caring father that Nicholas I brought to the Russian throne.

[19] S. W. Jackman, *Romanov Relations* (London, 1969), 4, 107, and passim.
[20] Grimm, *Alexandra Feodorovna*, 1:55.
[21] Shil'der, *Imperator Nikolai Pervyi*, 1:61–63.

CHAPTER NINE

Nicholas I and the Creation of a Dynastic Scenario

> May Alexander's epoch of largesse go on,
>
> In YOU, HE lives with us,
>
> Oh, TSAR-FATHER!
>
> Receive the people's vow of purest love . . .
>
> And YOU, HUSBAND, FATHER are fortunate,
>
> Tender BROTHER and obedient SON!
>
> And philanthropic, just,
>
> And enlightened RULER,
>
> Shine on the throne of renowned ANCESTORS . . .

> *Grigorii Okulov, "A Russian's Feelings on the Day of the Sacred*
> *Coronation of Emperor Nicholas Pavlovich," 1826*[1]

THE TWO SPHERES

If the grand duke Nicholas Pavlovich fit his mother's notion of the ideal husband, he hardly lived up to her expectations of education and cultivation. Maria Fedorovna, herself a product of the enlightenment, believed in civil education and mistrusted military training, which she saw running amok during Paul's reign. Nicholas was raised under the tough and unyielding supervision of officers from the Baltic provinces who instilled in him a German respect for discipline and authority. His first teachers were Miss Jane Lyon, a Scottish woman of pronounced anti-Polish views, and two Baltic noblewomen, Iulia Adlerberg and Charlotte Lieven. In 1800 Paul had appointed Count and General M. I. Lamsdorf to take charge of the education of his youngest sons, Nicholas and Michael. Lamsdorf immediately imposed a severe military regime on the boys. His notion of training and discipline was not complicated by enlightenment theories of the sensibility of children. He struck the boys with rulers and rifle-ramrods. Sometimes he would fly into a rage, seize the child who had angered him by the chest or collar and slam him against the wall until he was nearly unconscious.[2]

---

[1] Grigorii Okulov, *Chuvstvo russkogo v den' sviashchenneishego koronovaniia gosudaria imperatora Nikolaia Pavlovicha* (St. Petersburg, 1826).

[2] W. Bruce Lincoln, *Nicholas I: Emperor and Autocrat of All the Russias* (Bloomington, Ind., 1978), 50–54; M. Korf, "Materialy i cherty k biografii Imperatora Nikolaia I i k istorii ego tsarstvovaniia," *Sbornik Imperatorskogo Russkogo istoricheskogo obshchestva*, 98:22–23, 27–31.

Nicholas's early experience was of brutal barracks discipline. His education may have been stern and at times cruel, but it remained simple and uniform and free of the contradictions and pressures that had beset the early lives of Paul and Alexander. He grew up learning to respect his father's image and to admire everything Paul represented. He began to love the spare and simple world and the Germanic discipline he had been taught to obey. He felt an unwavering confidence in his own judgment and ideas. The young man not born to the throne gained the absolute confidence in authority that made him the exemplar of power for the Romanov house throughout the nineteenth century.

To be sure, Maria Fedorovna endeavored to give Nicholas a serious education and appointed noted scholars to teach him Latin, Greek, political economy, and law. But he showed little interest in these subjects. In 1809, when he was thirteen, Maria Fedorovna tried to isolate him from his surroundings, following the eighteenth-century notion that the influence of the environment could corrupt a young prince and turn his head from sound ideas. She removed both Nicholas and Michael from their friends and placed them under her personal supervision at Gatchina. There she sought to banish frivolity and military spectacles from their lives and compel them to devote themselves to their "university" studies.[3] But Nicholas proved a bored and surly pupil. The academician Heinrich Storch's lectures on political economy, Nicholas later recalled, put him to sleep. He described his eminent instructors in law, M. A. Balugianskii and V. G. Kukol'nik, as "the most insupportable pedants imaginable." The tedium of his lessons merely strengthened his longing for the military. He showed diligence and ability only in the study of military science. In 1814 he gave up alternating military and civil dress, as his mother had insisted, and began to appear only in military uniform.[4]

Nicholas and Michael longed to see combat against Napoleon, but their hopes were disappointed by their mother and the emperor, both of whom insisted that they remain in Russia until the end of hostilities. Their principal experience was celebrating the victory, particularly in large-scale parades, and the brothers lived with frustrated dreams of battle experience. They traveled to Paris in 1814, and again in 1815 for the parade at Vertus. At Vertus, they participated in the victory festivities as adult members of the family. In their debut as commanders, Nicholas, at age nineteen, and Michael, at seventeen, delighted in the rehearsals of the drill formations. On the first day, Nicholas was pleased that he was among only Russian officers. On the second, he commanded a brigade of the Grenadier's Division while his brother commanded the cavalry of the artillery. Their adjutant, Konovitsyn, reported to Maria Fedorovna that both had earned the respect of their troops. The mystique of Vertus, the translation of victory into spectacle that

---

[3] Lincoln, *Nicholas I*, 57–58.
[4] Ibid., 57; Korf, "Materialy," 73, 82–83.

reflected Providence, entranced Nicholas throughout his life. The parades at Vertus remained for him the prototypical demonstration of political power when he ascended the throne.[5]

The culmination of Nicholas's education, as planned by Maria Fedorovna, was for him to travel; two tours, one through Russia, the other to Europe, would acquaint the grand duke with the empire and with the world. Such trips fit the new inclination for monarchs to make themselves visible outside their palaces and capitals. An educational tour had been recommended by philosophes, such as Diderot, and was an important part of the program outlined by the German poet E. M. Arndt, whose work on the upbringing of a prince was well known in the Russian court (on Arndt, see below, chapter 11). Maria Fedorovna organized the journey in detail, giving specific instructions on what Nicholas was to see and how he was to behave. Her memorandum, outlining the plans, stated that the trip's principal goal was to enable the grand duke to learn about the condition of the Russian state.[6] She proposed, and Alexander agreed, that Nicholas was to visit governmental institutions where he would be allowed to question the officials about the functioning of their offices. She stressed that his inspections of the various areas had the purpose of learning about institutions, not inspecting them in order to pass judgment.

Maria Fedorovna stated most emphatically that the trip should not focus on military matters. Nicholas was to get to know his country, the state of each province, "its resources, its failings, the means to remedy them, to see all useful institutions of welfare, charity, science, factories, etc." The military knowledge he gained was to be no more than "a useful accessory." He was to keep a detailed journal of his experiences and make careful entries, for these would show his manner of seeing and judging and would help the emperor to form his own opinion of the grand duke's future use to the empire.

But the tour also had a ceremonial purpose: to introduce Nicholas to his subjects. Maria Fedorovna was extremely apprehensive about the impression Nicholas would leave. He would start out well, for "you are loved on the basis of hope." People had heard good things about him, "but this is the moment when you must consolidate this sentiment of affection: you must merit it by your kindness, the affability that should be evident in your manners, in your words." She warned him especially about his voice, "for in raising it too much, and allowing it full strength, it assumes an uncouth expression that resembles brusqueness, which must absolutely be avoided." Most of all, he should strive to capture the esteem of his compatriots. "Tell yourself, so to speak, that from province to province you will be judged."[7]

Nicholas's three-month tour in the spring of 1816, when he was ap-

---

[5] Shil'der, *Imperator Nikolai Pervyi*, 1:54–56.
[6] Ibid., 1:64–67, 573–75.
[7] Ibid., 1:577–78.

proaching his twentieth birthday, took him through central Russia to the Ukraine, the Crimea, and New Russia. Nicholas kept his "civil" and "military journals" faithfully, both of them in French, but otherwise seems to have paid little heed to his mother's words. Despite her admonitions, he viewed himself as an inspector, as a judge of what he saw, a young man not mindful of the opinions of society, but with his own views, which he did not question. The published extracts from his civil journal indicate his conviction that all problems could be solved by more assertive authority. He made numerous negative remarks about Poles, Jews, and Tatars. He commented on the weakness of the ties of the Polish nobles in Belorussia with the throne and on their poverty.

His notes on the Crimea describe the beauty of the landscape and stress the misery of the inhabitants: "There is nothing poorer and lazier than these southern Tatars." The wealth of the land was completely uncultivated, which prompted only proud expectations of the benefits of the Russian social system. "If the Crimea were not in Tatar hands, it would be completely different, for where there are landlords and Russian and Little Russian settlers, everything is different. There is grain, spacious gardens. In other words, they take advantage of the wealth of this blessed land." On occasion, he also remarked on economic measures, such as the building of a factory by a landlord to make productive use of household serfs' labor, or the possibility of making Odessa a free port to draw trade to the Black Sea.[8]

The same tone of censure characterizes his remarks in his military journal, which focuses primarily on physical conditions and drill. He remarks on the poor state of hospitals and barracks. He objects strenuously to the living accommodations of the regiments and the way the men were provided for. Otherwise, he devotes his journal to descriptions of drill and uniforms. He wrote of the town of Porkhov, in Pskov Province: "The combined battalion is really well trained. The officers are very firm in drill, the soldiers are trained fairly well, but the step is in general not sure. Among the Eger corps, it is worse. The men do not stand close in rows, they march in rows very badly, the drill is even worse." Baron Korf commented that his account did not "*concern a single essential matter of military organization, administration or the moral spirit and attitude of the rank and file.*" Indicatively, there was no mention of musketry practice.[9]

Nor did Nicholas seem to make an effort to win his servitors' hearts. The reports on his trip are reticent on his reception. News of Nicholas's trip appeared in *Severnaia Pochta* but with few indications of the impressions he had made. An account of his appearance at a ball in Novocherkassk briefly indicates that "taking part in the dances his incomparably sympathetic conduct brought those at the ball to indescribable rapture."[10] His guardian on the trip, Adjutant-General Count P. V. Golenishchev-Kutuzov, reported fa-

[8] Korf, "Materialy," 90–98; Lincoln, *Nicholas I*, 63–64.
[9] Korf, "Materialy," 95–96; Lincoln, *Nicholas I*, 63–64.
[10] *Severnaia Pochta*, August 12, 1816.

vorably on his conduct, indicating "that he had received excellent respect, devotion and love from all estates," but the descriptions of his visit give little sense of warmth. F. F. Vigel' described him as "uncommunicative and cold" in the years before his marriage. "Many regarded him unfavorably . . . To tell the truth absolutely no one liked him."[11] He was hardly the charming young grand duke conquering the hearts of those he met. But it was not Nicholas's inclination to court affections or perform a scenario of friendship. The tutelage of "Papa Lamsdorf" had instilled a respect for force, authority, and punishment that left him little disposed to seek approval or affection. It was this mode of behavior that he would display in unveiling his own scenario of power during the first days of his reign.

Nicholas's education concluded with a four-month tour of England in the fall of 1816 and the winter of 1817. A special memorandum written by Count Nesselrode, the foreign minister, informed him that each nation's political institutions were the result of its own historical experience and had to be protected from foreign borrowings. Nicholas took to the English aristocracy and the English court, and during his reign loved to play the English gentleman. But English political life, especially the clubs and demonstrations, repelled him. After England, he again visited Prussia, which was more to his taste. He was delighted when he was appointed chief of the Third Brandenburg Cuirassier Regiment and then led the regiment in review before the Prussian king.[12]

•

The passion for military review represented another feeling shared by Grand Duke Nicholas and Princess Charlotte. Charlotte felt none of the enlightenment wariness about military pursuits and display. When she crossed the frontier into Russia in June 1817, the sight of the guards' regiments welcoming her dispelled her homesickness. She wrote:

> I was delighted to see again the Semenovskii, Izmailovskii, and Preobrazhenskii Regiments which I remembered from a military review in Silesia . . . during the armistice of 1813. And when I saw the Chevalier Guards drawn up near the Admiralty, I could not restrain a small cry of pleasure because they reminded me of my beloved Guards of the Berlin Regiment. I did not even think that I would one day be the honorary commander of this regiment.[13]

Princess Charlotte, now baptized as Grand Duchess Alexandra Fedorovna, quickly became accustomed to her life in Russia. Although her Prussian manners seemed a bit brusque, as she herself was aware, those in the court quickly began to accept her, "when they saw my general benevolence." She and Nicholas spent the summer after the wedding enjoying dances and

[11] Shil'der, *Imperator Nikolai Pervyi*, 1:72; Lincoln, *Nicholas I*, 67.

[12] Ibid., 65–66.

[13] Ibid., 67; "Imperatritsa Aleksandra Fedorovna v svoikh vospominaniiakh," *Russkaia Starina* 88 (1898): 14–18.

games at Pavlovsk.[14] Her single unpleasant memory was her conversion to Russian Orthodoxy: "The change of religion cost me so much and oppressed my heart." She never found spiritual sustenance in orthodoxy. At heart, she remained Protestant; the master bedroom at Peterhof typically contained a European crucifixion and a Bible in English along with Russian icons placed there for Nicholas. Although, as empress, she faithfully observed orthodox rites and practices, she remained largely indifferent to religious questions and the activity of the church.[15]

The happiness of Nicholas's and Alexandra's marriage now became part of the scene that Maria Fedorovna constructed around herself, a contrast to the doleful family lives of Alexander and Constantine. The picture was completed when in April 1818, at the age of twenty-two, Nicholas became the first of his brothers to father a son and to make the dynasty a human reality. The birth of Alexander Nikolaevich in Moscow was another link between the Prussian and the Russian royal families. King Frederick William immediately awarded his grandson the order of the Black Eagle and set off for Moscow to serve as his godfather.[16]

Zhukovskii turned parenthood into a heroic attribute of the imperial family. His ode on the birth of Alexander Nikolaevich made the touching moment an event in the mythology of power.

> Enter our world, little one, welcome guest,
> Beholding you, knees bent,
> The young father before the saved mother,
> Speechless, sobs in the heat of love.

Motherhood, which figured little in eighteenth-century scenarios, became in Zhukovskii's verse a noble and romantic calling; maternal love was presented as a holy and uplifting force.

> How can one understand, in this incomprehensible hour,
> What has happened with your soul, young mother?
> Your soul beholds a new world.
> Your child, a heavenly messenger
> Has told your soul of a better life.
> Lit the purest hopes within it,
> Neither wishes nor joys,
> Are now for yourself,
> Swathed in diapers,
> Still without words, or eyes that see,
> In your eyes, he finds love;
> Like silence, his sleep is sublime,
> And the news of life has still not reached him.[17]

---

[14] Ibid., 19–24.

[15] Florent Gille, *A la mémoire de l'impératrice Alexandra Féodorovna* (Paris, 1864), 8; "Imperatritsa Aleksandra Fedorovna," 18–19, 23–24; A. Shemanskii and S. Geichenko, *Krizis samoderzhaviia; Petergofskii Kottedzh Nikolaia I* (Moscow, 1932), 35.

[16] S. S. Tatishchev, *Alexander II; ego zhizn' i tsarstvovanie* (St. Petersburg, 1903), 1:5.

[17] Zhukovskii, *Polnoe sobranie sochinenii*, 2:124–26.

Nicholas and Alexandra had now attained the happy, private life that represented an ideal of kingship in Europe during the restoration period. After the birth of their son, they moved into the Anichkov Palace. Nicholas had the chambers reconstructed in order to eliminate large halls and provide small rooms suitable for a quiet family life. He declared, "If someone asks you in what corner of the world true happiness hides, do me a favor and send that person to the paradise of Anichkov." Nicholas and Alexandra looked back on this period as the happiest time in their lives: "He and I, both of us were truly happy and content when we were alone in our rooms, very affectionate and tender," she wrote. "Both of us," she recalled "had a horror of everything that was *the court*." The happiness was interrupted only at a dinner in 1819, when Alexander stunned them with the suggestion that Nicholas would be his successor. "We felt as if struck by a bolt of lightening," Alexandra wrote. "The future seemed somber and without happiness."[18]

Their idyll dramatized the sharp division of sexual spheres, between the public and the private, that was underway in Europe in these years. It was the end of the eighteenth-century androgynous concept reflected in the ideal of a ruler who united male properties of power with female attributes of beauty and love, whose private life was engulfed in public obligations and duties beyond the ken of ordinary mortals. Catherine I, Elizabeth, and Catherine II could emulate men in the manner of goddesses in heroic achievements. The nineteenth century brought "the end of the old isomorphisms," what Thomas Laqueur called "the discovery of the sexes."[19] Empresses now distanced themselves from politics, and were sequestered in their own sphere as a symbol of the higher values that the government had to maintain. Alexandra vowed she would never utter the word *command*. Literature and the arts, not political thought, constituted her intellectual pastimes. While Nicholas intimidated, she endeared. She lived in a fairytale world, protected from the sordid and brutal exercise of power.

From the late eighteenth century, the ideal of marriage embodying romantic love had been set forth in European art and literature.[20] Nicholas and Alexandra exemplified this ideal, again presenting Russian monarchy as the realization of a current Western value. Their vision found expression in Caspar Friedrich's painting *On the Sailboat*, which they purchased in 1820 during a visit to Germany. A couple lies on the bow of a boat looking across the water toward the outlines of a medieval city, concealed in mist. They hold hands, spiritually united, facing a mysterious world from a spiritual distance, brought closer to each other by the expanse of the sea. *On the Sailboat* later hung on the living room wall of Nicholas's Cottage, the fam-

---

[18] I. N. Bozherianov, *Zhizneopisanie Imperatritsy Aleksandry Fedorovny, suprugi Nikolaia I* (St. Petersburg, 1898), iv; "Imperatritsa Aleksandra Fedorovna," 25, 52–54.

[19] Laqueur, *Making Sex*, chap. 5.

[20] On the beginnings of the spread of the romantic notion of marriage, see Lawrence Stone, *The Family, Sex, and Marriage in England, 1500–1800* (London, 1977), 284–87.

ily retreat with a view of the Gulf of Finland and Kronstadt (see below, chapter 12).[21]

On the stage of the Russian court, the private idyll turned into a new political idealization. As emperor, Nicholas's love for the empress signified something more than the feeling a husband has for his wife; connubial love was presented as a noble act of self-dedication and a model for his servitors' conduct at home and in the service. The metaphorical mode of eighteenth-century monarchy was replaced by the transformation of the life of a ruler into a romantic fairytale, a gratification of private wishes within the family. Nicholas, the stern officer, turns into the chivalric knight, whose undying love prompts acts of heroism and sacrifice.

The initial presentation of the idyll was the "divertissement" staged by King Frederick William in Berlin in 1821 on Thomas Moore's oriental fantasy, "Lalla-Rookh." In Moore's poem, Lalla-Rookh embarks on a voyage to meet the Prince of Bukharia. On the way she is entertained by the tales told by a young poet, which provided the subjects for the lavish *tableaux vivants*. At the end of the tales, she arrives at a lake, where she awaits her fiancé on the steps of his palace. The poet sheds his disguise and turns out to be the prince. Romantic love ends in wedlock. Thus ends a parable of a princess leaving home for happiness in a distant kingdom.

In the pageant, Alexandra herself played Lalla-Rookh, wearing a white and gold dress covered with pearls and jewels, and oriental slippers embroidered with emeralds. Nicholas played the prince, dressed in a blue Circassian-style coat, a green turban, and yellow oriental-style shoes (fig. 40). The romance unfolded against a background of oriental exotica, the men and women of (Indian) Bashkiria and Kashmir dressed in sumptuous costumes; the India of the poem was a romanticized expression of the "Eastern" myth of imperial power. The presentation in the form of *tableaux vivants*, according to the artistic code of the early nineteenth century, placed them in the sphere of art—a higher, ideal order depicted in the frozen poses of two-dimensional paintings. These, then, were captured in engravings reproduced in an album.[22] The spectacle, the album, and simultaneous German translation, greatly pleased the poet.[23]

The literary treatment of Alexandra presented an ideal love in the family without reference to Olympus. The family imitated fiction, and its members strove to live up to, or appear to live up to, their romantic models. The figure of Lalla-Rookh captured the role she was to play, and, when uttered at court,

[21] Sabine Rewald, ed., *The Romantic Vision of Caspar David Friedrich: Paintings and Drawings from the USSR* (New York, 1990), 14–15, 48–50. This exhibition catalog has useful essays by Robert Rosenblum and Boris I. Asvarishch.

[22] *Lalla Roûkh, Divertissement mêlé de chants et danses* (Berlin, 1822). On the use of two-dimensional representation as an artistic code, see Lotman, "The Theater and Theatricality as Components of Early Nineteenth Century Culture," in Lotman and Uspenskii, *The Semiotics of Russian Culture*, 165–69.

[23] Thomas Moore, *Lalla-Rookh: An Oriental Romance* (New York, 1868), 15–16.

40. Illustration of Grand Duke Nicholas Pavlovich and Grand Duchess Alexandra Fedorovna in costume for the performance of Thomas Moore's "Lalla-Rookh."

the name referred to her.[24] At the end of this evocation of a world of paradaisical beauty, she was reported as saying, with a sigh, "Is it then over? Are we at the close of all that has given us so much delight? And lives there no poet who will impart to others some notion of the happiness we have enjoyed this evening?"[25]

Indeed, Alexandra strove constantly to regain this happiness, and her life became an approximation of a fairytale. Just as Nicholas exemplified self-sacrifice, denying himself so he could make demands on others, she feigned happiness and gratification, her pleasure a constant expression of the love uniting the emperor with his elite and commending him to his people. Her ideal was set forth in a cycle of poems that Zhukovskii addressed to her as Lalla-Rookh. The poem, "The Appearance of Poetry in the Form of Lalla-Rookh," compares her to a "heavenly angel," the genius of pure beauty, the spirit of love, the spirit of song.

> Near her all our thoughts are song!
> And each sound of her speech,
> The smile of the lips, the movements of her face,
> Sigh, and glance, in her all is song.[26]

NICHOLAS'S ACCESSION AND THE DECEMBRIST INSURRECTION

The uprising of the guards on December 14, 1825, indicated both the sway and the limits of the utilitarian myth. The insurgent guardsmen, many from leading noble families, had accepted the premise of the sovereign's unlimited power to promote the betterment of his subjects. It was Alexander's failure to live up to their hopes that led them to take on the task for themselves, under the pretext of bringing Grand Duke Constantine to the throne. They would impose a new form of government, from above, whether constitutional monarchy or a republic. Although the Decembrists numbered only a small minority of the Russian nobility, their rebellion represented the first open rejection since 1730 of the Petrine myth that the emperor was the principal agent of secular progress. The severity of Nicholas's retribution and the vengeance expressed in his scenario created a rift in the nobility. The insur-

---

[24] In an omitted stanza of *Eugene Onegin*, Pushkin described Alexandra dancing the polonaise with the emperor, Alexander, while Onegin saw only his beloved Tatiana:

> And in the bright and rich hall,
> When into the hushed, and close crowd,
> Like a winged lily,
> Enters, swaying, Lalla-Rookh.
> Iu. M. Lotman, *Roman A. S. Pushkin "Evgenii Onegin":*
> *kommentarii* (Leningrad, 1980), 83–85

[25] Moore, *Lalla-Rookh*, 16.
[26] Zhukovskii, *Polnoe sobranie sochinenii*, 3:54–55.

rection and its aftermath divided those who adhered to the dynastic scenario from a small but growing number of educated noblemen who no longer looked upon the emperor as the transcendent embodiment of the state. After December 14, 1825, belief in the imperial scenario became a matter of political choice.

On the morning of December 14, the rebels assembled their troops on the Senate Square and took the oath to Grand Duke Constantine Pavlovich, whom they claimed would grant a constitution. If the Decembrists represented Alexander's liberal hopes, Nicholas followed his brother's example of severe military discipline and immediately sought to restore order. He tried, however, to avoid bloodshed. General Count M. A. Miloradovich, who had tried to calm the rebels, had been shot and killed by Peter Kakhovskii. Nicholas himself then rode out onto the square and in vain attempted to persuade the rebels to surrender. The metropolitan Serafim, holding the cross, announced that Constantine had abdicated and taken the oath of loyalty to Nicholas; but this prevarication also failed. The officers cried out that Constantine was under arrest and began to shout for Constantine. The situation deteriorated. The poet Küchelbecker tried to shoot Grand Duke Michael but his gun misfired. The construction workers on the roof of St. Isaac's Cathedral began to heave logs down on the loyal troops. Nicholas was afraid the insurrection would be taken up by "the rabble." He ordered a cavalry charge, but the horses slipped on the ice, and several of the Cavalier Guards were wounded by shots from the rebels. Finally, he issued the order to open fire, and rounds of artillery across the square sent the rebels into flight.

Only a few regiments mutinied on the morning of December 14, but the challenge to Nicholas's rule created an atmosphere of hostility, bitterness, and fear that would dominate his reign. It remained imprinted in Nicholas's mind as a traumatic moment that justified intensified surveillance and police persecution to combat a persistent specter of revolution. But the event that challenged his, and the dynasty's right to rule was, at the same time, the opportunity for him to justify his authority and to relegitimize monarchical authority in general.

In addition to suppressing the rebellion and wiping out the vestiges of opposition, Nicholas set about constructing an elaborate myth of the event. His manifestos and ceremonies following the uprising, the memoirs he left, his constant recollections of each moment of the day in private conferences assured that the heroic efforts of that day would not be forgotten. Each year, December 14 was celebrated with a Te Deum, and those who stood by him at the moment of danger became his constant comrades and advisers.

Nicholas used the Decembrist Rebellion to refurbish the ruler's image as conqueror and to put it at the service of the autocracy's defense, rather than its transformation. Nicholas's act of violence was perpetrated in behalf of the dynasty. The insurrection made it possible to present conservatism as a radical break, for Nicholas defined the Decembrist Movement as the embodiment of the Western, rationalistic views that his brother, Alexander, had also held. He rebelled against these Western doctrines, which he claimed had pervaded the nobility, and his violence hallowed the very fragile dynastic tradition that could perpetuate absolute monarchical power in Russia. He presented his triumph as the triumph of the Russian national spirit. Just as eighteenth-century monarchs defined their governance as resembling European monarchies, Nicholas would define his as distinctively Russian, as loyal to a nationally rooted tradition of authoritarianism. In crushing the rebellion, he heroically began a new era, loyal to a tradition presumably demonstrated by the failure of the rebellion.

To defend a dynastic tradition, one first had to be constructed, for it was the absence of clear directives about succession that had created the conditions for the revolt. Paul's Succession Law of 1797 remained in force, but Alexander's childlessness and Constantine's reluctance to rule made it largely irrelevant. Therefore, Alexander had reverted to the eighteenth-century principle of designation and had chosen Nicholas as his successor. In 1823 he signed a manifesto appointing Nicholas heir and placed copies of the document—together with two letters from Constantine indicating his intention to abdicate—in the State Council, the Senate, the Holy Synod, and the Assumption Cathedral in Moscow. But the act had not been promulgated, for reasons that remain inscrutable, and therefore had no legal force. At the moment of his death, it was known only to Arakcheev and A. N. Golitsyn, Metropolitan Filaret, Maria Fedorovna, and possibly to Nicholas himself.[27]

Nicholas at first endeavored to adhere to the law and took the oath to Constantine, who was in Warsaw, serving as commander-in-chief of the Russian armies. Sergei Mironenko has shown that Nicholas's initial impulse was to assume the throne, but he was dissuaded by General Miloradovich, who, as governor-general of St. Petersburg, insisted on observing the legal order of succession. The guards' regiments of the capital then swore loyalty to Constantine; this was a flagrant breach of the tradition for, previously, military forces had sworn their loyalty only *after* the civil authorities had done so.[28] Nicholas awaited Constantine's declaration of abdication. But Constantine remained enigmatically silent.

When Nicholas received news of an impending revolt, he embarked on a virtual coup d'état. He presented his accession manifesto to the State Council on the evening of December 13. The State Council approved the manifesto that evening. They had little choice. "Today, I request you to take the oath; tomorrow I shall command you," Nicholas declared. The statement, Bruce Lincoln has observed, set the tone of his relationship with the council for the course of his reign.[29] The next morning, members of the Senate and

---

[27] Mironenko, *Stranitsy tainoi istorii samoderzhaviia*, 74–85; Lincoln, *Nicholas I*, 22–26.
[28] Mironenko, *Stranitsy tainoi istorii samoderzhaviia*, 89–90.
[29] Lincoln, *Nicholas I*, 35.

the Holy Synod and the chiefs of the loyal guards' regiments swore the oath to Nicholas as Russian sovereign. The insurgent regiments on the square, paradoxically, were now the only defenders of the letter of the law on succession.

The accession manifesto masked the violation that Nicholas had perpetrated and affirmed continuity with past practice. In this respect, its message was the opposite of eighteenth-century accession manifestos, which sought to emphasize the complete break between reigns. The opening lines, written by Nicholas Karamzin, announced the emperor's grief at the loss of "Our Most Dear Brother," and "a Father and Sovereign who was Russia's benefactor for twenty-five years." Referring to his oath to Constantine, Nicholas declared that he had wished to "affirm Our respect for the fundamental law of the Fatherland on the order of succession to the Throne." He added that he wanted to "safeguard the basic law of the order of succession from any infringement in order to dispel the last doubt about the purity of Our intentions and to protect Our dear Fatherland from the slightest even momentary uncertainty about the Legitimate Sovereign." He cited the contents of the envelope that Alexander had prepared, the decree on his succession, and the letters written by Constantine indicating his intention to renounce the throne. But he insisted that these could have no effect until Constantine announced his abdication. The text of the manifesto contains the words, "Now having received this final announcement of the unswerving and irreversible will of His Highness," though no such announcement had arrived. The closing lines, also written by Karamzin, vowed that he would follow his brother's example, and declared "May Our reign be only a continuation of his reign." All future accession manifestos would contain similar declarations of affiliation with the previous ruler.[30]

Nicholas justified his violation of the dynastic order by his supreme loyalty to it. This seeming contradiction was concealed in his own dramatization of his acts as exploits of duty and self-sacrifice. Nicholas's memoir on his accession and the insurrection emphasizes that he took these steps not for his own benefit but in devotion to the existing order. When his mother urged that he bow before Constantine for allowing him to rule, Nicholas bridled. He asked her directly, he wrote in his memoir, why he should prostrate himself, "since I do not know which of the sacrifices is greater, that of the one who refuses or that of the one who accepts in such circumstances."[31] Nicholas understood his decision to turn the artillery on the rebels also as an act of renunciation. General Tol' and Vasil'chikov urged him to begin firing on the rebels. Nicholas claimed that the suggestion appalled him. He recalled, "I felt the necessity, but I confess, when the time came, I could not venture on such a measure and horror overcame me." "You want me to spill the blood of my subjects on the first day of my reign," he said to

---

[30] Shil'der, *Imperator Nikolai Pervyi*, 1:254–56, 642–44.
[31] "Iz zapisok imperatora Nikolaia I," *Byloe* 10 (1907/1910), 77.

Vasil'chikov. The general answered, "To save Your Empire." The words, Nicholas wrote, brought him to himself. "I saw that either I had to take on myself the spilling of the blood of a few, and save nearly *all*, or, *being merciful* to myself, to sacrifice the state."[32] Nicholas felt the necessity, but it required an act of self-abnegation, prompted by loyal aides at his side, to silence his scruples.

The other theme essential for a tale of heroic deliverance was that of beleaguered isolation, the lonely hero facing overwhelming forces of evil. Nicholas presented his account as if he, the new head of state, was virtually without allies. To be sure, Nicholas lacked ties in the court and did not know where to turn during the crisis. But his account dwells on his aloneness and magnifies his heroism in defeating the rebels. The news of the conspiracy, he wrote, left him dumbfounded and feeling himself completely alone. "Whom could I turn to, *I alone, completely alone, without advice!*"[33] He relates how he, the embattled and insecure young man, proceeded to act with courage and conviction to sacrifice his domestic peace in order to defend a right he believed was true. He then discovered his loyal allies, the institutions of government—the State Council, the Senate, and the Holy Synod—but most of all the generals who warned him of the conspiracy and were at his side on December 14—among them Miloradovich; General Count A. I. Chernyshev, Alexander I's aide-de-camp who brought the news of the conspiracy; Count Benckendorff; and General Prince I. V. Vasil'chikov, who had urged him to open fire. A print of the event published at the time shows Nicholas on horseback in the middle of the square, his adjutants at his side (fig. 41). They are in the foreground, dwarfing the regiments on the square and the Bronze Horseman.[34]

He found additional support in the loyal guards' regiments, especially the first battalion of the Preobrazhenskii Guards. He passed along the ranks and asked if they were ready to go wherever he commanded. They returned the robust cry, "We will do our best!" (*Rady starat'sia*). "A singular moment in my life." But it was the beautiful appearance of the tall, handsome, and self-possessed guardsmen that gave Nicholas the feeling that he was in his element. "No brush can depict the shapely, honorable and calm demeanor of this first battalion of the world at so critical a moment."[35]

Here, Nicholas is describing the inner core of his supporters, who stand by him at the moment of emergency and share his feeling of sacrifice for the cause. The generals who joined him would make up the majority of the investigating commission that passed judgment on the Decembrists and later occupied important positions in his court and government. The elite battalions of the Preobrazhenskii Regiment would remain his crack corps, whom he called on at other moments of duress and emergency to present an image

---

[32] Ibid., 86–87.

[33] Ibid., 79.

[34] Ibid., 79–80; Schil'der, *Imperator Nikolai Pervyi*, 1:261.

[35] "Iz zapisok imperatora Nikolaia I," 83.

41. *Nicholas I on Senate Square, December 14, 1825.* Lithograph by Riabtsov after a drawing by V. Sadovnikov.

of power and force. Nicholas I thus introduced a regime of conservatism by invoking the charismatic appeal of the conqueror whose selfless deeds in achieving victory won the loyalty and respect of his subjects. The new empress, Alexandra Fedorovna, immediately noticed the change; the man whom she embraced on the wooden staircase of the Winter Palace after the revolt seemed a different person.[36] The harrowing events of the accession had vested the grand duke with the qualities of an emperor.

•

Nicholas began the process of ceremonial confirmation of his rule after crushing the revolt, on the very day of the insurrection. He used the court and the drill field to give constant revalidation to the mythical grounding of his power. His ceremonies presented his dynastic scenario as a heroic triumph of good and morality, embodied in the imperial family, over the subversive forces of evil. The first performance took place late in the afternoon of the fourteenth. Nicholas brought his eight-year-old son Alexander before the Sapper Battalion, which had saved the imperial family from the insurgent Grenadiers' Regiment. Nicholas made clear that he and the heir were one. He asked the troops to love his son as they loved him. Then he placed Alexander in the arms of several cavaliers of the Order of St. George and, at his command, the first officers in each line rushed to the boy and kissed his hands and feet.[37]

---

[36] M. Korf, *Voshestvie na prestol Imperatora Nikolaia I* (St. Peterburg, 1857), 219–20.
[37] Ibid., 220.

42. *Nicholas I Presenting His Son, Alexander, to the Sapper Batallion, December 24, 1825.* Bas-relief on Nicholas I monument by N. Ramazanov.

This was the initial demonstration of the new importance of the principle of primogeniture in the life of the imperial house. It showed that the imperial family, rather than the emperor alone, represented the spirit and values of autocracy. The scene became an emblematic one during his reign. It was commemorated in popular pictures and on the bas-relief of the statue Alexander erected to his father in 1858 (fig. 42). That Alexander had stood at his father's side on the day of the rebellion was inscribed in his service list, along with the military honors he received on that day.

At 6:30 in the evening the formal prayer service, blessing the beginning of the new reign, took place in the palace church. Before the court, the family members enacted a scene of emotional exaltation and devotion that would be repeated frequently in the ceremonial settings of St. Petersburg. Metropolitan Serafim met the emperor and empress, the heir, and Grand Duke Michael with the cross. He then uttered the greeting to Christ, "Blessed be he who comes in the name of the Lord." The family members knelt before the altar. "What a scene!" one observer recalled. "The tsar and the empress cried inconsolably, and the public standing in the church, to put it simply, was sobbing." Then the emperor and empress kissed the cross. On their knees, they received the blessing and heard the prayer for the long life of the tsar. Again with tears, they asked for divine blessing for the reign. The dowager empress, shaken by the events, followed the service from the sacristy. At the end, the metropolitan addressed her with greetings.[38]

The event not only consecrated the victory, it revealed the pattern of response expected from those present, an emotional statement of solidarity with the ruler and his family. Baron Modest Korf, the author of the official account of the uprising, wrote: "No one among those attending this holy ceremony will ever forget its tender solemnity. All were shaken; all had tears in their hearts and in their eyes."[39] This was the first of many ceremonies of Nicholas's reign accompanied by august figures embracing one another with tears of joy and grief. Nicholas's elite expressed its allegiance as sentimental sharing in the feelings of the imperial family. The young tsar, Nicholas, who had evoked only antipathy required frequent ceremonial demonstrations of attachment and love.

In the eight months between his accession and his coronation, Nicholas staged two major ceremonial presentations that presented the basic principles of the new reign—the funeral and memorial services for Alexander I, and the manifesto announcing the sentences of the Decembrists. Both these occasions, while claiming fidelity to the past, signaled major innovations in the image of the autocrat and his relationship to the elite and the state. Both were publicized by manifestos and other ceremonial texts that left no doubt about the type of monarchical government Nicholas meant to introduce.

The commemoration of Alexander I that took place with the return of Alexander I's body and its burial in March 1826 marked a major change in the official celebration of death in Russia. After Peter the Great's funeral in 1725, such occasions had been observed discreetly, overshadowed by the celebration of deliverance. The memory of the previous, repudiated ruler would not be glorified or perpetuated. The single exception was Paul's ceremonies of reinterment for Peter III, which he used to restore his father to the dynasty. Alexander I, who in fact mourned his father, had to keep his feelings to himself in the midst of the euphoria accompanying his accession.

The limited symbolic importance of the funeral also reflected the predominant rationalist attitudes toward death and an afterlife in the eighteenth-century court. The eighteenth century was a period of relative indifference to the celebration and symbols of death, the mortal's passing away being regarded as less significant than his or her contribution to humanity.[40] Immortality was a secular immortality, attested to by the deceased's achievements as symbolized at the funeral in the battle gear, horses, standards, and the shields of the territories constituting the empire. Peter the Great's spirit lived on, but it lived on in his deeds and his posterity. His successors were not

---

[38] Ibid., 221; Prokhor Ivanov, "Mitropolit Serafim na Senatskoi ploshchadi 14ogo dekabria 1825 goda," *Istoricheskii Vestnik* 99 (1905): 166–70.

[39] Korf, *Voshestvie na prestol Imperatora Nikolaia I*, 221.

[40] On attitudes toward death in the seventeenth and eighteenth centuries, see Phillippe Ariès, *L'homme devant la mort* (Paris, 1977), 293–346.

honored with such tribute, for their reigns were characterized in somber tones of the dark age preceding the dawn of the new era of justice, peace, and prosperity.

With Nicholas's accession, the imperial funeral assumes a new importance as a statement of the continuity and sacred character of the dynasty itself. The solemnities in the capital were an international event renewing the feeling of solidarity displayed at Vertus. Prince William of Prussia stood at Nicholas's and Michael's side to meet the procession at Tsarskoe Selo, and he, along with the Prince of Orange and the Duke of Wellington, attended the funeral services in the Cathedral of Peter and Paul. The Hapsburg Court was represented by Arch-Duke Ferdinand d'Este. *Russkii Invalid* described the arrival of foreign representatives as a sign that they were showing "the proper honor to his holy memory with a unanimous expression of cordiality and respect to his august successor on the throne."[41]

The funeral cortege from the Kazan Cathedral, where the coffin lay in state, to the Cathedral of Peter and Paul took place on March 13, and was commemorated by the publication of a folio of engravings.[42] The procession followed the somewhat revised arrangements introduced for Paul I's funeral in 1801. The international and imperial pretensions of the house were expressed in additional coats of arms, the number having increased from thirty-two in Peter's procession to forty-seven. The character of the participants had also changed. Rather than military officers, officials of specified ranks, dressed in black cloaks and hoods, carried the standards and orders. The sequence of the groups and the positioning of the various ranks were illustrated on a scroll about three inches wide and nearly thirty feet long that was distributed before the procession.[43]

The processions and memorial observances were staged to recall Alexander as the victor over Napoleon. Two horses that had been with Alexander in Paris were led through the procession behind the "black knight," symbolizing mourning, and the banner of mourning. On March 19 a great parade of the guards commemorated the entry of Russian troops into Paris before a large crowd of spectators. The brilliant array of guardsmen marched by the emperor and his foreign guests twice. On that day, Nicholas issued a manifesto fulfilling Alexander's vow to distribute a silver coin minted in honor of the veterans in 1812, in this respect keeping the pledge of his accession manifesto to remain true to his brother's spirit.[44]

---

[41] Shil'der, *Imperator Nikolai Pervyi*, 1:396–99. The attention and publicity given to the funeral were also meant to stem rumors that the emperor had not died in Taganrog and that his body in fact was not in the coffin. But the glorification of his memory went far beyond efforts to confirm the fact of his death. On these rumors and the Fedor Kuzmich legend, see Mironenko, *Stranitsy tainoi istorii samoderzhaviia*, 97–99.

[42] *Opisanie pogrebeniia blazhennoi pamiati Nikolaia Iogo*, 68–73, contains a brief description of Alexander I's funeral procession and refers to these engravings.

[43] Kiselevskii fond, Bakhmeteff Archive, Columbia University.

[44] Shil'der, *Imperator Nikolai Pervyi*, 1:404–9.

Alexander's death was marked by the publication of memorial literature commemorating both his achievements and the tragic circumstances of his dying. Sergei Uvarov, the president of the Academy of Sciences, followed the eighteenth-century formula of extolling the emperor as a descending god. His eulogy borrowed themes from Prokopovich's funeral oration for Peter the Great. "It seemed that he was not subject to the general laws of Nature." Alexander was the superhuman figure capable of acting in every way in behalf of his subjects. "Neither military nor State concerns, in short nothing wearied Him. His brow shone with eternal youth. . . . Fifty million people prayed for His blessing from Heaven, from Which it seemed that He descended to us. We believed him invulnerable!"[45]

But the memorial literature published in the two years after Alexander's death expressed the new romantic notion of "a beautiful death," an exalted spiritual moment when the deceased entered the hereafter. The works dwell on the details of the deceased's last days, and especially the last moments.[46] The moment of death brings the emperor back into the family. The accounts describe the tender reconciliation of Alexander with the empress Elizabeth before his trip, as he arranges for her to convalesce at Taganrog. The emperor, who during his reign had regarded his wife as no more than a necessary appendage of office, now is depicted in terms of the new domestic scenario, as a caring husband filled with family feeling and concerned for familial obligations. Nicholas Danilevskii's *The Spirit of the Crowned Spouses: The Late Emperor Alexander I and Empress Elizabeth* presents Alexander's death as a dramatic moment of spiritual union. The empress urges him to seek solace in prayer. She kisses him on the brow and hand, after which he takes her by the hand, and declares, "I have never been in so comforting a situation as now. I thank you humbly!" The emperor died on November 19, 1825, "in the arms of his adored wife."[47] An engraving by I. Kulakov shows the deathbed scene, the empress sitting at his side in a plain dark dress, her hand raised above him (fig. 43).

But in the exalted spiritual mood of the time, death was only the prelude to a more lasting union in the hereafter. The empress Elizabeth expressed these thoughts in a letter to Maria Fedorovna, cited in Danilevskii's account and widely quoted in subsequent years: "Our Angel is in Heaven (*Notre ange est au ciel*) and I myself vegetate on earth! Who would have thought that I, feeble and sick, could survive Him? Mother! Do not abandon me for I am absolutely alone in this world of sorrows!" She declared that she would

[45] Quoted in Nikolai Mikhailovskii, *Dukh ventsenosnykh suprugov v boze pochivaiushchikh Imperatora Aleksandra Iogo i Imperatritsy Elizavety* (Moscow, 1829), 2:76–77.

[46] Ariès, *L'homme devant la mort*, 403–25. The memorial works include, in addition to the volume cited in note 45, *Poslednie dni zhizni nezabvennogo monarkha v boze pochivaiushego gosudaria Imperatora Aleksandra I* (St. Petersburg, 1827), also published in French translation, and Nikolai Danilevskii, *Taganrog ili podrobnoe opisanie bolezni i konchiny imperatora Aleksandra I* (Moscow, 1828).

[47] Mikhailovskii, *Dukh ventsenosnykh suprugov*, 3:25–26.

43. *Death of Emperor Alexander I.* Engraving by I. Kulakov.

not long survive him, and died the following May. In June, there was another cortege and funeral in St. Petersburg, also commemorated by the publication of a book of engravings. Danilevskii wrote in his preface that husband and wife died almost at the same time. "Their souls could not remain separate."

It is now the dynasty, the family, that attains immortality, a family union in the hereafter. The "cult of memory" of the dead monarch became an intrinsic part of scenarios of nineteenth-century Russian monarchy. If the memory of eighteenth-century rulers was consigned to a swift and inglorious oblivion, the memory of nineteenth-century rulers would be idealized by their successors and transformed beyond recognition. The sense of loss was presented as a shared national grief felt by the people for the deceased emperor and his family. *The Last Days of Life of the Unforgettable Late Tsar Emperor, Alexander I*, published in 1827, contained personal letters of grief of the anonymous author to his son and brother. "I do not weep, but sob that I have outlived him." Alexander's humble death became part of his idealization. "His death was quiet, like a retreat to peace after the painful labor of life." Official characterizations later elaborated on this theme. Nicholas Grech wrote in his biographical sketch of 1835, "His last gaze turned to the bright sky, then met with the gaze of his virtuous spouse, and his eyes closed forever." Although Russia enjoyed all earthly blessings, and loved its tsar, Grech wrote, "the sacred memory of Alexander still brings sincere tears to the eyes of his faithful subjects, faithful to his memory beyond the grave."[48]

•

If the ceremonies and evocation of death redefined the dynasty as a spiritual entity, the solemnities surrounding the sentencing of the Decembrists presented a new conception of the nature of the Russian monarchy and the service of the governmental elite. Since the reforms of Peter the Great, the Russian state had been defined as a Western state, drawing on a universal classical heritage and judged within a framework of Western intellectual categories. Nicholas sought to change this conception, but without abandoning the Western traditions of absolutism rooted in the Petrine state. He endeavored to define Russian monarchy as sui generis, impervious to the political conceptions of rule applied to other nations.

This view, of course, was a response to the spread of nationalism in Europe, and the idealist notion that each nation had its particular identity or spirit that distinguished it from others. In Nicholas's formulation, however, the national spirit expressed itself only in the autocratic state and the authoritarian inclinations indigenous to the Russian people. The symbolic significance of these views reached further. The redefinition of the meaning of autocracy eliminated analogy with foreign models as a device to idealize the monarch, thus precluding meaningful similarities with the West. The elevation and glorification of the monarch had to be placed in terms of himself; the emperor was immanent in the nation, and the nation was immanent in the autocracy and the emperor. The Decembrist Movement then could be dismissed as a contingent and alien contaminant that had to be ruthlessly expelled from the system. The sentencing of the convicted participants in the insurrection performed such a rite of expulsion.

The apparatus Nicholas instituted to pass judgment on the rebels immediately revealed his conception of the government. He informed the Count de La Ferronays shortly after December 14 that he would deal with the conspirators mercilessly. But he saw this not as his personal judgment: "The law dictates punishment, and I will not use my right of clemency for them. I will be implacable. I am obliged to give this lesson to Russia and to Europe."[49] He saw himself as enforcing impersonal rules of law: retribution would come not from him alone but from the state. Catherine II, Paul, and Alexander had disposed of their enemies personally, often in secret, banishing them to exile by exertion of their personal authority. Nicholas organized an Investigation Commission and an Investigation Tribunal to vest decisions in the forms of law. Both the commission and the tribunal consisted of those

[48] *Poslednie dni zhizni nezabvennogo monarkha*, 36–39; Nikolai Grech, *Biografiia Imperatora Aleksandra I* (St. Petersburg, 1835), 60–61.
[49] Shil'der, *Imperator Nikolai Pervyi*, 1:453–54.

members of the elite who had shown their loyalty to him. The Investigation Commission that issued the verdicts of guilty was made up of his adjutants; the tribunal that confirmed the verdicts and issued the sentences was composed of ministers, members of the State Council, and Senators. Following the Western pattern of administrative development, Nicholas set up state bodies, separate from himself, to deal with a problem of justice. But this separation remained completely formal. The members were beholden to him, the results were preordained, and Nicholas himself took an active part in the interrogations. The ostensible division between personal and administrative spheres in Nicholas's reign would result in subordination of the latter to the former and the sense that the state embodied the monarch's will.

To demonstrate the rectitude of his judgment, Nicholas had the report of the Investigating Commission, dated May 30, 1826, published in Russian, French, and English. The text, written by Dmitrii Bludov, elaborated a detailed history of the revolutionary movement. It emphasized that the uprising was a small conspiracy of those infected by foreign ideas. The report's conclusion foreshadowed both Nicholas's dynastic scenario and a doctrine of official nationality. The details of the events of December 14 "were marked by the violence of a few, and the signs of general zeal and sincere devotion to the Throne, and even more by a new example of the Tsars' valor, a hereditary trait of this most August house." Valor had now become a hereditary, rather than an individual trait of the sovereign, and the loyalty of the people was now not a response to the ruler's deeds, but a trait of the nation as a whole: "With the greatest grief and loathing, [Russia] (*Rossiia*) learned of the attempt of those intending to defile the Russian name (*imia Russkoe*), and sees with the rapture of gratitude that their criminal schemes and hopes were destroyed in one blessed moment."[50]

The Decembrists were subjected to severe retribution for their mistaken notion of the nation's destiny. Five were sentenced to quartering, thirty-one to beheading, and the rest to imprisonment. Nicholas commuted the sentences of the five to hanging, and of the thirty-one to imprisonment.[51] The harsh punishments drew a sharp line between the reigns of Alexander and Nicholas. Capital punishment had not been practiced under Alexander. It was rumored that the empress Elizabeth had interceded with Nicholas to plea for mercy and that at the last moment Nicholas would annul the death penalty. The execution of five of the leaders—M. P. Bestuzhev-Riumin, P. G. Kakhovskii, S. I. Murav'ev-Apostol, P. I. Pestel', and the poet K. F. Ryleev—and the exile of other young, attractive, and talented aristocrats confounded and shocked even conservative members of the elite.[52] It confuted the belief that the monarchy was becoming a milder, more humane institution that

---

[50] *Doneseniia sledstvennoi kommissii* (St. Petersburg, 1826), 79. The report was published at the Military Press of the emperor's *Glavny Shtab*.

[51] Lincoln, *Nicholas I*, 78–84.

[52] Shil'der, *Imperator Nikolai Pervyi*, 1:454.

would utilize its powers to achieve the good that elsewhere had come from conflict and violence.[53]

On the day of the executions, July 13, a memorial service on Senate Square consecrated the act of retribution. Troops lined up around the field chapel constructed next to the Bronze Horseman. Members of the court, led by the clergy, proceeded from the Admiralty Church to the square. The empress arrived in a carriage, Nicholas on horseback. After the service, the clergy blessed the troops with holy water. Nicholas described the solemnity as "the final duty of memory," "a purifying sacrifice for Russian blood shed for the faith, Tsar and fatherland on this very spot." A decree informed the army that the sentencing and executions had taken place "and your loyal regiments have been cleansed from the infection threatening you and all of Russia," and that a thanksgiving service had taken place "for the bestowing of the salvation of the state through you." In thanking "the courageous Russian armies," Nicholas felt able to speak as if "from the person of Russia." December 14 thus became another event, with the Napoleonic wars, that united the armed forces in the holy cause of defending Russia.[54]

The second decree issued on the occasion, the manifesto announcing the sentencing, presented Nicholas's concept of nationality and the state, in what Baron Korf called "the majestic program" of the new reign.[55] The manifesto shows the clear influence of Nicholas Karamzin, who, as his health was failing, continued to advise the young tsar. It began with the statement that the sentences had cleansed Russia of a festering infection—meaning the spread of ideas of constitutionalism and revolution. The intention of the Decembrists was not only criminal, the manifesto indicated, but was alien to the Russian people. "Neither in the characteristics nor the ways of the Russian is this design to be found. . . . The heart of Russia was and will be impervious to it." Here sounds the note of national distinctiveness that would be developed in the doctrine of official nationality. The Russian people are intrinsically dedicated to their ruler.

> In a state where love for monarchs and devotion to the throne are based on the native characteristics of the people, where there are laws of the fatherland and firmness in administration, all efforts of the evil-intentioned will be in vain and insane.

Love for monarchs, rooted in the national psyche, became the grounds for the violent defense of the emperor's power. Feeling created the bond between

[53] As, for example, in Speranskii's notions of introducing a constitution, which in the West were the result of "cruel transformations," and in Russia was "the benevolent inspiration of the supreme power" (Speranskii, *Proekty i zapiski*, 152–53).

[54] Shil'der, *Imperator Nikolai Pervyi*, 1:456–58.

[55] Ibid., 1:704–6; Korf, *Voshestvie na prestol Imperatora Nikolaia I*, 229; A. Kornilov, *Kurs istorii Rossii XIXv* (Moscow, 1918), 2:18–22. Kornilov and others have connected this manifesto with the coronation, but there is no reference to the coronation either in the title or the text of the manifesto.

tsar and people as it did between members of a family, and family as the basis of political solidarity was a central theme of the manifesto. The uprising prompted new signs of attachment uniting the estates. "Fathers did not spare their criminal sons, relatives repudiated the suspects and brought them to the court. We saw all estates united in one thought and one wish—the trial and punishment of the criminals." He assured the families of the revolutionaries that "the union of kinship endows its posterity with the glory of their deeds and is not besmirched by the dishonor of individual vices or crimes."

The manifesto indicated that the home education of noble children, usually conducted by foreign tutors, was at the root of the error of the revolutionaries. He warned that parents should turn their attention to "the moral upbringing (*nravstvennoe vospitanie*) of their children." The nobility should lead in the process of the improvement of Russia. "Just courts, the armed forces, the various branches of the government all need, all depend upon zealous and knowledgeable executors."

Nicholas set the goals for his elite. The improvement in the Russian state would occur "not from impudent dreams," but from the way "the institutions of the fatherland are gradually perfected, inadequacies are overcome, abuses are corrected." It would be based not on schemes from the West, which did not pertain, but on every "modest desire for the better." The political system of monarchy had become an incontrovertible attribute of Russian nationality, not to be judged by external standards or to be seen as a reflection of foreign models. The task of the nobility was to strive to become better officials who could improve Russia only by working within the autocratic system.

Nicholas's initial steps in the months after the insurrection revealed that he viewed the improvement of the governmental system as his own personal concern. He turned his own chancellery into an agency that would ensure that administrative offices followed his intentions, thus making himself the principal supervisor of the state's administrative machinery. Governors now were not to send reports on political matters to the Ministry of the Interior, but directly to the emperor's chancellery. In January 1826 he established the first and second sections of his chancellery. The First Section was charged with overseeing governmental appointments and other personnel matters. The Second Section had the seemingly intractable task of codifying Russian laws. He told the first head of the Second Section, Michael Balugianskii, "I want to put the full force and strictness of the laws at the base of the governmental system."[56] Under the direction of Michael Speranskii, the Second Section published the *Complete Collection of Laws* in 1830 and a *Digest of Laws* in 1832. Nicholas himself closely followed the work at each stage.

The Third Section of his chancellery, the political police, has come to characterize Nicholas's style of personal absolutism more than any other

---

[56] Shil'der, *Imperator Nikolai Pervyi*, 1:459.

organ of his rule. In June and July 1826 he brought the political police under his own purview and appointed Alexander Benckendorff head of the Third Section. The Third Section enabled him to exercise political and moral surveillance over the empire. The officials of the section, supported by a corps of gendarmes stationed in the provinces, sought to discover and extirpate oppositional thought and to inform the emperor of Russia's condition and state of mind. But the Third Section also spied on the administration itself, ensuring that officials were working with the loyalty and honesty that the tsar expected. It was a new "eye of the sovereign" that could extend the moral force of the emperor's person to the distant reaches of the empire.

At the same time, Nicholas made it clear that he was not giving up the process of reform. The July 13 Manifesto indicated that change could be pursued within the autocratic system, and he worked to remedy some of the grievances that the Decembrists revealed during their interrogations. He himself believed that serfdom was an evil, and he sought ways to improve the serfs' plight and to consider conditions for emancipation. The Committee of December 6, 1826, was the first of eleven secret committees established under Nicholas to consider changes in the status of the serfs and other governmental reforms. The work of these committees had few results, however, since the fear of disorders and rebellion discouraged measures that might call into question the very grounds of the authority of the nobility and the officialdom. The single significant reform instituted in Nicholas's reign was the introduction of new administrative and self-governing organs for the State Peasantry, by Count P. D. Kiselev, Minister of State Lands.

By the time of the coronation, Nicholas had presented himself as an able and conscientious servant of the state, completely devoted to improving the workings of the autocracy. There was nothing lofty or ethereal about him. The state he served was the emanation of his own imagination and will, and the model of devoted work he presented would provide a daunting ideal and a constant admonition for his servitors. A. V. Nikitenko, then a student at St. Petersburg University, wrote in his diary on November 8, 1826:

> The present tsar knows the science of ruling. They say he is weariless in his work, reviews everything himself, penetrates into everything. He is simple in his way of life. His severity to others is linked to his severity with himself. This of course is a rare feature in an autocratic sovereign. But he lacks what is most important, which is men who could be his true helpers. We have courtiers, but there are no ministers.[57]

THE CORONATION

The crushing of the Decembrist Insurrection and the severe punishments meted out to the revolutionaries validated Nicholas's claims as emperor. De-

[57] A. V. Nikitenko, *Dnevnik* (Leningrad, 1955), 1:34.

feating a menace to the fatherland by ruthless use of force, he had fulfilled the symbolic precondition for enthronement. He then proceeded to the stage of representation, to display his particular conception of rule as intrinsic to Russian monarchy and his person as the incarnation of supreme political power. The coronation consecrated his specific attributes and presented them in terms of a scenario of imperial power. It served its function of enshrining innovation in the traditional rituals and symbols of Russian monarchy.

The innovations introduced at Nicholas's coronation were indeed significant. Although the ceremonies and celebrations remained unchanged, the way they were performed and the associations attached to them by ceremonial texts gave the event a new meaning. It was the first "national" coronation that purported to draw on and express the distinctive historical traditions of the Russian people. It was the first coronation that involved the people as an active agent of acclamation after the ceremonies. The triple bow Nicholas made to the people from the Red Staircase on August 22, 1826, became, over the course of the century, a ceremony fixed in the tsarist repertoire, performed both at the coronation and during subsequent visits to Moscow. It came to be understood as an expression of the Russian national soul, displaying a bond between tsar and people that had existed since Muscovy.

The coronation now began to take on different functions. Eighteenth-century coronations had celebrated the successful aspirant to the throne as the champion of the general good, legitimizing dubious claims to succession. Nineteenth-century coronations, beginning with Nicholas's, consecrated the monarchy itself, as it was incarnated in the ruling dynasty of which the enthroned emperor was the god-chosen representative. Nicholas's scenario of power enshrined the principle of dynasty by glorifying his family as the ideal of both personal and political relationships for the Russian people. The members of the elite fade into the background of the coronation drama, leaving center stage to the emperor's family.

Nicholas I's coronation occurred two years after the coronation of George IV of England, and a year after the coronation of Charles X in France. All three events were reaffirmations of the hierarchical splendor of monarchy, as the rulers sought to rival the revolution as centers of popular sentiment. The English and French coronations were explicit efforts to recapture *ancien régime* France. George IV filled his palace with mementos of Louis XIV; he had his agents acquire the album for Louis XV's coronation in preparation for his own crowning. But his dream of re-creating French grandeur in the early nineteenth century suffered a debacle and his lavish coronation ended in a farce.[58] Charles X's coronation was a serious effort to recall the nation's medieval past. Romantic writers and artists put forth the Gothic as a na-

---

[58] Colley, *Britons*, 215; David Cannadine, "Splendor out of Court: Royal Spectacle and Pageantry in Modern Britain, c. 1820–1977," in Wilentz, *Rites of Power*, 212.

tional style. The eighteenth-century practice of covering the cathedral with a neoclassical decor was abandoned, and artists and writers stressed the national and historical significance of the Gothic style. The arches and galleries constructed for the event were designed to harmonize with the Gothic original.[59]

Charles X's coronation was an effort to adapt the French monarchy to the postrevolutionary period and to demonstrate popular support for the throne. The Vicomte de Chateaubriand's brochure, *Le Roi est mort, vive le Roi!*, presented the coronation as a way to forge the unity of France around Charles. The event was much larger than previous celebrations, made up of sixteen hundred invited guests compared to four hundred at the coronation of Louis XVI in 1775. The authorities carefully orchestrated shows of acclaim and assembled a force of fifteen battalions of infantry and eight cavalry squadrons to keep the people outside the cathedral during the rites.[60] The regime also used plays, poetry, and particularly the press to sing the praises of the monarchy. The royalist newspaper, *Quotidienne*, remarked on a "universal adherence" to the monarchy that promised a radiant future: "Royalism, devotion, fidelity, love of principles, and princes." The oppositional press, however, reported general public apathy to the celebration.[61]

Nicholas's coronation also emphasized the historical roots of Russian monarchy. The publicity of the event, moreover, suggests that Russia was following the example of both France and England in trying to use the press to win sympathy for the monarchy.[62] We witness a return of the ceremonial text, which now is a means to explain the dynastic and national meanings of the coronation solemnities. The accounts are written in the personal voice, the work of presumably independent authors. They were published in periodicals that were privately owned, though dependent on the state for subsidies and protection. Descriptions of the events appeared in journals, Pavel Svin'in's *Otechestvennye Zapiski* and M. T. Kachenovskii's *Vestnik Evropy*, and in Faddei Bulgarin's newspaper, *Severnaia Pchela*. In 1828 an illustrated album was issued in Paris with a brief French-language text explaining the coronation to a foreign audience.[63] The increasing publicity given to the

[59] Alain Charles Gruber, "Le décor des derniers sacres à Reims," in *Le sacre des rois*, 273–81; Francoise Waquet, *Les fêtes royales sous la restauration ou l'ancien régime retrouvé* (Geneva, 1981), 107–13, figure 66.

[60] Georges Clause, "Les réactions de la presse et de l'opinion au sacre de Charles X," in *Le sacre des rois*, 292, 294–95; Haueter, *Die Krönungen der französischen Könige*, 261.

[61] Clause, "Les réactions de la presse," 290, 298.

[62] On the French influence see, Charles A. Ruud, *Fighting Words: Imperial Censorship and the Russian Press, 1804–1906* (Toronto, 1982), 58–59, 63–64; on England, see Colley, "The Apotheosis of George III," 113–16.

[63] *Vues des cérémonies les plus intéressantes du couronnement de leurs Majestés Impériales l'empereur Nicholas Ier et l'impératrice Alexandra à Moscou* (Paris, 1828). The brief explanatory text was written by one Henry Graf, whom I have been unable to identify. V. A. Vereshchagin, in his *Russkie illiustrirovannye izdaniia XVIII i XIX stoletii* (St. Petersburg, 1898), 168, cites a Russian edition, but I have been able to find neither a copy of a Russian edition nor

coronation prefigures a dedicated effort to address broader layers of the educated public in Russia and to bring them into the sphere of the tsar's scenario (see below, chapter 11).

The most complete account was written by Svin'in, whose journal had published official reports of Alexander I's trips. Svin'in had served in the diplomatic corps—he worked in the Russian consulate in Philadelphia—and on administrative assignments within Russia. He was the author of travel books, among them one on his visit to North America and another on archaeological digs in Russia. He also was a trained artist, and the watercolors he executed on his trips were intended to accompany his texts. He had a poor reputation on the literary scene; contemporaries were critical that he wrote travel accounts about places they believed he had never visited. His rumored escapades as an official in Bessarabia provided Gogol with the plot for "The Inspector General." Svin'in also wrote two historical novels and was a collector of ancient Russian documents and works of art.[64] In any event, it was Svin'in's ability to embellish reality with the blandishments of fiction that enabled him to construct a description of the coronation filled with the precise personal meaning that the emperor intended.

In contrast to eighteenth-century descriptions, Svin'in's account places the ceremonies in the context of their historical development. It is entitled "Historical Description of the Most Sacred Coronation," and the first installment traces the evolution of the coronation from its presumed beginnings in the reign of Vladimir Monomakh. Svin'in emphasizes the persistence of the rituals, and notes to his text remind the reader of the origins of the various items used in the ceremonies.[65]

Svin'in's was the first description to present the coronation as a national tradition manifesting the monarch's historical ties with his people. A ceremony, previously elite in its participants and audience, now appears as one with mass resonance, with the people themselves playing a principal role. Svin'in gives full range to the personal voice of official sentimentalism in evoking the popular national upsurge for the tsar. He describes the entry procession on July 26 in epistolary form, writing with the pseudo-naive tone of a surprised observer. The Muscovites only wanted to see their tsar "to delight in the sight of his face." The Muscovites all wanted to say, "I saw the tsar up close." Now the enchantment, however, is not produced by the emperor's charm or beauty, as it had been with Alexander I. Rather, it is a

---

other references to it. The album lists 187 subscribers, including foreign ministers, companies, merchants, and Russian aristocrats, and was clearly published with the backing of the Russian government.

[64] See the useful introduction by Evgenia Petrova, in *Traveling Across North America 1812–1813; Watercolors by the Russian Diplomat Pavel Svinin* (New York, 1992), especially, 23–28, 33–37; *BE,* 29:151–52.

[65] "Istoricheskoe opisanie Sviashchennogo Koronovaniia i Miropomazaniia ikh Imperatorskikh Velichestv Gosudaria Imperatora Nikolaia Pavlovicha i Gosudaryni Imperatritsy Aleksandry Feodorovny," *Otechestvennye Zapiski* 31 (1827): 26–44.

historical property of the people: "Isn't it true that one has to be Russian or know very well the attachment of Russians to their tsars to understand these words? Russians have always honored their tsars and always cherished the happiness of coming close to them."[66] The reporter for *Severnaia Pchela* describes the exuberant welcome of the people as an emotional counterpoint to the sumptuous entry: "The external brilliance of the imperial procession was elevated and ornamented by the spiritual rapture (*dushevnym vostorgom*) of the zealous and faithful people, who with joyous tenderness (*radostnym umileniem*) in countless multitudes met the Great Sovereign within the walls of the First Throne city."[67]

Svin'in described the moving effect of the tsar's prayer at the Iberian Mother-of-God. As Nicholas prayed, his face revealed a sincere piety as he asked God to bless his state. He "prayed for our happiness, for the blessing of us." Then the procession moved to the Assumption Cathedral. Svin'in felt unable to express the feelings that overcame him when the tsar kissed the cross before the cathedral, "with the feelings of a Christian." The scene recalled dramatic historical events that the author believed had occurred at the cathedral's parvis—where Dmitrii Donskoi returned after the battle of Kulikovo, and Michael Romanov was exhorted by his people to accept the throne. Then, on the Red Staircase, their majesties were met by priests with the cross and holy water and members of the coronation committee who greeted them with bread and salt according to the ancient tradition. This ritual showed "the character of the virtues of the people and the gratitude to the Tsar who stands aloof from No one and honors the customs of his forefathers."[68]

Svin'in's account presented the entire imperial family as the object of popular affection. Nicholas rode down the avenue flanked by his brother, Michael; his brother-in-law, Prince Karl of Prussia; the Duke of Württemberg; and his son, Alexander.[69] But it was Alexander, not the emperor, who was endearing: "The kind Russian people admired the angelic charm of the Heir to the Throne with indescribable rapture." The author went on to point out that this "Royal Child" (*Derzhavnyi Mladenets*) was particularly dear to Muscovites because he was born in the Kremlin.

The members of Nicholas's elite now see their own devotion to the emperor reflected in the acclaim of the people, which justifies his firm assertion of power. One of those watching the procession was Dmitrii Bludov, a protégé of Karamzin and Zhukovskii, and now a state secretary to Nicholas. Bludov was one of the few civil servants to serve on the Investigating Commission for the Decembrist Insurrection. He described the coronation as an act of national unity; he may have been the first to use the phrase "union of

[66] "Moskovskiia sovremennye letopisi: perepiska izdatelia Otechestvennykh Zapisok," *Otechestvennye Zapiski* 27 (1826): 281–82.

[67] *Severnaia Pchela*, August 5, 1826.

[68] "Moskovskie sovremennye letopisi," 288–89.

[69] Ibid., 284.

tsar and people" that later became standard in official rhetoric: "Yesterday, we saw our monarch, who has succeeded so quickly in stirring so many hopes, arrive in the capital of the fatherland to receive the crown and scepter of his forefathers—to confirm his union with the people." Nicholas was worshiped by all Russians, Bludov believed, but especially by the poor.[70]

Bludov was particularly moved by the family scene. The dowager, the mother of two tsars, the emperor himself, the son, all seemed to ornament one another. He watched them proceed behind the clergy, who were holding gonfalons and crosses. Watching Nicholas prostrate himself before the Iberian Mother-of-God, Bludov recalled the events of 1812. Red Square was lined with Infantry of the Guard, and before the Kremlin walls the band played "God Save the Tsar"—the first time this anthem, with its English melody, was played in Moscow. The strains of the music, mixing with the tolling of the church bells, exalted him: "The effect was indescribable. It seemed that the words 'God Save the Tsar' resounded in all hearts. I assure you that at least for me, I felt something of a fever running through my heart and nerves—but a pleasant fever of hope. It was as if I more than ever before believed in the blessedness of Providence and the future happiness of Russia."[71]

With Nicholas's coronation, great reviews and maneuvers became an integral part of the coronation celebrations. They assumed the character of a ceremonial expression of the military's devotion to the imperial family. Military reviews took place frequently during the month between the entry procession and the coronation ceremonies. On July 30 a parade of more than fifty thousand troops paid homage to the dowager empress. The grand duke Alexander rode in his father's suite, on a magnificent steed. The eight-year-old galloped past the emperor, then charged up and stopped before him to the delight of the spectators. The son had paid deference to the father. Then, Nicholas led a detachment before his mother and saluted her, giving recognition to her personal and ceremonial preeminence in the house.[72] Nicholas took part in large-scale maneuvers of the Moscow army on August 15 and 16, which were summarized in Svin'in's articles. The maneuvers not only provided the troops with a useful exercise, but treated the many foreigners and other spectators to "a splendid spectacle, rare for the residents of Moscow."[73]

The feeling of the dynasty's unity was enhanced by the surprise arrival of the grand duke Constantine in Moscow. Constantine was peevish as usual, but Nicholas's deferential attention succeeded in calming him by the day of

---

[70] "Dva pis'ma gr. D. N. Bludova k supruge ego," *Russkii Arkhiv*, no. 5 (1867), 1046–47; on Bludov and sentimentalism, see Wortman, *The Development of a Russian Political Consciousness*, 143–49.

[71] "Dva pis'ma gr. D. N. Bludova k supruge ego," 1046–47.

[72] Tatishchev, *Alexander II*, 1:9–10; Maréchal de Marmont (Duc de Raguse), *Mémoires* (Paris, 1857), vol. 8: 118–19.

[73] "Istoricheskoe opisanie," 31:45–47.

the ceremony. A broadsheet printed at the time shows the three brothers, Nicholas, Constantine, and Michael, riding side by side, with the heir, Alexander, on horseback at Michael's side. On the day of the coronation, a manifesto was issued establishing the rules for a regency and designating Nicholas's "most kind" brother, Michael, regent, lest Nicholas die before the heir's majority.[74]

•

The accounts of the coronation reveal the new mode of presentation of official events that would dominate the ceremonial texts of Nicholas's reign. The author uses the personal voice of sentimentalism to express collective feelings not only of the elite but of the people themselves. Individual feelings are politicized and generalized to express adoration and worship of the emperor and his family. The author must attest to the overwhelming power of these feelings, which defy the capacities of the ordinary mortal. This results in the frequent resort to aporia, the confession of the artist's inability to express or describe what he wishes. Svin'in is unable to express the feelings that overwhelm him when he watches the tsar kiss the cross before the cathedral; Bludov finds the effect of the scene on Red Square indescribable.

The feelings gave rise to a rhetoric of sentimental devotion that became general in the official literature of Nicholas's reign. The words *vostorg* (rapture, enthusiasm) and *umilenie* (tender pity or pathos) conveyed the intensity of emotion of subject for monarch. Both were expressed by the shedding of tears. These words, borrowed from the religious as well as sentimentalist lexicon, carry the connotation of inspired fervent devotion. *Vostorg*, according to Dahl's dictionary, has a sense of rapture, of oblivion, "of self-forgetting and temporary renunciation of the world and its vanities." In Nicholas's reign, it expressed the sensuous merger of the subject with the sovereign and his family, a worship of and infatuation with their persons. Dahl defines *umilenie* as "a feeling of sweet pity, humility, grief, spiritual and joyous sympathy, benevolence." It was connected with the feeling of the Mother-of-God for the Christ child, depicted in *umilenie* icons. The word, above all, expresses the emotional bond, the sense of connection, between a figure that is lofty or powerful with one vulnerable or supplicant. It evokes the pathos of overcoming distance; in official discourse, a sense of sympathy between subject and sovereign. In Nicholas's reign, *umilenie* denoted the gratitude and love of the subject for the emperor who forsook his majestic reserve and showed human feelings, what B. I. Berman called, in reference to saints' lives, an "ecstasy of submission" (*vostorg poddanstva*).[75]

[74] *IGK, ts. Nik. I*, 219–20; V. I. Zhmakin, "Koronatsii russkikh imperatorov i imperatrits, 1724–1856," *Russkaia Starina* 38 (1883): 14. *PSZ*, no. 537, August 22, 1826.

[75] Vladimir Dal', *Tolkovyi Slovar' zhivogo velikorusskogo iazyka* (Moscow, 1955), 1:251, 4:493. George P. Fedotov, *The Russian Religious Mind* (Belmont, Mass., 1975), 1:393; Leonid Ouspensky and Vladimir Lossky, *The Meaning of Icons* (Crestwood, N.Y., 1989), 92–93; B. I. Berman, "Chitatel' zhitia," in *Khudozhestvennyi iazyk srednevekov'ia* (Moscow, 1982), 166–67, 179.

Svin'in uses these words to describe the heightened emotional state produced by the coronation ceremonies on August 22. In his portrayal, the coronation reveals the emperor's conquest of his subjects' hearts. The religious ceremonies consecrate the emperor's personal qualities as attributes of the office of emperor. Svin'in wrote:

> This high sacrament, uniting the Sovereign with his subjects, like a father with his children, took place under the sign of those lofty virtues, which, since his ascension to the throne, have conquered the hearts of Russians for God's Anointed, which astonish foreign peoples, and finally which serve as the most sacred guarantee, the firmest bulwark, of the prosperity and majesty of Russia.[76]

Dmitrii Zubarev opens his description with aporia to express his emotions on the "unforgettable day" of the coronation of the "Most Beloved and Most Just Monarch Nicholas Pavlovich and his God-Chosen Spouse":

> I feel my pen too weak to depict all the majesty of this sacred rite and the rapture of Russians (*Rossiiane*) at the sight of their worshiped Monarch and his Most August Spouse in all their Imperial brilliance.[77]

Svin'in focuses the account on the members of the imperial family; only they and their German relatives are identified by name. At 10:00 in the morning, walking under a rich canopy, carried by officials of the third and fourth ranks, the dowager empress in crown and purple led the first procession to the cathedral. At Maria Fedorovna's side were the heir, the emperor's sister, Grand Duchess Elena Pavlovna, and Alexandra's brother, Prince Karl, who led Alexander by the hand. Also under the canopy were Princess Marie of Württemberg, and the Duke and several princes of Württemberg, relatives of Maria Fedorovna.

After this procession had reached the cathedral and the august personages had been blessed by the bishops and taken their places, the emperor's procession commenced. The Cavalier Guards led the way; in July they had been placed under Alexandra's command and renamed "Her Majesty's Cavalier Guards." They were followed by masters of the court and masters of ceremonies, leading representatives of the estates—among them mayors of towns, and provincial marshalls of the nobility—and governmental institutions. Next followed the imperial regalia, borne by leading figures in the court, whom Svin'in does not identify. Behind another detachment of Cavalier Guards and the marshalls of the court, Nicholas himself walked bareheaded, beneath a canopy borne by sixteen lieutenant-generals and sixteen major-generals. At his side were his brothers, Constantine and Michael, an adjutant-general, and the commander of Cuirassier Regiment, with swords bared. Alexandra walked in the middle of the canopy with two assistants at

---

[76] "Istoricheskoe opisanie," 31:170–71.

[77] Dmitrii Zubarev, "O dne sviashchennogo koronovaniia i miropomazaniia Gosudaria Imperatora," *Vestnik Evropy*, no. 24 (December 1826): 279.

her side. Behind followed ladies of the court, and then a corpus of nobility, manufacturers, and representatives of the Moscow merchantry. The procession closed with another detachment of cavalry guards.

The figures of husband and wife dominate the author's attention: "All saw only The Monarch and his spouse, that August couple proceeding with the proper humility and piety to receive The Most Holy of Sacraments."[78] Svin'in evoked the drama of the meeting between clergy and the emperor and empress before the cathedral. At the parvis, the emperor was welcomed by the Holy Synod and other clerics who had just emerged from the cathedral, where they had pronounced the prayer for the emperor's long life. The officiating prelate, the Novgorod metropolitan, Serafim, presented Nicholas with the cross to kiss, and the Kiev metropolitan, Evgenii, sprinkled him with holy water. Then Filaret, the Moscow metropolitan, spoke of the tribulations of the recent months. He declared that Nicholas had delayed with his accession only to preserve the security of his tsardom. To console the young tsar for the troubles he confronted, he compared the emperor to Solomon, whose reign had also begun with difficulties. Nicholas would clear the land of the weeds, as Solomon had cleansed Israel. The speech, Svin'in reported, brought Nicholas to tears.[79]

Svin'in described the scene at the throne after the emperor and empress had entered. At their side were prominent officials and officers, and the highest clergy. The author remarked that their presence "attested that the Young Monarch was surrounded by wisdom, experience, merit, brought to the altar of faith and the fatherland." A footnote indicated that the emperor would be seated on the elaborate throne of Tsar Alexei Mikhailovich, studded with 876 large diamonds and more than a thousand rubies and emeralds. The throne of Alexei would be used and displayed as a great tsarist treasure at later coronations as well. The empress sat on the golden throne of Tsar Michael.[80]

After Nicholas had conferred crown and mantle on himself, the empress bowed before him, and, like Peter the Great and Paul, he placed the small crown on the empress's head. She fell to her knees "to a rising, general feeling of tenderness (*umilenie*)." He then placed the mantle on her shoulders and the chain of the Order of Andrew on her neck.[81]

Svin'in evoked the emotional response of the moment: "What rapture (*vostorg*) seized the hearts of those standing by, and all the inhabitants of Moscow, who had learned by the resounding bells and the cannon salvos that the Imperial Couple were invested with the purple and crowned!" But

---

[78] "Istoricheskoe opisanie," 31:183; S. Panchulidzev, *Istoria kavalergardov, 1724–1799–1899* (St. Petersburg, 1899), 1:58–59.

[79] "Istoricheskoe opisanie," 31:185–87.

[80] Ibid., 31:188–95; Bobrovnitskaia et al., *Gosudarstvennaia oruzheinaia palata*, 367–69.

[81] "Istoricheskoe opisanie," 31:195–98. The thrones of Michael and Boris Godunov were used at the coronations of Elizabeth and Catherine II. I have not been able to determine which thrones were placed in the cathedral for Paul's or Alexander's coronations.

he could not describe these feelings for the readers: "No, one had to see for himself all the moments of this Most Holy rite." Nonetheless, he did remark on the general feeling of *umilenie* when the dowager empress fell to her knees. Maria Fedorovna overflowed with rapture (*vostorg*): "All of Her thoughts, all of Herself, it seemed, was in the heavens from which the blessing descended upon the Head of Her Crowned Son." He then marveled over the feeling with which Nicholas kissed her and his brothers, Constantine and Michael.[82]

The Paris album also rhapsodized over the family drama. The embrace between the dowager and the young emperor was "shared by all those present with visible emotion." But Zubarev's account in *Vestnik Evropy* focused primarily on the embrace with Constantine, thus confirming the solidarity of the dynasty for the European audience: "Few of those present could hold back their tears, especially when the Emperor embraced the Tsarevich Grand Duke Constantine, who gathered at this moment the finest fruit of his noble sacrifices." The illustration in the album, entitled "The Crowning of Nicholas" (fig. 44), presented not the crowning but a scene of Constantine embracing Nicholas. An act of affection thus was used to show the tsesarevich's homage to his younger brother and to dispel the uncertainties about his abdication. The same scene was depicted in a popular print of the time.[83]

Nicholas's declamation of the prayer, on his knees, here identified as "the prayer of Solomon," moved everyone to tears: "Warm, sweet tears were the symbol of the unaffected sympathy (*umilenie*) of all upon hearing the prayer of the Crowned Tsar." Even "the representatives of foreign Powers," seemed touched, though they did not understand the words. Those in the congregation then fell to their knees with *vostorg* for the metropolitan's prayer. Svin'in described the liturgy in historical and familial terms. He used the pre-Petrine titles, tsar and tsaritsa, to describe the powerful impression left by Nicholas and Alexandra, who had received communion "with tenderness and reverence" (*s umileniem*). Again he expressed the individual emotions of those present. The powerful impression always produced by the liturgy on Christians, he wrote, was heightened by the sight of the tsar and tsaritsa, which, accompanied by the "heavenly" singing of the chorus, "submerged all present in sweet ecstasy, which suddenly was broken by rapture when this harmonious and majestic chorus intoned 'many years' three times!"[84]

The taking of communion also figured as a moment in a family imperial drama. Before he entered the sanctuary, Nicholas removed his sword and symbolically handed it to Constantine, demonstrating the trust that had come to unite the brothers; a moment, Benckendorff mentioned in his mem-

---

[82] Ibid., 31:196–99.

[83] *Vues*, 5; *IGK, ts. Nik. I*, 222; Zubarev, "O dne sviashchennogo koronovaniia," 287. Zubarev wrote, "The Most August Brothers embraced with a touching feeling of tender love and friendship, and held each other for several minutes."

[84] "Istoricheskoe opisanie," 31:205–9.

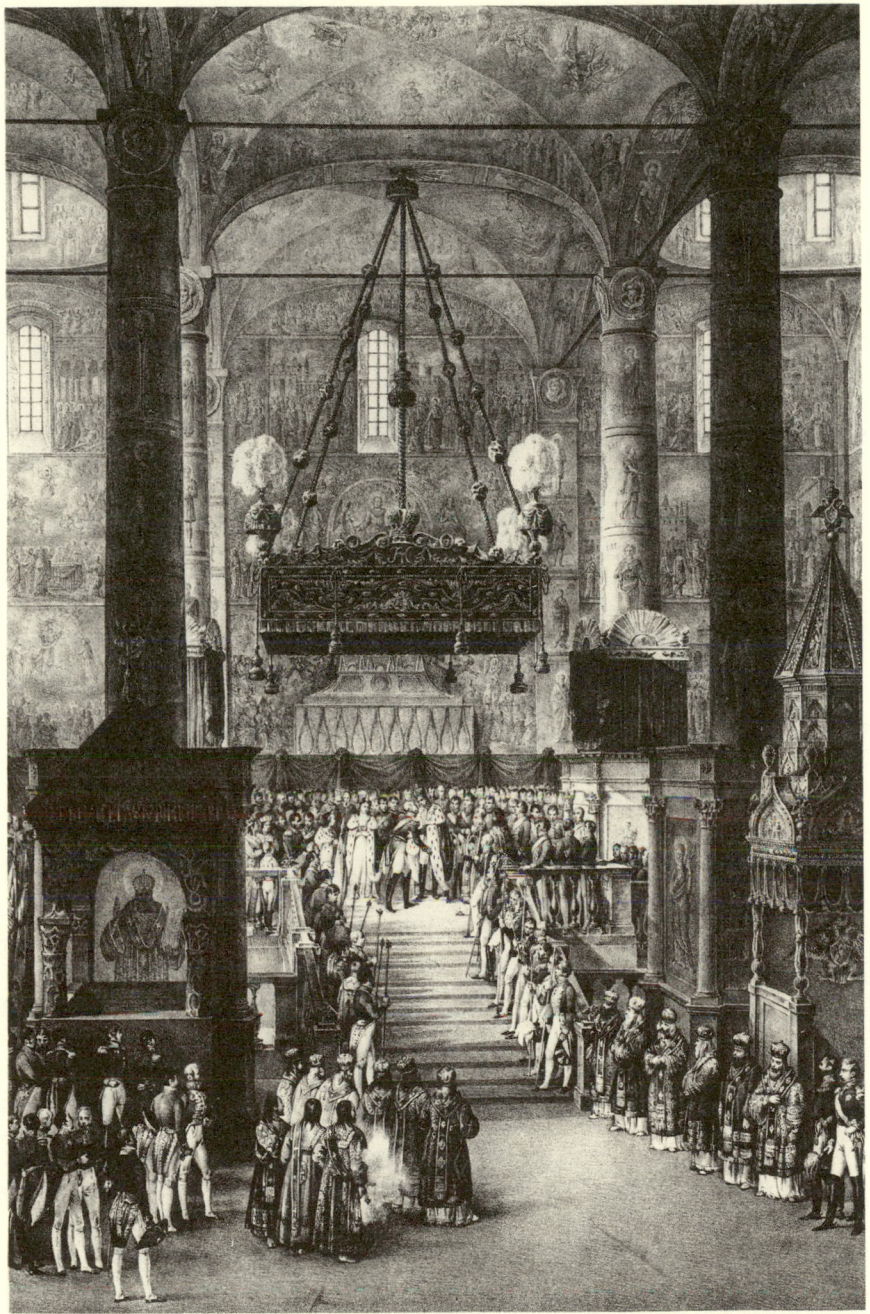

44. *Crowning of Nicholas I*. Lithographer, Louis Courtin. Artist, Victor Adam.

oirs, that evoked tears from all present. Alexandra received communion at
the Imperial Doors outside the sanctuary. Svin'in again described the feelings of the spectators. Seeing "the tender feelings" (*umilenie*) and reverence
of the couple in receiving the sacrament sent those present into "sweet ecstasy," broken only when the choir sang long life to the tsar three times.
"With what joy, without doubt, all present in the Cathedral repeated in their
souls, *long live the tsar!*" They then bowed three times to greet the tsar on
his coronation. At the end, they witnessed "the very most tender spectacle"
(*umilitel'neishee zrelishche*), the kissing of the members of the imperial family, "a spectacle moving every Russian to tears, seeing in this union, an example of high morality, the guarantee of the happiness and prosperity of the
fatherland."[85]

The spectacle fulfilled the literary and mythical expectations of the foreign
guests and the Russian official elite. The Duke of Raguse found the unity and
devotion of the family "one of the most beautiful things the imagination can
conceive."[86] Alexander Benckendorff recalled the family coming out of the
cathedral: "The incomparable face of the sovereign shone with beauty under
the valuable gems of the imperial crown. The young empress and the heir
near the empress-mother also attracted everyone's gaze. It was impossible
to imagine a more splendid family." Those in attendance gave their sympathy to the family by weeping—shedding tears of joy to share in the pathos
of the triumphant dynasty. Benckendorff remarked on the tears shed when
Nicholas handed his sword to Constantine Pavlovich. Bludov wept unabashedly when Maria Fedorovna embraced the emperor. The ceremony confirmed him in his faith: "I was again assured of the sweetness and the necessity of Faith, that every passion, even the most noble love of Fatherland, not
purified by religion, leads only to error and misfortune."[87]

Nicholas's coronation introduced scenes of family devotion and reconciliation to the solemn Byzantine rites. The family became a metonymic
expression of the constant, devoted, and pure feelings that attached servitors
and subject to the throne. The political bond was sustained by a mythical
bond of affection for the imperial family, which the dignitaries of Nicholas's
state would be expected to display at the proper occasions. The shedding of
tears of joy, and when necessary grief, became obligatory at court
ceremonies—a sign of loyalty and sharing in the tsar's family life, which
symbolized his moral and therefore political supremacy. The elite became
absorbed in the tsar's family, a family that exemplified the current European
ideal of dynastic monarchy and the current Russian ideal of utter dedication
to one's sovereign.

The culmination of the ceremonies portrayed by Svin'in occurred not in

[85] "Istoricheskoe opisanie," 31:199–202, 208–10; Marmont, *Mémoires*, 8:132–33;
Shil'der, *Imperator Nikolai Pervyi*, 2:6–7.

[86] Marmont, *Mémoires*, 8:132–33; Komarovskii, *Zapiski*, 256–57.

[87] "Dva pis'ma gr. D. N. Bludova k supruge ego," 1047; Shil'der, *Imperator Nikolai Pervyi*,
2:7.

the cathedral, but on the Kremlin square. The appearance on the square signaled the broadening of the ceremony's appeal, the absorption of those beyond the highest rank into the coronation ritual itself. In addition to the common people standing on the square, more than five thousand persons who could not fit into the crowded precincts of the cathedral watched patiently from grandstands. Among them were senators and lesser officials, foreigners, merchants, and deputies from Asiatic nationalities. Svin'in elaborated on the beautiful folk costumes of the Russians, the Circassians in their brilliant belts and pearls, the Kirgizy, Kabardintsy, Georgians, Armenians, Kalmyks, all in military costumes and exulting at the emperor's appearance. The gathering on the square stood for both nation and empire, which merged in the political entity of *Rossiia*. "It seemed that everything was assembled here that is attractive and glittering in Russia," he wrote.[88]

The appearance of the emperor in full regalia at the portal of the cathedral was an occasion for the author to describe feelings that he identified with those of the entire crowd: "How could one not be delighted in one's heart and soul at the sight of the Lord of half the universe, invested with virile beauty, health and all the gifts of nature marching in Purple and Crown, in one hand the Scepter, the other the Orb, accompanied by his August Brothers." There was no resisting the powerful transports of these feelings. "Each and everyone could hardly restrain his rapture (*vostorg*) and joyous exclamations at the appearance of His young Spouse, more radiant with Her heavenly charms and Angelic gentleness (*krotost'*) than the diamonds glittering on Her Crown."[89]

The dramatic climax occurred when Nicholas reached the top step of the Red Staircase as he returned to the palace. He then paused, turned to face the crowd, and bowed three times, once in each direction to the exultant people on the square. The act, which resembled the triple bow the emperor made before the imperial doors of the cathedral, was an unprecedented gesture of recognition and reciprocity.[90] The Russian emperor previously could receive but not acknowledge acclamation, for it was regarded as unseemly for his godlike person to seem beholden to ordinary mortals. We have seen how Alexander I, even in 1812, refrained from outward signs of recognition on the Red Staircase. Nicholas I reciprocated the feelings of those cheering him. Svin'in exclaimed, "I will say that this alone would be enough to win the hearts of the good Russian people, if they did not already belong to the Anointed of God."[91] Like the dignitaries in the cathedral, the people responded with the emotion appropriate to the scenario. Many of those present recalled an explosion of enthusiasm: "The joy of [the loyal subjects]

---

[88] "Istoricheskoe opisanie," 31:371–73.

[89] Ibid., 31:370–71.

[90] I have found no explanation for the appearance of the gesture at this coronation. It is suggested in Chakirov's volume that the triple bow was an imitation of the Byzantine acclamation, but no evidence for this conclusion is given (Chakirov, *Tsarskie koronatsii*, 108–9).

[91] "Istoricheskoe opisanie," 31:375.

knew no bounds at this solemn moment: loud unrelenting cries filled the air, innumerable caps flew upward, the crowd stirred noisily. Strangers embraced one another and many wept for joy."[92] And although those on the Kremlin grounds were especially selected, the members of the imperial family believed their acclaim to be sincere and representative of the nation. The empress was elated. "This dazzling Kremlin, on the clearest day, resounding with the cries of enthusiasm of this excellent Russian people! It was beautiful!" she wrote.[93]

Nicholas performed the triple bow at subsequent Kremlin processions, to the acclaim of the crowd described rhapsodically in the press. It was repeated by his successors, and by the end of the century came to be regarded as "an ancient Russian custom." The act both brought the people into the ceremonies on the day of the coronation and redefined the meaning of "love" in the relationship between throne and people. It acknowledged the principle of popular sovereignty, and immediately neutralized it, turning ceremonial acclamations into an expression of popular will.[94] Bowing, the tsar recognizes the love of the people as the source of his unlimited power, but the rhetoric of the text transforms the people's love into a historical justification for absolute monarchy. The exultant cries on the square become a symbolic substitute for institutionalized expressions of the will of the people. In the evening, after seeing the city of Moscow illuminated, and the crowds of people hailing the emperor in the street, Svin'in recorded his personal sense of the meaning of "the enchanting pictures of August 22, 1826." The feelings the ceremony evoked confirmed his confidence in "the unshakeable might of the Russian tsardom, where love for tsar and fatherland are not empty words but the highest of virtues."[95]

The Paris album also dwelled on the upsurge of popular feeling, indicating to a Western audience that it was the tsar rather than the Decembrists who represented the spirit of the people. The opening of the text explained that the coronation blessed "the bonds formed between monarch and people, by both the most sacred rights, and by gratitude, devotion, and limitless affection." While ignoring the triple bow, the author took the thunderous sounds of bells and cannon as "the great voice of the nation rising into the distance, towards the heavens, a concert of vows and homage." When Nicholas left the Assumption Cathedral, he was greeted with "thousands and thousands of cries of joy and enthusiasm." The text then returns to the family as a

[92] Ibid., 31:374–75; Zhmakin, "Koronatsiia russkikh imperatorov," *Russkaia Starina* (April 1883), 9; Marmont, *Mémoires*, 8:132–33; V. F. "Iz vospominanii byvshego gvardeiskogo sapera," *Russkii Vestnik* 72 (1867): 338–39.

[93] "Pis'ma Imperatritsy Aleksandry Fedorovny k V. A. Zhukovskomu 1817–1842." *Russkii Arkhiv*, no. 1 (1897): 499.

[94] The gesture could prompt criticism from those more fastidious than Nicholas about the tsar's debt to the people. See Cherniavsky, *Tsar and People*, 148–49, for Grand Duke Michael Pavlovich's anger at a report in *Severnaia Pchela* of the tsar's bowing from the Red Staircase in 1834.

[95] "Istoricheskoe opisanie," 31:395–96.

moral exemplar for the people. The tsar had, at his side, "his brothers, models of the most generous friendship," and the "wife that God has given him so that his subjects will know to seek the example of domestic virtues where the supreme rule of their duties to the state is found."[96]

The Paris album concluded with a description and lithograph illustration of Nicholas's and Alexandra's departure from Moscow. The emperor and empress sit in a four-horse calèche with only one servant beside them. Nicholas appears as a humble, simple person, close to the people, a scene that would be staged frequently during his reign. He tries to depart inconspicuously, but he and the empress could not escape "the expressions of devotion from the inhabitants of Moscow for their sovereigns, sentiments which are the characteristic trait of the Russian nation." Several individuals purportedly tried to jump on the splashboard of the vehicle to converse with them. The picture, the author wrote, showed the moment when the people bade farewell to their "adored parents who were departing from their numerous family."[97]

·

Svin'in noted both the national and imperial elements of the celebrations following the coronation. The ball for the highest governmental ranks in the Palace of Facets moved him to comment that the unique architecture and decoration of the halls, which recalled Muscovite Russia, stunned the eyes of those present. His description of the great masquerade, attended by nearly five thousand members of the nobility and merchantry and native leaders, emphasized the variety of ethnic types that constituted the empire. Viewing the scene from the balcony, the author observed the ladies' gowns sparkling in silver and gold. He saw "Asian ladies" in "sumptuous furs and valuable brocades."

But Svin'in's attention was drawn particularly to the Russian national costumes. Most of the women present were "dressed in Russian sarafans, with Russian bands (*poviazki*) and tiara hats (*kokoshniki*) on their heads, bathed, one might say, in pearls and diamonds." As they danced the polonaise, their "patriotic attire" (*otechestvennyi nariad*) transported him back to the times "when Russians were not ashamed of their splendid dress, proper for the climate, having a national character, and incomparably more beautiful than foreign dress." To confirm the universal acceptance of this "truth," Svin'in cited the opinion of an "enlightened foreigner," who declared his preference for these ladies to those dressed in the latest European fashion.[98] The Paris album also used the masquerade as an image of empire: "It seemed to have reunited everything that Europe and Asia had to offer in beauty, wealth, and pomp."[99]

[96] *Vues*, 1, 8–9.
[97] Ibid., 14.
[98] "Istoricheskoe opisanie," 32:26–34.
[99] *Vues*, 11.

Svin'in gave the first account of the gala theatrical performance in a Russian coronation description, emphasizing the importance of the imperial family's attendance of a Russian theater. The program included an opera, *The New Landlord*, and a ballet, *Cinderella*. But the principal performance was not on the stage but in the audience, which burst into wild acclaim for the imperial family—an expression "of the most vibrant ecstasy with loud applause and the exclamation, Hoorah!" Despite the charm of the show and the performers' skills, all eyes were turned to the imperial box, and the audience only noticed those parts of the opera "that could be connected with the feelings of the spectators at this time."[100]

The popular feast gave Svin'in an opportunity to elaborate on the robust and passionate qualities of the Russian people. He dwelled on the food, indicating the weight of the meat, and mentioning the sweet pies, apples, and the eighty loaves (*kalachy*) for each of the 240 tables. The ravenous appetites of the common people were cause for amusement. Once the white flag unfurled and announced the beginning of the feast, only a few minutes passed before every morsel of food had vanished. The tables and fountains also had disappeared, and only the soldiers had saved the grandstands. This rampage provided additional grounds to praise the people who cherished this event and so, "according to ancient tradition, wanted to bring their families even the tiniest sign of it. . . . Each of the common people held in his hand some trophy of his exploit: a basket, a barrel, a plate, a board, a shred of cloth, a rope, etc."[101]

The celebrations concluded on September 22, with fireworks at the buildings of the Cadets' Corps. The display was a reprise of the emperor's scenario. The initial scene of an alley of palm trees was explained as an "emblem of tranquillity and glory and of the length of the reign of His Imperial Majesty." The alley ended in a trophy of arms, supporting a pedestal with the blazing initials of the emperor and empress. Two genies soared above, and above them "the All-Seeing Eye of Providence lit with Its rays this symbol of the happiness of Russia."

The second display emphasized the theme of conquest. An explosion of light was followed, after a few minutes, by the appearance of a brilliantly illuminated triumphal arch with the inscription, "To the Pacifier (*Uspokoitel'*) of the Fatherland Nicholas the First." Over the arch appeared an allegorical figure of Russia, in a carriage, drawn by four horses. Her way was lit by two "Slavic horsemen" before whom soared Glory. Military trophies appeared between lit columns, and in the rear two gladiators sat upon steers they had slain, while horsemen raced across the expanse.[102]

The image of the pacifying tsar was expressed in the songs sung by the pupils of the Trinity Monastery during the imperial family's visit on Septem-

---

[100] "Istoricheskoe opisanie," 32:212–14.
[101] Ibid., 32:347–55.
[102] Ibid., 32:358–64; *Vues*, 13.

ber 25. The Christ image appears again, but now transformed to encompass the themes of dynasty and repressive force. The verses, released in a separate brochure in 1826, present Nicholas as Alexander resurrected, the blessed. But blessedness refers only to the crushing of opposition, a designation of strength rather than humility:

> When You began your rule,
> In the midst of widespread sedition,
> And stepped with calm majesty,
> With a spirit full of hope,
> Unyielding, like Mount Zion,
> With justice and mercy to the throne:
> The deeply-moved children of Russia,
> Drying the flood of tears,
> Cried, "He hath risen, he hath risen,
> ALEXANDER the blessed is in HIM."[103]

[103] *Pesnopeniia na vysochaischee . . . poseshchenie Sviato-Troitskiia Lavry i nakhodia-shcheisia v nei Moskovskoi Dukhovnoi Akademii* (Moscow, 1826), 7.

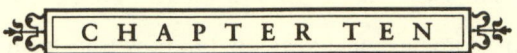

CHAPTER TEN

Epitomes of the Nation

The Emperor proceeded to their front, and to my astonishment, ma-
noueuvered the simple battalion. The firings, the common drill, and the
duties even of a sergeant-major, seemed perfectly familiar to them. The
recollections of these minutiae of instruction, and having them so entirely
at command, are surely very remarkable; and upon my commenting with
wonder on all this precision, I was informed by several of his officers that
in all the departments of the state, whether of justice, interior or foreign
affairs, finances, law, artillery, or marine services, the Emperor exhibited
equal proficiency. Now when this declaration was made by one and all
who surrounded him, and when one considers generally that ministers
and officers are too apt to raise themselves into importance by taking
credit for doing a great deal, one cannot but believe that the justice they
all render to the Emperor Nicholas is his due, and that he may be fairly
pronounced one of the most wonderfully gifted men of the age.

—*The [Third] Marquis of Londonderry,* Recollections of a Tour in the
North of Europe in 1836–1837[1]

These marvels inspired in the crowd an infectious admiration; in seeing
the triumph of the will of one man, and hearing the exclamations of
others, I myself began to become less indignant about the price of this
miracle. If I felt this influence after two days, how much should we indulge those men who are born and spend their life in the air of this
court, that is in Russia! For it is always the air of the court that one
breathes from one end of the empire to the other. . . . The emperor and
the court appear before Russians wherever there is
a man who obeys a man who commands.

—*Marquis de Custine,* La Russie en 1839[2]

[1] The Marquis of Londonderry, *Recollections of a Tour in the North of Europe in 1836–
1837* (London, 1838), 1:275.
[2] Marquis de Custine, *La Russie en 1839,* 2:140–41.

The Illusion of Omnipresence

Alexander I had sought to appear as an ordinary mortal, but his pretense to wisdom, kindness, and in the end godliness invited the metaphor of angel and the epithet "blessed" that lifted him into a higher realm. Nicholas showed what was possible for an ordinary human being, uplifted by a sense of duty. By the force of his will, he claimed to make things work, curb abuses, make the empire flourish, to give the impression, conveyed by the Marquis of Londonderry, of "one of the most remarkable men of his age." Allegory was disavowed in official rhetoric, because it was superfluous, or indeed insufficient. The emperor was all the more admirable and lofty because praise did not require embellishment. "The Russian Tsar (we speak without allegory, without exaggeration, without flattery) is the beneficial luminary of His land, nurturing everything, bringing life to everything," *Russkii Invalid* commented during the emperor's visit to Nizhnii-Novgorod in 1836.[3]

Nicholas's ascendancy was not metaphysical or aesthetic, but moral. His achievements showed what was possible for human beings and confirmed the failings of those who did not live up to his image. Nicholas sustained the symbolic preeminence of the autocrat not by elevating himself to celestial spheres but by abasing his subjects; he was a living reproach for the mortal weaknesses that prevented his servitors from working for the general good. Thus the figure of "first servant of the state," in Nicholas's person, kept and, paradoxically, enhanced the image of superordinate ruler whose person represented the Russian state.

Physically, Nicholas showed that a human being could resemble the gods. Anna Tiutcheva wrote that Nicholas's presence gave the imperial court its brilliance and majesty: "His inspiring and majestic beauty, his majestic bearing, the strict correctness of his Olympian profile, the gaze of command, everything ending with his smile of a condescending Jupiter—everything in him—recalled a god on earth, and all powerful commander; everything reflected his unshakeable conviction of his own calling." For the Marquis de Custine, too, Nicholas's appearance embodied a supreme authority: "His superb forehead, his traits which take after Apollo and Jupiter, his impassive physiognomy, imposing, imperious, his face more noble than mild, more monumental than human, exerts a sovereign power on anyone who approaches."[4]

Nicholas's charismatic appeal in this respect was immanent rather than transcendent: his person expressed qualities and values integral to this

---

[3] *Russkii Invalid*, September 21, 1836: 959–60.

[4] Anna Fedorovna Tiutcheva, *Pri dvore dvukh imperatorov*, 1:96; Custine, *La Russie en 1839*, 3:12.

world, or as was claimed, particular to Russia. In this respect, he adopted the manner of Frederick William III and other Western monarchs who appeared for their subjects as exemplars of virtue and the private life. The monarch strove to reflect the nation's essential characteristics. Presenting the charisma of immanence, official texts adopted new rhetorical strategies, revealed in the descriptions of Nicholas's coronation. They shift from figurative modes of presentation, which compare the emperor to universal images, to metonymic or more precisely synecdochical modes, which make of him the concrete expression of the nation. Ceremonies are given another meaning. Rather than expressions of otherworldly spheres, where godlike figures cavort and rejoice, they are presented as microcosms of Russia, exemplifying the attitudes toward authority and modalities of conduct, both official and private, that should prevail in the macrocosm of the empire.[5] The parade ground, the court, the meetings in the Kremlin become defined as epitomes of the nation.

In this equation, the macrocosm is defined in terms of the microcosm. The emperor, his family, the dynasty, the army and state epitomize the principal qualities of Russia and represent the whole. Here we see a kinship between political and symbolic representation. Both, Kenneth Burke has observed, invoke synecdoche to describe the identity between microcosm and macrocosm. All attempts to "represent" the general will of the people in parliamentary institutions involve a transfer of qualities to the representative body that stand for the people as a whole.[6] Likewise, the imagery of official nationalism claims to reflect the will of the people by making the tsar in his ceremonial appearances the representation of the whole. Nicholas, as was frequently stated during his reign, was "the embodiment of Russia."

In this case, the signifiers—Nicholas, his family, and their ceremonial appearances—engulfed the signified, Russia. Ceremonies and their representations in texts and pictures defined the nation in terms of the Westernized autocracy, of which Nicholas himself was the principal symbol. Nicholas's upbringing, tastes, and mannerisms were conspicuously German. "Even by blood," Custine observed, "Nicholas is German more than Russian."[7] While Nicholas encouraged national elements in the art, architecture, and music of his reign, he and his court presented themselves as part of the culture of international royalty.

But the contradiction of the foreigner presenting himself as most native of the Russians seemed paradoxical only to foreigners and radical critics. Nicholas merely reformulated the myth of conquest in contemporary terms. He, like his predecessors, was the Russian monarch who ruled because he appeared as foreign, but now this tradition was defined as peculiarly Rus-

---

[5] On the synecdoche as the expression of the identity of microcosm and macrocosm, see Kenneth Burke, "Four Master Tropes," in his *A Grammar of Motives and a Rhetoric of Motives* (Cleveland, Ohio, 1962), 508.

[6] Ibid.

[7] Custine, *La Russie en 1839*, 2:136.

sian. The doctrine of official nationalism propagated the notion that it was the Westernized ruler and state, adored by the common people, that constituted the distinguishing feature of Russia's experience. Uniqueness came from a political structure that remained faithful to universal principles of monarchy, the heritage of the Byzantine and Roman empires, from which Europe had fallen away, seduced by the philosophies of the enlightenment.

The relationship was expressed in the form of the tale of the calling of the Varangians, which achieved the status of canonical verity in Nicholas's reign. The historian, Michael Pogodin, elevated the event to the central moment of all of Russian history. In a lecture, delivered in the presence of then assistant minister of education, Sergei Uvarov, Pogodin declared, "The Varangians came to us, but *voluntarily chosen*, at least from the start, not like Western victors and conquerors—the first essential distinction in the kernel, the seed of the Russian State." The Russian people had invited their conquerors, and had obeyed and loved them; autocracy had national roots. In the West, conquest and conflict had brought national states into being and had become endemic to their history. The acceptance and worship of the supreme foreign ruler had become the distinguishing mark of the Russian people.[8] Uvarov was pleased by the lecture, and Pogodin's ideas contributed to the formulation of "official nationality," which Uvarov promulgated when he became minister the next year.

Norbert Elias showed that symbols in monarchy can become values in themselves. Louis XIV's court made the glory of the king a central value, and ceremonial presentations sought to elevate and extol him as the benefactor of the nation. The Baroque courts of Europe followed his example and glorified their sovereigns in a metaphorical frame. The central value of Nicholas's reign was loyalty, which was displayed in ceremonies of devotion to the heroic monarch. The people were recognized and then engulfed in demonstrations of loyalty. The principal feeling expressed at these ceremonies was gratitude to the ruler for his acts of self-sacrifice.

The events of December 14 established the paradigm for such demonstrations of loyalty. During his trips across the empire, on the parade ground and in the court, Nicholas reenacted the role of the embattled leader, assisted by a corps of dedicated followers, subduing contumacy, immorality, and human frailty in general. Lord Londonderry, Nicholas's guest at the court in 1836 and 1837, took these displays for sincere expressions of opinion. He wrote, "What rooted Nicholas in the affections of his people was the heroic courage and ability he displayed in seizing possession of the sceptre and the empire, at a moment when perfidy, confusion, and a band of traitors placed the Imperial diadem in jeopardy." Londonderry was convinced that Nicholas's acts "established him forever in the hearts of his people."[9]

---

[8] M. P. Pogodin, *Istoriko-kriticheskie otryvki* (Moscow, 1846), 6–8; N. L. Rubinshtein, *Russkaia istoriografiia* (Moscow, 1941), 261–65; P. Miliukov, *Glavnye techeniia russkoi istoricheskoi mysli* (Moscow, 1898), 1:365.

[9] The Marquis of Londonderry, *Recollections of a Tour*, 1:273.

Nicholas performed this scenario to emphasize his closeness, his immanence in the nation. He was both the "omnispective" monarch, who dominated by his attentiveness to all matters, state and private, and the omnipres-
ent monarch, whose person seemed to pervade the empire. The epigraphs at
the start of this chapter attest to Nicholas's relentless domination of his subjects' consciousness. Foreign visitors, whether adulatory, like Lord Londonderry, or critical, like the Marquis de Custine, described a Russian empire
dominated by the emperor's presence and personality. The literature about
Nicholas's travels through the empire, his strolls through St. Petersburg, created the image of a monarch who not only watched over his people, but
appeared among them. He gave the impression of involving himself in everything, from the writing of the laws to the design of buildings and the settling
of domestic disputes. In St. Petersburg, he received and examined the daily
reports of the police chief. Striding through the streets of the capital, he was
known to intervene in brawls and to instruct policemen on their duty.[10] His
ability to move among his own people was presented as a sign of their affection for him. *Russkii Invalid* wrote of his visit to Moscow in August 1836,
"The love of the people here stands near him like a vigilant general when
guards or other watch are completely removed."[11]

At moments of crisis, Nicholas appeared in public and reenacted the heroic scene of December 14. His acts, as lone hero appearing among his
people to crush the forces of subversion and ignorance, were quickly made
part of his mythology of rule. When the cholera epidemic struck Moscow in
the summer and fall of 1830, Nicholas appeared at the scene to take charge
of the measures needed to fight against the disease. He kissed the icon at the
Iberian chapel and was greeted at the Assumption Cathedral by the metropolitan Filaret. His appearance before the people had almost magical effects.
The crowds went wild, and Benckendorff wrote, "It seemed to all that the
disease itself would capitulate to his omnipotence." Filled with a sense of his
own mission, Nicholas courageously visited institutions. He, too, fell ill with
fever but quickly recovered.[12]

The steps Nicholas took to fight cholera, McGrew has shown, were of
little help. He merely criticized the quarantine commanders and the doctors
for their laxity in enforcing the emergency measures. But unlike Alexander
in 1824, Nicholas projected an aura of command and confidence. His personal confidence, the authority of the all-powerful tsar, and his sharing in
the danger consoled the population. An engraving of the time depicts
Nicholas's entry into Moscow on the Kremlin square. He sits stiff and stal-
wart in his carriage, while the mobs of surrounding people look up at him
adoringly. No sign of emotion is visible on his face, nor did it have to be (fig.

[10] M. A. Korf, "Iz zapisok Barona M. A. Korfa," *Russkaia Starina* 99 (1899): 272.
[11] *Russkii Invalid*, August 22, 1836: 851.
[12] Roderick E. McGrew, *Russia and the Cholera, 1823–1832* (Madison, Wis., 1965), 82;
Shil'der, *Imperator Nikolai Pervyi*, 2:306–7.

45. Nicholas I Arriving in Moscow during the 1830 Epidemic.
Contemporary engraving.

45). It was his presence alone that had the magical effect of restoring respect for authority. When the cholera began to abate, the newspaper, *Severnaia Pchela*, credited Nicholas with the result. He was presented as the heir to Peter the Great, the defender of European science who fought the superstitions of the "drunkards and fools" who refused to obey the rules of quarantine. He had gone to Moscow to oversee the measures against the disease and had appointed special governmental supervisors in St. Petersburg. When the cholera epidemic relents, the newspaper declared, the people will be convinced that they "owe the eradication of the infection and the restoration of health only to the *Tsar* and to those entrusted by him with power."[13]

When the epidemic struck St. Petersburg, the quarantine measures aroused protests from the populace. On June 23 Nicholas appeared before a rioting mob on *Sennaia* square, in a scene closely resembling that of December 14. Nicholas faced the crowd alone. He threw off his coat, then ordered the rioters to fall to their knees and cross themselves. He then scolded them, employing his characteristic logic that defiance proved disloyalty, and therefore the lack of a Russian spirit. "Remember what you did, remember that you aren't French, you aren't Poles, but Russians!" A report on the event

[13] *Severnaia Pchela*, July 15, 1831, July 16, 1831.

46. *Nicholas I Subduing Cholera Insurrection on Sennaia Square, St. Petersburg, 1831.* Bas-relief on Nicholas I monument by N. Ramazanov.

indicated that "they all fell to their knees and one could see that the majority of those present were repentant." Nicholas then shouted that he would punish wrongdoers, that he feared no one. "Remember my words! I will overcome everything." He rode through the square, stopping several times to tell the people to obey the governor-general.[14] The drama of the physical confrontation of a lone figure subduing the mob was caught in the bas-relief placed on the pedestal of Nicholas's statue in 1858. The emperor stands courageous and firm, unmoved before the crowd, a tower of certainty before the frightened mob at his feet (fig. 46).

Nicholas's appearances clearly emulated the image of Peter the Great, who intervened everywhere to demonstrate how things should be done. But the apparitions of the two emperors were of a different character and meaning. Peter appeared as an alien force coming from beyond who could be understood only in comparison with a god descended to earth. His superhuman talents and ruthlessness terrified his subjects and maintained the distance between him and them. Nicholas's subjects also cowered in his presence, but it was institutions and ceremonies that extended the force of his personality. He did not inflict punishment or engage in manual work himself.

Most important, Nicholas's scenario emphasized his closeness to the people, denying rather than magnifying the distance between the monarch and his subjects. The awe he inspired was the counterpart of love, the osten-

[14] Shil'der, *Imperator Nikolai Pervyi*, 2:600–601.

sibly voluntary dissolution of the subject's individuality in inspired devotion to the sovereign. Nicholas's presence among his people created a sense of connectedness by contiguity. Symbolic elevation occurs by making the scenes of contact metonyms for the political structure as a whole, and by presenting ceremonies and celebrations as synecdochical expressions of the people as a whole.[15]

The periodical press disseminated Nicholas's scenario to the population. Nicholas used the press to adapt the imagery of the Russian autocrat to a new era of nationalism and to establish a connection between monarch and nation. Following France's example, the government began to use the press not only to glorify the monarch but to give the illusion of widespread popular support. It developed the technique, used to publicize the coronation, of subsidizing private periodicals. In Nicholas's reign, the newspapers, *Severnaia Pchela* and *Russkii Invalid*, and the illustrated journal, *Russkii Khudozhestvennyi Listok*, brought knowledge of Nicholas's family and court to a broader reading public.[16]

Newspapers, which appeared several times a week, were particularly effective means to give the illusion of omnipresence. *Severnaia Pchela*, the first privately owned newspaper in Russia, had the largest circulation and broadest influence. Its publisher and editor, Faddei Bulgarin, showed both an ability to deal with the government and a sense of commercial enterprise. He was encouraged by the head of the chancellery of the Third Section, M. Ia. Von Vock. Von Vock, inspired by Louis Fouché, the minister of police under Napoleon and Louis XVIII, recognized the possibility of using the press to influence educated public opinion. The Third Section began to subsidize the publication of *Severnaia Pchela*, and Bulgarin and his future collaborator, Nicholas Grech, became semi-independent instruments of the government, what Belinskii later referred to as "the reptile press." In return, Bulgarin's newspaper was permitted to take up political questions forbidden to other periodicals.[17]

Severnaia Pchela strove to give the impression of an enthusiastic response to Nicholas's scenario beyond the precincts of the court. It was the most popular newspaper of its day, reaching a circulation of seven thousand in the 1830s and ten thousand during the Crimean War.[18] As Nurit Schleifman has shown, the newspaper was targeted at the minor officials who made up the lower ranks of the bureaucracy, as well as lesser gentry and merchants. The official orientation of the journal, moreover, increased over time. Govern-

[15] On connectedness, see Burke, "Four Master Tropes," 508–9.

[16] N. M. Lisovskii, "Periodicheskaia pechat' v Rossii, 1703–1903; statistiko-bibliograficheskii obzor russkikh periodicheskikh izdanii," in *Sbornik statei po istorii i statistike russkoi periodicheskoi pechati, 1703–1903* (St. Petersburg, 1903), 16–17.

[17] Ruud, *Fighting Words*, 58–59, 64–65; N. L. Stepanov, "'Severnaia Pchela' F. V. Bulgarina," in *Ocherki po istorii russkoi zhurnalistiki i kritiki* (Leningrad, 1950), 1:310–11.

[18] Ruud, *Fighting Words*, 64; V. G. Berezina, *Russkaia zhurnalistika vtoroi chetverti XIX veka (1826–1839 gody)* (Leningrad, 1965), 16–17.

mental decrees appeared in 5 percent of the issues in 1828, and in 40 percent in 1840. News of appointments appeared in 2 percent of the issues in 1828, and in 75 percent in 1840.[19]

The newspaper used the official sentimental voice to portray a sense of universal gratitude to the tsar for his deeds. The gratitude was complete and abject. The pages of the newspaper in the year 1830 are rich in examples. The January 7 issue begins by expressing a sense of gratitude for Nicholas's achievements of the previous year. The article praises the emperor for the victory over Turkey, and for the advancement of education, transportation, commerce, justice, and charity. There was no point in enumerating the emperor's many deeds, the author asserted; one had only to express thankfulness: "Every hour, every minute of the valuable life of our Monarch is marked by love for Russia, led by him to the height of enlightenment, power and glory." Nicholas asked only that his subjects, too, work for the general good. "We will be grateful: We will develop our capacities for the general good. We will join together in our labor and will deeply love Him, who for all his labors asks nothing besides our happiness."[20]

The newspaper described the public appearances of the emperor and his family as occasions to demonstrate the population's love and gratitude for a monarch who deigned to appear in their midst. An article of March 6, 1830, reported on a masquerade given by the minister of the court, P. M. Volkonskii, for their imperial majesties. The theme of the event was set by Gasparo Spontini's opera *Cortez*. The empress was dressed as the Mexican woman, Amarilla, her brother, Crown Prince William, came as Cortez, while the venerable Count S. S. Pototskii was Montezuma. The reporter observed that everyone noticed the gay spirit of the emperor, the empress, and the grand duke, Michael, and were touched at their kindly attentiveness to the guests. The gaiety, however, signified more than the pleasure of the moment; the reporter made the ball a symbol of feelings prevailing throughout Russia: "Sovereigns can act in this way where they are sure of the love of their subjects!"[21] This was one of many synecdochical expressions of the emperor's relations with his subjects described in *Severnaia Pchela*. A columnist in the May 30 issue marveled: "We will be grateful and frank. We are obliged to our Monarch for everything! Balls, masquerades, promenades, have been deemed worthy of the attendance of the Tsar and His Family, and have been transformed into national celebrations that leave the most pleasant of impressions on the soul."[22]

The image of Nicholas in the midst of a loving worshipful population was used to describe popular entertainments, the *balagany*. The author of an

---

[19] Nurit Schleifman, "A Russian Daily Newspaper and Its New Readership: *Severnaia Pchela* 1825–1840," *Cahiers du monde russe at soviètique* 29 (2): (April–June 1987): 127–44.

[20] *Severnaia Pchela*, January 7, 1830.

[21] Ibid., March 6, 1830.

[22] Ibid., April 17, 1830.

article about *balagany* during Holy Week admitted that few "of us" know about the simple people, "who are intelligent, kind and grateful." The people "judge by feeling, know and remember their benefactors." Nicholas was one of these because he had come to "participate in the gaiety of the people, to make Russians happy." The people felt, the author claimed, that "we cannot repay Him for his paternal love for Russia, except with tears of gratitude and zealous prayers to the Most High: God Save the Tsar!"[23] A report on the annual promenade at the park of Ekaterinhof commented: "Our Monarch, adoring of his children, deigned to participate in the pleasures of his subjects." In a scene reminiscent of their departure from Moscow, Nicholas and Alexandra rode in their phaeton in the midst of the people, without their suite. The people joyously ran after the carriage, trying to catch a glimpse of their faces.[24]

Moscow was the principal expression of national enthusiasm for the tsar, and *Severnaia Pchela* gave Nicholas's visits glowing accounts. The newspaper reported on the Muscovites' joyous response when he visited the city in March 1830.[25] Nicholas had "renewed the tradition of unexpected visits of his Great Ancestor, Peter." The Muscovites were especially joyous since they had not seen him since the coronation. Their response affirmed "the unchanging behest of Providence for our happiness." A long supplement, published on April 1, gave a detailed account of the emperor's visit.[26] It emphasized how pleased Nicholas himself was with his stay: "The bright, warm satisfaction of his gaze expressed this consoling thought with each of our glimpses of the SOVEREIGN who is our hope." Nicholas inspected the trade fair with especial attention. The account concluded with a description of the banquet given by the Moscow merchantry, where one of the merchants delivered a rousing speech proclaiming the Muscovites' and the Russians' love for their tsar that brought everyone present to tears: "It was touching to see how, without difference of rank and title, all hearts felt one thing, and all speeches expressed one thing."

Yet, these reports should not give the impression that *Severnaia Pchela* was denying the Western character of the Russian sovereign and his court. Quite the contrary, Russian monarchy deserved praise both for earning the love of the Russian people and epitomizing the highest level of Western manners and civilization. S. A. Vengerov accurately described the Russian newspaper of Nicholas's reign as "mainly a *chronicle of foreign life*."[27] Much of the space in *Severnaia Pchela* was devoted to foreign affairs and descriptions of events in foreign capitals. This emphasis sustained the newspaper's gen-

[23] Ibid.

[24] Ibid., May 3, 1830.

[25] Ibid., March 15, 1830.

[26] Ibid., April 1, 1830. The supplement is republished in Shil'der, *Imperator Nikolai Pervyi*, 2:565–71.

[27] S. A. Vengerov, "Ezhednevnaia pechat' kontsa doreformennoi epokhi," in *Sbornik statei po istorii i statistike russkoi periodicheskoi pechati, 1703–1903*, 104.

eral viewpoint that Russia was at the level of the West. Indeed, a theme in the newspaper was that although Russia had all the social blandishments of the West, they remained unknown to many because of the lack of coverage in the press. About a ball given by the St. Petersburg merchantry in 1825, an article boasted that "nothing more perfect is imaginable even in Paris or London."[28] St. Petersburg had masquerades and balls as lavish as those in Paris, but no one knew this because Russian journalists had previously not been allowed to attend. As a result, the reporter lamented, "all this remains without description, without lithographs." If the lavish masquerade given by Prince Volkonskii had taken place in Paris, he concluded, it would have been celebrated in poetry and prose, and the costumes illustrated in lithographs.[29]

Nicholas's extensive travel, much of it described in the press, heightened the sense of connectedness with the empire. The emperor gave the impression of being constantly on the move, with great impatience and haste. He insisted that the horses start out at a full gallop, the coach leaving in a burst of speed and a cloud of dust. "The emperor travels without interruption," Custine wrote. "He passes through at least five hundred places in a season." He spent one or two days in a provincial town, hurriedly inspecting institutions, reviewing troops, and avoiding ceremonial meetings and receptions.[30] He did not seek the mandate of public acclaim and, aside from parades, allowed himself little public exposure.[31]

Nicholas's connection with the life of the provinces was revealed by his attention to the appearance and condition of the towns he visited. He made his presence known by giving opinions and instructions, exercising rule on the spot. This was the image conveyed in the newspaper accounts of his tour of towns on the Volga in 1836. In Nizhnii-Novgorod, he inspected the fair. A report printed in both *Russkii Invalid* and *Severnaia Pchela* in August 1836 described the "splendid spectacle" of Nicholas's visit. The "Tsar Master"

---

[28] Shleifman, "A Russian Daily Newspaper," 137.

[29] *Severnaia Pchela*, March 6, 1830.

[30] A great number of horses suffered coronaries from the exertion, and after each trip the concessionaires submitted their often inflated bills. Horses were kept in readiness all along the emperor's route. A courier preceding the coach by an hour made sure the next team was in readiness, so that he could leave without delay (John Shelton Curtiss, *The Russian Army under Nicholas I* [Durham, N.C., 1965], 52–53). See also Custine, *La Russie en 1839*, 2:137; *IGK, ts. Nik. I*, 349; and A. V. Eval'd, "Rasskazy o Nikolae I," *Istoricheskii Vestnik* 65 (1896): 60–62.

[31] Benckendorff's journals of his travels with Nicholas from 1832 to 1837 describe the warm response the emperor received when he was recognized, but Nicholas did not tarry to enjoy the acclaim (Shil'der, *Imperator Nikolai Pervyi*, 2:647–764). Local officials and marshalls of the nobility nonetheless sought the opportunity to meet the tsar, and the minister of the interior had to issue strict rules limiting access to him. After 1845, only governors enjoyed the right of presentation during his trips. These rules produced some misunderstandings. One governor failed to appear at all to meet the emperor, which led to rules clarifying where such meetings were permissable (*IGK, ts. Nik. I*, 350–51; Finnish National Archive, "Delo kantseliarii finliandskogo general-gubernatora; o pravilakh i poriadkakh sobliudaemykh pri puteschestviiakh Gosudaria Imperatora i prochikh chlenov dvora, August 8, 1835").

(*Tsar-khoziain*) came "to survey the principal focus of trade and the meeting point of Europe and Asia." The merchants shouted as he passed through the humble stalls. But Nicholas was not there to receive acclaim. He observed the enormous variety of products from Europe, Siberia, and Asia. "All of this He wanted *to see for Himself.*"[32]

Having seen the town, Nicholas took steps to improve its appearance. He himself drafted plans for rebuilding the area of the booths at the fair and for new buildings along the embankment; the most scenic point would be occupied by a new residence for the military governor. One of the factors furthering the government's goals, *Russkii Invalid* explained in its September 9 issue, was the people's devotion to a sovereign who was concerned with "the tranquillity, the well-being, the wealth and the happiness of the people entrusted to him by God." In Kazan, Nicholas inspected schools, hospitals, and the university. In Simbirsk and Penza, he visited the gymnasiums and praised the boys for their attentive studies. Dmitrii Obolenskii, a distinguished official during the reign of Alexander II, recalled Nicholas's prepossessing appearance during a visit to a gymnasium in Kaluga in 1834. Obolenskii watched in amazement the common people mobbing the emperor's carriage. "The enthusiasm was sincere," Obolenskii wrote. "It powerfully affected my youthful imagination."[33]

Nicholas's visit to Simbirsk on August 22 and 23, 1836, was long remembered in the town. When Alexander I had visited Simbirsk in the fall of 1824, the reports told of the kindness and affection that the emperor had evoked from the townspeople. Nicholas, on the other hand, stormed through the institutions, terrifying the officials and the nobility with his criticisms. A memoir by a local resident, published in 1868, describes his effect on local society.[34] After the usual religious service and meeting with provincial dignitaries and officials, he proceeded forthwith to inspect the local garrison and hospital. The hospital did not meet with his approval, and he directly informed the local Bureau of Social Welfare (*Prikaz obshchestvennogo prizreniia*). When the governor announced that sums had been appropriated for a new jail, Nicholas angrily replied that they would be better spent on convict brigades. He swiftly went through other institutions, making comments and suggestions along the way.

Appearances were of great importance to Nicholas. He hoped to reconstruct provincial towns on the model of St. Petersburg and deplored the appearance of public buildings in Simbirsk, which, he claimed, lacked "a proper look." He criticized the design of the local trading arcade and other buildings that were being erected along the Volga. He had the work halted and gave precise instructions about the construction of new edifices, em-

---

[32] *Severnaia Pchela*, August 24, 1836: 767; *Russkii Invalid*, August 22, 1836: 851–53.

[33] *Russkii Invalid*, September 9, 1836: 919–20; September 21, 1836: 958–60; *Severnaia Pchela*, August 29, 1836: 785; September 1, 1836: 793. Dmitrii Obolenskii, "Dnevnik," Bakhmeteff Archive, Columbia University. Folder 1: 23.

[34] "Prebyvanie tsarstvennykh osob v Simbirskoi gubernii," *Sbornik istoricheskikh i statisticheskikh materialov o Simbirskoi gubernii* (Simbirsk, 1868), 152–55.

bankments, and a wharf. He ordered local officials to give the town square "a correct look" and to lay out a public garden. He told them to raze the old governor's mansion and build a new one on the embankment. He had especially critical remarks about the building occupied by the Simbirsk Noble Assembly, "which by its appearance did not correspond to its designation," and expressed confidence "that the nobility will not refuse to build a new one." He drew the changes he wished on a map of the town, which he gave to the governor and the Office of Routes of Communication. He also issued a decree ordering that the town erect a statue of Karamzin. He left the next day. "All the best buildings of the town and many other edifices were erected as a result of his supreme will," the Simbirsk resident wrote.

The Parade Ground as Epitome

Emperor Paul I had introduced the parade as a symbolic spectacle demonstrating the Western character and power of the Russian monarch. Alexander I had used parades to exemplify and confirm the Providential order that had brought the triumph of the forces of the godly; the military, and especially the guards' regiments, stood for the people who submitted to the divine force Alexander represented. Nicholas presented the parade as the principal epitome of the nation. The parade ground displayed the closeness of the emperor and his family to his military forces, which together epitomized the nation. The stunning discipline and subordination of Russian troops demonstrated the Russians' capacity not only to equal but to surpass the Western model of military organization, an ability inspired by their devotion to authority. The literary idiom of the time presented the displays of discipline not as triumphs of professional expertise, to which the monarch bore witness, but as spectacles of the monarch's personal authority and the Russian people's gift for obedience. Their obedience was portrayed as more than submission, as loyalty and love, an absorption of the person of the servitor into the person of his commander.

Parades became a central part of most holiday celebrations. Christmas Day—the anniversary of the expulsion of Napoleon's armies from Russia— was celebrated with Nicholas's inspection of the guards' regiments in the halls of the Winter Palace, then with a Te Deum for the war veterans. The parades accompanying the Blessing of the Waters, when weather permitted, became the center of a massive pageant in which the military engulfed the religious ceremony. All the divisions of the guards then spread out on Palace and Admiralty squares and along the embankment of the Neva, with the Preobrazhenskii Regiment nearby on the embankment. If the Neva was frozen, spectators crowded across the ice, pressing against the policemen to watch the ceremony.[35]

---

[35] *Russkii khudozhestvennyi listok*, no. 2 (1851).

Easter was marked by a great parade, followed by an exchange of greetings between the emperor and his troops. Baron Haxthausen described, with admiration, how the emperor, dressed in his uniform of the Don Cossacks, met and embraced soldiers selected from each of the regiments to bring him greetings. The military served as a symbol of all of Russia for Haxthausen, and he accepted the ceremonial act as the expression of genuine feelings of political solidarity: "It was a scene of striking grandeur . . . even the ruler of a quarter of the globe, the temporal protector and head of the Church, salutes the lowest of his subjects and acknowledges thereby the religious tie which binds him to his people by a community of faith, love and loyalty."[36]

Nicholas sustained this bond, in part, by instilling fear. He was ruthless, unforgiving, and draconian at meting out punishment. He was the all-seeing monarch. But unlike Western monarchs, he remained at the center of the stage, and his ubiquitous penetration itself became the subject of awe. His eyes haunted those who saw him; they seemed to reach everywhere, even into the servitor's soul. A lithograph of the time entitled *"un seul regard,"* reminded his subjects of his fierce, unswerving gaze. One officer wrote, "I have never again felt the glacial impression that the sight of the tsar made upon me." When Nicholas spoke, his "leaden eyes" remained fixed on those he addressed "as if he wanted to seek the secret thought at the bottom of their soul. . . . Of a colossal height, with an admirably handsome face, his eye, hard and penetrating, subjugated you [sic]." One officer found his left eye particularly fearsome. It was like "a red-hot nail," emitting a special piercing glow that left even courageous men trembling, and made some avert their gaze, and feel ashamed, "like a maiden."[37]

Nicholas held his head high in an artistic pose, and the innumerable portraits of him in military uniform catch his intimidating appearance. His eyes gaze off to the side with a look of imperturbable superiority. His neatly cut mustache frames his small thin lips that purse with a slight but detectable disdain. Like his behavior, his physiognomy was studied and intentional, fitting the pattern he thought would enhance his authority. "He expects always to be watched," the Marquis de Custine wrote. "He never forgets for a moment that he is being watched. You could even say that he wants to be the cynosure of all eyes."[38]

Fear was not the only or the principal bond between Nicholas and his officers. Nicholas aroused a feeling of love, a feeling that derived from a sense of utter subordination to his person, a dissolution of the individual in the embodiment of monarchical authority. It is this emotional attraction of

[36] Baron August Haxthausen, *The Russian Empire: Its People, Institutions and Resources* (London, 1856), 1:7.

[37] The Marquis of Londonderry, 1:208; Prince Joseph Lubomirski, *Souvenirs d'un page du tsar Nicolas* (Paris, 1869), 65; A. Karasev, "Levyi glaz Nikolaia vtorogo," *Istoricheskii Vestnik* 89 (1902): 106–8; M. A. Patkul', "Vospominaniia," *Istoricheskii Vestnik* 87 (1902): 840; N. K. Imeritinskii, "Iz zapisok starogo preobrazhentsa," *Russkaia Starina* 77 (1893): 321–22.

[38] Custine, *La Russie en 1839*, 2:102.

power that we lose in critical observations, like those of Custine. Nicholas represented a positive ideal that captivated by beauty and presence, and those who followed him did so in part because they were captivated. Vladimir Daehn, a guards' officer in the Sappers and later a governor, confessed to these feelings in his memoirs. In his late twenties, he served as an adjutant to Nicholas at Peterhof. He recalled the joy at being in the detachments that had the tsar as chief, a "joy—a delight which I am not in a state to describe: I loved him with all my loving soul—I could never get enough of him. My daily morning visit to the palace replaced all other pleasures for me."[39]

If Nicholas could punish with stern reproof and retribution, he could also show gratitude and recognition for faithful service. His personal attention bestowed importance and standing on an officer, the sense that that officer figured in the universe of the tsar. Nicholas gave signs that he knew of his servitors' existence. He had an amazing memory and knew the names of nearly all the guards' officers and of many of the pupils in the military training schools. Their meetings with him, especially when they were young, produced a sense of delight at the tsar's recognition of them, which they never forgot. The exchange of greetings and kisses with Nicholas at the Winter Palace was of special importance to them. One young man, serving as Nicholas's orderly at the Easter celebrations, wrote, "The tsar, with a contented look, taking me by the shoulder exchanged blessings with me (*pokhristovalsia so mnoi*), and my soul flew from my heels into seventh heaven. Ah what a happy moment in life this was, and how I wanted to experience it again, as an orderly."[40]

Nicholas established a rapport with the military by creating a sense of physical identity, of sharing a world of like appearance. He continued Alexander I's effort to make the parade ground an object of surpassing beauty. "Convinced that beauty was a sign of strength," the poet Afanasii Fet wrote, "the emperor Nicholas strove to attain in his strikingly disciplined and well-trained troops, who stunned European specialists, a nearly unconditional subordination and uniformity." Nicholas remarked with delight at the order of the troops he had reviewed at the camp of Voznesensk in 1837: "Everything shone with beauty and proper posture: the men, the horses, the dress, the harnesses, everything seemed to be made in one mold. . . . The troops received me with enthusiasm shining in their faces. I had no reason now to doubt the impression that this gathering of armies would make on foreigners."[41]

Nicholas felt a kinship with the artist who exercised power and control over reality, who shaped the world into an aesthetic order and excluded the

[39] V. I. Den', "Zapiski," *Russkaia Starina* 65 (1890): 79.

[40] M. O. Gershenzon, ed., *Epokha Nikolaia I* (Moscow, 1910), 15.

[41] A. Fet, *Moi vospominaniia* (Munich, 1971), reprint of Moscow 1890 edition, 1:iii; Shil'der, *Imperator Nikolai Pervyi*, 2:744.

unruly elements of human volition. He himself took lessons in engraving and left for posterity many copper plates he had made of the guards' regiments. Paintings and engravings of parades hung on his study wall.[42] He favored paintings produced by the "perspectival school" of art, in which men are reduced to lines of precisely disciplined troops in symmetrical formation who perform the drama of subservience, joining the emperor in overpowering the forces of disorder.

The construction of buildings in St. Petersburg followed the same spirit, continuing the project of re-creating Rome in St. Petersburg. George Knabe wrote, "Petersburg never looked more like Rome than under Nicholas, who decreed and confirmed triumphal arches, triumphal columns, decorative emblems of Roman swords and shields, standard facades going back, through Quarenghi and Palladio to the palaces and temples of imperial Rome." The governmental edifices spread out over large expanses, producing an impression of cold and forbidding uniformity, typified by the buildings leading down to the Aleksandrovskii Theater on Rossi's Theater Street. The center of St. Petersburg expressed discipline, subordination, whether military or administrative. St. Petersburg was to epitomize all of Russia, and no project for a governmental building anywhere in Russia could be undertaken without first passing the emperor's inspection.[43]

Nicholas liked to present himself as a Roman and appeared at many costume balls as a Roman warrior. A classical bust of him survives at the Gatchina Palace. But, Knabe observes, Nicholas knew no Latin and, unlike Paul and Alexander, had only a superficial acquaintance with classical history. The Roman persona was only one of several that he assumed, as he attempted to exemplify both classical and romantic inclinations in Russia. The classical architecture and statuary of St. Petersburg was neither Roman nor European, but, Custine opined, a grandiose Russian display of classical motifs exalting the image of sovereign, reflecting "not the love of art, but the self-love of man."[44]

Nicholas paid the same careful attention to his servitors' uniforms. He loved to spend hours sketching uniforms and drawing handsome guards' officers in graceful poses on still and stately horses.[45] Proper dress and demeanor was the essential sign of loyalty, showing an officer's identification with Nicholas's rule. The Preobrazhenskii Regiment, which had shown itself loyal to a man on December 14, provided the model of military appearance. He loved to wear the Preobrazhenskii and the Cavalier Guards' uniforms.

[42] Korf, "Iz zapisok," *Russkaia Starina* 98 (1899): 490–91; V. V. Shcheglov, *Sobstvennye ego imperatorskogo velichestva biblioteki i arsenaly* (Petrograd, 1917), 34.

[43] Knabe, "Rimskaia tema," 261; A. Benois and N. Lanceray, "Dvortsovoe stroitel'stvo Imperatora Nikolaia I," *Starye Gody* (July–September 1913), 178–80; Hamilton, *Art and Architecture of Russia*, 327–33.

[44] Knabe, "Rimskaia tema," 261; Custine, *La Russie en 1839*, 2:130.

[45] Shcheglov, *Sobstvennye ego imperatorskogo velichestva biblioteki i arsenaly*, 34; *IGK, ts. Nik. I*, 582.

"In these uniforms," he said, "I can always feel at peace with myself." Every year, at 1:00 P.M. on December 14, he visited the Preobrazhenskii barracks for a review and family reunion with the regiment.[46]

Nicholas heightened this sense of identification by favoring officers who resembled him. Tall and stately men were selected for the regiment and the best went into the "company of his majesty," those from the first Preobrazhenskii battalion, which guarded the Winter Palace. His company consisted of men of "masculine beauty," men who were tall, well built, "broadshouldered, healthy, true *bogatyri*." Nicholas once lined up with the men of "his company," and though he was six feet, two or three inches tall, ranked only eighteenth in height. The officers of the regiment shared Nicholas's sense of the importance of military appearance. The Preobrazhentsy on parade, one of them wrote, "crowned an army that by its martial look alone inspired full trust for all the eventualities in life."[47]

Rules on uniformity of hairstyles and grooming were strictly enforced. A decree of the minister of war in 1837 specified that hair was supposed to be cut on the forehead and the side, no longer than one-and-three-quarter inches, and from right to left. Although the rule was meant for lower ranks, it was presumed that officers would also comply. Infantry soldiers had to be seen in black hair and mustaches, whether natural or dyed. Beards, of course, were prohibited. Nicholas himself wore a mustache, and only military men were permitted to follow his example and to resemble the dashing figure of the emperor.[48]

Nicholas's own portraits presented the image of smart appearance and stern visage that was to serve as a model for the officer. Popular pictures (*lubki*) gave his image a broader, national character. Several portrayed his participation in the Turkish campaign of 1828. Nicholas, like Alexander, dreamed of commanding his army, to the dismay of his generals. He meddled in the strategic planning, insisting on simultaneous sieges of the Turkish forts of Varna, Silistria, and Shumla, what William C. Fuller describes as "one of the capital blunders of the campaign." He even took command briefly in 1828. But he quickly repaired to his camp at Braila, where he resumed his role as ceremonial commander.[49]

One *lubok* portrays him at the bivouac near a campfire with his suite at his side. In the background are other tents and campfires. Nicholas stands in a pose of implacable fortitude, a counterpart of Napoleon, while an adjutant salutes. Other pictures show him reviewing positions with his suite. The most striking is a popular print of Nicholas crossing the Danube, rowed by

[46] Curtiss, *The Russian Army under Nicholas I*, 51; Imeritinskii, "Iz zapisok," *Russkaia Starina* 77 (1893): 333; 104 (1900): 602.

[47] D. G. Kolokol'tsov, "Leib-Gvardii preobrazhenskii polk v vospominaniiakh ego starogo ofitsera, s 1831 po 1846 g.," *Russkaia Starina* 38 (1883): 293–94, 297.

[48] Imeritinskii, "Iz zapisok," *Russkaia Starina* 77 (1893): 537; Lubomirski, *Souvenirs*, 202; Curtiss, *The Russian Army under Nicholas I*, 47–48.

[49] Fuller, *Strategy and Power in Russia*, 251; Lincoln, *Nicholas I*, 124–25.

47. *Nicholas I Crossing the Danube*. Lubok.

ten Zaporozhets cossacks who had just gone over to the Russians. Nicholas stands in the boat, in the center of the picture, with his arm outstretched. The exaggeration gives him the proportions of a giant, dwarfing the row of the cossacks' heads, and dominating the landscape in the rear (fig. 47). The *lubki* give the emperor the allure of the *bogatyr'*, towering over the subjects who have recognized his suzerainty and ascendancy.[50]

The *bogatyr'*, the handsome, staunch, folk warrior of early Russia, became a common term of comparison for Nicholas and some of his robust and handsome adjutants. As *bogatyr'*, the Germanic figure of the emperor took on national traits. The *bogatyr'* was endowed with exaggerated beauty, size, strength, and exploits.[51] *Lubki* portrayed Nicholas in the characteristic pose of *bogatyr'* used to depict military heroes, such as Potemkin and Suvorov. He appears stiff and wooden on horseback, his steed's front hooves in the air, his right arm extended, sometimes with a sword, sometimes pointing into the distance. In the rear are usually scenes of battle, cavalry with their sabers raised, smoking cannons—or a row of soldiers in line.[52]

Officers were possessed by the sight of the tsar, and many strove to become

[50] *IGK, ts. Nik. I*, 250–51, 261, 264.

[51] Imeritinskii, "Iz zapisok," *Russkaia Starina* 104 (1900): 593; Lotman and Uspenskii, *The Semiotics of Russian Culture*, 242–43.

[52] See D. A. Rovinskii, *Russkie narodnye kartinki* (St. Petersburg, 1900), 151; Alla Sytova, *The Lubok, Russian Folk Pictures, 17th to 19th Century* (Leningrad, 1984), especially no. 73 of Suvorov (no background) and no. 96 of Major-General Alexander Seslavin (1839), with lines of soldiers in the rear.

his likeness. Since appearance denoted political disposition, the highest form of devotion was in imitation. The officers assumed Nicholas's intimidating pose and impressed their troops that no mistake or infraction could elude their gaze. Portraits show them with their mustaches cut like his, assuming his air of disdainful superiority and absolute control. Sleek, tall, and stiff, they took on Nicholas's punitive, menacing manner.

The officers who identified most closely with the emperor earned the favor of riding at his side as adjutant in his suite. Nicholas greatly expanded the imperial suite; he appointed 540 adjutants, compared to the 176 appointed by Alexander. His adjutants checked on command assignments at parades and undertook inspections of the troops to ensure their readiness. They performed guard duty for him in the palace, and accompanied him on his trips through Russia, which they helped to arrange. He regarded them as his comrades-in-arms and most trusted servitors, sending them as plenipotentiaries on special missions both of a civil and military nature. They even had the right to announce the tsar's oral decrees. Nicholas's adjutants filled the principal command positions in the three major armed conflicts in the first years of his reign: the Persian War of 1828, the Turkish War of 1828–1829, and the suppression of the Polish Rebellion in 1830 and 1831. He chose many of his ministers from their ranks.[53]

The parade ground revealed the unity of the military forces with the members of the imperial family. The appointment of the empress, of his brother Michael, and of his sons as heads of regiments strengthened the tie between officers and the family, weakening tendencies to professional autonomy in the military. Nicholas made special efforts to draw young noblemen into the life of his family. Junkers and cadets learned to regard the imperial family as their own. Grand Duke Michael, a stern martinet, was chief of military training schools from 1832 to 1849, and, despite his severity, was looked up to as a father by many of the guards' officers.[54] Nicholas delighted in organizing boys in military formations. They showed the continuity of his order, a reproduction of the parade ground in miniature. He displayed a paternal concern for the progress of the cadets and the pupils in the military training schools and took enormous pride in their marching skills. In the 1830s he formed a squadron of the cadets most adept at drill and delighted in showing them off to foreign visitors. Nicholas was especially proud of his sons, who often joined the cadets' exercises. During the 1840s he founded his own Preobrazhenskii "play regiments" for the grand dukes Nicholas and Michael, which he filled with sons of the aristocracy and important figures at court. Under the direction of old soldiers, the boys learned to dress and march properly and to build fortifications.[55]

---

[53] *IGK, ts. Nik. I*, passim; L. E. Shepelev, *Otmenennye istoriei*, 43–46; L. E. Shepelev, *Tituly, mundiry, ordena v rossiiskoi imperii* (Leningrad, 1991), 107–10.

[54] Curtiss, *The Russian Army under Nicholas I*, 185; E. P. Samsonov, "Vospominaniia," *Russkii Arkhiv* 1 (1884): 427–28. Samsonov remembered Michael's kindness and attentiveness to him.

[55] Lord Londonderry described Nicholas commanding a detachment of the cadets corps at a

The cadets and pupils in military schools were encouraged to see them-selves as members of the imperial family, sharing its fate and participating in its celebrations. They entertained the emperor and empress with parades and games during the annual summer camps near Peterhof. They exchanged pleasantries with Alexandra and received fruit and cakes from the young grand dukes. The climactic moment was the storming of the fountains at Peterhof, when the boys charged through the cascades of water to reach the imperial family and their entourage.[56]

The most favored joined in war games with the young heir and became his comrades (see below, chapter 12). When they grew up, they attended military maneuvers at Krasnoe Selo and met the imperial family at numerous balls, receptions, and theatrical performances. During social gatherings with the guards, Nicholas would recall the relatives of the officers, whose names he always remembered.[57] Worship for the imperial family became a tradition among generations of guards' officers who served the emperor. "In general," the Preobrazhenskii guards' officer, Imeritinskii, wrote, "the imperial family presented a lofty example of fraternal love, verging on self-renunciation."[58]

The bond of generations was the manifestation of the dynastic continuity Nicholas wished to establish in Russia. Nicholas frequently reaffirmed the significance of the family. On December 14, 1850, the twenty-fifth anni-versary of his reign, and on his assumption of the command of the Pre-obrazhenskii Regiment, he declared to the assembled officers, "You know what a strange occasion has bound us still closer together *and so we make up one common family, and my family all belongs to you as you all belong to me.*" He then pointed to the heir, Grand Duke Alexander, with his own sons near him. He continued, his voice breaking and tears in his eyes, "Here are three generations! Now you know who you will serve. Serve them as you have served me. I hope that your children will serve as you are serving me!" The regiment responded with a loud "Hoorah!"[59]

The press described military pageants as shows of mutual devotion be-tween the imperial family and the regiments of the guards. *Severnaia Pchela* reported a military holiday of the Izmailovskii Guards' Regiment attended by the grand duke Michael that was celebrated in June 1831, in the midst of military operations against Poland. The parade itself provided a diversion: after the "thunder of battle," it was pleasant "to calm the agitation of feel-ings at a spectacle of a simple military celebration." The author responded

---

half-hour drill in the Winter Palace after the ceremony of the Blessing of the Waters (The Mar-quis of Londonderry, 1:268–69). See also N. N. Murav'ev, "Zapiski," *Russkii Archiv* 2 (1894): 520–21; Lady Londonderry, *Russian Journal of Lady Londonderry, 1836–37* (London, 1973), 117; Gr. A. Olsufiev, "Poteshnye Imperatora Nikolaia Pavlovicha," *Russkii Arkhiv* 3 (1910): 443–45.

[56] Curtiss, *The Russian Army under Nicholas I,* 185; E. P. Samsonov, "Vospominaniia," 429–30.

[57] See, for example, Korf, "Iz zapisok," *Russkaia Starina* 101 (1900): 333.

[58] Imeritinskii, "Iz zapisok," *Russkaia Starina* 80 (1893): 274–76.

[59] Ibid., *Russkaia Starina* 104 (1900): 321–22.

with rapture to "the straight lines of this splendid army," to the "lively, healthy and virile look of the soldiers." Michael went through the ritual of drinking from the soldier's glass, and heard the exclamations of enthusiasm that were "testimony to that love that the ranks of the Guards Corps nurture in their hearts for the Ruling House and for the Brother of the worshiped Monarch of Russia!" The show of mutual recognition ends with the expression of sentiment, the *umilenie*, the tender recognition by the august figure for the show of affection. "We saw how tears of tenderness (*umilenie*) glistened in the eyes of *His Highness*, how He was moved so powerfully by the sincere, unanimous expression of universal love for Him!"[60]

•

The crushing of the Polish rebellion inaugurated a new era of triumphalism marked by great military displays recalling Alexander's victories and the spirit of Vertus. Massive maneuvers and parades celebrated Russia's invincibility at the unveiling of the Alexandrine column in 1834, the meeting of Russian and Prussian armies at Kalish in 1835, the twenty-fifth anniversary of the Napoleonic War at Voznesensk in Kherson Province in 1837, and the opening of the Borodino monument in 1839.[61] A series of publications recalled the glory of the wars, including Zhukovskii's poem "The Anniversary of Borodino," A. I. Mikhailovskii-Danilevskii's histories, and Lieutenant-General Khatov's account of Alexander I's review at Vertus.[62]

The first and most widely publicized of these glorifications of dynasty and nation was the dedication of Auguste Ricard de Montferrand's column to Alexander I. As many as 120,000 troops gathered in the capital on August 30, 1834, Alexander's name day, for a ceremony that marked the Alexandrine Column as a votive object in the emerging cult of dynasty. The principal published accounts, a brochure by Ivan Butovskii and an article by Vasilii Zhukovskii, described the spectacle as an epitome of the political order that had lifted Russia to the height of power and international prestige.[63]

For Butovskii, the setting, the imperial family, the lines of troops, represented the general relationship between the subjects and their sovereign. The setting was the massive palace square and the broad expanse to the north, "the enormous plain, that majestically spreads out before the eyes of the spectator." The statue of Peter the Great was then visible in the distance, on St. Isaac's Square; nearby was Rossi's majestic Senate and Synod arch. One

---

[60] *Severnaia Pchela*, June 26, 1831.

[61] A. G. Tartakovskii, *1812 god i russkaia memuaristika* (Moscow, 1980), 200–201.

[62] Ibid., 201–12; Khatov, *Dva znamenitye smotra voisk vo Frantsii*.

[63] Ivan Butovskii, *Ob otkrytii pamiatnika Imperatoru Aleksandru Pervomu* (St. Petersburg, 1834). Zhukovskii's account was published and unsigned in both *Severnaia Pchela* and *Russkii Invalid* (Vasilii Zhukovskii, "Vospominanie o torzhestve 30ogo avgusta 1834 goda," in *Severnaia Pchela*, September 8, 1834: 807–8; *Russkii Invalid*, September 9, 1834: 906–8). It was also printed in V. A. Zhukovskii, *Sochineniia* (St. Petersburg, 1902), 10:28–32.

could see Quarenghi's horse guards' manege, and the building of the military ministry, then the Winter Palace, and the noble arch of the general staff building. All of these were parts representing the whole; they made up the "foundation stones upon which our empire rests. The happiness and well-being of Russia flow from the marvelous buildings bordering the square."[64]

Butovskii conveys the personal significance of the event; for him it is a family holiday. In the morning, he tells the reader, he took his six sons to the palace where he met the emperor, the heir, and Michael Pavlovich on their way to the Nevskaia Lavra for the service for Alexander I's and the heir's saint day. At 11:00 A.M. Nicholas appeared on the square, cannon salvos sounded, and, at the third blast, columns of troops marched toward him. They quickly covered the entire vast expanse, "the brilliant Russian army, who by their smart, courageous, and fierce look would have stunned Alexander of Macedon, and would have been the envy of Caesar himself, and even of Napoleon."[65] Zhukovskii presents the parade as an emanation of the sovereign's power.

> The heavy measured step, shaking the soul, the calm approach of a force that was at once invincible and obedient. The army poured in in thick waves and submerged the square. But there was amazing order in this flood. The eyes beheld an innumerable and immense moving mass, but the most striking thing in this spectacle was something the eyes could not see: the secret presence of a will that moved and directed by a mere nod.[66]

The emperor, now standing at the side of his brother-in-law, Prince William of Prussia, bared his head, and prayed together with his entire army, "a spectacle that was at once touching and instructive," Butovskii wrote. Nicholas fell to his knees, followed by the entire army. When the Protodeacon uttered the prayer of Eternal Memory, the cloth fell, baring the column to public view. Nicholas then took command of the guard, and saluted the monument to the strains of band music and with loud shouts of "Hoorah!" from the crowd. The thunderous 248-gun salute that followed, accompanied by blaring music, struck Butovskii as a "frightening dream." The people crossed themselves and shed tears of tender pity (*umilenie*), while they gazed intently at the monument and Nicholas I standing before the column with lowered sword.[67]

Zhukovskii described the moment of common prayer as a condensed, microcosmic statement of Russian grandeur, silencing the writer's voice. Aporia alone could capture the moment.

---

[64] Butovskii, *Ob otkrytii pamiatnika*, 8–12.

[65] Ibid., 19–20.

[66] Zhukovskii, "Vospominanie o torzhestve 30ogo avgusta 1834 goda," *Severnaia Pchela*, September 8, 1834: 807.

[67] Butovskii, *Ob otkrytii pamiatnika*, 21–23; see also the description of the event in "Vospominaniia V. I Panaeva," *Russkaia Starina* no. 11 (1892): 292.

The miraculous fusion of earthly power reduced to dust, with the mysterious power of the cross, rising above it, and the invisible presence of that without name, expressing everything that is dear to us, something whispering to the soul, *"Russia, your past glory is your future glory"* and finally the touching word *eternal memory* and the name ALEXANDER, whereupon the drape fell from the column, followed by a thunderous prolonged *Hoorah*, combined with the sound of five hundred cannons, from which the air was transformed into a festive storm of glory . . . For the depiction of such moments there are no words and the very recollection of them destroys the gift of the one who describes.[68]

For Butovskii, the ceremony epitomized the emotional solidarity between people and monarch. The people on the square represented all the Russian people, united by pride in Russian military triumphs abroad and their relief and joy at the victory over the rebels. He described a "touching scene" that took place after the ceremony. "Common people" (*prostye liudi*) gathered at the monument and looked upon it with tenderness (*umilenie*), uttering the name of Alexander with tears in their eyes. They called him "their Angel, their Benefactor, their Little Father." Others brought their children to the column and spoke of "the kindness and majesty of Russian TSARS" and the glory of the Russian armies.[69]

The column itself was a blunt statement of Russia's exemplification of Western conceptions of empire (fig. 48).[70] Montferrand had designed the column after the Vendôme Column in Paris and Trajan's Column in Rome, but made sure that it stood taller than either of the others.[71] It was intended and presented as a symbol of the perfect state of Russia. The feelings of pride for a completed achievement that it inspired were quite remote from Alexander I's visionary dreams of the future. Zhukovskii compared the base of Falconet's statue of Peter the Great, "an ugly crag," to "the harmonious column that is the only one in the world of such height." The size and majesty of the object, he wrote, defied the poet's gifts.[72]

The statue on the monument, by Boris Orlovskii, glorified Alexander in Nicholas's idiom. Placed high atop the column—like the Roman emperors and Napoleon on their respective columns—the figure presents Alexander as an angel crushing a serpent. The angel, with Alexander's face, holds a cross, points to the heavens, and peers down at the square (fig. 49). If Peter

[68] Zhukovskii, "Vospominanie o torzhestve 30ogo avgusta 1834 goda," 807.

[69] Butovskii, *Ob otkrytii pamiatnika*, 23, 28.

[70] There is a fuller discussion of the monument in the context of tsarist statuary in my article, "Statues of the Tsars and the Redefinition of Russia's Past," forthcoming.

[71] The column, at 154 feet, was the largest in the world. Lest doubts linger, Montferrand included in his celebratory album scale drawings showing his column rising above the Napoleon, Trajan, Antonine, and Pompeian columns (A. Ricard de Montferrand, *Plans et détails du monument consacré à la mémoire de l'Empereur Alexandre* [Paris, 1836], iii, Plate 48; N. P. Nikitin, *Ogiust Monferran; proektirovanie i stroitel'stvo Isaakievskogo Sobora i Aleksandrovskoi Kolonny* [Leningrad, 1939], 243).

[72] Zhukovskii, "Vospominanie o torzhestve 30ogo avgusta 1834 goda," 807.

48. Alexandrine Column. Palace Square, St. Petersburg. Architect, A. Ricard de Montferrand. Drawing by Montferrand.

the Great appeared as a classical hero, Alexander assumed the incorporeal form of an angel. But he is a militant, not a gentle and endearing angel, whose spirit represents Russia's national triumph. It is a powerful expression of a divine force, an instrument of Providence acting in behalf of the nation. It is a statement of national destiny.[73]

The great column, Butovskii asserted, showed Alexander's firmness at the moment of doubt in 1812. "It seemed as if the Messiah came down to earth and announced to all peoples the beginning of eternal bliss." Enlightenment spread, luxury flourished, towns were built.[74] The theme of Alexander as national savior was stated most explicitly in a poem, "Feelings of a Youth at the sight of the Monument to Alexander the Blessed," printed in the newspaper, *Russkii Invalid*.

> Holding in your hands the sacred symbol,
> You gaze on us from on high;
> With the hand of the autocrat,

[73] Orlovskii had been directed to fashion an allegory expressing the triumph of Russia. Like Falconet, he insisted that the allegory be given concrete human form. "It is necessary that the idea of this allegory be expressed clearly, characteristically, and in a form proper to our era and national idea. Those were the conditions with which I harmonized my allegory, depicting an angel crushing a serpent with a cross" (I. E. Grabar' et al., *Istoriia russkogo iskusstva* (Moscow, 1964), vol. 8, pt. 2: 415.

[74] Butovskii, *Ob otkrytii pamiatnika*, 6–7, 33–34.

49. Statue of angel with face of Alexander I. Alexandrine Column, St. Petersburg.
Sculptor, Boris Orlovskii.

50. *Dedication of the Alexandrine Column*. Drawing by A. Ricard de Montferrand.

> You bless Holy Rus'.
> You are ours! In you I know
> The tsar savior of the universe!
> I stand as if charmed
> Enraptured by the visage of the Tsar.[75]

If the ceremony confirmed the political significance of the monument, pictures placed the ceremony in the mythical history of the dynasty. Montferrand's engraving turns the mortals on the square into objects of art, their order and submission reflecting the creative will of the monarch (fig. 50).[76] They are arranged in neat quadrilaterals over the expanse, the square surrounded by monumental classical edifices. The scene fades into the distance, giving the impression that it continues indefinitely, that Russia is an endless expanse of neoclassical squares filled with parades.

---

[75] *Russkii Invalid*, September 12, 1834): 920.

[76] Montferrand, Plate 44. Another, similar painting by Vasilii Raev is reproduced in small format in V. M. Glinka, *Russkii voennyi kostium*, 16. It is in the collection of the Russian Museum in St. Petersburg.

THE IMPERIAL COURT AS EPITOME

If the parade ground displayed the identity between the imperial family and the military, and by extension the nation, Nicholas's court revealed the bonds between the family and Russia's officialdom. In the first half of the nineteenth century, the imperial Russian administration grew—the number of officials rose fourfold from 1800 to 1856—and became increasingly educated and specialized. Bonds of personal devotion enabled the emperor to counteract rival claims of institutions and law that had favored the development of a professional bureaucratic ethos in the West. The ceremonies of Nicholas's court brought officials into the culture of dynastic monarchy and discouraged loyalty to the spheres of specialized competence characteristic of the European administrations that were Russia's ostensible models.[77]

Many of the civil servants who attended court functions were infected by the same feelings of awe, identification, and love as the officers of Nicholas's guards' regiments. Modest Korf typified the devotion of many Baltic noblemen to Nicholas. Korf, a state secretary engaged in the work of codification, felt Nicholas's spirit pervading all the workings of the state: "He gives meaning and color to everything. All the radii of the many-sided public activity converge on him." For Korf, as well as others, Nicholas's personality was compelling. The emperor radiated a charm, "some kind of bewitching power." Count Bludov, who served as state secretary, minister of the interior, and chief of the codification section of Nicholas's chancellery, also worshiped Nicholas and reacted strongly to his responses. He was beside himself on days he was to report to him; if well received, he pranced about like a child.[78]

Nicholas institutionalized his court, establishing a Ministry of the Court on August 26, 1826, the day of his coronation. The ministry administered court appointments, made arrangements for the disposition and attire of participants and guests, and circulated "ceremonials" (*tseremonialy*) that described the order of ceremonies. It also incorporated the emperor's cabinet, the office that managed the imperial family's finances, and the Appanage Department, which supervised their estates and palaces.

As before, the court included high officials, many of them from the titled aristocracy.[79] The highest appointments to court offices, such as marshall of the court, master of ceremonies, and keeper of the stable positions, were also

[77] P. A. Zaionchkovskii, *Pravitel'stvennyi apparat samoderzhavnoi Rossii XIX v.* (Moscow, 1978), 63–64; Torke, in *Das russische Beamtentum in der ersten hälfte des 19. Jahrhunderts* (Berlin, 1967), 134–35, estimates almost a threefold increase from 1805 to 1833. See Walter Pintner, "The Evolution of Civil Officialdom, 1755–1855," in Walter McKenzie Pintner and Don Karl Rowney, *Russian Officialdom: the Bureaucratization of Russian Society from the Seventeenth to the Twentieth Century* (Chapel Hill, N.C., 1980), 192.

[78] Korf, "Iz zapisok," *Russkaia Starina* 98 (1899): 373; 99 (1900): 505–6; Wortman, *The Development of a Russian Legal Consciousness*, 151.

[79] Forty-one of fifty-two of Nicholas's ministers came from the titled aristocracy (Lincoln, *Nicholas I*, 164).

bestowed on men with aristocratic titles and others with close associations with the tsar. They performed the usual functions of leading and directing ceremonies and state banquets, and managing the necessities and amenities of the emperor's life. Their responsibilities could be heavy, as attested to by the court composer and director of the Cappella, Alexei L'vov, who also served as *Gof-meister*. L'vov felt his life burdened by the routine of court ceremonies in addition to his particular service responsibilities. Nonetheless, he valued being close to the emperor and felt strongly attached to the members of the imperial family.[80]

Nicholas broadened membership in the court by granting the "court ranks" of chamberlain (*kamerger*) and junker of the chamber (*kameriunker*) to officials who had won favor. In this way he continued the process begun by Speranskii's law of April 3, 1809, which had made these ranks dependent on the holding of administrative office. He further limited court rank to civil officials of the eighth through the third ranks. Under Nicholas, all candidates for the ranks of chamber junker or chamberlain had to hold an administrative position and to be recommended for the appointment by their superiors.[81]

The court grew in numbers during Nicholas's reign, and more active officials from the administration were drawn into its activities. During the eighteenth century, the total number of court titles and ranks did not exceed a few dozen. In 1826 Nicholas set the total complement of chamberlains and junkers of the chamber at 48; by 1855, their numbers had risen to 382.[82] An examination of the "Directory of Ranks" of 1848 indicates that many leading officials of Nicholas's reign held court ranks and titles.[83] Nicholas issued rules for the duties incumbent on chamberlains and junkers of the chamber, ensured that they were fulfilled, and remarked on individuals' absences from important occasions. Such appointments could not be refused, and intellectuals like Pushkin and the Slavophile, Iurii Samarin, regarded them as a burden more than a reward.[84]

[80] Shepelev, *Otmenennye istoriei*, 112–20; Shepelev, *Tituly, mundiry, ordena*, 159–70; A. F. L'vov, "Zapiski," *Russkii Arkhiv* 2 (1884): 245–46; 3 (1884): 105.

[81] Shepelev, *Otmenennye istoriei*, 121–23; Shepelev, *Tituly, mundiry, ordena*, 170–74; N. E. Volkov, *Dvor russkikh imperatorov* (St. Petersburg, 1900), 24–31, 39.

[82] Shepelev, *Otmenennye istoriei*, 121–22; Volkov, *Dvor russkikh imperatorov*, 31–32.

[83] Leading officials who were chamberlains included Dmitrii Bludov, then chief of the Second Section; Modest Korf, the tsar's state secretary; Sergei Uvarov, the minister of education; Victor Nikitych Panin, the minister of justice; and Count Nesselrode, the minister of foreign affairs. L. A. Perovskii, minister of the interior and adjutant-general in the tsar's suite, was a *Gof-meister*. Further down the list, in the third civil service rank, future ministers such as G. G. Bibikov and A. M. Gorchakov, held the rank of chamberlain (*Spiski grazhdanskim chinam pervykh shest' klassov po starshinstvu* [St. Petersburg, 1848]).

[84] Volkov, *Dvor russkikh imperatorov*, 32–33; Shepelev, *Otmenennye istoriei*, 123. Iurii Samarin was aghast to learn that he had been appointed a junker of the chamber in 1846. To refuse would have meant exile to Viatka, he believed, and the end of his efforts to improve the Russian government (Iu. F. Samarin, *Sochineniia* [Moscow, 1911], 12: 173–74). I am indebted to Maia Rigas for this reference.

The award of ceremonial orders, such as the Order of St. George or the Order of Alexander Nevskii, also brought officials into court ceremonies. Nicholas's reform of the orders in 1842 designated the minister of the court the chancellor of orders and placed their administration under his own personal jurisdiction. It provided rules for the awarding of orders and the attendance of court functions by those designated the "cavaliers."[85] Cavaliers were expected to march in certain imperial processions. The most important functions for the orders were the annual feasts for the induction of cavaliers, which were preceded by a great procession and religious service. Feasts for the orders could be sumptuous affairs with two thousand to three thousand guests dining on elegant china service.[86]

At court, as in the military, exactitude and uniformity of dress were matters of great concern to Nicholas. At his accession, no single form of attire was required either for the court or for the civil service as a whole. Nicholas issued rules for the design and use of a court uniform. He also prescribed the women's court dress. A law of 1834 set strict rules for the colors, material, and style of the gowns worn by the different categories of ladies of the court, as well as for grand dukes and duchesses. The "Russian dress" that had been introduced by Catherine the Great was required at the most formal occasions, and Nicholas allowed no divergence from the official design. When, at one of the great balls of the 1840s, some of the ladies wore *kokoshniki* of flowers, he was enraged, and prohibited any deviations from the prescribed dress. Nonetheless, there remained leeway for lavish embellishment such as silver embroidery and gems.[87]

By complying with the dress rules of the court and attending official ceremonies, officials felt themselves inhabiting the same world as their sovereign. Court ceremonies were means for Nicholas to lift the leading cadres of the administration to the high levels of appearance and discipline that he believed characterized the military. The ceremony most expressive of the unity of the imperial court was the "great procession" (*bol'shoi vykhod*), which moved from the tsar's apartments in the Winter Palace to the great or small palace church on holidays. Participation in the processions, or even witnessing them from the halls of the palace, was a mark of an official's status.

At the "great processions," those with the highest standing had the right to assemble with the imperial family in Malachite Hall, adjacent to the im-

---

[85] On orders, see Helju Aulik Bennett, "*Chiny, Ordena,* and Officialdom," 172–75; Shepelev, *Otmennye istoriei,* 18–21; *BE,* 43:117–21.

[86] Imeritinskii, *Russkaia Starina* 104 (1900): 595–99; Lubomirski, *Souvenirs,* 216.

[87] Ladies holding court ranks and ladies-in-waiting wore a broach with a portrait of the empress on the right side of their chest. Ladies-in-waiting also wore on the left side the gold, diamond-studded "initials" (*shifry*) of the empress or of the grand-duchess whom they attended (Volkov, *Dvor russkikh imperatorov,* 28, 44–47, 93–96; Korf, "Iz zapisok," *Russkaia Starina* 99 [1899]: 294–95; John S. Maxwell, *The Czar: His Court and People* [New York, 1854], 251; Custine, *La Russie en 1839,* 2:147; Patkul', *Istoricheskii Vestnik* 88 [1902]: 445; Shepelev, *Otmennye istoriei,* 127–28).

perial chambers, before the procession; they entered "behind the Cavalier-Guards," the guards' regiment with the most extensive and illustrious ceremonial tradition. Great processions were led by court servants in livery—the *gof-fur'ery* and *kamer-fur'ery*. A ceremony master followed behind two rows of chamberlains and junkers of the chamber. Behind them marched high court officials in ascending order of seniority. The chief marshall of the court, swinging his diamond-studded mace, preceded the emperor and empress, who were followed by their suites, the heir, and other members of the imperial family. Ladies-in-waiting brought up the rear.[88]

In these processions, the hierarchy of tsars' servitors, dressed in brilliant uniforms, showed off the beauty and panache that gave Nicholas's power its luster. The Preobrazhenskii officer, N. K. Imeritinskii, describing a procession of 1851, was particularly struck by the physical height and beauty of the participants.[89] He called the generals, who now served Nicholas in high administrative positions, *bogatyri*; "an artist could paint from any of them the type of the ancient hero." Even the "civil ministers," who had risen through the civil service, were prepossessing. Count Panin, the minister of justice and a chamberlain, was also extraordinarily tall, and known for his feats of strength. His physical appearance was undoubtedly one of the features that impressed Nicholas and led to the count's swift rise in the civil service.[90]

•

The major holidays—New Year's Day, Easter, Nicholas's name day celebration, the empress Alexandra's birthday—became occasions to reaffirm the personal bond between the family and servitors. The doors of the palace were thrown open not only to the highest members of the elite but also to lesser-ranking civil servants, who could observe and marvel at the ceremonies of mutual devotion. These festivities gave the impression of being inclusive: in addition to the diplomatic corps and distinguished foreign guests, one could see merchants "in oriental caftans" and specially selected peasants. Such occasions presented what the empress's confidant, the writer and

[88] Shepelev, *Otmennye istoriei*, 128–30; Volkov, *Dvor russkikh imperatorov*, 145–48. This group who assembled "behind the Cavalier-Guards" included bearers of court titles, chamberlains, and junkers of the chambers, members of the State Council, senators, state secretaries, and honorary guardians, in addition to ladies of the court. Also allowed "behind the Cavalier-Guards" were the state secretaries to the emperor and cavaliers of the highest two orders—Andrei the First Called, and St. George.

Officials and officers lined up in the succeeding "parade rooms" in order of declining seniority, as specified in the announcements issued by the ministry of the court. Wives could attend only if they had been presented to the empress. On special occasions, the emperor would express his intention to stop and hold conversations after the processions. Then members of the suite, general-governors, and civil officials of the highest two ranks were allowed to meet with him in the room adjacent to his quarters.

[89] Imeritinskii, *Russkaia Starina* 104 (1900): 592–603.

[90] Ibid., 602.

pedagogue August Theodore Grimm, called "a miniature representation not only of the whole Russian realm, but also of Europe."[91]

The bringing of felicitations to the emperor and empress on these holidays dramatized the family relationship that was supposed to govern official relationships throughout the Russian state. The ceremony provided a model for all levels of the administration: on holidays, officials were obliged to bring greetings to their superiors and to attend church services with them, a requirement that Nicholas believed was part of their training in good manners.[92] On January 1, the imperial family would personally receive the line of visitors to the palace, a ritual that inaugurated each year. On Easter Sunday, they embraced and greeted each of the guests with the phrase "Christ has Risen"; by the end of the ceremony, wax from the hundreds of mustaches covered Nicholas's face. At personal and family celebrations, birthdays, name days, weddings, coming-of-age ceremonies, officials reaffirmed their solidarity with the dynasty.

The two most important of these were Nicholas's name day celebration and Alexandra's birthday celebration. These events were not described in the periodical press. But the numerous foreign memoirs written about them give vivid impressions of their atmosphere and of the involvement of the court and the officialdom in the display of the imperial family.[93] Nicholas's name day celebration took place on December 6 and marked the beginning of the winter social season in the capital after the imperial family's return to the Winter Palace. The elaborate reception was a rather anxious moment for

[91] Grimm, *Alexandra Feodorovna*, 2:31; Korf "Iz zapisok," *Russkaia Starina* 102 (1900): 287.

[92] Torke, *Das russische Beamtentum*, 206–7.

[93] The most revealing accounts were the memoirs of Lord Stuart, the Marquis of Londonderry; the memoirs of his wife, Lady Londonderry; and Custine's celebrated *La Russie en 1839*. Lord Londonderry, a half-brother of Viscount Castlereagh, was a former general who had retired from the British diplomatic corps. Highly conservative, very much the old soldier, he worshipped Nicholas and Russia, and his nomination by Robert Peel in 1834 to the ambassadorship to St. Petersburg brought forth such a storm of outrage from parliament that he was forced to withdraw. Instead, he and his wife embarked on a long journey with an extended sojourn in Russia. Both left memoirs, the Lord's more informative, the Lady's more elegantly crafted. Lord Londonderry was indeed a credulous guest, and, indeed, played the role of one of Nicholas's foreign apologists. With Grimm's memoirs, his recollections give a good sense of the response to the celebrations expected from a loyal servitor. See the introduction by W. A. L. Seaman and J. R. Sewell, in their edition of Lady Londonderry's memoir, *Russian Journal of Lady Londonderry, 1836–37* (London, 1973), 1–8.

Custine's renowned letters from Russia, published under the title *La Russie en 1839*, are of a quite different character. Custine himself was a writer and intellectual, and though politically conservative, adhered to values of individual integrity and culture that attracted him to intellectuals more than officials. His letters express the repugnance for despotism of a nobleman sympathetic to an independent aristocracy and to Polish independence. But they go beyond that and express a general distaste for the aesthetic immoderation and lack of classical balance of the Russian court, the exaggeration and performance that constituted one of the principal traits of Russian monarchy. On Custine, see George F. Kennan, *The Marquis de Custine and His Russia in 1839* (Princeton, N.J., 1971).

many of the court notables. Officers and officials brought their felicitations to their sovereign; Nicholas showed his gratitude by announcing generous awards of bonuses, titles, and promotions, which inevitably left some disappointed. He also distributed signs of his favor—rings, diamond-studded boxes, thimbles, imperial portraits.[94]

The name day celebration was an exercise in subordination that proved to outsiders the solidarity between Nicholas and his elite. There was no choral approval as in the eighteenth century, for there was no separation between the sovereign and the leading members of the court, the noble estate, and the administration who were obliged to attend this function. Lord Londonderry described the celebration in 1836 as a marvel of luxury and organization, attesting to the absolute devotion and obedience of all of Nicholas's subjects. In the first hall, he beheld *dames d'honneur* wearing long veils and the Russian cap, covered with jewels "as numerous as resplendent," presenting "a matchless *coup d'oeil*." In the adjoining halls stood members of the State Council, the senators bedecked in scarlet "with the richest gold embroidery," highly ranked civil servants and diplomats, "with light blue dress coats equally costly." In the last "magnificent apartment," Nicholas stood at the head of the room before the generals, the aides-de-camp, and officers of the armed forces grouped according to their unit.

The uniforms of "the cuirassiers, huzzars, dragoons and infantry of every denomination, Cossacks, Circassians, Georgians," the color and the glitter of the decorations in diamonds and "orders of all nations" dazzled the Marquis and impressed him with Nicholas's absolute mastery. The display of aesthetic taste attested to the power of the ruler to produce beauty through submission. "The admirable arrangement and order that reigned gave each his proper place, and without the least semblance of confusion. All appeared like clockwork, and I was never before so struck with the magical effect of order."[95]

The Marquis of Londonderry watched the spectacle of the procession with admiration and even envy. The imperial cortege approached with "at least one hundred *gentilhommes de la cour*, clothed in dark green and gold embroidery, far surpassing that on the full dress of our cabinet ministers." The emperor wore the uniform of the hetman of the cossacks, and the empress wore a full Russian gown with a red velvet and gold train, "her cap and gown a blaze of jewels." Her crown was surmounted by rows of pearls, "some of which were nearly as large as pigeon eggs." Then followed the heir, the grand duchesses, and the *demoiselles* of the court.

The elite showed their devotion by the ritual kissing of the empress's hand—the *baisemain*. After the mass, the empress, according to the custom for the tsar's name day, received these felicitations from the high nobility,

<hr />

[94] Grimm, *Alexandra Feodorovna*, 2:28–29.
[95] The Marquis of Londonderry, *Recollections of a Tour*, 1:250–52; Lady Londonderry, *Russian Journal*, 102.

officials, and others with access to the court. The *baisemain* began with the ladies; then the gentlemen followed. Both Lord and Lady Londonderry took the admirable order of the ceremony as an expression of allegiance that epitomized the attitudes of all Russians. Lady Londonderry wrote, "The pomp and splendor was [*sic*] surpassing but nothing was more beautiful than the devotion and affection shown to the Sovereign whom this great people, collectively and individually, look up to as a father."[96]

The ball in the evening also impressed foreign guests as a display of submission and coordination. The principal dance, the polonaise, was little more than a stately procession to musical accompaniment. The emperor, with a lady on his arm, and the empress, with a gentleman, led a long line of couples that wound through the palace. Its direction, Custine remarked, was "at the whim of the man who leads it." On the occasion of the emperor's name day, as on many of the imperial family's personal holidays, the polonaise lasted for most of the ball. Other steps tended to be executed with the same formality and stiffness. Nicholas himself did not enjoy dancing, and tended to approach it as ordered movement like parades. At the sign given by the conductor, the music began, and quadrilles moved "with the precision of exercises in triple time." Then everyone returned to his and her place and stood still. "A kind of automatic submission to these demands of etiquette was the best way to please the tsar," Prince Joseph Lubomirski wrote.[97]

The final and, for many, the culminating moment of the evening was the supper, which took place in a lush and exotic setting. This was the empress's "fairyland." In a winter garden, the guests dined on elegant service, before vessels of silver and gold, amid the aroma of immense orange trees whose stems had grown through the tables. The empress circulated around the hall according to Russian etiquette, chatting with each of the guests. The presence of orange trees in the midst of winter, as well as blacks in Moorish costume serving "every delicacy in the world," delighted the guests. The American, John Maxwell, wrote: "It rivals the enchantment of an eastern story." All those who attended such suppers invoked references to the exotic and legendary. The surroundings transported the visitor into a different reality, a world of fantasy and gratification of the senses, of "perfect enchantment," a "fairyland."[98]

The fairytale motif of the connubial love in the imperial family was the

---

[96] The Marquis of Londonderry, *Recollections of a Tour*, 1:252–55; Lady Londonderry, *Russian Journal*, 102, 104.

[97] In 1836, the ball, described by Lady Londonderry, was held a week later due to mourning over the death of the empress's aunt, Princess Radziwill. Lady Londonderry, *Russian Journal*, 110–11; Custine, *La Russie en 1839*, 2:142–43; Ol'ga Nikolaevna, *Son iunosti*, 94; Lubomirski, *Souvenirs*, 203; for observations on the social and literary roles of the polonaise, see Lotman, *Roman A. S. Pushkina, "Evgenii Onegin,"* 83–85.

[98] Grimm, *Alexandra Feodorovna*, 2:29; Maxwell, *The Czar*, 153; Lady Londonderry, *Russian Journal*, 110–11.

theme of the lavish festivities that took place at Peterhof each July, on the occasion of the empress's birthday. If the parade ground presented a paradigm of power, a simulacrum of the awesome state, the presentation of the family banished all signs of power, revealing scenes of concord, flawless beauty, unchanging youth. The empress was the center of admiration and love. Nicholas played the attentive husband, Alexandra the ideal wife and mother.

Nicholas had laid out Peterhof, which had been largely neglected by his predecessors, as a vast pleasure park. Palaces for members of the imperial family imitated Roman, Pompeian, French, and English styles of leisure homes. The grand duchess Olga received a Roman house, the grand duke Alexander a two-story palace with a French mansard roof. The thirty or so pavilions provided a variety of national settings for the empress to have breakfast and tea.[99] Before 1848, the July celebration of the empress's birthday was a massive popular holiday, open to large numbers of the public. Visitors from St. Petersburg crowded into the palaces, noble homes, and rooming houses, but these were insufficient to accommodate the influx.

The town and gardens, Grimm wrote, presented "the spectacle of a vast camp, a bivouac, a mass of carriages, of large and small tents with refreshments, cook-shops, rapidly run-up booths and beer-houses, while the interior of every carriage is used by the fashionable world as a dressing-room." Though the pretense was that Peterhof was open to the public, strict police surveillance controlled those admitted. Groups of peasants, judged reliable, attended the festivities, but when a few "beggars with children" slipped in, Nicholas demanded that they be immediately expelled.[100]

The celebrations began at the emperor's and empress's idyllic Peterhof residence, the "Cottage" (*Kottedzh*). Early in the morning, Nicholas had the empress awakened by music from the same military band that had welcomed her to Russia. As she prepared her toilet, Alexandra heard her favorite pieces, among them the overture to *Der Freischütz* and a waltz that the two had danced when they had first met in Berlin. From the Cottage, she rode past throngs of spectators. Before the lines of notables in the halls of the palace, she proceeded arm in arm with Nicholas to the church for a high mass. After the service, she received greetings and then appeared on the balcony of the palace before the elegant "public" of lavishly dressed ladies and handsome guards' officers in dress uniform. Those present sensed her charm and felt drawn into the family. The feelings of warmth and closeness dispelled the feeling of constraint one usually felt before royalty. A. I. Iakovleva, a lady-in-waiting for the grand duchess Maria Aleksandrovna,

---

[99] Benois and Lanceray, "Dvortsovoe stroitel'stvo," 186–93.

[100] Grimm, *Alexandra Feodorovna*, 2:44–46; Baronessa M. P. Frederiks, "Iz vospominanii," *Istoricheskii Vestnik* 71 (1898): 77; A. Shemanskii and S. Geichenko, *Krizis samoderzhaviia; Petergofskii Kottedzh Nikolaia I* (Moscow, 1932), 15–16, 60; Custine, *La Russie en 1839*, 3:95.

wrote: "Between the public and the imperial personages there was something kindred and close. The imperial family made the public the participant in its joys and pleasures. Everyone felt this and all were happy at meetings with the imperial family."[101]

The empress then left the balcony and sat in an equipage with the grand duchesses to review the troops of her Cavalier Guards' regiments. They marched before her in their white parade uniforms, their silver-colored helmets crowned with the Russian eagle. The emperor and the heir, wearing the same uniform, led the troops in a ceremonial march past her. Nicholas then stopped and bowed before her. Foreigners were charmed and moved by this scene. Two of them, the Frenchman Florent Gille—a confidant of the empress and tutor to the grand dukes—and the adjutant of the Swedish crown prince, Wolfgang Haffner, saw Nicholas perform the ceremony in the rain. The weather, Gille concluded, "only gave the Emperor an opportunity to offer proof of the sentiment in him." The emperor bowed like a chevalier before his lady, he observed. "Then with a double gesture, opening his arms and raising his eyes to the sky, he seemed to say, 'I have done everything I could.'" Haffner wrote that this "knightly spectacle" convinced him that Nicholas, in fact, was a European monarch, rather than "some kind of Asiatic sultan who sits on the throne, gives orders and receives expressions of respect from everyone."[102]

The evening was the occasion for a climactic extravaganza. The ball began at seven. The polonaise now was the only step. "This dance lasted the whole time," Haffner remarked, "perhaps because of the crowds of people." Custine described the emperor leading the procession for two or three hours with the grand duchesses and ladies of the court. At Peterhof the polonaise was not a ceremonious march but "a promenade to the sound of the instruments" through the Peterhof crowd, which parted to permit the procession through.[103]

Then began the illumination. In the half-light of the July night, the great Peterhof canal brilliantly reflected the glittering lamps, stunning the eyes of the guests. Custine said it required an Ariosto, the language of fairies, to describe the blazing lights arranged in fantastic forms, "flowers as large as trees, suns, vases, bowers of vines . . . obelisks, columns," everything glittering like diamonds. On the sea, small ships were lit with color. Twelve military bands played in different parts of the garden. At the end of the canal, the empress's initials burst into white flame surrounded by red, green, and blue, "a diamond crest, surrounded by colored gems." Custine was stunned, but reached a conclusion precisely opposite to that drawn by Haffner. Custine found what he had seen "too large to be real; it is the dream of

---

[101] Grimm, *Alexandra Feodorovna*, 2:47–49; A. I. Iakovleva, "Vospominaniia byvshei kamer-iungfery imperatritsy Marii Aleksandrovny," *Istoricheskii Vestnik* 31 (1888): 173.

[102] Gille, *A la mémoire de l'impératrice Alexandra Féodorovna* (Paris, 1864), 23–24; Wolfgang Haffner, "Tri nedeli v Rossii," *Istoricheskii Vestnik* 135 (1914): 261.

[103] Ibid., 262; Custine, *La Russie en 1839*, 3:93.

an enamored giant related by a mad poet." The extravaganza was another expression of Russia's Asiatic nature, only this too was not real; "this is Asia, not real Asia, modern Asia, but the fabulous Baghdad of *The Thousand and One Nights*, or the more fabulous Babylon of Semiramis."[104]

Shortly after the July 1 celebration, the imperial family customarily presented an open-air spectacle of family life. In front of the Cottage, they took tea in full view of the public, including peasants chosen by their landlords, who gazed on them "in silent devotion, as something sacred." The empress prepared and served the tea. Nicholas would rise and walk over to talk "with one of the most insignificant in the crowd," and Alexandra would invite one of them to take tea. The loyal Grimm expressed the intended meaning of this display: "Thus the greatest simplicity succeeds the utmost magnificence; yesterday the Empress of all the Russias was admired, but today the family of the Czar is honoured, the wife, the mother, in their quiet domestic life."[105]

Most foreigners found Nicholas's family life a sign of his Western, humanitarian character. To Londonderry, "the example afforded by the Imperial family of moral, conjugal, and domestic affection and happiness," was of "incalculable moral advantage" to the empire. The emperor's example of "conjugal bliss," Londonderry believed, led to the abandonment of liaisons and the absence of "light conduct" in the salons the lord had visited. "The emperor Nicholas is distinguished over all his predecessors for domestic virtues," Maxwell remarked. Grimm marveled that Nicholas favored those in service who had families, and sent the families gifts to place by their Christmas trees. This feeling showed that the imperial family, despite their lofty eminence, "were far more closely connected with their people than the most petty German prince with his subjects."[106]

Even Custine appreciated Nicholas's family sentiment: "His domestic virtues undoubtedly help him to govern, thus ensuring the esteem of the world, but he practices them, I believe, without calculation." But Custine was repelled by the theatrical display of domesticity and saw the motley social gathering of noblemen, peasants, and merchants as one more indication of despotism. The celebration was "a true bacchanal of absolute power." Nicholas was not saying to commoners that they were men like him, but saying to noblemen that they were slaves like the commoners, expecting all to gape in servile admiration. "To seek a simulacrum of popularity in the inequality of others is a cruel game, a despot's joke" from another era.[107]

Each response reveals one aspect of the image Nicholas was seeking to project. On the one hand, Nicholas's domesticity displayed the noble side of his character and allowed him to join with other mortals in affirming certain

[104] Ibid., 3:93–95.

[105] Ibid., 2:53; Shemanskii and Geichenko, *Krizis samoderzhaviia*, 15.

[106] The Marquis of Londonderry, *Recollections of a Tour*, 1:270–71; Maxwell, *The Czar*, 165; Grimm, *Alexandra Feodorovna*, 2:343–44.

[107] Custine, *La Russie en 1839*, 2:133–34, 3:66.

human and even humane values. On the other hand, he expected his servitors to worship his wife and children as they worshiped him, and to regard his joys and tragedies as their own—to make their sentiments a reflection of his own. In this respect, the domestic idyll, too, was a form of subordination, using current Western forms to display the daunting moral supremacy of the Russian emperor.

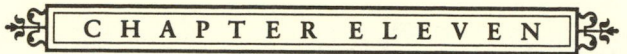

CHAPTER ELEVEN

Parents and Son

> Our Tsar, your Ruling Parent,
> Gave us a tablet of law,
> And this feat worthy of glory,
> Is wisdom, His altar.
>
> Praise to the Tsar! Praise to the Tsaritsa!
> She is the Mother of Russia's children,
> She is the light of day to them
> She is the blessing of the land!
>
> May their Power prosper,
> Like the ageless flower of paradise,
> And the resounding glory of NICHOLAS
> Pass to his posterity.
>
> And you our guest! A golden star
> The splendid son of The Great,
> Captivating Russians with tenderness
> Flower our young giant!

—Words to Polonaise by Michael Glinka, on the occasion of the visit of the grand duke and tsarevich, Alexander Nikolaevich, to the town of Smolensk, July 14, 1837[1]

"THE LORD OF THE COTTAGE"

An engraving by Thomas Wright after a painting by George Dawe completed not long after Nicholas's accession suggests the new importance of the emperor's family for the future of Russian monarchy. A portrait of the young grand duke, Alexander, is set in an oval frame surrounded by flowers between crowned portraits of his parents. The countenances of father, son, and mother dominate the sweep of the Winter Palace depicted below. The scene is illuminated by the sun, the traditional symbol of the benefactions of kingship and current symbol for the radiant future of the dynasty (fig. 51).[2]

[1] *Severnaia Pchela*, August 11, 1837: 712.
[2] *IGK, ts. Al. II, 9.*

51. *Emperor Nicholas I, Grand Duke Alexander Nikolaevich, and Empress Alexandra Fedorovna, 1826.* Engraving by Thomas Wright. Artist, George Dawe.

With great fanfare, Nicholas adopted the nineteenth-century European ideal of a separate family sphere, in which the hard-working ruler could find happiness and peace. Like previous scenarios, the domestic idyll was presented in absolute terms, as a flawless realization of Western values of domesticity, about which foreign visitors were expected to remark with admiration. Florent Gille wrote, in his eulogistic memoir to Alexandra, that Nicholas practiced the "moral cult of the woman," which Gille considered one of the essentially civilizing elements introduced by sovereigns in Christian society. The queen or empress became "the first woman of her empire, the predestined being, upon whom after the sovereign, regards have always been fixed."[3] Nicholas played the role of knight, shielding the delicate and beautiful woman from reality. Alexandra played the frail and exquisite damsel; her delicacy and her nervous tremble—traced unfailingly to the events of December 14—seemingly called out for protection. The emperor was the hero in a romantic tale, rather than a classical hero of battle or virtue.

The domestic scenario, however, was more than a romantic embellishment to the image of the tsar. It made the family a central symbol of the

[3] Gille, A la mémoire, 22.

moral purity of autocracy—the purest form of absolute monarchy. The association between domestic morality and autocratic government outlived Nicholas's reign and remained intrinsic to the image of Russian autocracy for the duration of the empire. To violate the principle of autocracy became tantamount to a biblical sin against the father, while violation of family morality would throw into doubt the moral foundations of autocratic rule. Nicholas introduced the forms of behavior, the ceremonies, the feelings of obligations that underlay the notion of dynastic autocracy in the nineteenth century.

This chapter examines the elaboration of the familial scenario in Nicholas's reign: first, in the romantic elevation of the empress; second, in the upbringing and presentation of the heir as defender of his father's traditions; and third, in the perpetuation of the domestic scenario with Grand Duke Alexander's marriage and family life. The dramatization of the tsar's family life ignored the distinction between private and public spheres. The private sphere provided a theatrical demonstration of obligations that were political as well as domestic, and Nicholas's family life became the object of his subjects' attention and even observation. Nicholas represented not only the good husband, but the most faithful and devoted husband of the realm whose spectacular displays of domesticity would earn him the admiration of all those in Russia and the West who shared the dominant familial morality.

Nicholas, in this way, fit the nineteenth-century image of the paterfamilias, but this was the scenario, the theater. There was rumored to be another side as well, however: the double standard permitting the husband secret liberties as long as he did not defile the beautiful idyll of the family. Whispered accounts told of his exercise of autocratic right over the daughters and wives of his servitors, which Tolstoi evoked in his story "Father Sergii." Later in his reign, when Alexandra was constantly ailing, Nicholas took himself a mistress, Varvara Nelidova. But this fact was carefully concealed from the court so that even the ladies-in-waiting learned of it only at Nicholas's death.[4] The emperor's straying did not figure in his display. Infidelity was no longer the sign of a monarch's virility and power.

In representations of the family, Alexandra epitomized maternal love and tenderness. The new scenario dispensed with the former reserve in the display of parental love. The close emotional relationship between Alexandra and her firstborn son, Alexander Nikolaevich, as well as her other children, appeared in the foreground for all to see. It symbolized the lofty spiritual and aesthetic bonds uniting members of the dynasty and uniting the dynasty with the state. Although the nursery staff watched over the children, the empress played with them, it was said, every day. When they grew up, she

---

[4] D. D. Blagoi, *Dusha v zavetnoi lire; ocherki zhizni i tvorchestva Pushkina* (Moscow, 1977), 415–16; Tiutcheva, *Pri dvore dvukh imperatorov*, 1:88–89, 179–80. It is difficult to determine how much substance there was to the rumors of infidelities. In any event, they are completely consistent with the pattern adopted by Nicholas of the display of family morality and the dual standard ascendant in the West.

drew them together in the evenings for family readings. Grand Duchess Olga Nikolaevna wrote that it was like "paradise" for the children to be near their mother. When she left, they were desolate: "If mother was away, we were like lost souls."[5]

Nicholas used the media of painting and engraving to disseminate his family idyll both to the elite and to a broader audience beyond the court. Portraits by English painters depicted the imperial family in the style of domestic portraiture perfected at the English court.[6] Paintings by George Dawe, rendered into engravings by his compatriot, Thomas Wright, presented royal personages for the first time in intimate family groups. One of these shows the empress sitting with the infant Olga Nikolaevna in her right arm, and the seven-year-old Alexander Nikolaevich grasping her gown on the left (fig. 52). Another is a garden scene: Alexander Nikolaevich, in a sailor suit, pushes his little sister Maria, wearing a bonnet with flowers, on a swing. Both have the innocent cherubic expressions of nineteenth-century beautiful children. Domestic scenes reached a wider audience in popular prints, such as one of the emperor adjusting his son's pillow, and another of a family gathering at Ekaterinhof.[7]

Alexandra was the center of this cult, irresistibly endearing, as tender and gracious as Nicholas was intimidating.[8] She was the passive recipient of affection, not like Maria Fedorovna—the bestower of maternal solicitude and succor upon the unfortunate. Although she continued to dispense charity, Alexandra insisted that her benefactions remain secret. According to Gille, she gave away two-thirds of her revenues to the indigent and unfortunate. But these deeds remained private, for they did not contribute to the public image of sublime isolation from the sufferings of this world.[9]

Her involvement in the charitable institutions established by Maria Fedorovna was likewise distant. To engage herself actively in their operations would have violated the division of male and female spheres and involved her in the sordid work of government. It would have given the hint of ambition, which, as Gille pointed out, she made every effort to avoid, and which in the early nineteenth century was regarded as an embarrassing trait for a member of the imperial family.[10] The institutions of the empress Maria were

---

[5] *IGK, ts. Al. II*, 9; I. N. Bozherianov, *Zhizneopisanie Imperatritsy Aleksandry Fedorovny* (St. Petersburg, 1898) 1:ix; Vel. Kn. Ol'ga Nikolaevna, *Son iunosti* (Paris, 1963), 34–37.

[6] On the meaning of two-dimensional representation, see Lotman, "The Theater and Theatricality," 165–69. On these developments in English and continental portraiture, see Simon Schama, "The Domestication of Majesty: Royal Family Portraiture, 1500–1850," *Journal of Interdisciplinary History* 17 (Summer, 1986): 155–83; Linda Colley et al., *Crown Pictorial: Art and the English Monarchy* (New Haven, Conn., 1990), 15.

[7] D. A. Rovinskii, *Podrobnyi slovar' russkikh gravirovannykh portretov* (St. Petersburg, 1886), 1:19–20; *IGK, ts. Al. II*, opp. 6.

[8] See the interesting remarks on the types of female behavior at the courts of Nicholas I in Alfred Rieber's introduction to Tiutcheva's diary and memoirs.

[9] Gille, *A la mémoire*, 37–51.

[10] Ibid., 27.

52. *Empress Alexandra Fedorovna, Grand Duke Alexander Nikolaevich, and Grand Duchess Olga Nikolaevna*. Engraving by Thomas Wright. Artist, George Dawe.

placed under the Fifth Division of Nicholas's own chancellery. Her role here, too, remained one of representation; every year she would appear at the charitable institutions she was supposed to supervise. Grimm emphasized the great courage that Alexandra and Nicholas showed in witnessing the poor, the ailing, and the insane. The mere sight of her was a benefaction, in this case for the unfortunates who were given the chance to worship their empress. "Her sympathy, her unostentatious, touching fondness of heart, only increased with the depths of distress, and those present felt greater reverence on seeing her there than in all the brilliancy of her throne." "The miserable" received her grace with far more gratitude than did the fortunate.[11]

Nicholas provided the picturesque setting for family life. He made Alexandra a gift of a section of Peterhof that he had received from Alexander I, and he named it "Alexandria" in her honor. Alexandria was laid out on the shore of the Gulf of Finland to resemble an English park. An alley of trees ran along a rivulet. Grimm wrote, "The Empress was thus insensibly reminded of the poetical landscapes of Matthison, like the pictures of Ruysdael, scarcely offering more than a quiet brook, enclosed by willows and maples—a bit of nature, modest though it be, that has the most pleasing effect on the mind in the immeasurable space of the Northern plains." He imagined her lingering there, holding the hands of one of her children, as if in a painting.[12]

The mansion Nicholas built for her at Alexandria, the Cottage, was designed by Adam Menelas, who had come to Russia from England to work with the architect, Charles Cameron, in 1784. Menelas took for his model the pseudo-Gothic country house of early-nineteenth-century England (fig. 53). Gothic motifs, abundant decorative pointed arches, and pediments and windows appear everywhere in the mansion. The dining room resembles a monastery refectory with ogee arches at the doorway, long tables, and high pointed chairs. A china clock on the living room mantel is a copy of the facade of Rouen Cathedral. A niche in the rear wall holds a statue of a Madonna and child by I. Vitali—a copy of a sculpture on the southern pediment of St. Isaac's Cathedral—recalling the ideal of Christian motherhood.[13]

Nicholas's scenario was preeminently eclectic, drawing on diverse elements of Western art and culture, with the confidence that their variety and diversity could only contribute to the appeal of the monarchy. Just as the unrelenting neoclassical style of St. Petersburg buildings expressed Nicholas's official persona, the Gothic home symbolized the sequestered private life set apart from the noisome everyday world. If in St. Petersburg, and in the more public Great Palace and upper park of Peterhof, Nicholas was the

---

[11] Grimm, *Alexandra Feodorovna*, 2:26–27.

[12] Ibid., 2:44.

[13] E. A. Borisova, *Russkaia arkhitektura vtoroi poloviny XIX veka* (Moscow, 1979), 84–86; see also the useful guidebook *Petrodvorets; Kottedzh* (Leningrad, 1986).

53. The Cottage (*Kottedzh*). Front view. Peterhof.

Roman or Prussian leader, hard and intimidating, at the Cottage he was the English country gentleman, genteel and chivalrous. In England, he liked to call himself "Lord of the Cottage."[14]

The Gothic revival house of early-nineteenth-century England, Marc Girouard has pointed out, became associated with Christianity and sociability. The style suggested a churchlike retreat from the detriment of the secular world. It evoked images of the novels of Walter Scott, popular in Russia no less than in Europe, and a setting for the displays of chivalry that identified the Russian emperor with the noble romantic sensibility Scott described in medieval England. The theme of the Cottage, the chivalric defense of the female sphere by the male force of arms, was represented in the device— composed by Zhukovskii—of a sword rising through a wreath of white roses, with the legend "For faith, tsar, and fatherland." It appears on a shield of turtle shell that hung over the door, and is repeated throughout the house. Nicholas presented the Cottage to Alexandra in 1829, after the victory over Turkey. A stone from the fortress of Varna, which he gave to her as a knightly token, was inserted above the doorway. He had two captured Turkish cannons placed before the main Alexandria gates.

[14] A. Shemanskii and S. Geichenko, *Krizis samoderzhaviia*, 11.

In the family scenario, medieval imagery uplifted the image of wife and mother. The white rose was first used as the empress's emblem at the Festival of the White Rose, a medieval pageant staged in Potsdam for Alexandra in 1829 by her father, King Frederick William, on her thirty-first birthday. The white rose was Alexandra's favorite flower; her friends called her *blanche-fleur*. At the festival, Alexandra, wearing a medieval robe with glittering diamonds and pearls and a crown of white roses, watched the jousting of German princes dressed as medieval knights. A silver cup from the tournament, designed by the German architect Karl Friedrich Schinkel as a trophy, stands in the living room of the Cottage.[15]

The family put on many medieval pageants, thus publicizing that it belonged to the chivalric culture of the West. Particularly popular were the "carousels," in which members of the imperial family, dressed in medieval costume, rode in a circle. The court journal for April 1834 reports that four of these were held in St. Petersburg in the first two weeks of the month alone.[16] The carousel staged in 1842 at Menelas's neo-Gothic arsenal at Tsarskoe Selo was probably the most elaborate and well known. Altogether seventeen members of the imperial family, as well as relatives, took part. Nicholas and Alexander dressed up in seventeenth-century armor and helmets from Nicholas's collection in the arsenal. The ladies' costumes were copies of robes taken from portraits of twelfth-century queens. The empress joined in the opening ceremonial march, led by Circassians in chain mail, weapon bearers, and the little grand dukes, Nicholas Nikolaevich and Michael Nikolaevich, as pages. Nicholas, the grand dukes and duchesses, and the duke of Luxembourg executed round dances on horseback. "The tsar and heir in knight's dress were incomparably majestic," Korf wrote in his diary.

The display was meant for the eyes of the public. A painting again placed the members of the family in the heroic company of those who appeared on canvases. A print from a rendering of the carousel by Horace Vernet was "sold everywhere," according to Modest Korf. Nicholas and Alexander Nikolaevich are shown riding in armor and plumed helmets on black horses (fig. 54). Alexandra sits on a white steed in the center. In the rear are the grand duchesses Olga and Alexandra Nikolaevna, the grand duke Constantine Nikolaevich, and the duke of Luxembourg.[17]

The Cottage, isolated at the edge of the sea in the midst of a private park, created the romantic setting for the tsar's display of private family life. The large living room window, where Friedrich's *On the Sailboat* hung, provided a magnificent view of the Gulf of Finland, with Kronstadt in the distance.[18]

---

[15] Marc Girouard, *Life in the English Country House: A Social and Architectural History* (New Haven, Conn., 1978), 273; Shemanskii and Geichenko, *Krizis samoderzhaviia*, 10–11, 18–19, 30–31; Gille, *A la mémoire*, 24–25.

[16] TsGIA, 516–120/2322–94: i, 6–28.

[17] Korf, "Iz zapisok," *Russkaia Starina* 100 (1899): 27–28; A. K. Annenkova, "Vospominaniia A. K. Annenkovoi, rozhdennoi Merder," *Nasha Starina*, no. 4 (1915): 381–82; *IGK, ts. Al. II,* opp. 72.

[18] Marquis Londonderry, *Recollections on a Tour,* 1:127.

54. *Family Carousel*, 1842, Tsarskoe Selo. Engraving from a painting by Horace Vernet.

Nicholas constantly declared his preference for the Cottage. He said to Lord Londonderry, "It is when I get there, just with my family, (for it holds no more,) that I am really happy." Alexandra said that she asked for a cottage as a retreat from the "massive gilt" of Peterhof, which she found insupportable. Official audiences did not take place at the Cottage, and only servants, tutors, and officials were allowed admission. Lord Londonderry expressed the desired impression that the Cottage was "a household of most domestic and affectionate intercourse."[19]

In fact, from the numerous statements of praise of the building, it is clear that the Cottage was an important public exhibition of private virtue, meant to be seen and to command obedient admiration. On certain days, observers, among them especially chosen peasants from the vicinity, were escorted up to the windows of the Cottage and allowed to peer in at the imperial family playing games in the living room; Nicholas acted as "the most obedient and deferential servant of the Peterhof lady." Despite its cozy English appearance, the Cottage was not a comfortable dwelling. The dampness from the swampy surroundings seeped into the house, penetrated the bones and lungs of the family and their servants. After rains, frogs would appear in the empress's boudoir, and mushrooms began to grow in her dressers. The children's room, on the top floor, became suffocating in the summer, in contrast to the coolness of palace apartments, and it is hardly surprising that when they came of age they received their own homes at Peterhof. Nicholas spent little time at the Cottage, rushing about to audiences and reviews, and Alexandra, once the children moved out, found it too large for her taste.[20]

The cultural life of the court also was in the empress's sphere, and here she set a tone of high seriousness (*ernst*). In the evenings she held a circle where she and her confidants read the sentimental and romantic literature of the day aloud. She was a lover of the theater and attended once or twice a week, often accompanied by the emperor and her children. The imperial family thus became theatergoers—in addition to holding occasional performances in the court. They arrived at performances without the customary ceremonial formalities.[21] In this way, the empress and the imperial family set another cultural pattern to be followed by the officialdom.

Alexandra was an active patron of the musical life of the court and the capital. She organized numerous family musicales, where she played the piano and Nicholas played the trumpet. At her suggestion, the composer, Alexei L'vov, founded an amateur court orchestra, which performed from 1834 to 1837. The renowned soprano, Henriette Sontag, the wife of the Sardinian ambassador, Rossi, was her friend, and performed frequently at the palace and in concert halls. Later, at the end of the 1830s, the empress's health began to suffer, and she kept more to herself. But concerts and musicales, comprising works principally by Western composers, continued to divert her and, at her instance, an Italian opera company was brought from Paris to perform during the winter season in Petersburg.[22]

[19] Ibid., 1:206, 128.

[20] Custine, *La Russie en 1839*, 3:113–14; Shemanskii and Geidchenko, *Krizis samoderzhaviia*, 28, 40; Tiutcheva, *Pri dvore dvukh imperatorov*, 1:138–39; 2:32–33; Frederiks, "Iz vospominanii," 78.

[21] Bozherianov, *Zhizneopisanie Imperatritsy Aleksandry Fedorovny*, 2:140.

[22] Grimm, *Alexandra Feodorovna*, 2:196–221; A. F. L'vov, "Zapiski," *Russkii Arkhiv* 22 (1884): 246–47.

Son and Pupil

In Nicholas's eyes, his firstborn son, Alexander, was the dynasty's hope for the future. He openly doted on the boy and watched closely over his education and military training. The father-son relationship encapsulated the broader fatherly relationship between monarch and servitors, and between servitors and subordinates. It was described in exalted rhetoric, consecrated in ceremonies, and displayed on tours through the empire. Such ties between father and son marked a sharp break from the Petrine ethos, reproduced by Catherine II and Paul, in which the son represented a potential rival, Absalom. In a letter of 1846 to Alexander, Zhukovskii expressed his wonder at the change: "When all historical epochs speak to us of the distrust of tsars for their heirs, and secret or open opposition of heirs to their fathers, we see here the most tender concern of the tsar about his son. This is not from political necessity alone, but from deep parental feeling." Zhukovskii believed that Nicholas's paternal feeling showed concern for both "the tenderly-beloved son and the happiness of the people, who are beloved of the tsar."[23]

The family scenario magnified the symbolic role of the heir, who represented both the moral and cultural preeminence of the imperial house and the future of the dynasty. His training for the throne, as a result, took on a critical urgency. The trust in education to mold an ideal ruler persisted from the eighteenth century, but in Nicholas's scenario the ideal assumed a different character. The heir was not to be presented with a philosophical ideal of civic virtue and accomplishment taken from classical antiquity, but an image of moral perfection. The boy's every step and misstep in the microcosm of the family had consequences for the macrocosm of the realm, as he was reminded by his instructors' rebukes and his father's icy stares. His training to rule took on a public character. In the study, in his personal relations, he was forever on view, an exemplar of the future.

As in the eighteenth century, the impetus for an heir's education came from the empress. In this case, it was the dowager Maria Fedorovna who took the initiative in planning and organizing her grandson's education. In 1826 she appointed Vasilii Zhukovsii as the chief tutor. For the heir's governor, her choice was Karl Karlovich Merder, a hero of 1812, a kindly, family man, respected in both government and literary circles. She gave Merder the tract, *Plan for the Education and Upbringing of a Prince*, written by the early-nineteenth-century German romantic poet Ernst-Moritz Arndt.[24] The *Plan* set forth the national, romantic concepts that informed the heir's upbringing and education.

Arndt had aspired to a constitution for Germany and drafted his program to prepare the future monarch to become the popular leader of his nation.

---

[23] V. A. Zhukovskii, *Sochineniia* (St. Petersburg, 1885), 6:508.
[24] I. I. Bozherianov, *Detstvo, vospitanie i leta iunosti Russkikh Imperatorov* (St. Petersburg, 1914), 99.

Not a remote figure seeking the truth in isolation, like the eighteenth-century philosophical ideal, the national monarch would understand his nation and become a part of it. In contrast to earlier pedagogical approaches that aimed to isolate the heir from parents and the corrupting milieu, Arndt's plan sought to bring the boy into the world as a sentient, social being. Princes, he asserted, were men and should be educated like other men. Arndt dismissed eighteenth-century misgivings, like La Harpe's, about the influence of favorites, and argued that princes must have friends. Contact with friends of his own age would teach the prince to determine which men were worthy of trust.

Unlike most eighteenth-century theories, Arndt's plan emphasized that the prince's parents were to play the principal role in raising their son as a humane and able individual. The mother was to provide an example of love, faith, and harmony: "In her live the dark and secret forces of God and nature." The father embodied the principle of necessity: "In him live the clear and ordered forces of God and nature." To the mother belonged faith and harmony; to the father, strength, order, the festive, and the fearful. "The mother is the shadow of infinite mildness, the father the shadow of infinite holiness; the mother is the picture of the inner, the father the picture of the outer world."[25]

Alexander II's upbringing appears to have conformed closely to Arndt's prescriptions. He was educated with friends of his age. Two aristocratic boys, Joseph Viel'gorskii and Alexander Patkul', joined Alexander when he began his lessons with Zhukovskii in the fall of 1827. The three studied, played, and fought together. They were instructed to treat Alexander on completely equal terms, and to address him not as "Your Highness," but "Alexander Nikolaevich." Later they accompanied him on his trips through Russia and Europe, and Patkul' became his adjutant. Alexander and his comrades also played with the cadets in various military schools and participated in their exercises. Prints and paintings depict such scenes. A watercolor shows a group of cadets marching along the road at the Peterhof camp, while Nicholas and Michael Pavlovich pass by in a carriage. The caption explains that Alexander is in the ranks.[26]

Nicholas was a stern embodiment of Arndt's principle of "necessity," enforcing the demands of reality. From an early age, Alexander learned the meaning of discipline from his father. The emperor rebuked and punished Alexander when he disobeyed his tutors. When Merder complained that Alexander had become surly and uncooperative, Nicholas redressed the boy: "You are not worthy to come to me after such conduct. You have forgotten that obedience is a sacred duty and that I can forgive everything but disobedience." Alexander was threatened with losing the right to wear his uniform

---

[25] E. M. Arndt, *Entwurf der Erziehung und Unterweisung eines Fürsten* (Berlin, 1813), 22–23, 31, 35–36, 48–52.
[26] E. P. Samsonov, *Russkii Arkhiv* 1 (1884): 430; *IGK, ts. Al. II*, opp. 41.

the following Sunday. Nicholas frequently withheld love. When Alexander disobeyed, Nicholas refused to kiss him. The boy then wept in desolation.[27] Other punishments were supper of only soup, confinement to his room, or losing a chance to go hunting. Alexander's diary from September to December 1830, when he was twelve, records his feelings of failure at meeting his teachers' and father's demands. On September 12 he was found inattentive in lessons and burst into tears. Merder declared that he was studying "without interest and strength of will." Merder's threats to bring him to his father led him to promise to change and never be inattentive again. On September 23 Merder forced Alexander to write a letter to his father, "not by my own choice," and in this, Alexander confessed, "I showed all my laziness."[28]

Alexander responded to failure and frustration with tears, angering Nicholas with conduct inappropriate for one who was supposed to show strength. Merder's diary tells how the slightest reproach or failure at studies made Alexander cry. When he was eleven, poor marks from Zhukovskii and other teachers reduced him to tears. He wept when Gille corrected his French spelling and again when Gille gave him the lowest grade of the three boys in geography. Most embarrassing were the war games Alexander played with his friend, Viel'gorskii, while his own parents watched. Viel'gorskii usually won, and then Alexander cried in disappointment, to his father's visible dismay. At the age of thirteen, Alexander was thrown from his horse and fell to the pavement unconscious. When he regained consciousness, he burst into tears. His father rebuked him for carelessness and lack of self-control.[29]

Alexandra was the mild and consoling mother of Arndt's educational plan, as indulgent as Nicholas was demanding. She sympathized with her son in his distress and allowed him to show his weakness. When his tears brought rebukes and anger, she gave him solace. She rewarded him for his fall from the horse with a full day in her company. She helped him avoid the regimen of his studies by taking him on walks or to the theater.[30]

•

Although there seems to be no direct evidence that Zhukovskii had read Arndt's tract, his notion of monarch as national leader corresponded to the German poet's ideas. Like Derzhavin, like Karamzin, Zhukovskii had summoned the heir at birth to be a "human being." But for him, the distinguish-

---

[27] K. K. Merder, "Zapiski K. K. Merdera, vospitatelia Aleksandra Nikolaevicha," *Russkaia Starina* 47 (1885): 40–41; M. A. Patkul, "Vospominaniia," *Istoricheskii Vestnik* 87 (1902): 840.

[28] "Aleksandr II; Dnevnik, 1830, (sent.-dek.)," TsGAOR, 678-1-274, 6, 7, 10–11.

[29] Merder, *Russkaia Starina* 45 (1885): 528, 530, 532, 535, 538–41; 47: 225–26, 238, 433.

[30] Ibid., 46:507; 47:224–25, 433; 48:504. On the relations between mothers and heirs in the nineteenth century, see my article, "The Russian Empress as Mother," in David L. Ransel, ed., *The Family in Imperial Russia: New Lines of Historical Research* (Urbana, Ill., 1978), 60–74.

ing feature of the ideal human being was not the acceptance of reason or the show of human sensibility. It was living for the people, understanding their needs and their sympathies. In the oft-quoted words of his ode on Alexander's birth in 1818, he declared:

> Yes, in his exalted sphere he will not forget,
> The most sacred of callings; to be a *human being*,
> To live for posterity in his people's majesty,
> For the good of *all*, *his own* to forget,
> Only in the free voice of the fatherland,
> To read his briefs with humility.[31]

For Zhukovskii, humility was the principal quality necessary for a national ruler to cultivate, for it enabled him to understand his people's wishes. He sought to make Alexander a moral hero whose heroism was shown in self-abnegation. Like Arndt, Zhukovskii admired the theories of Pestalozzi. He was particularly impressed by the Swiss pedagogue's belief that children should be raised as social beings, attentive to the needs of others, a sentiment expressed in the principle, "All for others, nothing for oneself," which was engraved on the monument at Yverdon.[32] Zhukovskii constantly reminded Alexander of the high calling he must assume. In a letter of 1832, he congratulated the grand duke on a victory over "the common hated enemy . . . called laziness." His ally was the feeling of "*dolzhnost*'" (duty or office), which would help him to conquer the talisman—"*moral worth*" (*nravstvennoe dostoinstvo*). The boy's moral education was not merely a matter of preparing his mind to exercise reason. It was a basis for the moral leadership of the people: "*The mob* can have *material* strength; but *moral* power is in the soul of *sovereigns*: for they can be active representatives of *justice* and *good*."[33]

Alexander Nikolaevich was the first Russian heir brought up to believe that the people's approval constituted an important moral basis of autocratic rule. Zhukovskii taught him that it was love that attached him to his subjects. The maxims that Alexander copied from Fénelon's *Télémaque* into his notebook emphasized that self-restraint and humility would endear him to his subjects: "Love your people as you love your children, savor the pleasure to be loved by them." Kings who sought to make themselves feared and harm their subjects were the scourge of the earth. The good king found his joy in the well-being of his people: "Not only do they obey him, but they love to obey him. He reigns in all hearts and everyone, rather than seeking to

---

[31] Zhukovskii, *Polnoe sobranie sochinenii*, 2:126.

[32] *Gody ucheniia ego Imperatorskogo Vysochestva Naslednika Tsesarevicha (Sbornik Russkogo Istoricheskogo Obshchestva)* 31 (St. Petersburg, 1881), xii–xiii; Bozherianov, *Detstvo, vospitanie i leta iunosti Russkikh Imperatorov*, 99. Zhukovskii recruited several of Alexander's tutors from the short-lived pension directed by Pastor Muralt, who was one of Pestalozzi's disciples.

[33] Zhukovskii, *Sochineniia*, 6:386–87.

overthrow him, fears to lose him, and is ready to give his life for him." The good king secured the submission of his servitors because he could "win their hearts."[34]

The education Zhukovskii arranged for the heir was very much a sentimental education, an education of the heart. The classical grounding of monarchy did not figure significantly in Alexander's instruction, as it had in Paul's and Alexander I's. In fact, Zhukovskii's initial program had included Latin language and classical writings, but Nicholas, who had suffered with Greek and Latin and identified classical thought with the French Revolution, objected. Like eighteenth-century pedagogues, Zhukovskii emphasized the importance of history, but he focused on the history of the Middle Ages, not classical antiquity, and the model he presented to Alexander was not the great monarchs of antiquity, but Prince Alexander Nevskii.

Zhukovskii conveyed his ideal through feelings and images rather than philosophical statement. He used the visual, two-dimensional idiom of his era. On New Year's Day, 1828, he gave a present of a painting to Alexander, who was then nine years old. The painting portrayed Alexander Nevskii, at about the boy's age, standing at the edge of a cliff and surveying his lands. Nevskii's pose, Zhukovskii explained in a letter to Alexander, revealed the inner resources that had made the prince great. At this point, Zhukovskii wrote, Nevskii had achieved nothing great, but already sensed who he was, what he should prepare for, and what was expected of him. Nevskii had climbed the cliff with great difficulty, and his diligence was rewarded by an enchanting scene: "Beyond the promontory there spread a vast plain, glittering in the rays of morning, strewn with human dwellings, decorated by the various creations of God." Everyone awaited the sun. Zhukovskii took this traditional symbol of monarchy as a symbol of the prince himself, who had been "designated by God to be the benefactor of the whole land, just as the sun was the benefactor of the whole land." Nevskii's beautiful soul sensed the meaning of what was before him, and, clasping his hands in prayer, he cried to the Lord "with submissive strength: '*Your will be done!*'" Zhukovskii described Nevskii to Alexander as his "invisible companion," "a special secret witness and judge of your acts."[35]

Three years later, Alexander set forth for his tutor the lessons he was supposed to learn from the painting. Nevskii had kept the promise he had made to God and himself on the promontory, Alexander wrote. "He became the model of Tsars and Heroes." He had achieved great victories as prince of Novgorod. "But History is even more surprised by his truly Christian humility." Nevskii's submissiveness before the Tatars was not a yielding to necessity, but an act of humility. Nevskii "forgot his dignity and humbly asked mercy for his subjects from the arrogant Tatar khans." It was for this politi-

---

[34] "Vypiski V. Kn. Aleksandra Nikolaevicha iz 'Telemaka' Fenelona, [1830–33]," TsGAOR, 678–1-198.

[35] Zhukovskii, *Sochineniia*, 6:375–76; *Gody ucheniia*, 167–68.

cal act, according to Alexander, that Nevskii was canonized—not for his religious faith or accepting the tonsure—"as a sign of gratitude for the self-sacrifice for the general good."[36]

The prince's virtue was in submission—to the will of God, to the will of the Tatars. Nevskii's military triumphs were left in the shadows. Zhukovskii's Nevskii was an alternative to Peter the Great. In a letter he wrote to Alexander in 1843, when the heir was approaching twenty-five, Zhukovskii defined autocracy as "only the highest degree of submissiveness to divine justice." He cited Peter the Great—an idol of Nicholas—as an example to be avoided, an example of rebellion against God. "Peter the Great, your great creator, left behind a pile of fragments. God does not endure a rival in his kingdom. He alone is the Creator, in time and in eternity." He wrote of "annihilation of the will" if autocracy was not to be a "rebellion against God." Two years later, on Alexander's name day, he again mentioned Nevskii as an example of submission, one "who laid down his soul for his people in fulfillment of the will of his heavenly tsar."[37]

The lesson was a continuation and yet a transformation of the didactic moralism of the eighteenth century. Like the tsarevich Khlor, like Telemachus, Zhukovskii's Nevskii appeared as an embodiment of self-restraint meant to show the boy the importance of controlling his impulses. But, in the meantime, the purpose of self-restraint had changed. A medieval prince and not a Roman emperor provided the ideal: reason and civic virtue no longer figured in the teacher's discourse and imagery. Instead, it was conscience and divine will that demanded renunciation. The eighteenth-century hero had restrained himself to give power to his reason, to rule according to the law and for the benefit of a public ideal. Controlling his passions, he became able to transform institutions. Zhukovskii's Nevskii was a tamed and subdued figure, whose grandeur came from a noble resignation. His humility enabled him to subordinate himself to the good of the land, the desires of the people.

This was an imperative that allowed the ruler to stand above institutions without changing them, and thus to preserve the moral supremacy of autocracy. Indeed, Zhukovskii's Nevskii was merely a poetic re-creation of the model of European monarch that was constantly set before the heir—his grandfather, Frederick William III of Prussia, whose principal achievement had been the courageous acceptance of defeat and humiliation in the war against Napoleon. Giving Alexander a biography of the king on his name day in 1843, Zhukovskii described the king's "bright, pure, just and blessed soul."[38] Frederick William remained an admired and beloved figure in the imperial family, especially for his grandson, Alexander.

The principle of humility dominated Alexander's religious lessons as well.

---

[36] Ibid., 493–94.
[37] Zhukovskii, *Sochineniia*, 6:461, 493–94.
[38] Ibid., 6:461.

His first instructor of religion, G. P. Pavskii, preached a life of Christian love. In his first lesson in 1826, Pavskii told the boy to take Christ as an example. On September 7, 1830, Alexander wrote in his diary, "We said that love is the striving for everything that is Divine." From Pavskii, he learned that Christ showed at each age how to live and "taught people to look inside themselves. In yourselves, he said to people, in your heart are found the treasures of life, '*The Kingdom of God is in you.*'" Christ taught the boy to look inside his heart to be sure that he did nothing to defy the will of his parents and that his teachers were happy with him.[39]

In 1834 Pavskii was replaced by the more conservative V. B. Bazhanov, under pressure from Filaret, the metropolitan of Moscow. Bazhanov instructed the children of the imperial family for the next thirty years and served as confessor to both Nicholas I and Alexander II. He preached love and obligation, but without Pavskii's emphasis on inner spirituality. For Bazhanov, a Christian's chief obligation consisted in love for his fatherland, which Bazhanov identified with Christian altruism. The obligations of the sovereign were divinely ordained. "The Supreme Ruler of the world, investing Him with power and force, entrusts Him with the care and direction of His millions of people, His brothers." This notion was to inspire the tsar with "fear and trembling," and a zealous concern for his obligations. The latter included respect for the laws, enlightenment, and protection of the security and well-being of his subjects. But Alexander had to do more than govern his subjects well, in the service of God. He had to protect the morality and piety of his people and serve as an exemplar of personal virtue. "The eyes of the whole people are turned to the Tsar, who by his merit and image is the Vicar of God on earth." He had to be a model of respect for religious teachings, propounded by the church, of Christian conduct, and to be "the best spouse, the best father of a family."[40]

Michael Speranskii's lectures to Alexander in 1837 are often credited with inspiring in Alexander the concern for law and legality that he later showed in his reforms. But Speranskii's lectures emphasized morality over law as the distinguishing and elevating feature of absolute monarchy—what he called "pure monarchy." In pure monarchies, the ruler achieved moral supremacy attained by the exercise of self-restraint in the interests of the people. Such self-restraint raised pure monarchy above mixed monarchies and republics, in which different "aristocracies" took power and struggled for their own particular advantage over the good of the whole people. The emperor's autocratic authority was limited by no other power on earth, Speranskii taught, but by the limits that the tsar himself establishes through treaties or his own words, which "should be for him immutable and sacred." "Law (*pravo*), and

---

[39] "Aleksandr II; Dnevnik, 1830 g.," 4; *Gody ucheniia*, 69–70; On Pavskii, see Petr Ivanov, "Zakonouchitel' imperatora Aleksandra IIogo i mitropolit Filaret," *Vozrozhdenie* 35 (September–October 1954): 148–64.

[40] *Gody ucheniia*, 105–8.

consequently autocratic law," Speranskii explained, "is law to the extent that it is based upon justice (*pravda*). Where justice ends and injustice begins, law ends and despotism begins." The autocrat was never subject to human courts and judgment, but always to the court of conscience and of God.[41]

The court of conscience and of God followed the heir through his daily life. Every moment of his life was lived under supreme unyielding, absolute judgment. His wayward impulses were constantly prompting admonitions from his governor and teachers. To become absolute ruler, Merder repeatedly stressed, the grand duke had to learn to obey, which, Merder emphasized in many of his reports, Alexander refused to do. Merder told the grand duke repeatedly that he must serve as a model in his compliance with rules if he wished to prescribe laws for others. Constantine Arseniev, his history tutor, warned him when he was thirteen that his work about Russia was exceedingly careless, and said, "I felt like crying from pity, knowing that you are the hope of Russia."[42]

Alexander's response was to propitiate with expressions of compliance and agreement. Indeed, he believed his father and his teachers were in the right and not only acknowledged their fairness, but pronounced their principles with great conviction. He said to Merder in May 1829, "I compare a man to a pupil, going from one school to the next. That pupil who surpasses his comrades in his studies has the right to expect an honorable place in the higher school. Having finished his moral education on earth, man moves to the next life and, consequently, occupies a place there by merit." Merder observed that it would be hard to find a young man who had such just ideas of his obligations as Alexander; he had never heard him utter an incorrect judgment. "But unfortunately it would be just as difficult to find a young man who had so little willpower over himself."[43]

From the age of nine to sixteen, Alexander was surly, arrogant, and lazy in his work. He showed no sign of developing the self-knowledge and self-discipline that Zhukovskii considered the center of man's education. During one of his fits of pique in 1829, Alexander said to Merder, "I wish I hadn't been born a Grand Duke." Merder rebuked him quickly, saying that he should thank God who had placed him on earth in such a way "that the well-being of millions of people depend on you."[44] Such exhortations only heightened Alexander's feelings of inadequacy, desperation, and helplessness. To spur him on, invidious comparisons were made with his comrades, particularly Viel'gorskii, who usually surpassed him in his studies and was a true model of good conduct.

At moments, Alexander felt moved to confess his own weakness, which brought forth further rebukes and pronouncements about the loftiness of his

[41] Ibid., 364–71.
[42] Merder, *Russkaia Starina* 45 (1885): 538–39; 46:489–90; 47:228.
[43] Ibid., 46:101, 490; 47:227–28.
[44] Ibid., 45:528.

station. In 1834 the ceremony of his majority on his sixteenth birthday (see below) frightened him, and he exclaimed, "It is too early." Pavskii replied that every young man had to achieve an exploit (*podvig*) of virtue, but he who was to become a tsar had to face an even greater challenge. "Imagine how much intelligence is necessary to harmonize the demands of millions of people and to show them the true and straight path to the goal, and imagine how much firmness is needed to keep them on that path!" Pavskii described the state as "a machine consisting of living and free links that are ready to leave their place at any moment if they are not held back by the strength of a will that is wise and just." The heir had to give an example of such a strong will. "Your designation is to rule over others. Show first your authority over yourself. Mastery over oneself is the best introduction to the science of government." He was told to emulate his father, whom Pavskii extolled as "a splendid example of wise activity." He urged Alexander again to keep the vow to invest himself in Christ and be his disciple.[45]

Pavskii framed the contradictory directives contained in the various admonitions and exhortations pronounced to the heir. Power and strength were to be proved by submissiveness and obedience. To become his father, the dominating fearsome emperor, he had first to become like Christ, humble and self-denying. But these were daunting images for the boy, and he felt himself forever falling short of the demands of an office he associated throughout his life with his father. He continued to profess the principles he heard in the classroom. The gap between his words and his actions as a child was perceived as dishonesty; when he became emperor, it was considered hypocrisy. But his lessons also instilled in him an acute sense of moral frailty. His teachers' constant admonitions and punishments impressed upon him the lesson that there existed a higher set of values that he did not completely understand and that he could never live up to. Unlike his father and his successors on the throne, he had a sense of humility; though a tsar, he could bow before prevalent ideals, and, taking the advice of others, admit the fallibility of power in order to win his people's love.

THE SON AS SYMBOL

In his public role, the heir experienced none of the difficulties of the classroom. He gained effortless successes at court and on the parade ground. Handsome, poised, adorable, he became the endearing symbol of the dynasty, proof of its survival and vitality. When paraded forth at the coronation at the age of eight, he was the center of attention, the embodiment of the familial monarchy. "All eyes were fixed on him," Merder wrote. "In the son of their tsar the subjects saw the guarantee of the future happiness of Russia."[46] With his mother, Alexander was a symbol and a surety of the

[45] *Gody ucheniia*, 99–101.
[46] Merder, *Russkaia Starina* 45 (1885): 347.

dynasty, a human embellishment to the superhuman force of Nicholas's autocracy. Both mother and son had the capacity to evoke love. Alexander's features, Grimm wrote, displayed "rather the gentle expression of his mother than the resolute look of the father." Merder remarked of his "sensitive and good heart." Alexander early mastered the devices of endearment. Merder wrote that he knew no other child his age who had "so much grace, dignity and amiability, or more beautiful manners than he."[47]

Engravings and paintings presented the beautiful child and the bond between mother and son to the elite. We see him as a tot, erect and distinguished in the uniform of the Pavlovsk Regiment, his sword planted to the ground toward the side, one leg stylishly before the other. He was often painted standing at the side of a bust of his namesake, Alexander I (fig. 55). He was portrayed in *lubki* as well, in 1828 in military uniform, at the side of his mother, and in 1831 in the uniform of his own Cuirassier's Regiment.[48]

Both empress and heir were cast in passive roles, objects of admiration for the Russian and European elite. They shared the burden of constant public representation, first expressed during the arduous ceremonies of coronation in the Assumption Cathedral. Alexandra Fedorovna showed sympathy when Alexander wept from fatigue, and he in turn wrote to Zhukovskii, "Thank God, Mama withstood that long ceremony."[49] Nicholas presented Alexander as his successor, and later as his "helper." He took every opportunity to show his son off as an obedient and adept soldier. At the age of two, Alexander could obey the order to come to attention. When he was three, Nicholas awakened him from his sleep to give a display of marching, while Nicholas himself, kneeling on the floor, beat time on a drum. At the age of eight, Alexander was already commanding grenadiers twice his size with aplomb and skill.[50]

For Nicholas, the heir was primarily a military figure, whose status would be designated by his military rank. From 1827, Nicholas announced a succession of appointments and promotions for his son that were then made known to all in newspaper statements and illustrations circulated to the court and the public. The process began in October 1827 with the naming of Alexander as honorary "Ataman of all the Cossack Hosts" and "Chief of the Don Regiment." The position of honorary ataman was presented as a direct personal bond between the imperial family and the cossacks. The bond was consecrated in an elaborate ceremony at Novocherkassk during the heir's 1837 trip (see below). Alexander II and his successors renewed these ties through the century, appointing the heirs cossack atamans and

---

[47] Ibid., 46:507; 47:38, 224–25, 433; 48:504; Grimm, *Alexandra Feodorovna*, 2:172.

[48] *IGK, ts. Al. II*, 12, 13, 16, 29, opp. 32; *IGK, ts. Nik. I*, 217.

[49] "Pis'ma Imperatritsy Aleksandry Fedorovny k V. A. Zhukovskomu, 1817–1842," *Russkii Arkhiv* 35 (1897): 498–99.

[50] N. I. Grech, "Neizdannoe mesto iz zapisok," *Russkii Arkhiv* 3 (1884): 58; I. N. Bozherianov, *Zhizneopisanie imperatritsy Aleksandry Fedorovny* 1:v; Maréchal Marmont (Duc de Raguse), *Mémoires* (Paris, 1857), 8:31.

55. Alexander II as heir in dress uniform. Engraving by O. Keselev.
Drawing by Gompelen Glukho-Nemoi.

sustaining what Robert McNeal called "the myth of tsar and Cossack."[51] An engraving portrays the young Alexander holding the *pernach*, the cossack mace, inside a medallion surrounded by standards, a cannon and cannon balls. A quatrain marked the event by hailing Alexander as the reincarnation of Alexander I and his father:

> The hope of Russians—Rare child!
> Grow, flourish, mature!
> In the days of war be a second Blessed One [Alexander I],
> In the Days of Peace, A Wise Nicholas![52]

On the death of the grand duke Constantine Pavlovich in June 1831, Alexander inherited the title of "Tsesarevich," the official title of the person next in line for the throne according to Paul's law of succession.[53] Nicholas issued a decree, declaring that "Our most beloved son" should henceforth be called "Sovereign Heir, Tsesarevich and Grand Duke" (*Gosudar' Naslednik, Tsesarevich i Velikii Kniaz'*). The decree was printed in the press and a series of pictures were executed that publicized Alexander's new title.[54] A *lubok* of 1831 shows him in a typical stylized equestrian pose; he wears a cuirassier's uniform, and looks dashing and heroic. At the bottom, among his various titles, the word *tsesarevich* is inscribed in bold capitals. Nicholas's family now held all of the titles and symbolic distinctions of the senior line, which provided the occasion to issue new pictures of the heir as loyal son. In a watercolor by Alexander Briullov, the heir stands at the center of a group of cadets in dress uniform at Peterhof in 1831. He is the tallest and most poised of the boys. His arm is on a staff; beside him is a waving standard. At his foot, sitting under the barrel of a cannon is his younger brother, Constantine Nikolaevich, not yet four years old. Merder reclines at the side. Lithographed copies of the painting were sent to all military schools (fig. 56).[55]

In his diary, Alexander recorded his delight with his promotions and the fancy new uniforms and ceremonies they entailed; these were signs of his entry into his father's world. On September 21, 1830, at the age of twelve, he participated in the celebration of the centenary of the Izmailovskii Regiment. He rode with Nicholas by the guardsmen on review and attended the prayer service and the banquet in the manege. "The entire ceremony was majestic," he wrote. On New Year's Day, 1834, he proudly appeared in the Great Procession through the halls of the Winter Palace in a red Cavalier Guard uniform. But the most thrilling moment was his appointment as flügel-adjutant to the emperor on the eve of his ceremony of majority. He awoke on the

---

[51] Robert H. McNeal, *Tsar and Cossack, 1855–1914* (Oxford, 1987), 1–5.

[52] *IGK, ts. Al. II*, opp. 46.

[53] A note to Paul's law specified, "The Title of Tsesarevich is always attached to that Individual who has been designated heir to the throne," which referred to Alexander Pavlovich. But Paul, with characteristic inconsistency, awarded it to Constantine later in 1797, for his bravery in war (*PSZ*, no. 17,906, April 5, 1797; *BE*, 75:114).

[54] *Severnaia Pchela*, September 7, 1831.

[55] *IGK, ts. Al. II*, 43.

56. *Tsarevich Alexander Nikolaevich with Cadets at Peterhof*. Lithograph of
a painting by A. Briullov.

morning of April 17, 1834, to see that the epaulettes on the ataman uniform
for the ceremony carried his father's initials and the braid, the aiguillette—
the decorations of a member of his father's suite (fig. 57). "At first I was
struck dumb, I couldn't believe my eyes from joy." When he appeared before
Nicholas, he heard his father say that "he wants to indicate by this that I
should prepare to be his helper."[56] During his father's reign, Alexander regarded his membership in the suite as a signal honor and distinction.

Later that year, in September 1834, he participated in the great parade
during the dedication ceremony of the Alexander I monument and described
the event in his diary. He dressed in a hussar uniform, for Alexander I had
appointed him chief of that regiment. He rode about the square giving orders according to his father's instructions. He recorded the event in the sentimental rhetoric of official texts. The procession around the column moved
him, "a solemn and touching moment," and the shouts of "Hoorah!" that
followed, and the troops moving "with surprising order," created "a picture
that cannot be described by the pen." "I stood the whole time in the Tsar's
suite," he wrote with pride.[57]

[56] "Aleksandr II; Dnevnik, 1830 g.," 9–10; "Aleksandr II; Dnevnik, 1834 g.," TsGAOR,
678–1-280, 1, 22–23.
[57] "Aleksandr II; Dnevnik, 1834 g.," 72–73.

57. *Alexander II as Most August Ataman*. Engraving from a painting by George Dawe.

Alexander's love for the parade ground became all absorbing. Zhukovskii watched with dismay as his charge followed the path of previous heirs. In October 1839 he entered a confession of failure in his diary:

> One cannot think of the casualness (*vetrenost'*) with which the Grand Duke's life is being sacrificed without a sign of indignation. And for what? To the imperial toy, which is improper for a tsar, harmful to Russia, and which kills all abilities of state. Since his return, the Grand Duke has been forced to command from morning till evening. Here we play at war and are fascinated with parades, while inside the state murdering and burning go on and there is no one to send to catch the brigands.[58]

•

Paul's Law of Succession of 1797 had set the majority of the *tsesarevich* at the early age of sixteen in order to ensure a smooth succession in the event of the ruling emperor's early death. Alexander was the first heir to reach that age under the law. To mark Alexander's sixteenth birthday, Nicholas introduced a new ceremony into the life of the imperial court—the taking of the oath of majority. Pronounced by Alexander and all future grand dukes when they came of age, the oath made the maintenance of autocracy a filial obligation, consecrated by God. Metropolitan Filaret of Moscow prepared an imposing ceremony in which the son, before the assembled elite of the Russian state, pledged obedience to his father, the autocrat, and to the laws of Russia.

Alexander's oath, composed by Michael Speranskii, was an emphatic statement of the unity of family feeling with autocratic government and the maintenance of the inviolability of the prerogatives of the father-sovereign. The purpose of the ceremony, Speranskii asserted, was to give religious sanction to the heir's future obligations. An oath, he wrote, "is an act of conscience and religion, by which he who vows summons God in witness to the sincerity of his promises and submits himself to His wrath and vengeance in case of violation."[59]

The ceremony took place on April 22, 1834, on Easter Sunday, which lent the event an especially sacred character—as it had the promulgation of the Succession Law. The oath was an important rite of passage for the boy, from a child to his father's helper, joining his father at least symbolically in the exercise of autocratic power. At midnight on New Year's Eve, 1834, Nicholas and Alexandra told their son that the coming year would be the most important of his life. Alexander wrote in his diary, "I feel its importance and will try to prepare myself as much as I can for this moment, for I know that even after it is over, the main task awaits me, that is to complete what has been begun. I ask the All-Powerful Father to give me strength to

---

[58] V. A. Zhukovskii, *Dnevniki V. A. Zhukovskogo* (St. Petersburg, 1901), 509.

[59] S. S. Tatishchev, *Imperator Aleksandr II, ego zhizn' i tsarstvovanie* (St. Petersburg, 1903), 1:62.

58. *Nicholas I Tells His Son of the Burden of the Tsar's Power.* Xylograph.

follow the example of my father in a worthy manner."[60] An engraving from wood shows Nicholas instructing Alexander on the "burden of the tsar's power," as the boy holds himself rigidly at attention (fig. 58).

On April 16 Nicholas took his son on a walk to the Peter-Paul Fortress. He told him of the difficulties he would encounter and urged him to turn to

[60] "Aleksandr II; Dnevnik, 1834 g." TsGAOR, 678–1-280, 1.

his father and mother for advice. "I will never forget this conversation," Alexander wrote in his diary. Nicholas initiated him in the cult of ancestors, the immortal unity of the dynasty. At the cathedral, father and son kissed the graves of Paul, Alexander I, and their spouses, and the grave of Constantine Pavlovich. Nicholas kissed his son and said, in French, "When I lie there, visit sometimes." "These words touched me so much that I could not contain my tears, and I prayed to myself that the All-Powerful God allow a long life to my dear father."[61] The next day Alexander received the epaulette and braids of a flügel-adjutant of Nicholas's suite.

The ceremony of the oath on April 22, 1834, in the Great Church at the Winter Palace was a major state occasion, described in a detailed account published in *Russkii Invalid* and *Severnaia Pchela*.[62] The account described those attending as "all of Russia," the symbolic representatives of the entire Russian state. On one side there stood arrayed the diplomatic corps, state councillors, and senators. Behind them were court officials, members of the emperor's suite, generals, state secretaries, and others with the right of entry "behind the Cavalier-Guards," and the mayor of St. Petersburg. They faced the wives of the diplomatic corps, and the ladies of the court. Deputies representing art, science, commerce, and industry were also present. Officers of the guards and lesser civil officials awaited in the adjoining halls. From Alexander's teaching staff, Zhukovskii, his mathematics instructor Edward Collins, and possibly others, attended.[63] The palace was so crowded that Pushkin had difficulty slipping through the back stairways to visit his aunt.[64]

While Metropolitan Serafim and other members of the Holy Synod awaited at the altar, the procession began. Minor court functionaries entered first, followed by gentlemen of the chamber and junkers of the chamber and other honorary court titles in ascending order of seniority. Then the chief marshall of the court, holding his mace, led in the emperor and empress, followed by their suite. Alexander entered before other members of the imperial family. Ladies-in-waiting and *Gof-meisteriny* brought up the rear.

The first part of the event, in the Great Church, was the taking of the oath as heir to the throne. After Metropolitan Serafim and other clergy met the imperial family with the cross and holy water, Nicholas led his son to the pulpit, before the life-giving cross and the gospels. Alexander, raising his right hand, delivered the oath. He vowed to serve and obey his father "in all respects" (*vo vsem*). He promised that he would not spare his life and would

---

[61] Ibid., 21.

[62] *Severnaia Pchela*, April 26, 1834: 365–66; *Russkii Invalid*, April 27, 1834: 407–8.

[63] I. A. Shliapkin, "Iz bumag odnogo iz prepodavatelei Aleksandra II," *Starina i novizna* 22 (1917): 15.

[64] My description is based on the newspaper accounts cited in footnote 62 above and *Vysochaishe utverzhdennyi tseremonial prisiagi Gosudaria, Naslednika, Aleksandra Nikolaevicha* (n.p., n.d.); Tatishchev, *Imperator Aleksandr II*, 1:63–65; Grimm, *Alexandra Feodorovna*, 2:89–91.

give his last drop of blood for Russia, the words of Peter the Great. He would defend the rights and power of "the autocracy of His Imperial Majesty" and would "assist the service of his majesty and the welfare of the state." He pledged to observe all the rulings of the throne and the laws of the imperial house. Finally, he called upon God "to guide and teach him in the great service" that had devolved upon him, words from the prayers of supplication at the coronation. At this point he broke down in tears, and tried several times to continue. The emperor and empress then embraced and kissed him.

Metropolitan Filaret, in a letter to Prince D. V. Golitsyn, described his feelings: "Kisses and tears reunited father, mother, and son. When my own absorption in this inspiring spectacle ended, and my own tears dried, I could see that all present were in tears."[65] Pushkin indicated in his diary that he had heard that those who did not weep made sure to wipe their eyes as well.[66] The ceremony was a reprise of the domestic scenario, and a display of feeling, whether real or feigned, showed participation in the spectacle of family solidarity.

The heir then signed the oath, and Count Nesselrode, the foreign minister, removed the document for safekeeping in the state archive. The first part of the ceremony concluded with the singing of a Te Deum, a 301-gun salute from the cannons of the Peter-Paul Fortress, and the tolling of the church bells of the capital. Then, after a prayer for the long life of the emperor, the imperial family received congratulations from the members of the Synod.

The tears and the family embrace were understood and presented in the sentimental idiom. The report published in *Severnaia Pchela* and in *Russkii Invalid*, following the sentimental ascription—and prescription—of emotion, evoked a general feeling of tenderness, of *umilenie*, which "penetrated all hearts." The dramatic climax was the embrace of parents and son. First, Nicholas kissed Alexander three times. Alexander wanted to hug his mother, but Nicholas reached her first. Then the emperor clasped both of them to him. "With this spectacle of all royal and human virtues, a reverent tremor of tenderness (*umilenie*) touched all hearts." The author of the newspaper accounts compared Alexander's tears to those of Michael Fedorovich when, as a boy, he had accepted the throne of Russia; the tears showed his understanding of the importance and greatness of the ritual. "May Your tears, Successor of the Great Tsars, be pleasing to God. May they be a guarantee of the goodness of Your soul and the happiness of Your Fatherland."

Alexander then proceeded to the second stage of the ceremony, the taking of his oath as military officer in St. George Hall. This was performed to an even larger assemblage than the civil oath. The imperial procession moved past rows of guard's officers to the hall, where cadets from the various military training schools, "the future defenders of the kingdom," were lined up

---

[65] Tatishchev, *Imperator Aleksandr II*, 1:63–64.
[66] A. S. Pushkin, *Dnevnik Pushkina, 1833–1835* (Moscow, 1923), 10.

along the walls. Generals stood on daises, while the same dignitaries present in the Palace Church arrayed themselves in hierarchical order beside the throne. On the two lowest steps of the throne, decorated with weapons and banners, officers of the guards held aloft their regimental standards. A company of the palace grenadier guards lined up in four platoons facing the throne.

To the rousing strains of the new national anthem, "God Save the Tsar" (see below, chapter 12), the emperor, empress, and tsarevich entered, ascended to the throne, and saluted the troops. Nicholas then stepped down and led Alexander to the lectern beneath the ataman's standard. There, Alexander pledged to serve the emperor faithfully, to obey all military regulations, and to oppose enemies of emperor and state firmly and courageously. The troops saluted, the standards were lowered before the throne, and the recessional began. In the halls of the palace, their majesties received congratulations from officials of the highest ranks and then retired to their chambers. In the evening, the capital was lit with festive illumination.

On the day of the ceremony, Nicholas issued an imperial manifesto that declared the oath an official state act, to be included in the recently published *Digest of Laws* and celebrated by Te Deums in the churches of the empire. Numerous gifts, awards, and bonuses were made to Alexander's tutors and other high government figures and officials. Alexander's promotion to flügel-adjutant was announced. To celebrate the event, Alexander declared that he "had the happiness to fulfill his first duty, taking before the throne of God the oath of fidelity to the Tsar parent, and in his person, the dear fatherland." He made gifts of fifty thousand rubles to the poor of both St. Petersburg and Moscow, and pronounced his thanks to both capitals. He addressed St. Petersburg, where he had spent his childhood, "where I learned to love Russia, and where finally I pronounced my sacred oath." Moscow he called "my dear native land"; "God gave me life in the Kremlin."[67]

The celebration continued through Holy Week. The next day there was a reception for the diplomatic corps, and Alexander met and received congratulations from foreign ambassadors and emissaries. A state dinner was held for the imperial family, dignitaries of the first three ranks, and those with court ranks and titles. Court officials offered toasts to the emperor, the heir, and the imperial house to the accompaniment of trumpet fanfares and kettledrums, and the roar of cannon salutes from the fortress. Holy Week ended with a great ball given by the St. Petersburg nobility in the mansion of chief master of the hunt, D. L. Naryshkin, which marked Alexander's first appearance as a member of Petersburg society.

The ceremony of the majority was a formal presentation of Alexander as a dynastic symbol expressing the unity of the governmental and social elite with the dynasty. The rhetoric of the writers close to the throne transformed him into a national symbol as well. A song Zhukovskii wrote for the occa-

---

[67] *Russkii Invalid*, May 1, 1834: 419; Tatischev, *Imperator Aleksandr II*, 1:65–66.

sion, set to music by Count Michael Viel'gorskii, presented Alexander's birth as an event dear to the nation, which Zhukovskii personified as a sentient, loving entity. From the heights of the Moscow Kremlin, the poem began, "the Russian Land" (*Russkaia zemlia*) had witnessed Alexander's birth. Years had passed quickly, and now, on the day of the resurrection, the "touching ritual" (*umilitel'nyi obriad*) was taking place in "Petrograd." Alexander embodied the unity between Moscow and Petersburg, the name now russified.

The ceremony revealed both generational solidarity and political solidarity. Father and son, dynasty and people, were united in the person of the heir. In the song written by Zhukovskii and Viel'gorskii, the son enters the cathedral, and raises his hands to heaven.

> Before him the father and ruler,
> The *tsar* receives the oath of his *son*.
> Hearken with a blessing,
> To the words of his young soul,
> And raise your arms to heavens,
> Faithful Russia, together with him.[68]

Another "Russian Song," by one B. Fedorov, appeared in *Russkii Invalid* on May 2. Fedorov used a group of boatmen rowing up the Neva to the palace as an expression of the joy of the nation as a whole. The boatmen, he imagined, provided the synecdochical voice of acclamation on the birthday of "the kind son." They sang to the tsar:

> Great is your Imperial joy,
> It spreads through all Holy Rus'.
> You have raised an Heir for Yourself,
> ALEXANDER, Your young son is Your hope!
> He is the comforting ray of the bright sun,
> Our dawn, our light from the great day!
> Glory to the Russian sun!
> Rejoice Father of the Fatherland![69]

THE TOUR OF THE EMPIRE

Alexander's tour of Russia after his nineteenth birthday, from April through December 1837, brought the dynastic scenario to the reaches of the empire. Accompanied by Zhukovskii and an adjutant of Nicholas, S. A. Iur'evich, he covered a distance of more than thirteen thousand miles. It was the longest tour of the empire by a tsar or heir and took him to regions, including parts of Siberia, never visited by a member of the imperial family.

The chief purpose of the trip was ostensibly instructional. It marked the

---

[68] V. A. Zhukovskii, *Polnoe sobranie sochinenii*, 4:22–23.
[69] *Russkii Invalid*, May 2, 1834: 424.

final stage of Alexander's education when, according to the educational theories of the day, the heir was "to become acquainted" with his future subjects. But it was also meant to acquaint the subjects of the tsar with the heir, to present him to them for the first time as an adult. Nicholas declared, in his "general instruction" for the trip, "The heir's journey has a dual role; to learn about Russia to the extent possible and to let himself be seen by his future subjects."[70] Following his mother's example, Nicholas gave specific directives about what Alexander was to do, whom he was to receive, where he was to stay, and what he was to wear. Alexander was to visit state institutions—hospitals, bureaus of social welfare—and barracks only if they were especially beautiful. Nicholas prescribed the sequence of events: religious services; dinners, mentioning which officials were to be invited; receptions of the nobility, officials, and troops. Alexander was to wear a frock coat in the coach while traveling, at other times ordinary uniforms. He was to appear in dress uniform only when he himself participated in a review. He could attend balls, but only in provincial towns. He was to dance the polonaise with a few of the distinguished ladies (*pochetnye damy*) of the province; he could partner young school girls in two or three quadrilles, but "no other dances," and was to leave no later than one or two in the morning, without waiting for the customary supper. He was to accept petitions and forward them to the proper individuals, and donate sums to the poor for which Nicholas assigned him five thousand rubles per town.[71]

The "personal instruction" that followed gave Alexander specific directives on how he was to present himself. It had the tone of an admonition on his public behavior. Many of the phrases repeated Maria Fedorovna's instruction for Nicholas's 1816 trip through the empire, which Nicholas must have consulted or recalled (see above, chapter 9). "Parting for the first time from the parental roof, you are, perhaps for the first time, placed before the court of your future subjects, in a test of your intellectual capacities." The trip was not meant to satisfy his curiosity or provide him pleasure, for "during the time that you are learning about your native lands, you yourself will be severely judged."[72]

Alexander should examine everything, for "*everything useful* must be important for you, and in addition you must learn about *the ordinary* to get a notion of the true state of things." Like Maria Fedorovna, Nicholas counseled caution in making judgments, for "you are traveling not to judge but to become acquainted with things, having seen them, *keeping them to yourself, for yourself*." When he reviewed the troops, he was not an inspector and so was not to make remarks but only convey his comments in private to the officers in charge.[73]

---

[70] The general and the personal instructions are included at the beginning of "Dnevnik V. Kn. Aleksandra Nikolaevicha vo vremia poezdki po Rossii, 1 maia–12 dekabria 1837," TsGAOR, 678-1-287.

[71] Ibid., 3–5.

[72] Ibid., 7.

[73] Ibid., 7–8.

Nicholas went into much greater detail than his mother on how the heir should develop ties with those he met and how he should inspire in them a sense of emotional closeness. "Be tender (*laskovat'sia*) with all—you must dispose them all to you, and make them attached to you (*priviazat'*)." He gave particular suggestions on the ways to win the affections of the particular estates. With the nobility, he was to conduct himself courteously (*uchtivo*), singling out those who had distinguished themselves by their previous service. He advised "tender, simple and polite conduct," with the merchants, singling out those known for their "virtuous and useful enterprises." The "simple people" (*prostoi narod*) required "accessibility." "Unaffected, tender conduct will make them attached" (*priviazhet ego*).[74] These were instructions for the role of kindly, humane, and sensitive son, not that of the autocratic father. But Nicholas predicted, and in a sense ordained, an enthusiastic reception:

> There is no doubt that you will be received everywhere with sincere joy. You will see the interior of Russia and will learn to honor our estimable, kind Russian people and Russian attachment (*priviazannost'*). But do not be blinded by this reception, even if you merit it. You will be received everywhere as their *Hope*. May God in his mercy help you to justify it.[75]

In this respect, Alexander's tour proved an enormous success. There was a festive atmosphere as Alexander passed from town to town. "One can say that the tsar has given Russia a general holiday, unique of its kind," Zhukovskii wrote.[76] Alexander entered each town amid crowds of people shouting "Hoorah!" Bands played the national anthem. According to Nicholas's schedule, Alexander received welcomes from the governor, the provincial marshall of the nobility and other eminent noblemen, the town clergy, and the highest civil and military ranks. He visited important historical sites, churches, and monasteries. He was shown schools and charitable institutions of the towns. He devoted much time to examining factories and "industrial exhibitions," where he demonstrated his and the government's interest in the economic development of the empire. He visited garrisons and reviewed the troops on parade. His sojourn usually concluded with a gala ball given by the provincial nobility.

The feeling of rapport during the trip was an act of mutual beholding. Towns along the way, many of which had never received an heir or emperor, primped for his inspection. Provincial governments had streets cleaned and weeded, public buildings painted, sidewalks, where they existed, repaired. Barrels along the streets, which contained water for use against fire, were painted and their contents, often putrid from standing, were replaced. Multicolored flags enlivened the dreary expanses of provincial streets. The pres-

[74] Ibid.
[75] Ibid., 8.
[76] Tatishchev, *Imperator Aleksandr II*, 1:73.

ence of the tsarevich broke the torpor of provincial towns by bringing them into the sphere of imperial attention. A reporter from Tver described the town as a backwater, or "a pretty postal station," until the heir arrived. There had been only "emptiness and boredom, boredom and emptiness!" The effect was most profound in Siberia. The inhabitants said of the visit, "Until then our region was Siberia, from that time it became Russia."[77]

From the beginning of his trip, Alexander captivated everyone with his beauty, tenderness, and charm, evoking personal affection for the imperial family. Memoirs of Alexander's visits to provincial towns unfailingly recall the effect of his beauty. "He was a real beauty (*krasavets*), cheerful, charming everyone with his unusual cordiality," a Saratov resident wrote.[78] Newspaper accounts, as well as memoirs of his visit, did not fail to describe his politeness and charm. The author of the letter from Tver reported conversations among the people who stood the entire night awaiting the sight of the tsar's face. "What a fine young man (*molodets*)! Clearly Russian blood runs in his veins! How ardently he prayed in church and bowed to the holy icons! How cordial (*privetliv*) to all!" When he met members of the nobility, officers, and officials, "the HEIR charmed each with his greeting, sowing in the hearts of all the seeds of love and devotion, which will yield a rich harvest in future generations." Departing from Ekaterinburg, he left the population "happy with the sight of his face and his kind, cordial manner, full of love and sympathy."[79]

Alexander showed his kindliness through acts of charity. Following his father's instruction, he gave 240,000 rubles to the needy and large sums to repair cathedrals and historical monuments. He received nearly sixteen thousand petitions of grievance to the tsar. In Siberia, he was touched by the lot of many of the exiles, including some of the Decembrists, and petitioned his father for a mitigation of their punishment. To the joy of Alexander's accompanying party, Nicholas informed his son that he would reduce many of the exiles' sentences. It was entirely his own compassion that moved Alexander to this act, Zhukovskii asserted. Seeing a crowd running behind the tsarevich's carriage, the poet wept and saw them as a symbol of the nation. "Run after him Russia, he is worthy of your love!" he repeated to himself.[80]

Severnaia Pchela made familial love a central theme in its reports of the heir's trip. The anonymous author of "A Letter from Tver," discussed above, told how, returning from a visit with Zhukovskii, he had heard peasant,

[77] V. A. Shompulev, "Poseshchenie Saratova Naslednikom Tsesarevichem Aleksandrom Nikolaevichem v 30-kh godakh XIX stoletiia," *Russkaia Starina* 138 (1909): 44; A. Mansurov, "Naslednik Tsesarevich Aleksandr Nikolaevich v gorode Kasimove," *Russkii Arkhiv* 2 (1888): 477–78; *Severnaia Pchela*, May 22, 1837: 443.

[78] Shompulev, "Poseshchenie Saratova," 45; Mansurov, "Naslednik Tsesarevich Aleksandr Nikolaevich," 478; *Severnaia Pchela*, July 17, 1837: 636; Iur'evich, "Dorozhnye pis'ma S.A. Iur'evicha," *Russkii Arkhiv* 1 (1887): 447.

[79] *Severnaia Pchela*, May 22, 1837: 443; June 10, 1837: 505–6.

[80] Tatishchev, *Imperator Aleksandr II*, 1:82–83.

merchant, and nobleman alike exclaiming with joy about the "paternal concern" of a tsar who had sent his son to learn about Russia.[81] A "Letter from Smolensk," quoted the lines, cited in the epigraph to this chapter, of the new polonaise by the "Smolensk landlord" Michael Glinka. The principal function of Alexander's journey, as Zhukovskii perceived, was ceremonial—to link the people to the tsar through the son. Everyone said, "the tsar is sending us his son; he respects his people and everyone's heart is full of gratitude," Zhukovskii wrote. In his letters to the empress, Zhukovskii emphasized widespread feelings of affection for the imperial family. He wrote of the exultant reception in Tver, "Everyone sees in this also the tender heart of the father who wants to share his love for his son with the fatherland and the caring heart of the tsar who ensures a happy future for his heir and his people in their mutual love, created by himself."[82]

Alexander's trip shows the development of the ceremonial mode revealed at the 1826 coronation—the appeal to the roar of popular approval in support of the stately silence of the Petersburg court. The "love" evoked by the heir was not the sublime, ethereal love for the angelic tsar displayed by Alexander I. The latter involved no compromise of the otherworldliness of imperial power, no recognition that the people was a political agent in itself, no love of the monarch for his people. Alexander II sought to generate an emotional mandate from the Russian people, a ceremonial equivalent to institutional representation, elaborated through the artifices of rhetoric and celebrated on the stage of the imperial court. The novelist and ethnographer, P. I. Mel'nikov-Pecherskii, in his *Travel Notes* of 1839, described the "ecstatic" (*voskhishchennyi*) people before the governor's house where Alexander stayed during his visit to the town of Perm. This was a feeling familiar to all Russians, he claimed. "Who of us does not know the way we Russians look upon our Tsars and their children; who of us has not felt that feeling of high rapture that seizes the Russian when he looks upon the Tsar or the Tsar's son! Only the Russian Tsar is called *God on earth*."[83]

Zhukovskii elaborated the rhetoric of closeness in his letters describing the trip. The trip was a love affair between Alexander and a personified Russian nation culminating in what he called an "all-national betrothal with Russia."[84] The young man gave indications of the susceptibility to public acclaim that would characterize him as emperor. After the tumultuous welcome in Tver, Zhukovskii observed, Alexander returned in the evening full of "a happy feeling of gratitude to the Russian people." Alexander recorded his satisfaction in his diary, "The people received me with astonishing cordiality." When he returned from the ball at eleven o'clock, he wrote, "the people accompanied me and shouted 'Hoorah!' like in Moscow." He noted the warmth of the greetings when he crossed the Volga. The people stood

---

[81] *Severnaia Pchela*, May 22, 1837: 443.

[82] Tatishchev, *Imperator Aleksandr II*, 1:74–75.

[83] P. I. Mel'nikov (Andrei Pecherskii), *Polnoe sobranie sochinenii* (St. Petersburg, 1898), 12:367.

[84] Tatishchev, *Imperator Aleksandr II*, 1:89.

shouting along the shores and roared their approval at his coach windows. Iur'evich wrote, "The splendid heart of our priceless voyager drinks the full cup of satisfaction, seeing how the Russian people receive him everywhere with unfeigned, sincere enthusiasm."[85]

•

Two events of Alexander's trip assumed special importance for the role Alexander was to play in his father's scenario—the visit to Moscow in July and August, and his installation as cossack ataman in Novocherkassk in October. The Moscow visit linked his personal appeal as heir born in Moscow with Russia's historical past. Metropolitan Filaret emphasized this theme in the welcoming speech he delivered on Alexander's arrival, which was printed in *Severnaia Pchela*. Alexander, Filaret declared, had now reached Moscow, the resting place of his ancestors: "Here You will come even more into contact with the heart of Russia and its vital force, which is an inherited love for hereditary tsars, repelling in previous centuries so many enemy forces. You will see it in its free play, in those waves of people striving toward You, in those enraptured (*vostorzhennykh*) gazes and solemn cries." An inherited, historical affection was the source of the ruler's authority. "May the love of Russians make Your task easy, inspired by love for Russia."[86] Michael Pogodin wrote an essay for Alexander explaining Moscow's role as political and religious center. Moscow preserved the national spirit, while St. Petersburg represented European influences. "That is why [Moscow] can be called the representative of Holy Rus'." Pogodin awaited Alexander's procession through the Kremlin, with the shouts of "Hoorah!" and the ringing of bells, as a great historical revelation. "May He [Alexander] gaze into these faces, and hearken to these sounds: he will hear in them, he will read our History in them more clearly than in any chronicle."[87]

When Alexander stopped and bowed from the Red Staircase to the people, Zhukovskii perceived the crowd's deafening shouts of "Hoorah!" as an expression of popular acclaim for the dynasty, embodied in the young heir. *Severnaia Pchela* described the people shouting happily, greeting the heir "with feelings of grateful love." The bowing from the Red Staircase, initiated by Nicholas in 1826, had already acquired the powerful hold of a historical tradition. Zhukovskii experienced a revelation during the visit to the Kremlin. He quivered with veneration, he wrote, hearing the words "tsar, heir, gratitude of the fatherland, and posterity" and gazing at the "young, magnificent tsesarevich, surrounded by the people, suddenly falling silent and weeping."[88]

[85] Zhukovskii, *Sochineniia*, 6:298–99; "Dnevnik V. Kn. Aleksandra Nikolaevicha vo vremia poezdki po Rossii, 1 maia–12 dekabria 1837," 15–16; Iur'evich, "Dorozhnye pis'ma," 1:442.

[86] *Severnaia Pchela*, August 3, 1837: 685.

[87] Pogodin, *Istoriko-kriticheskie otryvki*, 154–59.

[88] *Severnaia Pchela*, August 3, 1837: 685; Tatishchev, *Imperator Aleksandr II*, 1:84–85; Zhukovskii, *Sochineniia* (St. Peterburg, 1885), 6:308–9.

According to Nicholas's instructions, Alexander slept in the room where he was born and took historical tours of the city that identified his and the family's fate with Russia's past. Andrei Murav'ev, a specialist on religion and Muscovite antiquities, published an account of his excursions with Alexander to the sites of Moscow and its vicinity. Murav'ev described the young heir's visit to the relics and shrines of his ancestors. In the Novospasskii Monastery, Alexander proceeded slowly beneath a painting of his family tree, he wrote, "as if attaining at the end of this long genealogical chain that bright link to which he was predestined."[89]

Another dramatic moment was Alexander's meeting with his mother on August 3, after a separation of three months. An account by the popular, children's writer, Prince Vladimir L'vov, appeared in the September 27 issue of *Russkii Invalid*. L'vov described the scene of a moving embrace. The sun shone with bright rays. The empress and one of his sisters embraced him. "Let foreigners envy us!" L'vov wrote. "Let all Russia enjoy this spectacle and let it be repeated many, many times. Happy is the people whose ruling family gives such an example of love and friendship. Can the tears of joy and the cries of the suffering fail to strike a chord in their hearts?"[90]

After the Moscow sojourn, Alexander's route swung east to the Volga towns of Nizhnii-Novgorod and Simbirsk and Saratov, then west into the steppe region. *Russkii Invalid* gave special attention to his inspections of the gymnasia, where he gave out awards and, in Simbirsk, questioned the students on religion, grammar, and history and pronounced his satisfaction with their performance.[91] The empress also traveled south, and her visit, with the grand duchess Maria Nikolaevna to the Poltava Institute of Young Noble Ladies, provided another occasion to show the family's parental sympathy and concern. Her appearance there, *Severnaia Pchela* reported, was a scene of mutual affection between the empress and the girls. She remarked on the exceptional order in the institute. Her "kind attitude toward the children so charmed and enlivened them" that they refused to part with her. Then, to the girls' delight, the empress, "with angelic sympathy," wrote her initials on slips of paper, which were passed out to them, and left her gloves to the institute as a souvenir. All of this, the article concluded, attested to the purity of the feelings underlying their training, which was aimed at "inculcating the virtues, and the mutual love between themselves, and deep devotion to their Crowned Patrons ornamenting the All-Russian throne."[92]

The family was reunited at Voznesensk, in Kherson Province, where Nicholas staged the massive cavalry maneuvers that involved 350 squadrons. Nicholas's suite was joined by European royalty, including Archduke

[89] [A. N. Murav'ev], *Vospominaniia o poseshchenii sviatyni Moskovskoi Gosudarem Naslednikom* (St. Petersburg, 1838), 13.

[90] *Russkii Invalid*, September 27, 1837: 960.

[91] Ibid., October 18, 1837: 1039; October 19, 1837: 1042–43.

[92] *Severnaia Pchela*, October 25, 1837: 961–62.

Johann of Austria, Prince Adalbert and Prince August of Prussia, as well as an array of lesser German princes. Alexander took his place in his father's suite and assisted in the command, dutifully listing in his diary the names of all the regiments and their commanders, and the movements of his own troops. Like the annual maneuvers at Krasnoe Selo, the camp at Voznesensk provided the occasion for brilliant social events, balls, and dinners. At the parade on August 26, Alexander was appointed chief of the Regiment of Moscow Dragoons. During the celebration of his name day on August 30, he heard that he had received the village of Borodino as a gift from the emperor.[93]

The investiture ceremony at Novocherkassk in the steppes of New Russia on October 21 made the office of honorary ataman an attribute of the heir's hereditary right. It identified the devotion of the cossacks with the devotion of son to father, establishing a rite for all future heirs to the throne. Emperor and heir rode in ceremonial procession into Novocherkassk, the administrative center of the Don Host. The cossack leaders formed a circle around the cathedral; in the middle, the "appointed" (*nakaznyi*) cossack ataman conferred the *pernach*, one of the maces constituting the cossack insignia of power, on Nicholas, who then conferred it on Alexander. Nicholas explained the significance of the event. He declared that by appointing his son his ataman, he was giving "the most valuable pledge (*zalog*)" of his good will to them. "May this serve as proof of how close you are to my heart. When he replaces me, serve him as loyally as you served my ancestors and me. He will not forsake you." In his diary, Alexander described the ceremony and copied down his father's address. *Russkii Invalid* reported that "these words were impressed on the heart of each and every one of those present. General, but silent tenderness (*umilenie*). This then turned into the joyous cries of pure enthusiasm (*vostorg*) from the people."[94]

The next day, Alexander and Nicholas inspected a review of more than seventeen thousand members of the Host and in the evening attended a ball where he took part in several dances. From Novocherkassk, Alexander traveled to Moscow, and again received a warm and cordial welcome. He remained through the first week of December before his return to St. Petersburg. He attended lectures in anatomy at Moscow University; he was the first Russian heir to receive instruction at a university.[95]

[93] Tatishchev, *Imperator Aleksandr II*, 1:86–87; *Russkii Invalid*, September 16, 1837: 918–20; "Dnevnik V. Kn. Aleksandra Nikolaevicha vo vremia poezdki po Rossii, 1 maia–12 dekabria 1837," 62; "Zhurnal Ego Imperatorskogo Velichestva Gosudaria Imperatora Nikolaia Pavlovicha vo vremia Vysochaishei Prisutstviia v Gorode Voznesenska," TsGIA, 516–120/2322–133.

[94] *Russkii Invalid*, November 24, 1837: 1182–83; *Severnaia Pchela*, November 2, 1837: 989; Tatischev, *Imperator Aleksandr II*, 1:89; "Dnevnik V. Kn. Aleksandra Nikolaevicha vo vremia poezdki po Rossii, 1 maia–12 dekabria 1837," 95–96.

[95] "Dnevnik V. Kn. Aleksandra Nikolaevicha vo vremia poezdki po Rossii, 1 maia–12 dekabria 1837," 111–17.

Marriage and Family

Zhukovskii's phrase, "the all-national betrothal with Russia," signaled the beginning of the scenario of love that Alexander would use to present himself as popular, national monarch. It expressed the public character of his attraction; he was betrothed to Russia, having won her by his benevolence, charm, and beauty, and he responded warmly to the show of affection. Private attachments proved more troublesome. He was accustomed to swift conquests, easy adulation; long-term attachments palled and became burdensome. His betrothal to "Russia" made his betrothal to one fiancée problematical.

Alexander played the role of loyal and presentable son well. But the very extent of his subordination to his father and his strong filial feelings made it difficult for him to see himself as a father. The roles of adoring and faithful husband or doting father were not congenial to him. In the previous century, the ruler's marital behavior had not been an issue, but now, with the sovereign or future sovereign presented as a model for his servitors and subjects, Alexander's personal life threatened to clash with the image of the moral ascendancy of the Russian monarch.

To be sure, Alexander showed the proper intentions in striving to match his father's righteous example. But as in the classroom, this involved a struggle between duty and feelings, in which the former was only fleetingly the victor. Nicholas tried to show his son the importance of constancy, for straying, in his opinion, was dangerous as well as immoral. To dramatize this point, he took Alexander, then nineteen, to the syphilis ward of a hospital. He wanted to show him "the most horrible example of the effects syphilis had on men and women." Nicholas had been introduced to the same sight as a boy, and "the diseased people I saw so horrified me that I knew no woman until my marriage."[96]

Nicholas's admonition failed to discourage his son's amorous adventures. In 1838 Alexander became involved with a Fraulein Kalinovskaia, apparently with the encouragement of his uncle, the grand duke Michael. Nicholas expressed his anger in a letter to his wife, describing a conversation with his daughter, Maria Nikolaevna: "She, like me, says that [Alexander] is often very weak in character and loose at letting himself go." It was absolutely necessary that Alexander gain "more nerve." "He will be lost without that, since his task will be no easier than mine. And what has saved me? It isn't knowledge, poor devil that I am, but hope in God, and firm will to make things go and that is all." Alexander finally confessed his guilt, declaring that he was incapable of attachment to anyone but his friend, his father. Nicholas reminded him that "you belong not to yourself but your native land."[97] Alexander himself believed this and did not defend his behavior. At

[96] Korf, *Materialy*, 99–100.
[97] A. N. Savin, "Svatovstvo Tsesarevicha Aleksandra Nikolaevicha," *Pamiati Aleksandra Nikolaevicha Savina, 1873–1923* (Moscow, 1926), 61–65.

his mother's instance, he left the capital in order to forget Kalinovskaia. He wrote to Alexandra about his joy at reading his father's letters: "There has never been such a father for his children, an act of Providence, a friend."[98]

Under the circumstances, it became urgent to arrange the heir's marriage. The selection of a spouse was the purpose of his journey through Europe in 1839, when Alexander was introduced to the courts of Europe. His journey took him to Sweden, Denmark and Austria, as well as the Italian and German states. At each court, he surveyed the eligible damsels arrayed before him. The presentation followed the fairytale motif. This was not to be an arranged marriage: Alexander had to choose a spouse who suited his inclinations. And also as in fairytales, none of the most elegant or prepossessing candidates on his parents' list captured his fancy. Rather, it was a delicate and retiring princess not quite fifteen years old who caught his eye at the end of his trip. She was Princess Marie of Hesse-Darmstadt, who had been thought too young to be numbered among the eligible.[99]

As in a fairytale, Alexander's parents were not pleased. His choice particularly distressed his mother. It was an embarrassment for a Prussian princess to have as a daughter-in-law a princess from the lowly principality of Hesse-Darmstadt. To make matters worse, the princess's paternity was in doubt. Her mother and father had not been living together at the time of her conception, and her paternity, rumor had it, belonged to a chamberlain. For Nicholas, the champion of legitimacy, whether political or familial, this caused concern. In addition, Marie was in poor health. She suffered from serious colds and coughs that later were diagnosed as tubercular. But stopping the tsarevich's escapades outweighed these concerns. Nicholas knew when to yield to necessity, and preparations began for marriage.[100] Alexandra accepted the decision gracefully, and when she met the princess in Darmstadt, she was favorably impressed. She wrote in her diary that Marie was prettier than she had expected and, with time, would develop "lovely carriage" (*krasivaia osanka*).[101]

Once Alexander returned to Russia, he resumed his affair with Kalinovskaia. He even began to smoke, a habit that Nicholas could not abide. He neglected his work and lied about what he was doing. Enraged, Nicholas recalled the example of Peter the Great, and considered removing his son from the succession. The champion of dynasty began to doubt the principle of primogeniture of succession and, in a conversation with his aides, blamed the confusion at his accession on the precedence of the senior line. Alexander, like Peter the Great's son, Alexei, neglected the obligations and duties defined by his father and indulged his own personal sentiments. But the similarity ended there. Unlike Alexei, Alexander shared his father's image of

---

[98] Ibid., 70.

[99] Ibid., 70–74.

[100] Ibid., 75–83; Count Egon Corti, *The Downfall of Three Dynasties* (Freeport, N.Y., 1970), 8–9.

[101] Cited in the anonymous, "Zhizneopisanie Imperatritsy Marii Aleksandrovny; chast' 1aia, Mariia Aleksandrovna, tsesarevna, 1838–1854," TsGAOR, 641-1-113, 29.

the ideal ruler and was contrite. His sin was not rebellion but profligacy. When called to task, he fulfilled the role his father had assigned him.[102]

It was difficult for many to understand Princess Marie's appeal for the dashing prince. A sad and retiring girl, Marie had grown up neglected and isolated in the court of Hesse-Darmstadt, a small principality, ruled after 1820 as a constitutional monarchy with a bicameral legislature.[103] Marie's older sister, Elizabeth, had died in 1826. Her mother, Wilhelmina Louise of Baden, was the sister of Empress Elizabeth of Russia. Ignored by her husband, Wilhelmina Louise suffered an additional blow from her first daughter's death and paid little attention to Marie and her brother, Alexander of Hesse, who was a year older than his sister. The two grew up on their own in a small house at the beautiful palace of Heilenberg outside Darmstadt. They became very close, and later in life their letters would frequently recall their childhood happiness.[104]

The official version of Marie's life, however, emphasized the bond between mother and daughter. Wilhelmina Louise had provided a French classical education and instilled in her daughter an inclination to religious mysticism. She had died in 1836, and, however distant the relations between mother and daughter, her memory took on great significance in the context of the romanticizing of death. Marie claimed that she felt her mother watching over her from above and followed the advice she had received from her in childhood, especially in matters of faith.[105]

It was namely Marie's sad vulnerability that fit the chivalric role Alexander had learned to play. He was the knight protecting the helpless. He was attracted by her "modest charm." She awakened the feelings of pity and compassion he had been taught to display toward women, and especially toward his mother, who was constantly suffering from indispositions. Through the magic of his charm, he could lift the shy and melancholic princess to the dazzling heights of the Russian court.

In April 1840 Marie crossed the frontier into Russia and was escorted by her fiancé, accompanied by a detachment of cossacks, to St. Petersburg. She felt homesick for her native land, she wrote in a letter just after her arrival, but also "extremely attached to Russia." As with Alexandra Fedorovna, the military pageantry created a setting that was familiar and comfortable for the princess. She wrote in her letter that she was cheered by the strains of her favorite "Ernst-Ludwig march" and the sight of "rich pretty uniforms,"

---

[102] Savin, "Svatovstvo Tsesarevicha Aleksandra Nikolaeivicha," 87–98; N. N. Murav'ev, "Zapiski," *Russkii Arkhiv* 3 (1894): 499.

[103] On monarchical rule in Hesse-Darmstadt, see Eckhardt G. Franz, "Hof und Hofgesellschaft im Grossherzogtum Hessen," in Möckl, ed., 157–76.

[104] Corti, *The Downfall of Three Dynasties*, 2–3; Otto Hoetzsch, "Kaiserin Maria Alexandrovna von Russland, geb. Prinzessin Marie von Hessen-Darmstadt (1824–1880)," *Archiv für hessische Geschichte und Altertumskund*, Neue Folge, Band 21 (1940), 84–85; Alfred Börckel, *Hessens Fürstenfrauen von heilige Elizabeth bis zur Gegenwart in ihren Leben und Wirken dargestellt* (Giessen, 1908), 118–21.

[105] "Zhizneopisanie Imperatritsy Marii Aleksandrovny," 1–4.

for which she shared her fiancé's taste. "There were even Turks among them."[106]

Her gala entry into St. Petersburg on September 8, 1840, introduced her into the family scenario. Artillery salvos resounded at the moment she crossed the town line. Marie sat beside the empress in a golden carriage drawn by eight horses. She, the empress, and the grand duchesses all wore the "Russian dress." Hers was light blue with silver lace; the empress's was gold with maroon lace. Nicholas cut an imposing figure riding beside the carriage, and Alexander led the convoy of hussars while a brilliant suite followed behind. The merchants of the principal market (*Gostinnyi Dvor*) had covered the facade of the arcade with red cloth and extended carpets along the streets. On Vladimir Street people threw flowers. The roar of the crowd was deafening, according popular approval to the familial event. The diplomat, Nicholas Giers, recalled, "This was truly a national holiday fully expressive of the sincere love and devotion of the Russian people for their tsar. To be sure, one could not help being proud of him." Again, it was not Alexander's magnificence but his kindness that impressed the onlookers. Giers wrote, "One had to admire the affectionate character of the groom who was also on horseback on the other side of the carriage." The family stepped out for a brief service before the Kazan Mother-of-God at the Kazan Cathedral, then proceeded to the Winter Palace. When they came out on the balcony above the square, Alexander presented his bride to the populace. "A veritable roar rose from the crowd," Alexandra wrote in her diary, "Especially when Niks embraced me."[107]

The celebrations created the type of scene that delighted the empress. In the evening, the whole city was illuminated. Alexandra saw the lamplights on the Neva being lit from her bedroom in the palace, creating an enchanted world: "It was so pretty, fairy-like, that I doubted the reality of the present day." But she confessed that the role of Russian empress was not an easy one, and she worried for the frail princess entering the capital. As the symbol of the European birth and character of the house, the grand duchess had to exemplify majesty for the Western diplomats and visitors. She was proof that the dynasty belonged to the ceremonial world of the great monarchies. Alexandra believed that the fate of Russia hung on the appearance and manner of the empress.

> Yes, today I brought my successor into the capital, who will be here for many years when I will no longer be on this earth. So much will depend on her manner of bearing herself, her form of action, on her relations to dear Sasha. Yes, the good of the entire country depends upon her.[108]

[106] Ibid., 35–37.

[107] Ibid., 42; Charles and Barbara Jelavich, eds., *The Education of a Russian Statesman: The Memoirs of Nicholas Karlovich Giers* (Berkeley, Calif., 1962), 106–7; Annenkova, "Vospominaniia A. K. Annenkovoi," 380–81; *Severnaia Pchela*, September 10, 1840: 809.

[108] "Zhizneopisanie Imperatritsy Marii Aleksandrovny," 43.

The princess's reception at the theater allayed some of her doubts. "Our bride conquered the general sympathy of the public by her appearance, the pleasant expression of her eyes, and her simple manner," the empress wrote. *Severnaia Pchela* reported on how the audience "with reverent respect and sincere love" enjoyed the sight of the august personages, and "with rapture looked upon the Bride of the *Tsesarevich* flowering with youth, whose majestic and at the same time tender bearing, her splendid eyes and intelligent, pleasant and enchanting smile surpass all descriptions and portraits." The illuminations celebrated the return of the imperial family with the bride, and the acclaim showed the mutual love between people and family. The members of the imperial family, the article asserted, "saw, understood, felt our zeal, our love, our readiness to go this very minute to meet death for their welfare, and they replied with a gracious greeting, invaluable, sacred, that will be forever imprinted in our hearts." The tsar marked the event with a rescript to the Petersburg governor that was printed in *Severnaia Pchela*. Nicholas expressed his pleasure about the exemplary order and quiet in the city. "But dearer than anything for *His Imperial Majesty* was the cordial, *as if familial reception*, that deeply touched His Majesty as well as the Empress and Heir."[109]

Nonetheless, the sixteen-year-old girl had difficulties adjusting to her new position in the world. She often sat in her room and wept. Alexandra enforced a strict Prussian etiquette and remained intolerant of the more relaxed Hessian manners. After her arrival in St. Petersburg, Marie's face broke out in a rash, an affliction that would beset her at moments of tension throughout her life. She had to wear a veil and remained indoors for several weeks. Alexander was extremely caring and attentive in her distress, and apparently at this point she showed the first signs of reciprocating his affections.[110] In December 1840 she was anointed in the orthodox faith and renamed Grand Duchess Maria Aleksandrovna. She then passed the test of receiving the diplomatic corps, showing poise and elegance of bearing. Despite her shyness, she revealed what impressed Nicholas most, a talent for self-control.[111]

The wedding on April 16, 1841, was another fabulous spectacle meant to impress Europe with the extravagance at the disposal of the Russian emperor and the dynastic and national character of monarchical rule in Russia. After the ceremony, in the large palace church, Nicholas stepped out onto the palace balcony, facing the admiralty with Alexander and Maria at his side before a crowd of people. Both he and his son wore cossack uniforms. Nicholas marked the event by revising an article in the *Digest of Laws* to bestow on the wife of the heir to the throne the old Russian title of "Tsarevna," as well as that of "Grand Duchess," another of Nicholas's attempts to give the European monarchy a national look.

[109] Ibid.; *Severnaia Pchela*, September 12, 1840: 817.
[110] Tiutcheva, *Pri dvore dvukh imperatorov*, 1:77–78.
[111] Vel. Kn. Ol'ga Nikolaevna, *Son iunosti* (Paris, 1963), 129.

The wedding was hailed in *Severnaia Pchela* with lavish praises of family life that resemble the words of Vasilii Zhukovskii: "If family happiness is the greatest treasure of ordinary human life, then in the life of the Tsar it is a heavenly blessing." "The firm edifice of the people's well-being is built on domestic morals and the foundation stone of that edifice is the morals of the Tsar's family." The article went on to hope for the same type of "touching example of domestic happiness" in the family of the heir as was given by the tsar to the people.[112]

The next day, the emperor and empress, and the newlyweds, rode through the streets of the capital in carriages and were greeted by the shouts of onlookers. There followed a fortnight of celebrations. Numerous lavish balls took place. Forty-two thousand invitations were reputedly sent out for the ball given by the newlyweds. The festivities concluded with the great May parade, in which the grand duke commanded an infantry division. Maria was treated to the sight of a charge of forty regiments of cavalry who, at Nicholas's command, came to a halt a few yards away from the marquee.[113]

•

After the wedding celebrations, the couple left for a visit to Moscow. In 1781 Catherine II had forbidden the tsarevich, Paul, and the grand duchess, Maria Fedorovna, from visiting Moscow before their European trip; she feared for demonstrations in their behalf.[114] Now the heir represented an ally, not a rival of the sovereign, and the sojourn of Alexander and Maria Aleksandra initiated what would become a tradition followed by later heirs and their spouses. The newlyweds, the symbol of the vitality and the popularity of the dynasty, now received the acclamation of the Russian population. If the wedding itself was played to Europe, the visit to Moscow demonstrated the nation's acceptance of the marriage. Alexander expressed this feeling in a letter he wrote to Maria's sister-in-law, Elizabeth, just before their departure from St. Petersburg: "It is my native city that I am about to present her to and I am very much rejoicing. She will see with her own eyes how much in the heart of Russia [the people] are attached to their Sovereign and to His whole family."[115]

The memoirs of the poet, Afanasii Fet, give a sense of a young nobleman's perceptions of the popular response to the imperial family. He watched from a window as the procession came down Tver Boulevard. The emperor led the procession in a general's uniform, on horseback, "incomparably handsome, our Sovereign," followed by the heir. The bride rode in a carriage drawn by six snow-white horses given by the Hesse-Darmstadt prince. The scene of the throng of people mobbing the emperor, shouting resounding "Hoorahs!" and raising their right hands with a sign of the cross, "was engraved

[112] *Severnaia Pchela*, April 19, 1841: 334–35.
[113] Tatishchev, *Pri dvore dvukh imperatorov*, 1:111–12; Corti, *The Downfall of Three Dynasties*, 12.
[114] Shumigorskii, *Imperatritsa Mariia Fedorovna*, 1:174.
[115] Hesse State Archive, D-23–32/34.

in my mind," Fet wrote. The emperor ordered them away, but then over-whelmed by the shouts, let them come close. They kissed his boots and saddlecloth, as well as the horse itself. Fet was later told that when the police chief tried to stop the crush of the people, they answered, "What for? He himself is here!"[116]

With the marriage, the emperor, according to the *Law of the Imperial Family*, established the heir's court.[117] This provided Alexander with his own social world, where he and his wife held their own functions and drew together those close to him personally. Ideally, this world should have been more relaxed and private than the imperial court. But Nicholas brought the next generation into living arrangements resembling an extended family. Alexander and Maria had none of the freedom and privacy that Nicholas and Alexandra had enjoyed during the first years of their marriage at the Anichkov Palace. The young couple were immediately installed in the Winter Palace under the watchful eyes of the emperor and empress. Alexander's chambers adjoined his mother's; Nicholas's were on the floor above. "The members of the imperial family lived in close proximity," Tiutcheva wrote, "which created an intimate family life, at least as far as the habits of every-day life were concerned." Nicholas also watched over the care and upbring-ing of his grandchildren. He even forbade Maria Aleksandrovna from nurs-ing her firstborn, Alexandra, when the grand duchess expressed the wish to do so. He supervised the education of his grandsons Nicholas Alek-sandrovich (born, 1843) and Alexander Aleksandrovich (born, 1845) and took particular pleasure in following their military training.[118]

From nine to ten in the morning the family would gather around the em-press for morning coffee. Maria had to appear at Alexandra Fedorovna's daily gatherings of ladies, where she would work on crocheting or listen to readings of literature. She attended numerous audiences, dinners, presenta-tions, balls, and concerts and strictly observed the schedule of visits to mem-bers of the imperial family. At Tsarskoe Selo, life was more tranquil, but there, too, it was dominated by the empress. At Peterhof, they lived at the "Farm," not far from the Cottage on the Alexandria estate. Maria was con-stantly involved in the ceremonial and leisure activities of the imperial fam-ily, while Alexander was kept busy in the active military exercises in and around Peterhof.[119] Alexandra made sure that her daughter-in-law learned to act like an empress. During the wedding, she whispered to her, "I bless

[116] Fet, *Moi vospominaniia*, 195–96.

[117] Tatishchev, *Imperator Aleksandr II*, 1:113–14.

[118] Tiutcheva, *Pri dvore dvukh imperatorov*, 1:93–94. When their parents were abroad, Nicholas delighted in showing the boys how to skim rocks in the water, to climb fences, and to line up properly with the cadets. They attended the reviews at his side. See the vivid description of their summer together in S. A. Iur'evich, "Pis'ma ob avgusteishikh synoviakh Aleksandra II," unpublished typescript, Slavic and Baltic Division, New York Public Library.

[119] Tiutcheva, *Pri dvore dvukh imperatorov*; Iakovleva, *Istoricheskii Vestnik* 31 (1888): 164–69, 401–5; A. Benois and N. Lanceray, "Dvortsovoe stroitel'stvo Imperatora Nikolaia I," *Starye gody* (July–September 1913), 192–93.

59. *Alexander II as His Father's Adjutant*. Oil painting.

you in the name of your mother who at this moment is surely watching you and blessing you." Alexandra took over the role of Maria's mother, watching over her carriage, which, she wrote in her diary, "has become more majestic." She approved of her "beautiful toilet, chosen with such taste and refinement."[120]

[120] "Zhizneopisanie Imperatritsy Marii Aleksandrovny," 64.

Alexander continued his rise as Nicholas's subaltern. The marriage, on the eve of Alexander's twenty-third birthday, represented his true coming of age. Before the wedding, he was promoted to lieutenant-general in Nicholas's suite. The ceremony of majority had made him his father's helper; his marriage had made him a comrade-in-arms. On the birth of his first child in 1843, he was promoted to adjutant-general and could not contain his feelings of joy and gratitude. In 1844 he was appointed commander of all of the infantry of the guard. In 1846 he reached the rank of full General. On the death of his uncle, Grand Duke Michael, in 1849, he assumed the duties of commander of the Guard and Grenadier Corps and Chief of Military Schools. The portraits of the time show him proudly wearing the uniform of adjutant in his father's suite (fig. 59).[121]

Nicholas also sought to train Alexander in the work of government. On the day of his wedding, he was appointed to the State Council. In subsequent years, he served on the Committee of Ministers and state committees in charge of the Caucasus and major construction projects. He also participated in secret committees established to find ways to deal with the problem of serfdom. Nicholas entrusted Alexander with considerable authority over governmental matters during his absences from the capital; the first such occasion took place a little over a year after Alexander's wedding in the fall of 1842, when he was twenty-four years old. In fulfilling these assignments, Alexander gave no evidence of having views of his own. Indeed, his presence at state deliberations, like his reviewing of the troops, often tended to be ceremonial. According to one account, Alexander was not permitted to interrogate ministers, to express his opinion to the tsar at the State Council, or even to enter into discussions on state matters with ministers or other officials. So much was he under his father's personal domination that he left no opinion and made no statement before his own accession that differed in the least with his father's. He was truly his father's helper in service, devoted to the ideas of government and self-sacrifice that Nicholas embodied.[122]

---

[121] Tatishchev, *Imperator Alexandr II*, 1:110–11, 118; V. P. Marin, "Iz dnevnika babushki, 1842–46," *Nasha Starina*, no. 5 (1915): 419; *IGK, ts. Al. II*, 450, 461.

[122] Tatishchev, *Imperator Aleksandr II*, 1:116–17; Senator K. I. Fisher, "Zapiski," *Istoricheskii Vestnik* 113 (September 1908): 818–19.

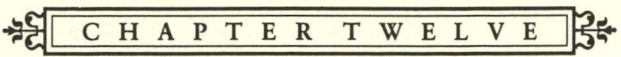

CHAPTER TWELVE

National Motifs

> Glory, Glory to our Russian Tsar!
> Given us by the Lord a Sovereign-Tsar!
> Moscow awaits you and our sacred Kremlin
> Appear before the people, our native father!
>
> Glory, Glory to our Russian Tsar!
> Given us by the Lord a Sovereign-Tsar!
> With great love and joy,
> All the people await the Chosen of God.
>
> Glory, Glory to our Russian Tsar!
> Given us by the Lord a Sovereign-Tsar!
> May your clan be immortal,
> May the Russian people flourish!
>
> —*From the Final Chorus of Michael Glinka's* Life for the Tsar

OFFICIAL NATIONALITY

The manifesto announcing the sentencing of the Decembrists had declared the national character of Russian monarchy: the Decembrists had committed not only the crime of rebellion, but also a violation of the will of the people, who were devoted to monarch and dynasty. The people's devotion turned the Petrine empire, with its Westernized official culture, into a national institution. This theme was announced with the coronation and promulgated in ceremony, the press, and in the doctrine of "official nationality" during Nicholas's reign. Nicholas himself felt a strong sense of Russia's difference from the West. He believed the institutions of monarchy protected the population's moral virtues, which distinguished Russia from Europe. He remarked to Korf in 1840, "If something is better there, then it is redeemed among us by something else, in other words, that our *imperfection* is in many respects better than their *perfection*. In general, then of course, we can learn something from foreigners about external life, but nothing about inner life—by that I mean family, home, as the English say."[1]

Nation, during the first half of the nineteenth century, carried romantic

---

[1] Korf, "Iz zapisok," *Russkaia Starina* 99 (1899): 290–91.

connotations of the importance of the people and history. German idealistic philosophy emphasized the existence of the spirit of a nation, reflected in its culture, institutions, and past. While such doctrines were hardly current at court, their implications were generally accepted. The European culture of the court and the state, consequently, had to be embellished with national attributes, indicating the elite's connection with Russian culture, abjured since Peter the Great. Foreign, Western attributes still signified power and authority, but now, when European states themselves boasted national traditions, the autocracy began to seek motifs demonstrating that Russia, too, had roots in a national culture and history.

Nicholas's nationalism, to a certain degree, was an effort to throw up a wall against the foreign influences that had caused rebellion in Russia. In 1827 he insisted that those who were sent abroad be "of pure Russian background," and in 1830 issued a decree that students between ten and eighteen must study in Russia.[2] At the same time, he introduced requirements for the study of Russian language in schools and universities. The university charter of 1834 favored the study of disciplines such as history, law, and philology with specifically Russian subject matter. Nicholas insisted on the use of Russian language at the imperial court.

The national character of the monarchy was also demonstrated by visible signs of the national, pre-Petrine history. Nicholas's reign marks the beginning of the active official encouragement of the discovery and preservation of artifacts of the past. The Kremlin cathedrals, the Assumption Cathedral in Vladimir, and the Romanov house in Kostroma are examples of the renovation undertaken, often not very successfully, in Nicholas's reign. But Nicholas also sought current expressions of the monarch's attachment to national culture. His reign witnesses a search for a national church architecture and a national music that would glorify the monarchy and show its closeness to the people. In Nicholas's scenario, the orthodox church, regarded in Alexander I's reign as little more than an impediment to universal Christian brotherhood, began to appear as the guardian of the national past, protecting autocracy from the pernicious doctrines emanating from the West.

But at the same time Nicholas remained true to the Petrine myth: national motifs embellished a heroic history of foreign domination. They were invoked to show the distinctive character of that domination. The historian, Michael Pogodin, had presented the tale of the calling of the Varangians, as both the primal historical expression and the prototype of the Russian people's acceptance of absolute rule (see above, chapter 10). The minister of education, Sergei Uvarov, who had listened approvingly to Pogodin's lecture on the tale, elaborated this notion into an ideological statement of official nationality in a circular of April 2, 1831. Just as Catherine the Great, in Article 6 of her *Nakaz*, had proclaimed that Russia was a European country, Uvarov asserted that Russia was distinct from Europe, which, we have seen,

[2] Lincoln, *Nicholas I*, 91–92.

had been a premise of Nicholas's policies and statements since the coronation.[3] The collapse of civil and religious institutions in Europe and the spread of revolutionary ideas, he wrote, had made it necessary to "find the principles which form the distinctive character of Russia, and which belong only to Russia; it was necessary to gather into one whole the sacred remnants of Russian nationality and fasten them to the anchor of our salvation."[4]

The principles Uvarov articulated formed the famous troika, "orthodoxy, autocracy, and nationality." They were proclaimed and defended, as Nicholas Riasanovsky has shown, by a score of official writers, contributing to such journals as *Severnaia Pchela* and *Moskvitianin*, and reflected the views of much of the educated public at the time.[5] Characteristically, the two initial components, orthodoxy and autocracy, were less principles than institutions or tropes—metonymic constructions that encapsulated the nation's spirit and past. The church, Uvarov declared, was "the guarantee of social and family happiness," and the Russian, devoted to his fatherland, "will agree as little to the loss of a single dogma of our Orthodoxy as to the theft of a single pearl from the Tsar's crown."[6] The Moscow metropolitan, Filaret, disseminated the notion of the historical role of the orthodox church as an ally of autocracy and the savior of Russia. "Nationality" expressed both the Russian people's devotion to the tsar, and the incomparable and unique power of that devotion. Russia was not Europe, namely because of the warm feelings that the Russian people displayed before their rulers from the moment of the calling of the Varangians.

THE NATIONAL STYLE IN CHURCH ARCHITECTURE: THE WORK OF CONSTANTINE THON

During Nicholas's reign, architecture, music, and ceremony were used to display the national identity of the monarchy. Church architecture served as a principal medium to demonstrate the role of the orthodox church in the history of the state. Churches became contemporary artifacts of the pre-Petrine past, disclosing the persistence of distinctive Russian motifs. Architecture took on a narrative historical function, realizing Nicholas Gogol's appeal for "an architectural chronicle" of Russia's past. Architects were expected to become archaeologists, recapturing in their designs images of the past that revealed the nation's spirit.[7]

[3] On Uvarov's intellectual development and bureaucratic career, see Cynthia H. Whittaker, *The Origins of Modern Russian Education: An Intellectual Biography of Count Sergei Uvarov, 1786–1855* (De Kalb, Ill., 1984), 10–84.

[4] Nicholas Riasanovsky, *Nicholas I and Official Nationality in Russia, 1825–1855* (Berkeley and Los Angeles, Calif., 1959), 73–74.

[5] Ibid., 76–78.

[6] Ibid., 74–75.

[7] Borisova, *Russkaia arkhitektura*, 17–29.

Nicholas's interest in pre-Petrine church architecture appeared while he was still a grand duke. At the time of his visit to Moscow in 1817, he visited Nikon's New Jerusalem and encouraged efforts to restore the monastery cathedral, which had fallen into disrepair. At his suggestion, the artist, M. N. Vorob'ev, was sent to Jerusalem to make drawings of the Church of the Holy Sepulcher in order to compare Nikon's cathedral to the original. Nicholas was pleased with the results in 1821, and, after he became tsar, frequently visited the artist in his studio and appointed him to his suite. Vorob'ev completed numerous paintings of the Jerusalem Cathedral, several of which were acquired by the imperial family. On his way to Jerusalem, he stopped in Constantinople, where he executed a series of scenes of the city and its major buildings. When exhibited in the Academy of Art from 1823 to 1827, the paintings familiarized Russians with their forgotten Byzantine heritage. In this respect, Byzantine architecture provided a national artistic alternative to the Gothic style.[8]

The struggle against Turkey, and Nicholas's vision of Russia as the defender of Christian shrines in the Holy Land, heightened his sense of identification with the Byzantine past. He pursued his interest with his usual unswerving determination. In 1827 the competition to create a model for the St. Catherine Church at the Kalinkin Bridge in St. Petersburg called for the creation of a building that "would attest to compatriots as well as to foreigners of the zeal of Russians for the orthodox faith." This, however, did not give the competitors a clear sense of what was desired. The architect, A. Mel'nikov, for example, pleading ignorance of the tsar's wishes, submitted three projects, one in Byzantine, one in ancient Roman style, and one in the manner of the Roman style of the Pantheon. None of the entries satisfied the emperor. Instead, he commissioned a project from Constantine Thon, a young architect of German-Russian extraction. Thon's project for the St. Catherine Church pleased the emperor greatly, and Thon's version of the national style became the model for church building in Nicholas's reign.[9]

Thon sought his prototype for national churches in what he called the "Byzantine style." He wrote in 1835, "[The] Byzantine style, having become intimately linked with elements of our nationality (*narodnost'*) from distant times, created our church architecture, examples of which we do not find in other countries."[10] But his initial projects, submitted in 1827, suggest a variety of styles, indicating that he, too, lacked a clear idea of what was expected. Thon presented several models of churches with large Byzantine domes. Some of his sketches followed the classical Russian five-cupola pat-

[8] P. N. Petrov, "M. N. Vorob'ev i ego shkola," *Vestnik iziashchnykh iskusstv* 6 (1888): 297–303; Borisova, *Russkaia arkhitektura*, 95.

[9] Borisova, *Russkaia arkhitektura*, 100–101, 277.

[10] Konstantin Ton, *Tserkvi, sochinennye arkhitektorom Ego Imperatorskogo Velichestva Professorom Arkhitektury Imperatorskoi Akademii Khudozhestv i chlenom raznykh akademii Konstantinom Tonom* (St. Petersburg, 1838), n.p.; E. I. Kirichenko, *Russkaia arkhitektura 1830–1910 godov* (Moscow, 1978), 117; Borisova, *Russkaia arkhitektura*, 93.

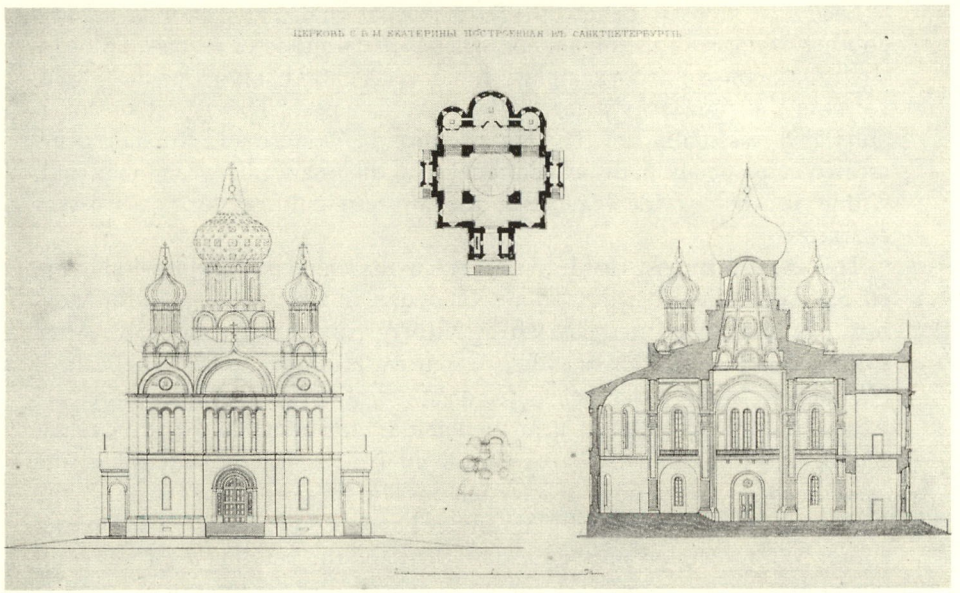

60. St. Catherine's Church, St. Petersburg. Architect, Constantine Thon.

tern, like the plans for the St. Catherine Church in St. Petersburg, and the Church of Peter-Paul at Peterhof. Others drew on the popular Russian national tradition of the tent church, with tent (*shater*) steeples, such as the project for a church for the horse guards' regiment. Finally, several of his churches combined cupolas or domes with tent belfries, in the manner of ancient Iaroslavl churches.[11] But the Byzantine style quickly assumed a specific meaning in Nicholas's mind: the five-cupola form of the Vladimir and Moscow Assumption cathedrals. The Building Ordinance of 1841 decreed this conception of Byzantine architecture as the official national style.[12]

The churches designed in Nicholas's reign combined the technological innovation of neoclassical architecture with stylistic elements of early Russian-Byzantine traditions. They typified the eclectic approach of Nicholas's reign, grafting national motifs onto a Western structure. The St. Catherine Church showed what came to be known as the "Thon style." The building, with its five-cupola form and tripartite wall division, bore a superficial resemblance to the five-cupola official style of the seventeenth century (fig. 60). The Muscovite exterior covered a large neoclassical structure—an enormous oblong nave and immense, elaborately decorated cupolas.[13]

[11] Konstantin Thon, *Tserkvi, sochinennye Konstantinom Tonom*; Konstantin Thon, *Proekty Tserkvei sochinennye arkhitektorom . . . Konstantinom Tonom* (St. Petersburg, 1844).

[12] I. Grabar', *Istoriia russkogo iskusstva* (Moscow, 1965), vol. 9, pt. 2, 261.

[13] Borisova, *Russkaia arkhitektura*, 102–105; A. Ialozo, "Konstantin Andreevich Ton," *Zodchii* 8 (1883), 1–10.

Nicholas's scenario defined the results as national. The "Thon style" was another example of metonymic or synecdochical mode of representation: a particular, constructed, exemplary case, here a church, stood for the whole, showing the monarchy's ties to the historical past. The aspect of contiguity also was significant. The juxtaposition of Western and Russian forms created an association, dispelled the sense of dissonance between them, and, within the official ideology, gave the Western cultural form a Russian character.

This effect was most visible in the principal architectural expression of the official nationality doctrine, Thon's Cathedral of Christ the Savior in Moscow. Thon inherited the task left by Vitberg (see above, chapter 8). After work on the construction of Vitberg's Sparrow Hills project had been halted, Nicholas announced that he wanted a cathedral "in ancient Russian taste." Accordingly, he chose a site near the Kremlin and assigned the work of designing the cathedral to Thon. Thon's final plans for the exterior of the cathedral were approved in 1832. Nicholas laid the cornerstone in 1837; the inscription on the stone read, "Alexander I bequeathed, Nicholas began execution." Construction started the next year, and the building itself was completed early in the reign of Alexander II, whereupon the interior decoration began. The dedication of the cathedral took place after the coronation of Alexander III in 1883.

The cathedral had the appearance of the five-cupola form of the Moscow-Vladimir style, but the resemblance was superficial (fig. 61). The most striking difference was in proportions. Nicholas abandoned Alexander's grandiose dreams of a gigantic temple to dwarf all other buildings. But he, too, associated grandeur with size, and as a monument to the 1812 war, its proportions had to be monumental. The intimate dimensions of Vladimir and even Moscow churches now were blown into huge dimensions to memorialize 1812 and the entire Russian past. The Cathedral of Christ the Savior, from the base to the cross, was about 340 feet. This meant that it stood more than a hundred feet higher than St. Sofia in Constantinople and was more than twice the height of Fioravanti's Assumption Cathedral, and more than three times that of the Vladimir Assumption Cathedral. It resembled a vastly enlarged and technically corrected modern replica of the old.[14]

Architectural historians have made clear the cathedral's structural similarity to neoclassical buildings. Arcades like those on the ancient churches of Vladimir decorated the external facades, but they adhered to the strictly symmetrical forms characteristic of the mid-nineteenth century. The building was patterned on the form of the St. Andrew's Cross, referring to the myth of Christian origin and universalistic destiny. The cupolas, except for their onion form, were more classical than Russian. The enormous central

[14] *Istoricheskoe opisanie postroeniia v Moskve khrama vo imia Khrista Spasitelia* (Moscow, 1869), 28; E. I. Kirichenko, "Arkhitekturnye ansambli Moskvy 1830–1860-kh godov," *Arkhitekturnoe Nasledstvo* (Moscow, 1976), 24:8; Louis Leger, *Moscou* (Paris, 1904), 78.

61. Cathedral of Christ the Redeemer, Moscow. Architect, Constantine Thon.

dome was typically neoclassical, while the four small cupolas were false, purely decorative in function. Their artificiality suggests the impulse to imitate one's own past, just as architects imitated Roman, medieval, and Renaissance models.[15]

Yet, Thon's contemporary rendering of a Russian original more than any other building expressed what was meant by "national." For Nicholas, there was no contradiction between national and universal; he saw Russian monarchy as the heir to the universal imperial tradition that he defended against the Turks. As such, it was the Russian Byzantine style that expressed Russia's adoption of the Byzantine tradition, which, unlike Western absolutism, according to the official nationality doctrine, had not begun its decline. If the spaciousness of the interior approached the vast interiors of Sofia in Constantinople more than the confined areas of a Russian church, this corresponded with Nicholas's urge to make the Russian emperor heir to the imperial heritage of Christendom. In this way, the architecture of the church erased the break between Petrine and Muscovite Russia and brought the history of early Russia into a universal perspective.

The wall paintings inside the cathedral and the bas-reliefs on the exterior

---

[15] Borisova, *Russkaia arkhitektura*, 106–108; Kirichenko, *Russkaia arkhitektura 1830–1910 godov*, 117–18; Hamilton, *The Art and Architecture of Russia*, 392.

walls illustrated the role of the orthodox church in the struggle for the unification of Rus' and the defeat of external enemies. If Vitberg's cathedral was meant to be a mystical symbol of Russia's providential victory, Thon's was a glorification of the church as the bearer of the divine word to Russia. The subjects for all the reliefs and most of the paintings were chosen by the metropolitan Filaret. The bas-reliefs, in neoclassical style, presented scenes from the Bible and Russian history that suggested parallels between sacred and military history. Reliefs on the south corners showed Abraham and David, returning victorious from battle. On the west corner, there were reliefs of Solomon and David with analogous scenes from Russia's past: St. Sergei blessing Dmitrii Donskoi before his departure on his campaign against the Tatars, and St. Dionysius blessing Minin and Pozharskii in 1612 before the struggle with the Poles. The Vladimir Mother-of-God, which had accompanied Russian armies at the battle of Borodino, was set in the arch above the central portal, while images of the sainted metropolitans of Moscow, Peter and Alexei, were placed in another arch. Both were depicted in scenes glorifying the Muscovite prince's construction of churches.[16]

The events of 1812 were portrayed in the cathedral's lower corridor. One painting showed an angel holding the Kazan Mother-of-God, which General Kutuzov venerated before departing to the army. Another showed the general's patron saint, Michael. The icon of St. Sergei of Radonezh was borne by an angel blessing Alexander I. A series of paintings illustrated the actual events of the fall and liberation of Moscow. They carried the message that victory in the Napoleonic war, the basis for Russia's present imperial grandeur, was the culmination of a pact between church and monarch sealed during the rise of Moscow.[17]

Thon's second major statement of nationality in architecture was not a church but his New Kremlin Palace. The palace, begun in 1838, complemented the restoration work that Nicholas initiated on the Terem Palace in the Kremlin and the St. Dmitrii Cathedral in Vladimir. The tsar scrutinized the initial plans for the palace, corrected the sketches, and made drawings indicating his own wishes.[18]

Thon's task was to fit a large, nineteenth-century palace into a seventeenth-century setting. Again he faced a problem of proportions, for the building was meant to hold the immense receptions and processions of the imperial court and yet had to fit with the modest size of the old Kremlin palaces and cathedrals. The palace contains approximately seven hundred rooms and halls, and the main facade is nearly four hundred feet long. The large St. George's Hall took up the right wing of the building, while the halls of the various

---

[16] *Khram khrista spasitelia v Moskve; chtenie dlia naroda* (Moscow, 1884), 1–13.

[17] Ibid., 41–42.

[18] S. P. Bartenev, *Bol'shoi Kremlevskii Dvorets; ukazatel' k ego obozreniiu* (Moscow, 1911), 24–25.

62. New Kremlin Palace, Moscow. Architect, Constantine Thon.
Drawing by N. Cherkasov.

orders filled the front and one side wing. These rooms had little national character; they were designed in a spirit of eclectic neoclassicism reminiscent of the Winter Palace after its 1837 restoration.[19]

Again it was the facade that introduced national motifs (fig. 62). Thon planned the tracery and arcade designs to blend with the churches and palaces around it. The reference now was not to Byzantine, but to seventeenth-century embellishments found on the old palace nearby.[20] The small windows decorated with surrounds of double arches and pendants add an odd medieval motif, borrowed from the frames on the windows of the Terem Palace, but, laid out symmetrically between colonnades on the vast facade, they give no hint of the organization of the rooms within. Thon's exterior dressed an opulent Petersburg palace in a national costume for Nicholas's festive appearances in Moscow.[21]

[19] Borisova, *Russkaia arkhitektura*, 114.

[20] G. Markova, *The Great Palace of the Moscow Kremlin* (Leningrad, 1981), pt. 2, 9.

[21] Ibid., pt. 1, 10–20; Borisova, *Russkaia arkhitektura*, 115–16; Kirichenko, "Arkhitektur-nye ansambli Moskvy," 8–10; A. Vel'tman, *Opisanie novogo Imperatorskogo dvortsa v kremle Moskovskom* (Moscow, 1851).

A National Anthem and a National Opera

During the first half of the nineteenth century nationality in music usually referred to the use of folk themes, and folk music suited neither Nicholas's tastes nor his imperial conception of nationality.[22] Nonetheless, he encouraged musical compositions that would glorify the monarch as the spirit of the nation. Such pieces assimilated distinctive Russian elements to the Western-type music he favored and dramatized his scenario with moving expressions of love for the tsar. The national anthem, "God Save the Tsar," and the opera, *A Life for the Tsar*, both written under his supervision, remained fixtures of tsarist ceremony until the demise of the empire. Their rousing strains created a national atmosphere around the monarch, a sense of uplift and inspiration identified later in the century as characteristically Russian.

A national anthem, which gave voice to the loyalty and devotion of subjects to their monarch, had an obvious appeal for Nicholas. It provided additional opportunities for exemplary demonstrations of the emotional bond between the people, represented by those present, and their sovereign. In the 1830s, France, Austria, and England had their own national anthems, and Russia used the English melody with Russian words. Nicholas told Benckendorff that the English music wearied him and that he regretted that Russia did not have its own anthem. After he returned from a journey to Austria and Prussia in 1833, he instructed a member of his suite, Flügel-Adjutant Alexei L'vov to compose a new anthem.[23]

A gifted musician, L'vov was a product of the military milieu of Alexander I and Nicholas I. The son of the director of the Court Cappella, he received his education at the Institute of Routes of Communication. He rose through the service as a military engineer, serving first under Arakcheev, then as an aide to Count Benckendorff in the corps of gendarmes. He accompanied Benckendorff with the imperial suite during the Turkish War, and, for the campaign, was decorated with the Vladimir ribbon and the medal of Anna "on the neck." Nicholas ordered L'vov then to accompany him on all his trips, as chief of clerical work in his suite. L'vov, in addition to being a reliable and presentable officer, knew Russian church music well, and Nicholas liked to sing hymns with him when they were away from home.[24]

At first, L'vov found the assignment daunting, especially when he thought of the "majestic" English anthem, the "original" French anthem, and the

[22] Malcolm Hamrick Brown, "Native Song and National Consciousness in Nineteenth-Century Russia," in Theofanis George Stavrou, ed., *Art and Culture in Nineteenth-Century Russia* (Bloomington, Ind., 1983), 63.

[23] A. F. L'vov "Zapiski," *Russkii Arkhiv* 2 (1884): 243; on national anthems as symbols, see Elisabeth Fehrenbach, "Über die Bedeutung der politischen Symbole im Nationalstaat," *Historische Zeitschrift*, vol. 213 (1971): 303–9, 315–20.

[24] A. F. L'vov "Zapiski," *Russkii Arkhiv* 2 (1884): 226–43; A. A. Bers, "Aleksei Fedorovich L'vov, kak muzykant i kompozitor," *Russkaia Starina* 102 (1900): 155.

"touching" Austrian anthem. In his memoirs, he told how he endeavored to write a song with broad appeal that could be used in all situations—"a majestic, powerful, emotional anthem, comprehensible to everyone, having the imprint of nationality, fit for the church, fit for the troops, fit for the people from the scholar to the ignoramus."[25] The sequence of his concerns is suggestive of the sources of his inspiration: he conceived of a melody that was solemn and ceremonial for church, parade ground, and, finally, the people of Russia.

L'vov took the text for the anthem from Zhukovskii's "Prayer of the Russian People," though in his memoirs he claims that Zhukovskii wrote the words to his music.[26] L'vov himself was a gifted composer of church music, and the anthem is very much a prayer set to music. Like most anthems of monarchies, it has the cadences of a hymn and surrounds the tsar's secular person with an aura of religious veneration. Yet, this is not a liturgical prayer that one would hear from the lips of a priest. It is the prayer of a poet, a secular address to the deity to protect the sovereign and Russia. The anthem expresses the servitor's deep attachment to the monarch. It calls on God to protect the tsar, powerful and sovereign, who rules for the glory of Russians and to strike fear into their enemies; to give long life to the tamer of the proud, the protector of the weak. God should protect the first power (*pervoderzhavnaia*), orthodox Rus', its armies, its peaceful leaders, and protectors of justice. Finally, the poet addresses Providence to grant blessings to Russia, the striving for good, humility in happiness, and patience in grief.[27]

The anthem delighted Nicholas and his family. At its first performance in 1833, by a chorus and two military bands, he demanded several reprises, and remarked, "C'est superbe." L'vov recalled an episode that occurred not long after the anthem's composition. The empress sat in her boudoir with the heir, her daughters at her side, and two courtiers in attendance. She and the children then softly began to sing "God Save the Tsar" as Nicholas descended the staircase. Nicholas wept at the strains of the anthem. He entered the room and ardently kissed his wife and children. "It is easy to imagine," L'vov wrote, "how we all were moved to the depths of our heart seeing true family happiness in the imperial house."[28]

Playing and singing of the stirring melody multiplied the opportunities to express adoration of the tsar and to give evidence of his symbolic presence. At its first public performance on Nicholas's name day, December 6, 1833,

[25] A. F. L'vov "Zapiski," *Russkii Arkhiv* 2 (1884): 243.

[26] The words of the anthem are identical, except for the first verse, to three verses of the "Prayer," which was published in 1818 as "Anthem sung by pupils of the St. Petersburg Gymnasium at the Public Examination." Considering the close relationship between the words and the music, it seems that L'vov may have had Zhukovskii's poem in mind when he composed the music (Zhukovskii, *Sochineniia* [St. Petersburg, 1885], 1:524).

[27] Zhukovskii, *Sochineniia*, 1:404–5; on the religious character of anthems in monarchies, see Fehrenbach, "Über die Bedeutung der politischen Symbole im Nationalstaat," 315–16.

[28] A. F. L'vov "Zapiski," *Russkii Arkhiv* 2 (1884): 247.

in the Bolshoi Theater in Moscow, the anthem was repeated three times. On Christmas Day of that year, military bands played it in all the halls of the Winter Palace, according to the emperor's own command. A week later, he decreed that it be performed at all parades and reviews, as well as at other ceremonial occasions.[29]

Public singing of the anthem in the theaters of Moscow became common soon after its introduction. The first public performance in St. Petersburg was on January 10, 1834, at the close of Catterino Cavos's opera, *Ivan Susanin*. The program declared that the entire troupe, accompanied by members of the regimental bands, would join in the new national anthem. A newspaper article of April 1834 told how an amateur concert concluded with rousing singing of the anthem, which was then repeated. The hymn spread quickly into the provinces so that by the heir's trip of 1837, he was greeted by its strains in most of the towns he visited.[30] Music, more than any other medium, translated political into personal feelings, identified the individual with the nation and the tsar. An article in *Severnaia Pchela* on May 3, 1840, declared that the anthem had "satisfied the needs of the Russian heart," by producing "an outpouring of national feelings." The music had a dual character, "religious and melancholy-tender." The anthem was "a musical study of the Russian character, *nationality*, in the full sense of the word."[31]

•

The composition of the opera *A Life for the Tsar* grew out of the discovery of the early seventeenth century as a period of national resurgence. The formation of a national militia and the convocation of an assembly of the land during "the time of troubles" provided a colorful theme for glorification of the Romanov monarchy. The most well-known works of this type took the form of exemplary tales of individual devotion to the throne. Michael Zagoskin's popular historical novel, *Iurii Miloslavskii or Russians in 1612*, presented a boyar, who broke his vow to the Polish king (induced by deception) to join the national militia in the cause of orthodoxy and a native tsar. The exemplary peasant was Ivan Susanin, the hero of Glinka's opera.

Unlike Iurii Miloslavskii, Ivan Susanin was an actual historical figure who lived on the Romanov estate of Domino in Kostroma Province. After the election by the Assembly of the Land, Michael Romanov was in hiding at the Ipat'ev Monastery in Kostroma from Polish detachments and brigands. Susanin fell captive to a band of Poles, who, according to the tale, tried to force him to reveal the whereabouts of Michael. Instead, he led his captors into the woods and paid with his life. When Michael ascended to the throne, he

---

[29] Ibid., 243–44; K. K. Shtakel'berger, "Russkii narodnyi gimn," *Istoricheskii Vestnik* 137 (1914): 118–19; Bers, "Aleksei Fedorovich L'vov," 147–48.

[30] Shtakel'berger, "Russkii narodnyi gimn," 121, 125–27.

[31] *Severnaia Pchela*, May 3, 1840: 389.

rewarded Susanin's son-in-law, Ivan Sobinin, and daughter, Antonida, and all their descendants with a deed to land in inheritance and an order that these lands in the village of Domino should be exempt from all taxation.[32]

The tale of a peasant sacrificing his life in the struggle against the invader enjoyed considerable popularity during the Napoleonic wars. But literature of an official character, loathe as it was then to suggest mass participation, avoided the subject. An extensive official album recommending heroic subjects for artists, published in 1807, included the major political figures of 1612 and 1613, but omitted mention of Susanin.[33] The opera *Ivan Susanin* by the court composer, Catterino Cavos, with a libretto by Prince Alexander Shakhovskoi, presents the Susanin story as a tale of peasant patriotism. Written in 1815, the libretto, in the genre of the "rescue opera," eliminates Susanin's death and supplies a happy ending, to match the outcome of 1812. A band of cossacks arrives at the last moment to save Susanin and avoid the note of tragedy. The opera thus dramatized the peasant's heroism but eliminated his sacrifice from the tale of national struggle.[34]

Susanin's exploit suited the sentimentalist imagery of Nicholas's scenario. One peasant's devotion stood for the devotion of all, became both the model and the substitute for the sympathies of the entire people. Emotion expressed on the individual level exemplified the political attitudes of a social group. Susanin was to the Russian peasants as Moscow was to all of Russia. The idea for the opera originated with Zhukovskii. Inspired by *Iurii Miloslavskii*, he had urged Zagoskin to write a novel about Susanin. The story, he remarked, had heroes "attractive to the imagination"; there would unfold "a picture bubbling with life." Zagoskin liked Zhukovskii's suggestion, but never wrote the novel. Four years later, when Glinka returned from abroad eager to write a national opera about the Russian past, Zhukovskii suggested the theme to him.[35]

Glinka's initial conception of the opera followed the patriotic myth of Susanin. His initial title was *Ivan Susanin, a Patriotic Heroic-Tragic Opera. . . .* He wanted the opening chorus to express the "strength and carefree fearlessness of the Russian people," and to express this sense musically, in "Russian measure and approximations that were drawn from rural subjects."[36] But the libretto was reshaped by the dictates of Nicholas's scenario into a story of personal devotion of the peasant to the tsar. It was written by a young Baron from Estland, Egor Rosen, who was then serving as the heir's

---

[32] "Potomki Susanina i selo 'Korobovo,'" *Prikhodskoe chtenie*, no. 35 (1913): 992.

[33] For a listing of the various versions of Susanin in the early nineteenth century, see Vl. Protopopov, *"Ivan Susanin" Glinki* (Moscow, 1961), 12–20.

[34] On the Cavos opera, see Protopopov, *"Ivan Susanin" Glinki*, 14; G. R. Seaman, *History of Russian Music* (New York, 1967), 146–48.

[35] Protopopov, *"Ivan Susanin" Glinki*, 16–17; M. I. Glinka, *Zapiski* (Moscow, 1930), 153–54.

[36] M. I. Glinka, "Pervonachal'nyi plan 'Zhizn' za Tsaria' 1835 g.," *Russkaia Starina* 30 (1881): 174–75.

personal secretary. Rosen was the author of several historical dramas in a conservative vein, none of them of note. Zhukovskii contributed the text of the final scene of the opera, including the famous "Glory" chorus. After the preparations were underway, Nicholas took a sympathetic interest in the opera. He appeared at rehearsals to make sure that Glinka was satisfied with the performers. Instructions came from high circles in the government, probably from Nicholas himself, to change the title from *Ivan Susanin* to *A Life for the Tsar*.[37]

Glinka accepted the revised conception of the opera with little ado. While he undoubtedly found the fulsome rhetoric of the libretto objectionable, Rosen adhered to Glinka's conception of the plot. As A. N. Rimskii-Korsakov remarked, Glinka's personality was essentially passive and amenable. He responded to prompting from others, then pursued his inspiration passionately in his music. After the success of the opera, he was not averse to accepting the position of director of the court choir.[38]

The result was an operatic masterpiece that presented the official view of the Russian peasant absolutely devoted to the person of the tsar. Glinka's opera lifts the tale of Susanin from the level of heroic adventure to tragedy. It was the scene in the woods and the death of Susanin that caught Glinka's imagination. Susanin's sacrifice is not only heroic, it is noble and reflects the selflessness of his person, which embodies the features of the official image of the peasant, generous, devoted, and passionate. The entire plot centers on the peasant's need for a tsar and the anguish the peasants felt when deprived of a tsar. The bond of the peasant and tsar is close and personal. In the first act, Susanin's daughter, Antonida, and her beloved, Ivan Sobinin, wish to wed. But there can be no wedding, Susanin insists, until there is a tsar.

> When the Lord gives us a Tsar,
> Then, immediately will be a happy wedding,
> A rich feast for all,
> We will rejoice for Rus'.[39]

The family and the army are the principal themes of the opera; both are absolutely devoted to the tsar. Susanin is the noble father figure, enforcing sacrifice on his family. Family feelings are entwined with the accession of Michael Romanov. In his initial plans, Glinka emphasized that the wedding should be a "family picture" (*Familiengemälde*). The chorus of peasants sings of Susanin's clan, that it may be happy in the Russian tsardom, and live "respected, beloved, and in honorable prosperity." There are expressions of affection in the family, and regret from Vania, the orphan boy, who lived with the Susanins and loves Antonida. The choruses, Glinka wrote, should

---

[37] Glinka, *Zapiski*, 176; A. A. Orlova, *Glinka v Peterburge* (Leningrad, 1970), 92; M. Livanova and V. Protopopov, *Glinka; tvorcheskii put'* (Moscow, 1955), 176.

[38] A. N. Rimskii-Korsakov, "Predislovie," Glinka, *Zapiski*, 8–17. For a full statement of the Soviet argument, see Protopopov, *"Ivan Susanin" Glinki*, 21–55.

[39] M. I. Glinka and Baron Rozen, *Zhizn' za Tsaria* (St. Petersburg, 1878), 17.

express "the quiet and sweet feelings of family happiness," in Russian measure in imitation of "ancient songs." When the peasants hear the news of the election, they ready the wedding feast and rejoice that Russia has a tsar.

The opera concludes with the fervent acclamation of the tsar, Michael, by the people of Moscow, projecting back to 1613 the exemplary national ceremony of Nicholaean Russia. The scene was written by Zhukovskii, but his text was modified considerably to suit the official character of the libretto. Crowds of people await the entry of the tsar on Red Square, on the roofs of surrounding buildings, and on the walls of the Kremlin. Michael himself does not appear in the original version, owing to the prohibition of portraying a Romanov tsar on the stage. The people sing the rousing "Glory" chorus, glory to Rus' and the tsar, and to the troops entering the city. After consoling Antonida and Sobinin for their loss, ensuring them that Susanin died for Rus', the chorus intones the final stirring verses of the opera, quoted in the epigraph to this chapter.[40]

Glinka's use of folk melodies and the folk idiom made *A Life for the Tsar* a truly national opera. Although composers such as Catterino Cavos and Alexei Verstovskii had drawn on folk themes to heighten the national motif of their opera, these had remained embellishments to fundamentally Western operatic structures. Glinka used folk melodies to create a national operatic idiom. Folk melodies provided the melodic structure and characteristic intonation for the music.[41] He thus succeeded in expressing a national idea and national musical themes in the form of the European grand opera.

Indeed, the folk melodies offended the tastes of many aristocrats and others unaccustomed to such breaches of classical form. Court circles were highly critical of music that drew on peasant melodies. It did not fit the elegant melodies they expected in grand opera. "Our serfs sing like the music we have heard here" was the comment of some in attendance. Bulgarin's famous characterization of the opera as "the music of coachmen" ("la musique des cochers") expressed the squeamishness about Russian music felt in high circles.[42] But the polonaise and mazurka from the opera soon became favorites at imperial balls.

Nicholas clearly approved of the theme and the libretto. His attitude to the music, however, is hard to determine. One eyewitness claimed that the emperor was in tears during the performance; a musician from the orchestra reported that he applauded only lightly, and since the Petersburg nobility took their sign from the royal box, their applause was also apathetic. Nicholas invited Glinka to the royal box for congratulations after the performance, a signal honor. But then he proceeded to criticize the scene in the

[40] Glinka and Rozen, *Zhizn' za Tsaria*, 76–82; Zhukovskii, *Polnoe sobranie sochinenii*, 4:24–25.

[41] On the importance of the folk element in Glinka, see Seaman, *History of Russian Music*, 171–76; Richard Taruskin, *Opera and Drama in Russia as Preached and Practiced in the 1860s* (Ann Arbor, Mich., 1981), 2; Protopopov, *"Ivan Susanin" Glinki*, 163–241.

[42] Ibid.; Orlova, *Glinka v Peterburge*, 101–3.

63. Ivan Susanin monument, Kostroma. Sculptor, Vasilii Demut-Malinovskii.
Drawing by V. Vasnetsov.

woods for showing the murder of Susanin on stage. The composer received a present of a thimble of topaz set in three rows of diamonds, having a value of four thousand paper rubles, as he recounts with considerable pride in his memoirs.[43] In any case, Glinka's opera became a fixture in the Imperial Opera's repertory, performed on major state occasions through the century.

Susanin's devotion to Michael was also commemorated by a monument erected in the town of Kostroma funded by donations from the nobility of the province. Nicholas approved the proposal in 1838, and the monument, by Vasilii Demut-Malinovskii, was completed in 1851 (fig. 63). The sculptor effectively rendered the official notion of the relationship between peasant and tsar. A column separates a figure of the peasant and a bust of tsar Michael wearing the Monomakh cap. The tsar and the peasant belong to different universes, but are bound by political faith. Michael, innocent and detached, looks into the distance. Susanin kneels at the base, devout and humble. The peasant shows emotion, what the sculptor described as the "spiritual transport of the patriot sacrificing himself for Russia." But it is not Russia, but his tsar, that the peasant worships, and it is this personal devotion that the statue conveys.[44] Susanin's ultimate heroism is in his death, and the relief shows the Poles, their swords lifted, ready to slaughter the helpless peasant. The act of violence, which perturbed Nicholas on the stage, is placed right before the eyes of the observer, as the central fact of the story. A peasant sacrifices his life for his tsar, while the savage act of the enemy justifies the strength of that bond and the remorselessness necessary to confront the enemy, the Poles.

FINAL VISITS TO MOSCOW

With the revolutionary events of 1848, the significance of Moscow as a symbol of the nation increased. The revolution only confirmed the sense that Europe was infirm and corrupt, while Russia, having escaped insurrections, remained strong in the defense of religion and monarchical legitimacy. The crushing of the Hungarian Revolution in June and July of 1849 thrust Nicholas forward as the defender of thrones and the opponent of liberation throughout Europe. The spread of revolution raised his fears that the infection might reach Russia. He wrote to Prince I. F. Paskevich in March 1848, "In general one cannot foresee anything; only God alone can save us from ruin."[45] He embarked on a series of measures, ranging from terminating deliberations on redefining relations between serfs and landlords, to the

---

[43] Glinka, *Zapiski*, 178–79, 462; *Russkaia muzykal'naia gazeta* (January 1897): 215–16.

[44] The sketch of the statue by Victor Vasnetsov is from *Vsemirnaia Illiustratsiia* (1872): 317. On the statue, see I. I. Shmidt, *Vasilii Ivanovich Demut-Malinovskii* (Moscow, 1960), 113–14; V. Ia. Lukomskii and G. Ia. Lukomskii, *Kostroma* (St. Petersburg, 1913), 308–9. The statue was demolished in the 1930s.

[45] Lincoln, *Nicholas I*, 296.

tightening of censorship restrictions. Steps were taken to increase the importance of religion in the university curriculum, and the teaching of philosophy was shifted to the theological faculty. Police surveillance intensified, and superiors in governmental offices were empowered to dismiss politically suspicious subordinates without trial or explanation. Travel abroad required the emperor's personal approval, which he was increasingly loathe to grant.

Fear of the West brought more strident assertions of Russia's national mission. Although Russia faced threats neither of invasion nor revolution, Nicholas's manifesto of March 14, 1848, proclaimed that "following the example of Our Orthodox forefathers, after invoking the help of God Almighty, we are ready to meet our enemies, wherever they may be, and not sparing Ourselves, We shall, in indissoluble union with our Holy Rus', defend the honor of the Russian name and the inviolability of Our borders." He thus proclaimed his solidarity with the nation, using the pre-Petrine term *Rus'* for Russia. The manifesto closed, "God is with us! Take heed, peoples, and submit for God is with us."[46]

The distinction between Holy Russia and Europe, monarchy and revolution, god and godlessness, took on increasingly messianic overtones during Nicholas's visits to Moscow in March and April 1849 and in August 1851. He used these appearances to reaffirm his connection with the nation's past by appearing at its national shrines. Closeness to the Muscovite past gave the European emperor something of the Muscovite character, distinguishing him from the West. The writer, Alexander Vel'tman, described Nicholas's visit of 1849 in the journal, *Moskvitianin*, as part of a providential design, beginning with the rise of Moscow in the thirteenth century: "When destruction and dissension have befallen the benighted West . . . we are under the shelter of the Creator of strength, well being and glory." He recalled the prophesy of the metropolitan, Peter, that the city of Moscow would triumph over its enemies and that Grand Prince Ivan I's clan would increase.[47]

But the fervent national rhetoric had perils. It stirred the expectations of Slavophile intellectuals like the Aksakovs for an autocracy purified of Western trappings and for a true union between tsar and people rather than ceremonial demonstrations of connectedness. Official writers, like the historian, Michael Pogodin, and Stephen Shevyrev, lost some of their restraint in describing the visit.[48] To them, the unity of tsar and people meant the rediscovery of cultural antecedents, the unity of the Petrine and Muscovite traditions. They were particularly inspired by the Kremlin procession and the roar of the throng when Nicholas bowed from the Red Staircase.

---

[46] *PSZ*, no. 22,087, March 14, 1848; Kornilov, *Kurs Istorii Rossii*, 2:101–2; Riasnovsky, *Nicholas I and Official Nationality in Russia*, 5.

[47] Alexander Vel'tman, "Osviashchenie novogo moskovskogo dvortsa v kremle," in the section "Moskovskaia letopis'," *Moskvitianin* (April 1849), 149–50; A. Vel'tman, "Torzhestvennyia prazdnestva, v novom imperatorskom kremlevskem dvortse," in "Moskovskaia letopis'," *Moskvitianin* (May 1849), 16. An abbreviated version of this article appeared in *Russkii Invalid*, no. 82 (1849).

[48] Riasanovsky, *Nicholas I and Official Nationality*, 137–38.

Pogodin described Nicholas's appearance at the Kremlin in 1849 in an article published in *Moskovskie Vedomosti*: "The square bubbles with people." All gazes fixed on the new palace where the imperial flag signaled the appearance of the emperor and empress. The bells of the Assumption Cathedral tolled loudly, then silenced, then began again. The officials and the metropolitan appeared.

> General anticipation. A sudden deafening ring, thunderous, solemn, filling the heart with harmonious joy. The tsar appeared on the porch! There he is, there he is! All heads were bared. . . . He bowed to the people; Hoor—ah! Hoor—ah! Hoorah! He has come down from the porch, taller than everyone, more visible than everyone. Behind him his firstborn son, the Heir, born in Moscow, is among us, his young sons . . . Hoorah! Hoorah! Hoorah![49]

Pogodin then recounted conversations that he ostensibly overheard in the crowd. The members of a carpenters' cooperative (*artel'*) vied with one another in expressing their love for the tsar. One said that he would stop the tsar in order to talk to him and "take a look." Another exclaimed, "By God's grace" ("*Nu spodobil Bog*").[50] The people, Pogodin explained, had an "organ" lacking in the educated groups in society, "a second vision," "a mysterious premonition," that enabled them to understand the truth and to worship the authority of their tsar. It was this feeling that distinguished Russian from European society, which was now shaken. A brief article Pogodin published in *Russkii Invalid* affirmed that the unity shown in Moscow was a display of the unity of estates in "holy Rus' tranquil and safe" behind the tsar and the imperial family.[51] Shevyrev expressed this feeling in a poem that appeared in the newspaper *Moskovskie Vedomosti* on the tsar's arrival in Moscow.

> The Tsar in the Kremlin before the shrines,
> And the people around him . . .
>
> . . . .
>
> The West! in storms and calm
> You look here:. . . . . .
>
> . . . .
>
> Here is the union of Tsar and people.[52]

The announced purpose of the journey to Moscow was the dedication of Thon's Kremlin palace. To dramatize the religious significance of the dedication, the ceremony was scheduled for Easter Sunday—the first observance of Easter in Moscow by an emperor since Paul's coronation in 1797. The emperor, accompanied by the imperial family, the suite, and other notables, proceeded through the ancient Hall of Facets to the small Church of the

---

[49] Nikolai Barsukov, *Zhizn' i trudy M. P. Pogodina* (St. Petersburg, 1896), 10:221–22.
[50] Ibid., 10:222.
[51] *Russkii Invalid*, April 29, 1849: 362.
[52] Barsukov, *Zhizn' i trudy M. P. Pogodina*, 10:224–25, 227–28. Ellipses in text.

Savior in the Terem Palace. After the mass, Filaret led the procession down forty steps into the sumptuous rotunda of the new palace. With priests carrying the altar cross and icon of the Don Mother-of-God, the procession moved through the halls of the palace, while the chorus sang "Christ has risen," and the clergy blessed each hall with holy water. Filaret intoned a prayer of blessing in the hall of St. Andrew.[53]

Vel'tman was the author of romantic novels and works on historical antiquities and archaeology. His description presented the ceremony in the heightened emotional tones of the sentimental scenario. While "the whole family of the Russian people" observed Easter Sunday, the heart of the realm, Moscow, "beat joyously, celebrating the Radiant Holiday with the Father and Mother of the Fatherland and their Blessed Family." He portrayed the preparations for the midnight mass as a magnificent spectacle, inviting aporia: "Description is weak before reality." The new palace was illuminated. "The Palace Giants—Grenadiers, like resurrected Russian *bogatyri*—stood guard at the entrances." Rows of carriages arrived; the people filled the two palaces and the squares. The notables of the government, courts, and military appeared as ornaments of a scene, as they awaited the imperial procession in the halls of the palace.[54]

The principal dramatic moment of Vel'tman's account was the Easter mass in the Church of the Savior, Tsar Alexei's private church built next to the Terem Palace for the "Icon not made by Human Hands." The historical and familial traditions were united. "It has been a long time since this ancient temple of the prayers of the *Tsar's Family* . . . has resounded with a similar Liturgy in the presence of *The Tsar Himself*, the *Tsaritsa*, and *the Tsar's Family*." Vel'tman used the early Russian title of "Tsaritsa" for the empress. The ringing of the bells and the shouts of "Christ has arisen" filled the air with joyous and grateful sentiment. "It seemed that a sea of sound ran between heaven and earth, the ground shook from the festive thunder of guns from the heights of the Kremlin. The Tsar exchanged the greeting 'Christ has risen' with the Tsaritsa and his family."

Vel'tman described greetings from the bemedaled members of the State Council, generals, court ladies, and those participating in the construction of the palace. After the service, the procession moved through the Catherine Hall into the Hall of the Cavalier Guards. There stood the front row of Cavalier Guards, "giants, in parade attire, in the helmets with soaring, two-headed eagles on top." At four in the morning, the ceremonies closed with prayers for the health and long life of their majesties. Vel'tman had little to say about the palace itself, which he described as "this elegant and magnificent Ancestral Home, built according to his [Nicholas's] own idea." He cited the emperor's statement that it "completely corresponds to the buildings

---

[53] On the procession, see A. F. L'vov "Zapiski," 3 (1884): 88–89, as well as the Vel'tman and Barsukov accounts cited above.

[54] Vel'tman, "Osviashchenie," 150

that surround it, which are sacred for us, and with those memories of past centuries and of the great events of the History of the Fatherland connected with those buildings."[55]

Nicholas used building and architecture to establish a sense of continuity with early Russia. Moscow intellectuals longed for such connection with the past. To mark the event, the historian, I. E. Zabelin, published a history of Moscow palaces, in which he lamented their neglect after Peter and the frequent fires that gutted parts of the Kremlin. Pogodin expressed his views in an essay, "Sketches from the Sojourn of the Tsar's Family in Moscow," which did not pass the censorship.[56] He stressed the striking change of Nicholas's image as he moved from the new palace to the old. In Thon's palace, he appeared as the European emperor. "Everywhere there is gold, silver, marble, silk! What columns, cornices, ceilings, floors and decorations! What an expanse enclosed between these walls! The gaze is lost in the endless perspective! Wealth, magnificence, glitter, glory!" He described the court, the brilliant uniforms, stars and medals, accoutrements of the European emperor rather than of the Russian tsar. Nicholas had to leave the new palace to capture his national persona.

> But are the Russian Tsar and the European Emperor two people? No, one! From the Vladimir Hall it is only a few steps to the Hall of Facets and the Red Staircase. Once he opens the door to the people, or even opens the window of Tsar Alexei Mikhailovich, all of Moscow, and with her all of Russia will see and hear him and answer, "The European Emperor is again the Russian Tsar."[57]

For Pogodin, the change of surroundings transformed the tsar's image and showed that two persons could inhabit the same body, exemplifying two cultures. The Easter ceremonies also endowed Nicholas with a Russian character. The procession through the halls and, most of all, the Easter greetings of "Christ has risen," "even in the St. George Hall," inspired the historian with a sense of the emperor's national feeling. This sense of a bond with the people was reinforced when Pogodin heard the crowds on the Kremlin square shout to Nicholas, "Christ has risen," and when he saw the emperor exchange the greeting with the people outside the manege.[58]

The celebrations in the days following the dedication placed Nicholas and his family in a national setting. Vel'tman's account made clear that the imperial family was the center of attention. The event had to be recorded, he wrote, in the annals of Moscow so as not to forget the "reverential transports of national feeling—to see and to hear the *Tsar*, to feast one's eyes on the good-hearted *Tsaritsa*, on the touching (*umil'naia*) beauty of *Her Children*; to delight at this model of family love and piety."[59]

[55] Ibid., 151–54.
[56] Barsukov, *Zhizn' i trudy M. P. Pogodina*, 10:230–31.
[57] Ibid., 10:234–35.
[58] Ibid., 10:222, 234–37.
[59] Vel'tman, "Moskovskaia Letopis,'" pt. 1 (May 1849): 18–19.

The final display of Russianness was a great masquerade in national costumes given by the governor-general of Moscow, Count Arsenii Zakrevskii, at his mansion. A masquerade of noblemen in Russian costume was hardly an innovation. From Peter's time, masquerades allowed the elite to play at appearing Russian. It gave them an occasion to relax their primary, official identity by relinquishing Western clothing, and assuming an ephemeral secondary role as native Russians. But in the midst of the national pretense of Nicholas's scenario, such a change of attire took on ambiguous meanings.[60] For nationalist and Slavophile intellectuals, the masquerade unveiled the primary identity of the Russian noblemen, enabling them to throw off their Western attire and manners and reveal their true selves.

The sense of masquerade as truth was set forth in a glowing account that Shevyrev published in the pages of *Moskvitianin*. A noble couple, wearing authentic Russian costumes, represented each of the fifty-two provinces of Russia. Before each couple marched a little boy, also dressed in native costume, carrying the seal of the particular province. The boys delighted the onlookers. Shevyrev marveled, "The children, the flower of the Russian nobility with the lovely charm of their age and their Russian costume, embellished the procession and gave its grave importance a sense of kindness, tenderness and joy." Numerous Russian historical figures also appeared, the *bogatyr'* Dobrynia, Ivan Susanin, Pozharskii, Ermak. The procession was opened, however, by a scene of Queen Elizabeth and her court. Shevyrev believed it completely appropriate that the English court of the sixteenth century should open a Russian masquerade. "Humble Russia yielded place to England, knowing that England marched first on the path of universal education."[61]

Songs and round dances followed the procession. "Modest wives and maidens placed their hands on the shoulders of majestic boyars and handsome young fellows," Shevyrev wrote. The display appealed to the Russian hearts of the court nobility. "At the sight of this spectacle, more than one shoulder under a heavy general's epaulet rose in pride from a familiar Russian feeling, and, of course more than one heart felt a Russian tremor."

After the procession they formed two lines, marched toward their majesties, their standards aloft. The little boy carrying the seal of Ufa Province, and dressed in Persian costume, was Peter Kropotkin. The anarchist thinker recalled the moment in his memoirs: "At a given signal all standards were lowered before the Emperor. The apotheosis of autocracy was made most impressive: Nicholas was enchanted." Shevyrev described Nicholas's expression: "The severe and thoughtful eyes of our Tsar cheered up at this Russian

---

[60] See Boris Uspenskii's remarks on the reversal of the values of Russian and foreign dress under Peter and the use of Russian dress in the eighteenth century as a form of amusement (B. A. Uspenskii, "Historia sub specie semioticae," 112).

[61] S. Shevyrev, "Russkii prazdnik dannyi v prisutstvie ikh imperatorskikh velichestv 9ogo i 11ogo aprelia," "Moskovskaia Letopis'," *Moskvitianin*, pt. 1 (April 1849): 26–28.

festival, and his bright smile expressed the happiness of His Russian heart."[62]

Thus, in Shevyrev's account, the sighs, tremors, and smiles of sympathy were sufficient demonstration of the Russian heart of both tsar and nobility. The aesthetic bond signified a national union, a theme emphasized the next evening, when the masquerade was repeated, at Nicholas's request, at the Moscow Noble Assembly. Shevyrev described the event as an expression of the emotional bond between the Russian nation and their tsar. At the end, their majesties displayed "warm joy" at the sight of the "external beauty of our Fatherland and at the striving of all of us for the idea of [the Fatherland] to unite with [*Their Majesties*]."

Shevyrev summoned Russians to heed Russia's call "to return to our Fatherland." "The time has come: not only in an outer but in an inner manner." Russians were not renouncing Western education. "But we will not follow it servilely. We are aware that we have *our own* special, cherished, forces, which have been given to us by God, History, and our land, and which we should not crush or distort by servile imitation."[63]

The display of Russian dress and sentiments encouraged Slavophile intellectuals in Moscow to hope for a return of the monarch to national culture and ways. Sergei Aksakov wrote: "The tsar has often delighted me with his glorious deeds. It seems that he never has come so close to the people as now, and the people with love, warmly and noisily, speak of him without interruption. This talk, like a stream of spring water flows across all of Rus'. Glory be to God!"[64] His son, Constantine Aksakov, along with several other Slavophiles, took the national sentiments further and appeared in public wearing a beard and Russian dress. For Constantine Aksakov there could be no discrepancy between a man's apparel and his heart. "Appearance makes, one might say, the tone of life. And 'it's the tone that makes the music' ('c'est le ton qui fait la musique')—the structure of life, that is what is most important."[65]

The response was not long in coming. On the first day of the masquerade, a circular from the Ministry of the Interior, issued to provincial marshalls of the nobility, announced that "the tsar is displeased that Russian noblemen wear beards." It went on to explain that in the West, beards signified "a certain type of ideas." "We do not have this here," it asserted. The tsar, it

---

[62] Shevyrev, "Russkii prazdnik dannyi," 28, 37; Barsukov, *Zhizn' i trudy M. P. Pogodina*, 10:242–50; L'vov "Zapiski," bk. 3, 89; Peter Kropotkin, *Memoirs of a Revolutionist* (Garden City, N.Y., 1962), 17–19. Kropotkin mistakenly recalls the year of the masquerade as 1851 and the seal he bore as Astrakhan rather than Ufa as the list appended to Shevyrev's account indicates. He also seems to have thought the designation as a page was a special favor to him rather than to all the boys who participated.

[63] Shevyrev, "Russkii prazdnik dannyi," 30–31.

[64] Barsukov, *Zhizn' i trudy M. P. Pogodina*, 10:238.

[65] Ibid., 10:251–52.

concluded, "considers that beards will interfere with noblemen's elective service."[66]

In Nicholas's Western frame of mind, beards signified not Russians but Jews and radicals. The official view identified the nation with the ruling Western elite, and the suggestion that there was another, contradictory measure of nation in the peasantry or the past intimated rebellion. Nicholas's shows of national spirit were meant to preserve, not to narrow the distance between the autocratic, noble elite and the ruled, to dramatize obedience as a spiritual quality of the nation. Authenticity, truth, other versions of the national past jeopardized the monologic universe of the imperial myth. The beard symbolized a coming together of elite and people in a national culture whose features were not defined by the autocratic power.

•

The visit to Moscow in August 1851 on the twenty-fifth anniversary of Nicholas's coronation carried an even clearer political message. A tumultuous reception at the Iberian Chapel was described in an article of one Mikhailov in *Severnaia Pchela*, which was reprinted in the illustrated journal, *Russkii Khudozhestvennyi Listok*. The crowds swarmed through the street awaiting the arrival at the Iberian Chapel. All the conversations Mikhailov reported were statements of absolute loyalty to the tsar and the system of autocracy and serfdom. The people were not gifted with eloquence but intelligence and a "pure heart not spoiled by false teachings." They uttered such phrases as, "Without a Tsar it is impossible to live for a minute"; "Everywhere a chief is necessary"; "Without lords we can't get along. . . . and the Tsar too can't get along without the lords, and the Tsar makes the lords, and God gives us a Tsar." An anonymous poem evoked the past of Moscow, which the author imagined, with all the tsar's ancestors resurrected before him. The people streamed to the Kremlin, the magnates from the Palace of Facets, and the tsar knelt before God in the Assumption Cathedral.

> Moscow! Moscow! Saints' benediction
> Prophesies your triumph . . .
> Stand firm, a precept for the people
> Of submissiveness before Tsars, and faith in the Divinity![67]

The procession from the Assumption Cathedral had now taken on central importance as a tradition hallowing the emperor's links with the pre-Petrine past and his remoteness from current European politics. An article in *Russkii Khudozhestvennyi Listok* traced the history of the procession from early Russia until Nicholas's appearance at the Kremlin on August 22, 1851,

[66] Ibid., 10:250–51; Knabe, "Rimskaia tema," 266.
[67] Mikhailov, "Moskva, 19-go Avgusta 1851 goda," *Russkii Khudozhestvennyi Listok* 31 (1851): 2; Barsukov, *Zhizn' i trudy M. P. Pogodina*, 9:502–3.

on the twenty-fifth anniversary of his coronation. The Kremlin, it began, had been the center of the religious life of the Muscovite tsar. On holidays, he appeared on the Red Staircase before his people in brilliant processions. After the capital moved to St. Petersburg, the love of the Russian people for their tsar only grew warmer. "Moscow people met their tsar, pressing toward him, like children to a father." The Kremlin square could be called "the open-air reception chamber of the Russian Tsars." "Russian Tsars admitted, without distinction, all their subjects and received the greetings of their love along their path to the sacred cathedrals, where the thanks and prayers for the salvation of Russia rose to Him on High."[68]

The author thus created a mythical past to substantiate an abiding bond between tsar and people. He described Alexander I's exultant reception at the Kremlin on July 12, 1812, adding features of Nicholas's scenario, such as the bow to the people, and "tears of tender pity (*slezy umileniia*)" glistening in Alexander's eyes. The rapt account of Nicholas's procession in 1851 placed him at the culmination of a history of demonstrative love that the people of Russia had for their emperor, which was personified in the people in the Kremlin. When Nicholas appeared, the square resounded with shouts of "rapture." The procession of the imperial family moved to the Assumption Cathedral "in the midst of blessing and joyful tears." On his return, their majesties stopped at the Red Staircase, and responded to the rapturous cries, with a "bow of love." Then the people "formed a single living wall, and the feelings of all of Russia echoed in the wholehearted hoorah with which Moscow responded to the tsar's bow." The author remarked that the spectacle could awaken memories of the past, but there was no room in "the Russian heart" at that moment: "So attractive was the present, so was everyone filled with feelings of reverent love for the *Sovereign* and *His* August House, joining in one wholehearted prayer for the well-being of *Tsar* and Russia!" An engraving of the scene, by the editor of the journal, Vasilii Timm, accompanied the text (fig. 64).[69]

Indeed, the past had little to do with these feelings, which were very much the product of the rhetoric and political narrative of Nicholas's scenario. Nicholas had inaugurated his reign with the first performance of the bowing as a ceremonial act. He had brought the people into imperial ceremonies, allowing them, too, to show acclamation for the monarchy whose rule had been challenged. By 1851, the ritual had become still more important, for it symbolized the distinction between the Russian people and the peoples of the West, who did not see their monarchs bow. As a result, the new ceremony had been turned into a tradition, showing the adoration of the people of Russia, personified by the people of Moscow, for their sovereigns, immanent in the nation's history. But their sovereigns still retained the external attri-

[68] B. F. "O tsarskikh vykhodakh," *Russkii Khudozhestvennyi Listok*, no 1 (1852): 1.
[69] Ibid., 2.

64. Kremlin procession of August 22, 1851. Lithograph by Vasilii Timm.

butes of the Western elite, the conquerors, and the pathos of the scene came from the mutual attraction of opposites, the grateful acceptance of the conquerors by the conquered. In this respect, the scene did recall the Russian past, though not so much the religious processions of Muscovy as the legendary summons to the princes beyond the sea to rule and bring order to the warring Slavic tribes of the ninth century.

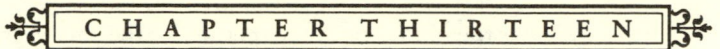
The Dissolution of the Scenario

He died like a worthy Descendant of Peter the Great and at the same
time as a true son, as a sincere member, of the Christian Church. The
unswerving strength, we dare to say even the sangfroid of the Tsar and
Warrior, the thought of his duties as Monarch, duties so grave, whose
weight was so burdensome, which he had sacredly fulfilled during the
thirty years he ruled his country, finally his tender love for the family by
blood, and his other, immense family, Russia. At this final moment,
everything fused into a single sentiment that surpassed,
embraced, and sanctified everything: Faith.

—*D. N. Bludov*, The Last Hours of the Life of Emperor Nicholas I[1]

The Persistence of Myth

From the fifteenth through the nineteenth centuries, Russian monarchs elevated their rule by the invocation and presentation of myth. In the eighteenth and nineteenth centuries, they were portrayed in an epic context and
credited with real or fictive achievements that justified the scope of their
power. Rulers and elite shared mythic expectations for each new ruler regardless of that monarch's personal attributes or disposition. These expectations shaped the attitudes of the heirs to the throne toward their future
powers and obligations. They grew up surrounded by ceremony and symbols indicating that it was their destiny to embody the cultural and political
grandeur of the Russian state. The education of the heirs, whatever the particular plans and goals of the tutors, was shaped by this setting. Western
ideals were to be realized in their purest, absolute form by a monarch working prodigies, sustaining the myth by displaying exemplary wisdom, courage, and beauty. These expectations perpetuated the notion of the sacred and
unlimited character of the power they would inherit.

The myth took on a life of its own, precluding the forms of elevation that
had evolved in the West. Michael Cherniavsky observed that the sophisticated legal distinction between the immortal body politic and the mortal
body of the ruler, a characteristic that was present to a greater or lesser
degree in various Western states, never took hold in Russia.[2] Kantorowicz's

---

[1] [D. N. Bludov], *Poslednie chasy Imperatora Nikolaia Pervogo* (St. Petersburg, 1855), 5;
[D. N. Bludov], *Les dernières heures de la vie de l'empereur Nicolas I* (Vienna, 1855), 4.
[2] Cherniavsky, *Tsar and People*, 84–91.

classic work showed that the notion of the perpetuity of the sovereign office, the immortality of the body politic, created a legal entity superior to the will and characteristics of individual monarchs.[3] In Russia, the monarchs themselves had to display the transcendent features of office by performances constantly reaffirming the myth. The troubled efforts of Paul I to establish an orderly succession in imitation of Western practices is a case in point. Such a law threatened his own and his successors' personal preeminence. A dynastic succession became rooted only during the reign of Nicholas I when the emperor mythologized the imperial family as the moral emblem of the empire.

The nobility shared in the charisma of otherness and dominance that surrounded their sovereign and joined in the performances of the myth. They participated in court ceremonies and celebrations and adopted their sovereign's notions of rule, as well as his literary, artistic, and architectural tastes. While not all members of the nobility shared the monarch's favors or predilections, those in the inner magic circle of power who did reflected his glory. The success of this effort is indicated by the deep and continuing personal attachment of Russian noblemen to the emperor into the nineteenth century, their persistent reverence for his image. This was a significant factor inhibiting movements toward the political autonomy of the Russian nobility and the development of a sense of professional autonomy in the administration and army during the nineteenth century.[4]

As a result, ceremonies borrowed from the West carried a mythic significance that they lacked or had lost in Europe: they demonstrated an abiding connection between the symbolic and real power of the Russian sovereign. The spectacles of the ruler's heroism and transcendence in the court and on the drill field celebrated the glories attained by monarchical rule—the prosperity of the realm, and, most concretely, the maintenance and expansion of the empire. At the same time, the flourishing of the empire gave substance to an imperial vision presented and extolled at court.

In Russia, the imperial myth took the form of an ongoing dramatization of the ruler's foreignness. In their scenarios of power, Russian emperors and empresses assumed varied guises—Roman emperor, Olympian god or goddess, Prussian king, leader of Christendom, angelic presence, doting paterfamilias. They claimed membership in the company of European monarchs by borrowing Western signs and images of sovereignty. The nobility also assumed foreign identities, adopted foreign styles, and boasted foreign lineages.

Such borrowing, to be sure, characterizes many monarchies with preten-

---

[3] On the concept of the perpetuity of the throne in the West, see Ernst H. Kantorowicz, *The King's Two Bodies: A Study in Medieval Political Theology* (Princeton, N.J., 1957), 383–450.

[4] For summaries of the discussions of the persistence of personal ties in the tsar, see Marc Raeff, "The Bureaucratic Phenomenon of Imperial Russia, 1700–1905," *American Historical Review* 84 (April 1979): 399–411; Daniel Orlovsky, *The Limits of Reform: The Ministry of Internal Affairs in Imperial Russia, 1802–1881* (Cambridge, Mass., 1981), 102–3; Wortman, *The Development of a Russian Legal Consciousness*, 270–78.

sions to power and prestige. The distinguishing feature of Russian symbolic development was the continuous and imperative nature of such borrowing, even after the empire had become a great and influential power. The appropriation and display of foreign signs in Russia carried a special meaning that it lacked or had lost in Europe. Foreignness established symbolic distance between the ruler and the ruling elite and the subject population. The constant appropriation of foreign symbols reaffirmed this distance and demonstrated the autonomous and unlimited power attached to the imperial office. The open, and often flamboyant displays of Byzantine or Western culture accentuated the inferior quality of the native population, who lived outside the heroic history of the ruling dynasty. The ceremonies of power—the coronation, the European advent, the court fête, and the parade—elevated the monarch in settings resembling distant realms: they were spectacular demonstrations of otherness, confirming the foreign and therefore exalted and sovereign character of the ruler and the elite.

The myth of foreignness set certain irresistible imperatives for each emperor or empress: imperial power had to be shown as advanced—humane or progressive in terms of current Western conceptions of monarchy. It had to appear unconstrained by local or private interests—to be unlimited. It had to appear universal, ruling extensive realms like the most glorious sovereigns of antiquity and the present. The myth itself dictated the defense of autocratic prerogatives, for there could be no grounds so compelling as to curb powers necessary to fulfill the epic demands of the imperial office. Formal legal definition of the extent of imperial power came only with the *Digest of Laws* in 1832.[5]

The rhetoric and imagery of the French Revolution posed a serious dilemma for imperial political imagery. The revolution elevated the people as the bearers of the sacral traits of rule, making them the creators of history, participants in their own myth, and united in an entity defined as the nation. The notions of popular sovereignty and the nation not only threatened the heroic image—the monarch with his elite as the only historical actors—but they also complicated the meaning of Westernness and foreignness. There were now competing models of governmental organization in the West, and absolute monarchy no longer appeared as the bearer of progress. Russian monarchs would continue to present themselves as exemplars of Western culture and rule, but their model was no longer the most advanced form of European government.

---

[5] The definition strains to force the image of the supreme and transcendent emperor into a legal frame. Article 1 of the *Digest of Laws* stated, "The Russian Emperor is an autocratic (*samoderzhavny*) and unlimited (*neogranichennyi*) Monarch. Obedience to His supreme authority (*verkhovnaia vlast'*) not only from fear but from conscience is the command of God Himself." The words *autocratic* and *unlimited*, the jurist N. M. Korkunov concluded, were synonymous and used only for greater "clarity." Indeed, the redundancy was an emphasis necessary to express a power that transcended individuals, institutions, traditions, and social groups (N. M. Korkunov, *Russkoe gosudarstvennoe pravo* [St. Petersburg, 1909], 1:210–13).

In Russia, the imperial myth precluded the very institutional arrangements that were becoming the practice in mid-nineteenth-century Europe. Prussian and Austrian rulers, while resisting constitutions, adapted to the times. They delegated responsibility to a chancellor or prime minister and increasingly left government in the hands of the administration. The separation of office from person assisted this change, for it allowed the throne to retain a symbolic role even when the ruler did little actual governing. In Russia, the obligations of the myth discouraged even such limited formal delegation of responsibility. The elevation of the monarch depended on his possession of absolute power. The nobility shared in power not by institutional means, but by drawing close to the person of the sovereign and participating in the scenarios that displayed him or her as sovereign. Until the Decembrists dedicated themselves to Western revolutionary ideals, there were few nobles who sought to curtail the emperor's power. Even Alexander I's young friends hoped to advance Russia along the path of reform by strengthening, not restricting, the emperor's authority.

Nicholas I renewed the image of conqueror, but now as lone and embattled defender of monarchy against the pernicious forces of revolution. Ceremony and rhetoric accommodated the new principles of popular sovereignty and nation. Nicholas presented nationality as an acceptance of domination by the Westernized elite, and Western humanitarianism as a display of domestic and personal virtue. The city of Moscow gave frequent ceremonial confirmation of the Russian people's devotion to their Westernized sovereign. Nicholas's eclectic scenario combined the universal and the native, the neoclassical and the romantic. In this way, he reconstituted the monologic universe that had been disrupted by Alexander I's wavering commitments. Art, music, and architecture confirmed and ornamented his scenario, creating a world insulated from reality and the exercise of administrative authority.

For the myth to retain its sway, the performance had to fulfill two conditions. First, it had to glorify Western values that commanded the allegiance of the elite. Second, it had to be sustained by military success, confirming the claims of imperial domination. By the end of Nicholas's reign, his scenario had failed on both counts. The influence of Western doctrine and the growth of educated cadres in the bureaucracy created a group of officials who looked to Europe for new models of government to deal with the ills of the existing system. Changes in the diplomatic balance and the new political forces unleashed by the revolutions of 1848 deprived Russia of a position of dominance and left it isolated on the international scene.

The officials who looked to the West, paradoxically, were a product of Nicholas's effort to introduce an educated officialdom drawn from the nobility. Nicholas hoped that trained loyal officials would be effective instruments of his will and would faithfully implement the laws codified at the beginning of the 1830s. A Western-type officialdom thus would help him realize his image of all-seeing sovereign supervising every level of the absolutist state. Contrary to his intentions, these officials began to look to the West as a model of legality, openness, and progressive change. In Prussia and other German states, they saw monarchies that had introduced liberal legal and administrative reforms and were beginning to heed the wishes of their subjects. They began to develop a notion of the professional dignity of the law that did not comport with the idealization of personal power expressed in official presentations.[6]

In the last years of Nicholas's reign, the sophisticated elite close to the imperial family—those traditionally most sensitive to current measures of foreignness—became increasingly skeptical of the presentations of the court. The "charm, acting on the imagination," which Tiutcheva described, turned into ennui with the preoccupation with trivial details of the imperial family's life. Tiutcheva wrote: "The immense significance and grandiose proportions that the most simple events like dinners, strolls, family meetings take on demand so much time, attention, and energy that there is nothing left for more serious matters. . . . Everything unplanned, and consequently, every living and vital impression, is erased from their life."[7]

In his last years, Nicholas himself betrayed diminishing confidence in the efficacy and popularity of his rule and began to show his father's characteristic suspiciousness of his servitors. The French ambassador, the Marquis de Castelbajac, observed in 1853: "The Emperor Nicholas has within himself the qualities of Peter the Great, Paul I and a medieval knight. But, as the years have passed, it is now the qualities of Paul I which rise more and more to the fore."[8] Nicholas transformed his father from an embarrassment, whose reign was to be passed over in silence, into an exemplar of strength and authority, whose vision had secured the greatness of Russia. The occasion to present this transformation was the dedication ceremony for I. P. Vitali's statue to the emperor Paul at Gatchina, on August 1, 1851, which Nicholas Grech described in *Russkii Khudozhestvennyi Listok*.

Paul stood "in a position of command, as if leading an army," Grech wrote. His bearing expressed "firmness, decisiveness, self-confidence." His face revealed "intelligence and nobility of soul."[9] Russians would see on the statue "the face of the Tsar who on the throne introduced love for order, respect for everything worthy of respect, strict justice and impartiality, the stern punishment of vice, the unlimited generosity for merit and virtue." The foreigner would also approach the statue and revere the Russian tsar who began a new period in the political history of Europe. With Paul's reign, Russia became the champion of international morality, the protector of

---

6 On this group in the nobility, see W. Bruce Lincoln, *In the Vanguard of Reform: Russia's Enlightened Bureaucrats, 1825–1861* (De Kalb, Ill., 1982), 41–76; Wortman, *The Development of a Russian Legal Consciousness*, 197–234.

7 Tiutcheva, *Pri dvore dvukh imperatorov*, 1:36, 95, 121.

8 Lincoln, *Nicholas I*, 291.

9 Nikolai Grech, "Otkrytie pamiatnika Imperatoru Pavlu Petrovichu v Gatchine," *Russkii Khudozhestvennyi Listok*, no. 32 (1851): 1.

peoples. During the eighteenth century, Russia had extended its boundaries and subdued foes by material force.

> But at the close of [the eighteenth century], Russia soared even higher, becoming not the conqueror, but the defender of peoples, using its frightening power for the magnanimous, selfless, assistance of the weak against the strong, of the oppressed against the oppressors, of the right against the perfidious, of the believers against the impious.

This Christian idea, Grech claimed, had first arisen in "the knightly soul of Emperor Paul." Although Paul's own efforts had not succeeded, Alexander had defended the idea in a war for the independence and well-being of Europe. Nicholas took up the cause again and "crushed the hydra of rebellion and dissent within the borders of an ally and preserved Europe from the disasters of anarchy and mutiny." Paul had thus become an example of "magnanimity and self-sacrifice, unheard of in history."[10]

The ceremony, performed on the holiday of the "Coming of the Virgins," on August 1, had the character of a private family event, given a broader meaning only by its publication and dissemination in the press. The Russian people, invoked so grandiloquently in previous ceremonies, were not mentioned in the description. Unlike the Alexander I dedication, there were no spectators. Nicholas's confessor, Bazhanov, led a procession of the cross to bless the waters in the Gatchina pond, followed by the Pavlovsk Guards' Regiment and several grand duchesses. The procession then moved to the monument, which the priests blessed with holy water, to the shouts of "Hoorah!" and cannon salutes from the artillery. After the religious procession returned to the palace, the guardsmen marched by the tsar.

Nicholas emphasized the dynastic significance of the ceremony by assigning his grandsons, the grand dukes Nicholas Aleksandrovich, age eight, and Alexander Aleksandrovich, age six, prominent roles in the ceremony. Vasilii Timm's lithograph makes the two boys the center of attention (fig. 65). In the foreground, the Pavlovsk guardsmen stand stiff and hold their heads high, displaying their characteristic pug noses. The emperor and his suite, including the heir, on horseback, look on from the rear. The slim figure of Nicholas Aleksandrovich occupies the center of the picture, leading a platoon. The tiny Alexander Aleksandrovich stands at attention with a rifle at his side, dwarfed by the large figures, and the monument. Thus three generations paid homage to the progenitor of the dynasty.[11]

The 1850s witnessed the erosion of Russia's prestige and influence abroad. The crushing of the Hungarian Revolution in 1849 saved the throne of the Austrian emperor, but it also identified Russia as the principal foe of progressive change and gave the monarchs of Central Europe an uncomfort-

---

[10] Ibid.
[11] Ibid.

65. Dedication of statue to Paul I, Gatchina, August 1, 1851. Lithograph by Vasilii Timm.

able sense of dependence on Russian armies. The Prussian and Austrian monarchs reached compromises with public opinion, leaving Russia alone among the great states as an absolute monarchy based on serfdom. Rather than the savior of Europe and Western Christian values, the Russian empire took on the aspect of a backward, obscurantist state, more Eastern than Western, whose might stemmed from a disregard rather than a defense of humane values. Even writers who were sympathetic to Russia, like Balzac, saw the Russians as different from Europeans, resembling Asians in their preference for obedience over freedom.[12]

When Russia's allies sought their interests apart from the system of alliances that was the legacy of the Congress of Vienna, Nicholas lost one of the key marks of authority in Russia—the claim to embody the universal values of monarchy. The Crimean War, which began in March 1854, brought the

[12] Honoré de Balzac, *Oeuvres complètes* (Paris, 1940), 40:654, 674–80. These were remarks in his "Letter on Kiev," written in 1847 during a visit to Russia.

moment of truth. Nicholas blundered into a war, determined to impose conditions on Turkey, only to find himself deserted by his erstwhile allies, Austria and Prussia. He had regarded the young emperor Franz Joseph as a son, had treated him sympathetically and defended his empire in 1849. Nicholas turned Franz Joseph's portrait to the wall, and wrote above it, in German, "the ingrate."[13]

The hypnotic power of Nicholas's scenario had blinded him to the true state of the Russian administration and armed forces. The illusion of omnipotence and omnipresence had disguised political and economic stagnation just when Europe had begun to develop rapidly and the dynamic effects of industrial development and freedom were making themselves felt. The police system of supervision, rather than assisting his all-seeing eye, had begotten elaborate paper pretenses of control that hid incompetence and peculation. At the same time, the triumphalist myth that had dominated military thinking since 1812 had led to a smug disregard of the problems of the Russian military. The excessive reliance on parade-ground training, the emperor's meddling in the conduct of war, the inadequate recruitment, the shortness of funds, the backwardness of technology had eluded the attention of the emperor and those near him.[14]

The setbacks in the Crimean War gave immediate notice that the vaunted might of Russia was illusory and that its government and economy lagged behind the West. Michael Pogodin now circulated a series of memoranda accusing the government of betraying Russia's national interest and pursuing a foreign policy that was too *European* in its objectives. The historian took the government to task for being insufficiently national, calling attention to a fundamental flaw in the official nationality doctrine. He claimed that the government had impoverished the people, and neglected education and the condition of the orthodox church, to suppress a revolutionary movement that threatened the West but that was alien to Russian historical tradition. His memoranda received a sympathetic hearing from many important figures in St. Petersburg, including the heir.[15]

Pogodin's memoranda, of course, did not mention the emperor, but the metonymic imagery of Nicholas's scenario identified him completely with the system. With the news of his setbacks, his own conviction that the autocracy was the embodiment of the nation also weakened. The daughter of Dmitrii Bludov, Lady-in-Waiting Antonina Bludova, wrote in her memoirs that the defeat meant "The destruction of everything that seemed so firmly founded, so sacredly established." Those close to Nicholas described him as suffering through sleepless nights, prostrating himself before the church, and, at each dispatch, weeping "like a child." In his last hours, he refused to

[13] Tiutcheva, *Pri dvore dvukh imperatorov*, 1:194–95.

[14] For an extended discussion of the problems of Nicholas's military leadership, see Fuller, *Strategy and Power in Russia*, 250–60.

[15] M. P. Pogodin, *Sochineniia* (Moscow, 1874), 4:245–71; A. A. Kornilov, *Obshchestvennoe dvizhenie pri Aleksandre II* (Paris, 1905), 4–6.

hear reports from the Crimea. Indeed, there were few at court who failed to realize that the Nicholaean system had outlived its time.[16]

THE DEATH OF AN EMPEROR

With the aura of invincibility gone, members of the elite began to question the system openly and place a value on breaking through image and pretense to find the truth. One of the first critiques of the old system came from the governor of Courland Province, Peter Valuev, who was a scion of an old noble family and a chamberlain in the imperial court. Valuev's memorandum of 1855 pointed to the very practices of ceremonial idealization and formality as the source of weakness and evil. He identified the distinctive feature of the Russian system as "a ubiquitous absence of truth." Paper formalities covered everything with falsehood. It was impossible to tell "what is real from what is merely apparent, justice from injustice or half-justice." Myth was merely a pretext for hypocrisy. "On the surface, there is glitter, beneath rot."[17]

It was Alexander II who would attempt to refurbish the Petrine myth with a new scenario adapted to the political universe of mid-nineteenth century Europe. The "hope" of Russia, dedicated to everything his father stood for, had to repudiate basic principles of his father's rule. But in the framework of a cult of dynasty, he also had to maintain an illusion of continuity. The initial statements of his reign intimated a scenario that, in contrast to those of the previous century, minimized the break with the previous reign and made the new reign seem a continuation of the old. Alexander's accession manifesto of February 18, 1855, declared his solidarity with his predecessors, with the pointed omission of his grandfather, Emperor Paul.

> Just as our Dear lamented Parent devoted all His Efforts, all the hours of His life, to the labors and cares for the welfare of His subjects, so We . . . take the sacred vow to have as a single goal the well-being of Our Fatherland. Guided and protected by Providence, which has called us to this Great service, may we establish Russia at the highest level of might and glory, and may we realize the constant wishes and intentions of Our August predecessors, Peter, Catherine, Alexander the Blessed, and our Unforgettable Parent.[18]

Nicholas's passing, like Alexander I's, was commemorated with an elaborate funeral procession. *Russkii Khudozhestvennyi Listok* published a detailed account of the funeral procession and lithographs of the ceremonies (fig. 66).[19] The extensive official description began with a detailed history of

[16] N. Ia. Eidel'man, *Gertsen protiv samoderzhaviia; Sekretnaia politicheskaia istoriia Rossii xviii–xix vekov i Vol'naia pechat'* (Moscow, 1973), 10–11.

[17] P. Valuev, "Duma russkogo," *Russkaia Starina* 70 (1891): 354.

[18] *PSZ*, no. 29,043, February 18, 1855.

[19] *Russkii Khudozhestvennyi Listok*, nos. 11, 12, 15 (1855).

66. *Funeral Procession of Nicholas I.* Lithograph by Vasilii Timm.

previous imperial obsequies, an indication that the celebration of the emperor's death had become a principal ceremony of dynasty, like the coronation.[20] A separate volume contained illustrations of all the various groups in the funeral procession to the Cathedral of Peter and Paul. For the first time, a newly devised Romanov coat-of-arms appeared in the procession, indicating that the royal house now had a historical emblem like Russian noble families. The device, composed from seventeenth-century Romanov personal emblems, consisted of a griffon holding a raised sword, set on the breast of the imperial Russian eagle.[21]

The presentation of Nicholas I's death transformed his image so as to preserve the dynastic tradition and maintain the aura of his transcendence. The eulogistic accounts created a new Nicholas, heroic, noble, and self-sacrificing, but devoid of the pretense of infallibility and omnipresence. It maintained the mystique of Russian monarchy, expressing the sense that the emperor would introduce significant institutional and social reforms without endangering his sacred prerogatives. The descriptions of Nicholas's

[20] *Opisanie pogrebeniia blazhennoi pamiati imperatora Nikolaia Igo s prisovokupleniem istoricheskogo ocherka pogrebenii tsarei i imperatorov vserossiiskikh i nekotorykh drugikh evropeiskikh gosudarei.*

[21] Ibid., 78–79; V. K. Lukomskii, "Gerb doma Romanovykh," in *Letopisi i litsevoi izbornik Doma Romanovykh* (Moscow, 1913), 2:109–14; Baron M. A. Taube, "K istorii Gerba Doma Romanovykh," *Gerboved* (1913): 109–17.

death prepared the way for the rapprochement with liberal society that began in the second half of the 1850s.

The accounts were issued, in part, to dispel rumors that Nicholas had ended his own life by taking poison.[22] *Russkii Khudozhestvennyi Listok* and *Severnaia Pchela* printed reports of Nicholas's illness and death.[23] The official presentation of the death was the work of Dmitrii Bludov, the loyal servitor who had hailed Nicholas's coronation, now an aged statesman. Bludov described Nicholas's death in a slim volume, *The Last Hours of Nicholas I*, which was published simultaneously in French, German, and English, as well as Russian. As the epigraph to this chapter indicates, Bludov used the deathbed scene to dramatize the emperor's secular and religious virtues.

Even as his illness progressed, Bludov wrote, the emperor allowed himself no indulgence, "devoting himself to work, day and night, and stealing his hours of rest from sleep." Nicholas's simple, austere study in the Winter Palace, depicted in a plate at the rear of the French volume, symbolized his self-denial. His camp bed, on which he purportedly preferred to sleep, is at the center, a striking symbol of his spirit of Spartan dedication. The furniture is sparse—besides the bed, a plain desk, a table in the rear, a small couch, a few tables and chairs.[24] Timm's lithograph in *Russkii Khudozhest-vennyi Listok* shows him on his deathbed, an image of modest self-denial (fig. 67).

Bludov portrayed Nicholas's courageous confrontation of death as a display of superhuman selflessness and dedication to duty in the company of his loving kin. When describing Nicholas's final conversation with Alexandra, Bludov invokes the sentimental mode: "In their tenderness, they spoke gently to each other. The conjugal affection which had embellished their long union, still ruled this last conversation." After Nicholas received the last sacraments, Alexandra embraced him.

> "Do you love me always as in the past?"
>
> "Do I love you!" he replied. "How could I not love you? The day we saw each other the first time, my heart told me that there is the Guardian Angel for your whole life and this prophesy of the heart has been fulfilled."[25]

[22] Eidel'man has discussed and analyzed the principal materials describing the circumstances of the death. The entries in the court journal, the *Kamer-fur'erskii Zhurnal*, were altered for reasons that remain unknown. Suspicions that he took poison arose almost immediately, given grounds by his deepening depression and dread of dying unawares. Charges were advanced that his personal physician, Martin Mandt, gave in to his requests for poison. The illegal press seized on this interpretation and published materials lending it credence. Eidel'man concludes that it is impossible to draw a definitive judgment on the basis of the available evidence (Eidel'man, *Gertsen protiv samoderzhaviia*, 9–20; Tiutcheva, *Pri dvore dvukh imperatorov*, 1:189).

[23] *Russkii Khudozhestvennyi Listok*, no. 12 (1855). This issue also reprints the *Severnaia Pchela* account.

[24] Bludov, *Poslednie chasy*, 7; *Les dernières heures*, 5.

[25] Bludov, *Poslednie chasy*, 10–11; Bludov, *Les dernières heures*, 7.

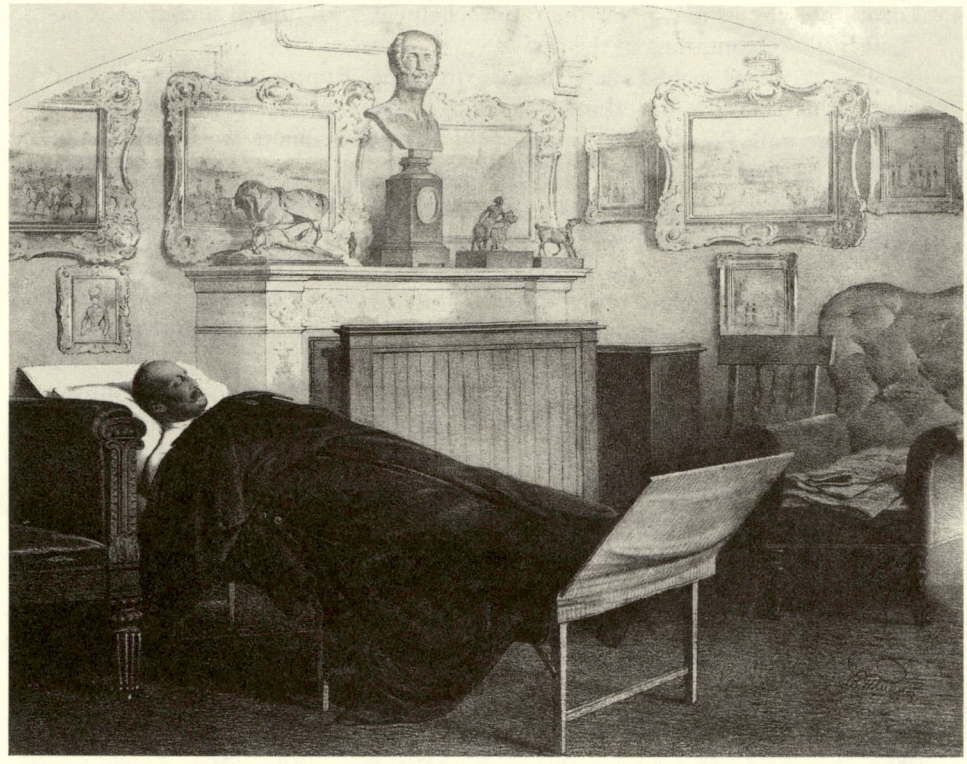

67. *Nicholas I on His Death Bed.* Lithograph by Vasilii Timm.

At the final parting, Nicholas pronounced his belief in the primacy and immortality of the family. He bade farewell to his wife and children and delivered his oft-repeated words to the heir, "Serve Russia."[26] Alexandra sobbed, "Why can't I die with you!" Nicholas replied, gesturing to the children, "You must live for them," then said to the children, "Live always, as at present, in the close union of family love."

Bludov's text combined glorification of dynastic continuity with a justification for change. After parting with his confidants, Nicholas called Alexander to his bedside. His last words to his son contained a poignant confession of defeat:

Having taken upon myself everything difficult and painful, I would have wished to leave you an Empire that was peaceful, happy, and flourishing. Providence has decided otherwise. Now I will pray for Russia and for you, who are, after Her, what I love above all in this world.[27]

[26] Bludov, *Poslednie chasy*, 18, 23; Bludov, *Les dernières heures*, 12, 15.
[27] Bludov, *Poslednie chasy*, 18–22; Bludov, *Les dernières heures*, 12–15. The account in *Russkii Khudozhestvennyi Listok* describes Nicholas's parting with his ministers *after* bading

Alexander II would follow the pattern of breaking with the previous reign, but with his father's blessing and with the claim, and probably the conviction, that his reforms were in accordance with his father's wishes. He strove to take on the image of a monarch championing Western ideals that Nicholas's scenario had condemned as alien to the Russian body politic. A creature of the Russian court, adoring of his father's person and principles, he sought to reconcile autocracy with the liberal model of mid-nineteenth-century Europe. His scenario, the tragic finale of the myth of foreignness, will be the subject of the first part of the second volume of this study.

---

farewell to Alexander. It also is more detailed and cites Alexander's parting words in response to Nicholas's confession of failure: "If I was destined to lose you, then I am certain that you will pray to Him for Russia, for all of Us, and for His sacred help to bear so heavy a burden." Then Nicholas responded, "Yes I always prayed to Him for Russia and all of You, and I will pray for Russia there" (*Russkii Khudozhestvennyi Listok*, no. 12 (1855).

BIBLIOGRAPHY

ARCHIVAL SOURCES

Bakhmeteff Archive. Columbia University. Kiselevskii fond.
Finnish National Archive. "Delo kantseliarii findliandskogo general-gubernatora."
Hesse State Archive. Maria Aleksandrovna Collection.
TsGIA. Fond 516—*Kamer-Fur'erskii Tseremonial'nyi Zhurnal*.
TsGAOR. Fond 678—Alexander II.
      Fond 641—Maria Aleksandrovna.

PRINTED SOURCES

Alef, Gustave. "The Adoption of the Muscovite Two-Headed Eagle: A Discordant View." In G. Alef, *Rulers and Nobles in Fifteenth-Century Muscovy*. London, 1983.

Alekseeva, M. A. "Brat'ia Ivan i Alexei Zubovy i graviura petrovskogo vremeni." In *Rossiia v period reform Petra I*, ed. N. I. Pavlenko. Moscow, 1973.

———. "Zhanr konkliuzii v russkom iskusstve kontsa XVII–nachala XVIII veka." In *Russkoe iskusstvo barokko; Materialy i issledovaniia*. Moscow, 1977.

———. *Graviura petrovskogo vremeni*. Leningrad, 1990.

Alexander I. *Perepiska Imperatora Aleksandra I s sestroi, Velikoi Kniaginei Ekaterinoi Pavlovnoi*. St. Petersburg, 1910.

Alexander, John T. "Favourites, Favouritism and Female Rule in Russia, 1725–1796." In *Russia in the Age of Enlightenment: Essays for Isabel de Madariaga*, ed. Roger Bartlett and Janet Hartley. New York, 1990.

———. *Catherine the Great: Life and Legend*. New York, 1989.

Alexandra Fedorovna, "Pis'ma Imperatritsy Aleksandry Fedorovny k V. A. Zhukovskomu, 1817–1842." *Russkii Arkhiv*, no. 1 (1897): 493–512.

———. "Imperatritsa Aleksandra Fedorovna v svoikh vospominaniiakh." *Russkaia Starina* 88 (1898): 5–60.

Androsov, S. O. "Skul'ptura letnego sada." In *Kul'tura i iskusstvo Rossii XVIII veka*, 44–58.

———. *Zapadnoevropeiskaia skul'ptura v Rossii petrovskogo vremeni; avtoreferat dissertatsii*. Moscow, 1990.

Anisimov, E. V. *Podatnaia reforma Petra Velikogo*. Leningrad, 1982.

———. *Rossiia v seredine XVIII veka; bor'ba za nasledie Petra*. Moscow, 1986.

———. *Vremia petrovskikh reform*. Leningrad, 1989.

Annenkova, A. K. "Vospominaniia A. K. Annenkovoi, rozhdennoi Merder." *Nasha Starina*, no. 4 (1915): 380–91.

Apostolidés, Jean-Marie. *Le roi machine; spectacle et politique au temps de Louis XIV*. Paris, 1981.

Ariès, Phillippe. *L'homme devant la mort*. Paris, 1977.

Arndt, E. M. *Entwurf der Erziehung und Unterweisung eines Fürsten*. Berlin, 1813.

Baehr, Stephen L. "'Fortuna Redux': The Iconography of Happiness in Eighteenth-Century Courtly Spectacles." In *Great Britain and Russia in the Eighteenth Century: Contacts and Comparisons*, ed. A. G. Cross. Newtonville, Mass., 1979.

——. "From History to National Myth: *Translatio imperii* in Eighteenth Century Russia." *Russian Review*, vol. 37, no. 1 (January 1978): 1–13.

——. *The Paradise Myth in Eighteenth Century Russia: Utopian Patterns in Early Secular Russian Literature and Culture.* Stanford, Calif., 1991.

Baiburin A. K., and A. L. Toporkov. *U istokov etiketa.* Leningrad, 1990.

Bakhtin, M. M. *The Dialogic Imagination.* Austin, Tex., 1981.

Baklanova, N. A. "Otrazhenie idei absoliutizma v izobrazitel'nom isskusstve pervoi chetverti XVIII v." In *Absoliutizm v Rossii (XVII–XVIIIvv)*, 492–507.

Balzac, Honoré de. *Oeuvres complètes.* Vol. 40. Paris, 1940.

Bardon, Françoise. *Le portrait mythologique à la cour de France sous Henri IV et Louis XIII; mythologie et politique.* Paris, 1974.

Baron, Samuel, ed. *The Travels of Olearius in 17th Century Russia.* Stanford, Calif., 1967.

Barsov, E. V. *Drevnerusskie pamiatniki sviashchennogo venchaniia tsarei na tsarstvo v sviazi s grecheskimi ikh originalami.* Moscow, 1883.

Barsukov, Nikolai. *Zhizn' i trudy M. P. Pogodina.* 22 vols. St. Petersburg, 1888–1910.

Bartenev, S. P. *Bol'shoi Kremlevskii Dvorets; ukazatel' k ego obozreniiu.* Moscow, 1911.

Bell, Catherine. *Ritual Theory, Ritual Practice.* New York, 1992.

Belozerskaia, N. "Tsarskoe venchanie v Rossii." *Russkaia Mysl'* 5 (1883): 1–48.

Bennet, Douglas Joseph, Jr. "The Idea of Kingship in Seventeenth Century Russia." Unpublished dissertation. Harvard University, 1967.

Bennett, Helju Aulik. "*Chiny, Ordena,* and Officialdom." In *Russian Officialdom; the Bureaucratization of Russian Society from the Seventeenth to the Twentieth Century*, ed. Walter McKenzie Pintner and Don Karl Rowney. Chapel Hill, N.C., 1980.

Benois A., and N. Lanceray. "Dvortsovoe stroitel'stvo Imperatora Nikolaia I." *Starye Gody* (July–September 1913): 172–97.

Berezina, V. G. *Russkaia zhurnalistika vtoroi chetverti XIX veka (1826–1839 gody).* Leningrad, 1965.

Bergholz, Friedrich Wilhelm von. *Dnevnik kammer-iunkera Berkhol'tsa.* 4 vols. Moscow, 1857–1860.

Berman, B. I. "Chitatel' zhitia." In *Khudozhestvennyi iazyk srednevekov'ia.* Moscow, 1982.

Bers, A. A. "Aleksei Fedorovich L'vov, kak muzykant i kompozitor." *Russkaia Starina* 102 (1900): 145–68.

Besançon, Alain. *Le tsarévitch immolé; la symbolique de la loi dans la culture russe.* Paris, 1967.

Beyrau, Dietrich. *Militär und Gesellschaft im vorrevolutionären Russland.* Cologne, 1984.

Biaudet, Jean Charles, and Françoise Nicod, eds. *Correspondance de Frédéric-César de la Harpe et Alexandre Ier.* Neuchatel, 1978.

Bil'basov, V. A. *Istoriia Ekateriny Vtoroi.* 2 vols. London, 1895.

Black, J. L. *Citizens for the Fatherland: Education, Educators and Pedagogical Ideals in Eighteenth Century Russia.* Boulder, Colo., 1979.

Blagoi, D. D. *Dusha v zavetnoi lire; ocherki zhizni i tvorchestva Pushkina.* Moscow, 1977.

Bludov, D. N. "Dva pis'ma gr.D. N. Bludova k supruge ego." *Russkii Arkhiv*, no. 5 (1867): 1046–47.

————. *Les dernières heures de la vie de l'empereur Nicolas I.* Vienna, 1855.

————. *Poslednie chasy Imperatora Nikolaia Pervogo.* St. Petersburg, 1855.

Bobrovnitskaia, I. A., et al. *Gosudarstvennaia oruzheinaia palata.* Moscow, 1988.

Bogdanovich, M. I. *Istoriia tsarstvovaniia Imperatora Aleksandra I i Rossii v ego vremia.* 6 vols. St. Petersburg, 1869.

Bogoslovskii, M. M. *Oblastnaia reforma Petra Velikogo.* Moscow, 1902.

————. *Petr I; Materialy dlia biografii.* Vol. 1. Leningrad, 1940.

Bolotov, A. *Zhizn' i prikliucheniia Andreia Bolotova opisannye samim im dlia svoikh potomkov, 1738–1795.* 4 vols. St. Petersburg, 1870–1873.

Börckel, Alfred. *Hessens Fürstenfrauen von heilige Elizabeth bis zur Gegenwart in ihren Leben und Wirken dargestellt.* Giessen, 1908.

Borisova, E. A. *Russkaia arkhitektura vtoroi poloviny XIX veka.* Moscow, 1979.

Borzin, B. F. *Rospisi petrovskogo vremeni.* Leningrad, 1986.

Bozherianov, I. *Detstvo, vospitanie i leta iunosti Russkikh Imperatorov.* St. Petersburg, 1914.

Bozherianov, I. N. *Zhizneopisanie Imperatritsy Aleksandry Fedorovny, suprugi Nikolaia I.* St. Petersburg, 1898.

Brown, Malcolm Hamrick. "Native Song and National Consciousness in Nineteenth Century Russia." In *Art and Culture in Nineteenth-Century Russia,* ed. Theofanis George Stavrou. Bloomington, Ind., 1983.

Brückner, A. *Istoriia Ekateriny vtoroi.* 3 vols. St. Petersburg, 1885.

————. "Puteshestvie Imperatritsy Ekateriny II v poludennyi krai Rossii v 1787 godu." *Zhurnal Ministerstva Narodnogo Prosveshcheniia,* pt. 2, vol. 162 (1872): 1–51.

Bruk, Ia. V. *U istokov russkogo zhanra; XVIII vek.* Moscow, 1990.

Brumfield, William Craft. *A History of Russian Architecture.* Cambridge, 1993.

Brunner, Otto. "Vom Gottesgnadentum zum monarchischen Prinzip." In *Das Königtum.* Lindau, 1956.

Brunon, Raoul. "Uniforms of the Napoleonic Era." In *The Age of Napoleon: Costume from Revolution to Empire, 1789–1815.* New York, 1989.

Burke, Kenneth. *A Grammar of Motives and a Rhetoric of Motives.* Cleveland, Ohio, 1962.

Burke, Peter. *The Fabrication of Louis XIV.* New Haven, Conn., 1992.

Bushkovitch, Paul A. "The Epiphany Ceremony of the Russian Court in the Sixteenth and Seventeenth Centuries." *The Russian Review,* vol. 49, no. 1 (January 1990): 1–18.

Butler, William E. "The *Nakaz* of Catherine the Great." *American Book Collector,* vol. 16, no. 5 (1966): 19–20.

Butovskii, Ivan. *Ob otkrytii pamiatnika Imperatoru Aleksandru Pervomu.* St. Petersburg, 1834.

Bychkov, A. "O svad'be Imperatora Petra Velikogo s Ekaterinoiu Alekseevnoiu." *Drevniaia i novaia Rossiia* 3 (1877): 323–24.

Cameron, Averil. "The Construction of Court Ritual: The Byzantine *Book of Ceremonies.*" In *Rituals of Royalty: Power and Ceremonial in Traditional Societies,* ed. David Cannadine and Simon Price. Cambridge, 1987.

Cannadine, David. "Splendor out of Court: Royal Spectacle and Pageantry in Modern Britain, c. 1820–1977." In *Rites of Power: Symbolism, Ritual and Politics since the Middle Ages,* ed. Sean Wilentz. Philadelphia, 1985.

Cassirer, Ernst. *The Philosophy of the Enlightenment.* Boston, 1951.

Catherine II, *Skazka o tsareviche Khlore.* St. Petersburg, 1787.

Chakirov, Nikita, ed. *Tsarskie koronatsii na Rusi.* New York, 1971.

Chartier, Roger. *Les origines culturelles de la révolution française.* Paris, 1990.

Cherniavsky, Michael. "Khan or Basileus: An Aspect of Russian Mediaeval Political Theory." In *The Structure of Russian History,* ed. Michael Cherniavsky. New York, 1970.

―――. "Russia." In *National Consciousness, History, and Political Culture in Early-Modern Europe,* ed. Orest Ranum. Baltimore, Md., 1975.

―――. *Tsar and People: Studies in Russian Myths.* New Haven, Conn., 1961.

Choiseul-Gouffier, Mme. la comtesse de. *Réminiscences sur l'empereur Alexandre Ier et sur l'empereur Napoléon Ier.* Paris, 1862.

Clark, Kenneth. *The Nude: A Study in Ideal Form.* Princeton, N.J., 1972.

Clause, Georges. "Les réactions de la presse et de l'opinion au sacre de Charles X." In *Le sacre des rois.* Paris, 1985.

Colley, Linda. "The Apotheosis of George III: Loyalty, Royalty and the British Nation, 1760–1820." *Past and Present,* no. 102 (February 1984): 94–129.

―――. *Britons: Forging the Nation, 1707–1837.* New Haven, Conn., 1992.

Colley, Linda, et al. *Crown Pictorial: Art and the English Monarchy.* New Haven, Conn., 1990.

Corti, Count Egon. *The Downfall of Three Dynasties.* Freeport, N.Y., 1970.

Cracraft, James. "Did Feofan Prokopovich Really Write *Pravda Volei Monarshei?*" *Slavic Review,* vol. 40, no. 2 (Summer, 1981): 173–94.

―――. "Feofan Prokopovich and the Kiev Academy." In *Russian Orthodoxy under the Old Regime,* ed. Robert L. Nichols and Theofanis George Stavrou. Minneapolis, Minn., 1978.

―――. *The Church Reforms of Peter the Great.* Stanford, Calif., 1971.

―――. *The Petrine Revolution in Russian Architecture.* Chicago, 1988.

Cross, Samuel Hazard, and Olgerd P. Sherbowitz-Wetzor, eds. *The Russian Primary Chronicle: Laurentian Text.* Cambridge, Mass., 1973.

Crummey, Robert O. *Aristocrats and Servitors: The Boyar Elite in Russia, 1613–1689.* Princeton, N.J., 1983.

―――. "Court Spectacles in Seventeenth Century Russia: Illusion and Reality." In *Essays in Honor of A. A. Zimin,* ed. Daniel Clarke Waugh. Columbus, Ohio, 1985.

Curtiss, John Shelton. *The Russian Army under Nicholas I.* Durham, N.C., 1965.

Custine, Marquis de. *La Russie en 1839.* 8 vols. Brussels, 1843.

Czartoryski, Adam. *Memoirs of Adam Czartoryski.* 2 vols. London, 1888.

Danilevskii, Nikolai. *Taganrog ili podrobnoe opisanie bolezni i konchiny imperatora Aleksandra I.* Moscow, 1828.

Day, Andrew. "The *Nakaz* and Catherinian Monarchy: A Historiographical Discussion." Unpublished paper.

Den, V. I. "Zapiski." *Russkaia Starina* 65 (1890): 55–90, 551–74, 655–80; 66 (1890): 49–71, 298–324, 577–608; 67 (1890): 161–94.

Derzhavin, G. R. *Sochineniia.* 9 vols. St. Petersburg, 1864–1883.

Dmitrieva, R. P. *Skazanie o kniaziakh vladimiriskikh.* Moscow, 1955.

Dollinger, Heinz. "Das Leitbild des Burgerkönigtums in der europäischen Monarchie des 19. Jahrhunderts." In *Hof, Kultur, und Politik im 19. Jahrhundert,* ed. Karl Ferdinand Werner. Bonn, 1985.

Doneseniia sledstvennoi kommissii. St. Petersburg, 1826.

Duffy, Christopher. *The Military Life of Frederick the Great.* New York, 1986.

Eidel'man, N. Ia. *Gertsen protiv samoderzhaviia; Sekretnaia politicheskaia istoriia Rossii xviii–xix vekov i Vol'naia pechat'.* Moscow, 1973.

———. *Gran' vekov; politicheskaia bor'ba v Rossii, konets XVIII–nachala XIX stoletiia.* Moscow, 1986.

Ekateriny II. *Sochineniia Imperatritsy Ekateriny II.* Vol. 2. St. Petersburg, 1901.

Elias, Norbert. *The Court Society.* Oxford, 1983.

Ermolaev, D. "Stikhi na vstuplenie v Parizh Gosudaria Imperatora." *Ruskoi Vestnik*, no. 10 (1814): 75–76.

Eval'd, A. V. "Rasskazy o Nikolae I." *Istoricheskii Vestnik* 65 (1896): 51–71, 322–53.

Faensen, Hubert, and Vladimir Ivanov. *Early Russian Architecture.* London, 1975.

Fatéev, A. "Le problème de l'individu et de l'homme d'état dans la personnalité historique de Alexandre I, empereur de toutes les Russies." In Russkii Svobodnyi Universitet v Prage, *Zapiski nauchno-issledovatel'skogo ob"edineniia* 3 (1936): 139–78; 5 (1937): 1–13.

Fauchier-Magnon, Adrien. *The Small German Courts of the Eighteenth Century.* London, 1958.

Fedotov, George P. *The Russian Religious Mind.* 2 vols. Belmont, Mass., 1975.

Fehrenbach, Elisabeth. "Über die Bedeutung der politischen Symbole im Nationalstaat." *Historische Zeitschrift*, 213 Band (1971): 296–357.

Fénelon, François. *Oeuvres complètes.* Vol. 6: *Les aventures de Télémaque.* Geneva, 1971.

Fet A. *Moi vospominaniia.* Moscow, 1890.

Fisher, Alan W. "Enlightened Despotism and Islam under Catherine II." *Slavic Review*, vol. 27, no. 4 (December 1968): 542–53.

Fisher, K. I. "Zapiski." *Istoricheskii Vestnik* 113 (September 1908): 792–821.

Flier, Michael S. "Emperor as Mythmaker: Ivan the Terrible and the Palm Sunday Ritual." Unpublished manuscript.

Florovsky, George. *Ways of Russian Theology.* Vol. 1. Belmont, Mass., 1979.

Foucault, Michel. *Discipline and Punish: The Birth of the Prison.* New York, 1979.

Franz, Eckhardt G. "Hof und Hofgesellschaft im Grossherzogtum Hessen." In *Hof und Hofgesellschaft in den deutschen Staaten im 19. und beginnenden 20. Jahrhundert*, ed. Karl Möckl. Boppard am Rhein, 1990.

Frederiks, Baronessa M. P. "Iz vospominanii." *Istoricheskii Vestnik* 71 (1898): 52–87, 454–84; 72 (1898): 49–79, 396–413.

Frideburg, G. K. *Portrety i drugie izobrazheniia Petra Velikogo.* St. Petersburg, 1872.

Fuller, William C., Jr. *Strategy and Power in Russia, 1600–1914.* New York, 1992.

Gasparov, B. M. *Poeticheskii iazyk Pushkina kak fakt istorii russkogo literaturnogo iazyka.* Vienna, 1992.

Geertz, Clifford. "Centers, Kings, and Charisma: Reflections on the Symbolics of Power." In *Rites of Power: Symbolism, Ritual and Politics since the Middle Ages*, ed. Sean Wilentz. Philadelphia, 1985.

———. *Negara: The Theatre State in Nineteenth-Century Bali.* Princeton, N.J., 1980.

Geldern, James von. "The Ode as a Performative Genre." *Slavic Review*, vol. 50, no. 4 (Winter, 1991): 927–39.

Gellner, Ernest. *Nations and Nationalism.* Ithaca, N.Y., 1983.

Gershenzon, M. O., ed. *Epokha Nikolaia I.* Moscow, 1910.

Giesey, R. E. "Inaugural Aspects of French Royal Ceremonials." In *Coronations:*

Medieval and Early Modern Monarchic Ritual, ed. Jànos M. Bak. Berkeley, Calif., 1990.

———. "Models of Rulership in French Royal Ceremonial." In *Rites of Power: Symbolism, Ritual and Politics since the Middle Ages*, ed. Sean Wilentz. Philadelphia, 1985.

Gille, Florent. *A la mémoire de l'impératrice Alexandra Féodorovna*. Paris, 1864.

Giraudo, Gianfranco. "*Car', carstvo*, et termes corrélatifs dans les textes russes de la deuxième moitié du XVIe siècle." *Da Roma alla Terza Roma* 3 (1983): 545–71.

Girouard, Marc. *Life in the English Country House: A Social and Architectural History*. New Haven, Conn., 1978.

Gleason, Walter J. *Moral Idealists, Bureaucracy, and Catherine the Great*. New Brunswick, N.J., 1981.

———. *The Political and Legal Writings of Denis Fonvizin*. Ann Arbor, Mich., 1985.

Glinka, M. I. "Pervonachal'nyi plan 'Zhizn' za Tsaria' 1835 g." *Russkaia Starina* 30 (1881): 173–80.

———. *Zapiski*. Moscow, 1930.

Glinka, M. I., and Baron Rozen. *Zhizn' za Tsaria*. St. Petersburg, 1878.

Glinka, Sergei. "Stikhi na pribytie Gosudaria Imperatora v Moskvu." *Ruskoi Vestnik*, no. 9 (1816): 5.

———. "Vospominanie o Moskovskikh proizshestviiakh v dostopamiatny 1812 god, ot 11 iulia do izgnaniia vragov iz drevnei Ruskoi Stolitsy." *Ruskoi Vestnik*, no. 9 (1814): 3–21.

———. *Zapiski o 1812 gode*. St. Petersburg, 1836.

Glinka, V. M. *Russkii voennyi kostium, XVIII-nachala XX veka*. Leningrad, 1988.

Gody ucheniia ego Imperatorskogo Vysochestva Naslednika Tsesarevicha (Sbornik Russkogo Istoricheskogo Obshchestva, 31). St. Petersburg, 1881.

Gol'dberg, A. L. "K predystorii idei 'Moskva- tretii rim.'" In *Kul'turnoe nasledie drevnei rusi; istoki, stanovlenie traditsii*. Moscow, 1976.

Golikov, I. I. *Deianiia Petra Velikogo, mudrogo preobrazatelia Rossii*. 15 vols. Moscow, 1837–1843.

Golovine, V. N. *Memoirs of Countess Golovine*. London, 1910.

Golovkine, Comte Fédor. *La cour et le règne de Paul Ier; portraits, souvenirs et anecdotes*. Paris, 1905.

Grabar', I., ed. *Istoriia russkogo iskusstva*. 6 vols. St. Petersburg, 1909.

———. *Istoriia russkogo iskusstva*. 13 vols. Moscow, 1953–64.

Grebeniuk, V. P. "Publichnye zrelishcha petrovskogo vremeni i ikh sviaz' s teatrom." In *Novye cherty v russkoi literature (XVII-nachalo XVIII v.)* Moscow, 1976.

Grech, N. I. *Biografiia Imperatora Aleksandra I*. St. Petersburg, 1835.

———. "Neizdannoe mesto iz zapisok." *Russkii Arkhiv* 3 (1884): 58.

———. "Otkrytie pamiatnika Imperatoru Pavlu Petrovichu v Gatchine." *Russkii Khudozhestvennyi Listok*, no. 32 (November 10, 1851): 1.

Grimm, A. Th. Von. *Alexandra Feodorovna, Empress of Russia*. 2 vols. Edinburg, 1870.

Gruber, Alain Charles. "Le décor des derniers sacres a Reims." In *Le sacre des rois*. Paris, 1985.

Guiomar, Jean Yves. *L'idéologie nationale; Nation, Représentation, Propriété*. Paris, 1974.

Gurvich, G. "*Pravda voli monarshei*" *Feofana Prokopovicha i eia zapadnoevropeiskie istochniki*. Iur'ev, 1915.

Haffner, Wolfgang. "Tri nedeli v Rossii." *Istoricheskii Vestnik* 135 (1914): 259–82.

Halperin, Charles J. *Russia and the Golden Horde: The Mongol Impact on Medieval Russian History.* Bloomington, Ind., 1985.

Hamilton, George Heard. *The Art and Architecture of Russia.* Kingsport, Tenn., 1983.

Hammer, Karl. "Die preussischen Könige und Königinnen im 19 Jahrhundert und ihr Hof." *Hof, Kultur, und Politik im 19 Jahrhundert,* ed. Karl Ferdinand Werner. Bonn, 1985.

Haueter, Anton. *Die Krönungen der französischen Könige im Zeitalter des Absolutismus und in der Restauration.* Zurich, 1975.

Haxthausen, Baron August. *The Russian Empire: Its People, Institutions and Resources.* 2 vols. London, 1856.

Hellie, Richard. *Enserfment and Military Change in Muscovy.* Chicago, 1971.

———. *Readings for Introduction to Russian Civilization: Muscovite Society.* Chicago, 1970.

Herzen, Alexander. *Byloe i dumy.* 2 vols. Moscow, 1962.

Himelfarb, Hélène. "Versailles, fonctions et légendes." In *Les lieux de mémoire,* ed. Pierre Nora, pt. 2, vol. 2. Paris, 1986.

Hobsbawm, E. J. *Nations and Nationalism since 1780: Programme, Myth, Reality.* Cambridge, 1990.

Hocart, A. M. *Kingship.* London, 1969.

Hoetzsch, Otto. "Kaiserin Maria Alexandrovna von Russland, geb. Prinzessin Marie von Hessen-Darmstadt, (1824–1880)." *Archiv für hessische Geschichte und Altertumskund,* Neue Folge, Band 21 (1940): 81–116.

Honour, Hugh. *Neo-classicism.* Middlesex, England, 1968.

Howes, Robert Craig, ed. *The Testaments of the Grand Princes of Moscow.* Ithaca, N.Y., 1967.

Hunt, Lynn. *Politics, Culture and Class in the French Revolution.* Berkeley, Calif., 1986.

Iakovleva, A. I. "Vospominaniia byvshei kamer-iungfery imperatritsy Marii Aleksandrovny." *Istoricheskii Vestnik* 31 (1888): 147–74, 393–413, 593–606.

Ialozo, A. "Konstantino Andreevich Ton." *Zodchii* (1883): 1–10.

Imeritinskii, N. K. "Iz zapisok starogo preobrazhentsa." *Russkaia Starina* 77 (1893): 313–39, 529–58; 78 (1893): 21–50; 80 (1893): 253–79; 104 (1900): 301–22, 589–609; 105 (1901): 559–77; 106 (1901): 567–86; 107 (1901): 189–99.

Imperator Aleksandr v Rige; maia 24, 25, i 26 chisl 1802 goda. St. Petersburg, 1802.

Istoricheskoe opisanie postroeniia v Moskve khrama vo imia Khrista Spasitelia. Moscow, 1869.

Istoricheskoe opisanie postroeniia v Moskve Khrama vo imia Khrista Spasitelia. Moscow, 1883.

Iur'evich, S. A. "Dorozhnye pis'ma S.A. Iur'evicha." *Russkii Arkhiv* 1 (1887): 441–68; 2 (1887): 49–72; 3 (1887): 171–216.

Ivanov, Petr. "Zakonouchitel' imperatora Aleksandra IIogo i mitropolit Filaret." *Vozrozhdenie* 35 (September–October 1954): 148–64.

Ivanov, Prokhor. "Mitropolit Serafim na Senatskoi ploshchadi 14ogo dekabria 1825 goda." *Istoricheskii Vestnik* 99 (1905): 166–170.

"Iz vospominanii byvshego gvardeiskogo sapera." *Russkii Vestnik* 72 (1867): 307–59.

Izbranneishiia cherty znamenitykh deianii, dostopamiatnykh deianii i dostopamiatnykh izrechenii ili anekdoty avgusteishego Imperatora Aleksandra I, mirotvortsa Rossii. Moscow, 1814.

"Izvestie o vysochaishem prebyvanii ego Imperatorskogo Velichestva na Zlatoustovskikh zavodakh." *Otechestvennye Zapiski* 20 (1824): 265–95.

Jackman, S. W. *Romanov Relations.* London, 1969.

Jackson, Richard. *Vive le roi!; A History of the French Coronation from Charles V to Charles X.* Chapel Hill, N.C., 1984.

Jelavich, Charles, and Barbara. *The Education of a Russian Statesman: The Memoirs of Nicholas Karlovich Giers.* Berkeley, Calif., 1962.

Jenkins, Michael. *Arakcheev.* New York, 1960.

Jones, Robert E. *The Emancipation of the Russian Nobility, 1762–1785.* Princeton, N.J., 1973.

Jouhaud, Christian. "Printing the Event: From La Rochelle to Paris." In *The Culture of Print: Power and the Uses of Print in Early Modern Europe*, ed. Roger Chartier. Princeton, N.J., 1989.

Kaganov, Grigorii. "'As in the ship of Peter.'" *Slavic Review*, vol. 50, no. 4 (Winter, 1991): 755–67.

Kahn, Andrew. "Readings of Imperial Rome from Lomonosov to Pushkin." *The Slavic Review*, vol. 52, no. 4 (Winter, 1993): 745–68.

Kalinin, B. N., and P. P. Iurevich. *Pamiatniki Leningrada i ego okrestnosti.* Leningrad, 1959.

Kallash, V. V. *Dvenadtsatyi god v vospominaniakh i perepiske.* Moscow, 1912.

Kämpfer, Frank. *Das russische Herrscherbild von den Anfangen bis zu Peter den Grossen.* Recklinghausen, 1978.

Kantorowicz, Ernst H. "Gods in Uniform." In his *Selected Studies.* New York, 1965.

———. "The 'King's Advent' and the Enigmatic Panels in the Doors of Santa Sabina." *Art Bulletin* 26 (1944): 207–31.

———. *The King's Two Bodies: A Study in Medieval Political Theology.* Princeton, N.J., 1957.

Kappeler, Andreas. *Russland als Vielvölkerreich; Entstehung, Geschichte, Zerfall.* Munich, 1992.

Karamzin, Nicholas. *Karamzin's Memoir on Ancient and Modern Russia*, ed. Richard Pipes. New York, 1969.

———. *Polnoe sobranie stikhotvorenii.* Moscow, 1966.

Karasev, A. "Levyi glaz Nikolaia vtorogo." *Istoricheskii Vestnik* 89 (1902): 106–8.

Karnovich, E. P. "Assamblei pri Petre Velikom." *Drevniaia i novaia Rossiia* 1 (1877): 81–82.

———. "Koronovanie gosudarei." *Russkii Arkhiv* 1 (1990): 33–63.

———. *Tsesarevich Konstantin Pavlovich.* St. Petersburg, 1899.

Kasinec, Edward, and Richard Wortman. "The Mythology of Empire: Imperial Russian Coronation Albums." *Biblion; The Bulletin of the New York Public Library*, vol. 1, no. 1 (Fall, 1992): 77–100.

Kaznakov, S. "Pavlovskaia Gatchina." *Starye Gody* (July–September 1914): 101–88.

Keenan, Edward. "Royal Russian Behavior, Style and Self-Image." In *Ethnic Russia in the USSR: The Dilemma of Dominance*, ed. Edward Allworth. New York, 1981.

Keep, John L. H. "The Military Style of the Romanov Rulers." *War and Society*, vol. 1, no. 2 (September 1983): 161–84.

————. "Paul I and the Militarization of Government." In *Paul I: A Reassessment of His Life and Reign*, ed. Hugh Ragsdale. Pittsburgh, Pa., 1979.

————. *Soldiers of the Tsar: Army and Society in Russia, 1462–1874*. Oxford, 1985.

Kennan, George F. *The Marquis de Custine and His Russia in 1839*. Princeton, N.J., 1971.

Khatov, Lieutenant-General. *Dva znamenitye smotra voisk vo Frantsii*. St. Petersburg, 1843,

Khram khrista spasitelia v Moskve; chtenie dlia naroda. Moscow, 1884.

Khrapovitskii, A. V. *Zhurnal Vysochaishego puteshestviia eia Velichestva Gosudaryni Imperatritsy Ekateriny II Samoderzhitsy Vserossiiskoi v Poludennye Strany Rossii v 1787 g*. Moscow, 1787.

Kirichenko, E. I. "Arkhitekturnye ansambli Moskvy 1830–1860-x godov." *Arkhitekturnoe Nasledstvo* 24 (1976): 3–19.

————. *Russkaia arkhitektura 1830–1910 godov*. Moscow, 1978.

Kizevetter, A. A. *Istoricheskie ocherki*. Moscow, 1912.

Kliuchevskii, V. O. *Sochineniia*. 8 vols. Moscow, 1956–1959.

Klochkov, M. V. *Ocherki pravitel'stvennoi deiatel'nosti vremeni Pavla I*. Petrograd, 1916.

Knabe, G. S. "Rimskaia tema v russkoi kul'ture i v tvorchestve Tiutcheva." In *Tiutchevskii Sbornik; stat'i o zhizni i tvorchestve Fedora Ivanovicha Tiutcheva*, ed. Iu. Lotman. Tallin, 1990.

————. *Voobrazhenie znaka; Mednyi Vsadnik Falkone i Pushkina*. Moscow, 1993.

Kobeko, Dmitrii. *Tsesarevich Pavel Petrovich, 1754–1796*. St. Petersburg, 1887.

Kollmann, Nancy Shields. *Kinship and Politics: The Making of the Muscovite Political System, 1345–1547*. Stanford, Calif., 1987.

————. "Ritual and Social Drama at the Muscovite Court." *Slavic Review*, vol. 45, no. 3 (Fall, 1986): 486–502.

————. "The Seclusion of Elite Muscovite Women." *Russian History*, pt. 2, vol. 10 (1983): 170–87.

Kolokol'tsov, D. G. "Leib-Gvardii preobrazhenskii polk v vospominaniiakh ego starogo ofitsera, s 1831 po 1846 g." *Russkaia Starina* 38 (1883): 273–311.

Komarovskii, E. F. *Zapiski*. St. Petersburg, 1914.

Korf, M. A. "Iz zapisok Barona M. A. Korfa." *Russkaia Starina* 98 (1899): 371–95, 511–42; 99 (1899): 3–30, 271–95, 480–515; 100 (1899): 25–58, 267–99, 481–521; 101 (1900): 25–56, 317–54, 545–88; 102 (1900): 27–50, 261–92, 505–27; 103 (1900): 33–55; 117 (1904): 59–78, 275–302; 118 (1904): 545–68.

————. "Materialy i cherty k biografii Imperatora Nikolaia I i k istorii ego tsarstvovaniia." *Sbornik Imperatorskogo Russkogo istoricheskogo obshchestva*, vol. 98.

————. *Voshestvie na prestol Imperatora Nikolaia I*. St. Peterburg, 1857.

Korkunov, N. M. *Russkoe gosudarstvennoe pravo*. 2 vols. St. Petersburg, 1909.

Kornilov, A. *Kurs istorii Rossii XIX v*. 2 vols. Moscow, 1918.

————. *Obshchestvennoe dvizhenie pri Aleksandre II*. Paris, 1905.

Korsakov, D. A. *Votsarenie Imperatritsy Anny Ioannovny*. Kazan, 1880.

Kotzebue, August. "Kratkoe opisanie Imperatorskogo Mikhailovskogo Dvortsa." *Russkii Arkhiv*, vol. 8, nos. 4–5 (1870): 969–98.

Krieger, Bogdan. "Erziehung und Unterricht der Königin Luise." *Hohenzollern Jahrbuch* (1910): 117–73

Kropotkin, Peter. *Memoirs of a Revolutionist*. Garden City, N.Y., 1962.

Kurbatov, V. Ia. *Peterburg.* St. Petersburg, 1913.

Lakier, A. B. *Russkaia Geral'dika.* Moscow, 1990.

Lanceray, N. "Arkhitektura i sady Gatchiny." *Starye Gody* (July–September 1914): 5–32,

———. "Po povodu Pavil'iona Venery," *Starye Gody* (July–September 1914): 192–93.

Langeron, Count A. "Russkaia armiia v godu smerti Ekateriny II." *Russkaia Starina* 83 (April 1895): 145–77.

Laqueur, Thomas. *Making Sex: Body and Gender from the Greeks to Freud.* Cambridge, Mass., 1990.

Latynin, F. "Otryvochnye vospominaniia." *Istoricheskii Vestnik* 116 (June 1909): 825–40.

Le Goff, Jacques. "A Coronation Program for the Age of Saint Louis: The Ordo of 1250." In *Coronations: Medieval and Early Modern Monarchic Ritual,* ed. Jànos M. Bak. Berkeley, Calif., 1990.

Le sacre de Louis XV, roi de France et de Navarre dans l'Église de Reims. Paris, 1732.

Le sacre et couronnement de Louis XVI, roi de France et de Navarre. Paris, 1775.

LeDonne, John P. *Absolutism and the Ruling Class: The Formation of the Russian Political Order, 1700–1825.* New York, 1991.

———. "Ruling Families in the Russian Political Order, 1689–1825." *Cahiers du Monde russe et soviétique,* vol. 38, nos. 3–4 (July–December 1987): 233–322.

———. *Ruling Russia: Politics and Administration in the Age of Absolutism, 1762–1796.* Princeton, N.J., 1984.

Lefevre, A. *O nadzirateliakh pri vospitanii iz Entsiklopedii.* St. Petersburg, 1770.

Leger, Louis. *Moscou.* Paris, 1904.

Leibniz, Gottfried Wilhelm. *De educatione Principis commentatio. Magazin für das Kirchenrecht die Kirchen und Gelehrten-Geschichte* 1 (1787): 177–96.

Leonard, Carol S. *Reform and Regicide: The Reign of Peter III of Russia.* Bloomington, Ind., 1992.

———. "The Reputation of Peter III." *The Russian Review,* vol. 47, no. 3 (July 1988): 263–92.

Lewitter, L. R. "Poland, the Ukraine and Russia in the 17th Century." *The Slavonic and East European Review,* vol. 27, no. 69 (May 1949): 414–29.

Likhachev, D. S. *Poeziia sadov; k semantike sadovo-parkovykh stilei; sad kak tekst.* St. Petersburg, 1991.

———. *Russkie letopisi.* Moscow, 1947.

Lincoln, W. Bruce. *In the Vanguard of Reform: Russia's Enlightened Bureaucrats, 1825–1861.* DeKalb, Ill., 1982.

———. *Nicholas I: Emperor and Autocrat of All the Russias.* Bloomington, Ind., 1978.

Lisovskii, N. M. "Periodicheskaia pechat' v Rossii, 1703–1903; statistiko-bibliograficheskii obzor russkikh periodicheskikh izdanii." In *Sbornik statei po istorii i statistike russkoi periodicheskoi pechati, 1703–1903.* St. Petersburg, 1903.

Livanova, M., and V. Protopopov. *Glinka; tvorcheskii put'.* Moscow, 1955.

Lomonosov, M. V. *Polnoe sobranie sochinenii.* Vol. 8. Moscow, 1959.

Londonderry, Lady. *Russian Journal of Lady Londonderry, 1836–37.* London, 1973.

Londonderry, The Marquis of. *Recollections of a Tour in the North of Europe in 1836–1837.* 2 vols. London, 1838.

Longworth, Philip. *The Three Empresses: Catherine I, Anne and Elizabeth of Russia.* London, 1972.

Lotman, Iu. M. *Roman A. S. Pushkin "Evgenii Onegin": kommentarii.* Leningrad, 1980.

Lotman, Iu. M., and B. A. Uspenskii, eds. *The Semiotics of Russian Culture.* Ann Arbor, Mich., 1984.

Lubomirski, Prince Joseph. *Souvenirs d'un page du tsar Nicolas.* Paris, 1869.

Lukomskii, V. Ia., and G. Ia. Lukomskii. *Kostroma.* St. Petersburg, 1913.

Lukomskii, V. K. "Gerb doma Romanovykh." In *Letopisi i litsevoi izbornik Doma Romanovykh* 2 (1913): 109–14.

L'vov, A. F. "Zapiski." *Russkii Arkhiv* 2 (1884): 225–60; 3 (1884): 65–114.

Madariaga, Isabel de. *Russia in the Age of Catherine the Great.* New Haven, Conn., 1981.

Magne, Émile. *Les fêtes en Europe au XVII siècle.* Paris, n.d.

Makarov, M. N. "Vospominaniia o koronatsii Aleksandra I." *Zaria* 3 (1870): 47–94.

Mansurov, A. "Naslednik Tsesarevich Aleksandr Nikolaevich v gorode Kasimove." *Russkii Arkhiv* 2 (1888): 476–79.

Marin, Louis. *Le portrait du roi.* Paris, 1981.

Marin, V. P. "Iz dnevnika babushki, 1842–46." *Nasha Starina,* no. 5 (1915): 411–25; no. 6 (1915): 526–40.

Markova, G. *The Great Palace of the Moscow Kremlin.* Leningrad, 1981.

Marmont, Maréchal de (Duc de Raguse). *Mémoires.* 9 vols. Paris, 1857.

Massie, Suzanne. *Pavlovsk: The Life of a Russian Palace.* Boston, 1990.

Materialy dlia istorii Imperatorskoi Akademii Nauk. Vol. 5. St. Petersburg, 1889; Vol. 7. St. Petersburg, 1895.

Matveev, V. Iu. "K istorii vozniknoveniia i razvitiia siuzheta 'Petr I—vysekaiushchii statuiu Rossii.'" In *Kul'tura i iskusstvo Rossii XVIII veka.* Leningrad, 1981.

Maxwell, John S. *The Czar: His Court and People.* New York, 1854.

McConnell, Allen. *Tsar Alexander I, Paternalistic Reformer.* New York, 1970.

McGrew, Roderick E. "A Political Portrait of Paul I from the Austrian and English Diplomatic Archives." *Jahrbücher für Geschichte Osteuropas,* Band 18, Heft 4 (December 1970): 503–29.

———. "Paul I and the Knights of Malta." In *Paul I: A Reassessment of His Life and Reign,* ed. Hugh Ragsdale. Pittsburgh, Pa., 1979.

———. *Paul I of Russia.* Oxford, 1992.

———. *Russia and the Cholera, 1823–1832.* Madison, Wis., 1965.

McNeal, Robert H. *Tsar and Cossack, 1855–1914.* Oxford, 1987.

Medvedkova, O. A. "Russkii paradnyi portret rubezha XVIII–XIX vekov: transformatsiia obraza." In *Aktual'nye problemy otechestvennogo iskusstva.* Moscow, 1990.

Meehan-Waters, Brenda. *Autocracy and Aristocracy: The Russian Service Elite of 1730.* New Brunswick, N.J., 1982.

Mel'gunov, S. *Dela i liudi Aleksandrovskogo vremeni.* Berlin, 1923.

Mel'nikov, P. I. (Andrei Pecherskii). *Polnoe sobranie sochinenii.* 14 vols. St. Petersburg, 1897–1898.

Menning, Bruce W. "The Emergence of a Military Administrative Elite in the Don Cossack Land, 1708–1836." In *Russian Officialdom: The Bureaucratization of Russian Society from the Seventeenth to the Twentieth Century,* ed. Walter McKenzie Pinter and Don Karl Rowney. Chapel Hill, N.C., 1980.

Merder, K. K. "Zapiski K. K. Merdera, vospitatelia Aleksandra Nikolaevicha." *Russkaia Starina* 45 (1885): 339–64, 527–54; 46 (1885): 87–106, 265–80, 481–510; 47 (1885): 27–44, 223–38, 429–44; 48 (1885): 503–22.

Merzliakov, A. *Oda na vseradostneishee koronovanie Blagochestiveishego Gosudaria Imperatora Aleksandra Pervogo.* Moscow, 1801.

Mikhailovskii, Nikolai. *Dukh ventsenosnykh suprugov v boze pochivaiushchikh Imperatora Aleksandra Igo i Imperatritsy Elizavety.* 3 vols. Moscow, 1829.

Miliukov, P. N. *Glavnye techeniia russkoi istoricheskoi mysli.* Vol. 1 (only one published). Moscow, 1898.

———. *Ocherki po istorii russkoi kul'tury.* 3 vols. Paris, 1930–1937.

———. "Verkhovniki i shliakhetstvo." In P. N. Miliukov, *Iz istorii russkoi intelligentsii.* St. Petersburg, 1903.

Miller, David B. "The Coronation of Ivan IV of Moscow." *Jahrbücher für Geschichte Osteuropas* 15 (1967): 559–74.

Mironenko, S. V. *Samoderzhavie i reformy; politicheskaia bor'ba v Rossii v nachale XIX v.* Moscow, 1989.

———. *Stranitsy tainoi istorii samoderzhaviia.* Moscow, 1990.

Moine, Marie-Christine. *Les fêtes à la Cour du Roi Soleil, 1653–1715.* Paris, 1984.

Monas, Sidney. "Anton Divier and the Police of St. Petersburg." In *For Roman Jakobson: Essays on his Sixtieth Birthday.* The Hague, 1956.

Montferrand, A. Ricard de. *Plans et détails du monument consacré à la mémoire de l'Empereur Alexandre.* Paris, 1836.

Moore, Thomas. *Lalla-Rookh: An Oriental Romance.* New York, 1868.

Moskva zlatoglavaia; religioznoe zodchestvo Moskvy v proshlom i nastoiashchem. Paris, 1979.

Muller, Alexander V. *The Spiritual Regulation of Peter the Great.* Seattle, Wash., 1972.

Murav'ev, A. N. *Vospominaniia o poseshchenii sviatyni Moskovskoi Gosudarem Naslednikom.* St. Petersburg, 1838.

Murav'ev, N. N. "Zapiski." *Russkii Arkhiv* 2 (1894): 449–536.

"Mysli pri chtenii Vysochaishego Manifesta ot 6 Dekabria 1813 goda," *Ruskoi Vestnik*, no. 11 (1814): 15–25.

Nadler, V. K. *Imperator Aleksandr I i ideia sviashchennogo soiuza.* 5 vols. Riga, 1886–1892.

Nakaz e.i.v. Ekateriny vtoryie . . . dannyi kommissii o sochinenii proekta novago ulozheniia. St. Petersburg, 1770.

Nelson, Janet. "The Lords anointed and the people's choice: Carolingian royal ritual." In *Rituals of Royalty: Power and Ceremonial in Traditional Societies*, ed. David Cannadine and Simon Price. Cambridge, 1987.

———. *Politics and Ritual in Early Medieval Europe.* London, 1986.

Neverov, O. Ia. "Pamiatniki antichnogo iskusstva v Rossii petrovskogo vremeni." In *Kul'tura i iskusstvo petrovskogo vremeni*, Leningrad, 1977.

Nicholas I. "Iz zapisok imperatora Nikolaia I." *Byloe* 10 (1907/1910): 77.

Nikitenko, A. V. *Dnevnik.* 3 vols. Leningrad, 1955–56.

Nikitin, N. P. *Ogiust Monferran; proektirovanie i stroitel'stvo Isaakievskogo Sobora i Aleksandrovskoi Kolonny.* Leningrad, 1939.

Nikolai Mikhailovich, Velikii Kniaz'. *General-Ad"iutanty Imperatora Aleksandra I.* St. Petersburg, 1913.

Nitsche, Peter. "Translatio imperii? Beobachtungen zum historischen Selbstverständnis im Moskauer Zartum um Mitte des 16. Jahrhunderts," *Jahrbucher für Geschichte Osteuropas* 35 (1987), 321–38.

Nol'de, B. "Zakony osnovnye v russkom prave." *Pravo*, no. 8 (1913): 448–61; no. 9 (1913): 524–41.

Obol'ianinov, N. S. *Katalog russkikh illiustrirovannykh izdanii, 1725–1860.* 2 vols. Moscow, 1914–15.

O'Brien, C. Bickford. *Russia under Two Tsars, 1682–1689: The Regency of Sophia Alekseevna.* Berkeley and Los Angeles, 1952.

Obstoiatel'noe opisanie torzhestvennykh poriadkov blagopoluchnogo vshestviia v tsarstvuiushchii grad Moskvu i sviashchenneishei koronovaniia eia Avgusteishego imperatorskogo velichestva vsepresvetleishiia derzhavneishiia velikiia gosudaryni Elisavet Petrovny, samoderzhitsy vserossiiskoi. St. Petersburg, 1744. Referred to in text as *Obstoiatel'noe opisanie.*

Okenfuss, Max J. "The Jesuit Origins of Petrine Education." In *The Eighteenth Century in Russia,* ed. J. G. Garrard. Oxford, 1973.

Okulov, Grigorii. *Chuvstvo russkogo v den' sviashchenneishego koronovaniia gosudaria imperatora Nikolaia Pavlovicha.* St. Petersburg, 1826.

Ol'ga Nikolaevna, Vel. Kn. *Son iunosti.* Paris, 1963.

Olsufiev, Gr. A. "Poteshnye Imperatora Nikolaia Pavlovicha." *Russkii Arkhiv* 3 (1910): 443–48.

Olshr, Giuseppe. "La Chiesa e lo Stato nel cerimoniale d'incoronazione degli ultimi sovrani Rurikidi." *Orientalia Christiana Periodica* 16 (1950): 267–302.

———. "La Chiesa e lo Stato nel cerimoniale d'incoronazione degli zar Romanov." *Orientalia Christiana Periodica* 18 (1952): 344–76.

Opisanie allegoricheskoi illiuminatsii predstavlennoi vo vseradostneishii den' koronatsii eia Imperatorskogo Velichestva Ekateriny Vtorye v Moskve pred Universitetskom dome v 1762 godu. Moscow, 1762.

Opisanie koronatsii e.v. imp. Ekateriny Alekseevny, torzhestvenno otpravlennoi v tsarstvuiuschchem grade Moskve 7 maiia 1724 gody. St. Petersburg, 1724; Moscow, 1725.

Opisanie koronatsii Eia Velichestva Imperatritsy i Samoderzhitsy Vserossiiskoi Anny Ioannovny torzhestvenno otpravelennoi v tsarstviushchem grade Moskve, 28 aprelia, 1730 g. St. Petersburg, 1730.

Opisanie pogrebeniia blazhennoi pamiati imperatora Nikolaia Igo s prisovokupleniem istoricheskogo ocherka pogrebenii tsarei i imperatorov vserossiiskikh i nekotorykh drugikh evropeiskikh gosudarei. St. Petersburg, 1856.

Opisanie poriadka derzhannogo pri pogrebenii blazhennyia vysokoslavnyia i vechno dostoineishiia pamiati . . . Petra Velikogo. St. Petersburg, 1725; Moscow, 1726.

Opisanie vseradostneishego vshestviia Blagochestiveishei Gosudaryni Imperatritsy Ekateriny Alekseevny v Sviatuiu-Troitskuiu Lavru. Moscow, 1762.

Opisanie vshestviia v Moskvu i Koronovaniia Gosudaryni Imperatritsy Ekateriny II. In *KFZ* 63 (1762). St. Petersburg, 185?. Referred to in text as *Opisanie vshestviia.*

"O prebyvanii Ego Velichestva Gosudaria Imperatora v Orenburge (Pis'mo k izdateliu)." *Otechestvennye Zapiski,* vol. 21 (1825): 404–27.

Orlov, A. S. "'Tilemakhida' V. K. Trediakovskogo." *XVIII Vek* (1935): 5–57.

Orlova, A. A. *Glinka v Peterburge.* Leningrad, 1970.

Orlovsky, Daniel. *The Limits of Reform: The Ministry of Internal Affairs in Imperial Russia, 1802–1881.* Cambridge, Mass., 1981.

Osmnadtsatyi vek, ed. P. Bartenev. 4 vols. Moscow, 1869.

Ostrogorskii, G. A. "Evoliutsiia vizantiiskogo obriada koronovaniia." In *Vizantiia, iuzhnye slaviane i drevniaia Rus', Zapadnaia Evropa.* Moscow, 1973.

Otechestvennaia voina 1812 goda v khudozhestvennykh i istoricheskikh pamiatnikakh iz sobranii Ermitazha. Leningrad, 1963.

Ouspensky, Leonid, and Vladimir Lossky. *The Meaning of Icons.* Crestwood, N.Y., 1989.

Ozouf, Mona. *Festivals and the French Revolution.* Cambridge, Mass., 1988.

Palmer, Alan. *Alexander I: Tsar of War and Peace.* New York, 1974.

Pamiatniki arkhitektury prigorodov Leningrada. Leningrad, 1983.

Panchenko, A. M. "Istoriia i vechnost' v sisteme kul'turnykh tsennostei russkogo barokko." *Trudy otdela drevnei russkoi literatury* 34 (1979): 189–99.

———. " 'Potemskie derevni' kak kul'turnyi mif." In *XVIII vek* 14 (1983): 93–104.

Panchulidze, S. *Istoriia kavalergardov, 1724–1799–1899.* 4 vols. St. Petersburg, 1899.

Panegiricheskaia literatura petrovskogo vremeni. Moscow, 1979.

Panin, N. I. "Vsepoddannaishee pred"iavlenie slabogo poniatiia i mneniia o vospitanii Ego Imperatorskogo Velichestva Pavla Petrovicha." *Russkaia Starina* 36 (1880): 315–30.

Papmehl, K. A. *Metropolitan Platon of Moscow (Petr Levshin), 1737–1812.* Newtonville, Mass., 1983.

Patkul', M. A. "Vospominaniia." *Istoricheskii Vestnik* 87 (1902): 31–55, 441–69, 837–54; 88 (1902): 39–56, 436–53, 851–79; 89 (1902): 38–66, 375–403, 700–36.

Pauzié, Geremie "Zapiski brillianshchika Poz'e." *Russkii Arkhiv*, no. 1 (1870): 42–127.

Pavlenko, N. I. "Idei absoliutizma v zakonodatel'stve XVIIIv." In *Absoliutizm v Rossii.* Moscow, 1964.

Pavlenko, N. I. *Petr pervyi.* Moscow, 1975.

Pavlov-Sil'vanskii, N. *Proekty reform v zapiskakh sovremennikov Petra Velikogo.* St. Petersburg, 1897.

Pesnopeniia na vysochaischee . . . poseshchenie Sviato-Troitskiia Lavry i nakhodiashcheisia v nei Moskovskoi Dukhovnoi Akademii. Moscow, 1826.

P''esy shkol'nykh teatrov Moskvy. Moscow, 1974.

Peterson, Claes. *Peter the Great's Administrative and Judicial Reforms: Swedish Antecedents and the Process of Reception.* Stockholm, 1979.

Petrodvorets; Kottedzh. Leningrad, 1986.

Petrov, P. "Khram Spasitelia v Moskve." *Zodchii* (1880): 30–31.

Petrov, P. N. "M. N. Vorob'ev i ego shkola." *Vestnik iziashchnykh iskusstv* 6 (1888): 297–303.

Pintner, Walter. "The Evolution of Civil Officialdom, 1755–1855." In *Russian Officialdom: The Bureaucratization of Russian Society from the Seventeenth to the Twentieth Century*, ed. Walter McKenzie Pintner and Don Karl Rowney. Chapel Hill, N.C., 1980.

Platon, (Mitropolit). *Pravoslavnoe uchenie ili sokrashchennaia khristianskaia Bogosloviia dlia upotrebleniia Ego Imperatorskogo Vysochestva Presvetleishego Vserossiiskogo Naslednika blagovernogo Gosudaria Tsesarevicha i Velikogo Kniazia Pavla Petrovicha.* Moscow, 1819.

Pogodin, M. P. *Istoriko-kriticheskie otryvki.* Moscow, 1846.

————. *Sochineniia.* Vol 4. Moscow, 1874.

Pommier, Édouard. "Versailles, l'image du souverain." In *Les lieux de mémoire,* ed. Pierre Nora, pt. 2, vol. 2. Paris, 1986.

Poroshin, Semen. *Zapiski.* St. Petersburg, 1881.

Poslednie dni zhizni nezabvennogo monarkha v boze pochivaiushego gosudaria Imperatora Aleksandra I. St. Petersburg, 1827.

"Potomki Susanina i selo 'Korobovo.'" *Prikhodskoe chtenie,* no. 35 (1913): 992.

"Prazdnestvo v Pavlovske, 17 Iunia 1814 goda." *Russkoi Vestnik* 13 (1814): 37–38.

"Prebyvanie Gosudaria Imperatora v Permi." *Otechestvennye Zapiski* 23 (1825): 316–21.

"Prebyvanie tsarstvennykh osob v Simbirskoi gubernii." In *Sbornik istoricheskikh i statisticheskikh materialov o Simbirskoi gubernii.* Simbirsk, 1868.

Priselkov, M. D. *Nestor, letopisets.* Petrograd, 1923.

Prokopovich, Feofan. *Slova i rechi pouchitel'nye, pokhval'nye, i pozdravitel'nye.* 2 vols. St. Petersburg, 1760–1761.

Protasov, A. Ia. "Dnevnye zapiski o vospitanii velikogo kniazia Aleksandra Pavlovicha." *Drevniaia i Novaia Rossiia* 3 (1880): 761–75.

Protopopov, V. *"Ivan Susanin" Glinki.* Moscow, 1961.

Prozorovskii, D. I. "Ob utvariakh pripisyvaemykh Vladimiru Monomakhu." *Zapiski otdeleniia russkoi i slavianskoi arkheologii Imperatorskogo russkogo arkheologicheskogo obshchestva* 3 (1882): 1–64.

Pumpianskii, L. V. "K istorii russkogo klassitsizma (Poetika Lomonosova)." *Kontekst* 14 (1982): 303–35.

————. "Lomonosov i nemetskaia shkola razuma." *XVIII vek; sbornik 14.* Leningrad, 1983.

Pushkin, A. S. *Dnevnik Pushkina, 1833–1835.* Moscow, 1923.

Puteshestvie ego Velichestva Gosudaria i Imperatora chrez Orlovskuiu guberniuu v 1823 godu. Orel, 1823.

Pypin, A. N. *Obshchestvennoe dvizhenie pri Aleksandre I.* Petrograd, 1918.

Raeff, Marc. "The Bureaucratic Phenomenon of Imperial Russia, 1700–1905." *American Historial Review* 84 (April 1979): 399–411.

————. "La jeunesse russe à l'aube du XIX siècle: André Turgenev et ses amis." *Cahiers du monde russe et soviétique* 8 (October–December 1967): 560–86.

————. *Michael Speransky: Statesman of Imperial Russia, 1772–1839.* The Hague, 1969.

————. *Origins of the Russian Intelligentsia: The Eighteenth Century Nobility.* New York, 1966.

————. *Plans for Political Reforms in Imperial Russia.* Englewood Cliffs, N.J., 1966.

Ragsdale, Hugh, ed. *Paul I: A Reassessment of His Life and Reign.* Pittsburgh, Pa., 1979.

Ransel, David. "An Ambivalent Legacy: The Education of the Grand Duke Paul." In *Paul I: A Reassessment of His Life and Reign,* ed. Hugh Ragsdale. Pittsburgh, Pa., 1979.

————. *Mothers of Misery: Child Abandonment in Russia.* Princeton, N.J., 1988.

————. *The Politics of Catherinian Russia: The Panin Party.* New Haven, Conn., 1975.

Rasmussen, Karen. "Catherine II and the Image of Peter I." *Slavic Review,* vol. 37, no. 1 (March 1978): 57–69.

Reddaway, W. F., ed. *Documents of Catherine the Great.* New York, 1971.

Reisman, Edward S. "The Absence of a Common-Descent Myth for Rus'." *Russian History / Histoire russe,* vol. 15, no. 1 (1988): 9–19.

Rewald, Sabine, ed. *The Romantic Vision of Caspar David Friedrich: Paintings and Drawings from the USSR.* New York, 1990.

Reynolds, Susan. "Medieval *Origines Gentium* and the Community of the Realm." *History,* vol. 68, no. 224 (October 1983): 375–90.

Rheinstein, Max, ed. *Max Weber on Law in Economy and Society.* New York, 1967.

Riasanovsky, Nicholas V. *The Image of Peter the Great in Russian History and Thought.* New York, 1985.

———. *Nicholas I and Official Nationality in Russia, 1825–1855.* Berkeley and Los Angeles, California, 1959.

Rieber, Alfred. "Bureaucratic Politics in Imperial Russia." *Social Science History,* vol. 2, no. 4 (Summer, 1978): 399–413, 407–8.

Riley, Patrick, ed. *The Political Writings of Leibniz.* Cambridge, 1972.

Robinson, A. N. *Bor'ba idei v russkoi literature XVII veka.* Moscow, 1974.

Rogger, Hans. *National Consciousness in Eighteenth-Century Russia.* Cambridge, Mass., 1960.

Roosevelt, Priscilla R. "Emerald Thrones and Living Statues: Theater and Theatricality on the Russian Estate." *Russian Review,* vol. 50, no. 1 (January 1991): 1–23.

Rosenblum, Robert, and H. W. Janson. *19th-Century Art.* New York, 1984.

Rovinskii, D. A. *Obozrenie ikonopisaniia v Rossii do kontsa XVII veka; opisanie feierverkov i illuminatsii.* St. Petersburg, 1903.

———. *Podrobnyi slovar' russkikh graverov XVI–XIXvv.* 4 vols. St. Petersburg, 1886–1889; 2 vols. St. Petersburg, 1888–1889; 2 vols. St. Petersburg, 1895.

———. *Russkie narodnye kartinki.* 2 vols. St. Petersburg, 1900.

Rubinshtein, N. L. *Russkaia istoriografiia.* Moscow, 1941.

Rudolph, Suzanne Hoeber, "Presidential Address: State Formation in Asia—Prolegomenon to a Comparative Study." *The Journal of Asian Studies,* vol. 46, no. 4 (November 1987): 731–46.

Ruud, Charles A. *Fighting Words: Imperial Censorship and the Russian Press, 1804–1906.* Toronto, 1982.

Sabatier, Gérard. "Imagerie héroique et sacralité monarchique." In *La royauté sacrée dans le monde chrétien,* ed. Alain Boureau and Claudio-Sergio Ingerflom. Paris, 1992.

Safonov, M. M. *Problema reform v pravitel'stvennoi politike Rossii na rubezhe XVIII i XIX vv.* Leningrad, 1988.

———. "Zaveshchanie Ekateriny II." Unpublished manuscript.

Sahlins, Marshall. *Islands of History.* Chicago, 1985.

Samsonov, E. P. "Vospominaniia." *Russkii Arkhiv* 1 (1884): 423–64; 2 (1884): 133–78.

Savin, A. N. "Svatovstvo Tsesarevicha Aleksandra Nikolaevicha." In *Pamiati Aleksandra Nikolaevicha Savina, 1873–1923.* Moscow, 1926.

Schama, Simon. "The Domestication of Majesty: Royal Family Portraiture, 1500–1850." *Journal of Interdisciplinary History* 17 (Summer, 1986): 155–83.

Schleifman, Nurit. "A Russian Daily Newspaper and Its New Readership: *Severnaia Pchela,* 1825–1840." *Cahiers du monde russe at soviétique,* vol. 29, no. 2 (April–June 1987): 127–44.

Schmidt, Albert J. *The Architecture and Planning of Classical Moscow: A Cultural History*. Philadelphia, 1989.

―――. "Architecture in Nineteenth-Century Russia: The Enduring Classic." In *Art and Culture in Nineteenth-Century Russia*, ed. Theofanis George Stavrou. Bloomington, Ind., 1983.

Schnapper, Antoine. "The King of France as Collector in the Seventeenth Century." *The Journal of Interdisciplinary History*, vol. 17, no. 1 (Summer, 1986): 185–202.

Scott, Richenda C. *Quakers in Russia*. London, 1964.

Seaman, Gerald R. *History of Russian Music*. New York, 1967.

Semenova, L. N. *Ocherki istorii byta i kul'turnoi zhizni Rossii; pervaia polovina XVIII v.* Leningrad, 1982.

Serman, I. Z. *Russkii klassitsizm; poeziia, drama, satira*. Leningrad, 1973.

Ševčenko, Ihor. "A Neglected Source of Muscovite Political Ideology." In Michael Cherniavsky, ed., *The Structure of Russian History*. New York, 1970.

Shakhmatov, M. V. "Gosudarstvenno-natsional'nye idei 'chinovnykh knig' venchaniia na tsarstvo moskovskikh gosudarei." *Zapiski russkogo nauchnogo instituta v Belgrade* 1 (1930): 245–78.

Shakhovskoi, Iakov Petrovich. *Zapiski*. St. Petersburg, 1872.

Shcheglov, V. V. *Sobstvennye ego imperatorskogo velichestva biblioteki i arsenaly*. Petrograd, 1917.

Shchukina, E. S. "O sozdanii medali v pamiat' vziatiia Azova raboty Ia. Boskama." In *Kul'tura i iskusstvo petrovskogo vremeni*, 159–62. Leningrad, 1977.

Shemanskii, A., and S. Geichenko. *Krizis samoderzhaviia; Petergofskii Kottedzh Nikolaia I*. Moscow, 1932.

Shepelev, L. E. *Otmennennye Istoriei; chiny, zvaniia i tituly v Rossiiskoi imperii*. Leningrad, 1977.

―――. *Tituly, mundiry, ordena v Rossiiskoi imperii*. Leningrad, 1991.

Shevyrev, S. "Russkii prazdnik dannyi v prisutstvie ikh imperatorskikh velichestv 9ogo i 11ogo aprelia." "Moskovskaia letopis'," *Moskvitianin* (April 1849): 26–41.

Shil'der, N. K. *Imperator Aleksandr Pervyi; ego zhizn' i tsarstvovanie*. 4 vols. St. Petersburg, 1897–1898.

―――. *Imperator Nikolai Pervyi; ego zhizn' i tsarstvovanie*. 2 vols. St. Petersburg, 1903.

―――. *Imperator Pavel Pervyi*. St. Petersburg, 1901.

Shishkov, Admiral A. S. *Zapiski, mneniia, i perepiska*. 2 vols. Berlin, 1870.

Shliapkin, I. A. "Iz bumag odnogo iz prepodavatelei Aleksandra II." *Starina i novizna* 22 (1917): 3–17.

Shmidt, I. I. *Vasilii Ivanovich Demut-Malinovskii*. Moscow, 1960.

Shmidt, S. O. "Obshchestvennoe samosozanie *noblesse russe* v pervoi treti XIX vv." *Cahiers du monde russe et soviétique*, vol. 34, nos. 1–3 (January–June 1993): 11–32.

Shompulev, V. A. "Poseshchenie Saratova Naslednikom Tsesarevichem Aleksandrom Nikolaevichem v 30-kh godakh XIX stoletiia." *Russkaia Starina* 138 (1909): 44–46.

Shtakel'berger, A. K. "Russkii narodnyi gimn." *Istoricheskii Vestnik* 137 (July 1914): 115–31.

Shumigorskii, E. S. *Imperator Pavel I; zhizn' i tsarstvovanie*. St. Petersburg, 1907.

——. *Imperatritsa Mariia Fedorovna, (1759–1828)*. Vol. 1 (only one published). St. Petersburg, 1892.

Silverman, Debora L. *Art Nouveau in Fin-de-siècle France: Politics, Psychology, and Style*. Berkeley, Calif., 1989.

Sizov, E. *"Voobrazheny podobiia kniazei"; stenopis' arkhangel'skogo sobora Moskovskogo Kremlia*. Leningrad, 1969.

Smirnov, Sergei. *Istoriia Moskovskoi Slaviano-Greko-Latinskoi Akademii*. Moscow, 1855.

Snegirev, I. M. *Ocherki zhizni Moskovskogo arkhiepiskopa Avgustina*. Moscow, 1848.

——. *Zhizn' Moskovskogo Mitropolita Platona*. 2 vols. Moscow, 1891.

Snyders, George. *La pédagogie en France au XVIIe et XVIIIe siècles*. Paris, 1965.

"Sobstvennoruchnyi imennoi ukaz i nastavlenie Imp. Ekateriny II gen.-an-shefu Nikolaiu Ivanovichu Saltykovu o vospitanii velikikh kniazei Aleksandra i Konstantina Pavlovichei." *Sbornik imperatorskogo russkogo istoricheskogo obshchestva* 27:307–20.

Solov'ev, S. M. *Istoriia Rossii s drevneishchikh vremen*. 15 vols. Moscow, 1959–1966.

Sontag, Susan, ed. *A Barthes Reader*. New York, 1983.

Spasskii, I. G. *Inostrannye i russkie ordena do 1917 goda*. Leningrad, 1963.

Speranskii M. M. *Proekty i zapiski*. Moscow, 1961.

Spiski grazhdanskim chinam pervykh shest' klassov po starshinstvu. St. Petersburg, 1848.

Stamm-Kuhlmann, Thomas "Der Hof Friedrich-Wilhelms III. von Preussen 1797 bis 1840." In *Hof und Hofgesellschaft in den deutschen Staaten im 19. und beginnenden 20. Jahrhundert*, ed. Karl Möckl. Boppard am Rhein, 1990.

Starobinski, Jean. *The Invention of Liberty, 1700–1789*. New York, 1987.

Stekl, Hannes. "Der Wiener Hof in der ersten Hälfte des 19. Jahrhunderts." In *Hof und Hofgesellschaft in den deutschen Staaten im 19. und beginnenden 20. Jahrhundert*, ed. Karl Möckl. Boppard am Rhein, 1990.

Stendar-Petersen, A. D. *Die Varägersage als Quelle der altrussischen Chronik*. Copenhagen, 1934.

Stepanov, N. L. "'Severnaia Pchela' F. V. Bulgarina." In *Ocherki po istorii russkoi zhurnalistiki i kritiki*. Vol. 1. Leningrad, 1950.

Stites, Richard. *Revolutionary Dreams: Utopian Vision and Experimental Life in the Russian Revolution*. New York, 1989.

Stone, Lawrence. *The Family, Sex, and Marriage in England, 1500–1800*. London, 1977.

Strong, Roy. *Splendor at Court: Renaissance Spectacle and the Theater of Power*. Boston, 1973.

Sturdy, D. "'Continuity' versus 'Change': Historians and English Coronations of the Medieval and Early Modern Periods." In *Coronations: Medieval and Early Modern Monarchic Ritual*, ed. János M. Bak. Berkeley, Calif., 1990.

Summerson, John. *The Architecture of the Eighteenth Century*. London, 1986.

Svin'in, Pavel. "Istoricheskoe opisanie Sviashchennogo Koronovaniia i Miropomazaniia ikh Imperatorskikh Velichestv Gosudaria Imperatora Nikolaia Pavlovicha i Gosudaryni Imperatritsy Aleksandry Feodorovny." *Otechestvennye Zapiski* 31 (1827): 27–59, 170–211, 369–96; 32 (1827): 23–52, 199–229, 347–84. Referred to in text as "Istoricheskoe opisanie."

————. "Moskovskiia sovremennye letopisi: perepiska izdatelia Otechestvennykh Zapisok." *Otechestvennye Zapiski* 27 (1826): 280–90.

Sytova, Alla. *The Lubok, Russian Folk Pictures, 17th to 19th Century.* Leningrad, 1984.

Szeftel, Marc. "The Title of Muscovite Monarch up to the End of the Seventeenth Century." *Canadian Slavic Studies*, vol. 13, nos. 1–2 (Spring–Summer, 1979): 65–66.

Tanner, Marie. *The Last Descendant of Aeneas: The Hapsburgs and the Mythic Image of Emperor.* New Haven, Conn., 1993.

Tartakovskii, A. G. *1812 god i russkaia memuaristika.* Moscow, 1980.

Taruskin, Richard. *Opera and Drama in Russia as Preached and Practiced in the 1860s.* Ann Arbor, Mich., 1981.

Tatishchev, S. S. *Alexander II; ego zhizn' i tsarstvovanie.* 2 vols. St. Petersburg, 1903.

Taube, Baron M. A. "K istorii Gerba Doma Romanovykh." *Gerboved* (1913): 109–17.

Ternovskii, F. *Religioznyi kharakter russkikh gosudarei XVIII veka.* Kiev, 1874.

Thaden, Edward C. *Russia's Western Borderland, 1710–1870.* Princeton, N.J, 1984.

Thon Konstantin. *Proekty Tserkvei sochinennye arkitektorom . . . Konstantinom Tonom.* St. Petersburg, 1844.

————. *Tserkvi, sochinennye arkhitektorom Ego Imperatorskogo Velichestva Professorom Arkhtektury Imperatorskoi Akademii Khudozhestv i chlenom raznykh akademii Konstantinom Tonom.* St. Petersburg, 1838.

Tikhomirov, M. N. *Rossiiskoe gosudarstvo XV–XVII vekov.* Moscow, 1973.

Tiutcheva, Anna Fedorovna. *Pri dvore dvukh imperatorov. Vospominaniia, Dnevnik, 1853–1882.* 2 vols. Moscow, 1928–1929.

Tokmakov, I. *Istoricheskoe opisanie vsekh koronatsii rossiiskikh tsarei, imperatorov i imperatrits.* Moscow, 1896.

Torke, Hans-Joachim. *Das russische Beamtentum in der ersten Hälfte des 19. Jahrhunderts.* Berlin, 1967.

Torzhestvo blagopoluchno sovershivshegosia v Moskve koronovaniia i miropomazaniia Blagochestiveishia Gosudaryni Imperatritsy Ekateriny Alekseevny . . . otpravlennoe Imperatorskoiu Akademieiu Nauk v publichnom sobranii 23 sentiabria, 1762. St. Petersburg, 1762.

"Torzhestvyiushchaia Minerva." *Moskvitianin*, no. 19 (October 1850), Otd. Nauki i khudozhestva, 109–128.

Traveling across North America 1812–1813: Watercolors by the Russian Diplomat Pavel Svinin. New York, 1992.

Treadgold, Donald W. *The West in China and Russia: Religious and Secular Thought in Modern Times.* 2 vols. Cambridge, 1973.

Troitskii, S. M. *Russkii absoliutizm i dvorianstvo v XVIII v.; formirovanie biurokratii.* Moscow, 1974.

"Tsarevich Pavel Petrovich; istoricheskie materialy khraniashchiesia v biblioteke dvortsa goroda Pavlovska." *Russkaia Starina* 9 (1874): 677–84.

Turner, Victor. *The Forest of Symbols: Aspects of Ndembu Ritual.* Ithaca, N.Y., 1967.

Uspenskii, B. A. "Tsar i Patriarkh: kharizma vlasti v Rossii (Visantiiskaia model' i eia russkoe pereosmyslenie)." In manuscript.

————. "Historia sub specie semioticae." In *Soviet Semiotics*, ed. D. P. Lucid. Baltimore, Md., 1977.

————. "Le perception de l'histoire et la doctrine 'Moscou-troisième Rome.'" In *La royauté sacrée dans le monde chrétien*, ed. Alain Boureau and Claudio-Sergio Ingerflom. Paris, 1992.

Van Gennep, Arnold. *The Rites of Passage*. Chicago, 1960.

Valuev, P. "Duma russkogo." *Russkaia Starina* 70 (1891): 349–60.

Vasil'ev, V. N. *Starinnye feierverki v Rossii*. Leningrad, 1960.

Vasiliev, A. A. "Was Russia a Vassal State of Byzantium?" *Speculum*, vol. 7, no. 3 (July 1930): 350–60.

Vel'tman, Alexander. *Opisanie novogo Imperatorskogo dvortsa v kremle Moskovskom*. Moscow, 1851.

————. "Osviashchenie novogo moskovskogo dvortsa v kremle." "Moskovskaia letopis'," *Moskvitianin* (April 1849): 149–54.

————. "Torzhestvennyia prazdnestva, v novom imperatorskom kremlevskom dvortse." "Moskovskaia letopis," *Moskvitianin*, pt. 1 (May 1849): 16–25.

Vengerov, S. A. "Ezhednevnaia pechat' kontsa doreformennoi epokhi." In *Sbornik statei po istorii i statistike russkoi periodicheskoi pechati, 1703–1903*. St. Petersburg, 1903.

Vereshchagin, V. A. *Russkie illiustrirovannye izdaniia XVIII i XIX stoletii*. St. Petersburg, 1898.

Veyne, Paul. *Les grecs, ont-ils cru à leurs mythes?; essai sur l'imagination constituante*. Paris, 1983.

Vigel', F. F. *Vospominaniia*. 7 vols. Moscow, 1864–1865.

Vilinbakhov, G. V. "K istorii uchrezhdeniia ordena Andreia Pervozvannogo i evoliutsiia ego znaka." In *Kul'tura i iskusstvo petrovskogo vremeni*. Leningrad, 1977.

————. "Osnovanie Peterburga i imperskaia emblematika." In *Semiotika goroda i gorodskoi kul'tury (Trudy po znakovym sistemam)*, vol. 18, ed. Iu. M. Lotman. Tartu, 1984.

————. "Otrazhenie idei absoliutizma v simvolike Petrovskikh znamen." In *Kul'tura i iskusstvo Rossii XVIII veka*. Leningrad, 1981.

————. "Sankt-Peterburg—Voennaia Stolitsa." *Nashe Hasledie*, no. 1 (1989): 17.

————. "Vsadnik russkogo gerba." *Trudy Gosudarstvennogo Ermitazha* 21 (1981): 117–22.

Vodoff, Wladimir. "Remarques sur la valeur du terme 'tsar' appliqué aux princes russes avant le milieu du XVe siècle." *Oxford Slavonic Papers* 11 (1978): 1–41.

Volkov, N. E. *Dvor russkikh imperatorov v ego proshlom i nastoiashchem*. St. Petersburg, 1900.

von Kruedener, Jürgen Freiherr. *Die Rolle des Hofes im Absolutismus*. Stuttgart, 1973.

Voronets, E. N. *Chetyrykhsotletie Rossiiskogo Gosudarstvennogo Gerba*. Kharkov, 1898.

Vues des cérémonies les plus intéressantes du couronnement de leurs Majestés Impériales l'empereur Nicholas Ier et l'impératrice Alexandra à Moscou. Paris, 1828.

Vysochaishe utverzhdennyi tseremonial prisiagi Gosudaria, Naslednika, Aleksandra Nikolaevicha. n.p., n.d.

Wackernagel, Rudolf H. *Der französiche Krönungswagen von 1696–1825*. Berlin, 1966.

Waquet, Françoise. *Les fêtes royales sous la restauration ou l'ancien régime retrouvé*. Geneva, 1981.

Whittaker, Cynthia H. *The Origins of Modern Russian Education: An Intellectual Biography of Count Sergei Uvarov, 1786–1855*. De Kalb, Ill., 1984.

———. "The Reforming Tsar: The Redefinition of Autocratic Duty in Eighteenth-Century Russia." *Slavic Review*, vol. 51, no. 1 (Spring, 1992): 77–98.

Wittram, Reinhard. *Peter I; Czar und Kaiser*. 2 vols. Göttingen, 1964.

Wolf, John B. "Louis XIV, Soldier-King." In *Louis XIV and the Craft of Kingship*, ed. John C. Rule. Columbus, Ohio, 1969.

Wolff, Robert Lee. "The Three Romes: The Migration of an Ideology and the Making of an Autocrat." *Daedalus*, vol. 88, no. 2 (Spring, 1959): 301–2.

Wortman, Richard S. *The Development of a Russian Legal Consciousness*. Chicago, 1976.

———. "The Russian Empress as Mother." In *The Family in Imperial Russia: New Lines of Historical Research*, ed. David L. Ransel. Urbana, Ill., 1978.

Wülfing, Wulf, Karin Bruns, and Rolf Parr. *Historische Mythologie der Deutschen*. Munich, 1991.

Yaney, George L. *The Systematization of Russian Government: Social Evolution in the Domestic Administration of Imperial Russia*. Urbana, Ill., 1973.

Yates, Frances. *Astraea: The Imperial Theme in the Sixteenth Century*. London, 1975.

Zabelin, I. E. *Domashnii byt russkikh tsarei v XVI i XVII st.* 2 vols. Vol. 1: Moscow, 1895. Vol. 2: Moscow, 1915.

———. *Domashnii byt russkikh tsarits v XVI i XVII st.* Moscow, 1901.

Zagoskin, N. P. *Imperator Pavel Pervyi v Kazani*. Kazan, 1893.

———. *Ocherki organizatsii i proiskhozhdeniia sluzhilogo sosloviia v do-petrovskoi Rusi*. Kazan, 1876.

Zaionchkovskii, P. A. *Pravitel'stvennyi apparat samoderzhavnoi Rossii XIX v.* Moscow, 1978.

Zaitsov, A. "Istoricheskaia spravka o naimenovanii 'Leib-Gvardiei.'" *Semenovskii Biulleten'* 20 (1950): 3–10.

Zenkovsky, Serge. "The Russian Church Schism." *Russian Review*, vol. 16, no. 4 (1957): 37–58.

Zhikharev, S. P. *Zapiski sovremennika*. 2 vols. Moscow, 1934.

Zhivov, V. M. "Gosudarstvennyi mif v epokhu Prosveshcheniia i ego razrushenie v Rossii kontsa XVIII veka." In *Vek Prosveshcheniia; Rossiia i Frantsia, Vipperovskie chteniia*. Moscow, 1989.

———. *Kul'turnye konflikty v istorii russkogo literaturnogo iazyka XVIII-nachala XIX veka*. Moscow, 1990.

———. "Kul'turnye reformy v sisteme preobrazovanii Petra I." Unpublished manuscript.

Zhivov, V. M., and B. A. Uspenskii. "Tsar' i Bog; semioticheskie aspekty sakralizatsii monarkha v Rossii." In *Iazyki kul'tury i problemy perevodimosti*, ed. B. A. Uspenskii. Moscow, 1987.

Zhmakin, V. I. "Koronatsii russkikh imperatorov i imperatrits." *Russkaia Starina* 37 (1883): 499–538; 38 (1883): 1–36.

Zhukovskii, V. A. *Dnevniki V. A. Zhukovskogo*. St. Petersburg, 1901.

———. *Polnoe sobranie sochinenii*. 9 vols. St. Petersburg, 1902.

———. *Sochineniia*. 6 vols. St. Petersburg, 1885.

Zhurnal poseshcheniia Moskvy ego Imperatorskim Velichestvom Aleksandrom I i kratkovremennogo prebyvaniia v cem pervoprestol'nom grade, v 1809. Moscow, 1810.

Zubarev, Dmitrii. "O dne sviashchennogo koronovaniia i miropomazaniia Gosudaria Imperatora." *Vestnik Evropy,* no. 24 (December 1826): 279–95.

Zyzykin, Mikhail. *Tsarskaia vlast' i zakon o prestolonasledii v Rossii.* Sofia, 1924.

CONTEMPORARY PERIODICALS

Otechestvennye Zapiski
Russkii Invalid
Russkii Khudozhestvennyi Listok
Ruskoi Vestnik
Sankt-Peterburgskie Vedomosti
Severnaia Pchela
Severnaia Pochta

Studies of the Harriman Institute

Soviet National Income in 1937 by Abram Bergson, Columbia University Press, 1953.

Through the Glass of Soviet Literature: Views of Russian Society, Ernest Simmons, Jr., ed., Columbia University Press, 1953.

Polish Postwar Economy by Thad Paul Alton, Columbia University Press, 1954.

Management of the Industrial Firm in the USSR: A Study in Soviet Economic Planning by David Granick, Columbia University Press, 1954.

Soviet Policies in China, 1917–1924 by Allen S. Whiting, Columbia University Press, 1954; paperback, Stanford University Press, 1968.

Literary Politics in the Soviet Ukraine, 1917–1934 by George S. N. Luckyj, Columbia University Press, 1956.

The Emergence of Russian Panslavism, 1856–1870 by Michael Boro Petrovich, Columbia University Press, 1956.

Lenin on Trade Unions and Revolution, 1893–1917 by Thomas Taylor Hammond, Columbia University Press, 1956.

The Last Years of the Georgian Monarchy, 1658–1832 by David Marshall Lang, Columbia University Press, 1957.

The Japanese Thrust into Siberia, 1918 by James William Morley, Columbia University Press, 1957.

Bolshevism in Turkestan, 1917–1927 by Alexander G. Park, Columbia University Press, 1957.

Soviet Marxism: A Critical Analysis by Herbert Marcuse, Columbia University Press, 1958; paperback, Columbia University Press, 1985.

Soviet Policy and the Chinese Communists, 1931–1946 by Charles B. McLane, Columbia University Press, 1958.

The Agrarian Foes of Bolshevism: Promise and Defeat of the Russian Socialist Revolutionaries, February to October, 1917 by Oliver H. Radkey, Columbia University Press, 1958.

Pattern for Soviet Youth: A Study of the Congresses of the Komsomol, 1918–1954 by Ralph Talcott Fisher, Jr., Columbia University Press, 1959.

The Emergence of Modern Lithuania by Alfred Erich Senn, Columbia University Press, 1959.

The Soviet Design for a World State by Elliot R. Goodman, Columbia University Press, 1960.

Settling Disputes in Soviet Society: The Formative Years of Legal Institutions by John N. Hazard, Columbia University Press, 1960.

Soviet Marxism and Natural Science, 1917–1932 by David Joravsky, Columbia University Press, 1961.

Russian Classics in Soviet Jackets by Maurice Friedberg, Columbia University Press, 1962.

Stalin and the French Communist Party, 1941–1947 by Alfred J. Rieber, Columbia University Press, 1962.

Sergei Witte and the Industrialization of Russia by Theodore K. Von Laue, Columbia University Press, 1962.

Ukranian Nationalism by John H. Armstrong, Columbia University Press, 1963.

The Sickle under the Hammer: The Russian Socialist Revolutionaries in the Early Months of Soviet Rule by Oliver H. Radkey, Columbia University Press, 1963.

Comintern and World Revolution, 1928–1943: The Shaping of Doctrine by Kermit E. McKenzie, Columbia University Press, 1964.

Weimar Germany and Soviet Russia, 1926–1933: A Study in Diplomatic Instability by Harvey L. Dyck, Columbia University Press, 1966.

Financing Soviet Schools by Harold J. Noah, Teachers College Press, 1966.

Russia, Bolshevism, and the Versailles Peace by John M. Thompson, Princeton University Press, 1966.

The Russian Anarchists by Paul Avrich, Princeton University Press, 1967.

The Soviet Academy of Sciences and the Communist Party, 1927–1932 by Loren R. Graham, Princeton University Press, 1967.

Red Virgin Soil: Soviet Literature in the 1920's by Robert A. Maguire, Princeton University Press, 1968; paperback, Cornell University Press, 1987.

Communist Party Membership in the U.S.S.R., 1917–1967 by T. H. Rigby, Princeton University Press, 1968.

Soviet Ethics and Morality by Richard T. De George, University of Michigan Press, 1969; paperback, Ann Arbor Paperbacks, 1969.

Vladimir Akimov on the Dilemmas of Russian Marxism, 1895–1903 by Jonathan Frankel, Cambridge University Press, 1969.

Soviet Perspectives on International Relations, 1956–1967 by William Zimmerman, Princeton University Press, 1969.

Krondstadt, 1921 by Paul Avrich, Princeton University Press, 1970.

Class Struggle in the Pale: The Formative Years of the Jewish Workers' Movement in Tsarist Russia by Ezra Mendelsohn, Cambridge University Press, 1970.

The Proletarian Episode in Russian Literature by Edward J. Brown, Columbia University Press, 1971.

Labor and Society in Tsarist Russia: The Factory Workers of St. Petersburg, 1855–1870 by Reginald E. Zelnik, Stanford University Press, 1971.

Archives and Manuscript Repositories in the U.S.S.R.: Moscow and Leningrad by Patricia K. Grimsted, Princeton University Press, 1972.

The Baku Commune, 1917–1918 by Ronald G. Suny, Princeton University Press, 1972.

Mayakovsky: A Poet in the Revolution by Edward J. Brown, Princeton University Press, 1973.

Oblomov and His Creator: The Life and Art of Ivan Goncharov by Milton Ehre, Princeton University Press, 1973.

German Politics under Soviet Occupation by Henry Krisch, Columbia University Press, 1974.

Soviet Politics and Society in the 1970's, Henry W. Morton and Rudolph L. Tokes, eds., Free Press, 1974.

Liberals in the Russian Revolution by William G. Rosenberg, Princeton University Press, 1974.

Famine in Russia, 1891–1892 by Richard G. Robbins, Jr., Columbia University Press, 1975.

In Stalin's Time: Middleclass Values in Soviet Fiction by Vera Dunham, Cambridge University Press, 1976.

The Road to Bloody Sunday by Walter Sablinsky, Princeton University Press, 1976; paperback, Princeton University Press, 1986.

The Familiar Letter as a Literary Genre in the Age of Pushkin by William Mills Todd, III, Princeton University Press, 1976.

Russian Realist Art. The State and Society: The Peredvizhniki and Their Tradition by Elizabeth Valkenier, Ardis Publishers, 1977; paperback, Columbia University Press, 1989.

The Soviet Agrarian Debate by Susan Solomon, Westview Press, 1978.

Cultural Revolution in Russia, 1928–1931, Sheila Fitzpatrick, ed., Indiana University Press, 1978; paperback, Midland Books, 1984.

Soviet Criminologists and Criminal Policy: Specialists in Policy-Making by Peter Solomon, Columbia University Press, 1978.

Technology and Society under Lenin and Stalin: Origins of the Soviet Technical Intelligentsia by Kendall E. Bailes, Princeton University Press, 1978.

The Politics of Rural Russia, 1905–1914, Leopold H. Haimson, ed., Indiana University Press, 1979.

Political Participation in the U.S.S.R. by Theodore H. Friedgut, Princeton University Press, 1979; paperback, Princeton University Press, 1982.

Education and Social Mobility in the Soviet Union, 1921–1934 by Sheila Fitzpatrick, Cambridge University Press, 1979.

The Soviet Marriage Market: Mate Selection in Russia and the USSR by Wesley Andrew Fisher, Praeger Publishers, 1980.

Prophecy and Politics: Socialism, Nationalism, and the Russian Jews, 1862–1917 by Jonathan Frankel, Cambridge University Press, 1981.

Dostoevsky and The Idiot: *Author, Narrator, and Reader* by Robin Feuer Miller, Harvard University Press, 1981.

Moscow Workers and the 1917 Revolution by Diane Koenker, Princeton University Press, 1981; paperback, Princeton University Press, 1986.

Archives and Manuscript Repositories in the USSR: Estonia, Latvia, Lithuania, and Belorussia by Patricia K. Grimsted, Princeton University Press, 1981.

Zionism in Poland: The Formative Years, 1915–1926 by Ezra Mendelshohn, Yale University Press, 1982.

Soviet Risk-Taking and Crisis Behavior by Hannes Adomeit, George Allen and Unwin Publishers, 1982.

Russia at the Crossroads: The 26th Congress of the CPSU, Seweryn Bialer and Thane Gustafson, eds., George Allen and Unwin Publishers, 1982.

The Crisis of the Old Order in Russia: Gentry and Government by Roberta Thompson Manning, Princeton University Press, 1983; paperback, Princeton University Press, 1986.

Sergei Aksakov and Russian Pastoral by Andrew A. Durkin, Rutgers University Press, 1983.

Politics and Technology in the Soviet Union by Bruce Parrott, MIT Press, 1983.

The Soviet Union and the Third World: An Economic Bind by Elizabeth Kridl Valkenier, Praeger Publishers, 1983.

Russian Metaphysical Romanticism: The Poetry of Tiutchev and Boratynskii by Sarah Pratt, Stanford University Press, 1984.

Ruling Russia: Politics and Administration in the Age of Absolutism, 1762–1796 by John LeDonne, Princeton University Press, 1984.

Insidious Intent: A Structural Analysis of Fedor Sologub's Petty Demon by Diana Greene, Slavica Publishers, 1986.

Leo Tolstoy: Resident and Stranger by Richard Gustafson, Princeton University Press, 1986.

Workers, Society, and the State: Labor and Life in Moscow, 1918–1929 by William Chase, University of Illinois Press, 1987.

Andrey Bely: Spirit of Symbolism, John Malmstad, ed., Cornell University Press, 1987.

Government and Peasant in Russia, 1861–1906: The Prehistory of the Stolypin Reforms by David A. J. Macey, Northern Illinois University Press, 1987.

The Making of Three Russian Revolutionaries: Voices from the Menshevik Past, Leopold H. Haimson, ed., in collaboration with Ziva Galili y Garcia and Richard Wortman, Cambridge University Press, 1988.

Revolution and Culture: The Bogdanov-Lenin Controversy by Zenovia A. Sochor, Cornell University Press, 1988.

A Handbook of Russian Verbs by Frank Miller, Ardis Publishers, 1989.

1905 in St. Petersburg: Labor, Society, and Revolution by Gerald D. Surh, Stanford University Press, 1989.

Alien Tongues: Bilingual Russian Writers of the "First" Emigration by Elizabeth Klosty Beaujour, Cornell University Press, 1989.

Iuzovka and Revolution, Volume I: Life and Work in Russia's Donbass, 1869–1924 by Theodore H. Friedgut, Princeton University Press, 1989.

The Menshevik Leaders in the Russian Revolution: Social Realities and Political Strategies by Ziva Galili, Princeton University Press, 1989.

Russian Literary Politics and the Pushkin Celebration of 1880 by Marcus C. Levitt, Cornell University Press, 1989.

Russianness: In Honor of Rufus Mathewson, Robert L. Belknap, ed., Ardis Publishers, 1990.

Soldiers in the Proletarian Dictatorship: The Red Army and the Soviet Socialist State, 1917–1930 by Mark von Hagen, Cornell University Press, 1990.

Ilya Repin and the World of Russian Art by Elizabeth Valkenier, Columbia University Press, 1990.

The Genesis of "The Brothers Karamazov" by Robert L. Belknap, Northwestern University Press, 1990.

Autobiographical Statements in Twentieth-Century Russian Literature, Jane Gary Harris, ed., Princeton University Press, 1990.

Folklore for Stalin by Frank Miller, M.E. Sharpe, 1990.

Vasilii Trediakovsky: The Fool of the "New" Russian Literature by Irina Reyfman, Stanford University Press, 1990.

Russia, Germany and the West from Khrushchev to Gorbachev by Michael Sodaro, Cornell University Press, 1990.

The Crisis of Russian Autocracy: Nicholas II and the 1905 Revolution by Andrew M. Verner, Princeton University Press, 1990.

Reforming Rural Russia: State, Local Society, and National Politics, 1855–1914 by Francis William Wcislo, Princeton University Press, 1990.

Remizov's Fictions, 1900–1921 by Greta N. Slobin, Northern Illinois University Press, 1991.

The Corporation under Russian Law, 1800–1917: A Study in Tsarist Economic Policy by Thomas C. Owen, Cambridge University Press, 1991.

Physics and Politics in Revolutionary Russia by Paul R. Josephson, University of California Press, 1991.

The Paradise Myth in Eighteenth-Century Russia: Utopian Patterns in Early Secular Russian Literature and Culture by Stephen Lessing Baehr, Stanford University Press, 1991.

Thinking Theoretically about Soviet Nationalities: Concepts, History and Comparison in the Study of the USSR, Alexander J. Motyl, ed., Columbia University Press, 1992.

The Post-Soviet Nations: Perspectives on the Demise of the USSR, Alexander J. Motyl, ed., Columbia University Press, 1992.